Fodor's 2014

CANCÚN AND THE RIVIERA MAYA

WELCOME TO CANCÚN AND THE RIVIERA MAYA

Mexico's Yucatán Peninsula remains enduringly popular with travelers, and there's little wonder why. Stellar attractions include the region's magnificent beaches and the extensive reefs off Cozumel and the southern Yucatán coast, as well as myriad Mayan ruins, the remains of a vast empire that ruled here long before the Spanish. Limestone pools called *cenotes,* great for a swim or dive, dot the countryside, even in Playa del Carmen. All-inclusive resorts predominate in Cancún, but luxurious retreats and simple guest houses also offer different kinds of hospitality.

TOP REASONS TO GO

★ **Coral Reefs:** Cozumel's are among the best, drawing both divers and snorkelers.

★ **Beaches:** Cancún's are busy and beautiful, the Riviera Maya's sugary soft and quieter.

★ **Mayan Ruins:** The pyramids of Chichen Itzá soar; Tulum overlooks a perfect beach.

★ **Nightlife:** Cancún and Playa del Carmen range from raucous to sophisticated.

★ **Spas:** Almost every big resort has a spa, and many are notable for their pampering.

★ **Nature:** Pockets of pristine beauty remain, despite widespread development.

Fodor's CANCÚN AND THE RIVIERA MAYA 2014

Publisher: Amanda D'Acierno, *Senior Vice President*

Editorial: Arabella Bowen, *Executive Editorial Director*; Linda Cabasin, *Editorial Director*

Design: Fabrizio La Rocca, *Vice President, Creative Director*; Tina Malaney, *Associate Art Director*; Chie Ushio, *Senior Designer*; Ann McBride, *Production Designer*

Photography: Melanie Marin, *Associate Director of Photography*; Jessica Parkhill and Jennifer Romains, *Researchers*

Maps: Rebecca Baer, *Map Editor*; David Lindroth *Cartographer*

Production: Linda Schmidt, *Managing Editor*; Evangelos Vasilakis, *Associate Managing Editor*; Angela L. McLean, *Senior Production Manager*

Sales: Jacqueline Lebow, *Sales Director*

Marketing & Publicity: Heather Dalton, *Marketing Director*; Katherine Fleming, *Senior Publicist*

Business & Operations: Susan Livingston, *Vice President, Strategic Business Planning*; Sue Daulton, *Vice President, Operations*

Fodors.com: Megan Bell, *Executive Director, Revenue & Business Development*; Yasmin Marinaro, *Senior Director, Marketing & Partnerships*

Editors: Alexis Crisman Kelly, Douglas Stallings

Writers: Marlise E. Kast, Marie Elena Martinez
Production Editor: Evangelos Vasilakis

ISBN 978-0-7704-3223-2

ISSN 2166-6253

SPECIAL SALES

This book is available at special discounts for bulk purchases for sales promotions or premiums. For more information, e-mail specialmarkets@randomhouse.com

PRINTED IN COLOMBIA

10 9 8 7 6 5 4 3 2 1

CONTENTS

MAPS

ABOUT THIS GUIDE

Fodor's Recommendations

Everything in this guide is worth doing—we don't cover what isn't—but exceptional sights, hotels, and restaurants are recognized with additional accolades. **Fodor'sChoice★** indicates our top recommendations. Care to nominate a new place? Visit Fodors.com/contact-us.

Trip Costs

We list prices wherever possible to help you budget well. Hotel and restaurant price categories from **$** to **$$$$** are noted alongside each recommendation. For hotels, we include the lowest cost of a standard double room in high season. For restaurants, we cite the average price of a main course at dinner or, if dinner isn't served, at lunch. For attractions, we always list adult admission fees; discounts are usually available for children, students, and senior citizens.

Hotels

Our local writers vet every hotel to recommend the best overnights in each price category, from budget to expensive. Unless otherwise specified, you can expect private bath, phone, and TV in your room. For expanded hotel reviews, facilities, and deals visit Fodors.com.

Restaurants

Unless we state otherwise, restaurants are open for lunch and dinner daily. We mention dress code only when there's a specific requirement and reservations only when they're essential or not accepted. To make restaurant reservations, visit Fodors.com.

Credit Cards

The hotels and restaurants in this guide typically accept credit cards. If not, we'll say so.

Top Picks

★ Fodor'sChoice

Listings

✉ Address

✉ Branch address

☎ Telephone

📠 Fax

🌐 Website

📧 E-mail

🎟 Admission fee

⏲ Open/closed times

[M] Subway

✥ Directions or Map coordinates

Hotels & Restaurants

🏨 Hotel

🛏 Number of rooms

🍽 Meal plans

✕ Restaurant

✍ Reservations

👔 Dress code

▭ No credit cards

[$] Price

Other

⇨ See also

☞ Take note

🏌 Golf facilities

1

EXPERIENCE CANCÚN

WHAT'S WHERE

2 Cancún. As the gateway to Riviera Maya, this thriving beach city is Mexico's most popular tourist destination, with a nightlife that has made it the Spring Break capital of the world. In the beach-front area known as "Zona Hotelera," high-rise resorts offer creature comforts. Hotels inland at Cancún's downtown "El Centro" are reasonably priced and will give a more authentic Mexican experience.

3 Isla Mujeres. A 30-minute jaunt across the water from Cancún, Isla Mujeres is light years away in temperament. This quaint fishing village is made up of dirt roads gener-ally traveled by golf cart, scooter, or bike. It's more laid-back, less crowded, and cheaper than almost any-where on the mainland.

4 The Caribbean Coast. The dazzling white sands and glittering blue waters of the Riviera Maya beckon everyone from snorkelers and sunbathers to spa goers and bird-watchers. Although most travelers visit for the sugary beaches, this region also offers the seaside ruins of Tulum, the jungle-clad pyramids of Cobá, and the sidewalk cafés of Playa del Carmen. Catering to families are the numerous theme parks, dolphin programs, and hidden cenotes. Some of the best spas in the world are located here.

5 Cozumel. The island is hugely popular with scuba divers and cruise-ship pas-sengers. Ever since Jacques Cousteau first made Cozu-mel's interconnected series of coral reefs famous in the 1970s, divers and snorkelers have flocked here. Giant ships ferry day-trippers to Cozumel. Avoid the crowds by visiting the island's windward side in search of crumbled monuments to the goddess Ixchel.

6 Yucatán and Campeche States. Mérida, the capital city of Yucatán State, is the cultural hub of the entire peninsula. Known for its weekend festivals, Mérida's restaurants, hotels, shops, and museums bring visitors back year after year. Near the remote north coast, you'll find shell-strewn beaches and charming villages. The state's major claim to fame, however, is its spectacular Mayan archi-tecture, including sites at Chichén Itzá and Uxmal.

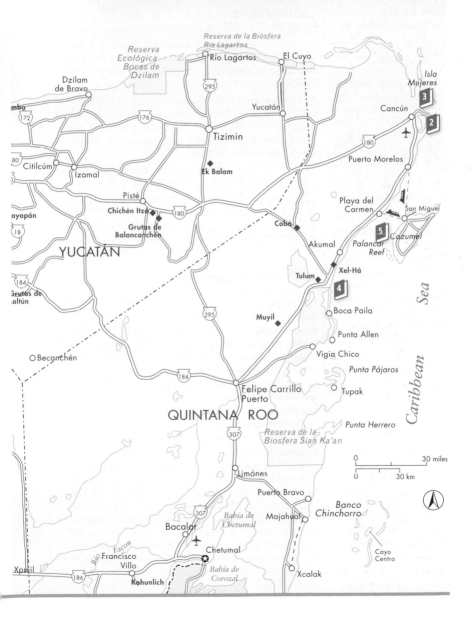

Reserva de la Biósfera
Ría Lagartos

Reserva
Ecológica
Boras de
Dzilam

Río Lagartos   El Cuyo

Isla
Mujeres

Dzilam
de Bravo

3

Yucatán   Cancún

mba
172

176   2

80   Tizimin   180

Puerto Morelos

Citilcúm   Izamal   Ek Balam

Playa del
Carmen   San Miguel

ayapán   Pisté
Chichén Itzá   180   Cobá

18   Grutas de
Balancanchén   5   Cozumel

Akumal   Palancar
Reef

YUCATÁN
184   Tulum   Xel-Há

Grutas de
.oltún   4

Muyil

Boca Paila

O Becanchén   Punta Allen

Vigia Chico

Punta Pájaros

Felipe Carrillo
Puerto   Tupak

QUINTANA ROO

Punta Herrero

Reserva de la
Biosfera Siah Ka'an

0   30 miles

0   30 km

Limónes

Puerto Bravo

Banco
Chinchorro

Bacalar   Majahual

Escon

Xpujil   Francisco
Villo   Chetumal

Bahía de
Corozal   Xcalak

Cayo
Centro

186   Kohunlich

Caribbean

Sea

THE YUCATÁN PENINSULA PLANNER

When to Go

High season lasts from late November through the first week in April, with Christmas holiday prices being up to 50% above regular rates. Beach resorts—particularly in Cancún—tend to fill up with college students during summer months and Spring Break (primarily February and March). You can save between 20% to 50% during low season (the day after Easter to mid-December). The closing months of Spring Break and summer (May and October) still offer plenty of sunshine.

Climate

From November through March, winter temperatures hover around 27°C (80°F). Occasional winter storms called *nortes* can bring blustery skies and sharp winds that make air temperatures drop and swimming unappealing. During the spring (especially April and May), there's a period of intense heat that tapers off in June. The hottest months, with temperatures reaching up to 43°C (110°F), are May, June, and July. The busiest part of Hurricane season—July through the end of September—is also hot and humid.

Getting Here

The Yucatán Peninsula has international airports in Cancún, Mérida, and Cozumel. Domestic airports are in Playa del Carmen, Chichén Itzá, Isla Holbox, Isla Mujeres, and Mahahual.

Few people travel to the Yucatán Peninsula by car, especially with the risks involved just south of the U.S. border. Those who do so will need a valid driver's license, a temporary car-importation permit, a car registration, a copy of the car title, and an FM-T form.

The most practical way to explore the Yucatán Peninsula is to fly to your region and rent a car for the duration of your stay. The best flight deals, however, are usually arriving and departing from the Cancún airport. Auto insurance is mandatory in Mexico, regardless of what travel-insurance package you have back home.

Getting Around

Compared to other parts of Mexico, the roads in the Yucatán Peninsula are nicely paved. Carretera 307 serves as the coastal route between Cancún and the Belize border, but this stretch of highway is known for its speed traps and large *topes* (speed bumps). Toll road 180, the four-lane highway from Cancún to Mérida, is nicely paved and has exits at major towns along the way. From Cancún, you can reach Mérida in about five hours, but you will pay close to $40 in tolls, an excellent investment in terms of time and ease of driving. Tolls must be paid in cash in pesos. Regardless of where you drive, be sure to arrive by sunset.

If you are nervous about driving, take a domestic flight to your ultimate destination; Aeroméxico and Mexicana travel to most places in Mexico. The cheapest way to get around is by bus. Luxury liners like ADO (⊕ *www.ado.com.mx*), Omnibuses de Mexico (⊕ *www.odm.com.mx*), and Primera Plus (⊕ *www.primeraplus.com.mx*) travel throughout the Yucatán Peninsula. *Colectivos* (mini-buses) run along Carretera 307 from Cancún to Tulum. Although affordable, traveling by bus means you'll have to either walk or organize additional transportation from the bus stop. Taxis will cost you about $20 per hour.

Festivals and Celebrations

Among the many Navidad (Christmas) events are *posadas*, during which families gather to eat and sing, and lively parades with colorful floats and brass bands, culminating December 24, on **Nochebuena** (*Holy Night*).

Carnaval festivities take place in February the week before Lent, with parades, floats, outdoor dancing, music, and fireworks; they're especially spirited in Mérida, Cozumel, Isla Mujeres, Campeche, and Chetumal.

Semana Santa is the most important holiday in Mexico. Reenactments of the Passion, family parties and meals, and religious services are held during this week leading up to Easter Sunday.

Since 1991, the **Cancún Jazz Festival**, held the last weekend in May at Oasis Resort, has featured such top musicians as Wynton Marsalis and Gato Barbieri.

Founder's Day, August 17, celebrates the founding of Isla Mujeres with six days of races, folk dances, music, and regional cuisine.

Día de Independencia (*Independence Day*) is celebrated throughout Mexico with fireworks and parties beginning at 11 pm on September 15, and continuing on the 16th.

Fiesta del Cristo de las Ampollas (*Feast of the Christ of the Blisters*) is an important religious event that takes place late September or early October, with daily mass and processions during which people dress in traditional clothing; dances, bullfights, and fireworks take place in Ticul and other small villages.

Ten days of festivities and a solemn parade mark the **Fiesta del Cristo de Sitilpech**, during which the Christ image of Sitilpech village is carried to Izamal. The biggest dances (with fireworks) are toward the culmination of the festivities on October 28.

Día de los Muertos (*Day of the Dead*), called Hanal Pixan in Mayan, is a joyful holiday during which graves are refurbished and symbolic meals are prepared to lure the spirits of family members back to earth for the day. Deceased children are associated with All Saints Day, November 1, while adults are feted on All Souls Day, November 2.

Money Matters

Mexican currency is the peso. When you arrive, it's a good idea to have smaller bills and some *centavos* (change) to pay for tips, bus fare, or taxis. Avoid having anything larger than a MX$50, because change is sometimes difficult to find. Do not accept damaged pesos, which are of no value to merchants or banks.

Traveler's checks can be changed at some banks for a processing fee. A passport is required when exchanging U.S. dollars or traveler's checks; foreign travelers may not exchange more than $1,500 U.S. dollars (cash) per person, per month into Mexican pesos. However, credit card transactions, traveler's checks, and non-U.S. foreign currencies are not affected by this law.

ATMs are the most convenient ways to get cash, are readily available, and charge the official exchange rate. Make sure your PIN has only four numbers, and inquire about foreign transaction fees processed by your U.S. bank. Larger resorts have ATMs on the premises, and most hotels will exchange dollars for pesos.

Most businesses accept major credit cards but may add a surcharge to compensate for their own hefty processing fee. In Mexico, American Express, Discover, and Diner's Club are not as readily accepted as Visa or MasterCard.

IF YOU LIKE

Spas

There are dozens of spa resorts scattered throughout the Yucatán Peninsula, primarily along the coast. Here decadent body treatments are offered in luxurious seaside settings. Some incorporate indigenous healing techniques into their services, using *temazcal* (an ancient Mayan sweat-lodge ritual), and plant extracts in aromatherapy facials. Others feature seawater and marine algae in mineral-rich thalassotherapy treatments; still others go the high-tech route with cutting-edge flotarium tanks, seven-jet Vichy massage tables, and Kinesis fitness machines. You won't have any trouble getting your pampering fix here—especially in the areas around Playa del Carmen and the rest of the Riviera Maya—but you'll likely pay top dollar for it.

The spas that get the most consistent raves include Punta Tanchacté's **Zoëtry Paraíso de la Bonita Resort and Thalasso.** Here you can soak away stress in specially built saltwater pools. **Mandarin Oriental** in Punta Maroma has relaxing, womblike flotation tanks and **Banyan Tree,** in Mayakoba, has a 12-step Rainforest Experience that combines hydrotherapy with infrared light to revitalize the body. The **Spa at JW Marriott,** Cancún, is justifiably famous for its Mayan-inspired treatments like the chocolate massage, ground-corn exfoliation, and chaya detoxification. At **The Tides,** in Punta Bete, it's hard to imagine a sweeter way to end the day than a honey massage.

Diving and Snorkeling

The turquoise waters of the Mexican Caribbean Coast are strewn with stunning coral reefs, underwater canyons, and sunken shipwrecks—all teeming with marine life. The visibility can reach 100 feet, so even on the surface you'll be amazed by what you can see.

Made famous decades ago by Jacques Cousteau, Cozumel is still considered one of the world's premier diving destinations. The **Mesoamerican Barrier Reef System (also known as the Great Mayan Reef),** just off the western coast, stretches some 32 km (20 miles)—and more than 100 dive operators on the island offer deep dives, drift dives, wall dives, night dives, wreck dives, and dives focusing on ecology and underwater photography.

Farther south, the town of Tankah is known for its **Gorgonian Gardens,** a profusion of soft corals and sponges that has created an underwater Eden. Near the Belize border, Mexico's largest coral atoll, **Banco Chinchorro,** is a graveyard of vessels that have foundered on the corals over the centuries. Experienced divers won't want to miss Isla Contoy's **Cave of the Sleeping Sharks.** Here, at 150 feet, you can see the otherwise dangerous creatures "dozing" in a state of relaxed nonaggression. From June to September, divers and snorkelers can swim with whale sharks, which can be up to 50 feet in length. These docile creatures migrate near the tropical waters of Isla Holbox and Isla Contoy.

The freshwater cenotes (sinkholes) that punctuate Quintana Roo, Yucatán, and Campeche states are also favorites with divers and snorkelers. Many of these are private and secluded, even though they lie right off the highways; others are so popular that they've become tourist destinations. At **Hidden Worlds Cenote Park** (on the highway between Xel-Há and Tankah), for example, you can float through cavernous sinkholes filled with stalactites, stalagmites, and rock formations.

Mayan Ruins

The ruins of ancient Mayan cities are magical; and they're scattered all across the Yucatán. Although **Chichén Itzá**, featuring the enormous and oft-photographed Castillo pyramid, is the most famous of the region's sites, **Uxmal** is the most graceful. Here the perfectly proportioned buildings of the Cuadrángulo de las Monjas (Nun's Quadrangle) make a beautiful "canvas" for facades carved with snakes and the fierce visages of Mayan gods. At the more easterly **Ek Balam**, workers on makeshift scaffolding brush away centuries of accumulated grime from huge monster masks that protect the mausoleum of a Mayan king. On the amazing friezes, winged figures dressed in full royal regalia gaze down.

At **Cobá**, the impressive temples and palaces—including a 79-foot-high pyramid—are surrounded by thick jungle, and only sparsely visited by tourists. In contrast, nearby **Tulum** is the peninsula's most-visited archaeological site. Although the ruins here aren't as architecturally arresting, their location—on a cliff overlooking the blue-green Caribbean—makes Tulum unique among major Mayan sites.

Farther afield, in Campeche State, the elaborate stone mural of **Balamkú** is hidden deep within another temple, sheltered from the elements for more than a millennium. Thousands of structures lie buried under the profuse greenery of Mexico's largest eco-corridor at the **Reserva de la Biosfera Calakmul**, where songbirds trill and curious monkeys hang from trees. These and other intriguing cities have been extensively excavated for your viewing pleasure.

Exotic Cuisine

Pickled onions tinged a luminous pink, blackened habanero chiles floating seductively in vinaigrette, lemonade spiked with the local plant called *chaya*—Yucatecan cuisine is different from that of any other region in Mexico. In recent years, traditional dishes made with local fruits, chiles, and spices have also embraced the influence of immigrants from Lebanon, France, Cuba, and New Orleans. The results are deliciously sublime.

Among the best-known regional specialties are *cochinita pibíl* and *pollo pibíl* (pork or chicken pit-baked in banana leaves). Both are done beautifully at **Hacienda Teya**, an elegant restaurant outside Mérida that was once a henequen hacienda. The *poc chuc* (marinated pork served with pickled onions and a plateful of other condiments) is delicious at **El Príncipe Tutul-Xiu**, an off-the-beaten-path and very authentic restaurant in the ancient Yucatán town of Maní. *Papadzules*—crumbled hard-boiled eggs rolled inside tortillas and drenched in a sauce of pumpkin seed and fried tomatoes—are a specialty at **Labná**, in Cancún's El Centro district.

In Campeche, a signature dish is *pan de cazón*, a casserole of shredded shark meat layered with tortillas, black beans, and tomato sauce; the best place to order it is at **La Pigua**, in Campeche City. The dish known as *tixin-xic* (fish marinated in orange juice and chiles and cooked over an open flame) is the dish of choice at Isla Mujeres' **Playa Lancheros Restaurant**.

CANCUN
TOP ATTRACTIONS

Cenotes

(A) For an underwater adventure, plunge into one of Mexico's sacred cenotes. These limestone pools are fed by subterranean springs that flow throughout the Yucatán. Rays of light illuminate these refreshing sinkholes; swim with the tiny fish that dart between the crevices. Experienced divers can explore the underwater tunnels that connect these hidden gems.

Tulum

(B) Although the Yucatán has plenty of ruins to choose from, none are quite as spectacular as those in Tulum. Skirting the ancient architecture is a powdery stretch of coastline that fades into four shades of turquoise water. South of the ruins are dozens of eco-lodges that operate on solar power, wind turbines, and recycled rainwater.

Isla Mujeres

(C) Find a shady spot under the arching palms of Playa Norte, a sugary beach on Isla Mujeres where time is nonexistent. Those who come here fall victim to the mañana mentality, spending days admiring tangerine sunsets while island life sweeps them away. Calm, warm waters make this aquatic paradise ideal for swimming, snorkeling, diving, or fishing.

Celestun Biosphere Reserve

(D) Located on a pristine beach west of Mérida, this 100,000-acre wildlife reserve has one of the largest colonies of flamingoes in North America, and more than 300 other species of birds. Flat-bottom boats float through the mangroves in search of turtles, crocodiles, cormorants, egrets, and herons. Nature lovers can take a break from bird-watching to enjoy the area's beaches, cenotes, or the sweet water springs of Baldiosera.

Chichén Itzá

(F) Considered one of the Seven Wonders of the World, this archaeological city is best known for its ancient Temple of Kukulcán. Also referred to as "El Castillo," the Mayan ruin stands a staggering 78 feet high and features a towering pyramid with four stairways. This surrounding area offers dozens of other archaeological sites as well as the famed Cenote Sagrado (Sacred Cenote).

Grutas de Loltun

(F) Roughly one hour southeast of Uxmal, these natural caverns show signs of man dating back to 800 BC. Illuminated pathways meander past stalactites, stalagmites, and limestone formations. Here you can admire the spectacular rays of light shining down on "musical" columns that are formed by the union of stalactites and stalagmites.

Playa del Carmen

(G) Located in the heart of Riviera Maya, Playa del Carmen has all the makings of a great vacation destination. Once a quiet fishing village, the town is booming with boutique hotels and open-air restaurants, making it one of the fastest-growing communities in Latin America. For a day of pampering, relax at one of the nearby luxury spas, or try zip-lining at Xcaret, a 250-acre ecological theme park.

Majahual and Xcalak

(H) Although a bit of a haul to get here, the colorful towns of Majahual and Xcalak are well worth the journey. This coastal paradise offers incredible offshore diving at Banco Chinchorro and the Mesoamerican Barrier Reef, the second longest in the world. Serious anglers will enjoy fly-fishing in the nearby saltwater flats of the peninsula.

FAQS

Do I need any special documents to get into Mexico?

You must have a valid passport to enter Mexico and to reenter the United States. Before landing in Mexico, you'll be given an FMT form (tourist card) to be stamped at immigration. Keep this card safe, because you'll need to present it when you leave the country.

How difficult is it to travel around the Yucatán?

It's relatively easy, thanks to improved roadways and domestic airlines offering daily flights to 10 destinations in the Yucatán. Mexico's bus system is an excellent way to travel around the country. Deluxe buses are more expensive, but have air-conditioning, reclining seats, movies, and fewer stops. Intercity transportation (used mainly by locals) is extremely reliable, and a great way to experience Mexican culture.

Are the roads as bad as they say?

Compared to other parts of Mexico, the roads in the Yucatán Peninsula are safe, flat, and well maintained. The main highway between Cancún and Belize, known as Carretera 307, is clearly marked and freshly paved. Even most secondary roads like those near Majahual are in decent shape, but tend to get pitted with potholes during and after the rainy season. Only in remote areas like Punta Allen will you find major potholes. Toll road 180 runs between Cancún and Merida and is by far your safest option. Throughout the peninsula, beware of unmarked *topes* (speed bumps) that can leave you airborne. Although road conditions have improved tremendously, avoid driving at night, since most areas lack street lighting.

What should I do when a police officer pulls me over?

Although not overly common in Riviera Maya, there are some police officers who expect bribes from drivers. When renting a car, ask the agency for a "Tourist Traffic Card," which can be handed to police upon receiving a traffic violation. This voucher allows you to pay the ticket at the car-rental agency when you return the car rather than having to spend several hours at the police station. It also helps eliminate corruption.

Should I get insurance on the rental car?

Yes! Regardless of what coverage you have from your credit card or travel insurance, you must (by law) have additional Mexican auto insurance to rent a car. This mandatory cost is around $12 per day, which is sometimes more than the daily rental fee if you happened to find a good deal online. When renting a car, make sure that your insurance coverage includes an attorney and claims adjusters who will come to the scene of an accident.

Should I consider a package?

Yes, packages that combine airfare, your hotel, and usually your airport transfers can be a good value in the Yucatán Peninsula. While guided tours aren't necessary, they are a good option if you prefer to travel with a group, and they can be arranged quite easily at your hotel's tour desk after your arrival. There's no need to book these in advance unless you are planning a particularly special trip.

Do I need a local guide?

Guides are helpful if you're visiting a wildlife area or an archaeological site where local knowledge or history is needed. Most wildlife guides will bring a telescope or binoculars and can locate

hidden animals and identify various species that the average traveler might overlook. If you do hire a guide, be sure to tip accordingly, since some (especially in rural areas) depend on tips as their main source of income.

Will I have trouble if I don't speak Spanish?

Si y no. If you stay within the main tourist areas, nearly everyone will speak English, and if they don't, someone nearby certainly will. In remote towns and areas less visited by travelers, you'll have to speak "Spanglish" or rely on a dictionary or phrase book.

Can I drink the water?

Better not. Tap water in Mexico is not potable. Most resorts and restaurants have purified water, but if you are concerned about a piece of contaminated ice ruining your vacation, then opt for bottled water.

Are there any worries about the food?

Most restaurants are clean and cater to fussy travelers. If you are sensitive to spicy food, you may have a difficult time at some of the more authentic Mexican restaurants. High-trafficked tourist areas will always have plenty of dining options, and coastal towns serve fresh-caught fish. If you visit a roadside market, unpeeled fruit or crunchy pork rinds are safe road-trip snacks. Unless you are in a nice restaurant, it's best to avoid uncooked vegetables, salads, rare meat, and milk products. Make sure that food is thoroughly cooked and hasn't been sitting under a heat lamp.

Do I need to get any shots?

Travelers visiting the Yucatán Peninsula do not need to get vaccinations or take any special medications. According to the U.S. Centers for Disease Control and Prevention, there's some concern about malaria along the Guatemala and Belize borders in the state of Quintana Roo.

Should I bring any medications?

To prevent bug bites, use insect repellent containing 10%–25% DEET. If you can bear the heat, wear long pants when you go out at night. It's a good idea to bring along antihistamine cream to keep you from scratching. Mild cases of diarrhea respond best to Imodium (known generically as Loperamide or Lomotil) or Pepto-Bismol, both of which you can buy over the counter. To avoid problems at customs, any prescription drugs you bring with you should be in their original pill bottle listed with printed identification. Over-the-counter medications are very expensive at resort gift shops, but in town you can find what you need at any local pharmacy.

Can I use my ATM card?

Yes. Most ATMs in Mexico accept U.S. credit and debit cards. Before your trip, make sure your PIN only has four numbers, since ATMs in Mexico do not recognize more digits. Foreign transaction fees can be high, as much as $10 per withdrawal.

Do most places take credit cards?

Outside of remote areas like Xcalak and Majahual, nearly all tourist-oriented businesses accept Visa and MasterCard, but some places charge 5% to 10% more for credit-card payments to help offset high processing fees. It's always a good idea to have at least some cash on hand.

YUCATÁN PENINSULA TODAY

Government

Yucatán is one of the 31 states (plus one federal district) that comprise Mexico's federal republic. The government consists of three branches: the executive, the legislative, and the judicial. The president of Mexico is elected to a one-time, six-year term by popular vote, and holds such extensive control that the position has been coined "the six-year monarchy." For more than 70 years, the country was ruled by the powerful PRI party (Institutional Revolutionary Party). The party abused its powers, including illegal landholding, charging the public for free services, bribery, and other forms of corruption. For the last half century, the opposition party, PAN (Partido de Acciòn Nacional) organized and slowly rose to power, making Vincente Fox the new president in 2000. Despite his efforts to reduce drug trafficking and corruption, a third political party, PRD (Partido de la Revolución Democrática) began to gain momentum as a voice for the poor. In 2006, the presence of three active political parties led to a hotly contested election and a marginal victory for PAN's Felipe Calderón, who began his presidential term amid widespread protests.

Like each of Mexico's 31 states, Yucatán is headed by a governor who serves a single, six-year term. Currently serving as governor until 2013 is Ivonne Pacheco, who previously served as the mayor of Dzemul and as a state senator. Though elected by a simple majority of the populace, the actual selection of state governors has historically been largely controlled by Mexico's presidents.

Much of Yucatán's revenue (like those of the other states) actually comes from the federal government. Such funding is then channeled to the mayors for distribution to their respective municipalities.

Economy

Before 1970, the Yucatán Peninsula relied solely on agriculture to support its economy, but in the 1980s, the region was successfully marketed as a travel destination, especially Cancún and the Riviera Maya. What were once small fishing villages are now bustling beach towns lined with luxury resorts. Each year millions of tourists are drawn to the area's beach resorts and archaeological sites; these attractions inject a steady cash flow into the economy. This influx of mass tourism created more jobs and a higher standard of living. Travelers have also shown more interest in local culture, and spurred the development of historical museums and exquisite Yucatán crafts, which have long been known for their quality workmanship. The Yucatán's economy is also helped by exports of up to 1,500 henequen products such as twine, rugs, and wall hangings. In the past, Yucatán's henequen had a global reputation of being "green gold." Sadly, the advent of similar man-made fibers destroyed the international market for henequen. Recently though, innovative entrepreneurs are using the plants to make other products, like alcohol and honey.

Tourism

In the late 1960s the Mexican government created a strategy to increase tourism in the Yucatán Peninsula, with Cancún selected as the primary destination. As a result, the city's population increased from 18,000 in 1976 to more than 500,000 in 2010. Growth has since expanded to neighboring regions, creating a solid infrastructure that has made the Yucatán Peninsula the most-visited destination in Mexico.

Today the country faces the challenge of protecting its natural resources while allowing development to continue. Cancún's beaches alone are lined with more than 150 towering hotels, many of which have contributed to coastal erosion. Fortunately, building restrictions are now in place in neighboring communities such as Playa del Carmen. Ecotourism in Tulum and most of Costa Maya has helped protect area wildlife and the natural surroundings.

Temporarily decreasing tourism were Hurricane Gilbert in 1988, Hurricane Wilma in 2005, and the state of the U.S. economy in 2010. Fortunately, these setbacks have not permanently affected tourism as the peninsula's driving force of economic development.

Religion

Although Mexico has no official religion, 89% of the population consider themselves Roman Catholic. Second only to Brazil, Mexico has more Catholics than anywhere else in the world, even though less than half attend church. Very few Maya people in the Yucatán Peninsula still practice traditional rituals of offerings and sacrifices of small animals. Central to the Maya religion is the idea of the duality of the soul, one part eternal, and the other supernatural. Only 7% of the population consider themselves Protestant, followed by Eastern Orthodox, Seventh-Day Adventists, Jehovah's Witnesses, and Mormons.

Sports

Soccer (or *fútbol* as they say in Spanish) is the most popular sport in Mexico. Locals have taken the game very seriously ever since it became a professional sport there in 1900. The country's most successful teams are Club Deportivo Guadalajara, Club América, Toluca, Cruz Azul, and Chivas.

Second to soccer is boxing, with Mexico's biggest knockout rival being Puerto Rico. After the United States, Mexico has produced the most boxing world champions. For more than 100 years, baseball has been popular in Mexico. There are 16 teams competing in the *Liga Mexicana de Béisbol* (Mexican Baseball League).

With more than 150 fairways dotting the country, golfing has gained notoriety among the locals, and has helped promote tourism with five professional tournaments, including the Mayakoba Golf Classic.

More traditional sports include bullfighting, Mexican wrestling (also known as *lucha libre*), and *charrería*, based on a series of Mexican equestrian events.

Cash Crops

Although tourism is the peninsula's main source of income, both agriculture and fishing are also great economic contributors. Before the tourism boom, production was limited to salt, mahogany, red cedar, and chicle (traditionally used for chewing gum). Until 1960 the main crop was henequen, an indigenous plant that produces sisal fiber used to make rope. Although not as lucrative as it once was, henequen is still manufactured in the north-central region. The peninsula's eastern area raises 65% of the state's livestock, while the southern region, near Peto and Tzucacab, is known for corn, citrus, sugarcane, and cattle. Today the Yucatán Peninsula exports more than 1,500 products, ranging from sponges and oranges to furniture and chocolates.

WEDDINGS AND HONEYMOONS

Imagine exchanging vows on a white sandy beach against a backdrop of swaying palms and the turquoise waters of the Caribbean. Your dream wedding can become a reality as long as you know the necessary steps to take when saying "I do" in Mexico.

Unfortunately, you'll need a lot more than just the wedding rings when organizing your tropical nuptials. Couples will need to bring passports, original birth certificates, tourist cards, and results of blood tests taken in Mexico two days before the wedding. Most clinics charge $150 per person for the required tests of RPR and HIV, and Thorax X-rays.

You also must have four witnesses at the ceremony, all of whom must be over 18 and have passports. If either the bride or groom was previously married, it's mandatory to wait a full year from the date that the divorce was final. Divorce papers must be translated into Spanish and notarized. In the case of a deceased spouse, you have to present a certified copy of the death certificate.

In Mexico the only marriages that are legally recognized are those that are conducted at the Oficina del Registro Civil (Civil Registers Office). The fee can be as much as $250, and you'll find that most people there don't speak English, so plan accordingly. Regulations vary from state to state in Mexico, so contact the Mexican Tourism Board for specifics about your desired wedding location.

Beautiful Backdrops

With so much to offer, the Yucatán Peninsula is one of the most sought-after spots for destination weddings. In fact, this growing trend in beachside nuptials has increased by 200% in the last decade. It's no wonder: the Caribbean coastline not only makes for an incredible backdrop, but it's also a great way to combine a wedding and honeymoon.

Surprisingly, exchanging vows in Mexico can be considerably cheaper than a traditional wedding back home. Some smaller hotels can organize beautiful ceremonies, including food and music, for under $5,000. If you book your entire wedding party at the hotel, special rates and upgrades are generally available, and you can have the entire place to yourselves. Between May and November, rates are at their lowest, but you might end up with a soggy ceremony, especially during hurricane months of August and September.

There are dozens of wedding planners and professional photographers in Cancún, Cozumel, Isla Mujeres, Mérida, and Playa del Carmen. Whether you choose a white sandy beach in Cozumel or a colorful hacienda in Mérida, there's no shortage of ceremony settings for your big day.

Honeymoons

The peninsula's countless treasures, ranging from Mayan ruins to fishing villages, make it a haven for honeymooners. Beach-bound newlyweds have plenty of resort options along Riviera Maya, many of which have luxury spas with treatments for two. Ideal for both weddings and honeymoons, Tulum offers ancient ruins, beautiful beaches, and dozens of eco-lodges willing to host simple weddings with vegetarian buffets and yoga classes between events. Other popular honeymoon spots are Isla Mujeres, where you can swim with nurse sharks, and Cozumel, with its excellent snorkeling and diving.

KIDS AND FAMILIES

Riddled with natural wonders, the Yucatán Peninsula has plenty of activities that the whole family can enjoy. The warm Caribbean waters are ideal for water sports such as swimming, snorkeling, and kayaking, and some areas even have roped-off sections designated for children. If you're vacationing in Cancún, beaches facing Bahía de Mujeres tend to have calmer waters and softer sand than those facing the Caribbean. Farther out, there may be undertows or riptides, so take note of warning signs and colored flags posted daily.

Kid-Friendly Activities

For teens, there are adrenaline-pumping water activities like Jet Skiing, banana boat rides, parasailing, and diving. Smaller children may prefer interactive programs like those available at Dolphin Discovery. There are locations in Cancún, Isla Mujeres, Cozumel, and Puerto Aventuras, and the tour includes encounters with manatees and sea lions, and a chance to swim with the dolphins.

For parents wanting to introduce their children to history, combine a tour of the Tulum ruins with a day at the beach, or opt for the Cobá ruins, where your entire family can explore jungle trails by mountain bike. Cancún's all-inclusive resorts have plenty to keep the kids busy, including swimming pools, children's programs, and on-site water sports. The nearby Isla Shopping Village has an interactive aquarium. Also located in Zona Hotelera is Plaza Kukulcán, an upscale mall with a game arcade and play area.

Isla Mujeres is home to El Garrafon National Park, where you can go snorkeling, swimming, hiking, or biking. To blend nature and education, visit the island's turtle farm, where you can see rescued turtle hatchlings and visit an on-site museum.

Choosing a Destination

Just 16 km (10 miles) south of Tulum, the Reserva de la Biosfera Sian Ka'an has hundreds of species of wildlife in their freshwater lagoons, mangrove swamps, and tropical forests. The beaches here are excellent for swimming, snorkeling, and camping.

The colorful city of Mérida has folkloric shows, free concerts, and open-air markets where local crafts are sold. South of Mérida are the impressive Grutas de Loltun, one of the largest cave systems on the Yucatán Peninsula.

The quaint fishing villages of Puerto Morelos and Puerto Aventuras are excellent for families and close to the 250-acre ecological theme park, Xcaret. Here families can experience a butterfly pavilion, bird aviary, bat cave, and dozens of water activities. Catering to adventure-seekers, the neighboring Xplor lets you swim in a stalactite river, ride in an amphibian-vehicle, or soar across the park on the longest zip-line in Mexico. At the entrance to Puerto Morelos is Croco-Cun, an animal farm where you can feed monkeys and hold baby crocodiles.

To escape the heat, families can take a dip in one of the hundreds of cenotes that dot the peninsula. These freshwater pools are ideal for snorkeling and swimming. For a day of horseback riding, Rancho Loma Bonita has tours along the beach or on the jungle trails near Playa del Carmen. Although known for its snorkeling and diving, Cozumel also offers horseback riding, mini-golf, and fishing expeditions.

GREAT ITINERARIES

CANCÚN AND DAY TRIPS

Cancún is the place where you'll likely start your visit. If sunbathing, water sports, and parties that last until the wee hours of the morn are what you're after, you won't need to set foot outside the Zona Hotelera (or even your resort). If you're staying for a week or so, though, you should definitely check out some of the attractions that are an easy day-tripping distance from Cancún.

■**TIP→** Driving is the best way to see the peninsula, especially if your time is limited. However, there's nothing in this itinerary that can't be accessed by either bus or taxi.

Days 1 and 2: Arrival and Cancún

After arriving at your hotel, spend your first day or two doing what comes naturally: lounging at the hotel pool, playing in the waves, parasailing, and going out for dinner and drinks. If you start to feel restless your second day, you can head to the Ruinas del Rey, go tequila tasting at La Destileria, or take a ride into El Centro (downtown Cancún) to browse the shops and open-air markets along Avenida Tulum and grab some authentic and delicious Mexican food.

Day 3: Cozumel or Isla Mujeres

Spend the day visiting one of the islands off Mexico's Caribbean Coast. If beach-combing and a laid-back meal of fresh seafood under a *palapa* (thatched roof) sound appealing, take a ferry from the Embarcadero Dock at Playa Linda and head for Isla Mujeres. If you like underwater sea life, drive or take a bus south from Cancún to Puerto Morelos, where you can catch a boat over to Cozumel. There are more than 100 scuba and snorkeling outfits on the island, all of which run trips out to the spectacular Meso-american Barrier Reef.

Day 4: Playa del Carmen and Xcaret

In the morning, pack your bathing suit and towel, take a taxi to the Xcaret bus station near Playa Caracol, and catch a 9:45 bus to this magical nature park. You can easily spend an entire day here snorkeling through underwater caves, visiting the butterfly pavilion, sea-turtle nursery, and reef aquarium, and (if you reserve a spot early) bonding with dolphins. Alternatively, get up early and take a rental car south along Carretera 307 toward Playa del Carmen, about an hour and a half away. Once you arrive, head to Avenida 5 along the waterfront where you can choose from dozens of places to lunch. If you want to splurge, try the ceviche or the namesake specialty at Blue Lobster. Then spend the afternoon either wandering among the shops and cafés and watching the street performers, or else jump in the car and head 10 minutes south of town to Xcaret.

Days 5 and 6: Tulum and Cobá

If you have the time, it's worth spending a day at each of these beautiful Mayan-ruin sites near Playa del Carmen; each is entirely different from the other. Cobá, which is about a half-hour's drive west of Tulum, is a less-visited but spectacular ancient city that's completely surrounded by jungle. Tulum, the only major Mayan site built right on the water, has less-stunning architecture, but a dazzling location overlooking the Caribbean. After picking through the ruins, you can take a path down from the cliffs and laze for a while on the fabulous beach below. Be warned, though: since Tulum is just a 45-minute drive south from Playa, it's the Yucatán's most popular Mayan site.

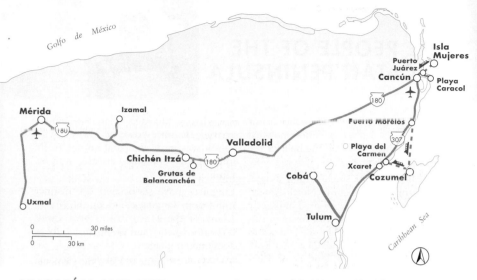

YUCATÁN AND THE MAYAN INTERIOR

If you have more than a week to spend on the peninsula, you're in luck. You'll have time to visit some of the most beautiful— and famous—ruin sites in the country, and to explore some authentic-Mexican inland communities that feel worlds away from the more touristy coast.

Day 7: Valladolid and Chichén Itzá

Get up early, check out of your hotel, and make the drive inland along Carretera 180 toward the world-renowned Chichén Itzá ruins. Stop en route for a late breakfast or early lunch in Valladolid, about 2½ hours from Cancún. One of the best places to go is the casual eatery at Cenote Zaci, where you can also swim in the lovely jade-green sinkhole. Continue another half hour to Chichén Itzá and check into one of the area hotels (the Hacienda Chichén is a terrific choice). Then spend the afternoon exploring the site before it closes at 5 pm. Visit El Castillo; check out the former marketplace, steam bath, observatory, and temples honoring formidable Mayan gods. Chill for an hour or two before the light-and-sound show, then turn in after dinner at your hotel.

Days 8 and 9: West to Mérida

Either take an easterly detour for an on-the-hour tour at the limestone caverns of Grutas de Balancanchén, or head immediately west on Carretera 180 for the hour-long drive to Mérida. After checking into a hotel in the city (Villa Mercedes is an especially delightful choice), wander the zócalo and surrounding streets. Spend the next day shopping, visiting museums, and enjoying Mérida's vibrant city scene.

Days 10 and 11: East to Cancún and Departure

The drive from Mérida or Uxmal back to Cancún will take you some five or six hours on Carretera 180, so if you're flying out of Cancún airport the same day, get an early start. Otherwise, if you can afford to take your time, stop at the lovely town of Izamal on the way back. At this charming town, famous for its bright yellow buildings, you can take a horse-drawn carriage tour of artisans' shops, visit the stately cathedral, or climb to the top of crumbling Kinich Kakmó pyramid. Arrive in Cancún in the afternoon, take a last swim on the sugar-sand beach before dinner, and get a good night's sleep at your hotel before your departure the next day.

THE PEOPLE OF THE YUCATÁN PENINSULA

The Maya people, whose ancient ruins have made the Yucatán a world-renowned attraction, also make up the bulk of the area's population.

The Maya are the single largest indigenous group on the entire North American continent. Although predominantly located on the Yucatán, members of this group have also settled in other Mexican states such as Campeche, Quintana Roo, Tabasco, and Chiapas. Outside of Mexico, the Maya can be found in Guatemala, Belize, Honduras, and El Salvador. Their total population is estimated at about 7 million, with 1.2 million living on the Yucatán Peninsula.

The Maya are rightfully proud of their history, which dates back to a period immediately following the rise of the Olmec culture. After the fall of the Olmecs, the Maya rose to power and settled in the Yucatán Peninsula, where they developed several city-states including that of Chichén Itzá.

Mayan architecture, much of it ceremonial in nature, has been archaeologically classified as dating back some 3,000 years. Well-preserved hieroglyphics found in the Yucatán trace the presence of the Maya to 200 BC or before. More than 100 ancient Maya ruins still exist today, many of them drawing travelers from around the world to the Yucatán each year.

These ancient and mysterious ruins clearly show that the Maya were once a regional superpower, and that Maya nobles had widespread influence. This remarkable group inhabited the Yucatán Peninsula long before the arrival of the Spanish.

The Spanish fought to colonize the Yucatán well into the 1500s. The first attempt took place in 1527, but it was only 20 years later, in 1546, that the Spanish saw victory. But long before the Spanish arrived, the once-powerful Mayan civilization was in decline, and no one really knows why—possibly disease, war, or famine.

Linguists have associated 24 distinct indigenous languages among the Maya. Many of the Maya in this area speak "Yucatec Maya" and use Spanish only as a second language.

The Maya continue to blend the elements of their ancient worship practices and rituals (minus the human sacrifice) with more-contemporary religious practices. Many still wear traditional clothing, and construct the oblong, thatch-roof houses of their forebears. The Mayan passion to preserve their long history can be seen in the highly valued handicrafts that they create with the same skill and artistry as their ancestors.

CANCÚN

WELCOME TO CANCÚN

TOP REASONS TO GO

★ **Dancing the night away:** Salsa, cumbia, reggae, mariachi, hip-hop, and electronic music dizzy the air of the Zona Hotelera's many nightclubs.

★ **Exploring the nearby Mayan ruins:** Trips to remarkable sites like Tulum, Cobá, and Chichén Itzá can easily be accomplished in a day.

★ **Getting wild on the water:** Rent Jet Skis, a Windsurfer, or a kayak, and skim across the sea or Laguna Nichupté.

★ **Browsing for Mexican crafts:** The colorful stalls of Mercado Veintiocho will certainly hold something that catches your eye.

★ **Indulging in local flavor:** Dishes like lime soup and *poc chuc* (pork with achiote and onions) and drinks like tamarind margaritas pay respect to traditional cuisine.

1 El Centro. Cancún's mainland commercial center, known as El Centro, provides an authentic glimpse into modern-day Mexico and a colorful alternative to the Zona Hotelera. Many of the restaurants scattered throughout this downtown area offer surprising bursts of culture and Mexican flavor. With more than 800,000 permanent residents, Cancún is full of shops, cafés, and open-air markets that cater mainly to locals. Although the majority of tourists choose to bask on the beaches of Cancún, those who venture into the heart of El Centro will be glad they did—prices are much more reasonable and the food is outstanding.

2 The Zona Hotelera Norte. A separate northern strip called Punta Sam, north of Puerto Juárez, is sometimes referred to as the Zona Hotelera Norte (Northern Hotel Zone). This area is quieter than the main Zona, but there are some newer resorts, marinas, and restaurants. This is also a good launching point for those heading to the nearby Isla Mujeres.

3 The Zona Hotelera. Ideal for those wanting to stay local, the Hotel Zone is structured along a 22½-km

(14-mile) stretch known as Kukulcán Boulevard. On the Caribbean side, dozens of resorts and condominiums tightly line the beachfront like a row of Legos. On the inland side, Laguna Nichupté is home to water sports, shopping malls, seafood restaurants, and golf courses. At the northern tip of this main thoroughfare, near Punta Cancún, is a pack of nightclubs, discos, and bars—a nighttime favorite for those who like to party.

GETTING ORIENTED

Over the past three decades, Cancún has turned into the Miami of the south, with international investors pouring money into property development. The main attractions for most travelers to Cancún lie along the Zona Hotelera—a 22½-km (14-mile) barrier island shaped roughly like the number 7. To the east is the Caribbean, and to the west you'll find a system of lagoons, the largest of which is Laguna Nichupté. Downtown Cancún—aka El Centro—is 4 km (2½ miles) west of the Zona Hotelera on the mainland.

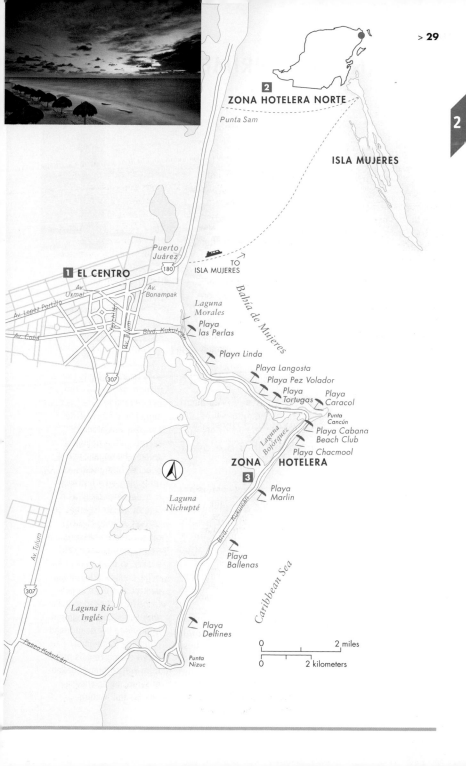

2

ZONA HOTELERA NORTE

Punta Sam

ISLA MUJERES

Puerto Juárez

1 EL CENTRO

180

TO
ISLA MUJERES

Av. Uxmal   *Av. Bonampak*

Av. López Portillo

Av. Cobá

Blvd. Kukulcán

Laguna Morales

Playa las Perlas

Bahía de Mujeres

307

Playa Linda

Playa Langosta
Playa Pez Volador
Playa Tortugas   **Playa Caracol**

Punta Cancún

Playa Cabana Beach Club

Playa Chacmool

ZONA HOTELERA

Laguna Bojorquez

3

Playa Marlin

Laguna Nichupté

Blvd. Kukulcán

Playa Ballenas

Av. Tulum

307

Laguna Río Inglés

Playa Delfines

Caribbean Sea

Paseo Kukulcán

Punta Nizuc

0   2 miles
0   2 kilometers

MEXICAN FOOD PRIMER

The varied culinary characteristics of each region make it difficult to define "Mexican food" as a whole. Its complexity and diversity is a direct result of the ingredients that are available within each region.

Still, there are overlapping ingredients used in the majority of regions throughout the county. The most frequently used spices are chile powder, cumin, oregano, cilantro, epazote, cinnamon, and cocoa. Chipotle, a smoke-dried jalapeño chile, is common, as are tomatoes, garlic, onions, and peppers. Rice is the most common grain, but corn, beans, and chiles are considered the cornerstones of Mexican cuisine.

The Spanish introduced rice, wheat, olive oil, nuts, cinnamon, wine, and parsley, and a variety of animals including cattle, chickens, goats, sheep, and pigs. These ingredients were incorporated with indigenous corn-based dishes, beans, turkey, fish, vanilla, chocolate, and fruits such as guava, pineapple, and papaya, giving us what we now know as Mexican food.

JUST DESSERTS

Locally grown fruits like mango, mamey, cherimoya, pomegranate, tuna (cactus apple), and strawberries are delicious alone or served with a dollop of cream and sugar. Stewed peaches and guavas are refreshing on a hot summer day, especially with a side of *nieves* (sherbet or sorbet). Among Mexico's most common desserts are *tres leches* (sponge cake soaked in three types of milk), churros (fried-dough pastry), and *arroz con leche* (rice cooked in milk with sugar and cinnamon). *Capirotada* (Mexican bread pudding), traditionally eaten during Lent, is made from French bread soaked in syrup, sugar, cheese, raisins, and walnuts.

REGIONAL CUISINES

Mexican food is much more than burritos, tacos, and rice and beans. Traditional recipes reach far beyond these stereotypical dishes, varying by region as a result of the climate, geography, local ingredients, and cultural differences among the inhabitants.

Yucatán Peninsula. Characterized by its Mayan heritage, the Yucatán Peninsula has a strong European influence due to its connection with the continent and its geographical distance from Mexico City. Specialties of the region include *cochinita pibil* (seasoned pork colored with annatto seed and wrapped in banana leaves), turkey with black stuffing, and *papadzules* (tortillas filled with hard-boiled eggs and topped with a pumpkin seed sauce). Unique to Yucatán's cooking is the earthen pit oven where meats are slowly cooked with *recado negro* or *chilmole* (a blend of dried chiles that are set aflame and ground with spices to create a paste).

Mexico City and Environs (including Puebla). Largely influenced by the rest of the country, Mexico City still has original dishes such as *carnitas* (braised or roasted pork), *menudos* (tripe stew), and *pozole* (pork and hominy soup). Mexico City is also known for its incredible cheeses, tamales, and yellow-corn tortillas. The favored *mixiote* (mutton wrapped in maguey leaves) is slowly

steam-baked in a pit oven. Puebla produces various species of cacti including maguey and nopal, which can be eaten as a vegetable (de-spined, of course) or used to make juices and sorbets. Puebla is best known for *mole poblano* (thick, chocolate-tinged sauce) and *chiles en Nogada* (stuffed chiles topped with a walnut cream sauce).

Oaxaca. With a strong pre-Hispanic influence, the state of Oaxaca has the second-highest percentage of indigenous residents in Mexico, exceeded only by the Yucatán. *Gusanos de maguey* (worms) and chapulines (grasshoppers), which were originally indigenous foods, are fried and eaten like roasted peanuts or sprinkled onto tacos. Oaxaca takes pride in its assortment of chiles, including yellow and black *chilhuacles, costeños,* and the large, light green *chiles de agua.*

Veracruz. Spanning the coast of the Gulf of Mexico, the cuisine here is characterized geographically by fish and seafood. It is also one of the most versatile agricultural regions of Mexico. Nut- and seed-based sauces are very popular, as are spicy chicken and vegetable dishes. Spanish influence is evident in the *pescado a la Veracruzana,* fish made with tomato sauce, capers, and olives.

(*Left*) Cancún's famous seafood. (*Top*) Steaming white pozole. (*Bottom*) Salsa verde goes with just about everything.

Updated by
Marie Elena
Martinez

Cancún is a great place to experience 21st-century Mexico, because it has everything you'd want in a vacation: shopping, sports, spas, and beaches. Here you'll find five-star resorts, exceptional food, Mexican culture, and natural beauty within minutes of the world-famous Mayan ruins. That said, there isn't much that's quaint or historic in this distinctively modern city, many of whose residents have embraced the accoutrements of urban middle-class life—cell phones, Internet, cable TV—that are found all over the world.

Most locals live on the mainland in the part of the city called El Centro and work in the posh Zona Hotelera, whose main drag is called Boulevard Kukulcán. Kilometer markers alongside Boulevard Kukulcán indicate where you are, starting from Km 1 near El Centro to Km 20 at the southern tip of Punta Nizuc. The area in between consists entirely of hotels, restaurants, shopping complexes, marinas, and time-share condominiums. Most travelers base themselves in this 22½-km (14-mile) stretch of paradise, unless the charm of El Centro's city life trumps the beach.

The party atmosphere of Zona Hotelera has inevitably earned it the title "spring break capital of the world." Dozens of bars and nightclubs cater to college students just south of Punta Cancún at Km 9. Fortunately, this late-night/early-morning scene is contained within a small area, far from the larger resorts. Although Cancún is a magnet for youth on the loose, families are drawn to the limitless water sports, pristine beaches, and children's activities including theme parks, live entertainment, and dolphin programs.

For authentic Mexican food at some of the best hole-in-the-wall cantinas, travel west of Avenida Tulum (El Centro's main street) to Yaxchilán. The more upscale area of El Centro is east of Tulum to Avenida Bonampak. Although El Centro is less visited by travelers than Zona

Hotelera, the downtown area holds cultural gems that will remind you that you really are in Mexico.

PLANNING

TIMING

There's a lot to see and do in Cancún—if you can force yourself away from the beach, that is. Understandably, many visitors stay here a week, or longer, without ever leaving the silky sands and seductive comforts of their resorts. If you're game to do some exploring, though, it's a good idea to allow an extra two or three days for day trips to nearby eco-parks and archaeological sites.

WHEN TO GO

The sun shines an average of 253 days a year in Cancún. The months between December and April have nearly perfect weather, with temperatures hovering around 84°F during the day and 64°F at night. May through September are much hotter and more humid, with temperatures that can top 97°F. The rainy season starts in mid-September and lasts until mid-November, bringing afternoon downpours that can last anywhere from 30 minutes to two hours. El Centro's streets often get flooded during these storms, and traffic can grind to a halt.

High season for Cancún starts at the end of November and lasts until the first week in April. Between December 15 and January 5, hotel prices are at their highest, and may rise as much as 30% to 50% above regular rates. If you plan to visit during Christmas, spring break, or Easter, you should book at least three months in advance.

If you have travel-date flexibility, you can save 20% to 50% on accommodations during **low season** (the day after Easter through mid-December). The closing months of spring break and summer (May and October) still offer plenty of sunshine, and you won't have to rub elbows with other travelers on the beach.

Although costs drop from August to October, travelers might return home waterlogged rather than tanned. Lower prices and pleasant weather are available during the **shoulder season** from October 1 to December 15. Keep in mind that winter's strong north winds tend to eat away at the beaches, uprooting surface sea kelp. Less sand and choppy waters may result in overcrowded swimming pools.

GETTING HERE AND AROUND
AIR TRAVEL

The Aeropuerto Internacional Cancún is 16 km (9 miles) southwest of the heart of Cancún and 10 km (6 miles) from the Zona Hotelera's southernmost point. There are direct flights from some major U.S. cities, with some flights connecting in Mexico City. It's simple to get to or from the airport: buses leave every hour from Cancún Airport to downtown Cancún, or you can take taxis or *colectivos* (mini-buses).

BICYCLE TRAVEL

Cancún is not the sort of place you can get to know on foot, although there's a bicycle and walking path that starts downtown at the beginning of the Zona Hotelera and continues through to Punta Nizuc. The beginning of the path parallels a grassy strip of Boulevard Kukulcán decorated with reproductions of ancient Mexican art.

BUS TRAVEL

For farther-flung destinations, buses leave El Centro's terminal for all parts of Mexico. *Autobuses del Oriente,* or ADO, is one of the oldest bus lines in Mexico and offers regular first-class service to Puerto Morelos and Playa del Carmen every 15 minutes from 4 am until midnight. Tickets, available outside Terminal 2 Baggage Claim, are less than $10 one-way. Playa Express has express buses that leave from a small terminal across from the main bus station every 10 minutes for Puerto Morelos and Playa del Carmen. Mayab Bus Lines has second-class buses leaving for destinations along the Riviera Maya every hour.

Bus Contacts Autobuses del Oriente (ADO) ☎ *998/884-5552* ⊕ *www.ado. com.mx.* **Mayab Bus Lines** ☎ *998/884-5552.* **Playa Express** ☎ *998/887-6782.* **Terminal de Autobuses** ✉ *Pino Mz. 23 Sm 56, between Avs. Tulum and Uxmal, Sm 23* ☎ *998/884-5552.*

CAR TRAVEL

If you are planning to visit only Cancún, you don't need to (and probably shouldn't) rent a car. But if you want to explore the region, a car can be convenient, though expensive. Be sure to read our extensive guidelines regarding road conditions, insurance requirements, and costs (*see* ⇨ *Car Travel in Travel Smart*) so that you can make an informed decision regarding whether renting a car is for you.

Car Rental Contacts Adocar Rental ✉ *Plaza Nautilus, Blvd. Kukulcán, Km 3.5, Zona Hotelera* ☎ *998/849-4233* ⊕ *www.adocarrental.com.* **Avis** ✉ *Aeropuerto Internacional Benito Juárez, Zona Hotelera* ☎ *998/886-0221* ⊕ *www.avis.com.* **Hertz** ✉ *At Cancún Airport, Carretera de Cancún Chetumal, Km 22* ☎ *999/911-8040, 800/405-7000 toll-free* ⊕ *www.hertz.com.* **Mónaco Rent a Car** ✉ *Av. Yaxchilán 65, Lote 5, Sm 25* ☎ *998/884-6540* ⊕ *www.monacorentacar.com.*

TAXI TRAVEL

Taxi rides within the Zona Hotelera cost $6–$10; between the Zona Hotelera and El Centro they run $8 and up; and to the ferries at Punta Sam or Puerto Juárez, fares are $15–$20 or more. You can always find a taxi in Cancún, but make sure you check the fare before accepting a ride. A list of rates can be found in the lobby of most hotels or you can ask the concierge. Keep in mind it's also easy and cheap to get around Cancún by bus.

ESSENTIALS

BANKS AND CURRENCY EXCHANGE

In 2010, Mexican authorities passed a law stating that foreign travelers may not exchange more than $1,500 U.S.D. (cash) per person per month into Mexican pesos. Mexican travelers are also limited to $1,500 U.S.D. cash per person, per month, with the added restriction of no more than $300 U.S.D. cash per day. Other methods of payment, including credit cards, traveler's checks, and non-American foreign currencies, are not affected by this new law.

When exchanging foreign currency at banks and hotels in Mexico, you must show your passport. Most banks have ATMs where you can withdraw local currency, or you can pay for services with a debit or credit card without restrictions. There's no limit on the number of purchases or the amount of each individual transaction. It is recommended to have Mexican pesos on hand shortly after you arrive in Cancún, especially if you intend to use public transportation or pay cash during your trip.

EMERGENCIES

Contacts Green Angels (for highway breakdowns) ☏ *078*. **Hospital Amat (emergency hospital)** ✉ *Av. Náder 13, Sm 2* ☏ *998/887–4422*. **Hospital de las Americas** ✉ *Avs. Bonampak and Nichupté, next to Plaza las Américas, Sm 7* ☏ *998/881–3400, 998/881–3434 for emergencies*. **Municipal Police** ✉ *Av. Xcaret, Sm 21, Cancún* ☏ *998/884–1913*.

VISITOR INFORMATION

Cancún Convention and Visitors Bureau (*CVB*). The Cancún Convention and Visitors Bureau has lots of information about area accommodations, restaurants, and attractions. ✉ *Zona Hotelera, Blvd. Kukulcán, Km 9, Cancún Center* ☏ *998/881–2745* ⊕ *www.cancun.travel*.

HOTELS

A growing number of Cancún hotels are now encouraging people to make their reservations online. Some allow you to book rooms on their websites; even hotels without their own sites usually offer reservations via online booking agencies such as ⊕ *www.docancun.com* and ⊕ *www.cancuntoday.net*. Since hotels customarily work with several different agencies, it's a good idea to shop around online for the best rates before booking.

Besides being convenient, booking online can often get you a 10% to 20% discount on room rates. The downside, however, is that there are occasional breakdowns in communication between booking agencies and hotels. You may arrive to find your Spanish-speaking front-desk clerk has no record of your online reservation, or only has a room that's different from the one you specified. To prevent such mishaps from ruining your vacation, be sure to print out copies of all your Internet transactions, including receipts and confirmations, and take them with you.

When booking a hotel online, be sure to ask if the hotel is currently undergoing renovation. Early-morning construction can be a painful wake-up call for Cancún party animals.

DINING AND LODGING PRICES

Prices in the restaurant reviews are the average cost of a main course at dinner or, if dinner is not served, at lunch; taxes and service charges are generally included. Prices in the hotel reviews are the lowest cost of a standard double room in high season, excluding taxes, service charges, and meal plans (except at all-inclusives). Prices for rentals are the lowest per-night cost for a one-bedroom unit in high season.

SAFETY

Cancún is one of the safest cities in Mexico. Reported violence generally takes place 2,090 km (1,300 miles) from Cancún on the northern border of Mexico, the same distance from New York to Texas. Don't be surprised to see Tourist Police patrolling the Hotel Zone, especially during the holidays and high season when security is increased. The C4 Surveillance and Rescue Center monitors the tourist area through video cameras installed in strategic points throughout the city, and an emergency 911 call center is now in place. Visitors are still advised to exercise caution and use common sense while traveling.

TOURS

GENERAL TOURS

Mayaland Tours. Tours to Mérida, the Uxmal ruins, and the flamingo park at Celestún are available. Self-guided tours to Tulum and Cobá can also be arranged; the agency provides a car, maps, and an itinerary. The agency can also help with accommodations. ✉ *Calle Robalo 30, Sm 3* ☎ *998/887–2495, 877/240–5864 in U.S.* ⊕ *www.mayaland.com.*

Olympus Tours. Specializing in tours around Cancún, the agency can book your reservations to Xcaret, Xel-Há, and other local adventure parks. ✉ *Av. Yaxchilán, Lote 13, Sm 17, Mza 2* ☎ *998/881–9030, 786/338–9358 in U.S.* ⊕ *www.olympus-tours.com.*

BOAT TOURS

Kolumbus Tours. Eco-excursions to Isla Contoy are available Tuesday, Thursday, and Sunday on a replica boat of the *Pinta*. A daily combination tour to Isla Contoy and Isla Mujeres is also offered on board the *Maltese Falcon*. ✉ *Punta Conoco 36, Sm 24* ☎ *998/884–5333, 800/715–3375 toll-free in Mexico* ⊕ *www.kolumbustours.com.*

Sea Passion Catamaran. Day trips (which includes a buffet lunch, open bar, and snorkel equipment) to Isla Mujeres, the Riviera Maya, and Tulum are available with this agency. ✉ *El Embarcadero, Blvd. Kukulcán, Km 4.5, Zona Hotelera* ☎ *998/849–5573* ⊕ *www.seapassion.net.*

BREATHING BUBBLE TOURS

B.O.B. (Breathing Observation Bubble) Cancún. B.O.B. Cancún lets you sit on a machine resembling an underwater motor scooter, and steer your way through the reef while wearing a pressurized helmet that lets you breathe normally ($75). ✉ *El Embarcadero, Blvd. Kukulcán, Km 4.5, Loc E-3, Zona Hotelera* ☎ *998/849–4440* ☉ *Closed Sun.*

ECOTOURS

Eco Colors. Bike tours, butterfly- and bird-watching adventures, as well as kayaking, diving, and snorkeling eco-adventures can be booked through Eco Colors. ✉ *Calle Camarón 32, Sm 27* ☎ *998/884–3667* ⊕ *www.ecotravelmexico.com.*

Reserva Ecológica El Edén. Reserva Ecológica El Edén offers a wide variety of tours that investigate the biodiversity of the surrounding region. ✉ *Teocaltiche 207, Sm 45, M4 L3, El Centro* ☎ *998/880–5032* ⊕ *www. reservaeleden.org.mx.*

SUBMARINE TOURS

AquaWorld's Sub See Explorer. This "floating submarine" is a glass-bottom boat that submerges halfway into the water. ✉ *Blvd. Kukul-cán, Km 15.2, Zona Hotelera* ☎ *998/848–8327, 877/730–4054 in U.S.* ⊕ *www.aquaworld.com.mx.*

2

EXPLORING

The best way to explore Cancún is by hopping on one of the public buses that run between the Zona Hotelera and El Centro. The cost is 75¢ no matter how far you go. Taxis from the Zona to El Centro cost anywhere from 150 pesos ($12) to 250 pesos ($20) each way. A more affordable alternative is to catch a north-bound bus to the Kukulcán–Bonampak intersection, which marks the beginning of El Centro. From here, you can explore by foot or flag down a taxi to your area of choice. A taxi to almost anywhere within El Centro costs around 40 pesos ($3). If you want to get a taste of downtown culture, start at the colorful Mercado Veintiocho or Parque de las Palapas. To return to the Hotel Zone, take a taxi to the Chedraui on Avenida Tulum and then catch a bus that passes every few minutes toward the Hotel Zone. (Don't be alarmed if a man in a clown suit roams the aisle in search of money: at night the buses come alive with all sorts of amateur performers, from accordionists to jugglers, hoping to earn a few pesos.) The year 2012 saw the opening of Museo Maya, a modern new exhibition within the hotel zone that showcases the area's archeological history. One of Cancún's few "sights," it's definitely worth a visit if you have the time.

> **WORD OF MOUTH**
>
> "You will not entirely 'beat' the college students by going to Mexico In mid-February (instead of going in March). Canadian universities (colleges) have what is called reading week in mid-February, and it is sort of the equivalent of spring break. The students head south by the thousands during that week, and Cancún is one of their primary destinations." —succeed

South of Punta Cancún, Boulevard Kukulcán becomes a busy road and is difficult for pedestrians to cross. It's also punctuated by steeply inclined driveways that turn into the hotels, most of which are set back at least 100 yards from the road. The lagoon side of the boulevard consists of scrubby stretches of land alternating with marinas, shopping centers, and restaurants. ■**TIP**➜ Because there are so few sights, there are no orientation tours of Cancún: just do the local bus circuit to get a feel for the island's layout. The buses run 24 hours a day, and you'll rarely have to wait more than five minutes.

When you first visit El Centro, the downtown layout might not be self-evident. It's not based on a grid but rather on a circular pattern. The whole city is divided into districts called Super Manzanas (abbreviated Sm in this book), each with its own central square or park. In general, walks through downtown are somewhat unpleasant, with whizzing cars, corroding pathways, and overgrown weeds. Sidewalks disappear for brief moments, forcing pedestrians to cross grassy inlets and thin strips of land separating four lanes of traffic. Few people seem to know exactly where anything is, even the locals who live in El Centro. When exploring on foot, expect to get lost at least once and enjoy it—you may just stumble on a courtyard café or a lively cantina.

TOP ATTRACTIONS

Fodor's Choice
★

Cancún Underwater Museum. Combining art and nature, Sculptor Jason de Caires Taylor has created underwater museums (known locally as MUSA) off the shores of Punta Cancún, Punta Nizuc, and Manchones Reef in Isla Mujeres. His main body of work features more than 400 lifelike statues that serve as artificial reefs to attract marine life. The displays have conveniently been placed in shallow areas for viewing by divers, snorkelers, and glass-bottom boats. Acting as a restoration project, this artificial habitat also helps restore the natural reefs that have suffered damage over the years. ⊠ *Punta Cancún, Punta Nizuc, and Manchones Reef in Isla Mujeres, Cancún and Isla Mujeres* ⊕ *www. underwatersculpture.com* 🖼 *Free.*

El Centro. Nearly two decades ago, downtown Cancún was the place to be after a day at the beach. The once-barren Hotel Zone had very limited dining options, so tourists strolled the active streets of Avenida Tulum, Yaxchilán, and Parque de las Palapas. With the emergence of luxury resorts and mass tourism, a major shift brought the focus back to the Hotel Zone. Today many visitors are unaware that the downtown area even exists, while others consider "downtown" to be the string of flea markets near the convention center. In reality, El Centro's malls and markets offer a glimpse of Mexico's urban lifestyle. Avenida Tulum, the main street, is marked by a huge sculpture of shells and starfish in the middle of a traffic circle. This iconic Cancún sculpture, which many locals refer to as "el ceviche," is particularly dramatic at night when the lights are turned on. El Centro is also home to many restaurants and bars, as well as **Mercado Veintiocho** (Market 28), an enormous crafts market just off Avenidas Yaxchilán and Sunyaxchén. For bargain shopping, hit the stores and small strip malls along Avenida Tulum.

Museo Maya De Cancún. Opened in December 2012, this modern, new museum in the Zona Hotelera sits in the middle of a small, lush jungle of excavated local ruins. Air-conditioned second-floor exhibits, accessible by elevator, showcase Mayan artifacts such as pottery, jewelry, and stone-carved scripts from various eras of civilization. While there is much to see, signage is mostly in Spanish. On a sunny day, be sure to wander the grounds adjacent to the museum. The admission fee ($5) is taken in Mexican pesos, so be sure to have proper currency for entry. ⊠ *Blvd. Kukulcán, Km 16.5, Zona Hotelera* ☎ *998/885–3842* 🖼 *$5* ⊙ *Daily 9–5.*

Ruinas el Rey. Large signs on the Zona Hotelera's lagoon side, roughly opposite Playa Delfines, point out the small Ruins of the King. Although much smaller than famous archaeological sites like Tulum and Chichén Itzá, this site (commonly called El Rey) is worth a visit, and makes for an interesting juxtaposition of Mexico's past and present. First

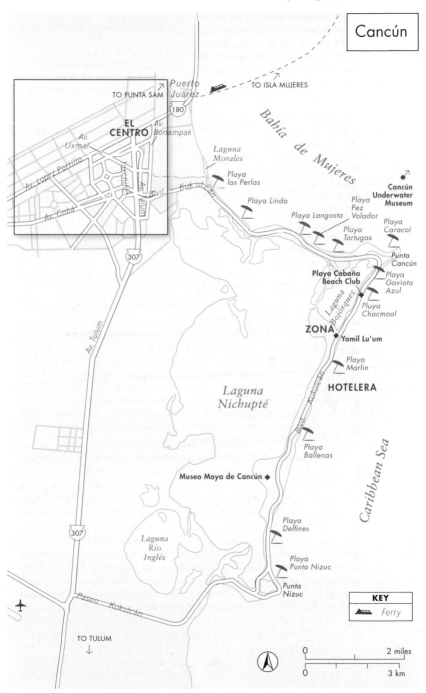

Cancún

2

TO PUNTA SAM
Puerto Juárez
TO ISLA MUJERES

EL CENTRO
Av. Bonampak
Av. Uxmal
Av. López Portillo
Av. Cobá
Blvd. Kukulcán

Bahía de Mujeres

Laguna Morales

Playa las Perlas

Playa Linda

Playa Langosta

Playa Pez Volador

Cancún Underwater Museum

Playa Tortugas

Playa Caracol

Punta Cancún

Playa Cabaña Beach Club

Playa Gaviota Azul

Laguna Bojórquez

Playa Chacmool

ZONA ◆ **Yamil Lu'um**

Playa Marlin

HOTELERA

Laguna Nichupté

Blvd. Kukulcán

Av. Tulum

Caribbean Sea

Playa Ballenas

Museo Maya de Cancún ◆

Playa Delfines

Laguna Río Inglés

Playa Punta Nizuc

Punta Nizuc

TO TULUM

KEY
Ferry

Paseo Kukulcán

0		2 miles
0		3 km

entered into Western chronicles in a 16th-century travelogue, the ruins weren't explored by archaeologists until 1910, and excavations didn't begin until 1954. In 1975, archaeologists began restoration work on the 47 structures with the help of the Mexican government.

Dating to the 3rd to 2nd century BC, El Rey is notable for having two main plazas bounded by two streets. (Most other Mayan cities contain only one plaza.) Originally named Kin Ich Ahau Bonil, Mayan for "king of the solar countenance," the site was linked to astronomical practices. The pyramid is topped by a platform, and inside its vault are paintings on stucco. Skeletons interred at the apex and at the base indicate the site may have been a royal burial ground. In 2006, workmen unearthed an ancient Mayan skeleton on the outskirts of the park. ⊠ *Blvd. Kukulcán, Km 17, Zona Hotelera* ☎ *998/849–2880* ⌨ *$3.50* ⊘ *Daily 9–5.*

Yamil Lu'um. Located on Cancún's highest point (the name means "hilly land"), this archaeological site is on the grounds of the Park Royal Cancún and Westin Lagunamar, which means that nonguests can only visit from the beach side. The concierges at either hotel may let you enter through their property if you ask nicely, but otherwise head to Playa Marlín and you can admire the ruins from a distance. Although it consists of two structures—one probably a temple, the other probably a lighthouse—this is the smallest of Cancún's ruins. Discovered in 1842 by John Lloyd Stephens, the ruins date from the late 13th or early 14th century. Keep an eye out for roaming iguanas. ⊠ *Blvd. Kukulcán, Km 12, Zona Hotelera* ⌨ *Free* ⊘ *Daily 9–5.*

> **BUSES MADE EASY**
>
> In conjunction with the Cancún tourist board, Autocar and Publicar have published an excellent pocket guide called "TheMAP" that shows all the bus routes to points of interest in Cancún and the surrounding area. TheMap is free and easiest to find at the airport. Some of the mid-range hotels carry copies, and if you're lucky you may find one on a bus.

BEACHES

Beaches that are not maintained by hotels have seaweed on their shores. All beaches can be reached by public transportation; just let the driver know where you are headed.

For those with young children, it's best to head to the beaches facing Bahía de Mujeres at the top of the "7." They tend to be less crowded and more sheltered than beaches on the Caribbean side. Wide beaches and shallow waters make the northern tip ideal for those wanting to snorkel or swim. Forming the right side of the "7" are beaches facing the Caribbean Sea. Here riptides and currents can be somewhat dangerous, especially when the surf is high. For snorkeling, it's best to head to the southern end of Boulevard Kukulcán near the Westin Hotel. In the saltwater lagoon, motorized Jet S Playa Gaviota Azul (literally "Blue Seagull Beach," but also commonly called City Beach) is the first beach on the Caribbean's open waters. Here the waves break up to six feet

ECOTOURS

The 500,000-acre Reserva Ecológica El Edén, 48 km (30 miles) northwest of Cancún, is in the area known as Yalahau. The reserve was established by one of Mexico's leading naturalists, Arturo Gómez-Pompa, and his nephew, Marco Lazcano-Barrero, and is dedicated to research and conservation. It offers excursions for people interested in exploring wetlands, mangrove swamps, sand dunes, savannas, and tropical forests. Activities include bird-watching, animal-tracking, stargazing, and archaeology. You must call to make an appointment before you visit. Rates are $75 per person for a full-day visit. If you're not into roughing it, these trips aren't for you.

Eco Colors runs adventure tours to the wildlife reserves at Isla Holbox and Sian Ka'an, and to remote Mayan ruin sites. The company also offers bird-watching, kayaking, camping, and biking excursions around the peninsula. They operate day trips (starting at $109), five-day trips (starting at $495), and seven-day trips (starting at $1,450).

Eco Colors (⊠ *Calle Camarón 32, Sm 27* ☎ *998/884-3667* ⊕ *www. ecotravelmexico.com*).

Reserva Ecológica El Edén (⊠ *Teocaltiche 207, Sm 45, M4 L3, El Centro* ☎ *998/880-5032* ⊕ *www. reservaeleden.org.mx*).

during the winter months, making it one of the few surfing spots in Cancún. If you need a break from the waves and want to be pampered in the sand, head right up a short flight of steps to Playa Cabaña Beach Club. Kids and speedboats rule the waters by day and adult crocodiles wade the banks by night.

The beaches listed here are organized by location, beginning on the northwest side of the "7" facing Bahía de Mujeres, and continuing down along the Caribbean side toward Punta Nizuc.

■**TIP→** Don't swim when the black danger flags fly; red and yellow flags indicate that you should proceed with caution, and green or blue flags mean the waters are calm. Most likely, you will always see a red flag posted on the shores.

Playa Ballenas. Also known as Whale Beach, this is a raw stretch of sand and crystal water at Km 14.5 between Sandos Cancún and Cancún Palace. Jet skiers often zoom through the water, and the strong wind makes the surf rough. The beach is open to the public, and parking and beach access are available at Calle Ballenas. **Amenities:** parking; water sports. **Best for:** walking; windsurfing. ⊠ *Blvd. Kukulcán, Km 14.5, Zona Hotelera.*

Playa Caracol. Playa Caracol (Snail Beach), the last "real" beach along the east–west stretch of the Zona Hotelera, is near Plaza Caracol and the Xcaret dock. Located at Km 8.5, the whole area has been eaten up by development, in particular the high-rise condominium complex next to the entrance. This beach is also hindered by the rocks that jut out from the water to mark the beginning of Punta Cancún, where Boulevard Kukulcán turns south. There are several hotels along here and a few sports rental outfits. It's also the launching point for trips to

Contoy Island. **Amenities:** water sports. **Best for:** windsurfing. ⊠ *Blvd. Kukulcán, Km 8.5, Zona Hotelera.*

Playa Gaviota Azul (*Blue Seagull Beach*). Heading down from Punta Cancún onto the long, southerly stretch of the island, Playa Gaviota Azul (literally "Blue Seagull Beach," but also commonly called City Beach) is the first beach on the Caribbean's open waters. Here the waves break up to six feet during the winter months, making it one of the few surfing spots in Cancún. If you need a break from the waves and want to be pampered in the sand, head right up a short flight of steps to Playa Cabaña Beach Club at Km 9.5 behind the City Discotheque, where travelers can enjoy the full resort experience without booking into a hotel. (It's also the only beach club open to the public.) Facilities include 32 beach cabanas, each equipped with misting machines and a personalized sound system. The $10 entrance fee also includes access to the multilevel swimming pool, sundeck, restaurant, and sushi bar. Chances are you'll never want to leave your cabana. There is paid parking at Plaza Forum or minimal street parking in front of Krystal Cancún. **Amenities:** food and drink; parking; toilets. **Best for:** partiers; swimming. ⊠ *Blvd. Kukulcán, Km 9.5, Zona Hotelera* ☎ *998/848–8380* ⚏ *$10* ☉ *Daily 9–5.*

Playa Chacmool. Located at Km 10 on Boulevard Kukulcán, Playa Chacmool can be accessed through the beach entrance across the street from Señor Frog's. As at Playa Caracol, development has greatly encroached on Chacmool's shores. There are a lot of rocks, but the water is a stunning turquoise and the beach is close to shopping centers and the party zone, so there are plenty of restaurants nearby. The short stretch to the south has gentler waters and fewer rocks. Public changing rooms are also available. The clear, shallow water makes it tempting to walk far out, but be careful—there's a strong current and undertow. **Amenities:** food and drink; toilets; water sports. **Best for:** partiers. ⊠ *Blvd. Kukulcán, Km 10, Zona Hotelera.*

Playa Delfines. Located near Ruinas del Rey at Km 18, where Boulevard Kukulcán curves into a hill, Playa Delfines (Dolphin Beach) is one of the last beaches before Punta Nizuc. Hotels have yet to dominate this small section of coastline, and there's an incredible lookout over the ocean. On a clear day you can see at least four shades of blue in the water, though swimming is treacherous unless a green flag is posted. This resort-free area has plenty of sand and surfers, and it's one of the few places in Cancún where you can take surfing lessons. Although decent waves roll in during hurricane season, they seldom hit "epic" status. At best, you might find choppy, inconsistent surf here and at Playa Chacmool and City Beach. Those seeking more than just a ripple should avoid the placid northern beaches, where Isla Mujeres lies just offshore. **Amenities:** parking. **Best for:** solitude; surfing. ⊠ *Blvd. Kukulcán, Km 18, Zona Hotelera.*

FAMILY **Playa Langosta.** Small, placid Playa Langosta (Lobster Beach), which has an entrance at Boulevard Kukulcán's Km 5, has calm waters that make it an excellent place to swim. There's a dock (mainly used by Dolphin Discovery) that juts out in the middle of the water, but swimming areas are marked off with ropes and buoys. The safe waters and gentle waves make this a popular beach with families as well as Spring Breakers. Next to the beach is a small building with a restaurant, an ice-cream shop, and an ATM. On weekends, you'll be lucky if you can find a spot on the sand. **Amenities:** food and drink; toilets. **Best for:** swimming. ⊠ *Blvd. Kukulcán, Km 5, Zona Hotelera.*

FAMILY **Playa las Perlas.** Playa las Perlas (Pearl Beach) is the first heading east from El Centro along Boulevard Kukulcán. Located at Km 2.5, between the Cancún mainland and the bridge, it's a relatively small

WORD OF MOUTH

"Some of the beaches in Cancún have eroded and some have strong waves, so check carefully. The hotels in the hotel zone that are on the top of the '7' would be your best choice since they sit on a very nice stretch of beach in a cove and are within walking distance of shops, clubs, and restaurants. There's also a convenient bus stop that can take you further down the Hotel Zone." —KVR

beach on the protected waters of the Bahía de Mujeres, and is popular with locals. There are several restaurants lining the sand, but most of the water-sports activities are only available to those staying at the nearby resorts like the Imperial las Perlas or Holiday Inn Cancún Arenas. There's a small store beside Imperial las Perlas where you can buy sanwiches and drinks if you want to have a beach picnic. **Amenities:** food and drink; lifeguards. **Best for:** swimming. ⊠ *Blvd. Kukulcán, Km 2.5, Zona Hotelera.*

Playa Linda. At Km 4 on Boulevard Kukulcán, Playa Linda (Pretty Beach) is where the ocean meets the freshwater of Laguna Nichupté to create the Nichupté Channel. Restaurants and changing rooms are available near the launching dock. There's lots of boat activity along the channel, and the ferry to Isla Mujeres leaves from the adjoining Embarcadero marina, so the area isn't safe for swimming, although it's a great place to people-watch, with a 300-foot rotating scenic tower nearby that offers a 360-degree view. **Amenities:** food and drink; parking; toilets. **Best for:** solitude. ⊠ *Blvd. Kukulcán, Km 4, Zona Hotelera.*

Playa Marlin. Playa Marlin (Marlin Beach), at Km 13 along Boulevard Kukulcán, is a seductive stretch of sand in the heart of the Zona Hotelera, accessible via a road next to Kukulcán Plaza. Despite its turquoise waters and silky sands, the waves are strong and the currents are dangerous. If this beach is crowded, you can walk in either direction to find quieter spots. There's also a small tent where you can rent boogie boards, snorkel equipment, and motorized sports equipment. Although there are currently no public facilities, you can always walk over to Kukulcán Plaza if you need a restroom. **Amenities:** water sports. **Best for:** solitude; snorkeling; surfing; walking. ⊠ *Blvd. Kukulcán, Km 13, Zona Hotelera.*

FAMILY **Playa Pez Volador.** The calm surf and relaxing shallows of Playa Pez Volador make it an aquatic playground for families with young children. Marked by a huge Mexican flag at Km 5.5, the wide beach is popular with locals, as many tourists tend to head to the more active Playa Langosta. Sea grass occasionally washes ashore here, but by early

Playa Cabaña Beach Club on Playa Gaviota Azul is the only public full-service club in Cancún.

morning it is cleared away by the staff of the neighboring Casa Maya Hotel. **Amenities: none. Best for:** swimming. ⊠ *Blvd. Kukulcán, Km 5.5, Zona Hotelera.*

Playa Punta Nizuc. On the southern tip of the peninsula at Km 24, Playa Punta Nizuc is the most isolated and deserted beach in Cancún. Far from the crowds and party scene, this area has no amenities to speak of other than those available to guests at the nearby Wet 'n Wild Water-park (Km 25). The lack of beach-traffic helps keep the white sands clean and the waters sparkling, except when sea grass washes onto the sand. This is a great place to collect seashells or swim, since waves only crash here on stormy days. There's plenty of street parking on Boulevard Kukulcán, but make sure you bring water, snacks, sunscreen, and an umbrella for shade, since this beach is about as barren as they come. Bordered by jungle to the south, Playa Punta Nizuc can be accessed directly from Boulevard Kukulcán. The nearest hotel with amenities (for guests only) is Club Med Cancún. **Amenities:** parking. **Best for:** solitude; swimming. ⊠ *Blvd. Kukulcán, Km 24.*

Playa Tortugas. Playa Tortugas (Turtle Beach) eroded greatly after Hurricane Wilma. There's now a restored sandbank at the entrance around Km 6.5 on Boulevard Kukulcán. The water is deep and the swimming is excellent, so many people come here to sail, snorkel, kayak, paraglide, and ride Wave Runners. The nicest section of this beach is on the far right, just past the rocks. The sand can get very crowded, especially because this is where people usually grab a drink or snack before catching the ferry to Isla Mujeres. Locals from El Centro will spend their entire weekend here, so if you are looking for isolation, it's best to head

Cancún's History

The Maya, Cancún's original inhabitants, arrived centuries ago, and their descendants remain in the area to this day. During the golden age of Mayan civilization, also called the Classic Period, this part of the coast remained sparsely populated as other parts of the peninsula were developing trade routes and building enormous temples and pyramids. Consequently, Cancún never developed into a major Mayan center. Excavations at El Rey ruins in what is now the Zona Hotelera have showed that the Maya communities that lived here around AD 1200 simply used this area for burial sites. Even the name given to the area was not inspiring: Cancún means "nest of snakes" in Mayan.

When the Spanish conquistadores began to arrive in the early 1500s, much of the Mayan culture was already in decline. Over the next three centuries the Spanish largely ignored coastal areas like Cancún, which consisted mainly of low-lying scrub, mangroves, and swarms of mosquitoes, and focused instead on settling inland where there was more economic promise.

Although it received a few refugees from the War of the Castes, which engulfed the entire region in the mid-1800s, Cancún remained more or less undeveloped until the middle of the 20th century. By the 1950s, Acapulco had become the number-one tourist attraction in the country—and had given the Mexican government its first taste of tourism dollars. When Acapulco's star began to fade in the late 1960s, the government hired a market-research company to determine the perfect location for developing Mexico's next big tourist destination. Guess where they picked?

In April 1971, Mexico's president, Luis Echeverría Alvarez, authorized the Ministry of Foreign Relations to buy the island offshore of Cancún and the surrounding region. With a $22 million development loan from the World Bank and the Inter-American Development Bank, the transformation of Cancún began. At the time there were just 120 residents, most of whom worked at a coconut plantation. By 1979 Cancún had become a resort of 40,000, attracting more than 2 million tourists a year. Today, more than 800,000 people live here, and the city has become Mexico's most lucrative source of tourism income. The recently opened Museo Maya showcases the evolution of the region and its archeological timeline. Set in the middle of the bustling hotel zone, attractions include both indoor exhibits and outdoor ruins.

elsewhere. Don't be fooled by the name—this spot is seldom frequented by *tortugas*. **Amenities:** food and drink; water sports. **Best for:** partiers; snorkeling; swimming. ⊠ *Blvd. Kukulcán, Km 6.5, Zona Hotelera.*

WHERE TO EAT

Be aware that restaurants that line Avenidas Tulum and Yaxchilán are often noisy and crowded, and gas fumes make it hard to enjoy alfresco meals. Many of the finer restaurants and boutiques are on Avenida Bonampak, making it the continuation of Boulevard Kukulcán. The

Spend a romantic evening at Le Basilic.

restaurants in the Parque de las Palapas, just off Avenida Tulum, serve expertly prepared Mexican food. Famous for its taco scene, El Centro's Avenida Yaxchilán caters mainly to large groups and budget travelers. Deeper into the city center, you can find fresh seafood and traditional fare at Mercado Veintiocho (Market 28). Dress is casual in Cancún, but many restaurants do not allow bare feet, short shorts, or bathing suits, and require shirts. At upscale restaurants, pants, skirts, or dresses are required. Large breakfast and brunch buffets are among the most popular meals in the Zona Hotelera, with prices ranging from $10 to $25 per person. Most restaurants in Cancún open for lunch around 2 pm and generally stay open until midnight.

⚠ Most upscale resorts in Zona Hotelera purify their tap water; however, ask in advance whether it's safe to drink.

ZONA HOTELERA

$$$ ✗**Cambalache.** This Argentinean steak house is rustic yet elegant, with
ARGENTINE dark wooden tables and arched brick ceilings. The house cocktail, *cleri-cot*, made from red wine, sparkling cider, and fresh fruit, is prepared at your table. For starters, try the traditional empanadas (turnovers stuffed with spinach and cheese). Although tenderloin steak is the most popular choice here, the lamb threaded on skewers and grilled over a brick fire is also delicious. Be sure to leave room for *alfajor*, a crisp pastry dessert layered with caramel and pecans. The tango music coupled with views of Coral Negro Market give this restaurant an international flair, and help you forget that you're inside a shopping mall. With enough room for 350 people, the dining room tends to get rather loud at night,

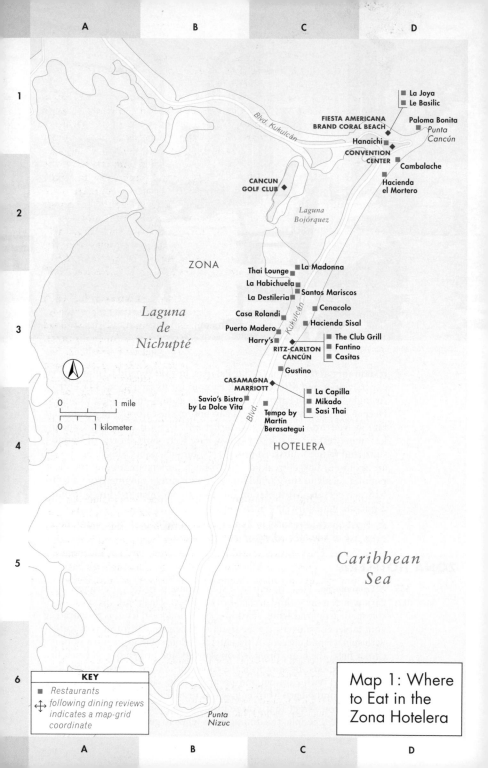

Map 1: Where to Eat in the Zona Hotelera

and there's no outdoor seating. $ *Average main: $25* ✉ *Blvd. Kukulcán, Km 9 at Plaza Forum, Zona Hotelera* ☎ *998/883–0902* ⊕ *www.cambalacherestaurantes.com* ✛ *1:D2.*

$$$$
SWISS
Fodor'sChoice
★

✗ **Casa Rolandi.** The secret to this restaurant's success is its creative handling of Swiss and Italian cuisine. Be sure to try the *carpaccio de pulpo* (thin slices of fresh octopus), the cheese fondue, or the mesquite-grilled rib eye. Appetizers are also tempting: there's puff bread from a wood-burning oven and a salad and antipasto bar. For something with a bit more local flavor, try the black ravioli stuffed with lobster or the restaurant's specialty *Gamberoni dei Re Maya:* jumbo shrimp baked in banana leaves and topped with a special Mayan sauce. Entrées are served under silver domes, including the chef's specials that change monthly. The restaurant also has an extensive wine list and a wine bar. The beautiful dining room and attentive service might make you want to stay for hours, and there are pleasant lagoon views from the spacious patio. $ *Average main: $30* ✉ *In front of Royal Sands, Blvd. Kukulcán, Km 13.5, Zona Hotelera* ☎ *998/883–2557* ⊕ *www.rolandi.com* ✛ *1:C3.*

$$$$
SEAFOOD

✗ **Casitas.** Sink your toes into the sand at Cancún's only on-the-beach restaurant where the impeccable service matches the incredible setting. The romantic ambiance caters to couples, and many of the seafood dishes are created for two. Silk curtains drape *palapas* (open-air huts), each centered with an illuminated table adorned with seashells. For a delicious sampling, try the seafood platter of shrimp, oysters, tuna tartar, king crab, and lobster tail. A variety of steaks and salads are also available. For a little bit of everything, ask for the tasting menu. The mini dessert shooters are the perfect way to extend your dinner-with-a-view; be sure to head to oceanfront beds after your meal to relax and digest. Call ahead, since the restaurant is at the mercy of the weather. $ *Average main: $95* ✉ *Ritz-Carlton Cancún, Retorno del Rey 36, Blvd. Kukulcán, Km 13.5, Zona Hotelera* ⊕ *www.ritzcarlton.com* ⌂ *Reservations essential* ◔ *No lunch* ✛ *1:C3.*

$$$
ITALIAN

✗ **Cenacolo.** Brick oven pizza and pasta, handmade in full view, have made this fine Italian restaurant a favorite. Appetizers include beef or octopus carpaccio that practically melt in your mouth and a light calamari. There are more than 15 pasta dishes to choose from, including a delicious lobster ravioli filled with ricotta cheese and served in a white-wine sauce. The restaurant also has a small wine cave with a romantic table for two (reserve this section in advance). Although it's inside a mall, the restaurant's main dining room is elegant, with stained-glass panels on the ceiling and live piano music. $ *Average main: $20* ✉ *Kukulcán Plaza, Blvd. Kukulcán, Km 13, Zona Hotelera* ☎ *998/885–3603* ⊕ *www.cenacolo.com.mx* ◔ *No lunch* ✛ *1:C3.*

$$$$
INTERNATIONAL
Fodor'sChoice
★

✗ **The Club Grill.** The Club Grill has re-created the upscale ambience of the swank 1960s with such details as a martini lounge, tuxedoed waiters, and live jazz complete with a double bass. A five-course tasting menu, paired with boutique Mexican wines, changes monthly. The dining room here is romantic and quietly elegant, with rich wood, fresh flowers, crisp linens, and courtyard views. The contemporary menu changes every three months, but might include starters like caramelized scallops and truffle corn soup, or main courses like tequila duck. For dessert, try the soufflé trio served with cups of liquid chocolate, coconut cream and Grand Marnier sauce. Like a waiters' ballet, the delivery of domed silver platters is synchronized among the servers, making the entire dining experience an unforgettable one. To cap the evening, women are given a red rose and a box of truffles. Reservations are recommended. [$] *Average main: $40* ✉ *Ritz-Carlton Cancún, Blvd. Kukulcán, Km 13.5, Retorno del Rey 36, Zona Hotelera* ☎ *998/881–0822* 🌐 *www.ritzcarlton.com* ✍ *Reservations essential* 👔 *Jacket required* ⏲ *Closed Mon.* ✥ *1:C3*

$$$$ MEDITERRANEAN ✕ **Fantino.** Reflecting Mexico's rich Spanish heritage, this Mediterranean restaurant lives up to its reputation as one of the country's finest. Grandeur hits a peak in this ballroom setting, with long-stemmed roses and hand-painted ceiling frescoes that subtly match the fine English china. Each guest, referred to by name, is treated to the sounds of live piano music, and the velvet walls mounted with candelabras are only overshadowed by the red satin curtains and ocean views. Each course is paired with its own wine. Designed to play with the senses, appetizers moisten the palate in preparation for the seven-course tasting menu. Divine dishes include watermelon salad with buffalo mozzarella, sautéed foie gras with berries, and vanilla braised veal cheek with squash gnocchi. All ingredients are hand selected from local farms or air-freighted to the hotel. Just when you think you've seen it all, the waiter wheels over the candy cart, featuring 10 glass towers of handmade sweets. Reservations are recommended. [$] *Average main: $75* ✉ *Ritz-Carlton Cancún, Blvd. Kukulcán, Km 13.5, Zona Hotelera* ☎ *998/881–0822* 🌐 *www.ritzcarlton.com* ✍ *Reservations essential* 👔 *Jacket required* ⏲ *No lunch. Closed Sun.* ✥ *1:C3*

$$$$ ITALIAN ✕ **Gustino.** From the moment you walk down the dramatic entrance staircase, you know you're in for a memorable dining experience. The circular dining room has artistic lighting and views of the wine cellar and open-air kitchen. The *gamberetti al aglio* (sautéed shrimp with garlic) appetizer is a standout, as are the tagliatelle in truffle sauce and seafood risotto entrées. Other memorable dishes include the sea bass baked in wax paper and the braised veal with prosciutto and wild mushrooms. The service here is impeccable, and saxophone music adds a dash of romance. A private dining area can hold up to 14 guests. [$] *Average main: $40* ✉ *JW Marriott Resort, Blvd. Kukulcán, Km 14.5, Zona Hotelera* ☎ *998/848–9600, 998/848–9600* 🌐 *www.gustinocancun.com* ✍ *Reservations essential* ⏲ *No lunch* ✥ *1:C3.*

$$$$ MEXICAN ✕ **Hacienda el Mortero.** As one of Cancún's first restaurants, the main draw is the setting: a replica of a 17th-century traditional hacienda, complete with courtyard fountain, flowering garden, and a strolling mariachi band. Although there's nothing outstanding on the traditional Mexican menu, the tortilla soup is very good and the chicken fajitas and rib-eye steaks are tasty. Fish lovers may also like the *pescado Veracruzana* (fresh grouper prepared Veracruz-style with olives, garlic, and fresh tomatoes). Sunday brunch ($18) is served from 9 to 2. This is a popular restaurant for large groups, so be warned: it can get boisterous, especially once guests begin sampling the 110 types of tequila. [$] *Average*

main: $45 ✉ *Next to Krystal Hotel Cancún, Blvd. Kukulcán, Km 9, Zona Hotelera* ☎ *998/848–9800* 🕒 *No lunch Mon.–Sat.* ✣ *1:D2*

> **WORD OF MOUTH**
>
> "There are a handful of restaurants at La Isla Mall that overlook the large lagoon. It looks great during sunset, since the sun sets behind the lagoon."
> —CancunWithMe

$$$$ MEXICAN 🍴 **Hacienda Sisal.** Built to resemble a sprawling hacienda, this restaurant is warm and intimate, with comfortable high-backed chairs and Mexican paintings. Menu highlights include the goat-cheese and mango salad, Tampico chicken breast, New York steak with stuffed pepper, and annatto-seasoned grilled pork chops. Traditional dances from Mexico and the Caribbean are performed on various weeknights in the restaurant's patio section. Children eat free on Tuesday nights. There's a breakfast buffet from 8 to 2 on Sunday, which is the only day when Hacienda Sisal opens early. [$] *Average main: $25* ✉ *Royal Sands Resort, Blvd. Kukulcán, Km 13.5, Zona Hotelera* ☎ *998/848–8220* 🌐 *www.haciendasisal.com* 🕒 *No lunch* ✣ *1:C3.*

$$ SUSHI **Fodor's Choice** ★ 🍴 **Hanaichi.** It might look like a hole-in-the-wall, but this small Japanese restaurant has some of the best sushi in Cancún, and is frequented by Mexico's best chefs. Across from bustling Plaza Caracol you'll find skilled Japanese chefs preparing sashimi, nigiri, and every type of sushi roll imaginable. House specialties include the Copan Roll (deep fried shrimp wrapped in cucumber) and the Cancún Roll (stuffed with eel and scallops). There is a sushi bar on the ground floor and an intimate dining area with a few tables upstairs. Granted, you might not hear crashing waves or feel the sand under your toes, but you'll have an authentic Japanese experience for a fraction of what you might pay down the road. It's best to know your sushi if you dine here though, since the menu is written in Spanish and Japanese. [$] *Average main: $12* ✉ *Blvd. Kukulcán, Km 9* ☎ *998/883–2804* 🌐 *www.hanaichicancun.com* ✣ *1:D1.*

$$$$ STEAKHOUSE 🍴 **Harry's.** On the lagoon across from the Ritz-Carlton, this steak house is easy to spot by the line of luxury cars at valet parking. High-profile locals and visitors alike are drawn to the Vegas–meets–Beverly Hills style of this flashy and contemporary establishment. The dimly lit interior is dominated by onyx and marble, with cedar beams and railings adding a touch of warmth. Its creators traveled the world for two years in search of the best trends in culinary art. The result is a spectacular menu featuring glazed duck, king salmon, Maine lobster, and USDA Kobe beef served with aged Vermont cheddar cheese. If you can get past the glass meat cooler in the lobby, the concept is impressive—all steaks are aged in-house for 21–28 days, and then grilled and broiled to perfection. Be sure to save room for Mini Indulgences, six tasty desserts served in shot glasses. The waitstaff deliver a tower of cotton candy with the check. (Try not to faint when you see the total; this place is pricey.) All the stone indoors creates echoes, so the outdoor seating is recommended. [$] *Average main: $50* ✉ *Blvd. Kukulcán, Km 14.2, across from Ritz-Carlton, Zona Hotelera* ☎ *998/840–6550* 🌐 *www.harrys.com.mx* ✣ *1:C3.*

Wagons set up along the waterfront in Cancún sell toys and other wares.

$$$$ STEAKHOUSE 🍴 **La Capilla.** Nestled in the belly of a brick cavern, this Argentine steak house is dimly lighted with wrought-iron chandeliers dramatically suspended from wooden beams. The flavorful menu features Kobe beef carpaccio, lobster tail, *arrachera* steak, and herb-crusted rack of lamb. In the center of the circular dining area is Cancún's most extensive salad bar, with exotic cheeses, grilled vegetables, Italian prosciutto, and seven types of olive oil. The creations of Chef Javier Carcamo are served on iron skillets with skewered vegetables and roasted garlic. Be sure to check out the international wine cave, home to more than 200 types of wine. Vegetarians may want to look elsewhere. Reservations are recommended, except for during breakfast hours when a buffet is served from 6:30 to 11:30 am. [$] *Average main: $35* ✉ *CasaMagna Marriott, Blvd. Kukulcán, Km 14.5, Zona Hotelera* ☎ *998/881–2000* 🌐 *www.marriott.com* 🕒 *No lunch.* ✥ *1:C3*

$$$$ MEXICAN 🍴 **La Destileria.** Be prepared to have your perceptions of tequila changed forever. In what looks like a Mexican hacienda, complete with an *alambique* (tequila distillery), you can sample from a list of 100 varieties—in shots or superb margaritas—and also visit the on-site tequila museum and store. The traditional Mexican menu focuses on fresh fish and seafood. Other highlights include the *molcajete de arrachera* (a thick beef stew served piping hot in a mortar), and the Talla-style fish fillet from a traditional Acapulco recipe. Midday (1–5 pm) diners can enjoy tequila tasting, appetizers, and a house cocktail for just $8. Be sure to leave room for the caramel crepes, a signature Mexican dessert. Reservations are recommended. [$] *Average main: $23* ✉ *Blvd. Kukulcán, Km 12.65, across from Plaza Kukulcán, Zona Hotelera* ☎ *998/885–1086, 998/885–1087* 🌐 *www.ladestileria.com.mx/cancun* ✥ *1:C3.*

2

$$$$ ✕**La Habichuela Sunset.** Following a 35-year success in El Centro, this
CARIBBEAN lagoon-side eatery opened a second outpost in the bustling Zona
Hotelera. Catering to tourists with its kitschy Mayan live music show
(complete with fire eaters) on Wednesday and Friday at 8, the multilevel
dining area features a dramatic staircase leading down to an archaeological dig covered by a glass floor. Blending modern and Mayan designs,
the restaurant has an outdoor patio with a small stream and illuminated
trees. Popular appetizers include the lime soup or Caesar salad prepared
tableside. The soft-shell crab tacos and garlic shrimp are frequently
seen coming from the kitchen, as is the breaded fish served with tamarind and mango sauce. Although known for their fresh fish, they also
offer chicken, steak, and pasta at inflated prices. Dessert lovers will
enjoy the butterscotch crepes and Mayan coffee. $ *Average main: $30*
✉ *Blvd. Kukulcán, Km 12.6, Zona Hotelera* ☎ *988/840–6240* ⊕ *www.
lahabichuela.com* ✛ *1:C3.*

$$$$ ✕**La Joya.** The dramatic interior of this restaurant has three levels of
MEXICAN stained-glass windows, a fountain, artwork, and beautiful furniture
from central Mexico. The food is traditional but creative. The grilled
beef prepared Tampíqueña-style is especially popular, as is the catch
of the day wrapped in maguey leaves. Those with lighter appetites
will want to try the tortilla soup or seafood appetizer of shrimp, scallops, and squid. Performances (Wednesday–Friday 7:30–8:30 pm) by
folk dancers and a mariachi band add to the ambience. There's also a
cocktail lounge where you can have a drink or cigar before, or after,
dinner. $ *Average main: $25* ✉ *Fiesta Americana Grand Coral Beach,
Blvd. Kukulcán, Km 9.5, Zona Hotelera* ☎ *998/881–3200* ☾ *Closed
Mon.* ✛ *1:D1*

$$$$ ✕**La Madonna.** This dramatic-looking restaurant is a great place to enjoy
ITALIAN a selection of 180 martinis, as well as Italian food with a "creative Swiss
twist." Guests are dwarfed by a massive reproduction of the *Mona Lisa*
and towering Greek sculptures that frame the three-story restaurant.
For starters, try the pan-seared mozzarella wrapped in prosciutto. You
can also enjoy classics like fettuccine with shrimp in a grappa sauce,
mussels in white wine with saffron cream, and veal parmigiana served
on a bed of homemade basil pasta. Cheese and chocolate lovers can try
one of the chef's traditional fondues. The lychee martini is a tad expensive but worth it. In addition to the ground level patio, there's a pleasant terrace on the third floor. $ *Average main: $40* ✉ *La Isla Shopping
Village, Blvd. Kukulcán, Km 12.5, Zona Hotelera* ☎ *998/883–2222*
✛ *1:C2.*

$$$$ ✕**Le Basilic.** If heaven had a restaurant, this would be it. Arched bay
MEDITERRANEAN windows, checkered marble floors, live jazz, and exquisite garden views
create the backdrop for this ideal spot for couples. The 14 chestnut
tables surround a sunken gazebo where long-stemmed orchids bloom
under glass. The restaurant doubles as a gallery where paintings by
local artists are propped on easels, and, each Friday and Saturday from
7 to 10 pm, an artist paints while you dine. The dishes here—created
by French chef Henri Charvet—are served beneath silver domes by
pleasant tuxedoed waiters. The menu changes every four months, but
it is always comprised of French-Mediterranean cuisine, from fresh

tuna and sea scallops to seared duck and roasted lamb. As a keepsake, guests are presented with a box of French truffles and elegant recipe cards recapping the bill of fare. The dress code is elegant, reservations are recommended, and children are not allowed. Since this restaurant is rather intimate, expect quality service, meaning that some people might feel uncomfortable being watched by attentive waiters. $ *Average main: $35* ⊠ *Fiesta Americana Grand Coral Beach, Blvd. Kukulcán, Km 9.5, Zona Hotelera* ☎ *998/881–3200* ⊕ *www.lebasiliccancun.com* ⌳ *Reservations essential* ⌂ *Jacket required* ⊙ *No lunch. Closed Sun.* ✢ *1:D1*

$$$$ ✗ **Mikado.** Sit around the teppanyaki tables and watch the utensils fly
JAPANESE   as the showmen chefs here prepare steaks, seafood, and vegetables. The menu includes Japanese specialties such as *futo-maki* (large sushi rolls) and panfried sea bass. The sushi, tempura, grilled salmon, and beef teriyaki are all feasts fit for a shogun. For added flavor, several dishes are infused with sake or braised with Sapporo beer, like the oriental short ribs served with crispy onions. Unlike most restaurants in Cancún, however, there's no outdoor seating or scenic view. $ *Average main: $30* ⊠ *CasaMagna Marriott, Blvd. Kukulcán, Km 14.5, Zona Hotelera* ☎ *998/881–2036* ⊕ *www.mikadocancun.com* ⊙ *No lunch* ✢ *1:C3.*

$$$$ ✗ **Paloma Bonita.** Replicating three regions of Mexico, this vibrant set-
MEXICAN   ting features stone fountains, handcrafted furniture, and colorful linens imported from the western state of Michoacan. Waiters dressed in sombreros dance between the tables while women in traditional costumes serve olive bread from wicker baskets. This is one of the best places in the Hotel Zone to get authentic Mexican cuisine—so be adventurous! Traditional fare like *moles enchiladas* (stuffed corn tortillas covered with thick chocolate and chile sauce) is fabulous here—and if you're unsure about what to order, the waiter will explain the different chiles used in many of the dishes. Treat your palate to *queso fundido Oaxaca,* a specialty of bubbling cheese dripping from a stone pot onto handmade tortillas. The glass-enclosed patio with its water view is a great place to linger over tequila or a *tamarindo margarita.* The live music here is Norteño style. Unlike the neighboring nightclubs, this lively atmosphere will remind you that you are in Mexico. Meals are on the heavy side, so come with an appetite. $ *Average main: $30* ⊠ *Dreams Cancún Resort & Spa, Blvd. Kukulcán, Km 9, Punta Cancún, Zona Hotelera* ☎ *998/848–7082* ⊙ *No lunch* ✢ *1:D1.*

$$$$ ✗ **Puerto Madero.** Modeled after the dock warehouses that have been
STEAKHOUSE converted into modern restaurants in the famed Argentine port city
Fodor's Choice Puerto Madero, this steak-and-seafood house gets rave reviews from
★   locals. It's the small touches that make this an unforgettable dining experience, like fresh bread served in leather baskets and martini reserves chilled in miniature ice buckets. The grilled octopus bathed in olive oil is exceptional, and the Big Rib Eye generously serves two people. The Alaskan halibut steak, also a crowd pleaser, is prepared with white wine, shallots, and fresh pepper. No matter what you order, be sure to request a side of *papas infladas* (potatoes fried until they're puffed)— bite down and they crackle on your tongue. Adding to the cosmopolitan ambience is a fun-loving staff, most of whom have been there over 15 years. If the restaurant is too loud inside, ask for a table outside on the

patio overlooking the lagoon. Reservations are recommended on weekends. [$] *Average main: $30* ✉ *Blvd. Kukulcán, Km 14.1, Zona Hotelera* ☎ *998/885–2829* 🌐 *www.puertomaderorestaurantes.com* ✣ *1:C3.*

$$ MEXICAN 🍴 **Santos Mariscos.** The most reasonably priced eatery in the Hotel Zone, serving surprisingly good food, this restaurant is a tribute to masked wrestling champion El Santo. Colorfully decorated with retro furnishings like rainbow lawn chairs and sculptures of the Virgin Mary holding plastic roses, a bright red bar dominates the downstairs, and there's an upstairs dining area with a small outdoor patio. Frequented by locals who work in the Hotel Zone, this eatery serves great shrimp tacos with seven types of sauces. For those who want an alternative to the traditional flour tortilla, try the fried cheese taco. The *tamarindo* margaritas are also very refreshing. Located just south of La Isla Shopping Village, this kitschy cantina is marked by a string of Christmas lights dangling over the patio. This is not a fine-dining restaurant, so don't be surprised if the one waiter on staff serves your table in stages. [$] *Average main: $12* ✉ *Blvd. Kukulcán, Km 12.7, Zona Hotelera* ☎ *998/840–6300* ✣ *1:C3.*

$$$$ THAI 🍴 **Sasi Thai.** Despite the street-facing views, this open-air restaurant has one of the most pleasant settings in Cancún. Six thatch-roof cabanas—each housing four tables—are staggered on a hill and dimly lighted with cubed candles and marble lanterns. Plank floors lead to a bamboo bar where fruity mojitos and martinis are prepared. The menu features traditional Thai cuisine such as spring rolls, pork dumplings, red duck curry, and pad thai with chicken or shrimp. The mango crème brûlée with ginger sorbet makes it worth a special visit to this outdoor eatery. [$] *Average main: $26* ✉ *Casa Magna Marriott, Blvd. Kukulcán, Km 14.5, Zona Hotelera* ☎ *998/881–2092* 🌐 *www.sasi-thai.com* ✣ *1:C3.*

$$$$ ITALIAN 🍴 **Savio's Bistro by La Dolce Vita.** It's the 30-year success of this downtown restaurant that draws people in, but it's the fresh seafood, homemade pasta and warm atmosphere that keep them here. As one of the newer eateries to join the Hotel Zone, this fine Italian restaurant has an elegant dining room and multilevel patio overlooking Laguna Nichupte. Request a table on the palapa-covered terrace, dimly lit by candles and woven lanterns. (Note that smoking is permitted outside.) Keep a lookout for the resident alligator that occasionally pops his head out of the lagoon. For an exceptional meal with a view, try the signature Boquinete Dolce Vita, a local snapper encased in puff pastry and topped with shrimp and mushrooms. Breads and pizzas are baked inside a brick oven and sprinkled with fresh ingredients like arugula and grape tomatoes. The shrimp lasagna is creamy and flavorful, and the wines are remarkably affordable. Gluten-free pastas are also available. Drop by on Friday night for live jazz, but be patient because service is not this restaurant's strongest suit. [$] *Average main: $25* ✉ *Blvd. Kukulcán, Km 15, Zona Hotelera* ☎ *998/885–0161* 🌐 *www.ladolcevitacancun.com* ✣ *1:B4.*

$$$$ ECLECTIC Fodor's Choice ★ 🍴 **Tempo by Martin Berasategui.** This elegant restaurant in the Paradisus Cancún is the latest Caribbean offering from acclaimed Spanish chef Martin Berasategui. The stylish white dining room is enhanced by mirrored columns, leather chairs, orchid floral accents, and white-gloved

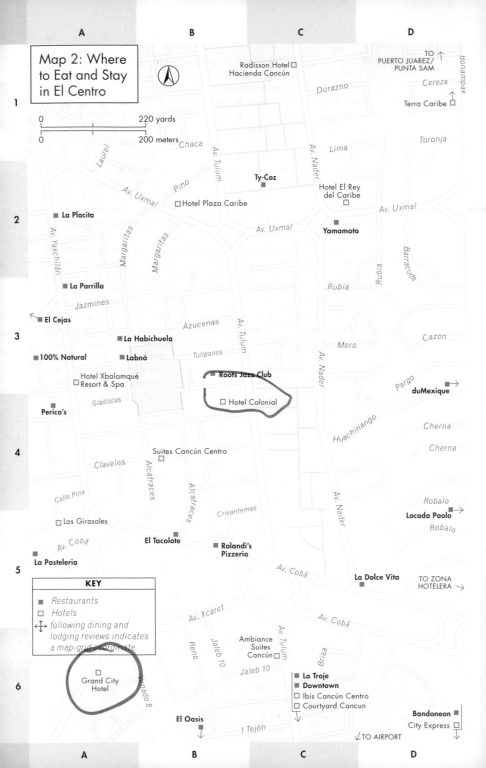

Map 2: Where to Eat and Stay in El Centro

KEY
- ■ Restaurants
- □ Hotels
- ↔ following dining and lodging reviews indicates a map-grid coordinate

0 ————— 220 yards
0 ————— 200 meters

TO PUERTO JUAREZ/ PUNTA SAM

□ Radisson Hotel Hacienda Cancún

Terra Caribe □

■ Ty-Coz

□ Hotel Plaza Caribe

Hotel El Rey del Caribe □

■ La Placita

■ Yamamoto

■ La Parrilla

■ El Cejas

■ La Habichuela

■ 100% Natural

■ Labná

Hotel Xbalamqué □ Resort & Spa

■ Roots Jazz Club

□ Hotel Colonial

duMexique ■→

■ Perico's

Suites Cancún Centro □

□ Los Girasoles

■ El Tacolote

■ Rolandi's Pizzeria

Locada Paolo ■→

■ La Pasteleria

La Dolce Vita ■

TO ZONA HOTELERA →

Ambiance Suites Cancún □

■ La Troje
■ Downtown
□ Ibis Cancún Centro
□ Courtyard Cancun

□ Grand City Hotel

Bandoneon ■
City Express □

■ El Oasis

↓ TO AIRPORT

service unmatched in Cancún. The adults-only culinary experience begins with a trio of butter (mustard, avocado, salt) that accompanies fresh-baked bread. A seven-course tasting menu is a wonder for the palate, and wines from around the world, chosen by talented sommelier Carlos Duarte, match each note of the meal. Though à la carte options are available, the tasting, which might include offerings like potato and prosciutto croquettes, baby squid-stuffed tomatoes, and veal tenderloin with potato, bacon, and truffle sauce, is highly recommended. Savor each artfully presented dish, but save room for dessert and the requisite finishing touch: delectable petit fours. Though guests at the all-inclusive Paradisus pay a surcharge for their meal, nonguests are welcomed and encouraged. [$] *Average main: $40* ✉ *Paradisus Cancún, Blvd. Kukulcán, Km 16.5, Zona Hotelera* ☎ *998/881/1100* 🌐 *www.paradisus.com* ✍ *Reservations essential* 🕒 *No lunch* ⊕ *1:C4.*

2

$$$$ THAI 🍴 **Thai Lounge.** Expect a truly unique dining experience from the moment you walk into this garden oasis. After all, not many restaurants have a dolphin aquarium in the bar area. The individual huts with thatch roofs provide an intimate setting to sample spicy Thai dishes like roasted duck in coconut red curry, and the house favorite, a deep-fried fish fillet prepared with ginger, garlic, and a tamarind chile sauce. The bill of fare also features such traditional dishes as shrimp curry, Thai salad, and spicy chicken soup. Call ahead to reserve one of the palapa casitas perched over the water on stilts for an unbeatable Cancún dining experience. There are only 17 tables, so reservations are highly recommended. [$] *Average main: $25* ✉ *Plaza la Isla shopping center, Blvd. Kukulcán, Km 12.5, Zona Hotelera* ☎ *998/176–8070* 🌐 *www.thai.com.mx* 🕒 *No lunch* ⊕ *1:C3.*

EL CENTRO

$$$$ ARGENTINE 🍴 **Bandoneon.** From the moment you enter the restaurant, you might think you've taken a "right" turn and ended up in Buenos Aires. Every detail replicates the streets of Argentina, right down to the cobblestone floors, the dramatic tango music, and the indoor market that offers wine and pasta. The walls are adorned with antique *bandoneons* (concertinas, similar to the accordion) and paintings of tango dancers. In the center of the restaurant are two enormous lighthouse structures, guarding more than 100 Argentinean wines. The overwhelming menu includes starters like smoked marlin and charcoal-grilled provolone cheese. In addition to beef, Bandoneon also serves salads, pasta, fish, and chicken. The sizzling rib-eye steak is extremely tender and succulent, but if you're health-conscious, ask for a leaner cut. If you still have room for dessert, try the brandy-soaked cake roll with caramel filling and dark chocolate sauce. With 160 seats, this place can get a bit chaotic at times, and reservations are recommended. [$] *Average main: $30* ✉ *Av. Bonampak at Nichupté, El Centro* ☎ *998/889–9500* 🌐 *www.bandoneonrestaurantes.com* ⊕ *2:D6.*

$$ ECLECTIC 🍴 **Downtown.** This urban bistro brings a touch of New York into the heart of El Centro. Warehouse meets Zen in the informal yet sophisticated dining room, which has cement floors, exposed air ducts, dim light from dangling light bulbs, red velvet cushions, and a chicle tree enclosed in glass. Lack of detail on the chalkboard menu might deliver a pleasant surprise: the nondescript mac-and-cheese or steak-frites are both rather gourmet. The goat-cheese pizza and duck pâté with red onion marmalade are excellent starters—follow with a lamb burger topped with tzatziki. This is a great place to grab a hearty breakfast since all the sausages, breads and marmalades are made in-house. You can watch the chefs at work in the open kitchen; there's also a lounge area with relaxing music and powerful martinis. $ *Average main: $15* ✉ *Av. Xpuhil, Sm 19, Mza 2, Lote 24, El Centro* 🖀 *998/883–9800* ⊕ *downtownrestaurantcancun.com* ⊗ *Closed Mon.* ✛ *2:C6*

$$$

FRENCH

Fodor'sChoice

★

✗ **duMexique.** Discreetly located on the bustling Avenida Bonampak, this hidden gem bears no resemblance to an ordinary restaurant. Chef Alain Grimond and his wife Sonya have converted their home into an intimate dinner-party setting to create a dining experience unlike any other. Doubling as a gallery, the dining room features modern art, a grand piano, and a crystal chandelier that casts spectrums of light onto the pristine ceiling. Accommodating only 20 guests per evening, the restaurant begins the ritual with martinis in the tropical garden, decorated with tiki torches, dark rattan furniture, glass lanterns, and microsuede cushions. The French menu (featuring five appetizers, five entrées, and four desserts) changes daily and is seldom repeated. Selections might include duckling with risotto or entrecôte with wine sauce. By calling ahead, you can request *soufflé de huitlacoche*, a delicacy made from mushrooms that grow on cornstalks. A fusion for the eye and palate, each course is a masterpiece of presentation. Be sure to visit the kitchen, where the awards of master chef Grimond are on display. $ *Average main: $30* ✉ *Av. Bonampak 109, Sm 3, El Centro* 🖀 *998/884–5919* ⚏ *Reservations essential* ⊗ *No lunch. Closed Sun.* ✛ *2:D3*

$

SEAFOOD

✗ **El Cejas.** The seafood is fresh at this open-air eatery, and the clientele is lively—often joining in song with the musicians who stroll among the tables. If you've had a wild night, try the *vuelva a la vida*, or "return to life" (conch, oysters, shrimp, octopus, calamari, and fish with a hot tomato sauce). The kitchen serves crab (stuffed, steamed, or fried) and whole-fried fish that is crispy on the outside and moist on the inside. The ceviche and the spicy shrimp soup are also good, though the quality can be inconsistent. A favorite with El Centro locals, this no-frills eatery is casual and easy on the wallet, so don't expect to be pampered. It's inside the bustling Mercado 28. $ *Average main: $10* ✉ *Mercado Veintiocho, on southwest end, Loc 90–100, Sm 26, El Centro* ✛ *2:A3.*

$$

SEAFOOD

✗ **El Oasis.** This appropriately named eatery offers a welcome escape from El Centro's busy streets. A small wooden bridge leads the way into a palapa, which is colorfully decorated with turquoise chairs, mosaic flooring, seashell lamps, and a bamboo bar. Diners can relax to the sounds of a cascading waterfall, skirted by palm trees and tropical plants. House specials include grilled seafood with rice; fish fillet with coconut cream or smaller dishes like ceviche and aguachiles (spicy lime shrimp). Many of the seafood dishes can be prepared with your choice of mango, tamarind, or guava salsa. This spot is popular with the locals; menus are in Spanish, and the staff doesn't speak much English. $ *Average main: $10* ✉ *Prolongación Yaxchilan, Sm 17, Mza 2, Lote 3,*

El Centro ☎ *998/884–4106* ⏲ *No dinner* ✥ *2:B6.*

$ MEXICAN 🍴 **El Tacolote.** A great place to stop for lunch or after a night on the town, this popular *taquería* (taco stand) sells delicious fajitas, grilled kebabs, burritos, and all kinds of tacos. The salsa, which comes with every meal, is fresh and *muy picante* (very hot). Ask for the two-person *parrillada,* a hearty sampler of barbecued meat, served with all the beer you can guzzle in one hour. Portions are large and far from "light," so come with an appetite, especially if you order the stuffed chiles smothered with cheese, salsa, and beans. A mariachi band plays nightly at 8. [$] *Average main: $7* ✉ *Av. Cobá 19, Sm 22, El Centro* ☎ *998/887–3045* ✥ *2:B5.*

WORD OF MOUTH

"For good eats you will have to venture into downtown. Fairly easy to do via bus. Once outside the Hotel Zone, use taxis to get around. In downtown, you pretty much pay 20 to 30 pesos for the places you would want to go." —CancunWithMe

$$ MEXICAN Fodor's Choice ★ 🍴 **Labná.** Yucatecan cuisine reaches new and exotic heights at this Mayan-themed restaurant, with fabulous dishes prepared by chef Elviro Pol. The *papadzules* (tortillas stuffed with eggs and covered with pumpkin sauce) are a delicious starter; for an entrée, try the *poc chuc* (tender pork loin in a sour orange sauce) or *longaniza de Valladolid* (traditional sausage from the village of Valladolid). Finish off your meal with some *maja blanco* (white pudding), and Xtabentun-infused Mayan coffee. You may want to linger and enjoy the trio that performs traditional Mexican music Friday through Sunday evenings. Owned by the same team as La Habichuela, this spot serves the most authentic food. [$] *Average main: $10* ✉ *Av. Margaritas 29, Sm 22, El Centro* ☎ *998/892–3056* ✥ *2:A3.*

$$$$ ITALIAN 🍴 **La Dolce Vita.** This grande dame of Cancún restaurants delivers on the promise of its name (which means "the sweet life" in Italian). In business since 1983, this local favorite has candlelit tables and discreet waiters who will make you feel as if you've been transported to Italy. The Italian fare includes homemade pizzas and pastas such as Bolognese-style lasagna, veal scaloppini, and calamari steak in shrimp and lobster sauce. The wine list is excellent, and the dessert truffle is a must for chocolate lovers. Be patient when waiting for your order, though, as good food takes time to prepare. The owners recently opened a second location (featuring the same menu) in the Hotel Zone called Savio's Dolce Vita. [$] *Average main: $25* ✉ *Av. Cobá No. 87, El Centro* ☎ *998/884–3393* 🌐 *www.ladolcevitacancun.com* ✥ *2:D5.*

$$$ CARIBBEAN 🍴 **La Habichuela.** Elegant yet cozy, the much-loved "Green Bean" has an indoor dining room, as well as an outdoor area full of Mayan sculptures and local trees and flowers. Open since 1977, the spot is named after the famous *crema de habichuela* (a rich, cream-based vegetable soup) or the *cocobichuela* (lobster and shrimp in a light curry sauce served inside a coconut). Seafood lovers will get their fix with Caribbean lobster tail or giant shrimp prepared 10 different ways. The menu also features chicken, pasta, and grilled shish kebabs. Finish off your meal with *Xtabentun*, a Mayan liqueur made with honey and anise. If you prefer

to stay in the Hotel Zone, La Habichuela Sunset recently opened to much tourist fanfare, but the food's much better at this Centro location, and prices are slightly less. $ *Average main: $20* ✉ *Av. Margaritas 25, Sm 22, El Centro* ☎ *998/884–3158* ⊕ *www.lahabichuela.com* ✛ *2:A3.*

$$$ ✕ **La Parrilla.** With its flamboyant live mariachi music and energetic wait-
MEXICAN   ers, this place is a Cancún classic. The menu isn't fancy, but it offers good, basic Mexican food. Two reliably tasty choices are the mixed grill (chicken, steak, shrimp) and the grilled Tampiqueña-style steak. Combining entertainment and cuisine, waiters flame broil lobster, salmon, shrimp, and filet mignon directly at your table. Offered are 30 different taco dishes as well as sizzling fajitas and thick burritos. Choose from a wide selection of tequilas to accompany your meal. Reservations are recommended. $ *Average main: $16* ✉ *Av. Yaxchilán 51, Sm 22, El Centro* ☎ *998/287–8118* ⊕ *www.laparrilla.com.mx* ✛ *2:A3.*

$ ✕ **La Pasteleteria.** This cheery café and bakery has comfortable *equipales*
CAFÉ   (rustic Mexican chairs) to plop into as you sample terrific soups, salads, and pizzas. The crepes are what keep the locals coming back for more (the turkey-breast crepe makes a perfect lunch), as well as a variety of sumptuous pastries baked on-site. For travelers with a sweet tooth, this is the best place to buy a delectable dessert or grab a smoothie. The strawberry shortcake is exceptional. Somewhat difficult to find, this downtown gem is on the bustling Avenida Cobá near Walmart. $ *Average main: $8* ✉ *Guanabana Mza 15, Av. Cobá 7, past Av. Labna, Sm 25, El Centro* ☎ *998/193–1150* ☽ *No dinner* ✛ *2:A5.*

$$ ✕ **La Placita.** The menu is simple but tasty at this brightly decorated
MEXICAN   downtown fixture, where plastic tables and chairs are scattered around an outdoor grill. For those who want a more formal setting, the same menu is served indoors with colorful linens and Mexican music to match. The mixed grill of sausage, steak, and pork chops is a stand-out, as are the glorious barbecued ribs and the tequila shrimp. A local favorite since 1987 is the *arrachera* (flank steak) served with a basket of warm tortillas. A selection of tasty pastas and salads is also available. A cold beer makes a perfect accompaniment, and the banana flambé is the ideal way to complete a meal. $ *Average main: $12* ✉ *Av. Yaxchilán 12, Sm 22, El Centro* ☎ *998/884–0407* ⊕ *www.laplacita.com.mx* ✛ *2:A2.*

$$$ ✕ **La Troje.** From the moment you enter the garden patio, you'll feel as if
ECLECTIC   you've stumbled onto a local hideaway. Potted ferns hang from wooden
Fodor'sChoice   beams in this charming setting that's fashioned around oak trees that
★   pierce through the bamboo roof. A brick staircase leads into the main dining area, where Chef Ana Cano and her two daughters prepare homemade pastas, pizzas, baguettes, and crepes, as well as chicken and beef dishes. The vast, colorful menu melds French, Italian and Mexican flavors and features 21 different salads, all with the distinctive flavors of fruits, nuts, cheeses, and tangy dressings. For a local favorite, try the grilled chicken stuffed with spinach, apricots, and cream cheese; or one of the many pasta specials. Early birds can enjoy the full breakfast menu, which includes blended smoothies and fresh-squeezed juices. $ *Average main: $15* ✉ *Av. Acanceh, Sm 15, Mz 3, Lote 3, El Centro* ☎ *998/887–9556* ⊕ *www.latrojedecancun.com* ✛ *2:C6.*

$$$ ITALIAN 🍴 **Locanda Paolo.** Flowers and artwork lend warmth to this sophisticated restaurant, and the staff's attentive without being fussy. The Italian cuisine includes linguine with lobster and angel hair pasta with seafood, and a list of meat and fish specials. Despite the formal setting, the staff is laid-back and seems to know everyone who walks in the door, most of whom are locals who've been dining at the restaurant for more than 20 years. On any given night, many of Chef Paolo Ceravolo's dishes are specials that do not appear on the menu; most are colorful and innovative, such as hot, coiled bread rolls interlaced with piquant mushrooms and eggplant. The international wines are a major draw for locals, as are the specialty lasagnas, which are revised regularly. [$] *Average main: $19* ✉ *Av. Bonampak 145, on corner of Calle Jurel, Sm 3, El Centro* ☎ *998/887–2627* 🌐 *www.locandapaolo.com* 🕒 *No lunch* ✥ *2:D5.*

$$ VEGETARIAN 🍴 **100% Natural.** You'll be surrounded by plants and modern Mayan sculptures when you eat at this open-air restaurant. Start the day with one of their signature omelets and a *bebida inteligente* ("intelligent drink"), which combines fruit juice with ginseng. The lunch menu has soups, salads, pastas, and other vegetarian items. Sandwiches, soy burgers, and stuffed pitas are prepared with fresh-baked breads, or for those craving meat, there's grilled chicken prepared fajita-style. Mexican and Italian specialties are also available. The neighboring 100% Integral shop sells whole wheat breads and other goodies. [$] *Average main: $10* ✉ *Av. Sunyaxchén 62, Sm 25, El Centro* ☎ *998/884–0102* 🌐 *www.100natural.com* ✥ *2:A3.*

$$$ MEXICAN 🍴 **Perico's.** Okay—it's a tourist trap. But it's a really fun one, albeit a dated one. Bar stools are topped with saddles, and waiters dressed as revolutionaries serve flaming drinks and desserts while mariachi and marimba bands play (loudly). Every so often everyone jumps up to join the conga line; your reward for galloping through the restaurant and nearby streets is a free shot of tequila. With 300 seats, this place can sometimes feel a bit empty. The Mexican menu (tacos, seafood, fajitas, kebabs) is passable, but the real reason to come is the nonstop party. For a photo op, stop in the lobby, where you can try on authentic Mexican clothing and pose with props like sombreros and ponchos. [$] *Average main: $20* ✉ *Av. Yaxchilán 61, Sm 25, El Centro* ☎ *998/884–3152* 🌐 *www.pericos.com.mx* ✥ *2:A4.*

$$ PIZZA 🍴 **Rolandi's Pizzeria.** A Cancún landmark for more than 35 years—with outposts in nearby Isla Mujeres, Cozumel, and Playa del Carmen—Rolandi's continues to draw crowds with its scrumptious wood-fired pizzas. There are 20 varieties to choose from and their most popular dish, Pizza Del Patrón, is topped with tomatoes, prosciutto, arugula, and mascarpone cheese. The calzones are smothered with olive oil and packed with fresh ingredients like asparagus, mushrooms, and ham. Homemade pasta dishes like the veal-stuffed ravioli or vegetable lasagna are also very good. Check their website for discounts on your next visit. [$] *Average main: $10* ✉ *Av. Cobá 12, Sm 5, El Centro* ☎ *998/884–4047* 🌐 *www.rolandipizzeria.com* ✥ *2:B5.*

$$ ECLECTIC 🍴 **Roots Jazz Club.** Locals and tourists mingle here to enjoy contemporary jazz and flamenco music (piped in during the afternoon but live at night). The performances are the main attraction, but there's also

an eclectic, international menu of salads, soups, sandwiches, and pastas. The tables nearest the window, along the quaint pedestrianized Avenida Tulipanes, are the best place to tuck into your *chíchí* (chicken breast stuffed with ham and veggies) or German sausage, because the stage area tends to get crowded. This candlelit venue also frequently hosts local art events. $ *Average main: $15* ✉ *Av. Tulipanes 26, Sm 22, El Centro* ☎ *998/884–2437* ⊕ *www.rootsjazzclub.com* ⊗ *No lunch. Closed Sun.–Wed.* ✛ *2:B3*

$ ✗ **Ty-Coz.** Tucked behind the Comercial Mexicana grocery store and
CAFÉ   across from the bus station on Avenida Tulum, this inexpensive restaurant serves croissants and freshly brewed coffee (available starting at 6 am) that make for a delicious breakfast. At lunchtime, stop in for a huge sandwich stuffed with all the deli classics, but be prepared to wait a while since lines can get long. There are also a few vegetarian items on the menu. Pictures of France adorn the walls of the small dining room. The company has recently branched out to offer "Ty-Coz Express" locations, usually connected to local gas stations or convenient stores, and abundant in the hotel zone. $ *Average main: $6* ✉ *Av. Tulum, Sm 2, El Centro* ☎ *998/884–6060* ⊕ *www.tycozmexico.com.mx* ▬ *No credit cards* ⊗ *Closed Sun.* ✛ *2:C2*

$$$ ✗ **Yamamoto.** As the oldest Japanese restaurant in Cancún, Yamamoto
JAPANESE   has some of the best sushi in downtown Cancún. In addition to sashimi, there's a menu of traditional Japanese dishes like chicken teriyaki and tempura for those who prefer their food cooked. Large groups can order combination platters of sushi, sashimi, *kushikatsu*, and *gyoza*. The dining room is tranquil, with Japanese art and bamboo accents, but you can also call for delivery to your hotel room. $ *Average main: $17* ✉ *Av. Uxmal 31, Sm 3, El Centro* ☎ *998/887–3366* ⊕ *www.yamamoto-cancun.com* ✛ *2:C2*.

WHERE TO STAY

You might find it bewildering to choose among Cancún's many hotels, not least because brochures and websites make them sound—and look— almost exactly alike. For luxury and amenities, the Zona Hotelera is the place to stay. In the modest El Centro, local color outweighs facilities. The hotels here are more basic and much less expensive than those in the Zona. If you want to be in the heart of the action, northern hotels near Punta Cancún are within walking distance of the nightclubs. Quieter properties are located at the southern end of Boulevard Kukulcán and in the residential streets between El Centro and the Hotel Zone at Laguna Nichupté near the Pok-Ta-Pok Golf Course.

PRICES

Many hotels have all-inclusive packages, as well as theme-night parties complete with food, beverages, activities, and games. Mexican, Italian, and Caribbean themes seem to be the most popular. Take note, however, that the larger the all-inclusive resort, the blander the food (and the more watered-down the cocktails). For more memorable dining, you may need to go somewhere else and essentially pay for food you're not eating. Expect high prices for food and drink in most hotels. Many of the more exclusive hotels are starting to enforce a "no outside food or drink" policy, so discretion is advised.

Many of the larger and more popular all-inclusives will no longer guarantee an ocean-view room when you book your reservation. If this is important to you, check that all rooms have ocean views at your chosen hotel, or book only at places that will guarantee one. Be sure to bring your confirmation information with you to prove you paid for an ocean view room. Also be careful with lost wristband fines and towel charges, since many of the resorts have started charging up to $150 per day for lost wristbands and $25 for unreturned towels. Be sure your towel returns are duly noted by the pool staff. When checking out, make sure the hotel hasn't tacked on excessive phone or minibar expenses, as some tend to do. ■ **TIP→ At check-in, ask if your all-inclusive rate includes tips—some resorts are now automatically adding 15% gratuities—and "resort fees," which tend to be hidden supplementary charges.**

For expanded reviews, facilities, and current deals, visit Fodors.com.

PUNTA SAM

The area north of Cancún is slowly being developed into an alternative hotel zone, known informally as the Zona Hotelera Norte. This is an ideal area for a tranquil beach vacation, because the shops, restaurants, and nightlife of Cancún are about 30 minutes away by cab. If you decide against an all-inclusive plan, be sure to factor in about $40 in cab fees (each way) from Punta Sam to Cancún restaurants.

$$$$ RESORT ALL-INCLUSIVE **The Beloved Hotel.** As one of the area's only boutique-style all-inclusives, this modern hotel is stylishly decorated in creams and whites, and offers the perfect balance between luxury and comfort. **Pros:** great food; maid service three times daily; spacious bathrooms. **Cons:** cold pool; swim-up bar is in the shade; small bed pillows; see-through door to toilet offers no privacy. [$] *Rooms from: $600* ✉ *Vialidad Paseo Mujeres, Mz1, Lote 10, Sm 3, Zona Continental de Isla Mujeres* ☎ *998/872–8730* 🌐 *www.belovedhotels.com* ⇆ *109 rooms* 🍴 *All-inclusive* ✥ *3:A1.*

$$$$ RESORT ALL-INCLUSIVE **Excellence Playa Mujeres.** North of mainland Cancún, this adults-only resort has redefined the all-inclusive concept. **Pros:** beautifully sculpted grounds; relaxation spa. **Cons:** repetitive restaurant menus; far removed from activity outside resort; no children under 18. [$] *Rooms from: $600* ✉ *Prolongacíon Bonampak s/n, Punta Sam, Lote Terrenos 001, Mza 001, Sm 003, Zona Continental de Isla Mujeres* ☎ *866/540–2585 toll-free in U.S., 998/872–8600* 🌐 *www.excellence-resorts.com* ⇆ *450 rooms* 🍴 *All-inclusive* ✥ *3:A1.*

$$$ RESORT ALL-INCLUSIVE **Villa del Palmar.** Blending Mayan and modern architecture, this five-star resort is like having your personal home transported to the beaches of Mexico. **Pros:** free nonmotorized sports equipment; daily shuttle to Cancún's Hotel Zone; within walking distance to ferry dock for Cozumel and Isla Mujeres; great service. **Cons:** neighboring construction; seaweed in the water; timeshare pitch. [$] *Rooms from: $200* ✉ *Carr Punta Sam, Km 5.2, Zona Continental de Isla Mujeres* ☎ *998/193–2600, 877/845–3795* 🌐 *www.villapalmarcancun.com* ⇆ *125 rooms, 290 suites* 🍴 *Multiple meal plans* ✥ *3:A1.*

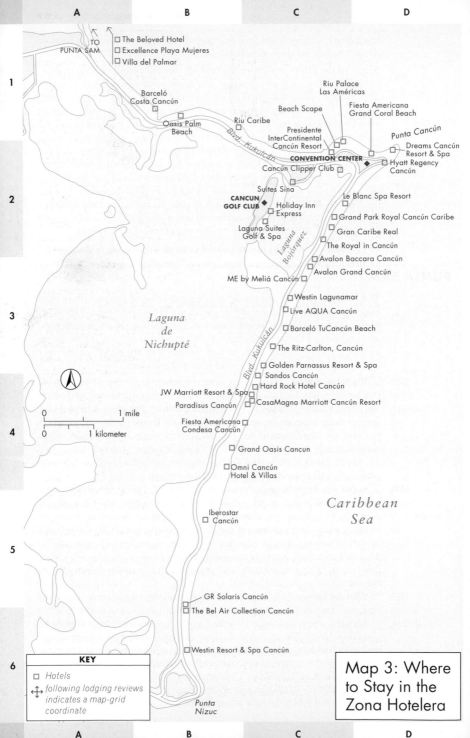

A   B   C   D

1

TO
PUNTA SAM

☐ The Beloved Hotel
☐ Excellence Playa Mujeres
☐ Villa del Palmar

Barceló
Costa Cancún
☐

Oasis Palm
Beach
☐

Riu Caribe ☐

Riu Palace
Las Américas

Beach Scape

Fiesta Americana
Grand Coral Beach

Presidente
InterContinental
Cancún Resort

Punta Cancún

Dreams Cancún
Resort & Spa

CONVENTION CENTER ◆

Hyatt Regency
Cancún

Cancún Clipper Club ☐

Blvd. Kukulcán

2

Suites Sina

CANCUN
GOLF CLUB ◆

Holiday Inn
Express

Laguna Suites
Golf & Spa

ME by Meliá Cancún ☐

Le Blanc Spa Resort

☐ Grand Park Royal Cancún Caribe

☐ Gran Caribe Real

☐ The Royal in Cancún

☐ Avalon Baccara Cancún

☐ Avalon Grand Cancún

Laguna
Bojórquez

☐ Westin Lagunamar

☐ Live AQUA Cancún

3

Laguna
de
Nichupté

☐ Barceló TuCancún Beach

☐ The Ritz-Carlton, Cancún

☐ Golden Parnassus Resort & Spa

☐ Sandos Cancún

☐ Hard Rock Hotel Cancún

JW Marriott Resort & Spa ☐

Paradisus Cancún ☐

☐ CasaMagna Marriott Cancún Resort

Blvd. Kukulcán

0   1 mile
0   1 kilometer

Fiesta Americana
Condesa Cancún ☐

4

☐ Grand Oasis Cancun

☐ Omni Cancún
Hotel & Villas

Caribbean
Sea

Iberostar
Cancún ☐

5

GR Solaris Cancún
☐ The Bel Air Collection Cancún

☐ Westin Resort & Spa Cancún

6

KEY
☐ Hotels
⬍ following lodging reviews
     indicates a map-grid
     coordinate

Punta
Nizuc

Map 3: Where
to Stay in the
Zona Hotelera

A   B   C   D

ZONA HOTELERA

$$ HOTEL

[H] **Avalon Baccara Cancún.** Amid the towering resorts with sleek, modern interiors that line the Zona Hotelera, the Avalon Baccara stands out for its small size and rustic Mexican design. **Pros:** refreshing home-like setting unlike all-inclusive–resort style; artistically unique. **Cons:** no children under 18; small pool and patios; steep driveway can be dangerous and there are only three parking spaces. [$] *Rooms from: $112* ✉ *Blvd. Kukulcán, Km 11.5, Zona Hotelera* ☎ *998/881–3900* 🌐 *www.avalonbaccaracancunresort.com* 🛏 *8 rooms, 19 suites* 🍴 *No meals* ⊕ *3:C2.*

$$ RESORT

[H] **Avalon Grand Cancún.** Doubling as a time-share property, the Avalon Grand Cancún is slightly overshadowed by newer Cancún properties, but still has everything you need to have a pleasant vacation. **Pros:** guests have access to facilities at nearby sister resort Avalon Baccara and Avalon Reef on Isla Mujeres; reasonable rates; meal plan available. **Cons:** Wi-Fi costs extra; understaffed; small step between bedroom and bathroom can be dangerous; rooms could use some upgrades. [$] *Rooms from: $150* ✉ *Blvd. Kukulcán, Km 11.5, Zona Hotelera* ☎ *998/848–9300, 800/774–0040 toll-free from U.S.* 🌐 *www.avalongrandcancun.com* 🛏 *39 rooms, 80 suites* 🍴 *Multiple meal plans* ⊕ *3:C3.*

$$$ RESORT ALL-INCLUSIVE FAMILY

[H] **Barceló Costa Cancún.** Ferries to Isla Mujeres are just steps away from this resort, as it neighbors one of Cancún's main piers, El Embarcadero. **Pros:** great for kids; close to Embarcadero; good water-sports center. **Cons:** no air-conditioning in lobby; small beach area; check-in/out times are chaotic in the lobby area. [$] *Rooms from: $204* ✉ *Blvd. Kukulcán, Km 4.5, Zona Hotelera* ☎ *998/849–7100, 800/227–2356 toll-free in U.S.* 🌐 *www.barcelo.com* 🛏 *358 rooms* 🍴 *All inclusive* ⊕ *3:B1.*

$$$ RESORT ALL-INCLUSIVE

[H] **Barceló TuCancún Beach.** Just behind the massive Kukulcán Plaza and about a half mile down the road from La Isla, this resort is an ideal location for mall addicts. **Pros:** near two of Cancún's biggest malls; wide range of activities for children and adults. **Cons:** extra fees for use of Wi-Fi and safes; only half of rooms have ocean view; blue walls and lobby murals make this hotel feel dated. [$] *Rooms from: $204* ✉ *Blvd. Kukulcán, Km 13.5, Zona Hotelera* ☎ *998/891–5900, 800/227–2356 in U.S.* 🌐 *www.barcelo.com* 🛏 *316 rooms, 16 villas* 🍴 *All-inclusive* ⊕ *3:C3.*

$$ HOTEL

[H] **Beach Scape Kin-Ha Villas & Suites.** This condo hotel is a wonderful place for families thanks to its tranquil beach and relaxed atmosphere. **Pros:** all rooms have balconies; peaceful location; one of the best beaches in Cancún. **Cons:** no elevator in the three-story hotel; no children's programs; charge for Wi-Fi. [$] *Rooms from: $145* ✉ *Blvd. Kukulcán, Km 8.5, Zona Hotelera* ☎ *998/891–5400* 🌐 *www.beachscape.com.mx* 🛏 *80 rooms, 50 suites* 🍴 *Breakfast* ⊕ *3:C2.*

$$ RESORT ALL-INCLUSIVE

[H] **The Bel Air Collection Cancún.** The design scheme at this strikingly chic and tranquil resort is unlike that of any other hotel along Boulevard Kukulcán. **Pros:** luxurious spa; all-inclusive plan available; aesthetically pleasing hotel. **Cons:** no kids under 12; far from party zone; open-air lobby can be very wet and windy during rainy season. [$] *Rooms from: $150* ✉ *Blvd. Kukulcán, Km 20.5, Zona Hotelera* ☎ *998/193–1770*

2

🌐 *www.belaircollection.com* 🛏 *136 rooms, 19 suites* 🍴 *Multiple meal plans* ✥ *3:B6.*

$ HOTEL 🏨 **Cancún Clipper Club.** Right next to the Zona Hotelera's main hub of shops and clubs, this hotel still manages to feel secluded because it's set back from Boulevard Kukulcán. **Pros:** decent rates; close proximity to lots of activities. **Cons:** no beach; Wi-Fi in common areas only; $100 fine for lost safe key. [$] *Rooms from: $75* ✉ *Blvd. Kukulcán, Km 9, Zona Hotelera* ☎ *998/891–5999* 🌐 *www.clipper.com.mx* 🛏 *71 rooms, 71 suites* 🍴 *Multiple meal plans* ✥ *3:C2.*

$$$ RESORT FAMILY 🏨 **CasaMagna Marriott Cancún Resort.** Sweeping grounds and arched walkways that lead up to the six-story building will make you forget you're at a Marriott. **Pros:** more culturally traditional than most Marriotts; excellent Thai restaurant; gorgeous views from most rooms; on-site wedding planner and car rental. **Cons:** geared to groups and conventions, which account for 60% of the hotel's business; no designated pool for children; Wi-Fi ($15/day) can be spotty. [$] *Rooms from: $189* ✉ *Blvd. Kukulcán, Km 14.5, Zona Hotelera* ☎ *998/881–2000, 800/900–8800* 🌐 *www.marriott.com* 🛏 *414 rooms, 38 suites* 🍴 *Multiple meal plans* ✥ *3:C4.*

$$$$ RESORT ALL-INCLUSIVE FAMILY 🏨 **Dreams Cancún Resort & Spa.** Surrounded on three sides by ocean, this resort provides stunning panoramic views of the Caribbean. **Pros:** dolphin aquarium; excellent beach access; family theme nights. **Cons:** swimming with dolphins costs extra; lobby extremely crowded during check-in hours; charge to use Wi-Fi. [$] *Rooms from: $450* ✉ *Blvd. Kukulcán, Km 9.5, Punta Cancún, Zona Hotelera* ☎ *998/848–7000, 866/237–3267 in U.S.* 🌐 *www.dreamsresorts.com* 🛏 *345 rooms, 34 suites* 🍴 *All-inclusive* ✥ *3:D2.*

$$$$ RESORT ALL-INCLUSIVE FAMILY 🏨 **Fiesta Americana Condesa Cancún.** This hotel is easily recognized by the 118-foot-tall palapa that covers its lobby. **Pros:** friendly staff; scheduled activites on the hour; smaller pools designated for children. **Cons:** hallways get slippery when it rains; sound carries between floors; popular with tour groups. [$] *Rooms from: $430* ✉ *Blvd. Kukulcán, Km 16.5, Zona Hotelera* ☎ *998/881–4200* 🌐 *www.fiestaamericana.com/cancun* 🛏 *476 rooms, 26 suites* 🍴 *All-inclusive* ✥ *3:B4.*

$$$$ RESORT Fodor's Choice ★ 🏨 **Fiesta Americana Grand Coral Beach.** If luxury's your bag, you'll feel right at home at this distinctive all-suites hotel, which is more upscale than Cancún's other Fiesta Americana properties. **Pros:** enormous pool with three swim-up bars; complimentary kids' club; business center has private offices; excellent service. **Cons:** pool water is chilly; too big for some; Wi-Fi costs extra. [$] *Rooms from: $550* ✉ *Blvd. Kukulcán, Km 9.5, Zona Hotelera* ☎ *998/881–3200* 🌐 *www.fiestamericanagrand.com* 🛏 *602 suites* 🍴 *No meals* ✥ *3:D2.*

$$$ RESORT ALL-INCLUSIVE 🏨 **Golden Parnassus Resort & Spa.** The rooms at this all-inclusive, adults-only resort are warmly decorated with sunset colors, fruit baskets, and rich wood furnishings; some rooms even have private hot tubs. **Pros:** free shuttle to sister property Great Parnassus Resort & Spa; evening entertainment; great tiki bar. **Cons:** no kids under 18; no Internet; thin towels and poor lighting in the dated rooms. [$] *Rooms from: $200* ✉ *Blvd. Kukulcán, Km 14.5, Retorno San Miguelito Lote 37, Zona*

Hotelera ☎ *998/287–1400* 🌐 *www.parnassusresorts.com* 🛏 *214 rooms* 🍴 *All-inclusive* ✣ *3:C3.*

$$$$ RESORT ALL-INCLUSIVE FAMILY 🏨 **Gran Caribe Real.** There's no such thing as a standard room at this all-suite resort, where the most basic option is a spacious junior suite with a sofa bed, sitting area, flat-screen TV, and balcony. **Pros:** wide array of activities; gym has yoga and spin classes. **Cons:** room decor uninspired; mediocre restaurants; pools tend to get crowded. [$] *Rooms from: $329* ✉ *Blvd. Kukulcán, Km 11.5, Zona Hotelera* ☎ *998/881–7340, 800/760–0944 in U.S.* 🌐 *www.realresorts.com* 🛏 *487 suites* 🍴 *All-inclusive* ✣ *3:C2.*

$$$$ RESORT ALL-INCLUSIVE 🏨 **Grand Oasis Cancún.** This multistructure hotel, comprised of a main building simply called Pyramid and two side buildings, is right next door to sister property and Spring Break mecca Oasis Cancún, how ever this property prohibits spring breakers and is geared more toward families. **Pros:** enormous pool area; lively atmosphere. **Cons:** $4 charge for use of room safe; large grounds require fair amount of walking; too boisterous for some. [$] *Rooms from: $350* ✉ *Blvd. Kukulcán, Km 16.5, Zona Hotelera* ☎ *888/774–0040 in U.S., 998/881–7000* 🌐 *www.grandoasiscancunresort.com* 🛏 *765 rooms* 🍴 *All-inclusive* ✣ *3:B4.*

$$$ RESORT ALL-INCLUSIVE 🏨 **Grand Park Royal Cancún Caribe.** There's a wide variety of accommodations at the Grand Park Royal, and most have ocean views. **Pros:** most rooms face ocean; excellent pool areas. **Cons:** Wi-Fi and gym cost extra; reservations required at restaurants. [$] *Rooms from: $190* ✉ *Blvd. Kukulcán, Km 10.5, Zona Hotelera* ☎ *998/848–7800* 🌐 *www.park-royalhotels.com* 🛏 *311 rooms* 🍴 *All-inclusive* ✣ *3:C2.*

$$$$ RESORT ALL-INCLUSIVE 🏨 **GR Solaris Cancún.** More upscale than its Royal Solaris sister property in Cancún, this resort is somewhat focused on adults. **Pros:** lighted tennis court; water-sports marina across from sister property; fully equipped free gym. **Cons:** pool area can get noisy; loud Mexican music in the lobby; private Jacuzzis are exposed to neighbors; Wi-Fi costs extra. [$] *Rooms from: $267* ✉ *Blvd. Kukulcán, Km 18.5, Zona Hotelera* ☎ *998/848–8400* 🌐 *www.hotelessolaris.com* 🛏 *306 rooms* 🍴 *All-inclusive* ✣ *3:B5.*

$$$$ RESORT ALL-INCLUSIVE 🏨 **Hard Rock Hotel Cancún.** Opened in 2012, this property fits right into Cancún's lively and energetic atmosphere. **Pros:** kids' and teens' center; two tennis courts; excellent Japanese restaurant. **Cons:** some rooms lack ocean views; no water sports. [$] *Rooms from: $450* ✉ *Blvd. Kukulcán, Km 14.5, Zona Hotelera* ☎ *998/881–3600* 🌐 *www.hardrockhotels.com* 🛏 *601 rooms, 24 suites* 🍴 *All-inclusive* ✣ *3:C4.*

$ HOTEL 🏨 **Holiday Inn Express.** Within walking distance of the Cancún Golf Club, this hotel caters to business travelers and tourists seeking an affordable alternative to the pricey resorts. **Pros:** good rates; free shuttle to beach. **Cons:** simple rooms; no elevator; not on the beach. [$] *Rooms from: $65* ✉ *Paseo Pok-Ta-Pok, Lotes 21 and 22, off Blvd. Kukulcán, Km 7.5, Zona Hotelera* ☎ *998/883–2200, 888/465–4329 in U.S.* 🌐 *www.hiexpress.com/cancunmex* 🛏 *119 rooms* 🍴 *Breakfast* ✣ *3:C2.*

$$$$ RESORT 🏨 **Hyatt Regency Cancún.** Situated on the tip of Punta Cancún, this 14-story hotel offers the best views in Zona Hotelera. **Pros:** excellent views; on-site beauty salon and car rental; great restaurants. **Cons:** no children's programs; bathrooms have showers only; Wi-Fi occasionally

drops. $ *Rooms from: $265* ⊠ *Blvd. Kukulcán, Km 8.5, Zona Hotelera* ☎ 998/891–5555 ⊕ *www.cancun.regency.hyatt.com* ⮑ *287 rooms, 8 suites* ⭘ *Multiple meal plans* ✥ *3:D2.*

$$$$
RESORT
ALL-INCLUSIVE
⛯ **Iberostar Cancún.** Formerly a Hilton, the Caribbean plays a central role at this all-inclusive resort, with ocean views from all standard guest rooms and junior suites. **Pros:** outstanding beachfront villas; tasteful decor; angled pool area gets all-day sunshine. **Cons:** only one heated pool; rooms and overall resort decor hasn't been updated since Hilton ownership. $ *Rooms from: $500* ⊠ *Blvd. Kukulcán, Km 17, Zona Hotelera* ☎ 998/881–8000 ⊕ *www.iberostar.com* ⮑ *426 rooms, 23 suites, 82 villas* ⭘ *All-inclusive* ✥ *3:B5.*

$$$$
RESORT
Fodor's Choice
★
⛯ **JW Marriott Cancún Resort & Spa.** This is the best place to experience luxury, Cancún style, plus good service. **Pros:** top-notch service; huge spa; iPod docks; artificial reef. **Cons:** lacks the festive mood of other hotels along the strip; breakfast buffet costs $28. $ *Rooms from: $300* ⊠ *Blvd. Kukulcán, Km 14.5, Zona Hotelera* ☎ 998/848–9600, 888/813–2776 ⊕ *www.marriott.com* ⮑ *448 rooms, 74 suites* ⭘ *No meals* ✥ *3:C4.*

$$$$
HOTEL
ALL-INCLUSIVE
⛯ **Laguna Suites Golf & Spa.** Framing the fairway of Pok-Ta-Pok Golf Course, this tranquil resort is comprised of 12 white-stucco buildings, each housing four spacious suites. **Pros:** free shuttle to the beach every hour; quiet location; access to golf course; all-inclusive plan available; neighboring laundromat is convenient. **Cons:** menu is very repetitive if you select all-inclusive package; no children's activities; bathrooms have showers only; mosquitoes in common areas. $ *Rooms from: $280* ⊠ *Paseo Pok Ta Pok #3, Zona Hotelera* ☎ 998/891–5252 ⊕ *www.lagunasuites.com.mx* ⮑ *48 suites* ⭘ *Multiple meal plans* ✥ *3:C2.*

$$$$
RESORT
ALL-INCLUSIVE
Fodor's Choice
★
⛯ **Le Blanc Spa Resort.** An airy and modern hotel with refined white-and-beige minimalist decor, Le Blanc Spa is the most upscale of the Palace Resort properties, and perhaps the most luxurious all-inclusive resort in Cancún. **Pros:** aesthetically pleasing design; excellent spa; butler service; great food. **Cons:** no kids; pricey; some rooms have small French balconies only. $ *Rooms from: $600* ⊠ *Blvd. Kukulcán, Km 10, Zona Hotelera* ☎ 998/881–4740 ⊕ *www.leblancsparesort.com* ⮑ *222 rooms, 38 suites* ⭘ *All-inclusive* ✥ *3:C2.*

$$$$
RESORT
ALL-INCLUSIVE
Fodor's Choice
★
⛯ **Live AQUA Cancún.** You won't find raucous Spring Breakers or screaming kids at this ultra-stylish Mexican-owned Hotelera Posadas property, which mostly attracts luxury-minded thirtysomething sun worshippers. **Pros:** huge suites; all rooms have oceanfront views; extensive spa services; free yoga classes offered daily. **Cons:** aromatherapy scents in public spaces can be strong; only one restaurant is open for lunch; no kids under 18. $ *Rooms from: $600* ⊠ *Blvd. Kukulcán, Km 12.5, Zona Hotelera* ☎ 998/881–7600, 888/782–9722 ⊕ *www.feel-aqua.com* ⮑ *335 rooms, 36 suites* ⭘ *All-inclusive* ✥ *3:C3.*

$$$$
RESORT
ALL-INCLUSIVE
Fodor's Choice
★
⛯ **ME by Meliá Cancún.** The ME takes the chic flavor of a trendy boutique hotel and blows it up to the grand scale of a large resort. **Pros:** great for young couples; amazing contemporary design; pet-friendly; 24-hr gym. **Cons:** not ideal for kids; watered-down cocktails; $150 charge per day for lost all-inclusive wristband; reservations needed for restaurants. $ *Rooms from: $450* ⊠ *Blvd. Kukulcán, Km 12, Zona*

Live AQUA Cancún

Hotelera ☎ 998/881–2500 🌐 www.me-cancun.com 🛏 348 rooms, 71 suites 🍴 All-inclusive ⊕ 3:C3.

$$$$ RESORT ALL-INCLUSIVE FAMILY 🏨 **Oasis Palm Beach.** Within walking distance of El Embarcadero, this all-inclusive family resort sits in prime location if you're looking to take a boat to Isla Mujeres. **Pros:** great location; access to Grand Oasis Cancún golf course; good for families. **Cons:** pool is shaded most of the day; the only Jacuzzi is at the spa and it costs extra; small TVs. [$] *Rooms from: $250 ✉ Blvd. Kukulcán, Km 4.5, Zona Hotelera ☎ 998/848–7500 🌐 www.oasishotels.com 🛏 468 rooms, 2 suites 🍴 All-inclusive ⊕ 3:B1.*

$$$$ RESORT ALL-INCLUSIVE 🏨 **Omni Cancún Hotel & Villas.** After undergoing a $17 million renovation in 2007, this 12-story hotel has definitely moved up a notch or two in Cancún's hotel hierarchy. **Pros:** all-inclusive plan available; tons of scheduled activities; educational programs at Kid's Club; on-site ATM. **Cons:** crowded pool area; time-share sales pitches in the lobby; Wi-Fi costs extra. [$] *Rooms from: $350 ✉ Blvd. Kukulcán, Km 16.5, Zona Hotelera ☎ 998/881–0600 🌐 www.omnihotels.com 🛏 259 rooms, 19 suites, 23 villas 🍴 Multiple meal plans ⊕ 3:B4.*

$$$$ RESORT ALL-INCLUSIVE 🏨 **Paradisus Cancún.** Having been remodeled from a Gran Melia to a Paradisus in November 2012, this enormous beachfront hotel resembles a modern Mayan temple, complete with atriums topped by pyramid-shaped skylights. **Pros:** all-inclusive plan available; privacy of Royal Service; golf course. **Cons:** lacks intimacy due to size; Internet costs extra for non–Royal Service guests; top-shelf alcohol and minibar snacks are not part of all-inclusive plan; some restaurants require reservations. [$] *Rooms from: $400 ✉ Blvd. Kukulcán, Km 16.5, Zona Hotelera ☎ 998/881–1100 🌐 www.paradisus.com 🛏 678 suites 🍴 Multiple meal plans ⊕ 3:C4.*

$$$$ RESORT 🏨 **Presidente InterContinental Cancún Resort.** This landmark hotel boasts one of the best beaches in Cancún, and it has a contemporary and clean look to it that includes the swanky lobby with a tequila bar. **Pros:** short walk to shops and restaurants; virtually current-less beach is great for families; tower rooms renovated in 2010. **Cons:** focus on business travelers and conventions; Wi-Fi and in-room coffee costs extra; palm trees block ocean view in some lower level rooms. [$] *Rooms from: $249 ✉ Blvd. Kukulcán, Km 7.5, Zona Hotelera ☎ 998/848–8700 🌐 www.intercontinental.com/cancun 🛏 267 rooms, 22 suites 🍴 No meals ⊕ 3:C2.*

$$$$ RESORT Fodor's Choice ★ 🏨 **The Ritz-Carlton, Cancún.** Outfitted with crystal chandeliers, beautiful antiques, and elegant oil paintings, this hotel's elegant style is so European that you may well forget you're in Mexico. **Pros:** progressive dinners allows guests to sample three restaurants in one night; tennis center offers private lessons; impeccable service. **Cons:** conservative atmosphere for the Hotel Zone; expensive; parking costs extra. [$] *Rooms from: $459 ✉ Blvd. Kukulcán, Km 13.5, Retorno del Rey 36, Zona Hotelera ☎ 998/881–0808 🌐 www.ritzcarlton.com 🛏 365 rooms, 50 suites 🍴 No meals ⊕ 3:C3.*

$$$$ RESORT ALL-INCLUSIVE 🏨 **Riu Caribe.** Despite renovations in 2012, this hotel still retains some of its Mayan themes in the main lobby, like the pyramid-shape architectural design and striking stained-glass Mayan calendars on the high

JW Marriott Cancún

The Ritz-Carlton, Cancún

ceiling. **Pros:** tennis courts; large beach and pools; recently renovated; use of facilities at neighboring Riu Palace. **Cons:** beach and pool areas can get crowded; no room service; a far walk to the clubs and shops. $ *Rooms from: $350* ⊠ *Blvd. Kukulcán, Km 5.5, Zona Hotelera* ☎ *998/848–7850* ⊕ *www.riu.com* ⤴ *445 rooms, 61 suites* ⦿ *All-inclusive* ✛ *3:B1.*

$$$$
RESORT
ALL-INCLUSIVE

🍽 **Riu Palace Las Américas.** A colossal eight-story property at the north end of the Zona, the Palace is visually stunning and different from the modern, minimalist resorts that dot the Zona Hotelera. **Pros:** spacious suites; access to sister properties Riu Cancún and Riu Caribe. **Cons:** small pools and tiny beach; not much sun by the pool or beach by late afternoon; some rooms smell musty. $ *Rooms from: $500* ⊠ *Blvd. Kukulcán, Km 8.5, Zona Hotelera* ☎ *998/891–4300* ⊕ *www.riu.com* ⤴ *372 junior suites* ⦿ *All-inclusive* ✛ *3:C1.*

$$$$
RESORT
ALL-INCLUSIVE

🍽 **The Royal in Cancún.** Luxury is the focus at this high-end, adults-only resort (age 16+), where all 288 suites have mahogany furniture, Jacuzzis, ocean views, balconies with hammocks, and "magic boxes" that allow room service to be delivered without ever opening the door. **Pros:** two-person Jacuzzis in suites; ocean view from all suites and spa. **Cons:** adults only; time-share sales pitch in the lobby; sleepless nights for rooms near the pool and lobby. $ *Rooms from: $500* ⊠ *Blvd. Kukulcán, Km 11.5, Zona Hotelera* ☎ *998/881–5600* ⊕ *www.realresorts.com.mx* ⤴ *288 suites* ⦿ *All-inclusive* ✛ *3:C2.*

$$$$
RESORT
ALL-INCLUSIVE

🍽 **Sandos Cancún.** Though it sits high on a hill tucked away from the main boulevard, this refined yet relaxed hotel, an artful blend of art deco and Mayan styles, gets mixed reviews under the new management—the former Le Méridien Cancún Resort and Spa was purchased by Sandos in the summer of 2012. **Pros:** near one of Cancún's best malls; large fitness center; all rooms have ocean or lagoon views; tastefully decorated. **Cons:** Wi-Fi costs extra; some rooms are small; shady pool by early afternoon. $ *Rooms from: $500* ⊠ *Blvd. Kukulcán, Km 14, Retorno del Rey, Lote 37, Zona Hotelera* ☎ *998/881–2200, 866/336–4083* ⊕ *www.sandos.com* ⤴ *214 rooms* ⦿ *All-inclusive* ✛ *3:C4.*

$
HOTEL

🍽 **Suites Sina.** On a quiet residential street off Boulevard Kukulcán, these economical suites are in front of Laguna Nichupté and close to the Pok-Ta-Pok golf course. **Pros:** ideally situated on the lagoon; affordable. **Cons:** 10-minute walk from beach; no elevator; loud a/c. $ *Rooms from: $80* ⊠ *Club de Golf, Calle Quetzal 33, turn right at Km 7.5 after golf course, Zona Hotelera/El Centro* ☎ *998/883–1017* ⊕ *www.suitessinacancun.com* ⤴ *4 rooms, 36 suites* ⦿ *No meals* ✛ *3:C2.*

$$$$
RESORT
ALL-INCLUSIVE
FAMILY

🍽 **The Westin Resort & Spa Cancún.** On the southern end of the Zona Hotelera, this hotel is quite secluded; you'll get privacy, but have to drive to get to shops and restaurants. **Pros:** two beaches; a natural reef great for snorkeling; all-inclusive plan available. **Cons:** extra charge for use of amenities like Internet and spa; only rooms in the Royal Tower have breakfast and cocktails included in the rate. $ *Rooms from: $300* ⊠ *Blvd. Kukulcán, Km 20, Zona Hotelera* ☎ *998/848–7400* ⊕ *www.westin.com/cancun* ⤴ *362 rooms, 17 suites* ⦿ *Multiple meal plans* ✛ *3:B6.*

$$$$
RESORT
FAMILY

☷ **Westin Lagunamar.** This recently renovated timeshare property is centrally located across from La Isla shopping center. Pros: beautiful infinity pool; all the comforts of home; great for families. Cons: timeshare pitch; Wi-Fi signal drops in areas; no all-inclusive plan. $ *Rooms from: $269* ⊠ *Blvd. Kukulcán, Km 12.5, Zona Hotelera* ☎ *998/891–4200* ⊕ *www.starwoodhotels.com* ⇗ *143 rooms* ⦿*No meals* ⊕ *3:C3.*

EL CENTRO

$
HOTEL

☷ **Ambiance Suites Cancún.** Branding itself as "your home and office," this modern hotel caters mostly to business executives. Pros: convenient location within El Centro; good value. Cons: unfriendly staff; far from the beach. $ *Rooms from: $97* ⊠ *Av. Tulum 227, Sm 20, El Centro* ☎ *998/892–0392* ⊕ *www.ambiancecancun.com* ⇗ *48 rooms* ⦿*Breakfast* ⊕ *2:C6.*

$
HOTEL

☷ **City Express.** Across the street from Plaza las Américas, this bright-yellow hotel is mostly geared toward business travelers and those passing through Cancún. Pros: great value; clean rooms; children under 12 years stay free. Cons: neighboring shopping mall creates street traffic; 15-minute drive to the beach; bland decor. $ *Rooms from: $82* ⊠ *Av. Nichupté, Sm 8, Mza 1, Lote 4, El Centro* ☎ *998/881–1930* ⊕ *www.cityexpress.com.mx* ⇗ *124 rooms, 4 suites* ⦿*Breakfast* ⊕ *2:D6.*

$$
HOTEL

☷ **Courtyard Cancún.** The draw of this deluxe property is that it's five minutes from the international airport with free round-trip airport shuttle service. Pros: free Wi-Fi; complimentary shuttle service to and from airport; ATM in hotel. Cons: astronomical phone charges; far from Cancún center and beaches. $ *Rooms from: $109* ⊠ *Blvd. Luis Donaldo Colosio, Km 12.5, Sm 301, Carretera Cancún-Aeropuerto* ☎ *998/287–2200* ⊕ *www.marriott.com/cuncy* ⇗ *195 rooms, 6 suites* ⦿*No meals* ⊕ *2:C6.*

$
HOTEL
Fodor's Choice
★

☷ **Grand City Hotel.** This modern budget hotel offers large, pleasant rooms, each with a flat-screen TV, wireless Internet, iPod dock station, minibar, microwave, and private bath. Pros: best budget hotel in Cancún; newly renovated. Cons: street noise; restaurant closes early. $ *Rooms from: $73* ⊠ *Av. Yaxchilán 154, Sm 20, across street from Red Cross, El Centro* ☎ *998/193–3580* ⊕ *www.grandcity-hotel.com* ⇗ *18 rooms* ⦿*Breakfast* ⊕ *2:A6.*

$
HOTEL

☷ **Hotel Colonial.** A charming fountain and garden are at the center of this hotel's colonial-style buildings. Pros: good location; friendly staff; affordable. Cons: no pool; sound carries; no elevator; website photos wrongly imply that property is on or near the beach. $ *Rooms from: $50* ⊠ *Av. Tulipanes 22, Sm 22, El Centro* ☎ *998/884–1535* ⊕ *www.hotelcolonialcancun.com* ⇗ *46 rooms* ⦿*Breakfast* ⊕ *2:B4.*

$ HOTEL 🏨 **Hotel El Rey del Caribe.** Thanks to the use of solar energy, a water-recycling system, and composting toilets, this unique hotel has very little impact on the environment—and its luxuriant garden blocks the heat and noise of downtown. **Pros:** tranquil atmosphere; eco-friendly; affordable spa; airport transportation ($35); free Wi-Fi. **Cons:** simple and musty rooms; no elevator; mosquitoes in the common areas. [$] *Rooms from: $85* ✉ *Av. Uxmal 24, at Náder, Sm 2A, El Centro* ☎ *998/884–2028* 🌐 *www.elreydelcaribe.com* 🛏 *31 rooms* 🍴 *Breakfast* ✥ *2:C2.*

$ HOTEL Fodor's Choice ★ 🏨 **Hotel Xbalamqué Resort & Spa.** A refreshing retreat from the bustling streets of El Centro, this hotel has a lobby adorned with a palapa roof, waterfalls, tropical birds, and stone flooring. **Pros:** only downtown hotel with (small) spa, beauty salon, and yoga studio on-site; good El Centro location. **Cons:** street noise audible from front rooms; Wi-Fi connection drops; limited parking spaces. [$] *Rooms from: $80* ✉ *Av. Yaxchilan 31, Sm 22, Mza 18, El Centro* ☎ *998/193–2720* 🌐 *www.xbalamque.com* 🛏 *80 rooms, 11 suites* 🍴 *Breakfast* ✥ *2:A3.*

$ HOTEL Fodor's Choice ★ 🏨 **Ibis Cancún Centro.** Within walking distance of Las Américas Shopping Center, this hotel is perfect for mixing business with pleasure at a very reasonable price. **Pros:** 15 minutes from the airport; clean, bright rooms; great rates. **Cons:** no pool; mainly caters to business and budget travelers. [$] *Rooms from: $65* ✉ *Av. Tulum y Nichupte, Sm, 11 M2 L3, El Centro* ☎ *998/272–8500* 🌐 *www.ibishotel.com* 🛏 *190 rooms* 🍴 *No meals* ✥ *2:C6.*

$ HOTEL 🏨 **Los Girasoles.** Set back on one of El Centro's few quiet streets, this pleasant hotel is within walking distance of the city's main avenues and shopping centers. **Pros:** very affordable; blackout curtains block sunlight; laundry facilities; centrally located. **Cons:** no decent views or balconies; no elevator; rooms are slightly musty. [$] *Rooms from: $45* ✉ *Calle Pina 20, Sm 25, El Centro* ☎ *998/887–3990* 🌐 *www.losgirasolescancun.com.mx* 🛏 *17 rooms* 🍴 *No meals* ✥ *2:A5.*

$$ HOTEL 🏨 **Radisson Hotel Hacienda Cancún.** A stimulating change from the street on which it lies, this hacienda-style building is strikingly hip and sleek. **Pros:** state-of-the-art gym equipment; business center with Internet access. **Cons:** east-facing rooms tend to have street noise; lights in rooms are movement triggered. [$] *Rooms from: $100* ✉ *Av. Náder 1, El Centro* ☎ *998/881–6500* 🌐 *www.radisson.com* 🛏 *237 rooms, 11 suites* 🍴 *Multiple meal plans* ✥ *2:C1.*

$ HOTEL 🏨 **Suites Cancún Centro.** You can rent suites or rooms by the day, week, or month at this quiet hotel. **Pros:** in the heart of downtown Cancún; near many restaurants and bars; clean and affordable. **Cons:** no elevator; not much of a social scene at hotel. [$] *Rooms from: $85* ✉ *Calle Alcatraces 32, Sm 22, next to Parque de las Palapas, El Centro* ☎ *998/887–5833, 998/887–5655* 🌐 *www.suitescancun.com.mx* 🛏 *42 rooms, 27 suites* 🍴 *No meals* ✥ *2:B4.*

$ HOTEL 🏨 **Terra Caribe.** Far from the Hotel Zone chaos, this Mediterranean style property is one of the best deals in El Centro. **Pros:** daily shuttle to the beach; comfortable beds; polite staff; free Wi-Fi. **Cons:** no views; lukewarm water in the Jacuzzi; far from the beach. [$] *Rooms from: $45* ✉ *Av. Lopez Portillo # 70, at Av. Bonampak, El Centro* ☎ *998/880–0448* 🌐 *www.terracaribe.com* 🛏 *42 rooms* 🍴 *No meals* ✥ *2:D1.*

NIGHTLIFE

We're not here to judge: we know that most people come to Cancún to party. If you want fine dining and dancing under the stars, you'll definitely find it here. But if your tastes run more toward bikini contests, all-night chug-a-thons, or cross-dressing Cher impersonators, rest assured: Cancún has plenty of those, too.

■**TIP➔** If you want to avoid rowdy spring breakers, stay clear of "open-bar" establishments and chain restaurants like Margaritaville, Señor Frogs, and Planet Hollywood. You're likely to find them packed with party animals on the loose.

BARS

ALL-PURPOSE BARS

Many of these spots daylight as restaurants, but after sunset the party kicks up with pulsating music and waiters who don't so much encourage crowd participation as demand it. Just remember, it's all in good fun.

Carlos 'n Charlie's. At Carlos 'n Charlie's waiters will occasionally abandon their posts to start singing or performing comical skits. It's not unusual for them to roust everyone from their seats to join in a conga line before going back to serving food and drinks. ⊠ *Blvd. Kukulcán, Km 9, Forum by the Sea Mall, Zona Hotelera* ☎ *998/883 4468* ⊕ *www.carlosandcharlies.com/cancun.*

Jimmy Buffett's Margaritaville. You can enjoy a cheeseburger in paradise, along with live music, drinks, and games, at Jimmy Buffett's Margaritaville. Of course, you'll especially like this place if you're a parrothead. ⊠ *Plaza Flamingo, Blvd. Kukulcán, Km 11.5, Zona Hotelera* ☎ *998/885–2376* ⊕ *www.margaritaville.com.mx.*

Planet Hollywood. Planet Hollywood has a nightly show of bartenders juggling liquor bottles, and during the day, this is one of the best spots to catch the sports game on TV. DJs begin playing music at 8 pm. The dance floor is warmed up by a laser light show. ⊠ *Plaza la Isla, Blvd. Kukulcán, Km 12.5, Zona Hotelera* ☎ *998/883–1936* ⊕ *www.planethollywood.com.*

Señor Frog's. Known for its over-the-top drinks, Señor Frog's serves up foot-long funnel glasses filled with margaritas, daiquiris, or beer, which you can take home as souvenirs once you've chugged them dry. Needless to say, Spring Breakers adore this place and often stagger back night after night. ⊠ *Blvd. Kukulcán, Km 9.5, Zona Hotelera* ☎ *998/883–3454* ⊕ *www.senorfrogs.com/cancun.*

GAY BARS

Karamba Bar. A variety of drag shows with the usual lip-synching and dancing celebrity impersonations are put on every Wednesday and Thursday at Karamba Bar, a large open-air disco and club that's known for its stage performers. On Friday night the Go-Go Boys of Cancún entertain, and strip shows are on weekends. The bar opens at 10:30 pm and the party goes on until dawn. Cover charges range $5–$8. ⊠ *Av.*

Tulum 9 and corner of Azuenas, Sm 22, El Centro ⊕ www.karambabar. com ⊗ Closed Mon.

Picante Bar. The oldest gay bar in Cancún, Picante Bar has been operating for over 15 years. Doors open at 10 pm and close at 7 am, and there's no cover. ✉ *Plaza Galerias, Av. Tulum 20, Sm 5, El Centro* ☎ *998/897–2138* ⊗ *Closed Mon. and Tues.*

SPORTS BARS

Champions Sports Bar & Grill. Champions Sports Bar & Grill has a giant TV screen and 26 smaller monitors on which to watch all kinds of sporting events. You can also play pool here and dig in to American-style grub, or enjoy karaoke at night. ✉ *CasaMagna Marriott Cancún Resort, Blvd. Kukulcán, Km 14.5, Zona Hotelera* ☎ *998/881–2000.*

WINE BARS

El Rincón del Vino. El Rincón del Vino is a popular wine and tapas bar where you can enjoy the sounds of live *trova*, rumba, flamenco, and jazz music. The bar has 250 varieties of *vino* hailing from the world's top wine-making regions, and tapas like *tortilla española* (a potato omelet) and *chistorra* (a Spanish sausage) that range $6–$12. It's open from 6 pm to midnight Tuesday through Saturday. ✉ *Av. Náder 88, El Centro* ☎ *998/898–2446* ⊗ *Closed Sun. and Mon.*

DANCE CLUBS

Cancún wouldn't be Cancún without glittering discos, which generally start jumping around 10:30 pm (though some open at around 9) and often carry on until 6 am. As the hours roll on, clothes peel off and frenzied dancing seems to quake the building and the floor beneath. Most clubs offer open-bar tickets ($35–$70) that cover admission and unlimited drinks until 3 am. This is the way to go if you plan on having more than a couple of drinks. If you stay past 3, however, you'll have to pay by the drink. You can also pay a lower cover charge of $10–$20 and buy drinks separately. Typical prices range from $3 for a shot to $8 for a cocktail. Although every spot seems to be pumping by midnight, especially during March and April, the most popular clubs include Coco Bongo, Dady'O, The City, and Sweet Club.

The City. The City is a giant party complex with a daytime water park; at night there's a cavernous dance floor with stadium seating and several large bars selling overpriced drinks. Dancing and live shows are the main draw, as well as a Tuesday-night beach party and bikini contest. This is by far the loudest club in the Zona Hotelera, so don't be surprised if you go home with your ears ringing. Doors open at 10 pm. ✉ *Blvd. Kukulcán, Km 9.5, Zona Hotelera* ☎ *998/848–8385* ⊕ *www. thecitycancun.com.*

Coco Bongo. The wild, wild Coco Bongo has no chairs, but there are plenty of tables that everyone dances on and capacity for 1,800 people. There's also a popular show billed as "Las Vegas meets Hollywood," featuring celebrity impersonators and an amazing gravity-defying acrobatic show with an accompanying 12-piece orchestra. After the shows, the techno gets turned up to full volume and everyone gets up

Continued on page 84

TEQUILA AND MEZCAL—¡SALUD!

If God were Mexican, tequila and mezcal would surely be our heavenly reward, flowing in lieu of milk and honey. Before throwing back your first drink, propose a toast in true Mexican style and wave your glass accordingly— *"¡Arriba, abajo, al centro, pa' dentro!"* ("Above, below, center, inside!")

Historians maintain that, following the Spanish conquest and the introduction of the distillation process, tequila was adapted from the ancient Aztec drink *pulque*. Whatever the true origin, Mexico's national drink long predated the Spanish, and is considered North America's oldest spirit.

When you think about tequila, what might come to mind are spaghetti-Western-style bar brawls or late-night teary-eyed confessions. But tequila is more complex and worldly than many presume. By some accounts it's a digestive that reduces cholesterol and stress. Shots of the finest tequilas can cost upward of $100 each, and are meant to be savored as ardently as fine cognacs or single-malt scotches.

Just one of several agave-derived drinks fermented and bottled in Mexico, tequila rose to fame during the Mexican Revolution when it became synonymous with national heritage and pride. Since the 1990s tequila has enjoyed a soaring popularity around the globe, and people the world over are starting to realize that tequila is more than a one-way ticket to (and doesn't necessitate) a hangover.

Harvesting agave in Jalisco.

TEQUILA AND MEZCAL 101

Harvesting blue agave to make tequila.

WHICH CAME FIRST, TEQUILA OR MEZCAL?

Mezcal is tequila's older cousin. Essentially, all tequila is mezcal but only some mezcal is tequila. The only difference between tequila and mezcal is that the tequila meets two requirements: 1) it's made only from blue agave (but some non-agave sugar can be added) and 2) it must be distilled in a specific region in Jalisco or certain parts of neighboring Guanajuato, Michoacán, Nayarit, and Tamaulipas. Unlike tequila, all mezcal must be made from 100 percent agave and must be bottled in Mexico.

CHOOSE YOUR LIQUOR WISELY

Your first decision with tequila is whether to have a *puro* or a *mixto*. You'll know if a bottle is *puro* because it will say so prominently on the label; if the words "100% *de agave*" don't appear, you can be sure you're getting *mixto*. Don't be fooled by bottles that say, "Made from agave azul," because all tequila is made from agave azul; that doesn't mean that cane sugar hasn't been added. Popular wisdom holds that *puro* causes less of a hangover than mixto, but we'll leave that to your own experimentation.

Even among *puros*, there's a wide range of quality and taste, and every fan has his or her favorite. For sipping straight (*derecho*), most people prefer *reposado*, *añejo*, or extra *añejo*. For mixed drinks you'll probably want either a *blanco* or a *reposado*.

Herradura

TEQUILA TIMELINE

Aztec ritual human sacrifice as portrayed on the Codex Magliabechiano.

Pre-Columbian	Aztecs brew pulque for thousands of years; both priests and the sacrificial victims consume it during religious rituals.
1600	The first commercial distillery in New Spain is founded by Pedro Sanches de Tagle, the father of tequila, on his hacienda near the village of Tequila.
1740	*Mezcal de Tequila* earns an enthusiastic following and King Philip V of Spain grants José Antonio Cuervo the first royal license for a mezcal distillery.

THE MAKING OF MEZCAL

[1] To make both mezcal and tequila, the agave may be cultivated for as long as ten years, depending on growing conditions and the variety of plant.

[2] When the agave is ripe, the leaves, or *pencas*, are removed and the heavy core (called a *piña*, Spanish for "pineapple," because of its resemblance to that fruit) is dug up, [3] cut into large chunks, and cooked to convert its starches into sugars.

[4] The *piñas* are then crushed and their juice collected in tanks; yeast is added and the liquid ferments for several days.

After the fermentation, the resulting *mosto* generally measures between 4 and 7 percent alcohol. [5] Finally it's distilled (usually twice for tequila, once for mezcal). This process of heating and condensing serves to boost the alcohol content. [6] And finally, the alcohol is aged in barrels.

While the process is the same, there are a few critical differences between tequila and mezcal. Mezcal is made in smaller distilleries and still retains more of an artisanal quality; mezcal magueys are grown over a wider area with more diverse soil composition and microclimate, giving mezcals more individuality than tequila. Lastly, the *piñas* for mezcal are more likely to be baked in stone pits, which imparts a distinctive smoky flavor.

The World's Columbian Fair in Chicago, 1893.

1800s As the thirst for mezcal grows, wood (used to fire the stills) becomes scarce and distilleries shift to more efficient steam ovens.

1873 Cenobio Sauza exports mezcal to the United States via a new railroad to El Paso, Texas.

1893 ***Mezcal de Tequila*** (now simply called "tequila") receives an award at Chicago's Columbian Exposition.

TEQUILA COCKTAILS

Margarita: The original proportions at Rancho La Gloria were reportedly 3 parts tequila, 2 parts Triple Sec, and 1 part lime juice, though today recipes vary widely. In Mexico an orange liqueur called Controy is often substituted for the Triple Sec. The best margaritas are a little tart and are made from fresh ingredients, not a mix. Besides deciding whether you want yours strained, on the rocks, or frozen, you have dozens of variations to choose from, many incorporating fruits such as strawberry, raspberry, mango, passion fruit, and peach. To salt the rim or not to salt is yet another question.

Sangrita: The name meaning "little blood," this is a very Mexican accompaniment, a spicy mixture of tomato and orange juice that's sipped between swallows of straight tequila (or mezcal).

Tequila refresca: Also very popular in Mexico, this is tequila mixed with citris soft drinks like Fresca, or Squirt. Generally served in a tall glass over ice.

Tequila Sunrise: Invented in the 1950s, this is a distant runner-up to the margarita, concocted from tequila, orange juice, and grenadine syrup. The grenadine sinks to the bottom, and after a few refills you might agree that the resulting layers resemble a Mexican sky at dawn.

Bloody Maria: One to try with brunch, this is a bloody Mary with you-know-what instead of vodka.

DID YOU KNOW?

Aging mezcal and Tequila imparts a smoothness and an oaky flavor, but over-aging can strip the drink of its characteristic agave taste.

TEQUILA TIMELINE

Mexican revolutionaries

1910–1920 During the Mexican Revolution, homegrown tequila becomes a source of national pride, associated with the hard-riding, hard-drinking rebels.

1930s Federal land reforms break up the great haciendas and Mexico's agave production slumps by two thirds. To make up for the shortfall, the government allows distillers to begin mixing non-agave sugars into their tequila. This blander drink, called mixto, is better suited to American tastes and sales surge.

TEQUILA AND MEZCAL VOCABULARY

pulque: an alcoholic drink made by the Aztecs

mexcalmetl: Nahuatl word for agave

mixto: a type of tequila that is mixed with non-agave sugars

puro: tequila made with no non-agave sugars

reposado: aged between two months and a year

añejo: aged between one and three years

extra añejo: aged longer than three years

blanco: tequila that is aged less than two months

joven: young tequila, usually a mixto with colorings and flavors

caballito: tall shot glass

pechuga: mezcal flavored with raw chicken breast

cremas: flavored mezcal

aguamiel: agave juice

piña: the agave core

salmiana: a type of agave

pencas: agave leaves

mosto: fermented agave before it is distilled

gusano: the larva found in mescal bottles

WHAT'S WITH THE WORM

Some mezcals (never tequila) are bottled with a worm (*gusano*), the larva of one of the moths that live on agave plants. Rumor has it that the worm was introduced to ensure a high alcohol content (because the alcohol preserves the creature), but the truth is that the practice started in the 1940s as a marketing gimmick. The worm is ugly but harmless and the best mezcals are not bottled *con gusano*.

IN FOCUS TEQUILA AND MEZCAL—¡SALUD!

2

Early 1940s — The history of mixology was forever altered when Carlos Herrera invented the margarita for American starlet Marjorie King.

2004 — The agave fields around Tequila become a UNESCO World Heritage Site.

Agave fields

CHOOSING A BOTTLE

Reposado (rested)

Silver

Añejo (mature)

Corralejo

BUYING TEQUILA

There are hundreds of brands of tequila, but here are a baker's half dozen of quality *puros* to get you started; generally these distillers offer blanco, reposado, añejo, and extra añejo.

Corralejo—An award winner from the state of Guanajuato, made on the historic hacienda once owned by Pedro Sanchez de Tagle, "the father of tequila" and birthplace of Miguel Hidalgo, the father of Mexican independence.

Corzo—Triple distilled, these tequilas are notably smooth and elegant.

Don Julio—This award-winning tequila, one of the most popular in Mexico, is known for its rich, smooth flavor; the *blanco* is especially esteemed.

Espolón—A relative newcomer founded only in 1998, this distiller has already won several international awards.

Herradura—This is a venerable, popular brand known for its smoky, full body.

Patrón—Founded in 1989, this distiller produces award-winning tequilas. The *añejo* is especially noteworthy for its complex earthiness.

Siete Leguas—Taking their name ("Seven Leagues") from the horse of Pancho Villa, a general in the Mexican Revolution, these quality tequilas are known for their big, full flavor.

TYPES OF TEQUILA AND MEZCAL

Three basic types of tequila and mezcal are determined by how long they've been aged in oak barrels.

Blanco (white) is also known as *plata* or silver. It's been aged for less than two months.

Reposado ("rested") is aged between two months and a year.

añejo ("mature") is kept in barrels for at least a year and perhaps as long as three. Some producers also offer an extra *añejo* that is aged even longer.

Herradura

Don Julio

Gusano Rojo

BUYING MEZCAL

As for enjoying mezcal, it can be substituted in any recipe calling for tequila. But more often it's drunk neat, to savor its unique flavor. Like tequila, straight mezcal is generally served at room temperature in a tall shot glass called a *caballito*.

Some producers now add flavorings to their mezcals. Perhaps the most famous is *pechuga*, which has a raw chicken breast added to the still, supposedly imparting a smoothness and subtle flavor. (Don't worry, the heat and alcohol kill everything.) Citrus is also a popular add-in, and *cremas* contain flavorings such as peaches, mint, raisins, or guava, along with a sweetener such as honey or *aguamiel* (the juice of the agave).

Part of the fun of mezcal is stumbling on smaller, less commercial brands, but here are a few recognized, quality producers. Most make *blancos, reposados,* and *añejos,* and some offer extra *añejos,* flavored mezcals, and *cremas* as well.

El Señorio—Produced in Oaxaca the traditional way, with stone ovens and a stone wheel to crush the *piñas*.

El Zacatecano—Founded in 1910 in the northern state of Zacatecas; in a recent competitive tasting, their añejo was judged the best in its category.

Gusano Rojo—This venerable Oaxaca distillery makes the number-one-selling mezcal in Mexico. Yes, there's a worm in the bottle.

Jaral de Berrio—From Guanajuato, this distiller uses the *salmiana* agave. Their *blanco* recently garnered a silver medal.

Real de Magueyes—From the state of San Luis Potosí, these fine mezcals are also made from the local *salmiana* agave. Try the flavorful añejo.

Scorpion—More award-winning mezcals from Oaxaca. Instead of a worm, there's a scorpion in the bottle.

Cancún meets Vegas at the Coco Bongo.

to get down. Doors open at 10:30 pm. ⊠ *Blvd. Kukulcán, Km 9.5, across street from Dady'O, Zona Hotelera* ☎ *800/841–4636 toll-free in Mexico* ⊕ *www.cocobongo.com.mx* ✉ *$20; $60–$70 for open bar and shows.*

Dady'O. Dady'O has been around for a while, but it's still very "in" with the younger set. A giant screen projects music videos above the always-packed dance floor, while laser lights whirl across the crowd. During Spring Break the place gets even livelier for the Hawaiian Bikini contests. No cover charge for women on Wednesday. ⊠ *Blvd. Kukulcán, Km 9.5, Zona Hotelera* ☎ *998/883–3333* ⊕ *www.dadyo.com.mx* ✉ *$20; $45 for open bar.*

Mambo Café. Mambo Café features some of the city's hottest live bands and DJs playing tropical music, making it the ideal disco to practice your salsa and merengue steps. There is no cover on Wednesday and Thursday nights. ⊠ *Plaza Hong Kong, Loc 31, Sm 20, El Centro* ☎ *998/884–4536* ⊕ *www.mambocafe.com.mx* ✉ *$5 cover.*

Sweet Club. Sweet Club draws a high-energy crowd that likes entertainment along with their drinks. Live bands usually start off the action, followed by DJs spinning dance tracks into the wee hours of the morning. Girls drink free on Monday and Wednesday; wet body contests are on Sunday; and hot leg contests are on Thursday. Winners take home $2,000 in cash and prizes. Doors open daily at 10 pm. ⊠ *Blvd. Kukulcán, Km 9.5, Zona Hotelera* ☎ *998/883–3333* ⊕ *www.sweetclub.com* ✉ *$20; $45 for open bar.*

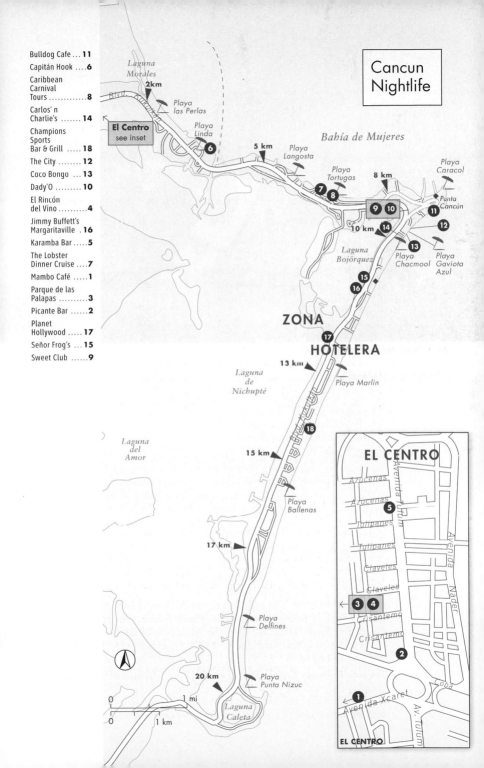

Cancun
Nightlife

Laguna
Morales

2km

Blvd.

El Centro
see inset

Playa
las Perlas

Playa
Linda

6

5 km

Bahía de Mujeres

Playa
Langosta

Playa
Tortugas

8 km

Playa
Caracol

7

8

9 10

Punta
Cancún

11

12

10 km

14

Playa
Chacmool

13

Playa
Gaviota
Azul

Laguna
Bojórquez

15

16

ZONA

HOTELERA

17

13 km

Playa Marlin

Laguna
de
Nichupté

Laguna
del
Amor

18

15 km

Playa
Ballenas

17 km

Playa
Delfines

0   1 mi

0   1 km

20 km

Playa
Punta Nizuc

Laguna
Caleta

EL CENTRO

Azucenas

Avenida Tulum

5

Azucenas

Tulipanes

Tulipanes

Avenida Nader

Claveles

Claveles

3 4

Crisantemo

Crisantemo

2

1

Avenida Xcaret

Av. Tulum

Cobá

EL CENTRO

Dady'O has been around for a while but is still a hotspot.

DINNER CRUISES

Sunset boat cruises that include dinner, drinks, music, and sometimes dancing are popular in Cancún—especially among couples looking for a romantic evening and visitors who'd rather avoid the carnival atmosphere of the clubs and discos.

FAMILY **Capitán Hook.** On the Capitán Hook, watch a private show aboard a replica of an 18th-century Spanish galleon, then enjoy a lobster or steak dinner and drinks as the ship cruises around at sunset. The three-hour trip takes place 7:30–10:30 pm, but you must arrive 30 minutes before departure. ⊠ *El Embarcadero, Blvd. Kukulcán, Km 4.5, Zona Hotelera* ☎ *998/849–4451* ⊕ *www.capitanhook.com* ✉ *Adults $82–$92; children $41* ☉ *Daily 7:30–10:30 pm.*

FAMILY **Caribbean Carnival Tours.** Caribbean Carnival Tours start off on a large two-level catamaran at sunset. There's an open bar for the sail across to Isla Mujeres; once you reach shore, you'll join in a moonlight calypso cookout and a full dinner buffet, followed by a Caribbean carnival show and dancing. You can choose between the Pirate or Caribbean theme for your sailing experience. ⊠ *Playa Tortugas, next to Dos Playas Hotel, Blvd. Kukulcán, Km 6.5, Zona Hotelera* ☎ *998/884–3760* ⊕ *www.caribbeancarnaval.com* ✉ *$67–81; children $33.50–$40.50* ☉ *Daily 6–11 pm.*

The Lobster Dinner Cruise. The Lobster Dinner Cruise offers tranquil, couples-only cruises on a 62-foot galleon. A fresh lobster dinner is served while the sun sets over Laguna Nichupté; afterward, the boat continues to cruise so you can stargaze. No children under 14. ⊠ *Agua*

Tours Marina, Blvd. Kukulcán, Km 6.5, in front of Playa Tortugas, Zona Hotelera ☎ *866/393–5158 in U.S., 800/727–5391 toll-free in Mexico* ⊕ *www.thelobsterdinner.com* ✉ *$89* ☯ *Daily 5 pm and 8 pm.*

LIVE MUSIC

2

Bulldog Cafe. Bulldog Cafe has an all-you-can-drink bar, live rock groups, the latest dance music, and an impressive laser light show. The stage here is large, and some very well-known bands have played on it, including Guns n' Roses and Radiohead. Another, somewhat bawdier draw is the private hot tub, where you can have "the Jacuzzi bikini girls" scrub your back. Naturally, this place is popular with young Spring Breakers. Although street promoters will try and sell you a Bulldog wristband for $50, you can usually talk them down to half that. ✉ *Krystal Cancún hotel, Blvd. Kukulcán, Km 9, Zona Hotelera* ☎ *998/848–9850* ⊕ *www. bulldogcafe.com* ✉ *$50.*

Parque de las Palapas. To mingle with locals and hear great music for free, head to the Parque de las Palapas. Every Friday night at 7:30 there's live music that ranges from jazz to salsa to Caribbean; lots of locals show up to dance. On Sunday afternoon the Cancún Municipal Orchestra plays. ✉ *Bordered by Avs. Tulum, Yaxchilán, Uxmal, and Cobá, Sm 22, El Centro.*

SHOPPING AND SPAS

The *centros comerciales* (malls) in Cancún are fully air-conditioned and as well kept as similar establishments in the United States or Canada. Like their northerly counterparts, they also sell just about everything: designer clothing, beachwear (including raunchy T-shirts aimed at the spring-break crowd), sportswear, jewelry, music, video games, household items, shoes, and books. Some even have the same terrible mall food that's standard north of the border. Prices are fixed in shops. They're also generally—but not always—higher than in the markets, where bargaining is a given. Perfumes in Cancún are considerably less expensive than at home and even than at the duty-free shops at the airport. Of course tequila is a bargain here as well, but make sure you buy at the supermarket rather than at a souvenir shop.

There are many duty-free stores selling designer goods at reduced prices, sometimes as much as 30% or 40% below retail. You can find hand-woven textiles, leather goods, and handcrafted silver jewelry, although prices are higher than in other cities and the selection is limited.

Shopping hours are generally weekdays 10–1 and 4–7, although more stores are staying open throughout the day rather than closing for siesta. Many shops keep Saturday-morning hours, and some are now open on Sunday until 1. Centros comerciales tend to be open daily at 9 or 10 am to 8 or 9 pm.

GALLERIES

Casa de Cultura. Serious collectors visit Casa de Cultura for regular art shows featuring Mexican artists. ✉ *Prolongación Av. Yaxchilán, Sm 25* ☎ *998/884–8364* ⊕ *www.culturaencancun.blogspot.com.*

Dorfman's Art Gallery. Dorfman's Art Gallery features Mayan-inspired and environmentally themed sculptures and paintings by local artists and brothers Renato and Adán Dorfman. ✉ *Plaza Kukulcán, Blvd. Kukulcán, Km 13, Zona Hotelera* ☎ *998/887–2402, 998/840–6734* ⊕ *www.renatodorfman.com.*

> **AVOID TORTOISESHELL**
>
> Refrain from buying anything made from tortoiseshell. The *carey*, or hawksbill turtle from which most of it comes, is an endangered species, and it's illegal to bring tortoiseshell products into the United States and several other countries. Also be aware that there are some restrictions regarding black coral. For one, you must purchase it from a recognized dealer.

El Pabilo Cafe. El Pabilo is a downtown café that showcases Mexican painters and photographers on a rotating basis. ✉ *Av. Yaxchilán 3, Sm 7* ☎ *998/892–4553.*

GROCERY STORES

Chedraui. This is a popular superstore with six locations. ✉ *Av. Tulum 57, at Av. Cobá, El Centro* ☎ *998/884–1024* ⊕ *www.chedraui.com.mx* ✉ *Plaza las Americas, Av. Tulum 260, Sm 7* ☎ *998/887–2111.*

Costco. If you're a member in the States, you can visit Costco in Mexico. ✉ *Avs. Kabah and Yaxchilán, Sm 21* ☎ *998/881–0265.*

Mega Comercial Mexicana. One of the major Mexican grocery-store chains, Mega Comercial Mexicana has three locations. The most convenient is at Avenidas Tulum and Uxmal, across from the bus station; its largest store, farther north on Avenida Kabah, is open 24 hours. ✉ *Avs. Tulum and Uxmal, Sm 2* ☎ *998/884–3330* ✉ *Avs. Kabah and Mayapan, Sm 21* ☎ *998/880–9164* ⊕ *www.comercialmexicana.com.*

Sam's Club. Sam's Club has plenty of bargains on groceries and souvenirs. ✉ *Paseo Kukulcán entre Palenque y Yaxchilán, Sm 21, Mza. 2, Lote 2* ☎ *998/881–0200* ⊕ *www.samsclub.com.*

Super Aki. This is a smaller grocery store downtown. ✉ *Av. Xel-Há, Lote 1, next to Mercado Veintiocho, Sm 28* ☎ *998/884–2812.*

Walmart. Just like in the U.S., Walmart is a popular shopping spot to find beach supplies, snacks, and necessities you forgot to pack. ✉ *Av. Cobá, Lote 2, Sm 21* ☎ *998/884–1383* ⊕ *www.wal-mart.com.mx.*

■**TIP→** The few grocery stores in the Zona Hotelera tend to be expensive. It's better to shop for groceries downtown.

MARKETS AND MALLS

ZONA HOTELERA

Coral Negro. Next to the convention center, this open-air market has about 50 stalls selling crafts and souvenirs. It's open daily until late evening. Everything here is overpriced, but bargaining does work. Stalls deeper in the market tend to have better deals than those around the market's periphery. ✉ *Blvd. Kukulcán, Km 9, Zona Hotelera.*

Forum-by-the-Sea. This three-level entertainment and shopping plaza in the Zona features brand-name restaurants, upscale clothing boutiques, a food court, and chain stores, all in a circuslike atmosphere. For Spring Breakers the main draws are the nightclubs, Coco Bongo, and Hard Rock Cafe, identified by the massive guitar at the mall entrance. The bungee trampolines set up here during high season are especially popular with children. You will also find several ATMs here. ✉ *Blvd. Kukulcán, Km 9.5, Zona Hotelera* ☎ *998/883–4428.*

La Isla Shopping Village. The glittering, ultratrendy, and ultraexpensive La Isla Shopping Village is on the Laguna Nichupté under chic, white canopies. A series of canals and small bridges is designed to give the place a Venetian look. In addition to more than 200 shops, the mall has a marina, a disco, restaurants, and movie theaters. There's also an interactive aquarium where you can swim with the dolphins and feed the sharks. ✉ *Blvd. Kukulcán, Km 12.5, Zona Hotelera* ☎ *998/883–5025* ⊕ *www.laislacancun.com.mx.*

Plaza Caracol. North of the convention center, the two-story Plaza Caracol houses chain stores like Sunglass Island, Benetton, and Ultrafemme, along with souvenir and jewelry shops and pharmacies. This mall has 100 shops, as well as a food court, a Starbucks, and a Häagen-Dazs ice cream shop where free Wi-Fi is available. ✉ *Blvd. Kukulcán, Km 8.5, Zona Hotelera* ☎ *998/883–4760* ⊘ *Closed weekends*

Plaza El Zócalo. It may look small from the entrance, but Plaza El Zócalo has about 60 stalls where you can find traditional Mexican handicrafts, silver jewelry, and handmade sandals. It also houses four restaurants—including Mextreme, which still sports a banner announcing its claim to fame as a set in the 1980s movie *Cocktail.* ✉ *Blvd. Kuckulcán, Km 9, Zona Hotelera.*

Plaza Flamingo. This is a small mall that houses around 80 different shops that sell mainly clothing, jewelry, and souvenirs. The main attractions here are the chain restaurants Jimmy Buffet's, Margaritaville, Outback Steakhouse, and Bubba Gump, which fill up with partiers during Spring Break. ✉ *Blvd. Kukulcán, Km 11.5, across from Hotel Flamingo Resort & Plaza, Zona Hotelera* ☎ *998/883–2855* ⊕ *www.flamingo.com.mx.*

Plaza Kukulcán. Plaza Kukulcán is a large, upscale mall with around 100 shops and four restaurants. The Luxury Avenue section of the mall offers brand names from Cartier, Fendi, and Burberry to Coach. While parents shop, kids can enjoy the game arcade and play area. The mall hosts art exhibits and other cultural events. If you fell in love with the European clothing chain Mango on your last trip to Paris, swing by the branch here. ⊠ *Blvd. Kukulcán, Km 13, Zona Hotelera* ☏ *998/193-0161* ⊕ *www.kukulcanplaza.com.*

Plaza la Fiesta. In from the convention center, Plaza la Fiesta has 20,000 square feet of showroom space and more than 100,000 different products for sale. Probably the widest selection of Mexican goods in the Hotel Zone, it includes leather goods, silver and gold jewelry, handicrafts, souvenirs, and swimwear. There are some good bargains here, so get ready to negotiate. ⊠ *Blvd. Kukulcán, Km 9, Zona Hotelera.*

EL CENTRO

There are lots of interesting shops downtown along Avenida Tulum between Avenidas Cobá and Uxmal; however, by and large the greater proportion of stores in El Centro are geared toward the needs of locals rather than tourists. The most interesting shops for travelers may be in Plaza Bonita; otherwise, there are better options available in the Zona Hotelera.

Cancún Gran Plaza. Cancún Gran Plaza offers jewelry shops, fashion boutiques, and major department stores such as Sanborns and Walmart. There are also cinemas, cafés, and restaurants in the shopping mall, which is mainly frequented by El Centro residents. ⊠ *Av. Nichupté, Mza 18, Lote 1, Loc 24, 30 and 62A, Sm 51, El Centro* ⊙ *Daily 9–9.*

Ki Huic. The oldest and largest of Cancún's crafts markets is Ki Huic. It's open daily 9 am to 9 pm and houses about 100 vendors. ⊠ *Av. Tulum 17, between Bancomer and Bital banks, Sm 3* ☏ *998/884-3347.*

FodorśChoice
★ **Mercado Veintiocho** (*Market 28*). Just off Avenidas Yaxchilán and Sunyaxchén, this is the largest open-air market in Cancún. In addition to a few small restaurants, here you'll find around 100 stalls selling many of the same items found in the Zona Hotelera but at half the price. Expect to be bombarded by aggressive vendors trying to coax you into their shop. This is a great place to haggle, and usually you can end up paying half of the initial asking price. ⊠ *Off Avs. Yaxchilán and Sunyaxchén, next to Walmart.*

Parque Lumpkul. Parque Lumpkul is a small park with a hippy vibe. Vendors sell their wares Wednesday through Sunday, but Friday and Saturday are the best nights to go. There are only about 20 tables, but you can find bargains on beautiful handmade jewelry with unusual stones, as well as hand-painted clothes. There are sometimes music and artistic performances on market days. ⊠ *Between Av. Margaritas and Calle Azucenas, Sm 22, El Centro.*

Paseo Cancún. Paseo Cancún was developed by the same company that owns La Isla in the Zona Hotelera, so it has the same open-air design with modern white canopies throughout. Here you'll find a small ice-skating rink, a movie theater, a bowling alley, a pet store, a food court, several cafés, and around 60 stores. ⊠ *Av. Andrés, Sm 39, El Centro* ☏ *998/872-3735.*

Plaza Bonita. A small outdoor plaza attached to Mercado Veintiocho (Market 28), Plaza Bonita has many wonderful specialty shops carrying Mexican goods and crafts. ⊠ *Av. Xel-Há 1 and 2, Sm 28* ☏ *998/884-6812* ⊕ *www.plazabonita.com.mx.*

2

Plaza Hong Kong. Plaza Hong Kong seems strikingly out of place with it massive pagoda structure. Here you'll find Mexican handicrafts, souvenir shops, and a restaurant appropriately named Hong Kong. There is also a babysitting service available in the mall. ⊠ *between Labná and Av. Xcaret, Sm 35, Mza 2, Lote 6, El Centro* ☎ *998/887–6315.*

Plaza Hollywood. You'll find several small boutiques and restaurants at this strip mall, as well as a bank, post office, and Starbucks. For the wine connoisseur, there is La Europea Wine Market, which carries a wide selection of imported cheeses and meats, as well as Mexican reds. ⊠ *Av. Xcaret at Rubi Cancún, El Centro* ☎ *998/887–3187.*

Plaza Las Américas. This is the largest shopping center in downtown Cancún. Its 50-plus stores, three restaurants, two movie theaters, video arcade, fast-food outlets, and several large department stores will—for better or worse—make you feel right at home. This mall is intolerably crowded on weekends. ⊠ *Av. Tulum, Sm 4 and Sm 9* ☎ *998/887–3863.*

Plaza Las Avenidas. Far from the Hotel Zone, this shopping area is most convenient for those staying in El Centro. There are gift shops, fast-food restaurants, cafés, nightclubs, and a karaoke bar. You'll also find a drugstore and a bakery on the premises. ⊠ *Av. Yaxchilán, Sm 35, N.C-2, El Centro* ☎ *998/887–7552.*

Ultrafemme. Ultrafemme is a popular downtown store that carries duty-free perfume, cosmetics, and jewelry. It also has branches in the Zona Hotelera at Plaza Caracol, Plaza las Americas, Plaza Kukulcan, and La Isla Shopping Village. The downtown store is open daily 9:30 am–9 pm. ⊠ *Av. Tulum 111 at Calle Claveles, Sm 21* ☎ *998/884–1402* ⊕ *www. ultrafemme.com.*

SPAS

JW Marriott Spa. This 35,000 square-foot spa has breathtaking ocean views and Mayan-inspired treatments like chocolate massages, ground corn exfoliations, or chaya detoxifications. Choose from one of 13 invigorating facials including the pumpkin enzyme treatment or the cucumber green tea facial. Women will enjoy "Precious Stones and Flowers" which begins with a detoxifying marine mask followed by flower petals and crystals placed over energy points to bring balance and harmony to the body. The JW Spa even offers specialized treatments for men, golfers, couples, and teens. ⊠ *JW Marriott, Blvd. Kukulcán, Km 14.5* ☎ *998/848–9700.*

Kayantá Spa. The intimate Kayantá Spa at the Ritz-Carlton offers a "Deep Blue Peel," a massage and body-scrub combo that involves marine extracts, seaweed, bergamot and jojoba oil. The avocado and yogurt wrap will leave your skin feeling silky smooth, but you won't go wrong with a plain, old massage. ⊠ *Ritz-Carlton, Blvd. Kukulcán, Km 14, Zona Hotelera* ☎ *998/881–0808.*

Fodor's Choice ★ **Le Blanc Spa.** The most luxurious spa in Cancún, Le Blanc's massive facility takes pampering to a whole new level. Arrive early and linger in one of the many dimly lighted relaxation rooms, nibble on fresh cookies and *agua fresca* flavored with hibiscus or cucumber, or take a circuit in the hydrotherapy pools. Indulge in a vast array of treatments from facials and body wraps to intensive four-handed couples massages in oversize suites. Nonguests can use the resort on a day pass when booking treatments at the spa. If you're in the market for serious relaxation, Le Blanc is not to be missed. ⊠ *Le Blanc Resort, Blvd. Kukulcán, Km 10, Zona Hotelera* ☎ *998/881–4740* ⊕ *www.leblancsparesort.com.*

SPORTS AND THE OUTDOORS

BOATING AND SAILING

There are lots of ways to get your adrenaline going on the waters of Cancún. You can arrange to go parasailing (about $50 for 10 minutes), waterskiing ($70 per hour), or jet skiing ($70 per hour, or $80 for Wave Runners). Paddleboats, kayaks, catamarans, and banana boats are readily available, too. Jungle boat tours, which usually last from 2 to 2½ hours, are also popular, for around $60 per person.

AquaWorld. AquaWorld rents boats and water toys like Aqua Twister, a high-speed boat that fishtails 270 degrees. They also offer parasailing and submarine tours. ⊠ *Blvd. Kukulcán, Km 15.2, Zona Hotelera* ☎ *998/848–8327* ⊕ *www.aquaworld.com.mx.*

El Embarcadero. The marina complex at Playa Linda, El Embarcadero is the departure point for ferries to Isla Mujeres and several tour boats. ⊠ *Blvd. Kukulcán, Km 4, Zona Hotelera* ☎ *998/849–7343.*

Marina Barracuda. Marina Barracuda rents out Wave Runners and offers daily jungle tours ($66), as well as charter boats (starting at $200 an hour) and big game fishing trips (starting at $440 for four hours) for parties of six. ⊠ *Blvd. Kukulcán, Km 14, in front of Ritz-Carlton, Zona Hotelera* ☎ *998/885–2444* ⊕ *www.marinabarracuda.com.*

Marina Punta del Este. Marina Punta del Este has Wave Runners and offers jungle tours that leave every hour from 9–3. They also offer catamaran tours, which start at $66. ⊠ *Blvd. Kukulcán, Km 10.3, Zona Hotelera* ☎ *998/883–1210* ⊕ *www.puntaestemarina.com.*

FISHING

Some 500 species—including sailfish, wahoo, bluefin, marlin, barracuda, and red snapper—live in the waters off Cancún. You can charter deep-sea fishing boats starting at about $380 for four hours, $470 for six hours, and $550 for eight hours. Rates generally include a captain and first mate, gear, bait, and beverages.

Asterix Tours. With an emphasis on nature conservation, Asterix is the only tour company permitted to visit Isla Contoy and the underwater gardens of Isla Mujeres. Tours to Isla Contoy ($90 per person) depart at 9 am and return at 5:30 pm on Tuesday, Thursday, and Saturday. They also offer nighttime "party fishing" trips that cost $78 per person and include dinner and drinks. ⊠ *Blvd. Kukulcán, Km 5.5, Zona Hotelera* ☎ *998/886–4270* ⊕ *www.contoytours.com.*

Water Sports in Cancún

With the Caribbean on one side and the still waters of Laguna Nichupté on the other, it's no wonder that Cancún is one of the water-sports capitals of the world. The most popular activities are snorkeling and diving along the coral reef just off the coast.

Both kiteboarding and windsurfing are popular, although the waves are not as constant as on Mexico's Pacific coast. For the avid beach-break surfer, the sandbars are best at Playa Delfines, Chamol, and City Beach. Thirty-two kilometers (20 miles) south of Cancún are several point breaks off the coast of Puerto Morelos and Punta Brava.

If you want to view the mysterious underwater world but don't want to get your feet wet, a glass-bottom boat or "submarine" is the ticket. You can also fish, sail, jet ski, or parasail.

Because the beaches along the Zona Hotelera can have a strong undertow, always respect the flags posted in the area. A black flag means no swimming at all. A red flag means you can swim but only with extreme caution. Yellow means approach with caution, while green means water conditions are safe. You'll most likely always see a red flag and seldom a green one, even when the water is calm.

Unfortunately, there's very little wildlife to see in the Laguna Nichupté, so most advertised jungle tours are glorified Jet Ski romps where you drive around fast, make a lot of noise, and don't see many animals. American crocodiles still reside in these waters though, so don't stand or swim in the lagoon.

Although the coral reef in this area is not as spectacular as farther south, there's still plenty to see. It's quite common to spot angelfish, parrotfish, blue tang, and the occasional moray eel. To be a good world citizen, follow the six golden rules for snorkeling or scuba diving:

1. Don't throw any garbage into the sea, as the marine life will assume it's food, an often lethal mistake.

2. Never stand on the coral.

3. Secure all cameras and gear onto your body so you don't drop anything onto the fragile reef.

4. Never take anything from the sea.

5. Don't feed any of the marine animals.

6. Avoid applying sunblock or tanning lotion just before you visit the reef.

FISHING AND DIVING COMBOS

Scuba Cancún. Scuba Cancún also offers deep-sea fishing and diving. Prices are $550 for a four-hour fishing trip, $650 for six hours, and $800 for an eight-hour expedition. ⊠ *Blvd. Kukulcán, Km 5, Zona Hotelera* ☎ *998/849–7508, 998/849–4736* ⊕ *www.scubacancun.com.mx.*

GO-CARTS

FAMILY **Go Karts Cancún.** About 10 minutes south of Cancún, speed demons can get their fix at Go Karts Cancún. There's a racetrack where Honda-engine go-carts reach speeds of up to 80 kph or 50 mph (there are also slower carts for children). Your choice of cart determines the price, but standard go-carts begin at $13 per 10-minute race session. For the experienced driver, motorcycles and V8 Nascars are also available by the hour. If you don't have a vehicle to get here, a taxi ride should run $10 to $15 from downtown (and considerably more from the Zona Hotelera). Buses leave every 20 minutes from the downtown terminal and cost about $1.20. Check to make sure your bus is not a direct route and will let you off. ⊠ *Carretera Cancún–Aeropuerto, Km 7.5, Residencial Campestre* ☎ *998/882–1275, 998/882–1246* ⊙ *Tues.–Sun. 10–6.*

GOLF

Cancún Golf Club at Pok-Ta-Pok. Many hotels offer golf packages that can considerably reduce your greens fees at Cancún golf courses. Cancún's main golf course is at Cancún Golf Club at Pok-Ta-Pok. The club has fine views of both sea and lagoon; its 18 holes were designed by Robert Trent Jones Jr. It also has two practice greens, three tennis courts, a pro shop, and a restaurant. The greens fees go from $145 to $175, and include your cart, food, and beverages; club rentals are $45, shoes $15. ⊠ *Blvd. Kukulcán, Km 7.5, Zona Hotelera* ☎ *998/883–1230* ⊕ *www. cancungolfclub.com.*

Iberostar Cancún. There's only one 18-hole championship golf course in Cancún and it's at the recently opened Iberostar. Lying along the Nichupté Lagoon, the course has a practice facility with driving range and putting green. The 16th hole overlooks the Mayan Ruinas del Rey. Greens fees are $199 ($159 for hotel guests), carts included. ⊠ *Iberostar, Blvd. Kukulcán, Km 17, Zona Hotelera* ☎ *998/881–8016* ⊕ *www. iberostar.com.*

Moon Spa & Golf Club. Moon Spa & Golf Club has three 9-hole courses. The 18-hole greens fee, which includes a cart, food, and drink service, is $260. If you're staying at the Moon Palace, inquire about the hotel's all-inclusive golf package. ⊠ *Carretera Cancún-Chetumal, Km 340, Sm 40 about 15 mins from airport* ☎ *998/881–6000* ⊕ *www. palaceresorts.com.*

Paradisus Cancún. The 9-hole executive course at the new Paradisus Cancún forms a semicircle around the property and looks out onto the lagoon. The greens fee is $35, but the course is for the exclusive use of hotel guests. ⊠ *Paradisus Cancún Resort, Blvd. Kukulcán, Km 16.5, Zona Hotelera* ☎ *998/881–1100* ⊕ *www.paradisus.com.*

Playa Mujeres Golf Club. The newest course in Cancún is the Playa Mujeres Golf Club. Designed by Greg Norman, this 18-hole, par-72 course is within the 930-acre Playa Mujeres Resort in Punta Sam. Practice facilities include a driving range, two putting greens, and a short game area. You can also arrange for individual and group instruction. Greens fees run from $230 to $290. ⊠ *Playa Mujeres Beach Resort, Prolongación Bonampak, Punta Sam* ☎ *998/887–7322, 998/892–0874* ⊕ *www.playamujeresgolf.com.mx.*

Puerto Cancún Golf. Puerto Cancún Golf, designed by Tom Weiskopf, is an 18 hole, championship golf course in Puerto Cancún that stretches

Cancún has quite a few enviable courses.

out over 185 acres and has ocean views and two holes that play on the marina. ⊠ *Blvd. Kukulcán, Km 1.5, Zona Hotelera* ☎ 998/898–3306 ⊕ *www.puertocancun.com.*

Riviera Cancún Golf. Designed by Jack Nicklaus, this 18-hole golf course has ocean views and a Mexican-style clubhouse that's surrounded by mangroves. A 30% discount is available for guests of all Palace Resorts. All others pay $200 greens fees, or $120 after 2 pm. ⊠ *Blvd. Kukulcán, Km 25, Zona Hotelera* ☎ 998/193–2010 ⊕ *www.palaceresorts.com.*

SCUBA DIVING AND SNORKELING

The snorkeling is best at Punta Nizuc, Punta Cancún, and Playa Tortugas, although you should be careful of the strong currents at Tortugas. You can rent gear for about $10 per day from many of the diving places as well as at many hotels.

Scuba diving is popular in Cancún, though it's not as spectacular as in Cozumel. Look for a scuba company that will give you lots of personal attention. (Smaller companies are often better at this than larger ones.) Regardless, ask to meet the dive master, and check the equipment and certifications thoroughly. ■**TIP→** A few words of caution about one-hour courses that many resorts offer for free: such courses do not prepare you to dive in the open ocean—only in shallow water where you can easily surface without danger. If you've caught the scuba bug and want to take deep or boat dives, prepare yourself properly by investing in a full certification course.

FAMILY **Aqua Fun.** Aqua Fun offers a two-hour tour of the mangroves that costs $66 per person and includes snorkeling at the Punta Nizuc reef. Daily tours take place at 9 am, noon, and 3 pm. Reservations must be made in advance. ✉ *Blvd. Kukulcán, Km 16.5, Zona Hotelera* ☎ *998/885–2930* ⊕ *aquafun.com.mx.*

FAMILY **AquaWorld.** AquaWorld has a day-trip snorkeling excursion to Isla Mujeres for $77 per person. This operation also offers one-tank dives for $72 and two-tank dives starting at $77, as well as dive trip to MUSA the underwater museum. Dive explorations of boat wrecks cost $85, and three-day dive packages cost $266. ✉ *Blvd. Kukulcán, Km 15.2, Zona Hotelera* ☎ *998/848–8327* ⊕ *www.aquaworld.com.mx.*

FAMILY **Marina Barracuda.** Sightseeing and snorkeling starts at $80 per hour (for 5 people) and includes snorkeling equipment, life jackets, and refreshments. ✉ *Blvd. Kukulcán, Km 14, Zona Hotelera* ☎ *998/885–2444* ⊕ *www.marinabarracuda.com.*

Marina Punta del Este. Located right in front of the Grand Park Royal Cancún Caribe, Marina Pinta del Este has dives that last from 3½ to 4 hours and cost $72 if you are certified or $88 if you need a lesson. Wreck dives are $79. Daily lessons begin at 9 am and 1 pm. ✉ *Blvd. Kukulcán, Km 10.3, Zona Hotelera* ☎ *998/883–1210* ⊕ *www. puntaestemarina.com.*

Scuba Cancún. Scuba Cancún specializes in diving trips and offers NAUI, CMAS, and PADI instruction. It's operated by Tomás Hurtado, who has more than 60 years of experience. Two-tank dives start at $68, one-tank dives start at $54, and they take place in the afternoons. ✉ *Blvd. Kukulcán, Km 5, Zona Hotelera* ☎ *998/849–7508* ⊕ *www. scubacancun.com.mx.*

Solo Buceo. Solo Buceo charges $55 for one-tank dives, $70 for two-tank dives, and $90 for twilight diving every Tuesday and Thursday. They also have NAUI, FMAS, CMAS, and PADI instruction (lessons run $90–$240). ✉ *Blvd. Kukulcán, Km 9.5, Zona Hotelera* ☎ *998/883–8979* ⊕ *www.solobuceo.com.*

ISLA MUJERES

WELCOME TO ISLA MUJERES

TOP REASONS TO GO

★ **Getting away from the crowd:** Although Isla Mujeres is just across the bay from Cancún, the peace and quiet make it seem like another universe.

★ **Exploring the southeastern coast:** Bump along in a golf cart where craggy cliffs meet the blue Caribbean.

★ **Eating freshly grilled seafood:** For some reason it always tastes best under a beachfront *palapa* (thatch roof) at lovely Playa Norte.

★ **Diving with "sleeping sharks":** They dwell in the underwater caverns off Isla.

★ **Taking a boat trip to Isla Contoy:** On this even smaller island, more than 70 species of birds make their home.

1 The Western Coast. Midway along the western coast of Isla you can glimpse the lovely Laguna Makax. At the lagoon's southeastern end are the shady stretches of Playa Tiburón and Playa Lancheros. At Isla's southernmost tip is El Garrafón National Park.

2 Playa Norte. With its waist-deep turquoise waters and wide soft sands, Playa Norte is the northernmost beach on Isla Mujeres, and the most beautiful. Most of the island's resorts and hotels are located here, and the town center and historic cemetery are both just a short walk away.

3 El Pueblo. Directly in front of the ferry piers, El Pueblo is Isla's only town. It extends the full width of the island's northern end, sandwiched between sand and sea to the south, west, and northeast. The *zócalo* (main square) is the hub of Isleño life.

GETTING ORIENTED

Isla Mujeres is still quiet by Riviera Maya standards, with a small-town feel that makes it a great escape from Cancún. (Don't mention that to locals, who will tell you that the influx of big hotels has changed it forever.) Just 8 km (5 miles) long and 1 km (½ mile) wide, its landscapes include flat sandy beaches in the north and steep rocky bluffs to the south. The liveliest activities here are swimming, snorkeling, exploring the remnants of the island's past, drinking cold beer, eating fresh seafood, and lazing under palapas.

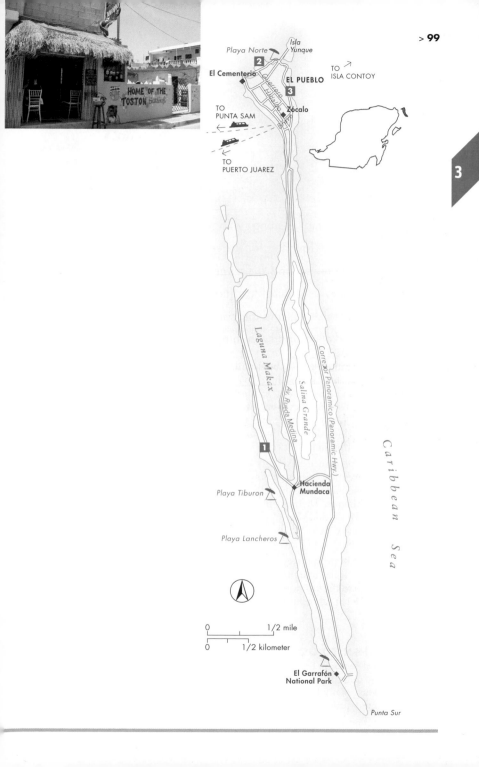

Playa Norte

Isla Yunque

2

El Cementerio

EL PUEBLO

3

TO ISLA CONTOY

TO PUNTA SAM

Zócalo

TO PUERTO JUAREZ

3

Laguna Makax

Corredor Panoramico (Panoramic Hwy.)

Salina Grande

Av. Rueda Medina

1

Caribbean Sea

Playa Tiburon

Hacienda Mundaca

Playa Lancheros

0 ——— 1/2 mile

0 ——— 1/2 kilometer

El Garrafón National Park

Punta Sur

Updated by
Marie Elena
Martinez

Once a small fishing village, colorful Isla Mujeres has become a favorite for travelers seeking natural beauty, island serenity, and a slower pace of life—all without compromising its cultural traditions. Winter months offer excellent sportfishing, and the calm surrounding waters are great for snorkeling and swimming year-round.

During high season, boatloads of visitors pop over from Cancún for a taste of the island life. The midday rush is a boon for vendors and hagglers offering every kind of service from braided hair to beach massages. By late afternoon, though, the masses disappear and return to their big-city nightlife and the comforts of the mainland. Those who stay behind discover that on Isla Mujeres, worldly concerns fade with the setting sun.

Isla's permanent residents include nearly 100 Canadian and American expats (most operating hotels and restaurants) and 15,000 Maya, many of whom earn a living selling fish at the docks or plates of food outside their homes. There are plenty of opportunities to practice your Spanish, and you'll find that most locals beam when you try. Taxi drivers are genuinely interested in sharing details of the island's history and telling you about their families who were born and raised here.

The minute you step off the boat, you'll get a sense of how small Isla is. The sights and properties are strung along the coasts, and there's not much to the interior except for two saltwater marshes where the Maya harvested salt centuries ago.

PLANNING

WHEN TO GO

High season in Isla Mujeres begins the week before Christmas and continues until the day after Easter. Rates are highest during July and August, when many Europeans head to Mexico for the sunshine. Prices also jump during Thanksgiving week and over spring break (between early

March and late May), when U.S college students flock to neighboring Cancún for the party scene.

Low season starts the day after Easter and continues until mid-December, during which prices may drop as much as 50%.

Some of the **best deals** can be found in early November, after the rainy season has passed and before the crowds have arrived.

Isla enjoys its best weather between November and May, when temperatures usually hover around 80°F. June, July, and August are the hottest and most humid months, with daytime highs routinely over 95°F. A few festivals and holidays are worth keeping in mind while you're planning your trip: the Sol a Sol Regatta in late April; Founder's Day on August 17; the Day of the Virgin de la Caridad del Cobre, patron saint of local fishermen, on September 9; the Day of the Dead from October 31 to November 2; and the Feast of the Immaculate Conception from December 1 to 8. Be sure to book well in advance if you're planning to visit on any of these days.

TIMING

Although most mainland travelers only visit Isla for the day, it's definitely worth spending the night if you're looking for a mix of culture, tranquillity, good food, and island life. In a single afternoon you can visit all the best beaches and major attractions. You may even have enough time to snorkel or swim.

GETTING HERE AND AROUND

BICYCLE AND SCOOTER TRAVEL

Most scooter rental places charge $25–$35 a day, or $8–$11 per hour, depending on the vehicle's make and age. Rueda Medina, directly across from the dock, is lined with scooter shops where rentals start at $10 per hour or $25 per day (9–5) or $35 for 24 hours. You can also rent bicycles on Isla, but keep in mind that it's hot here and the roads have plenty of speed bumps. Don't ride at night, as many roads don't have streetlights. Those scooter shops also offer bike rentals starting at $10 per day for beaters and $18 per day for fancy three-speeds. Most bike rental companies provide helmets but not safety reflectors, so it might be wise to pack a headlamp or flashlight if there's a possibility you might ride after dark. ■TIP➡ Scooters and golf carts are the most popular modes of transportation on Isla.

BOAT AND FERRY TRAVEL

Isla ferries are actually speedboats that run between Puerto Juárez on the mainland and the island's main dock. The *Miss Valentina,* the *Ultramar,* and the *Caribbean Lady* are small air-conditioned cruisers that can make the crossing in just under 20 minutes. A one-way ticket costs $3.50, and the boats leave daily every 30 minutes from 5:30 am to 8:30 pm, with a late ferry at 11:30 pm for those returning from partying in Cancún. You can also choose to take a slower open-air ferry, which takes about 45 minutes but costs only $1.60 per person, running from 5 am to 6 pm.

Fast ferries to Isla's main dock also leave from two places in Cancún's Zona Hotelera: El Embarcadero marina complex and the Xcaret office complex at Playa Caracol, just across from Plaza Caracol Shopping Mall. The voyage costs $10–$15 round-trip and takes about 30 minutes. Although you don't need a car on Isla Mujeres, there is a car ferry that leaves from Punta Sam, a dock north of Puerto Juárez. The ride takes about 45 minutes, and the fare is $1.50 per person and $18–$26 per vehicle, depending on the size of your car.

GOLF CART TRAVEL

Golf carts are another fun way to get around the island, especially if you're traveling with kids. Ciro's Motorent has an excellent choice of flatbed golf carts, which cost approximately $50 for 24 hours depending on the season. Pepe's Moto Rental has a large fleet of carts (starting at $55 for 24 hours) and mopeds (from $25 per day).

Contacts Ciro's Motorent ⊠ *Av. Guerrero Norte 14, at Av. Matamoros* ☎ *998/877–0568.* **Gomar** ⊠ *D'Gomar Hotel, Av. Rueda Medina #150, at Calle Nicolas Bravo* ☎ *998/877–0541* ⊕ *www.hotelgomar-islamujeres.com/golfcar.php.* **Pepe's Moto Rental** ⊠ *Av. Hidalgo 19, and Av. Matamoros* ☎ *998/877–0019.*

HOTELS

There are several Internet-based rental agencies that can help you rent a home on the island: ⊕ *www.islabeckons.com*, for example, lists fully equipped apartments and houses (and also handles reservations for hotel rooms); ⊕ *www.morningsinmexico.com* offers smaller and less expensive properties. Most rental homes have fully equipped kitchens, bathrooms, and bedrooms. You can opt for a house downtown or a more secluded one on the eastern coast.

DINING AND LODGING PRICES

Prices in the restaurant reviews are the average cost of a main course at dinner or, if dinner is not served, at lunch; taxes and service charges are generally included. Prices in the hotel reviews are the lowest cost of a standard double room in high season, excluding taxes, service charges, and meal plans (except at all-inclusives). Prices for rentals are the lowest per-night cost for a one-bedroom unit in high season.

SAFETY

There's little crime on this small island, making it an excellent choice for visitors traveling alone. Common-sense precautions do apply: stay clear of drugs; don't leave personal items unattended on the beach or in a golf cart; and lock your hotel room when you leave. Dehydration is one of the biggest safety concerns, so drink plenty of bottled water and order beverages without ice unless you're at a restaurant that uses purified water. Be careful when driving along the narrow roads, especially since many have gravel surfaces and potholes.

VISITOR INFORMATION

Tourist office. The tourist office, located directly across from the ferry pier, is open weekdays 9–4 and has lots of general information about the island. ⊠ *Av. Rueda Medina 130, across from pier* ☎ *998/877–0307, 998/877–0767* ⊕ *www.isla-mujeres.com.mx.*

ESSENTIALS

BANKS AND CURRENCY EXCHANGE

It's best to arrive at Isla Mujeres with pesos, or you can exchange money at the "cambio" window at the Ultramar ferry dock in Cancún. While most businesses accept U.S. dollars, be prepared to receive change back in pesos at a subjective exchange rate. On the island there are ATMs at the San Francisco Super Express store on the town square, the 7-Eleven, and at the HSBC across from the ferry port. These machines tend to run out of money on weekends and holidays, and lines are long.

Island banks will no longer exchange U.S. dollars to Mexican pesos, but there are many "casa de cambio" (exchange houses) that will—in fact, they're the only option. Few places on Isla Mujeres, including banks, will accept traveler's checks, and a minority of establishments (although this number is growing) accept credit cards, mostly MasterCard and Visa. (Expect to pay an additional 5% service fee.)

Contacts Cunex Money Exchange ⊠ *Av. Francisco Madero 12A, at Av. Hidalgo* ☎ *998/877–0474.* **HSBC** ⊠ *Av. Rueda Medina, # 3, across from ferry port, El Pueblo* ☎ *998/877–0005* ☽ *Open weekdays 8:30–6 , Sat 9–2.* **Monex Exchange** ⊠ *Av. Morelos 9, Lote 4.*

TOURS

There aren't any tours of the island itself; this is a place to explore at your own pace. Most "island tours" are actually trips around the island, including catamaran party boats or open-bar ferries. Local travel agents can help guide you through Isla's activities.

Contacts Mundaca Travel ⊠ *Av. Hidalgo No. 15-A, Isla Mujeres* ☎ *998/877–0025* ⊕ *www.mundacatravel.com.* **Viajes Prisma** ⊠ *Av. Rueda Medina 9C* ☎ *998/877–0938.*

EXPLORING

To get your bearings, picture the island as a long fish: the head is the southeastern tip, the tail is the northwest prong. Eight kilometers (5 miles) long and 1 km (½ mile) wide, Isla Mujeres is easy to explore in a single day. If you take your time, however, you'll discover that the island is not a destination to be rushed. The virtually car-free dirt roads are best traveled by golf cart, scooter, or bike. ⚠ Before leaving the rental agency, check your scooter and golf cart for scratches and dings. You may even want to take a photo for additional proof of the original condition. Otherwise, you'll pay dearly for any damage that was not noted prior to your rental agreement. If you're staying at one of the remote hotels on the southern tip, a taxi will take you from one end of the island to the other for $6.

If you want to tour the island by golf cart, start by looping the island exterior, stopping midway at the southernmost tip. Here you can walk down to the rocky shores where waves crash at your feet. The views from Punta Sur are magnificent, and the temple of Goddess Ixchel is worth a visit. Head back north and explore the tiny streets and colorful neighborhoods on the outskirts of town, with a stop at the excellent

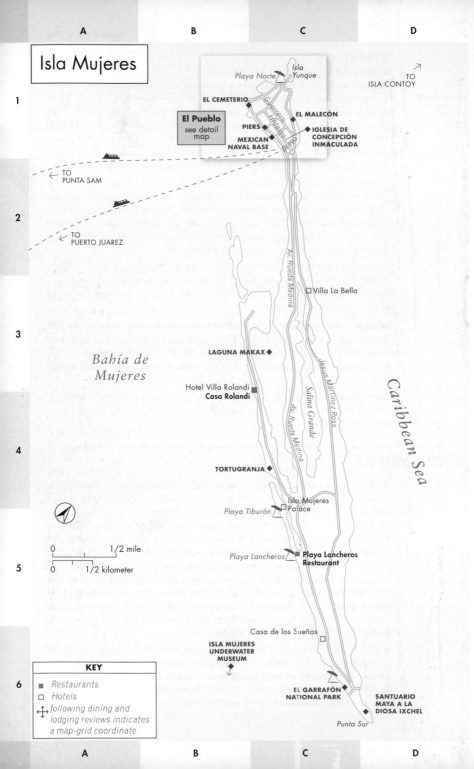

Mango Café for lunch. If you prefer the beach, relax at peaceful Playa Lancheros on the island's west side and see the area's dolphins, turtles, or nurse sharks before enjoying a traditional Mayan lunch at Playa Tiburón. Finish your tour with a sunset cocktail at Playa Norte before heading downtown for dinner and live music. ■TIP→ To learn more about the history of Isla's famous sites, check out Hear & There, an audio tour available at Casa el Pio.

3

TOP ATTRACTIONS

FAMILY **El Garrafón National Park.** Despite the much-publicized "Garrafón Reef Restoration Program," much of the coral reef at this national marine park is dead, the result of hurricanes, boat anchors, and too many careless tourists. There are still colorful fish, but many of them will come near only if bribed with food. Although there's not much for snorkelers anymore, the park does have kayaks, restaurants, bathrooms, and a gift shop. Be prepared to spend $85 for the basic package called "Royal Garrafón," which includes snorkeling gear, breakfast, lunch, kayaks, transportation from Cancún, a bike tour, and an open bar. Another option is Dolphin Discovery ($115–$175), where you can use the parks amenities and swim with dolphins. ■TIP→ The Beach Club Garrafón de Castilla next door is a much cheaper alternative; the snorkeling is at least equal to that available in the park. The club is open to everyone, and a day pass is 50 pesos. You can take a taxi from town. The park is home to the **Santuario Maya a la Diosa Ixchel,** the sad vestiges of a Mayan temple once dedicated to the goddess Ixchel. A lovely walkway around the area remains, but the natural arch beneath the ruin has been blasted open and "repaired" with concrete badly disguised as rocks. The views here are spectacular, though: you can look to the open ocean, where waves crash against dramatic cliffs on one side and the Bahía de Mujeres (Bay of Women) on the other. On the way to the temple there's a cutesy Caribbean-style shopping center selling overpriced jewelry and souvenirs, as well as a park with brightly painted abstract sculptures. The ruins (open daily 9–5) are near the old lighthouse, where the road turns northeast into the Corredor Panorámico. It costs $3 to visit just the ruins and sculpture park, but this is included with admission to El Garrafón. ✉ *Carretera El Garrafón, 6 km (3¾ miles), Mza 41, Lote 12, Sm 9, Punta Sur, southeast of Playa Lancheros* ☎ *998/193–3360, 866/393–5158 toll-free from U.S.* ⊕ *www.garrafon.com* ✉ *$85* ⊙ *Daily 10–5.*

OFF THE BEATEN PATH

When exploring the southeastern tip of Isla Mujeres, be sure to visit the unique seashell-shape house located on Corredor Panorámico. Owned by artist Octavio Ocampo, the house resembles an enormous conch shell both inside and out.

Who Was Ixchel?

Ixchel (ee-*shell*) is a principal figure in the pantheon of Mayan gods. Sometimes called Lady Rainbow, Ixchel is the goddess of childbirth, fertility, and healing, and is said to control the tides and all water on earth. Originally married to the earth god Voltan, Ixchel fell in love with the moon god Itzamna, considered the founder of the Maya because he taught them how to read, write, and grow corn. When Ixchel became his consort, she gave birth to four powerful sons known as the Bacabs, who continue to hold up the sky in each of the four directions.

Often portrayed as a wise crone, Ixchel can be seen wearing a skirt decorated with crossbones and a crown of serpents while carrying a jug of water. The crossbones are a symbol of her role as the giver of new life and keeper of dead souls. The serpents represent her wisdom and power to rejuvenate, and the water jug alludes to her dual role as both a benign and destructive deity. Although she gives mankind the continual gift of water—the most essential element of life—according to Mayan myth Ixchel also sent floods to cleanse the earth of wicked people who had stopped thanking the gods. She is said to give special protection to those making the sacred pilgrimage to her sites on Cozumel and Isla Mujeres.

Iglesia de Concepción Inmaculada (*Church of the Immaculate Conception*). In 1890 local fishermen landed at a deserted colonial settlement known as Ecab, where they found three identical statues of the Virgin Mary, each carved from wood with porcelain face and hands. No one knows where the statues came from, but it's widely believed they were gifts from the Spanish during a visit in 1770. One statue went to the city of Izamal in the Yucatán, and another was sent to Kantunikin in Quintana Roo. The third remained on the island. It was housed in a small wooden chapel while this church was being built; legend has it that the chapel burst into flames when the statue was removed. Some islanders still believe the statue walks on the water around the island from dusk until dawn, looking for her sisters. You can pay your respects daily 10–11:30 am and 7–9 pm, or attend prayer services (in both English and Spanish) throughout the week. ⊠ *Avs. Morelos and Bravo, south side of zócalo.*

NEED A BREAK?

It's a small island, but there are several small shops selling gelato and homemade ice cream.

Cool Homemade Ice Cream. Cool has more than a dozen flavors, and is the only island shop that makes 100% natural ice cream. Be sure to try the coconut. ⊠ *Hidalgo 18.5.*

Gelateria Monte Bianco. Gelateria Monte Bianco is run by an Italian couple who have lived on the island since 2005. They serve a wide variety of gelato flavors, as well as desserts like tiramisu. ⊠ *Av. Matamoros 20* ▭ *No credit cards* ⊙ *Closed Sun.*

Fodor's Choice **Isla Mujeres Underwater Museum.** Combining art and nature, sculptor
★ Jason de Caires Taylor (*www.underwatersculpture.com*) has created
"underwater museums" off the shores of Punta Cancún, Punta Nizuc,
and Manchones Reef near Isla Mujeres. Locally known as MUSA
(Museo Subacuático de Arte), his main work features more than 400
lifelike statues that serve as artificial reefs to attract marine life. The
displays have conveniently been placed in shallow areas for viewing
by divers, snorkelers, and glass-bottom boats. The unusual artificial
habitat also helps restore the natural reefs that have suffered damage
over the years. Most local dive shops can organize excursions to the
site ($70–$75). ⊠ *Punta Cancún, Punta Nizuc, and Manchones Reef
in Isla Mujeres, Cancún and Isla Mujeres* ☎ 998/578–7097 ⊕ *www.
musaislamujeres.com* 🖥 *Free.*

FAMILY **Tortugranja** (*Turtle Farm*). This scientific station, run by the Mexican
government in partnership with private funding, works to conserve
the endangered sea turtle. You can see rescued hatchlings in three large
pools or watch larger turtles in sea pens. There's also a small museum
with an excellent display on turtles and their ecosystem. From May
through October you can join the staff in collecting and hatching eggs,
and in the fall you can help release baby turtles. ⊠ *Take Av. Rueda
Medina south of town; about a block southeast of Hacienda Mundaca,
take right fork (smaller road that loops back north called Sac Bajo);
entrance is about ½ km (¼ mile) farther, on left, Carretera Sac Bajo
Km 5* ☎ 998/888–0705 🖥 *$3* ☉ *Daily 9–5.*

WORTH NOTING

El Cementerio. Isla's cemetery is on Avenida López Mateos, the road that
runs parallel to Playa Norte. Many of the century-old gravestones are
covered with carved angels and flowers, with the most elaborate and
beautiful marking the graves of children. Hidden among them is the
tomb of the notorious Fermín Mundaca de Marechaja, a 19th-century
slave trader—often billed more glamorously as a pirate—who carved
his own skull-and-crossbones gravestone with the ominous epitaph: "As
you are, I once was; as I am, so shall you be." Ironically, his remains
actually lie in Mérida, where he died. The monument is tough to find—
ask a local to point out the unidentified marker. ⊠ *Av. Lopez Mateos.*

Laguna Makax. Pirates are said to have anchored their ships in this
lagoon while waiting to ambush hapless vessels crossing the Spanish Main. Today the lagoon houses a local shipyard and provides a
safe harbor for boats during hurricane season. It's off Avenida Rueda
Medina, about 2½ km (1½ miles) south of town, two blocks south of
the naval base.

BEACHES

Despite being surrounded by water, Isla Mujeres really has only three
beaches suitable for visitors: Playa Norte on the north end, and Playa
Lancheros and Playa Tiburón on the west side. With its crystal-clear
water, Playa Norte is generally tranquil and better for swimming than

CLOSE UP

Isla's History

The name Isla Mujeres means "Island of Women," although no one knows who dubbed it that. Many believe it was the ancient Maya, who were said to use the island as a religious center for worshipping Ixchel, the Mayan goddess of rainbows, the moon, and the sea, and the guardian of fertility and childbirth. Another popular legend has it that the Spanish conquistador Hernández de Córdoba named the island when he landed here in 1517 and found hundreds of female-shape clay idols dedicated to Ixchel and her daughters. Still others say the name dates from later, the 17th century, when visiting pirates stashed their women on Isla before heading out to pillage the high seas. (Legend has it that both Henry Morgan and Jean Lafitte buried treasure on Isla, although no one has ever found any pirate's gold.)

It wasn't until 1821, when Mexico became independent, that people really began to settle on Isla. In 1847, refugees from the War of the Castes fled to the island and built its first official village of Dolores, which was welcomed into the newly created territory of Quintana Roo in 1850. By 1858 a slave trader-turned-pirate named Fermín Mundaca de Marechaja began building an estate that took up 40% of the island. By the end of the century the population had risen to 651, and residents had begun to establish trade with the mainland, mostly by supplying fish to the owners of chicle and coconut plantations on the coast. In 1949, the Mexican navy built a base on Isla's northwestern coast. Around this time the island also caught the eye of some wealthy Mexican sportsmen, who began using it as a vacation spot.

Tourism flourished on Isla during the latter half of the 20th century, partly due to the island's most famous resident, Ramón Bravo (1927–98). A diver, cinematographer, ecologist, and colleague of Jacques Cousteau, Bravo was the first underwater photographer to explore the area. He discovered the now-famous Cave of the Sleeping Sharks and produced dozens of underwater documentaries for American, European, and Mexican television. Bravo's efforts to maintain the ecology on Isla has helped keep development here to a minimum. Even today, Bravo remains a hero to many *isleños* (ees-*lay*-nyos); his statue can be found where Avenida Rueda Medina changes into the Carretera El Garrafón, and there's a museum named after him on nearby Isla Contoy.

eastern beaches facing the Caribbean, which are susceptible to strong winds and riptides and have very little sand. The southern part of the island has several secluded beaches, but they too are dangerous due to exposed reefs and strong currents and are often littered with sea grass and ocean debris.

In 2008, high winds and stormy seas stole nearly 30 yards of Isla's sandy beaches. (Many say the beaches hadn't yet recovered from Hurricane Wilma in 2005.) The local government is slowly working to replenish the sand.

Playa Norte (North Beach). Playa Norte (North Beach) is easy to find: simply head north on any of the north–south streets in town until you hit

Playa Norte is a superb beach for relaxing under an umbrella.

this superb beach. The turquoise sea is as calm as a lake here, though developers have arrived and the area no longer has a secluded feel. The small cove between Avalon Reef Club and the Caribbean is the nicest section. Although relatively shallow, the water flows directly from the open sea, making this protected area cool and clean. Play a game of beach volleyball or enjoy a drink at one of the area's palapa bars, where wooden swings take the place of bar stools; **Buho's** is especially popular with locals and tourists, as $5 lounge chairs come with a free drink ticket. Lounge chairs and hammocks at **Sergio's** are free for customers, but to relax in front of **Maria del Maria** in a lounge chair will cost you $3. **Na Balam** charges a whopping $10 for one chair and umbrella. **Amenities:** food and drink; toilets. **Best for:** swimming. ⊠ *Along northern end of island, just before Avalon Reef Club at Calle Zazcil-Há.*

FAMILY **Playa Lancheros (Boatman's Beach).** There are two beaches between Laguna Makax and El Garrafón National Park. Playa Lancheros (Boatman's Beach) is a popular spot with an open-air restaurant where locals gather to eat freshly grilled "tikin-xic" (whole fish marinated with adobo de achiote and sour oranges, then wrapped in a banana leaf). This beach has grittier sand than its neighbor Playa Norte, but more palm trees. The calm water makes it perfect for children, although it's best if they stay close to shore, since the bottom drops off steeply. The souvenir stands are fairly low-key, renting kayaks, canoes, and beach toys.

WORD OF MOUTH

"Isla is very REAL and there are places to stay that suit every budget. The north beach is very safe—good choices in restaurants, many quite casual." —Fanjoy

Isla's Salt Mines

The ancient salt mines in Isla's interior were worked during the postclassic period of Mayan history (roughly AD 1000–1500). Salt was an important commodity for the Maya, who used it not only for preserving and flavoring food but also for making armor. Since the Maya had no metal, they soaked cotton cloth in salt until it formed a hard coating.

There's little to see today: simply two shallow marshes called Salina Chica (small salt mine) and Salina Grande (big salt mine) with murky water and quite a few mosquitoes at dusk. Since both of the island's main roads (Avenida Rueda Medina and the Corredor Panorámico) pass by them, you can have a look on your way to other parts of Isla.

Most bars and restaurants will give you access to beach chairs, umbrellas, and facilities provided you order a drink. There's also a small pen with tame *tiburones gatos* (nurse sharks). You can swim with them or just get your picture taken for $2. **Amenities:** food and drink; toilets; water sports. **Best for:** snorkeling. ⊠ *Bahia de Mujeres, on western side of island, near Hacienda Mundaca.*

Playa Tiburón (Shark Beach). Like Playa Lancheros, Playa Tiburón (Shark Beach) is on the west side of the island facing Bahía de Mujeres, and so its waters are also exceptionally calm. Once a respite from the crowds, this has become a more developed beach, with a large, popular seafood restaurant (through which you actually enter the beach) that serves burgers, hot dogs, and fish. There are several souvenir stands selling the usual T-shirts, as well as handmade seashell jewelry. On certain days you can find women who will braid your hair or give you a henna tattoo. This beach also has two sea pens with sleepy and relatively tame nurse sharks. Swim with them for $2 or just snap a photo. **Amenities:** food and drink; toilets. **Best for:** snorkeling; swimming. ⊠ *West side of Isla Mujeres, facing Bahía de Mujeres, near turtle farm.*

WHERE TO EAT

Dining on Isla is a casual affair, and much more affordable than in neighboring Cancún. Restaurants tend to serve simple food like seafood, pizza, salads, and Mexican dishes. Fresh ingredients and hospitable waiters make up for the island's lack of elaborate menus and master chefs. It's cash-only in most of the restaurants. If credit cards are accepted, you'll most likely pay an additional 5% service charge.

Though informal, most indoor restaurants do request that you at least wear a shirt and shoes. Some outdoor terrace and palapa restaurants also require shoes and some sort of cover-up over your bathing suit.

It's customary in Mexico for the waiter to bring the bill only when you ask for it (*"la cuenta, por favor"*). Always check to make sure you didn't get charged for something you didn't order, and to make sure the addition is correct. The "tax" on the bill is often a service charge, a sort of guaranteed tip.

EL PUEBLO

$$ ✕**Amigos.** This easy-to-miss café is
ECLECTIC a great spot for breakfast, offering delicious omelets and strong early-morning coffee. Once you settle at one of the street-side tables, the staff treats you like an old friend. The friendly vibe also makes Amigos a local favorite. Though it used to be known mainly for its superb pizza, the restaurant serves a little bit of everything from fish and meat to vegetarian dishes. Pastas are also a favorite here, as well as grab-and-go Mexican staples. $ *Average main: $11* ⊠ *Av. Hidalgo 19, between Avs. Matamoros and Abasolo* ☎ *998/877–1338* ✛ *C4.*

$$$ ✕ **Angelo.** Named for its Italian chef
ITALIAN Angelo Sanna, this charming bistro on Hidalgo's busy main strip is done up with soft lighting and a wood-fired oven. Go here for the pizza; they have a thin crispy crust and are quite delicious. A large selection of Italian classics round out the menu. Try their famous wood-oven lasagna or mussels steamed in white wine. Angelo, who has lived and worked in Isla Mujeres for more than 15 years, is a hospitable host and a great source of local information. Open late, Angelo will serve pizzas to the local bars if you're hungry at the end of a long night. $ *Average main: $20* ⊠ *Av. Hidalgo 14* ☎ *998/877–1273* ✛ *B4.*

$$ ✕ **Bistro Français.** The name of this casual restaurant is somewhat
BISTRO deceiving. Though French dishes like chicken *cordon bleu* or *coq au vin* can be found on the menu (which is painted on the wall in bright colors), the grilled fish and pasta specials are the real reason to visit. Breakfast is particularly good, featuring tasty fruit salads and fluffy French toast. The apple crepes with maple cream might just inspire repeat visits. Victor, the owner, makes it a point to ensure that each of his diners has a good experience. The deck overlooks the bustling street, so you can watch the world go by. $ *Average main: $14* ⊠ *Av. Matamoros 29, between Juárez and Hidalgo* ⊟ *No credit cards* ⊗ *No breakfast Sat.* ✛ *B4*

$ ✕ **Café Cito.** This cheery, seashell-decorated place was opened in 1988
CAFÉ as one of Isla's first cafés, and it's still one of the best breakfast spots on the island. The menu includes fluffy pancakes, fresh waffles, fruit-filled crepes, and egg dishes, as well as great cappuccino and espresso,

Dining on the island is a casual and friendly affair.

and every breakfast comes with complimentary coffee or tea. The fresh-squeezed OJ is a great way to start the day, and don't miss the pineapple-coconut marmalade. Lunch specials are also available daily. [$] *Average main: $6* ✉ *Avs. Juárez and Matamoros* ☎ *998/877–1470* 💳 *No credit cards* 🕒 *No dinner* ⊕ *B4.*

$$ ECLECTIC Fodor's Choice ★

🍴 **Café Mogagua.** Whether you're sitting at one of the wooden tables, on a comfortable couch, or on a street-facing lounger, this open-air café and restaurant has a relaxed and comfortable vibe. Packed for breakfast and lunch, the menu ranges from Mexican classics like chilaquiles and *huevos divorciados* (eggs with chile sauce), to pizza and grilled meats and fish later in the day. An all-purpose establishment, you can stop in to play board games, have a glass of wine with a friend, or spend time on your laptop, thanks to the organic coffee from Chiapas and free Wi-Fi. [$] *Average main: $11* ✉ *Av. Juárez at Madero, El Pueblo* ☎ *998/877–0127* ⊕ *C4.*

$$ MEXICAN

🍴 **Don Chepo.** Grilled meats (tacos, fajitas, and steaks) are the draw at this lively restaurant that resembles a small hacienda, one of the best places on the island for Mexican food. Inside, the focal point is the large and well-stocked bar, where you can chat with other visitors or enjoy the (sometimes live) mariachi music. Tables outside are perfect for watching all the downtown action on Hidalgo Street. The *arrachera,* a fine cut of beef grilled to perfection and served with rice, salad, baked potato, warm tortillas, and beans, is a reliably excellent choice, as is the chile relleno. The cocktails are strong and pair well with the ceviche, and a 2-for-1 happy hour is honored all day long. [$] *Average main: $12* ✉ *Avs. Hidalgo and Francisco Madero* ☎ *998/877–0165* ⊕ *C4.*

$$ MEXICAN

🍴 **Fayne's Bar and Grill.** The vibe at this brightly painted spot is hip and energetic. Best known for its terrific cocktails (don't miss the mango margaritas), this funky restaurant serves island fare such as garlic shrimp, ceviche enchiladas, stuffed calamari, and grilled snapper. There's live music nightly starting at 8. [$] *Average main: $15* ✉ *Av. Hidalgo 12A, between Avs. Mateos and Matamoros* ☎ *998/877–0528* 🌐 *www.faynesbarandgrill.com* ✥ *B4.*

$$$ MEXICAN

🍴 **Fenix.** Formerly known as Zazil Ha, this beachside restaurant at the trendy Na Balam Hotel is clustered under big, shady palms, but for more intimate dining you can ask to be seated upstairs under a palapa roof. Homemade breads, yogurt, and granola make breakfast a treat. Later in the day the kitchen serves innovative vegetarian fare, like salads with coconut, mango, and mint vinaigrette, as well as traditional Mexican dishes and a killer burger. Musicians from Mexico, Cuba, and the Caribbean often play during the weekends, turning the restaurant into an after-hours island hotspot. [$] *Average main: $17* ✉ *Na Balam Hotel, Calle Zazil-Há 118* ☎ *998/881–4770* 🌐 *www.nabalam.com* ✥ *B2.*

$$ MEXICAN

🍴 **Fredy's Restaurant & Bar.** This family-run restaurant specializes in simple fish, seafood, and traditional Mexican dishes like fajitas and oven-baked shrimp. There isn't much here in the way of decor—think plastic chairs and tables—but the staff is friendly, the food is fresh, the beer is cold, and the value is good. The tasty daily specials are a bargain and attract both locals and visitors. [$] *Average main: $11* ✉ *Av. Hidalgo, between Avs. Matamoros and Lopez Mateo* ☎ *998/810–1691* 🌐 *www.fredys.myislamujeres.com* 🕑 *No lunch Mon.* ✥ *B4*

$$$ ARGENTINE

🍴 **L'Argentina Grill.** Famous for its perfect location in the exact center of Hidalgo, this boisterous restaurant and bar offers both Mexican and Argentine dishes. There are more than 150 entrées on the menu, including lamb, filet mignon, and an assortment of fish, from mahimahi to salmon. Portions are huge and revolve around meat and fish, but there are salads and pasta for vegetarians. For a quiet table away from the lively street, head indoors to the restaurant's lounge bar that's open until 1 am. [$] *Average main: $17* ✉ *Corner of Av. Hidalgo and Matamoros, El Pueblo* ☎ *998/214–1349* ✥ *B4.*

$ MEXICAN
Fodor's Choice ★

🍴 **Loncheria La Lomita.** Don't judge a restaurant by its setting. This hole in the wall, with its red plastic tables and chairs, is a perennial local favorite. Prepare yourself for enormous portions, starting with the beloved *sopa de frijoles* (black bean soup made with onions, tomatoes, lime and fresh cheese). Moist fish fillets are cooked in a bed of oil and herbs and wrapped in a sheet of foil. If you only try one dish, make it the chile relleno: stuffed chiles lightly battered and fried and served with a side of pickled cabbage and rice. [$] *Average main: $7* ✉ *Av. Juarez Sur No. 25-B, El Pueblo* 💳 *No credit cards* 🕑 *Closed Sun.* ✥ *D5*

$$ ITALIAN

🍴 **Mamma Rosa.** In the heart of downtown, on one of the island's busiest corners, this Italian restaurant is one of the more popular eateries on Isla Mujeres. The menu, which consists mostly of pizzas and pastas, also features hearty Angus beef and tasty grilled snapper. The spinach-and-ricotta tortellini is a pasta favorite, and their heaping Caesar salad is big enough for two. Try to grab outdoor seating on the sidewalk (it's perfect for people-watching), but if you can't, the exposed dining area is charming, with arched ceilings, yellow walls, and black-and-white photographs. Save room for the homemade tiramisu. $ *Average main: $14* ✉ *Av. Hidalgo at Matamoros Centro, Downtown* ☎ *998/190–0713* ⊕ *www.mammarosaisla.com* ⊗ *No lunch* ✛ *C4.*

$
CAFÉ

✕ **Mañana Restaurant & Bookstore.** It's hard to miss this bright fuchsia restaurant with a yellow sun stretching its rays over the front door. But you won't want to pass up the great breakfasts, including excellent egg dishes, fresh baguettes, and Italian coffee. Salads, homemade burgers (meat or vegetarian), and fresh fruit shakes are served at lunch; the banana-granola shake is amazing. If you're in a hurry, you can grab a quick snack like falafel and hummus at the outdoor counter, but because there's a bookstore on-site, you may end up lounging on a couch and reading after your meal. $ *Average main: $6* ✉ *Av. Guerrero 17* ☎ *998/877–0555* ▭ *No credit cards* ⊗ *No dinner. Closed Sun.* ✛ *C4*

$$
SEAFOOD

✕ **Minino's Cocteleria.** If you're looking to dine on the waterfront with sand between your toes, Minino's is the place to go. This no-frills spot serves fresh fish tossed in ceviche (shrimp, octopus, conch, or mixed varieties) or simply grilled. During the afternoons, you can watch local fishermen bring their catch back to shore while you sip on a beer and lazily nosh on small plates like fish tacos. For those who like it hot: the *pico de gallo* is delicious but incredibly spicy, so watch how much you add to your plate. $ *Average main: $12* ✉ *Av. Rueda, El Pueblo, Isla Mujeres* ☎ *998/274–0159* ▭ *No credit cards* ✛ *B5.*

$$
MEDITERRANEAN
Fodor's Choice
★

✕ **Olivia.** The delightful dishes at this sexy Mediterranean restaurant are combinations of Moroccan, Greek, and Turkish flavors based on owners Lior and Yaron Zelzer's family recipes. Everything from the freshly baked spanakopita to the flaky baklava is made from scratch in the open-air kitchen. Start with the Greek or Moroccan tapas and move onto house favorites like the *shawarma* pita wrap filled with grilled chicken, hummus, tahini, and fried eggplant, or the *mafrum,* a blend of potatoes stuffed with ground beef in a Moroccan red sauce. The setting is casual yet romantic, with tiki torches lighting the way to a tropical garden where rustic tables sit beneath a palapa roof. A visit to Olivia's isn't complete without a bowl of homemade cherry ice cream. $ *Average main: $12* ✉ *Matamoros 11, between Juárez and Medina, El Pueblo* ☎ *998/877–1765* ⊕ *www.olivia-isla-mujeres.com* ⊗ *No lunch. Closed Sun. year-round and Mon., Apr.–Nov.* ✛ *B4*

$$
SEAFOOD

✕ **Picus Coctelería.** Kick off your shoes and settle back with a cold beer at this charming beachside restaurant right near the ferry docks. You can watch the fishing boats come and go while you wait for some of the freshest seafood on the island. The grilled fish and grilled lobster with garlic butter are both magnificent, as are the shrimp fajitas—but the real showstopper is the mixed seafood ceviche, which might include conch, shrimp, abalone, fish, or octopus. $ *Average main: $11* ✉ *Av. Rueda Medina, 1 block northwest of ferry docks* ☎ *998/129–6011* ✛ *B5.*

$
CUBAN
Fodor's Choice
★

✕ **Qubano.** This delightful Cuban restaurant is owned by vivacious chef Vivian Reynaldo, who seems to know everyone in town. Her rich Hungarian potatoes, a recipe handed down from her mother, have been known to leave customers speechless, while the grilled *tostones* sandwiches, which use fried plantains instead of bread, are topped with a finger-licking onion-and-orange sauce and can't be missed. Meat lovers will relish the juicy hamburgers stuffed with goat cheese and served with yucca fries. Lunch salads are topped with fresh ingredients like garbanzo beans, avocado, and jicama. There are also several vegetarian dishes as well as freshly squeezed juices. The simple setting, with tables both inside and outside of the turquoise-color shack, is cozy, pleasant, and welcoming. [$] *Average main: $6* ✉ *Plaza Los Almendros, Av. Hidalgo* ☎ *998/214–2118* ▭ *No credit cards* ✥ *C4.*

$$$ ITALIAN 🍴 **Sardinian Smile.** Despite the cheesy name (there is an outpost in Sardinia), this cozy addition to the busy Avenida Hidalgo strip has quickly become the most authentic Italian restaurant on the island, serving handmade pastas like fettuccine with clams or a spicy *arrabiata* sauce to happy crowds. Hearty lobsters and juicy steaks add protein to a carbohydrate-rich menu Always ask about the daily catch; the snapper baked in wine and olive oil is divine. Though service can be slow, it's worth it when the food arrives; just order a glass of Italian wine and await your feast. [$] *Average main: $18* ✉ *Near main plaza, Av. Hidalgo, El Pueblo, Isla Mujeres* ☎ *998/163–6850* ✥ *C4.*

$ MEXICAN 🍴 **Sergio's Playa Sol.** More of a beach bar than a formal restaurant, Sergio's dabbles in typical Mexican beach fare like chicken nachos, creamy guacamole, and savory fish kebabs. You can easily spend the whole day here, ending your visit with the beautiful sunset. There are free hammocks, beach chairs, and umbrellas for customers, along with what may be the best margaritas on the island. The kitchen closes at 5 pm. [$] *Average main: $8* ✉ *North end of Rueda Medina on Playa Norte* ☎ *998/705–3250* ▭ *No credit cards* ✥ *A4.*

$$ SEAFOOD 🍴 **Sunset Grill.** Recently remodeled, this is the perfect place to savor the sunset. A covered dining terrace with large picture windows overlooks the sea, while soft music and candlelight add to the romantic ambience. Grab a table outside and you can take a dip in the ocean between your appetizer and main course. The dinner menu has a wide range of dishes, including favorites like grilled tuna steak, coconut shrimp, and Parmesan-crusted fish fillet. For lunch, the kitchen offers Mexican favorites like tacos and quesadillas, but also fries up a great burger. Service is very good, and there's live music nightly. [$] *Average main: $17* ✉ *Av. Rueda Medina, North End, Condominios Nautibeach, Playa Norte* ☎ *998/877–0785* 🌐 *www.sunsetgrill.com.mx* ✥ *A4.*

ELSEWHERE ON THE ISLAND

$$$ NORTHERN ITALIAN Fodor's Choice ★ 🍴 **Casa Rolandi.** This quietly sophisticated hotel restaurant has an open-air dining room connected to a deck overlooking the water. Tables are set with beautiful linens, china, and cutlery, making Casa Rolandi the most upscale and romantic restaurant on the island. The northern Italian menu here includes the wonderful carpaccio *di tonno alla Giorgio* (thin slices of tuna with extra-virgin olive oil and lime juice), along with excellent pastas. Even the simplest dishes, such as angel-hair pasta in tomato sauce, are delicious. For something different, try the saffron risotto or the *costolette d'agnello al forno* (lamb chops with a thyme infusion). The sunset views, of course, are spectacular. [$] *Average main: $20* ✉ *Hotel Villa Rolandi, Laguna Mar, Sm 7, Mza 75, Lotes 15 and*

16 ☎ 866/754–0452 toll-free from U.S. ✛ C3

$$
CUBAN
✕ **El Varadero.** Located off the beaten path in a weathered fisherman's cottage with a palapa roof, this local favorite is the perfect place for delicious, reasonably priced seafood. It's known for its fresh mojitos, but the family-style plates of garlic fish (grilled or fried) is the real reason to visit. The day's catch changes regularly, ranging from grouper to lobster, and don't miss the creole sauce if it's being served. Cuban specialties like *tostones* and sandwiches round out the menu options at this relaxed, charming island spot. $ *Average main: $13* ✉ *Colonia Electricistas* ☎ 998/877–1600 ☾ *Closed Mon.* ✛ D5

WORD OF MOUTH

"It's very easy to get around. Taxis from one end of the island to the other run you about $5. Golf cart rentals for the day are around 45 dollars and available a few blocks from the ferry dock. The town center bustles at night. I don't think I ever had a bad meal there." —ontariogirl

$
ECLECTIC
Fodor's Choice
★
✕ **Mango Cafe.** Warm and inviting with wooden tables and colorful chalkboards announcing the day's *agua frescas*, this 10-table hotspot is a must if you're looking for an unbeatable breakfast or lunch in Isla Mujeres. The owner, Polo Avila, is a delight, serving up playfully inspired takes on classic dishes using Mexican ingredients and flavors. Standouts are a bacon-egg-and-cheese-stuffed chile poblano, coconut French toast, and eggs Benedict topped with local *chaya* (a cousin of spinach). Portions are massive, so be sure to go hungry. A self-serve coffee bar guarantees you always get a refill for your cup of joe. $ *Average main: $9* ✉ *Payo Obispo, Lot 1, Isla Mujeres* ☎ 998/274–0118 ⊕ *www.mangocafeislamujeres.com* ✛ D5.

$
SEAFOOD
✕ **Playa Lancheros Restaurant.** If you want to savor one of the island's most authentic meals, take a short taxi ride to this casual eatery under a big palapa roof on the beach of the same name. It's right on the sand, so it's no surprise that the kitchen takes pride in serving the freshest fish. The house specialty is the Yucatecan *tikin xic*, fish marinated in a sour-orange sauce and cooked in a banana leaf over an open flame; this is cooked to order and can take up to 45 minutes. There are also delicious tacos, fresh guacamole, and spicy salsa. The food (served 10 am–7 pm) may take a while to arrive, so bring your swimsuit and take a dip while you wait. On Sunday there's music, dancing, and the occasional shark wrestler. $ *Average main: $7* ✉ *Playa Lancheros where Av. Rueda Medina splits into Sac Bajo and Carretera El Garrafón* ☎ 998/877–0340 ✛ C5.

WHERE TO STAY

Many of Isla's smaller hotels don't accept credit cards, and some add a 5%–10% surcharge if you use one. Isla has also been tightening up its cancellation policy, so check with your hotel about surcharges for changing reservations. ⌨ Before paying, always ask to see your room to make sure everything is satisfactory—especially at the smaller hotels.

A growing number of Isla hotels are now encouraging people to make their reservations online. Some allow you to book rooms right on their websites, but even hotels without their own sites usually offer reservations via online booking agencies, such as 🌐 *www.docancun.com* and 🌐 *www.lostoasis.net*. **■TIP→ Be sure to ask whether construction is taking place nearby; it's often the reason a hotel lowers its rates, but the savings may not be worth the disruption.**

Booking online is certainly convenient, and can often get you a 10% to 20% discount on room rates. The bad news, though, is that there may be an occasional breakdown in communication between a booking agency and a hotel. **■TIP→ If you do end up booking online, be sure to print out copies of all your Internet transactions, including receipts and confirmations, and bring them with you.**

For expanded reviews, facilities, and current deals, visit Fodors.com.

EL PUEBLO

$$ RESORT 🏨 **Avalon Reef Club.** This resort sits on a tiny island called Isla Yunque, and is connected to the northern tip of Isla Mujeres by a long wooden bridge. **Pros:** beautiful location; calm bay. **Cons:** constant sales pitches; some rooms lack views; hotel could use a renovation; non-filtered tap water. [$] *Rooms from: $117* ✉ *Calle Zazcil Há s/n 7, Isla Yunque* ☎ *998/999–2050, 888/515–2154 toll-free from U.S.* 🌐 *www.avalonvacations.com* 🛏 *74 rooms, 6 suites, 49 villas* 🍴 *Multiple meal plans* ✥ *B1.*

$ HOTEL Fodor's Choice ★ 🏨 **Casa el Pio.** Off the town square, this boutique hotel—owned by a graphic designer and hair stylist—is bursting with character, charm, and creativity. **Pros:** unlimited fresh drinking water; spotless property; MP3 audio tour available detailing sites of Isla Mujeres. **Cons:** no restaurant; no housekeeping or check-ins on Sunday; lacks 24-hour service; Wi-Fi in common areas only. [$] *Rooms from: $72* ✉ *Av. Hidalgo 3, between Bravo and Allende* ☎ *998/229–2799* 🌐 *www.casaelpio.com* 🛏 *4 rooms* 🍴 *No meals* ✥ *D4.*

$ B&B/INN 🏨 **Hotel Belmar.** This hacienda-style hotel has cozy rooms that are decorated with Mexican artwork, saltillo floors, talavera tile bathrooms, and French doors that lead to small balconies. **Pros:** clean and comfortable; near shops and restaurants. **Cons:** some street noise; no elevator. [$] *Rooms from: $67* ✉ *Av. Hidalgo Norte 110, between Avs. Madero and Abasolo* ☎ *998/877–0429* 🌐 *www.hotelbelmarisla.com* 🛏 *10 rooms, 1 suite* 🍴 *Breakfast* ✥ *C4.*

$$ HOTEL 🏨 **Hotel Playa la Media Luna.** This breezy palapa-roofed bed-and-breakfast lies along Half Moon Beach, just south of Playa Norte. **Pros:** rooms have balconies; nearby beach is calm and shallow. **Cons:** inhospitable staff; hotel needs renovating; lost safe key costs $50 and lost towel costs $10. [$] *Rooms from: $125* ✉ *Sección Rocas, Punta Norte, Lote 9/10* ☎ *998/877–0759* 🌐 *www.playamedialuna.com* 🛏 *22 rooms* 🍴 *Breakfast* ✥ *C2.*

$ HOTEL 🏨 **Hotel Plaza Almendros.** This little hotel is right in the center of the action, close to all the restaurants and bars on Avenida Hidalgo. **Pros:** central location; family-friendly atmosphere. **Cons:** can be noisy;

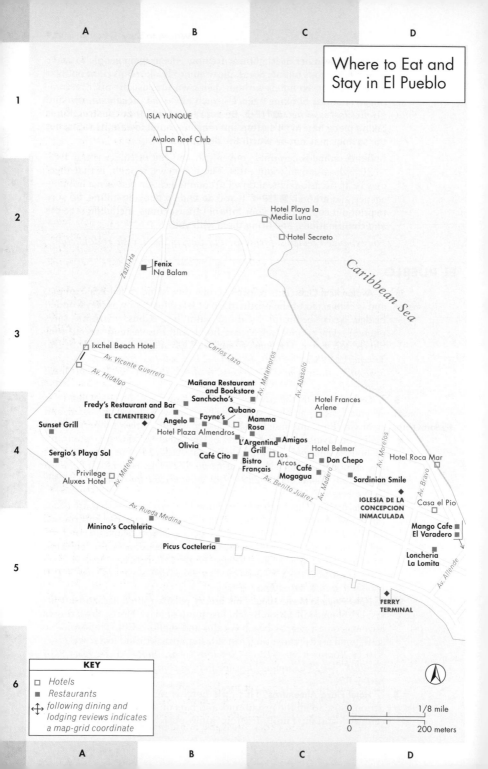

Where to Eat and Stay in El Pueblo

ISLA YUNQUE

Avalon Reef Club □

Hotel Playa la Media Luna □

□ Hotel Secreto

Caribbean Sea

Fenix ■
Na Balam

Zazil-Ha

□ Ixchel Beach Hotel
□

Av. Vicente Guerrero

Carlos Lazo

Av. Hidalgo

Av. Matamoros

Av. Abasolo

Mañana Restaurant ■
and Bookstore
Sanchocho's ■

Hotel Frances
Arlene

Fredy's Restaurant and Bar ■
EL CEMENTERIO ◆

Qubano ■

Sunset Grill ■

Angelo ■ Fayne's ■

Mamma ■
Rosa

Hotel Plaza Almendros □

Olivia ■

L'Argentina ■ Amigos ■
Grill

Hotel Belmar

Av. Morelos

Sergio's Playa Sol ■

Café Cito ■

□ Los
Arcos

□ Don Chepo ■

Hotel Roca Mar □

Bistro ■
Français

Café ■
Mogagua

Privilege
Aluxes Hotel □

Av. Mateos

Av. Benito Juárez

Av. Madero

Sardinian Smile ■

Av. Bravo

Casa el Pio
□

Av. Rueda Medina

IGLESIA DE LA
CONCEPCION
INMACULADA ◆

Mango Cafe ■
El Varadero ■

Minino's Cocteleria □

Loncheria
La Lomita

Av. Allende

Picus Cocteleria ■

FERRY ◆
TERMINAL

KEY

□ Hotels
■ Restaurants
⬦ following dining and
lodging reviews indicates
a map-grid coordinate

0   1/8 mile

0   200 meters

basic and musty rooms. $ *Rooms from: $75* ✉ *Av. Hidalgo, Lote 14* ☎ *998/877–1217* ⊕ *www.hotelplazaalmendros.com* 🖥 *39 rooms* 🍴 *No meals* ✢ *B4.*

$$ 🛏 **Hotel Roca Mar.** You can smell, hear, and see the ocean from the simply furnished, blue-and-white guest rooms at this hotel. **Pros:** steps away from the water; friendly and helpful staff; free purified water and coffee in the lobby. **Cons:** glass-walled bathrooms lack privacy; town-facing rooms do not have a/c; no elevator; Wi-Fi in common areas only. $ *Rooms from: $110* ✉ *Calle Nicolas Bravo and Abasolo* ☎ *998/877–0101* ⊕ *www.rocamar-hotel.com* 🖥 *30 rooms, 2 suites* 🍴 *Multiple meal plans* ✢ *D4.*

HOTEL

$$$$ 🛏 **Hotel Secreto.** It's beautiful. It's famous. It's très chic. **Pros:** in-room massage and facials; pool overlooks ocean; peace and quiet; renovated fitness center. **Cons:** not good for children; books up in advance; no restaurant. $ *Rooms from: $250* ✉ *Sección Rocas, Lote 11, Half Moon Beach* ☎ *998/877–1039* ⊕ *www.hotelsecreto.com* 🖥 *12 rooms* 🍴 *Breakfast* ✢ *C2.*

HOTEL

Fodor's Choice ★

$$ 🛏 **Ixchel Beach Hotel.** The location—on a beach with clear, calm water—is unbeatable. **Pros:** beautiful location; reasonable rates; complimentary beach chairs. **Cons:** small pool; no meals. $ *Rooms from: $120* ✉ *Playa Norte, Calle Guerrero, Sm 1* ☎ *998/999–2010, 800/638–5061 toll-free from U.S.* ⊕ *www.ixchelbeachhotel.com* 🖥 *117 rooms* 🍴 *No meals* ✢ *A3.*

RENTAL

$ 🛏 **Los Arcos.** In the heart of downtown, this hotel is a terrific value. **Pros:** reasonable rates; spacious rooms; near restaurants and shops. **Cons:** some linens feel worn; sparse furnishings; no elevator; street noise. $ *Rooms from: $80* ✉ *Av. Hidalgo 58, across from Amigos restaurant between Abasolo and Matamoros* ☎ *998/877–1343* ⊕ *www.suites-los-arcos.myislamujeres.com* 🖥 *12 rooms* 🍴 *No meals* ✢ *C4.*

HOTEL

$$$ 🛏 **Na Balam.** Elegant without being pretentious, this tranquil hotel is a true sanctuary. **Pros:** good restaurant; beautiful beach; 24-hour security. **Cons:** not all rooms are on the beach; mosquitoes at night. $ *Rooms from: $200* ✉ *Calle Zazil-Há 118* ☎ *998/881–4770* ⊕ *www.nabalam.com* 🖥 *35 rooms* 🍴 *Multiple meal plans* ✢ *B3.*

HOTEL

$$$ 🛏 **Privilege Aluxes.** Perched on the sugary shores of Playa Norte, this five-story resort is the largest and one of the newest properties on the island. **Pros:** excellent location; all-inclusive meal plan available; Wi-Fi on the beach. **Cons:** some rooms have cemetery views and noise from neighboring school; watered-down cocktails; small spa; standard rooms lack tubs. $ *Rooms from: $190* ✉ *Av. Adolfo Lopez Mateos* ☎ *998/848–8470* ⊕ *www.privilegehotels.com* 🖥 *124 rooms* 🍴 *Multiple meal plans* ✢ *A4.*

RESORT
ALL-INCLUSIVE

ELSEWHERE ON THE ISLAND

$$$$ 🛏 **Casa de los Sueños.** Walking into the open-air sunken lobby of this gorgeous spot feels like walking into a friend's fabulous vacation hacienda; colorful and cozy, yet modern and chic, this used to be Isla's best-kept secret, but with a recent renovation, it will be soon be Isla's hardest booking. **Pros:** intimate, secluded atmosphere; iPod docking stations; no children under 14. **Cons:** not for families; far from town;

HOTEL

Fodor's Choice ★

Casa de los Suenos

Casa el Pio

Internet in common areas only. $ Rooms from: $275 ⊠ Carretera a Garrafón, Fracc. Turquesa lote 9 A and B, Isla Mujeres ☎ 998/888–0370, 877/372–3993 toll-free from U.S. ⊕ www.casasuenos.com ↴ 10 suites ⦿ Breakfast ✛ C6.

$$$$ ⛆ **Hotel Villa Rolandi.** The luxury
HOTEL starts with the private yacht that delivers you to this hotel's lagoon dock from Cancún's Embarcadero Marina, and continues throughout your entire stay. **Pros:** attentive staff; great ocean views; luxurious touches like fragrant towels and bathrobes. **Cons:** expensive; property feels dated; must drive to reach the main town; young children not allowed. $ Rooms from: $500 ⊠ Fracc. Laguna Mar, Sm 7, Mza 75, Lotes 15 and 16, Carretera Sac–Bajo ☎ 998/999–2000 ⊕ www.villarolandi.com ↴ 35 suites ⦿ Some meals ✛ C3.

$$$$ ⛆ **Isla Mujeres Palace.** With its restaurants, beach, and pool, this all-
RESORT inclusive hotel makes it tempting to never leave the property. **Pros:** large
ALL-INCLUSIVE pool; comfortable rooms; good service. **Cons:** far from downtown; no children under 18; only one restaurant. $ Rooms from: $500 ⊠ Carretera Garrafón, Km 4.5, Mza 62, Sm 8 ☎ 998/999–2020 ⊕ www.palaceresorts.com ↴ 62 rooms ⦿ All-inclusive ✛ C4.

$$ ⛆ **Villa La Bella.** Located on the eastern coast, this romantic B&B is one
B&B/INN of the most laid-back spots on the island. **Pros:** welcoming owners; relaxing atmosphere; tasty breakfasts. **Cons:** taxi ride from downtown; kids under 18 not allowed. $ Rooms from: $150 ⊠ Carretera Perimetral al Garrafón ☎ 998/888–0342 ⊕ www.villalabella.com ↴ 6 rooms ⦿ Breakfast ✛ C3.

NIGHTLIFE

This sleepy island has a surprisingly healthy nightlife scene, with a variety of options to choose from. Most bars close by midnight, but the party continues at the nightclubs until 2 or 3 am. The majority of venues are within downtown's four-block radius, with a few others along Playa Norte. The proximity makes barhopping on foot perilously convenient.

BARS

Buho's. Buho's has three palapa beach bars with swings and hammocks where you can pass away the day with a tropical drink or ice-cold beer. There's even a large TV for sports fans. From 5 to 7, take a seat at the bar and enjoy happy-hour sunset. For $5, you can rent a Buho's lounge chair on Playa Norte, which includes a free nonalcoholic beverage. ⊠ Av. Carlos Lazo 1, at Cabanas Marina del Mar on Playa Norte ☎ 998/877–0179 ⊘ 10 am–midnight.

Café del Mar. Designed by renowned architect Lluís Güell, Café del Mar is an Ibiza-inspired beach bar that plays chill-out music by day and has live music at night. The fish tacos are a perfect cerveza accompaniment. Try to stop by for the gorgeous sunset. ⊠ *Av. Adolfo Lopez Mateos, at Privilege Aluxes in front of Playa Norte* ☎ *998/848–8473* ⊙ *Daily 10–10.*

La Adelita. La Adelita is a popular spot for enjoying reggae, salsa, and Caribbean music while trying out over 150 varieties of tequila and cigars. ⊠ *Av. Hidalgo Norte 12A.*

Sanchocho's. If you're looking for a place to watch a game, you'd be wise to settle in for 2-for-1 beer specials and root for your team at this lively sports bar. Multiple big screen TVs broadcast various games throughout the day. ⊠ *Av. Hildalgo, at Matamoros, El Pueblo, Isla Mujeres.*

DANCE CLUBS

Bar OM. Bar OM is a small, eclectic bi-level lounge offering wine, organic teas, and self-serve draft-beer taps. Chill out to the sounds of acid jazz, bossa nova, and reggae. ⊠ *Av. Matamoros, at Juárez.*

SHOPPING

Aside from seashell art and jewelry, Isla produces few local crafts. Still, the streets are filled with souvenir shops selling cheap T-shirts, garish ceramics, and seashells glued onto a variety of objects. Amid all the junk you may find good Mexican folk art, hammocks, textiles, and silver jewelry. Most stores are small family operations that don't take credit cards, but everyone gladly accepts American dollars. Stores that do take credit cards sometimes tack on a fee to offset the commission they must pay. Hours are generally Monday through Saturday 10–1 and 4–7, although many stores stay open during siesta hours (1–4).

BOOKS

Mañana Bookstore. This friendly shop is the island's only English-language bookstore, offering two-for-one trades (no Harlequin romances) and renting out board games. You can have something to eat and then settle in on the couch for some reading. Used books can either be traded or exchanged for food credit at the café. ⊠ *Av. Guerrero 17* ☎ *998/877–0555.*

CRAFTS

Artesanías Arcoiris. Artesanías Arcoiris has Mexican blankets and other handicrafts. The staffers here also braid hair. ⊠ *Avs. Hidalgo and Juárez.*

Artesanías Market. Many local artists display their works at the Artesanías Market, where you can find plenty of bargains. For custommade clothing, visit **Hortensia**—the last stall on the left after you come through the market entrance. Choose from bright Mexican fabrics and then pick a pattern for a skirt, shirt, shorts, or a dress. They'll sew it

Some impressive catches are to be had off the coast of the island.

Sociedad Cooperativa Turística. Sociedad Cooperativa Turística is a fishermen's cooperative that rents boats for a maximum of four hours and six people ($150). An island tour with lunch costs $55 per person. ⊠ *Av. Rueda Medina at Contoy Pier* ☎ 998/887–0800.

SNORKELING AND SCUBA DIVING

Most local dive spots are described in detail in *Dive Mexico* magazine, available in many local shops. Coral reefs at El Garrafón National Park have suffered tremendously from a variety of factors, some unavoidable (hurricanes) and some all-too-avoidable (boats dropping anchors onto soft coral, a practice now outlawed). Some good snorkeling can be found near Playa Norte on the north end.

Isla is a good place for learning to dive, since dive areas are close to shore. Offshore, there is excellent diving and snorkeling at Xlaches (pronounced *ees*-lah-chayss) reef, due north on the way to Isla Contoy. One of Contoy's most alluring dives is a cave full of sharks off the northern tip. Discovered by a local fisherman, the cave was extensively explored by Ramón Bravo, a local diver, cinematographer, and Mexico's foremost expert on sharks. It's a fascinating 150-foot dive for experienced divers only.

At 30–40 feet deep and 3,300 feet off the southwestern coast, the coral reef known as **Manchones** is a good dive site. During the summer of 1994, an ecological group hoping to divert divers and snorkelers from El Garrafón commissioned a 1-ton, 9¾-foot bronze cross, which was later sunk here. Named the Cruz de la Bahía (Cross of the Bay), it's a tribute to everyone who has died at sea. Another option is the Barco

Shhh . . . Don't Wake the Sharks

The underwater caverns off Isla Mujeres attract reef sharks, a dangerous species. Once the sharks swim into the caves they enter a state of relaxed nonaggression seen nowhere else. Naturalists have two explanations, both involving the composition of the water inside the caves, which contains more oxygen, more carbon dioxide, and less salt than usual.

According to the first theory, the decreased salinity causes the parasites that plague sharks to loosen their grip, allowing the remora fish (sharks' personal vacuum cleaners) to eat the parasites more easily. Perhaps the sharks relax to make the cleaning easier, or maybe it's the aftereffect of a good scrubbing. Another theory is

that the caves' combination of fresh- and saltwater produces a euphoria similar to the "nitrogen narcosis" scuba divers experience on deep dives.

Whatever the sharks experience while "sleeping" in the caves, they pay a heavy price for it. A swimming shark breathes automatically and without effort as water flows through its gills, but a stationary shark must laboriously pump water to continue breathing. If you dive in the Cave of the Sleeping Sharks, be cautious: many are reef sharks, the species responsible for the largest number of attacks on humans. Dive with a reliable guide and be on your best underwater behavior.

L-55 and C-58 dive, which visits World War II boats 20 minutes off Isla Mujeres' coast.

DIVE SHOPS

Most dive shops offer a variety of packages with rates depending on the time of day, location, and the number of tanks.

Corey Diving. This popular PADI dive shop also offers whale-watching, fishing, and snorkeling excursions. One-tank reef dives begin at $55, deep dives at $75, and two-tank cenote dives at $140. ⊠ *Av. Matamoros #13-A, off Juárez, Isla Mujeres* ☎ *998/877–0763* ⊕ *www. careydivecenter.com.*

Sea Hawk Divers. Sea Hawk Divers runs reef dives from $50 (for one tank) to $65 (for two tanks). Special excursions to the more-exotic shipwrecks and the MUSA underwater museum cost $75 to $95. The PADI courses taught here are highly regarded. For nondivers there are snorkel trips that depart at 9:30 and 2:30 daily. ⊠ *Av. Arq. Carlos Lazo, just before Playa Norte* ☎ *998/877–1233* ⊕ *www.sea-hawk-divers.myislamujeres.com.*

Squalo Adventures. One of the more official dive shops on the island, this PADI-certified outfit offers full scuba courses, as well as one-tank ($59) and two-tank ($69) dives to local sites including the MUSA underwater museum. ⊠ *Madero 10, off Hidalgo* ☎ *998/877–0607* ⊕ *www. squaloadventures.com.*

SIDE TRIP TO ISLA CONTOY

30 km (19 miles) north of Isla Mujeres.

The national wildlife park and bird sanctuary of Isla Contoy (Isle of Birds) is just 6 km (4 miles) long and less than 1 km (about ½ mile) wide. The whole island is a protected area, with visitor numbers carefully regulated to safeguard the flora and fauna. Isla Contoy has become a favorite among nature lovers who come to enjoy its unspoiled beauty. Sand dunes rise as high as 70 feet along the east coast, which is edged by black rocks and coral reefs. The west coast is fringed with sand, shrubs, and coconut palms.

More than 70 bird species—including gulls, pelicans, petrels, cormorants, cranes, ducks, flamingos, herons, doves, quail, spoonbills, and hawks—fly this way in late fall, some to nest and breed. Although the number of species is diminishing, partly as a result of human traffic, Isla Contoy remains a treat for bird-watchers.

The island is rich in sea life as well. Snorkelers will see brilliant coral and fish, while 5-foot-wide manta rays are visible in the shallow waters. All around the island are large numbers of shrimp, mackerel, barracuda, flying fish, and trumpet fish. In December, lobsters pass through in great (though diminishing) numbers on their southerly migration.

GETTING HERE AND AROUND

The trip to Isla Contoy takes about 45 minutes to 1½ hours, depending on the weather and the boat, and costs $40–$60. Everyone landing has to purchase a $5 authorization ticket, though this is usually included in the cost of a guided tour. The standard tour begins with a fruit breakfast on the boat and a stopover at Xlaches reef on the way to Isla Contoy for snorkeling (gear is included in the price). As you sail, your crew trolls for the lunch it will cook on the beach: anything from barracuda to snapper. (Beer and soda are also included.) While the catch is being barbecued, you have time to explore the island, snorkel, check out the small museum and biological station, or just laze under a palapa.

The island is officially open to visitors daily 9–5:30, and overnight stays aren't allowed. Other than the birds and the dozen or so park rangers who live here, the island's only residents are iguanas, lizards, turtles, hermit crabs, and boa constrictors. You can read more about Isla Contoy at ⊕ *www.islacontoy.org.*

TOUR OPERATORS

Sociedad Cooperativa Isla Mujeres. Sociedad Cooperativa Isla Mujeres offers daily boat trips from Isla Mujeres to Isla Contoy Pier at Rueda Medina for 6 to 12 people. ⊠ *Contoy Pier, Av. Rueda Medina* ☎ *998/ 877–0800.*

4

THE CARIBBEAN COAST

WELCOME TO THE CARIBBEAN COAST

TOP REASONS TO GO

★ **Visiting Mayan ruins with a Caribbean view:** The ruins at Tulum, only an hour south of Playa del Carmen, are a dramatic remnant of a sophisticated pre-Columbian people with an eye for real estate—the site overlooks the Caribbean, in one of Mexico's classic postcard views.

★ **Casting for bonefish:** These elusive shallows-dwellers, off the Chinchorro Reef near the Reserva de la Biosfera Sian Ka'an, can match wits with even the most seasoned fly-fisher.

★ **Relaxing at a spa:** The Riviera Maya is flush with luxurious spa resorts to indulge your every whim, and then some.

★ **Snorkeling with parrotfish and spotted eagle rays:** The turquoise waters of the Puerto Morelos Maritime National Park, just off the Yucatán's east coast, are teeming with protected marine life.

★ **Exploring the inland jungle:** South of Rio Bec, you might glimpse howler monkeys, coatimundis, and Yucatán parrots in the thick, unspoiled forest.

1 The Riviera Maya. The coastal communities along the Caribbean run the gamut from sleepy fishing villages and glitzy resort enclaves to the eco-friendly town of Tulum, a historic Mayan trading center reinvented as a hippie-chic beach hangout. The pyramids at Cobá are surrounded by jungle, where birds and monkeys call overhead. Stunning, sweeping, white-sand beaches draw scuba divers, snorkelers, anglers, bird-watchers, and beachcombers.

2 Reserva de la Biosfera Sian Ka'an. This 25-year-old nature reserve protects thousands of wildlife species, including monkeys, coatimundis, and jaguars. Coastal mangrove forests dotted with *cenotes* (sinkholes) give way to dense inland vegetation in 1.3 million acres of wilderness.

3 The Costa Maya. Once a no-man's-land stretching south of Felipe Carrillo Puerto to Chetumal, the Costa Maya is now being circled by a pack of hungry developers. Although droves of cruise passengers descend on the newly built port of Puerto Costa Maya, it's still possible to enjoy a sleepy, sunbaked, economical Mexican vacation here, off the beaten path.

184

Caobas

Rio Bec

CAMPECHE

Kohunlich

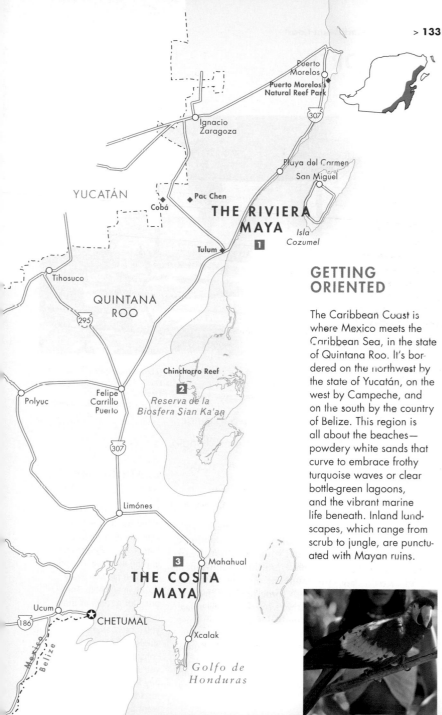

Puerto
Morelos
Puerto Morelos's
Natural Reef Park

307

Ignacio
Zaragoza

Playa del Carmen
San Miguel

YUCATÁN

Pac Chen

Cobá

**THE RIVIERA
MAYA**

1

Isla
Cozumel

Tulum

4

Tihosuco

**QUINTANA
ROO**

295

Chinchorro Reef

2

*Reserva de la
Biosfera Sian Ka'an*

Felipe
Carrillo
Puerto

Polyuc

307

Limónes

3   Mahahual

**THE COSTA
MAYA**

Ucum

186

CHETUMAL

Xcalak

*Golfo de
Honduras*

GETTING ORIENTED

The Caribbean Coast is where Mexico meets the Caribbean Sea, in the state of Quintana Roo. It's bordered on the northwest by the state of Yucatán, on the west by Campeche, and on the south by the country of Belize. This region is all about the beaches—powdery white sands that curve to embrace frothy turquoise waves or clear bottle-green lagoons, and the vibrant marine life beneath. Inland landscapes, which range from scrub to jungle, are punctuated with Mayan ruins.

TOP RESORTS

Champagne greetings, private butlers, beach-front massages—and that's just to say hello. The Riviera Maya's luxury resorts strive to outdo one another with over-the-top amenities, ranging from tequila tastings to in-room chefs to personal Range Rovers.

(Above) The Viceroy Riviera Maya. (Opposite top) Banyan Tree Hotels & Resorts. (Opposite bottom) Rosewood Mayakoba.

The lion's share of Riviera Maya hotel rooms are in vast, all-inclusive beachfront resorts. (All-inclusive sometimes really includes all your costs—but sometimes not. Read the fine print.) They usually have multiple restaurants, swimming pools, and entertainment options, and are popular with families—although some top-end properties don't allow children. Whether you choose to relax poolside or on the beach in a sun bed with built-in mist sprayers, chances are you'll spend a good part of your trip admiring the ocean view. In fact, it's rare to find a resort that is not perched on the white sands of the Caribbean. Nearly all resorts (and many public beaches) along the Riviera Maya are accessible only through security gates off Carretera 307.

DEATH OF THE ALL-INCLUSIVE?

A crop of new resorts along the Riviera Maya takes pampering to a higher level. By eliminating the all-inclusive option, they can provide every luxury imaginable. The price for a room at these resorts is exorbitant and you'll be charged for every single indulgence you consume. But in the end, you'll get exactly what you pay for, rather than paying for something you don't want or won't use.

BANYAN TREE

Named for the Banyan tree that centers the property, the focus of this Asian-style resort is the award-winning spa. The service here is unparalleled, and the location is downright surreal. Designed to blend with their natural surroundings, some villas are built on stilts over the mangroves, while others rest on the white sandy beaches of the Caribbean. For the ultimate in relaxation, every villa has a private pool, sundeck, and pavilion.

4

ROSEWOOD MAYAKOBA

Pushing the boundaries of luxury, this exquisite resort spills across 20 acres of crystal clear lagoons. Nestled under a canopy of mangroves, rooms are spacious (some 3,200 square feet) and include outdoor showers, plunge pools, garden baths, rooftop sundecks, and private docks from which guests are transported throughout the property by boat. Reminiscent of Venice, roads are replaced by water canals that wind from the limestone lobby to the pristine beaches. The 17,000-square-foot spa is on its own private island.

THE VICEROY RIVIERA MAYA

Tucked in the forest of Riviera Maya, this luxury refuge embraces nature with 41 sumptuous villas surrounded by waterfalls and jungle at the edge of the sea. On arrival, guests are greeted with a coconut-lemongrass cocktail and then escorted to their suites by private butlers. Bougainvillea petals create a natural path from your private plunge pool into the *palapa* (thatch-roof) villa with its garden terrace and outdoor shower. Unlike many properties in the area, the Viceroy introduces guests to the environment and traditions of Mexico with tequila tastings, diving courses, and Mayan rituals.

ZOËTRY PARAÍSO DE LA BONITA

This small, all-suites, all-inclusive resort really does include everything in the price, which is a welcome change from the big resorts that promise everything and often come up short. With an attentive staff and well-designed, attractive rooms, it's the kind of luxurious retreat where you really can settle in and enjoy yourself. It's among the closest Riviera Maya resorts to Cancún's airport.

Updated
by Marlise
Kast-Myers

Mexico's Caribbean coastline can be divided into two sections: developed coast and wild coast. The northern stretch from Punta Tanchacté to Punta Allen—the Riviera Maya— has the most sights and accommodations, and includes some of the Yucatán's most beautiful ruins and cenotes. The southern stretch, between Punta Allen and Chetumal, is where civilization thins out. Here in the "Costa Maya" you'll find the most alluring landscapes, including the pristine jungle wilderness of the Reserva de la Biosfera Sian Ka'an.

Wildlife has been affected by the development of coastal resorts. Thanks to the federal government's foresight, however, 1.6 million acres of coastline and jungle have been set aside for protection as the Reserva de la Biosfera Sian Ka'an. Whatever may happen elsewhere along the coast, this preserve is a haven for the wildlife and the travelers who seek the Yucatán of old.

PLANNING

WHEN TO GO

Peak Season: November–April. The coastal weather is heavenly, with temperatures of 80°F and near-constant ocean breezes. Rates reflect increased demand from sun-starved northerners, especially in Playa del Carmen. During Christmas week, hoteliers tack on as much as $200 a night—so if you're planning a Christmas vacation, you'd do well to book six months in advance.

Off Season: June, September, and October. September and October bring the worst weather, with frequent rain, mosquitoes, and the risk of hurricanes. There's also often rain in June. Breezes disappear, and humidity soars, especially inland. But if you're looking for a spa getaway and don't mind the weather outside, hotel rates can drop on the Caribbean Coast by as much as 50% in the low season.

Sweet Spot: May, July, and August. Low-season prices and sunny skies make late spring and midsummer a great time to save on airfares and hotels, while having beaches to yourself.

TIMING

Five days will give you enough time to enjoy the beach and explore many of the best parts of the Caribbean Coast. If you use Playa del Carmen as a base, you can easily take day trips to the Xcaret theme park or Tulum's beachfront Mayan ruins. Don't miss swimming at Xel-Há or one of the numerous cenotes along Carretera 307. The beaches at Paamul and Xpu-Há are also within driving distance, as is the Mayan village of Pac Chen, the ruins at Cobá, and the Reserva de la Biosfera Sian Ka'an.

GETTING HERE AND AROUND

CAR TRAVEL

The entire coast from Cancún to Chetumal is connected by one highway, the Carretera 307. Between Cancún and Tulum it's four divided lanes, and after Tulum it's two, but it's in excellent condition the whole way. (A section of the highway sometimes is not referred to as the 307 but by the towns it connects: Carretera Playa del Carmen-Tulum, Carretera Tulum-Chetumal.) Because this is the only road connecting cities, towns, parks, and jungle attractions, expect to spend a lot of time on it to see the region. Addresses along the highway but outside of towns are usually referred to by kilometer mark on small white upright signs at the side of the road.

If you want to explore beyond your accommodations, you'll need a rental car. Be aware that some roads off the highway are bumpy or potholed, and the road between Mahahual and Xcalak in the extreme south can be challenging after heavy rain.

Driving: The most dangerous place on the Caribbean Coast may be the road. Carretera 307 is in excellent shape, but secondary roads can develop a serious case of the potholes. Combine that with poor lighting, unexpected speed bumps, and the occasional big crab skittering across the tarmac, and you've got ample reason to drive slowly and carefully. Speed bumps, called topes, deserve special mention: they range from well-built and marked tarred hills to a simple but effective thick rope lain across the tarmac. When they're marked, you'll see a yellow or white sign showing bumps or reading TOPE. Often, however, they're not, so use caution and watch the road.

Obey speed limits: Police radar and sudden decreases in speed limits are easy traps for travelers. Should you get pulled over, hand over your license and expect to get it back the next day, when you pay your ticket at the police station. Most police officers are honest, but some will pull you over just to see if you'll pay them to avoid the hassle—don't fall for it. In many cases you'll get off with a warning when you make it clear you're prepared for the paperwork. A new program to combat police corruption by providing car renters with a two-strikes-free Tourist Travel Card is still in experimental stages, but when fully implemented, it will be a free pass for your first two minor traffic offenses.

Ask at your rental counter. ⇨ *Check out our Travel Smart chapter for rules of the road if you plan on driving.*

Precautions: Before your trip, purchase travel insurance, monitor the weather, and notify your embassy and credit card company of your whereabouts. Make a copy of your passport and leave your travel itinerary with a friend or family member. To avoid unwanted situations, steer clear of remote locations, travel with a partner, and refrain from driving long distances at night.

HOTELS

There's lodging for every taste and budget here, from giant all-inclusive luxury resorts to small family-run cabanas on the beach. Most resorts are in remote areas. If your resort doesn't provide good shuttle service, you'll want to rent a car to visit local sights or restaurants. Staying at beach areas in Playa del Carmen, Akumal, or Tulum will allow you to explore on foot from your hotel. Smaller hotels and inns are often family-run. Stay in one of them and mix with the locals.

RESTAURANTS

Restaurants here vary from quirky beachside affairs with outdoor tables and palapas to more-elaborate and sophisticated establishments. Dress is casual at most places, so leave your tie and jacket at home. Smaller cafés and fish eateries may not accept credit cards or traveler's checks, especially in remote beach villages. Bigger establishments and those in hotels normally accept plastic. Many restaurants add *propinas* (tips) to the bill; look for a charge for *servicio*. If tips aren't included, a 15% gratuity is standard. It's best to order fresh local fish—grouper, dorado, red snapper, and sea bass—rather than shellfish like shrimp, lobster, and oysters, since the latter are often flown in frozen from the Gulf. Playa del Carmen has the largest selection of restaurants.

DINING AND LODGING PRICES

Prices in the restaurant reviews are the average cost of a main course at dinner or, if dinner is not served, at lunch; taxes and service charges are generally included. Prices in the hotel reviews are the lowest cost of a standard double room in high season, excluding taxes, service charges, and meal plans (except at all-inclusives). Prices for rentals are the lowest per-night cost for a one-bedroom unit in high season.

SAFETY AND HEALTH

With its massive resorts and tourist-oriented beach towns, the Caribbean Coast is free of most big-city dangers. Though increasingly urban, Playa del Carmen is generally safe in tourist areas, and extensive police patrols keep it that way. Between 2011 and 2013, Playa del Carmen experienced a slight rise in crime outside the major resort areas, most of it associated with criminal groups. Regardless of this increase in reported crime, Playa del Carmen is still more secure than most North American cities and remains among the safest areas in Mexico for tourists. Resorts all have 24-hour security guards, and most have in-room safes. Thanks to advances in water purification, food safety has made great strides in the last decade, but Mexicans drink bottled water and you should, too. However, there's no need to worry about ice—it's made from purified water virtually everywhere. Look for the barrel-shaped industrial cubes, just to be sure.

ESSENTIALS

BANKS AND CURRENCY EXCHANGE

Foreigners may not exchange more than $1,500 U.S.D. (cash) per person, per month into Mexican pesos. Mexican travelers are also limited to $1,500 U.S.D. cash per person, per month, with the added restriction of no more than $300 U.S.D. cash per day. Most banks along Carretera 307 have ATMs where you can withdraw local currency, or you can pay for services with a debit or credit card without restrictions. There's no limit to the number of purchases or the amount of each individual transaction. We recommend having Mexican pesos on hand, especially if you intend to use public transportation, leave tips, or pay cash during your trip.

TOURS

Contacts **Alltournative.** Alltournative offers eco-friendly adventures for travelers of all ages and fitness levels. ⊠ *Carretera 307, Km 287, near Playacar, Playa del Carmen* ☎ *984/803–9999, 877/437–4990 from U.S.* ⊕ *www.alltournative. com.* **Hilario Hiler.** Hilario Hiler, who is fluent in Spanish, Mayan, and English, customizes tours of Mayan villages, ruins, and the jungle. ⊠ *La Jolla, Casa Nai Na, 3rd fl., Akumal* ☎ *984/875–9066* ✍ *hilariohiler@gmail.com.* **Maya Sites Travel Services.** Maya Sites Travel Services uses archaeologists and other experts to lead inexpensive tours of Maya archaeological sites. ☎ *505/255–2279, 811/620–8715 in U.S.* ⊕ *www.mayasites.com.*

VISITOR INFORMATION

For additional information on the Caribbean Coast, you'll find information on several useful websites.

For updated information on Playa del Carmen and the Riviera Maya, *Playa Maya News* (⊕ *playamayanews.com*) has details on leading restaurants, nightlife, and real estate. They also provide resources on trip planning, private tours, and sailing charters. Meaning "white road" in Maya, Sac-Be.com provides current information on everything from local beaches to environmental issues in Riviera Maya and Costa Maya. This resourceful website Yucatan Today provides travel information about Merida, Valladolid, Campeche and Yucatan State. The monthly magazine also features maps and articles about the region.

Contacts **Playa Maya News** ⊕ *www.playamayanews.com.* **Sac-Be** ⊕ *www. sac-be.com.* **Yucatan Today** ⊠ *Calle 39 #483, Mérida, Yucatán* ☎ *999/927–8531* ⊕ *www.yucatantoday.com.*

THE RIVIERA MAYA

This region is full of treasures, from spectacular white-sand beaches and offshore reefs to some of the peninsula's most beautiful Mayan ruins. Unsurprisingly, it's also a region full of tourists, who come from around the world to bask in the sun and soak up the unique Mayan-Mexican-international culture. The Riviera Maya, from Punta Tanchacté in the north down to Punta Allen in the south, has more than 23,000 hotel

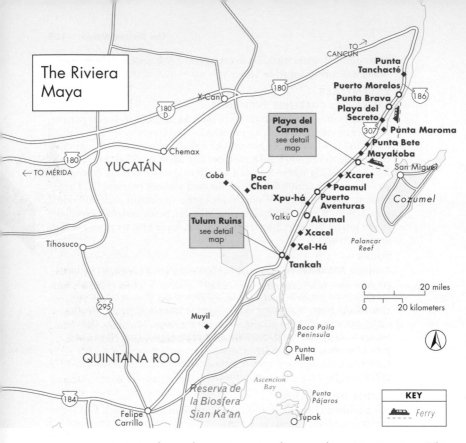

The Riviera Maya

rooms and countless restaurants, shops, and tourist attractions. This frenzy of building has forced many beachside Mayan communities to relocate to the inland jungle, from which residents commute to work in the hotels.

Discovering the Riviera Maya is easy. One road, the Carretera 307, will take you everywhere you want to go. The well-paved conduit is an easy way to cover long distances between sights, but on your journey there's little to see beyond road signs, gas stations, and the monumental resort entrances marking access roads. Although exploring the Riviera Maya is about the soft sway of palms along sparkling sands, it's also about the highway miles you'll cover to get there.

It's worth noting that while all beaches in Mexico are open to the public, access is not guaranteed. This means that when a resort snatches a prime beachfront site, it can effectively block access to nonguests. This is not uncommon in the Riviera Maya.

PUNTA TANCHACTÉ (BAHÍA PETEMPICH)

23 km (14 miles) South of Cancún.

The Riviera Maya region technically starts at Punta Tanchacté (pronounced tan-chak-*te*), also known as Bahía Petempich, with small hotels on long stretches of beach caressed by turquoise waters. Historically a fishing village, this area has recently been overtaken by Puerto Morelos's growth, and now there are new hotels and resorts here as well. Just 20 minutes south of Cancún, Punta Tanchacté is quieter than neighboring towns but still close to the action.

GETTING HERE AND AROUND

Driving south on Carretera 307, turn left at Km 27.5. Heading north on Carretera 307, turn right at Km 328. Driving south on Carretera 307, turn left at Km 27.5. The entrance is marked by a large gate reading "Bahía Petempich." This community of resorts does not offer any facilities other than those that are available within the hotels. The nearest shops, restaurants, banks, and clinics are in Cancún and Puerto Morelos.

WHERE TO STAY

For expanded reviews, facilities, and current deals, visit Fodors.com.

$$$$
RESORT
ALL-INCLUSIVE
FAMILY

Azul Beach Hotel. On a beautiful beach, this all-inclusive hotel has ocean views, lush grounds, and *palapa*-covered walkways. **Pros:** intimate setting; excellent service; good food. **Cons:** Wi-Fi costs extra; lots of seaweed on the beach; limited number of beach cabanas; proximity to neighboring mangroves can produce an unpleasant sulfur odor and attract mosquitoes. $ *Rooms from: $434* ⊠ *Carretera 307, Km 27.5* ☎ *998/872–8080* ⊕ *www.karismahotels.com* ↝ *145 rooms, 2 villas* ⦿ *All-inclusive.*

$$$$
HOTEL
ALL-INCLUSIVE
Fodor's Choice
★

Zoëtry Paraíso de la Bonita. A pair of stone dragons guards the entrance to this eclectic, all-inclusive resort, and spacious two-room suites—all with sweeping sea and jungle views—take their inspiration from a grand notion of Italy, with cast-stone columns and sunken marble baths big enough for a party. **Pros:** attentive staff; tasteful room design; every room has ocean view. **Cons:** no evening entertainment; mediocre lunch; no kids' club. $ *Rooms from: $688* ⊠ *Carretera 307, Km 328* ✛ *Turn on highway at signs for Secrets Silversands; follow road about 2 miles for gate to Paraíso de la Bonita* ☎ *998/872–8314* ⊕ *www.zoetryparaisodelabonita.com* ↝ *90 suites* ⦿ *All-inclusive.*

SPAS

Thalasso Center & Spa. The 22,000-square-foot spa at the Zoetry Paraíso de la Bonita resort is the only certified thalassotherapy spa in the Riviera Maya, meaning many of its treatments use seawater to wash your cares away. The extensive menu features body wraps, holistic treatments, saltwater hydrotherapy, and proto-Mayan *temezcal* rituals. Although most treatments involve getting wet, you'll also find healing dry remedies like wraps, facials, massages, and acupuncture. Spa products infused with sea kelp and marine mud are said to eliminate toxins. Acupuncture, tai-chi, yoga, and Mayan healing practices are available upon request. ⊠ *Zoetry Paraíso de la Bonita Resort, Carretera Cancún-Chetumal, Km 328* ☎ *984/872–8300* ⊕ *www.zoetryresorts.com/paraiso/spa.html.*

PUERTO MORELOS

8 km (5 miles) south of Punta Tanchacté, 32 km (20 miles) north of Playa del Carmen.

At the edge of a mangrove-tangled jungle pushing up to the shore, Puerto Morelos is one of the few coastal towns on the Riviera Maya that's maintained a measure of authenticity. Although it's become a favorite of Canadian and American expat artists, painters, and poets, it's still essentially a salty Mexican seaside village. Nothing here has been prettied up for the gringos, and tourist traps are few and far between. With a wide selection of restaurants, a variety of nearby hotels and a good road connecting the town with the highway, it's a great base for exploring the region.

Environmental laws and building restrictions have so far kept growth under tight control. This has prevented Puerto Morelos from becoming the next Cancún or Playa del Carmen—which many locals consider a blessing. Although these are not the turquoise waters of Cancún, they are calm and safe. However, if a spectacular beach is a key part of your vacation plans, consider staying at a resort north or south of town.

Where Puerto Morelos shines is out at sea: the superb coral reef only 1,800 feet offshore is an excellent place to explore with a snorkel or scuba tank. This thriving reef and the surrounding mangrove forests are a protected national park, so you'll need to visit with a licensed guide. Home to 36 species of birds, the park is a draw for bird-watchers. (The mangroves are also a haven for mosquitoes—bring repellent, especially after dusk.) ■TIP➔ Architecture fans shouldn't miss the bizarre cartoon castle at the corner of Niños Heroes and Morelos, a carved, curvy, leaning tree-house fantasy that has to be seen to be believed.

GETTING HERE AND AROUND

Puerto Morelos is 36 km (22 miles) south of Cancún. It's the first major town on Carretera 307. When the center of the road rises up to an overpass, stay right and turn left underneath, then just follow the road 2 km (1 mile) east. This will take you directly to the town square and lighthouse. You can also reach Puerto Morelos by turning at the paved road at Croco-Cun Zoo off Carretera 307 at Km 31. This paved road dead-ends at the entrance to Excellence Resort, where you will turn right and follow the road to the center of town. You can explore this downtown area by foot, but those staying on the outskirts of Puerto Morelos will find a rental car convenient.

Downtown is essentially the sprawling town square, bordered by Avenida Rafael Melgar at the beach, Avenida Rojo Gomez parallel, and Avenidas Tulum and Morelos to the south and north respectively. The square verges on the water, where you'll find a visitor information booth next to Pelicanos restaurant on the right. Steps to the left take you down to the beach. The taxi stand is at the northeast corner of the square at Morelos and Rojo Gomez. Avenida Niños Heroes, where you'll find John Gray's Kitchen and the way out of town to La Ceiba del Mar Resort, is the next street inland, parallel to Avenida Rojo Gomez.

Taxi Contacts Taxi Service ☎ *998/871–0090.*

EXPLORING

FAMILY **Croco-Cun Zoo.** The biologists running the Croco-Cun Zoo, an animal farm just north of Puerto Morelos, have collected specimens of many of the reptiles and some of the mammals indigenous to the area. They offer immensely informative tours—you may even get to handle a baby crocodile or feed a monkey. Be sure to wave hello to the 500-pound crocodile secure in his deep pit. ⊠ *Carretera 307, Km 31* ☎ *998/850–3719* ⊕ *www. crococunzoo.com* ⊠ *$26* ☉ *Daily 9–5.*

Yaax Che Jardín Botánico del Dr. Alfredo Barrera Marín (*Dr. Alfredo Barrera Marín Botanical Garden*). South of Puerto Morelos, the 150-acre Yaax Che Jardín Botánico del Dr. Alfredo Barrera Marín is the largest botanical garden in Mexico. Named for a local botanist, the garden exhibits the peninsula's plants and flowers, which are labeled in English, Spanish, and Latin. The park features a 130-foot suspension bridge, three observation towers, and a library equipped with reading hammocks. There's also a tree nursery, a remarkable orchid and epiphyte garden, an authentic Mayan house, and an archaeological site. A nature walk goes directly through the mangroves for some great birding. More than 220 species have been identified here (be sure to bring the bug spray, though). Spider monkeys can usually be spotted in the afternoons, and a tree-house lookout offers a spectacular view—but the climb isn't for those afraid of heights. The park is open daily from 8 am; last entry is at 4. It's closed Sunday May through November. ⊠ *Carretera 307, 1 km south of Puerto Morelos* ⊕ *Entrance is from northbound side of highway. From southbound side, turn around after town* ☎ *998/206–9233* ⊠ *$10* ☉ *Mon.–Sat. 8–4.*

BEACHES

When you arrive in Puerto Morelos, don't be disappointed by the rocky beaches, blankets of seaweed, and boats that dock ashore; this place's claim to fame is the remarkable snorkeling just offshore, on a 100-foot-wide reef where underwater caves are filled with abundant sea life. There are plenty of beaches in Puerto Morelos; the best one is two blocks north of the square. They're rarely crowded, except on Sunday, when Cancún locals visit the area for a weekend escape.

Puerto Morelos Main Beach. For a day of sand and sea, head to the narrow stretch of beach two blocks north of the square in front of Ojo de Agua Hotel. A snack at their restaurant will give you access to beach amenities. Walk just north of the hotel for better snorkeling. Park on the town square or the streets just adjacent. **Amenities:** food and drink. **Best for:** snorkeling. ⊠ *North of town square.*

WHERE TO EAT

$$
SOUTH
AMERICAN

✕ **Al Chimichurri.** The smoky aromas of a South American *parillada* waft down the street from this Uruguayan barbecue joint every night. Heaping portions of short ribs, flank steak, and *chorizo*, start you off; crepes with "flaming apple" or *dulce de leche* finish nicely. Tables are set off the street, in a pleasant walled courtyard. $ *Average main: $8* ✉ *Av. Javier Rojo Gomez between Tulum and Isla Mujeres, across from Posada Amor* ☎ *998/192–1129 cell, 998/252–4666* ⊕ *www.alchimichurri.com* ⊟ *No credit cards* ☾ *No lunch. Closed Mon. and all of Sept.*

> ## A SACRED JOURNEY
>
> In ancient times Puerto Morelos was a point of departure for pregnant Maya women making pilgrimages by canoe to Cozumel, the sacred isle of the fertility goddess, Ixchel. Remnants of Mayan ruins survive along the coast here, although none of them have been restored.

$$
MEXICAN

✕ **El Pirata.** A popular spot for breakfast, lunch, dinner, or just a drink from the bar, this restaurant is just off Puerto Morelos's town square. If you have a hankering for American food, you can get a good hamburger with fries here. Daily specials include *pozole*, a broth made from cracked corn, chicken, chiles, and bay leaves and served with tostada shells—but there are always tasty tacos and fresh seafood on order. $ *Average main: $10* ✉ *Calle Javier Rojo Gomez, 200 meters north of town square* ☎ *998/251–7948* ⊟ *No credit cards.*

$$$
INTERNATIONAL
Fodor'sChoice
★

✕ **John Gray's Kitchen.** This restaurant—from a former Ritz-Carlton chef—right next to the jungle draws a regular crowd of Cancún and Playa locals. Using only the freshest ingredients—from local fruits and vegetables to seafood right off the pier—Gray works his magic in a comfortable and contemporary setting that feels more Manhattan than Mayan. Don't miss the delicious tender roasted duck breast with tequila, chipotle, and honey. Another great option is coronado, a local white fish grilled to perfection and served with pesto and cilantro. The menu changes weekly so repeat guests are always in for a treat. $ *Average main: $18* ✉ *Av. Niños Heroes, 1 block north of Av. Morelos, on jungle side* ☎ *998/871–0665* ⊕ *www.johngraysrestaurants.com* ☾ *Closed Sun. No lunch.*

$
MEXICAN

✕ **La Playita.** Two blocks north of the town square, this "restaurant" is actually made up of plastic tables and chairs shaded by mismatched tarps and umbrellas. What it lacks in charm is more than made up for by the food and prices. This is where locals go for seafood soup, fried fish, shrimp tacos, ceviche, and fresh guacamole. Entrées come with a side of rice and shredded lettuce, but plan to either practice your Spanish or use sign language since this family-run business focuses more on quality cooking than it does on customer service. This is the perfect place to sink your toes in the sand and enjoy a refreshing rice-milk *horchata*. Just watch out for the mosquitoes at dusk, and eat early because the restaurant closes by 8. $ *Average main: $8* ✉ *Av. Rafael Melgar, Sm 02, Mza 03, Lote 02* ⊟ *No credit cards.*

$
BAKERY

✕ **Le Café D'Amancia.** This colorful local hangout on the corner of the main plaza is the best place in town to grab a seat and a cup of coffee and a pastry to munch as you watch the world go by. The fruit smoothies are delicious, as is the homemade apple pie. Most menu items are organic, and there is free Wi-Fi if you happen to travel with a computer or smart phone. $ *Average main: $4* ✉ *Av. Tulum at Rojo Gomez* ☎ 998/206–9242 ═ *No credit cards.*

$$ ✕ **Pangea.** Abutting the plaza at the beach, Pangea has it all: breakfast,
ECLECTIC lunch, and dinner served on an umbrella-shaded terrace overlooking the sea, and live music and eclectic entertainment until late. Daily menus— all prepared with organic ingredients and without preservatives—may include grilled fresh tuna, vegetarian lasagna, or shrimp kebabs, and there's fresh ginger-lemongrass tea and pancakes for breakfast. Evening menus are themed according to the show, thus, Middle Eastern food for belly dancing night and Spanish tapas for flamenco. The owners came from Mexico City in the early 1990s and are a great source for tips and local gossip. $ *Average main: $12* ✉ *Av. Morelos at water* ☎ 998/159–5241 *cell.*

$$$ ✕ **Pelicanos.** Enjoy the fresh, well-prepared seafood on the shaded patio
SEAFOOD at this family-owned restaurant in the heart of town. Try the fresh fish prepared *al ajo* (in a garlicky butter sauce). The fried shrimp, served in a coconut shell, melds sweet and salty, while the massive margaritas pack a powerful punch. On a small dock, the restaurant offers a variety of four-hour day trips that include fishing, snorkeling, and cooking the daily catch at the restaurant. $ *Average main: $18* ✉ *Av. Rafael Melgar at Av. Tulum, on main square at beach* ☎ 998/871–0014.

$ ✕ **Posada Amor.** This restaurant, the oldest in Puerto Morelos, has
MEXICAN retained a loyal clientele for nearly four decades. In the dining room with its picnic-style wooden tables and benches, the gracious staff serves up terrific Mexican and seafood dishes, including a memorable whole fish dinner and a rich seafood bisque. The Sunday buffet is also delicious. Salsa lessons are offered Friday nights at 9. $ *Average main: $6* ✉ *Avs. Javier Rojo Gómez between Isla Mujeres and Tulum* ☎ 998/871–0033.

WHERE TO STAY

For expanded reviews, facilities, and current deals, visit Fodors.com.

$$ ⊡ **Casa Caribe.** Opened in 2011, this charming hacienda-style B&B five
B&B/INN minutes from the town square and opposite the main beach has five
Fodor's Choice large rooms with king-size beds, ocean views from private terraces with
★ hammocks. **Pros:** free filtered water; great breakfasts; lovely staff. **Cons:** not all rooms have a/c; proximity to the mangroves attracts bugs; no pool; four-night minimum. $ *Rooms from: $121* ✉ *Av. Rojo Gómez, 768* ☎ 998/251–8060 *in Mexico, 512/410–8146 in U.S.* ⊕ *www. casacaribepuertomorelos.com* ⤴ *5 rooms* ⦿ *Breakfast.*

$$$$ ⊡ **Dreams Riviera Cancún.** Opened in 2010, this sprawling resort offers
RESORT a wide range of activities, nice rooms with both mangrove and ocean
ALL-INCLUSIVE views, and a good albeit expensive spa. **Pros:** family-friendly; children
FAMILY under 12 years stay free; hydrotherapy circuit at the spa garden. **Cons:** Internet costs extra; only 40% of rooms have ocean view; hallway noise can be heard in rooms. $ *Rooms from: $450* ✉ *Calle 55, Sm 11, Mza 4, Puerto Morelos* ☎ 998/872–9200 ⊕ *www.dreamsresorts.com* ⤴ *486 rooms* ⦿ *All-inclusive.*

$$$$ RESORT ALL-INCLUSIVE **Excellence Riviera Cancún.** Just 15 minutes from Cancún Airport, this large, luxurious, adults-only resort is centered on a wonderfully indulgent spa and six meandering pools. **Pros:** caters to honeymooners; plenty of pool lounging space; rooms have private hot tubs for two. **Cons:** cold pools; thin walls; mediocre food; no children under 18. [$] *Rooms from: $454* ✉ *Carretera 307, Km 324, north of Puerto Morelos* ☎ *998/872–8500* 🌐 *www.excellence-resorts.com* 🛏 *440 rooms* 🍴 *All-inclusive.*

$ RENTAL **Hotelito y Studios Marviya.** The breezy king studios at this small hotel near the beach have large tile baths and terraces with hammocks and views of the ocean or mangroves, but not all have microwaves, TVs, or a/c. **Pros:** multilingual staff; pool. **Cons:** three blocks to town center; must book for a week or more; no bathroom amenities. [$] *Rooms from: $120* ✉ *Avs. Javier Rojo Gómez and Ejercito Mexicano* ☎ *998/871–0049* 🌐 *www.marviya.com* 🛏 *10 studios* 🍴 *No meals.*

SHOPPING

BOOKS

Alma Libre Bookstore. Alma Libre Bookstore has more than 20,000 titles in stock. You can trade in your own books for 25% of their cover prices here and replenish your holiday reading list. It's open daily from November through May, from 10:30 to 8. Owners Robert and Joanne Birce are also great sources of information on local happenings. ✉ *Av. Tulum, 3* 🌐 *www.almalibrebooks.com.*

CRAFTS AND FOLK ART

Colectivo de Artesanos de Puerto Morelos (*Puerto Morelos Artists' Cooperative*). The Colectivo de Artesanos de Puerto Morelos is a series of palapa-style buildings where local artisans sell their jewelry, hand-embroidered clothes, hammocks, and other items. You can sometimes find real bargains. It's open daily from 8 am until dusk. ✉ *Avs. Javier Rojo Gómez and Isla Mujeres.*

Ixchel Jungle Market & Spa. This nonprofit organization generates income for Maya women and their families. The market, held every Sunday between December and April from 9:30 to 1, features traditional dances, regional foods, and handmade crafts sold by Maya women dressed in embroidered dresses. The spa offers traditional Mayan treatments such as deep-tissue massage and body wraps with aloe vera or chocolate fresh from the cacao. It's open Tuesday through Saturday by appointment only, with bookings available at 10, 12, 2, and 4. ✉ *Calle 2* ☎ *998/208–9148* 🌐 *www.mayaecho.com* 🕒 *Closed Mon.*

SPORTS AND THE OUTDOORS

ADVENTURE TOURS

FAMILY **Selvática.** Selvática, just outside the center of Puerto Morelos, offers tours over the jungle on more than 3 km (2 miles) of zip-lines. The entire tour will take you a little over two hours, so you'll be glad to have a snack afterward in the on-site cafeteria. The full trip takes four hours including the transfers and costs $99. Advance reservations are required. ✉ *Carretera 307, Km 321, 19 km (12 miles) from turnoff* ☎ *998/898–4312, 866/552–8826 toll-free from U.S.* 🌐 *www.selvatica.com.mx* 🕒 *Closed Sun.*

The Viceroy Riviera Maya

Zoëtry Paraíso de la Bonita

COOKING SCHOOLS

The Little Mexican Cooking School. Learn how to cook authentic Mexican cuisine from the trained chefs at Casa Caribe's culinary school. After participating in the hands-on making of seven to eight dishes, you can enjoy the meal you've just prepared. Cooking classes ($122) are offered Tuesday through Saturday, from 10 to 3:30, by reservation only. ⊠ *Casa Caribe, Av. Rojo Gomez 768, 3.5 blocks north of town square, Puerto Morelos* ☎ *998/251–8060, 512/410–8146 in U.S.* ⊕ *www.thelittlemexicancookingschool.com.*

FISHING

Los Pelicanos. Pelicanos, a downtown restaurant, offers four-hour tours that include fishing, snorkeling, and cooking up the catch of the day. The tour costs are from $250 for a 27-foot boat to $300 for a 31-foot boat. Drinks and snacks on the boat are included. ⊠ *Av. Rafael E. Melgar, Lote 2* ☎ *998/871–0014.*

SCUBA DIVING

Almost Heaven Adventures. Almost Heaven Adventures, the oldest dive shop in the area, is the only one owned and operated by locals. Snorkeling trips cost $55, and two-tank reef dives cost $70. Night tours are especially popular in summer, so book at least a day in advance. ⊠ *Av. Javier Rojo Gómez, Mza 2, Lote 10* ☎ *998/846–8009, 998/871–0230* ⊕ *www.almostheavenadventures.com.*

Diving Dog Tours. Diving Dog Tours runs snorkeling trips at various sites on the Great Mesoamerican Reef for $30 per person. ☎ *998/848–8819, 303/325–3986* ⊕ *www.puertomorelosfishing.com.*

PUNTA BRAVA

24 km (15 miles) north of Playa del Carmen.

Punta Brava is a long, winding sweep of sand strewn with seashells. The only direct access to this beach area is through the security gate at the El Dorado Royale resort. Past the entrance is a tropical jungle and more than a mile of coastline at Punta Brava Beach. In an effort to calm the powerful waves, the resort has built artificial sandbars along the shore. Not only are these burlap sacks an eyesore, but also they have eliminated one of the few spots in the area where bodysurfing was once possible.

GETTING HERE AND AROUND

If you're heading north from Playa del Carmen, turn right into El Dorado Royale gate at Km 45. Currency exchange is available within El Dorado Royal Resort. Otherwise, the nearest banks, medical facilities, and police stations are 8 km (5 miles) north in Puerto Morelos.

WHERE TO STAY

For expanded reviews, facilities, and current deals, visit Fodors.com.

$$$$
RESORT
ALL-INCLUSIVE

El Dorado Royale. This beachfront resort has been overshadowed by its newer neighbors, but the staff is friendly, and the location—amid 500 acres of lush jungle—is just as alluring as ever, and it was remodeled in 2012. **Pros:** on-site health bar with fruit smoothies and health foods; sprawling property; on-site ATM; green practices. **Cons:** gym crowded in the morning; slow room service; no kids under 18; rocky beach. $ *Rooms from: $450* ✉ *Carretera 307, Km 45* ☎ *998/872–8030* 🌐 *www.eldorado-resort.com* 🛏 *698 rooms* 🍴 *All-inclusive.*

PLAYA DEL SECRETO

23 km (14½ miles) north of Playa del Carmen.

The secret is out—the half-mile stretch of white sand at Playa del Secreto is one of the most beautiful coastal communities in Riviera Maya. Surrounded by jungle and Caribbean waters, the protected shores are a favorite nesting ground for giant leatherback sea turtles, weighing up to 300 pounds. From May through October, early risers can watch baby turtles struggle from their shells and skitter down to the sea. The bordering jungle is home to foxes, deer, crocodiles, wild boars, and even jaguars. Bird-watching is excellent here with species ranging from wild parrots and hawks to kingfishers and black-necked stilts.

4

Playa del Secreto is midway between Cancún and Playa del Carmen, meaning that nightclubs, shopping, and restaurants are less than 20 minutes away.

GETTING HERE AND AROUND

From Cancún, take Carretera 307 south. Approximately 10 km (6 miles) past Puerto Morelos, turn left at Km 312 on to the Playa del Secreto road that leads to the beach. For those staying at the Valentin resort, there's a designated entrance off Carretera 307 at Km 311. Because only private villas and a resort make up this beach community, there are no restaurants, shops, or services available. The nearest are north in Puerto Morelos.

BEACHES

Playa del Secreto. Free of rocks, sea grass, and drop-offs, Playa del Secreto is perfect for swimming, kayaking, or snorkeling. On windy days the waves are large enough for boogie boarding or bodysurfing. At the nearby reef, divers can get down with lobster, octopus, crabs, and turtles. The powdery white sand makes it great for long walks on the beach and gathering shells. The stretch near Valentin Imperial Maya is especially clean, with clear warm water where fish come to eat out of your hand. Dotting the shore are vacation rentals and a private community of homeowners, meaning that there is no public access to this beach other than through the private roads off Carretera 307. Despite the fact this is a public beach, nonhotel guests will be turned away at security gates. That also means that there are no public facilities other than those offered exclusively to guests. **Amenities:** none. **Best for:** snorkeling; swimming; walking. ✉ *Carretera 307, Km 311, 15 minutes south of Cancún Airport* ✥ *Beach can be accessed by hotel guests through private road off Carretera 307.*

WHERE TO STAY

For expanded reviews, facilities, and current deals, visit Fodors.com.

$$$$ RESORT ALL-INCLUSIVE 🏨 **Valentin Imperial Maya.** Nestled in the thriving mangrove forests of Playa del Secreto, this adults-only, all-inclusive resort is one of the few hotels in the region that still embraces Mexican tradition. **Pros:**

impeccable service; enormous pool; authentic Mexican coffee; pillow menu; free Internet. **Cons:** evening entertainment disappointing; no kids under 18. $ *Rooms from: $454* ✉ *Carretera 307, Km 311.5* ☎ *984/206–3660* ⊕ *www.valentinmaya.com* ⌁ *524 rooms; 16 suites* ⦿ *All-inclusive.*

PUNTA MAROMA

23 km (14 miles) north of Playa del Carmen, 48 km (29 miles) south of Cancún.

The waters of this protected bay stay calm even on blustery days, and the enchanting beach ranks among Mexico's finest. A string of resorts has taken advantage of its enviable position—Maroma Secrets, Catalonia Playa Maroma, and the Maroma Resort & Spa, as well as the Blue Diamond Resort, halfway between Punta Bete and Punta Maroma. Access resorts through the security gate marked with a Peacock mural just beyond the Burger Bar fast-food joint. Unfortunately, nonguests of the resorts will not be able to access the beach since the only entry point is through the main security gate.

GETTING HERE AND AROUND

Driving south from Cancún, take Carretera 307 to the east (left) turnoff at Km 306.5. Heading north from Playa del Carmen, turn right into the Punta Maroma gate at Km 51. Signs (and a security guard) will point you to the beach or the resort of your choice. Blue Diamond Resort is accessed by way of a private entrance at Km 298.8 off Carretera 307.

ESSENTIALS

Because Punta Maroma is a gated community rather than a developed town, the only available facilities are within the resorts themselves. The closest shops and restaurants are 10 minutes south in Playa del Carmen or 15 minutes north in Puerto Morelos. For shops, restaurants, banks, and emergency facilities, head to Playa del Carmen.

BEACHES

Punta Maroma. Punta Maroma is one of the most beautiful beaches in Mexico. The coastline is immaculate, with deep white sand that feels like powdered sugar between your toes, while the water is crystal clear and free of rocks—this a great place to bodysurf the small waves that crash onshore. Just 10 minutes off the coast of the Blue Diamond Resort, you'll find terrific diving. Hotels supply plenty of lounge chairs and umbrellas, as well as excellent beach service and activities like volleyball, yoga—even remote-control boat racing. Unfortunately, this beach can only be accessed by way of the security gate on Carretera 307 that leads to Maroma Secrets, Catalonia Playa Maroma, and Maroma Resort & Spa. Unless you plan to visit this beach by boat or stay at one of these resorts, you are probably out of luck. **Amenities:** food and drink; lounge chairs; volleyball; toilets (all for resort guests only). **Best for:** bodysurfing; diving; walking. ✉ *Carretera Federal 307, Km 306.*

WHERE TO STAY

For expanded reviews, facilities, and current deals, visit Fodors.com.

Almaplena Resort

Escencia Seaside Estate

$$$$ RESORT ALL-INCLUSIVE **Blue Diamond Riviera Maya.** Blending Mayan and Asian traditions, this all-inclusive resort is on the south end of Maroma Beach, midway between Punta Bete and Punta Maroma. **Pros:** golf carts available for exploring property; huge rooms; excellent service. **Cons:** only three restaurants; spa treatments are overpriced; no children under 18. [$] *Rooms from: $364* ✉ *Carretera Federal 307, Km 298.8* ☎ *984/206–4100* 🌐 *www.bluediamondrivieramaya.com* 🛏 *128 rooms* 🍴 *All-inclusive.*

$$$$ RESORT **Maroma Resort & Spa.** Connecting jungle and beach, a labyrinth of paths wind through the grounds at this elegant Mayan-themed hotel, where butterflies and parrots fly and the scent of flowers fills the air. **Pros:** nearly every room has an ocean view; exceptional beach; great place to escape the crowds; programs for children. **Cons:** not much entertainment; difficult to find from the highway. [$] *Rooms from: $765* ✉ *Carretera 307, Km 306* ✣ *From Carretera 307, look for peacock mural and Burger Bar restaurant just outside security entrance. There's no other sign* ☎ *998/872–8200, 866/454–9351 in U.S.* 🌐 *www.maromahotel.com* 🛏 *30 rooms, 34 suites, 1 villa* 🍴 *Multiple meal plans.*

SPAS

Kinan Spa. At the Maroma resort, the Kinan spa offers treatments based on ancient Mayan healing, including alignment of treatment rooms based on celestial energies, and a mud bar, to smear yourself dirty in the sauna or steam room. Signature treatments include the Kinan Ritual (a wrap and exfoliation), the Acai Body Treatment, and the Mayan Temazcal Ritual that combines ancient traditions, chants and meditation. ✉ *Maroma Resort, Carretera 307, Km 51* ☎ *998/872–8200* 🌐 *www.maromahotel.com.*

Spa at Blue Diamond. Exclusively for guests of the Blue Diamond resort, this 25,000 square-foot spa merges ancient Mayan philosophy with Asian healing rituals. Both the design and philosophy of the spa are inspired by the Mayan healing elements of water, air, fire and earth. Signature treatments include Four Hand Harmony (four-hands massage), Temazcal Ceremony (ritual guided by a Mayan Shaman), and the Peace Stone Ritual (a stone massage to balance energy levels). Among spa favorites are the body scrubs and wraps made with chocolate and coffee. Body treatments, ranging from one to six hours, take place in jungle palapas, Thai suites, or in garden villas. For travelers who have spent too many days basking in the sun, try the sunburn remedy wrap and hydrating facial. ✉ *Blue Diamond Riviera Maya, Carretera Federal 307, Km 298, Punta Bete* ☎ *984/206–4100* 🌐 *www.bluediamondrivieramaya.com.*

PUNTA BETE (XCALACOCO)

10 km (6 miles) north of Playa del Carmen, 55 km (34 miles) south of Cancún.

Beyond Punta Maroma, a river spills into the sea, dividing the coastline. South of the split, Playa Xcalacoco (scala-coco) is a 7-km-long (5½-mile-long) beach dotted with bungalows, small, exclusive resort hotels, and thatch-roof restaurants, backing into dense jungle. The beach is beautiful, a more natural extension of Playa del Carmen, but the shore can be rocky. All hotels here supply water shoes for swimming, and the Viceroy has a dock to enter deeper water. Punta Bete is simply a beach area with few shops, bars, or restaurants outside of the hotels, although there's an OXXO convenience store and a pizzeria on the way to Le Rêve.

GETTING HERE AND AROUND

There's no public transportation in Punta Bete, and taxis seldom pass. The best way to reach this beautiful beach area is by car. From Carretera 307, turn at the huge sign for the Princess Resort, at Km 296, to reach Petit Lafitte, Cocos Cabanas, the Viceroy, and the beach. (To reach Le Rêve, you'll have to take the road about 100 yards south, marked with a blue sign for Azul Fives condos.) Once you reach the water, you can walk along the beach to Playa del Carmen in 1 to 1½ hours.

BEACHES

If long walks on the beach are your thing, you'll love the 10-km (6-mile) stretch from Playa Xcalacoco to Playa del Carmen. Although delightfully deserted, the beach itself is not the area's best; the sand is somewhat coarse and often draped in sea grass. There's decent snorkeling, however, and the isolation is unbeatable. Plus, it's a way to explore Playa from Xcalacoco without bumping over the jungle road.

WHERE TO STAY

For expanded reviews, facilities, and current deals, visit Fodors.com.

$$ B&B/INN **Cocos Cabanas.** Tranquillity and seclusion are the name of the game in these cozy bungalows a stone's throw from the beach. **Pros:** good pizza; friendly staff; all units have a/c; gorgeous beach. **Cons:** a bit of a drive from Playa del Carmen; not on beach; Wi-Fi in common areas only. [$] *Rooms from: $95* ✉ *Carretera 307, Km 296, Playa Xcalacoco* ✣ *Take paved road at Princess Resort and follow signs. Turn left onto dirt road. Cocos Cabanas is on your right* ☎ *998/874–7056* 🌐 *www.cocoscabanas.com* 🛏 *6 rooms* 🍴 *Breakfast.*

$$$$ HOTEL **Le Rêve Hotel & Spa.** At the end of a quarter mile of a bumpy dirt road, this intimate resort makes the perfect place for a secluded, romantic getaway. **Pros:** stylish feel; all rooms have balcony or garden; free use of kayaks, iPad, and snorkel gear. **Cons:** access road full of potholes; small resort means few amenities; expensive meals; Wi-Fi in common areas only. [$] *Rooms from: $320* ✉ *Playa Xcalacoco Fraccion 2A, Carretera 307, Km 295, 49 km (31 miles) from Cancún, Playa del Carmen* ✣ *From Carretera 307, turn at Azul Fives highway sign and follow signs* ☎ *984/109–5660* 🌐 *www.hotellereve.com* 🛏 *25 rooms* 🍴 *No meals.*

$$$ RESORT FAMILY **Petit Lafitte.** This warm, family-friendly resort named after the famous pirate is made up of multiunit cabanas and newer bungalows on the beach's north end that are more private and charming. **Pros:** peaceful atmosphere; on-site library; kids love the small animal refuge; on-site dive center; fabulous staff. **Cons:** rocky beach, mosquitoes; no TVs or phones in newer bungalows. [$] *Rooms from: $240* ✉ *Carretera 307, Km 296* ✣ *From Carretera 307, turn onto paved road for Princess Resort and follow signs to Petit Lafitte* ☎ *984/877–4000* 🌐 *www.petitlafitte.com* 🛏 *30 rooms, 21 bungalows* 🍴 *Some meals.*

$$$$ RESORT Fodor's Choice ★ **The Viceroy Riviera Maya.** Formerly the Tides, Punta Bete's most luxurious jungle-beach resort is still as romantic, private, and exotic as the it ever was. **Pros:** romantic and private; great food; luxurious villas. **Cons:** bugs in jungle setting; hidden service charges; rocky beach; no children under 16; the welcome Mayan blessing is not for everyone. [$] *Rooms from: $720* ✉ *Playa Xcalacoco, Carretera 307, Km 296* ✣ *From Carretera 307, turn onto paved road for Princess Resort and follow signs to the Viceroy* ☎ *800/578–0281* 🌐 *www.viceroyrivieramaya.com* 🛏 *41 villas* 🍴 *Multiple meal plans.*

TEQUILA TASTINGS

Viceroy Riviera Maya (☎ *983-877-3000* 🌐 *www.viceroyhotelsandresorts.com*) offers tequila tastings daily at 5, 6, and 9 daily. Top-shelf brands like Don Julio and Herradura are paired with four types of ceviche. The resort's maestro *Tequilero* will reveal the secrets and history behind this local favorite, and can prepare Mezcal tastings upon request. By reservation only.

SPAS

Wayak Spa. Although not as grandiose as most spas in Riviera Maya, the Wayak Spa (meaning "the dreamer") utilizes natural surroundings to create an unparalleled pampering experience. From the shaman who greets you with a purifying waft of cobal smoke to the treatment rooms oriented toward sun, moon, and stars, this small spa makes a point of reminding you that you're in the land of the Maya. Opt for massages in jungle palapa huts surrounded by waterfalls (and mosquito curtains) or a purifying steam bath with a heavenly oculus. Client favorites include the honey and citrus scrub or the seaweed body wrap. For something unique, try the black lava treatment that infuses minerals in a three-step process including a body scrub, hydration, and a heated wrap. ✉ *Viceroy Riviera Maya Resort, Carretera 307, Km 296, Playa Xcalacoco* ✣ *From Carretera 307, turn onto paved road at Princess Resort and follow signs to the Viceroy* 🌐 *www.viceroyhotelsandresorts.com.*

MAYAKOBA

6 km (4 miles) north of Playa del Carmen, 70 km (44 miles) south of Cancún.

Mayakoba (meaning "village of water") is home to four of the world's most exclusive resorts, connected by a network of canals that inspire its tagline "the Venice of the Caribbean." The 1,600-acre enclave supports mangrove forest, freshwater lagoons, beach dunes, and sunken cenotes. It's also home to a variety of wildlife, including monkeys, turtles, crocodiles, manatees, and flamingos. Here spas are perched amid jungle treetops, and boats drift between limestone waterways. Cars are banned here, and transportation is limited to golf carts, bicycles, and thatch-roof boats.

GETTING HERE AND AROUND

The only way to reach this resort community is by car. If you're heading south from Cancún, take Carretera 307 to the east turnoff at Km 298. The entrance is marked by a large metal gate with silver lettering reading "Mayakoba." Security guards will direct you to the property of your choice. Access to hotels, restaurants, spas, and the golf course are permitted by reservation only. Those who are not staying at one of the Mayakoba resorts may not visit the spas, restaurants, and golf course only without an advance appointment or reservation. Otherwise, prepare to be turned away at the security gate.

WHERE TO EAT

$$$$ ECLECTIC 🍴 **El Puerto.** Featuring lagoon views, this restaurant is just past the main lobby at Fairmont Mayakoba and is open to the public—if you're not a guest at the hotel, arrive early to explore the grounds, on a sunset boat tour that winds through Mayakoba's waterways. Then get ready to feast, on molecular-gastronomy-engineered dishes like foie gras terrine with vanilla reduction, burnt peach, brioche bread, and sweet wine jelly. Savory veal cheeks can be served with unique sides like truffle mac-and-cheese or guajillo chile mushrooms. More traditional are desserts, including a bitter chocolate fondant with pear ice cream. All ingredients are local, organic, and sustainable, including the lobster from Sian Ka'an Biosphere. Those with specific diet restrictions should peruse the Lifestyle Cuisine Menu, specializing in macrobiotic, raw and vegan diets. [$] *Average main: $35* ✉ *Fairmont Mayakoba, Carretera Federal, Km 298* ☎ *984/206–3000* 🌐 *www.fairmont.com* ✍ *Reservations essential* 🕒 *Closed Mon.*

WHERE TO STAY

For expanded reviews, facilities, and current deals, visit Fodors.com.

$$$$ RESORT 🏨 **Banyan Tree Mayakoba.** This Thai chain has brought its own traditions to Mexico's Riviera with stunning results: in addition to vaulted ceilings, lounge areas, dining rooms, private gardens, and Talavera earthenware sinks, all rooms have outdoor bathtubs and private 376-foot swimming pools—a unique perk. **Pros:** all-villa resort; top-notch spa; excellent food; world-class service. **Cons:** no sign of Mexico; no kids' club; fee to use bicycles on property; not many activities. [$] *Rooms from: $780* ✉ *Carretera Federal, Km 298* ☎ *984/877–3688* 🌐 *www.banyantree.com* 🛏 *107 rooms* 🍽 *No meals.*

$$$$ RESORT ALL-INCLUSIVE Fodor's Choice ★ 🏨 **Fairmont Mayakoba.** Set under a mangrove canopy, this sprawling luxury resort sets new standards in the Riviera Maya for sustainability and comfort. **Pros:** all-inclusive plan available; free shuttle to neighboring properties; bird-watching tours; cooking classes and beer tastings. **Cons:** Internet costs $20 per day; some rooms lack water views; 20-minute walk from the lobby to the ocean; no Jacuzzi at pool area. [$] *Rooms from: $399* ✉ *Carretera Federal 307, Km 298* ☎ *984/206–3000* 🌐 *www.fairmont.com/mayakoba* 🛏 *367 rooms, 34 suites* 🍽 *Multiple meal plans.*

$$$$ RESORT FAMILY Fodor's Choice ★ 🏨 **Rosewood Mayakoba.** From the moment you set foot on the palapa-roofed boat that brings you to your room's private dock, the Rosewood transports you to an exotic world. **Pros:** free kids' club; complimentary bottle of tequila in rooms; extraordinary spa; check-in takes place on the boat. **Cons:** narrow beach; limited food options; seven-night minimum stay during holidays. [$] *Rooms from: $900* ✉ *Carretera Federal,*

Fairmont Mayakoba

Rosewood Mayakoba

Km 298 ☎ *984/875–8000* ⊕ *www.rosewoodmayakoba.com* ⌁ *128 suites* ⧯ *No meals.*

SPAS

Banyan Tree Spa. Built over freshwater lagoons, the Banyan Tree Spa draws on centuries-old Asian traditions. The therapists (most of whom are from Thailand) begin with a heavenly footbath, followed by your choice of Asian-flavored healing treatments, including scrubs with turmeric, lemongrass or green tea. Treatments take place in private pavilions, each with its own steam room, shower, and outdoor Jacuzzi enclosed by bamboo walls. Unique to Banyan Tree are its signature Rainmist Steam Bath and the romantic couples' Rainforest Experience, that combines hydrotherapy with infrared light to release tension and revitalize the body. ⊠ *Banyan Tree Resort, Carretera 307, Km 298* ☎ *984/877–3688* ⊕ *www.banyantree.com.*

Sense Spa. Rosewood's 17,000-square-foot spa is on its very own jungle-covered island. Wooden walkways lead to a swimming pool and limestone cenote, which is fed by subterranean springs. Many treatments, such as the temazcal ritual and the Mayakoba ancient massage, incorporate the Mayan tradition of aligning the energies of the body in rhythmic harmony. Nonguest visitors can book a treatment, then enjoy the spa facilities, including the gym, sauna, Jacuzzi, plunge pool, and the eucalyptus steam room for free. ⊠ *Rosewood Mayakoba, Carretera 307, Km 298* ☎ *984/875–8000* ⊕ *www.rosewoodhotels.com.*

Willow Stream Spa. It's easy to lose yourself (literally) within this enormous 37,000 square foot spa at the Fairmont Mayakoba. Signature treatments are the Mexican stone massage, the Mayan clay massage, the Cha Chac Rain ritual (a massage that takes place on a seven-jet Vichy table) and Honey in the Heart (a honey body mask and massage). Weary travelers will want to try the Jet Lag Recovery, an aromatherapy bath and massage that purports to reverse the negative effects of flying and time zone changes. After a gym workout, ease your muscles at the rooftop vitality pool. ⊠ *Fairmont Mayakoba, Carretera 307, Km 298* ☎ *984/206–3000* ⊕ *www.fairmont.com/mayakoba-riviera-maya/.*

PLAYA DEL CARMEN

68 km (42 miles) south of Cancún.

Welcome to the party! "Playa" is one of Latin America's fastest-growing communities, with a population of more than 135,000 and an international flavor lent by the *Estadounidenses* (United States citizens), Canadians, and Europeans who have moved here since the early 1990s. The eminently walkable downtown, full of lively bars, restaurants, beach clubs, shops, and hotels is one of the few places on the Riviera Maya where you can have a car-free vacation.

Sun and swim at trendy beach clubs by day, then drink and dance at nightclubs until the sun comes up and start all over again. In between, there's an enjoyable array of diversions along Avenida 5, a pedestrian-only cobbled street that is the town's main drag. Its southern section, from about Calle 4 to Constituyentes, is busy, noisy, and sometimes rowdy—the place to go for nightlife, tequila shots, and souvenir shopping. Its quieter, more upscale northern end, north of Constituyentes up to about Calle 38, is the place for chic cafés and stylish boutiques. Rapid development means a decline in Mexican culture, with chain stores and cheap souvenirs emerging on every corner (Starbucks junkies can easily get their fix.)

The club scene is a major draw in the South Beach of Mexico. The action is on Calle 12, lined with nightclubs and lively young things ready to set the night afire. Most clubs are open-air, so this part of town gets very noisy until very late—something to keep in mind if you're planning to stay downtown, and actually want to sleep. The north end of Avenida 5 is quieter at night. Since Fifth Avenue's pedestrian zone ends at Calle 32, you might encounter street noise from cars (rather than people) if you stay north of here. By day, Playa's lively beach clubs are packed with travelers lounging in the sun or dancing to the sounds of a live DJ.

Although building-height restrictions have helped to keep Playa from turning into the next Cancún, you'll have to leave town to get off the beaten path. Most of the area is developed, most recently by a slew of all-inclusive resorts opening up on the city's outskirts. If you plan on leaving the town center, be aware of your surroundings. A slight increase in criminal activity was reported in 2012, most of which occurred outside major resort areas.

GETTING HERE AND AROUND

Driving from Cancún airport, follow the signs on Carretera 307. Shortly before town, take the overpass up and descend at the Avenida Constituyentes exit. Turn left under the overpass and follow Constituyentes into town.

Buses traveling south from Cancún stop at Playa del Carmen's bus terminal at Avenida 20 and Calle 12, a short walk from downtown and the main drag, Avenida 5, known as "la Quinta." Buses headed to Cancún from Playa del Carmen use the main bus terminal at Avenida Juárez and Avenida 5. ADO runs express, first-class, and second-class buses to major destinations. You can hire taxis in Cancún to go as far as Playa del Carmen—price is about $55 for the one-hour drive. Shared vans from Cancún airport generally cost $80 for a six-person van, or $120 for a 10-person van; if you're traveling with a group or even find some other Playa-bound travelers at the airport, a van can be a good way to go.

The town is set up on a grid system that's easy to navigate, if you know the rules. North–south avenidas are numbered in multiples of five, with Avenida 1 along the beach, and then moving westward through Avenidas 5, 10, 15, 20, and so on. East-west calles are even numbers only, starting with Calle 2 and progressing northward through 4, 6, 8, and so on. The Playacar resort development is south of the numbered calles, starting at Avenida Juárez, but is of little interest outside of its large beachfront luxury resorts, a golf course, and the small shopping mall Plaza Playacar. To get there from Cancún, stay on the highway past the Constituyentes exit and turn left after the overpass at the Playacar sign.

■**TIP→** In Playa del Carmen, parking is prohibited at yellow curbs. If you're ticketed, your license plate will be taken to a nearby police station and returned only after the fine has been paid.

Bus Contacts ADO ☎ *984/873–0109* ⊕ *www.ado.com.mx.*

Car Rental Contacts Avis ⊠ *Plaza Playacar, Paseo Xaman-Ha Mzn 25, Local 207, Playacar* ☎ *984/873–3843* ⊕ *www.avis.com.*

ESSENTIALS

Currency Exchange Banamex ⊠ *Av. Benito Juárez, between Avs. 20 and 25* ☎ *984/873–0825* ⊠ *Av. 10 at Av. 12, Sm 30* ☎ *984/873–2947.* **Bancomer** ⊠ *Av. Juárez between Calles 25 and 30* ☎ *984/873–0356.*

Tours Tierra Maya Tours ⊠ *Av. 5 and Calle 6* ☎ *984/873–1385* ⊕ *www. tierramayatours.com.*

BEACHES

Playa del Carmen is as famous for pristine beaches as it is for thriving nightlife. Its trendy beach clubs, all of which are located in central Playa del Carmen, are the best of both. The combination of DJ music, cocktails, and twentysomethings makes these open-air bars a can't-miss for young singles. Outside of resorts, they're also the only places you'll find beach amenities.

There are beach clubs all the way from Calle 8 to Calle 46, with the hottest at Mamita's and Kool beach between Calles 26 and 30. (In between, you can also find little ad-hoc massage places for about $25/hour.) The southern beaches of Playacar up to the ferry dock at Avenida Benito Juárez are shored up against erosion with buried sandbags, but there's still a sharp drop-off from the beach level to the water—beaches north of the ferry dock are more level. Although all local beaches are technically open to the public, those in Playacar are difficult to access since they are dominated by all-inclusive resorts. You also won't find any beach clubs in Playacar. Coco Beach, where Calle 46 meets the ocean at Canibal Royal Beach Club, is popular with snorkelers drawn to the outer Chunzubul Reef. For deserted beaches, head even farther north, where the waves are small and the water is shallow.

Although Playa's beaches lack protective outer reefs, the strong wind and waves make these areas great for water sports. All of Playa's beaches are open to the public, with various access points staggered between the hotels on Avenida 5. Snorkeling here's a bust. For a real underwater adventure, organize a tour with one of the local dive companies that will take you to outer reefs and cenotes.

Mamita's Beach. This stretch of beach north of the ferry dock, from Constituyentes to Calle 38, is known to locals as Mamita's, although it also encompasses Kool beach club and the Royal and Mahekal hotels. Independent of the main beach's dropoff (and the sandbags that are sometimes visible there), it's a lovely straight stretch of flat sand and clear water, which you'll share with lots of other visitors. The tradeoff is that Wave Runners, which are largely absent from the main beach, are very present here. It's a good spot for fun in the sun with the amenities of the beach clubs. But this is not the place for seclusion and quiet.

Amenties: food and drink; toilets; water sports. **Best for:** partiers; swimming. ⊠ *Beach between Constituyentes and Calle 38, Playa del Carmen.*

Playa del Carmen Main Beach. Playa del Carmen's most central section of beach stretches from the ferry docks up to Calle 14 at Gran Porto Real, a swath of deep white sand licked by the turquoise water. The beach and water are clean, but there is some boat traffic that makes swimming less idyllic. Snorkelers aren't likely to see much in these waters. But you can't beat it for convenience: countless bars and restaurants are a short walk away on Fifth Avenue, masseurs compete (discreetly) to knead out your kinks, and it's easy to find a dive shop ready to take you out to sea. The closer you get to the ferry docks, the more people you'll find. If you're looking for seclusion, head farther north outside Playa del Carmen. **Amenities:** food and drink; water sports. **Best for:** swimming; walking. ⊠ *Calle 14 and beach.*

BEACH CLUBS

Canibal Royal. Playa's most urbane beach club is set apart from the crowd in more ways than one. It's north of town at Calle 48 and the beach, and its retro-1950s architecture and eclectic music selection make it a destination in itself. The beach area is equipped with plenty of lounge chairs, and there's a rooftop bar with a plunge pool and sundeck. Expect to pay around $15 for a chair and umbrella; fees are generally waved for those who spend a minimum of $15 on food or drinks. For a stylish lunch, try braised octopus or a tarte flambé. There's also a juice bar and full cocktail menu featuring their signature rosemary *caipiroska* (vodka with lime and sugar). **Amenities:** food and drink; toilets. **Best for:** partiers. ⊠ *Calle 48 and beach, in front of Elements Condominiums and next to Grand Coco Bay, Playa del Carmen* ☎ *984/803–4506* ⊕ *www.canibal-royal.com* 🍽 *$15 food/drink minimum* ⊙ *Daily 10–10.*

Indigo Beach. Cure your morning hangover with the breakfast buffet ($15) at this beach club located beside El Taj Condo Hotel. The restaurant serves fresh fusion cuisine that blends Italian, Asian, and Mexican dishes. Lounge chairs and beach beds are plentiful, and there are changing rooms, outdoor showers, and oversized towels for your convenience. A section of this beach is used as a launching point by small fishing boats, but the view is still lovely and there is plenty of space to lounge. As you enter the water, you'll feel about 20 feet of coral stone before the bottom transitions to smooth sand. The morning yoga and tai chi classes are a great way to start the day. **Amenities:** food and drink; showers; toilets. **Best for:** walking. ⊠ *Calle 14 at beach* ☎ *984/879–3919* ⊕ *www.indigobeach.com.mx* ⊙ *Daily 8–5:30.*

Kool Beach. Private cabanas, a fashionable restaurant, a happening bar, and a vast terrace with a view make this one of Playa's favorite beach clubs. Guests can relax in the VIP area while a DJ spins trance and techno beside the freshwater pool. With two bars, a massage palapa, supply store, and a private catamaran, this beach club caters to the pampered traveler. This premier lounge spot is next to Mamitas, where Calle 28 meets the beach; both are main venues for the occasional festivals that draw international DJs to town. **Amenities:** food and drink; toilets. **Best for:** partiers. ⊠ *Calle 28 and beach, Zona Federal Maritima*

☎ *984/803–1961* ⊕ *www.koolbeachclub.com.mx* ▨ *$7 chairs, $12 beds* ☉ *Daily 8–5.*

Mamita's Beach Club. Accessible by way of Calle 28, this is Playa's hottest spot to catch some rays. For $3 you can rent an umbrella or chair, and $20 will get you a king-size bed in the sand. A day in the sun can get pricey, though; expect to pay around $12 for a cocktail and $5 for a beer while listening to a famous DJ or conversing with young singles. Facilities include a dive shop, swimming pool, lounge bar, and dressing room. Guests can also enjoy beach volleyball or swim in the small club pool. **Amenities:** food and drink; toilets; water sports. **Best for:** partiers. ✉ *Calle 28 and beach, Playa del Carmen* ☎ *984/803–2867* ⊕ *www. mamitasbeachclub.com* ▨ *Chairs $3, umbrellas $3, bed $20, lockers $5, towels $5* ☉ *Daily 8:30–6.*

Mosquito Beach Club. An extension of the Mosquito Beach Hotel, this trendy beach club is often utilized by guests from neighboring hotels without beach access or a swimming pool. For a flat $20 fee you can lounge on a comfy beach bed, nap under a huge umbrella, or take a dip in the pool. This modern hot spot has an amazing view of the water and a restaurant that serves Mexican food until 4 (the bar is open until 7 pm). DJs spin chill-out music throughout the day, but unlike some of the other loud beach clubs, here you can still have a conversation. Towels and lockers are not offered. **Amenities:** food and drink; showers; toilets. **Best for:** swimming; walking. ✉ *Calle 8 and beach* ☎ *984/873–0001 Mosquito Beach Hotel* ⊕ *www.mosquitobeachhotel. com* ▨ *$20* ☉ *Daily 8–7.*

Zenzi. This beach club and restaurant is one of the few spots in Playa del Carmen open every day from morning (7:30) to late (2 am). Take a dip in the ocean and then catch some rays on one of the sun beds or chaise longues. When the sun goes down, there is live music, shows, and salsa lessons (Thursday) on the beach. The fish tacos and daily happy-hour specials make it difficult to ever leave. **Amenities:** food and drink; toilets. **Best for:** partiers; swimming. ✉ *Calle 10 and beach* ☎ *984/803–5738* ⊕ *www.zenzi-playa.com.*

WHERE TO EAT

$$
MODERN
MEXICAN

✕ **Aldea Corazón.** Playa's most dramatically sited restaurant sits atop a small cenote, in a vast jungly garden full of strangler vines and Mayan ruins—right in the middle of Avenida 5. Designed in accordance with Maya building practices, it's a feast for the eyes, with living "green walls" covered with plants, a bar that's built on a stone wall, and the park in back that makes for a romantic setting at night (bring bug spray). A menu full of dressed-up Playa standards—fresh fish, chicken mole, jicama tacos, guacamole—takes second place to the setting, but it's a worthwhile meal nonetheless. $ *Average main: $17* ✉ *Av. 5, between Calle 14 and Calle 16* ☎ *984/803–1942* ⊕ *www.aldeacorazon. com* ✚ *C4.*

$$
THAI

✕ **Babe's Noodles & Bar.** Photos and paintings of old Hollywood pin-up models share decor space with a large stone Buddha at this Swedish-owned Thai restaurant, known for its fresh and interesting fare cooked to order. Try the spring rolls with peanut sauce, or the Korean sesame

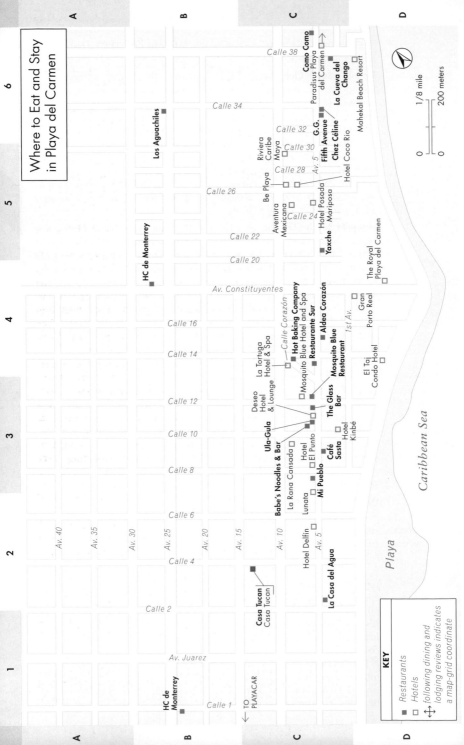

Where to Eat and Stay in Playa del Carmen

Caribbean Sea

Playa

TO PLAYACAR

Av. Juarez

Av. 40
Av. 35
Av. 30
Av. 25
Av. 20
Av. 15
Av. 10
Av. 5
1st Av.
Av. 5

Calle 1
Calle 2
Calle 4
Calle 6
Calle 8
Calle 10
Calle 12
Calle 14
Calle 16
Av. Constituyentes
Calle 20
Calle 22
Calle 24
Calle 26
Calle 28
Calle 30
Calle 32
Calle 34
Calle 38
Calle Corazón

HC de Monterrey

Los Aguachiles

HC de Monterrey

Casa Tucan
Casa Tucan

La Casa del Agua

Hotel Delfin

Lunata

Babe's Noodles & Bar

La Rana Cansada

Mi Pueblo

Hotel El Punto

Café Sasta

Ula-Gula

Deseo Hotel & Lounge

Hotel Kinbé

The Glass Bar

La Tortuga Hotel & Lounge

Hot Baking Company

Mosquito Blue Hotel and Spa

Restaurante Sur

Mosquito Blue Restaurant

Aldea Corazón

El Taj Condo Hotel

Gran Porto Real

The Royal Playa del Carmen

Yaxche

Aventura Mexicana

Be Playa

Hotel Posada Mariposa

Riviera Caribe Maya

Hotel Coco Rio

G.G.

Chez Céline

Fifth Avenue

Paradisus Playa del Carmen

La Cueva del Chango

Como Como

Mahekal Beach Resort

0   1/8 mile
0   200 meters

KEY
■ Restaurants
□ Hotels
↕↔ following dining and lodging reviews indicates a map-grid coordinate

noodles, made with chicken or pork, veggies, chile, sesame and peanut cream, and wash it all down with a refreshing lemonade, blended with ice and mint. [$] *Average main: $10* ✉ *Calle 10, between Avs. 5 and 10* ☎ *984/879–3569* 🌐 *www.babesnoodlesandbar.com* 🕒 *Closed Mon.* ✥ *C3*

$ CAFÉ 🍴 **Café Sasta.** This sweet little café serves good espresso drinks and a wide variety of teas, along with bagel sandwiches, fruit, yogurt, and pastries. Try the coconut muffin. [$] *Average main: $3* ✉ *Av. 5, between Calles 8 and 10* ☎ *984/166–0193* 💳 *No credit cards* ✥ *C3.*

$ ECLECTIC 🍴 **Casa Tucan.** The refined Italian, Swiss, and Greek dishes at this sidewalk cheapie are top-notch, with fresh ingredients and homegrown herbs. The spanakopita and vegetarian lasagna are especially good, as are the burgers and seafood options. About half the menu is vegetarian. There's additional seating on the rooftop terrace. [$] *Average main: $9* ✉ *Calle 4, between Avs. 10 and 15* ☎ *984/873–0283* 🌐 *www.casatucan.de* ✥ *C2.*

$$ FRENCH Fodor's Choice ★ 🍴 **Chez Céline.** Take one bite of Céline's chocolate croissants, and you'll think you've died and gone to Paris. Fresh-baked breads and pastries bring honor to France, especially exquisite desserts like the lemon tart and crème brûlée. Classic bistro fare like quiche lorraine or vols-au-vent make for a light lunch *comme il faut.* Streetside tables back into a small pétanque court, where you can bowl away the afternoon. The restaurant is open until 11 pm daily. [$] *Average main: $6* ✉ *Av. 5 and Calle 34* ☎ *984/308–3480* 🌐 *www.chezceline.com.mx* ✥ *C6.*

$$ MEDITERRANEAN Fodor's Choice ★ 🍴 **Como Como.** This small but intimate Mediterranean restaurant is perhaps the most popular eatery on Playa's Fifth Avenue. It's where locals and travelers in-the-know go for perfectly *al dente* homemade pasta. Top orders range from squid ink tagliatelle with clams to seared tuna with tamarind sauce. For an imaginative starter, try the white tuna carpaccio topped with apple, ginger, beet, fresh mint, and lime salad. Most dishes can be modified for vegetarians. Prepare for the triumphant moment when a chocolate fondant reaches your table, resulting in the inevitable words, "I shouldn't really, but I'm on vacation." The restaurant doesn't open until 1 pm, but it's open until 11:30 nightly. [$] *Average main: $17* ✉ *Av. 5 between Calles 38 and 40* ☎ *984/859–1646* 🌐 *www.comocomo.mx* 🕒 *No lunch Mon.* ✥ *C6*

$$$ ITALIAN 🍴 **G.G.** The giant photos of a nightclubbing Sophia Loren on the wall capture the essence of this Italianissimo hot spot. Take in the newest part of Avenida 5 from G.G.'s spacious stone terrace. The cool lounge music gets progressively louder as the evening wears on. Although the extensive menu covers everything from tuna tartare and filet mignon to sesame-crusted shrimp and crispy calamari, the star here is the impeccable pasta, handmade in the restaurant's upstairs kitchen lab by the chef, an Italian import himself. [$] *Average main: $15* ✉ *Av. 5, between Calle 32 and 34, next to Chez Céline* ☎ *984/879–3387* 🌐 *www.ggfifthavenue.com* ✥ *C6.*

$$$$ MEDITERRANEAN 🍴 **The Glass Bar.** Right in the heart of Fifth Avenue, the restaurant formerly known as Di Vino takes its inspiration from the regional cuisines of Italy. Rough brick walls, wooden floors, and chalkboards inscribed with the daily specials lend a Continental flavor, as do house-made

breads and pastas, including gnocchi and spaghetti with mussels and clams. For local seafood, try the panfried scallops and grilled octopus; for something farther out to sea, try Chilean sea bass served with grape and ginger reduction. The desserts here are said to be the best in Playa, especially the bitter chocolate cake with homemade ice cream. Large groups can reserve the Imperial Table for 18; the street-level patio is the best place to sit if you want to people-watch. The bar is open until 2 am. [$] *Average main: $25* ✉ *Av. 5 and Calle 12* ☎ *984/803–1270* 🌐 *www.theglassbar.com.mx* ✥ *C3.*

$ MEXICAN 🍴 **HC de Monterrey.** Follow your nose to this Mexican grill house, where locals gather for some of the best-tasting steak in town. Far from romantic, the open-air restaurant is filled with the sounds of mariachi music blaring from the radio; a mounted bull's head hangs above the plastic tables and chairs. The main draws are the huge cuts of beef, pork, and chicken served with baskets of corn tortillas, baked potatoes, and ripe avocados. There are two locations in central Playa del Carmen. [$] *Average main: $6* ✉ *Calle 1, between Avs. 20 and 25* ☎ *984/116–4260* 🌐 *www.hcdemonterrey.com.* [$] *Average main: $6* ✉ *Constituyentes, between Avs. 25 and 30, across from Mega Grocery Store* ☎ *984/155–1955* 🌐 *www.hcdemonterrey.com* 💳 *No credit cards* ✥ *B4*

$ CAFÉ 🍴 **Hot Baking Company.** This cheap streetside breakfast café opens at 7 am, and it's one of the few places where you can get breakfast before early-morning sightseeing. Known for Mexican egg dishes like the chile-and-cheese omelet, which will get your day off to a spicy start, Hot also serves more pedestrian packaged muffins and pastries. Salads and sandwiches are available at lunch and dinner. If vacation funds are running low, you can grab a light dinner here since the kitchen stays open until 10:30 pm. [$] *Average main: $7* ✉ *Calle 14 Norte, between Avs. 5 and 10* ☎ *984/879–4520* 🌐 *www.hotbakingcompany.com* ✥ *C4.*

$$$$ SEAFOOD 🍴 **La Casa del Agua.** From the street-level bistro, a dramatic staircase leads to a small cocktail bar and dining room overlooking Fifth Avenue. A stone waterfall is the focal point in the dining room illuminated by wrought-iron chandeliers, where the open layout provides nearly every table with a breeze from the water. Start with the crispy scallops marinated in lime and served over Champagne risotto. Among other menu favorites are sesame-seared blue-fin tuna with portobello mushrooms, and cocinita pibil ravioli, a lighter take on Yucatecan achiote-roasted pork. Remarkably flavorful short ribs are cooked for eight hours in black beer, Dijon mustard, red wine, and honey. [$] *Average main: $25* ✉ *Av. 5 and Calle 2* ☎ *984/803–0232* 🌐 *www.lacasadelagua.com* ✥ *C2.*

$$ MEXICAN 🍴 **La Cueva del Chango.** This Playa institution, in a funky jungle garden with fountains, palmettos, and a rambling koi pond, is Playa del Carmen's favorite breakfast spot. The well-prepared, authentic Mexican selections include soft enchiladas with an excellent mole, sprinkled with sesame seeds; homemade empanadas with *huitlacoche* corn truffle; a seductively spicy habanero cream soup; and classic *chilaquiles*, a tortilla-and-egg scramble that will have you skipping lunch. It's popular for lunch and dinner as well. [$] *Average main: $8* ✉ *Calle 38, between Av. 5 and beach* ☎ *984/147–0271* 🌐 *www.lacuevadelchango.com* 💳 *No credit cards* 🕓 *No dinner Sun.* ✥ *C6*

$$ MEXICAN 🍴 **Los Aguachiles.** This upscale taquerìa is an anchor of Playa's alternative culinary scene, reimagining tacos sautéed in olive oil and topped with cucumber or strawberry-habanero salsa. Local favorites include shrimp tacos with "black gold" (beans), fish ceviche with green salsa, and fish tacos wrapped in your choice: corn tortilla, flour tortilla, or a giant leaf of Bibb lettuce. It's an in-the-know spot for lunch, at either its original location or at the Canibal Royal beach club, but it's only open until 7, so only very early diners can eat there in the evening. [$] *Average main: $10* ✉ *Calle 34 at Av. 25* ☎ *984/142–7380* 💳 *No credit cards* ✥ *B6.*

$$ MODERN MEXICAN 🍴 **Mi Pueblo.** Skip the tourist traps and hit Mi Pueblo for dressed-up, down-home Mexican food. The 33 dishes on the menu are taken from the culinary traditions of 33 Mexican cities, including Monterrey's *corcholatas callejeras*, sweet and soft, bite-size blue corn tortillas with beans, avocado, sour cream, and guajillo pepper. Other top picks are the creamy, crispy Mexico City–style quesadillas with corn and *rajas* (pepper strips) and a killer *mole poblano* from Puebla, where the owner trained as a chef. Go up the stairs and sit in back to watch the cooks make fresh corn tortillas in a traditional Talavera-tiled open kitchen. Daily Happy Hour starts at 5, and a live mariachi can be heard nightly from 7:30 to 9. This is a great spot to grab a margarita or mojito and watch Playa in action. [$] *Average main: $18* ✉ *Av. 5 at Calle 8* ☎ *984/803–0332* 🌐 *www.mipuebloplaya.com* ✥ *C3.*

$$$$ ITALIAN 🍴 **Mosquito Blue Restaurant.** See and be seen in the open dining room of this fashionista hot spot right in the middle of Avenida 5's action. Top selections include linguine with truffle oil and duck, fig-crusted rack of lamb, and the citrus shrimp with lemongrass, avocado mousse, and serrano; the tasting menu is delivered from the Italian chefs on a three-tiered glass tower. If you brought Manolos, this is the place to wear them. [$] *Average main: $30* ✉ *Av. 5, between Calles 12 and 14* ☎ *984/873–0001* 🌐 *www.mosquitoblue.com* ⏲ *No lunch* ✥ *C3.*

$$$$ ARGENTINE **Fodor's Choice** ★ 🍴 **Restaurante Sur.** This two-story enclave of food from the Pampas region of Argentina is a trendy spot. Dine outside on the garden terrace or in the intimate upstairs dining room. Entrées come with four sauces, dominant among them is *chimichurri*, made with oil, vinegar, and finely chopped herbs. You can start off with meat or spinach empanadas or Argentine sausage, followed by a sizzling half-pound *vacio* (flank steak), and finish your meal with hot soufflé with ice cream. [$] *Average main: $28* ✉ *Av. 5, between Calles 12 and 14, on corner of Calle Corazon* ☎ *984/803–2995* 🌐 *www.restaurantsur.com* ✥ *C4.*

$$$ ECLECTIC 🍴 **Ula-Gula.** A sceney streetside bar attracting a well-heeled crowd is the front man for the breezy, open-air restaurant upstairs. The creative, oddball menu can't decide if it's Asian, Mediterranean, or Mexican, vacillating between tamarind salmon and sushi, lamb hamburgers and pork tacos. Most people come for the drinks, which include a famous cucumber martini. [$] *Average main: $12* ✉ *Av. 5 and Calle 10* ☎ *984/879–3727* 🌐 *www.ula-gula.com* ⏲ *Closed Mon. No lunch* ✥ *C3.*

WHERE TO STAY

For expanded reviews, facilities, and current deals, visit Fodors.com.

PLAYA DEL CARMEN

$$ HOTEL
Aventura Mexicana. This small inn three blocks from the beach is a work of art, with Mexican decor, batik wall hangings, and rustic wood-frame beds. **Pros:** spotless; friendly staff; spacious rooms. **Cons:** uncomfortable beds; unimaginative breakfasts. [$] *Rooms from: $90 ✉ Calle 24, between Avs. 5 and 10 ☎ 984/873–1876 🌐 www.aventuramexicana.com 🛏 49 rooms 🍴 Breakfast ✥ C5.*

$$ HOTEL
Be Playa. This funky boutique hotel melds together retro vintage with a touch of modern, starting with the red vinyl couches in the lobby all the way up to the exceedingly cool rooftop pool bar, where tables and chairs wade in the water. **Pros:** creative design; good views from rooftop bar; reasonably priced rooms. **Cons:** four blocks from the beach; rooms don't have ocean views; bland breakfast. [$] *Rooms from: $130 ✉ Calle 26 between Avs. 5 and 10 ☎ 984/803–2243 🌐 www.beplaya.com 🛏 23 rooms 🍴 Breakfast ✥ C5.*

$ HOTEL
Casa Tucan. For the price, it's hard to beat this funky hotel in a lush courtyard garden a few blocks from the beach. **Pros:** multilingual staff; on-site car-rental agency; exceptional restaurant. **Cons:** some rooms lack air-conditioning. [$] *Rooms from: $60 ✉ Calle 4, between Avs. 10 and 15 ☎ 984/873–0283 🌐 www.casatucan.de 🛏 24 rooms, 4 apartments, 10 cabanas 🍴 No meals ✥ B2.*

$$$ HOTEL
Deseo Hotel & Lounge. This trendy but comfortable adults-only hotel is known for its cutting-edge design. **Pros:** contemporary decor; friendly staff; comfortable beds; films shown nightly. **Cons:** small pool; no kids under 16 allowed. [$] *Rooms from: $265 ✉ Av. 5 and Calle 12 ☎ 984/879–3620 🌐 www.hoteldeseo.com 🛏 12 rooms, 3 suites 🍴 Breakfast ✥ C3.*

$$$$ RENTAL
Fodor's Choice ★
El Taj Condo Hotel. The elegant, curvy building on the beach at Indigo Beach Club is a collection of stylish condo rentals, with bells and whistles starting at Indonesian lamps and spacious stone showers and going all the way up to private Jacuzzis and sea views. **Pros:** on beach; private kitchens; 10% discount for seven-plus night stay; free phone calls included. **Cons:** units are mostly two- and three-bedroom; units outside of main building have no sea view; three-night minimum stay. [$] *Rooms from: $295 ✉ Calle 14 at beach ☎ 984/879–3919, 866/479–2738 from U.S. 🌐 www.eltaj.com 🛏 57 units 🍴 No meals ✥ D4.*

$$$ RESORT ALL-INCLUSIVE FAMILY
Gran Porto Real. The family-friendly sister hotel to the Royal (which is just next door) has downtown Playa's best accommodations for the schoolyard set. **Pros:** kids under 5 years stay free; central location; good breakfast buffet. **Cons:** gaudy style; touts in lobby; least attractive part of beach. [$] *Rooms from: $280 ✉ Av. Constituyentes 1, at beach ☎ 984/873–4000 🌐 www.realresorts.com 🛏 287 rooms 🍴 All-inclusive ✥ D4.*

$ HOTEL
Hotel Coco Rio. A tropical garden beckons near the entry to this small hotel on a tree-lined street in Playa's north end. **Pros:** pleasant staff; charming setting, great value. **Cons:** no breakfast; no views. [$] *Rooms from: $70 ✉ Calle 26, between Avs. 5 and 10 ☎ 984/879–3361 🌐 www.hotelcocorio.com 🛏 13 rooms, 5 suites 🍴 No meals ✥ C5.*

$ B&B/INN
Hotel Delfín. This simple, well-priced hotel is covered with ivy and looks fresh and smart, making it a good option for travelers on a budget who don't need to be directly on the beach. **Pros:** quiet setting; central

location. **Cons:** no common areas; no restaurant or bar; not all rooms have a/c; lots of steps to climb (and no elevator). $ *Rooms from: $70* ⊠ *Av. 5 and Calle 6* ☏ *984/873–0176, 518/672–7235 in U.S.* ⊕ *www. hoteldelfin.com* ⟿ *15 rooms* ⊚⏐ *No meals* ✛ *C2.*

$$ ⊡ **Hotel El Punto.** The glass-floored corridors of this modern hotel, each
HOTEL inlaid with strips of bamboo, lead to well-appointed rooms with king-size beds (illuminated from beneath) that have enormous headboards and bathrooms made of marble and sapote wood. **Pros:** contemporary decor; great lounge bar; rooms have espresso machines. **Cons:** not all rooms have ocean view; no elevator; no kids under 15. $ *Rooms from: $150* ⊠ *Av. 5 and Calle 8* ☏ *984/803–0288* ⊕ *www.hotelelpunto.com* ⟿ *16 rooms* ⊚⏐ *Breakfast* ✛ *C3.*

$$ ⊡ **Hotel Kinbé.** An interesting fusion of Mayan and contemporary decor,
HOTEL this small, stylish place (which means "path to the sun") is set in a tropical garden steps from the beach. **Pros:** great value; free access to nearby Indigo Beach Club. **Cons:** small rooms; rustic decor is not family-friendly; strict cancellation policy. $ *Rooms from: $85* ⊠ *Calle 10 Norte, between Avs. 1 and 5* ☏ *984/873–0441, 984/873–0443* ⊕ *www. kinbe.com* ⟿ *19 rooms, 10 suites* ⊚⏐ *Breakfast* ✛ *C3.*

$ ⊡ **Hotel Posada Mariposa.** Although it has few facilities, this hotel is still
HOTEL a great value, with impeccable rooms set around an open-air garden courtyard where trees grow past the third floor. **Pros:** cozy setting; good shuttle service; discount to Mamita's Beach Club. **Cons:** hard beds; Wi-Fi only in lobby; though promised by 2014, at this writing no room phones, pool, or gym. $ *Rooms from: $140* ⊠ *Av. 5 No. 314, between Calles 24 and 26* ☏ *984/873–3886* ⊕ *www.mariposagrouphotels.com* ⟿ *18 rooms, 5 suites* ⊚⏐ *Breakfast* ✛ *C5.*

$ ⊡ **La Rana Cansada.** Close to the downtown action yet far enough away
HOTEL to have a peaceful feel, this little hotel has enough creature comforts to keep most budget travelers happy, but the cheapest rooms may be too basic for some tastes. **Pros:** lively bar; free purified drinking water; clean rooms. **Cons:** hard beds; east rooms sometimes lack hot water; poor ventilation. $ *Rooms from: $60* ⊠ *Calle 10 between Avs. 5 and 10* ☏ *984/873–0389* ⊕ *www.ranacansada.com* ⟿ *14 rooms, 1 suite* ⊚⏐ *No meals* ✛ *C3.*

$$$ ⊡ **La Tortuga Hotel & Spa.** Mosaic stone paths wind through lovely gar-
B&B/INN dens, and colonial-style hardwood furnishings gleam throughout at this inn on a quiet side street. **Pros:** some rooms have rooftop terraces; lovely grounds; outstanding breakfast. **Cons:** late-night street noise; no kids under 18; spotty Internet. $ *Rooms from: $160* ⊠ *Calle 14 and Av. 10* ☏ *984/873–1484, 800/822–3274* ⊕ *www.hotellatortuga.com* ⟿ *45 rooms, 6 junior suites* ⊚⏐ *Breakfast* ✛ *C4.*

$$ ⊡ **Lunata.** An elegant entrance, Spanish-tile floors, and hand-tooled
B&B/INN furniture from Guadalajara greet you at this classy inn. **Pros:** prime location; impeccable rooms; intimate setting. **Cons:** street-facing rooms tend to be noisy; mediocre breakfast; mosquitoes in common areas. $ *Rooms from: $135* ⊠ *Av. 5 between Calles 6 and 8* ☏ *984/873–0884* ⊕ *www.lunata.com* ⟿ *10 rooms* ⊚⏐ *Breakfast* ✛ *C3.*

$$$$ RESORT Fodor's Choice ★ 🏨 **Mahekal Beach Resort.** With candy-colored, palapa-roofed bungalows and a great location—on the sand but just two blocks from the town's upscale northern end—this may be the perfect beach resort. **Pros:** private patios with hammocks; excellent service; billiards and Ping-Pong. **Cons:** no evening entertainment; narrow beach; no amenities; mediocre food; sulfur smell after the rain. [$] *Rooms from: $400* ✉ *Calle 38, at beach* ☎ *984/873–0611, 877/235–4452* 🌐 *www.mahekalplaya.com* 🛏 *121 cabanas* 🍴 *Some meals* ✥ *D6.*

$$$$ HOTEL 🏨 **Mosquito Blue Hotel and Spa.** Easily Playa's most stylish property, this is the digs for the nightclubbing tropical jet set. **Pros:** access to Mosquito Beach Hotel's chic beach club; billiards; access to nearby fitness center. **Cons:** area tends to get loud at night; kids under 14 not allowed; breakfast included in the rate during high season only. [$] *Rooms from: $242* ✉ *Calle 12, between Avs. 5 and 10* ☎ *984/873–1245* 🌐 *www.mosquitoblue.com* 🛏 *44 rooms, 1 suite* 🍴 *Breakfast* ✥ *C3.*

$$$$ RESORT ALL-INCLUSIVE 🏨 **Paradisus Playa del Carmen.** This Playa all-inclusive offers flash and class in a Vegas-meets-cruise ship environment with 14 restaurants, 11 bars, and nearly 1,000 rooms scattered between two buildings. **Pros:** complimentary cell phones at check-in; beautiful swim-up rooms; plenty of activities for kids. **Cons:** hot tubs are cold; rocky beach; 10-minute drive from downtown Playa del Carmen; not all restaurants are open to children. [$] *Rooms from: $300* ✉ *Av. 5 and Calle 112* ☎ *984/877–3900* 🌐 *www.paradisus.com* 🛏 *512 rooms at Esmeralda, 394 rooms at La Perla* 🍴 *All-inclusive* ✥ *C6.*

$$ HOTEL 🏨 **Riviera Caribe Maya.** It may not have the bells and whistles of other Playa hotels, but this small property, on a quiet street two blocks from the beach, is very pleasant. **Pros:** breezy rooms; outstanding pool area; huge bathrooms. **Cons:** hard mattresses; Wi-Fi in common areas only; no restaurant. [$] *Rooms from: $80* ✉ *Calle 30 and Av. 10* ☎ *984/873–1193* 🌐 *www.hotelrivieramaya.com* 🛏 *21 rooms, 4 suites* 🍴 *Breakfast* ✥ *C5.*

$$$$ RESORT ALL-INCLUSIVE 🏨 **THE Royal Playa del Carmen.** If you're looking for the royal treatment, this is the place, from butler service and iPad check-in to in-room Jacuzzis and liquor bars. **Pros:** on Playa's best beach; live entertainment evenings; great spa. **Cons:** the largest property in central Playa del Carmen; most rooms face the garden rather than the ocean; no kids under 16. [$] *Rooms from: $467* ✉ *Av. Constituyentes, No. 2, and beach* ☎ *984/877–2900* 📠 *984/877–2999* 🌐 *www.realresorts.com* 🛏 *513 rooms* 🍴 *All-inclusive* ✥ *D4.*

PLAYACAR

South of downtown Playa del Carmen, the upscale gated community of Playacar is home to a string of all-inclusive resorts, beachfront condos, and rental properties. It also features an 18-hole golf course and the small open air mall, Plaza Playacar. A paved bike path skirts the tree-lined streets of the development, past private neighborhoods, all the way north to downtown Playa and south to the adventure parks Xplor and Xcaret. For those not staying in Playacar, it is of little interest since most of the action takes place along Avenida 5.

La Tortuga Hotel & Spa

$$$$ RESORT ALL-INCLUSIVE FAMILY

🏨 **Iberostar Tucan and Quetzal.** This unique all-inclusive resort has preserved its natural surroundings—among the resident animals are flamingos, turtles, toucans, peacocks, and monkeys. **Pros:** oceanfront rooms; tropical setting; bicycles for guests; tax and tips included in rate. **Cons:** food lacks variety; small beach; water at swim-up bar can be chilly; Wi-Fi costs extra. [$] *Rooms from: $500* ✉ *Av. Xamanha, Playacar* ☎ *984/877–2000* 🌐 *www.iberostar.com* 🛏 *730 rooms* 🍴 *All-inclusive.*

$$$$ RESORT ALL-INCLUSIVE

🏨 **Riu Palace Riviera Maya.** This enormous all-inclusive serves its luxury with an extra helping of glitz, but its breathtaking beach and exceptional service are what really shine. **Pros:** sports bar open nonstop; friendly staff; lots of scheduled activities. **Cons:** need to make dinner reservations in advance at certain restaurants; no poolside service; hallways echo at night; always seem to be piles of luggage in the lobby. [$] *Rooms from: $450* ✉ *Av. Xaman-Ha, Lote #9 and #10, Playacar* ☎ *984/877–2280* 🌐 *www.riu.com* 🛏 *460 rooms* 🍴 *All-inclusive.*

$$$$ RESORT ALL-INCLUSIVE

🏨 **Royal Hideaway.** Art and antiques from around the world fill the lobby, and streams, waterfalls, and fountains fill the grounds of this 13-acre resort on a stretch of pristine beach. **Pros:** romantic setting; attentive service. **Cons:** no children under 13; cold pool; roaming beach vendors can be bothersome. [$] *Rooms from: $457* ✉ *Av Xaman-Ha, Lote #6, Playacar* ☎ *984/873–4500, 800/858–2258* 🌐 *www.royalhideaway.com* 🛏 *194 rooms, 6 suites* 🍴 *All-inclusive.*

Playa del Carmen remains less developed and more pedestrian-friendly than Cancún.

NIGHTLIFE

The Riviera Maya Jazz Festival splashes cool on Playa's music scene, every year in the last week of November. ⊕ *www.rivieramayajazzfestival.com.*

Alux. Inside a cavern, Alux has a bar, disco, and restaurant. Live DJs spin everything from smooth jazz to electronica until 2 am. ⊠ *Av. Juárez, between 65 and 70* ☎ *984/147–1563* ⊕ *www.aluxrestaurant.com.*

Bar Ranita. Bar Ranita, attached to the Rana Cansada Hotel, is a favorite among rowdy expats. The prices are unbeatable, and the margaritas pack a powerful punch. ⊠ *Rana Cansada Hotel, Calle 10 between Avs. 5 and 10* ☎ *984/873–0389* ⊕ *www.ranacansada.com.*

CoCo Bongo. Following the success of its sister property in Cancún, CoCo Bongo has flying acrobats, bar-top conga lines, live bands, and DJs mixing everything from rock to hip-hop. The cover charge includes unlimited drinks. ⊠ *Calle 10 at Av. 10* ☎ *984/803–5939* ⊕ *www. cocobongo.com.mx* ⧈ *$60–$70* ⊙ *Closed Sun.*

Deseo Lounge. DJs spin chill-out music as black-and-white Mexican film classics are projected on the wall at the rooftop Deseo Lounge (otherwise known as the Hotel Deseo's pool bar), famed for its icy-cool cucumber martinis. ⊠ *Hotel Deseo, Av. 5 at Calle 12* ☎ *984/879–3620* ⊕ *www.hoteldeseo.com.*

Diablito Cha Cha Cha. Miami-chic with retro white patent leather chairs and a palapa roof, Diablito Cha Cha Cha serves up sushi and DJ tunes as late as 3 am. ⊠ *Calle 12, between Avs. 5 and 1* ☎ *984/803–3695* ⊕ *www.diablitochachacha.com.*

Kartabar. Kartabar's hookah-smokers puff on tobacco flavored apple, strawberry, and mango that wafts away into the open tropical night. On weekends, belly dancers weave their way between the tables. ⊠ *Calle 12 at Av. 1, Playa del Carmen* ☎ *984/873–2228* ⊕ *www.kartabar.com.mx.*

Kitxen. An anchor of Playa's live music scene, cool Kitxen features bands from Mexico and the Caribbean playing everything from rock to reggae. Cash only. ⊠ *Av. 5, between Calle 20 and Constituyentes.*

La Bodeguita del Medio. Graffiti-styled La Bodeguita del Medio, a franchise of the famous Havana outpost, features live Cuban music nightly. ⊠ *Av. 5 and Calle 34* ☎ *984/803–3951* ⊕ *www.labodeguitadelmedio.com.mx.*

La Santanera. La Santanera's international DJs and a young, cosmopolitan crowd groove to electronic music until very late at this "underground disco cantina." For a breath of fresh air, head upstairs to the rooftop lounge for cool drinks and chill-out music. ⊠ *Calle 12 between Avs. 5 and 10* ☎ *984/803–2856* ⊕ *www.lasantanera.com* 🖅 *$8* ⊙ *Closed Mon.*

Los Dioses de la Arena. Ironic urbanites down oddball *micheladas*—beer cocktails— flavored with strawberry and chiles while they take in live wrestling matches, in this pseudo-dive bar dedicated to Mexico's most pseudo-dive sport. ⊠ *Calle 38 at Av. 5.*

Mandala. Mandala is the newest, biggest, loudest and most expensive party spot on Calle 12. This trendy venue is divided into a street-level bar, a rooftop terrace, and a dance club, each with its own DJ spinning everything from house and hip-hop to disco and techno. ⊠ *Calle 12, between Avs. 1 and 5* ☎ *984/879–4189* ⊕ *www.mandalanightclub.com* 🖅 *$12, $45 for open bar.*

SHOPPING

Avenida 5 between Calles 4 and 38 has the Riviera Maya's best shopping. Small galleries sell original folk art from around Mexico, clothing boutiques offer everything from chic bikinis to tacky tees, and there are stores dedicated to Mexican specialties as varied as silver, chocolate, and tequila. Mexico's upscale Liverpool department store puts in an appearance at Calle 14, and you'll find international brand names like Diesel and Havaianas scattered up and down the avenue.

BOOKS

Mundo Librería–Bookstore. Mundo Librería–Bookstore has an extensive selection of books on Mayan culture, along with used English-language books. Profits from all English-language books here are donated to Mexican schools to buy textbooks. ⊠ *Calle 1 Sur No. 189, between Avs. 20 and 25* ☎ *984/879–3004, 984/109–1566 at Plaza las Américas in Playa del Carmen.*

CLOTHING

Uca Luca. In-the-know locals go to Uca Luca for the beach's most fashionable bikinis, pareos, and dresses for lunching in the shade. ⊠ *Av. 5, between Calle 36 and 38.*

CRAFTS

Fodor's Choice **Ah Cacao.** This modish chocolate shop sells Mexico's finest, in bars,
★ tablets, soaps, massage oils, and brownies. There's another branch
at the corner of Avenida 5 and Calle 30. ☒ *Av. 5 and Constituyentes*
☎ *984/803–5748* ⊕ *www.ahcacao.com.*

Artevelas. Artevelas sells the outsize, handmade candles that you see
lighting the night so elegantly in Playa's restaurants and hotels. ☒ *Av.
1, between Calles 14 and 16* ☎ *984/267–3420* ⊕ *www.artevelas.com*
☉ *Closed Sun.*

Hacienda Tequila. Hacienda Tequila sells 480 different types of tequila
and kitschy Mexican crafts and souvenirs. Free tastings are available,
and there's an exhibit that walks you through the world of agave booze.
☒ *Av. 5 and Calle 14* ☎ *984/803–0821.*

La Hierbabuena Artesanía. At La Hierbabuena Artesanía, owner Melinda
Burns offers a collection of fine Mexican clothing and crafts. ☒ *Av. 5,
between Calles 8 and 10* ☎ *984/873–1741.*

La Sirena. La Sirena sells edgy folk art, from *lucha libre* wrestling col-
lages to painted ceramic skulls. ☒ *Av. 5 and Calle 26* ☎ *984/803–3422.*

JEWELRY

Ambar Mexicano. Ambar Mexicano has jewelry crafted of Chiapan amber
by a local designer. ☒ *Av. 5, between Calles 4 and 6* ☎ *984/873–2357.*

MALLS

Paseo del Carmen. Paseo del Carmen is an open-air, upscale shopping
mall with a number of boutiques, including Diesel, Ultrafemme, and
American Apparel. Seattle-coffee lovers can get their fix at the Starbucks
that dominates the center of the mall. A cobblestone path makes this
mall one of the area's most popular and pleasant shopping destinations.
☒ *Av. 10 and Calle 1* ☎ *984/803–3789.*

Plaza Las Américas. Plaza Las Américas is a family-friendly mall featuring
restaurants, shops, and cinemas. ☒ *Carretera 307* ☎ *984/109–2161.*

Plaza Playacar. This Mexican-colonial style outdoor mall in Playacar sells handcrafts, clothes, jewelry, and specialty items like Tequila
and cigars. Of course, there is also a Starbucks. ☒ *Paseo Xaman-Há,
past main entrance of Playacar, Playacar* ☎ *984/873–0006* ⊕ *www.
plazaplayacar.com.*

SPORTS AND THE OUTDOORS

ADVENTURE TOURS

Alltournative. Alltournative will have you feeling like Indiana Jones in no
time. Trips, which range in price from $99 to $129, focus on ecological
preservation and Mexican culture. You can kayak through a lagoon,
snorkel in a cenote, or zip-line above a lush jungle. The company also
organizes trips to Mayan communities on expeditions to Cobá. ☒ *Carretera Federal 307, Km 287, near Playacar* ☎ *984/803–9999* ⊕ *www.
alltournative.com.*

Punta Venado. South of Playa del Carmen, Punta Venado offers adventure tours in all-terrain vehicles or on horseback. The 4 km (2½ miles)
of isolated coastline are great for snorkeling and kayaking. Packages

range from $50 to $60. ✉ *Carretera Federal 307, Km 278, Calica* ☎ *998/887–1191.*

FITNESS CENTERS

The Gym. Playa's most complete workout is to be had at this vast and well-equipped gym, which offers a full complement of cardio, weights, and classes from spinning to yoga. Day passes cost $15. ✉ *Av. 1 Norte #255, between Constituyentes and Calle 16* ☎ *984/873–2098* ⊕ *www. thegymplaya.com.*

GOLF

Casa Club de Golf. Playa del Carmen's golf course is an 18-hole, par-71 championship course designed by Nick Price. The greens fee is $165; there's also a special twilight fee of $120. ✉ *Grand Coral Riviera Maya Resort, Carretera 307, Km 294* ☎ *984/109–6020* ⊕ *www. grandcoralrivieramaya.com.mx.*

Playacar Golf Club. The Golf Club at Playacar has an 18-hole course; the greens fee is $200 and the twilight fee $120 after 1 pm. ✉ *Paseo Xaman-Há, near Riu Palace, Playacar* ☎ *984/873–4990.*

SCUBA DIVING

Abyss. The PADI and SSI-affiliated Abyss offers introductory courses and dive trips ($50 for one tank, $70 for two tanks). They also run dives in Tulum, as Cenote Dive Center. ✉ *Av. 1, between Calles 10 and 12* ☎ *984/873–2164* ⊕ *www.abyssdiveshop.com.*

Cenote Dive Center. The virtual office of Playa del Carmen's Abyss specializes in Tulum dives. ✉ *Av. 1, between Calles 10 and 12* ☎ *984/876–3285* ⊕ *www.cenotedive.com.*

Mexico Blue Dream. Mexico Blue Dream provides custom snorkel tours in Playa, Laguna Yal-Ku, Akumal, and nearby cenotes, as well as dive trips to Cozumel. Trips start at $35. ✉ *Between Av. 1 and Mamitas Beach* ☎ *984/803–0660* ⊕ *www.mexicobluedream.com.*

Tank-Ha Dive Center. Playa's original dive outfit, Tank-Ha Dive Center has PADI-certified teachers and runs diving and snorkeling trips to the reefs and caverns. A one-tank dive costs $45; for a two-tank trip it's $65. Dive packages are also available, as well as trips to Cozumel. ✉ *Calle 10, between Avs. 5 and 10* ☎ *984/873–0302* ⊕ *www.tankha.com.*

Yucatek Divers. PADI-affiliated Yucatek Divers offers cenote dives, dive packages, and instruction. A one-tank introductory course costs $95; the four-day, five-dive beginner certification course is $410. ✉ *Av. 15, between Calles 2 and 4* ☎ *984/803–2836* ⊕ *www.yucatek-divers.com.*

SKYDIVING

SkyDive. Thrill seekers can take the plunge high above Playa in a tandem sky dive (where you're hooked up to the instructor the whole time). SkyDive shoots video of your freefall ($150) for proof that you did it. Jumps take place every hour and cost $250. Reserve at least one day in advance. ✉ *Plaza Marina 32, next to Señor Frog's, at Cozumel ferry* ☎ *984/873–0192* ⊕ *www.skydive.com.mx.*

XCARET

6 km (4 miles) south of Playa del Carmen.

Once a sacred Mayan city and port, Xcaret (pronounced *ish*-car-et) is now home to two theme parks on a gorgeous stretch of coastline. The 250-acre ecological theme park, simply known as "Xcaret," is the coast's most heavily advertised attraction. Billed as "nature's sacred paradise," it has a network of buses, its own published magazines, and a collection of stores. Just 2 km (1 mile) from Xcaret is a newer adventure park, Xplor, a sister property targeted at extreme adventure seekers.

GETTING HERE AND AROUND
Xcaret and Xplor are 56 km (35 miles) south of Cancún International Airport and 6 km (4 miles) south of Playa del Carmen. The entrance for both parks and Occidental Grand Xcaret Resort is at Km 282 on Carretera 307.

EXPLORING

FAMILY **Xcaret.** Among the most popular attractions are the Paradise River raft tour that takes you on a winding, watery journey through the jungle; the Butterfly Pavilion, where thousands of butterflies float dreamily through a botanical garden while New Age music plays in the background; and an ocean-fed aquarium where you can see local sea life drifting through coral heads and sea fans.

The park has a Wild Bird Breeding Aviary, nurseries for both abandoned flamingo eggs and sea turtles, and a series of underwater caverns that you can explore by snorkeling or snuba (a hybrid of snorkeling and scuba). A replica Mayan village includes a colorful cemetery with catacomb-like caverns underneath; traditional music and dance ceremonies (including performances by the famed *Voladores de Papantla*—the Flying Birdmen of Papantla) are performed here at night. But the star performance is the evening "Spectacular Mexico Night Show," which tells the history of Mexico through song and dance.

The list of Xcaret's attractions goes on and on: you can visit a dolphinarium, a bee farm, a manatee lagoon, a bat cave, an orchid and bromeliad greenhouse, an edible-mushroom farm, and a small zoo. You can also visit a scenic tower that takes you 240 feet up in the air for a spectacular view of the park.

The entrance fee covers only access to the grounds and the exhibits; all other activities and equipment—from sea treks and dolphin tours to lockers and swim gear—are extra. The $109 Plus Pass includes park entrance, lockers, snorkel equipment, food, and drinks. You can buy tickets from any travel agency or major hotel along the coast. ⊠ *Carretera 307, Km 282, Xcaret* ☎ *800/292–2738 in Mexico, 888/922–7381 in U.S.* ⊕ *www.xcaret.com* ⊠ *$79 Basic Pass; $109 Plus Pass* ☉ *Daily 8:30 am–9:30 pm.*

FAMILY **Xplor.** Designed for thrill seekers, this 125-acre park features underground rafting in stalactite-studded water caves and cenotes. Swim in a stalactite river, ride in an amphibian vehicle, or soar across the park on 13 of the longest zip-lines in Mexico. The price includes all food, drink, and equipment. ⊠ *Carretera 307, Km 282* ☎ *984/147–6560,*

888/922–7381 in U.S. 🌐 *www.xplor.travel* 🎟 *$109* 🕒 *Mon.–Sat. 8:30–5.*

WHERE TO STAY

For expanded reviews, facilities, and current deals, visit Fodors.com.

$$$$ RESORT ALL-INCLUSIVE [T] **Occidental Grand Xcaret.** In such an enormous all-inclusive hotel it's surprising to find the excellent, personal service that you get here. **Pros:** pleasant lagoon; easy access to Xcaret; free scuba course. **Cons:** time-share sales reps give you the hard sell; small beach; squawking parrots in the lobby; Internet costs extra. [$] *Rooms from: $375* ✉ *Carretera Federal 307, off Puerto Juárez, Km 282, Xcaret* ☎ *984/871–5400* 🌐 *www.occidentalhotels.com* 🛏 *724 rooms, 45 suites* 🍴 *All-inclusive.*

WORD OF MOUTH

"We flew into Cancun and rented a car. . . . Driving was a breeze and we had no trouble. We stayed [in a time share]. We drove to Tulum one day to see the Mayan ruins. On the same day we swam in a cenote in Hidden Worlds. Both were very interesting and not to [be] miss[ed]. We drove to Playa Del Carmen three times. . . . Overall, we had a fabulous time."

—sdtravels

PUERTO AVENTURAS

26 km (16 miles) south of Playa del Carmen.

GETTING HERE AND AROUND

Puerto Aventuras is a 20-minute drive south of Playa del Carmen along Carretera 307. Taxis are stationed at the small parking area near the marina outside the Omni hotel. You can also find them parked outside all major hotels. Taxis from Playa del Carmen cost about $20.

ESSENTIALS

Currency Exchange **Money Exchange** ✉ *Calle Punta Celis, next to Omni.* **Santander - ATM** ✉ *North end of Marina, below Museo CEDAM.*

EXPLORING

Puerto Aventuras is the most Americanized of all the Riviera Maya's resorts, a 900-acre gated community and golf course more reminiscent of coastal Florida than Mexico. This has its advantages if you want to speak English exclusively and have the option to eat American food. The main beach in front of the Omni hotel is glorious, but the town itself is not particularly scenic. Its orientation around a small marina makes it very manageable and walkable, a place where you can let older kids go off by themselves for the afternoon. The main marina is closed off to boat traffic and is instead home to Dolphin Discovery's dolphins and sea lions, which are fun to watch from the waterside restaurants and benches. The main visitor center is just before the town center, on the main road on the right as you enter Puerto Aventuras.

Museo CEDAM. The Museo CEDAM displays coins, sewing needles, nautical devices, clay dishes, and other artifacts from 18th-century sunken ships, recovered by members of the Mexican Underwater Expeditions Club. The club was founded in 1959 by Pablo Bush Romero, who later went on to found the nearby town of Akumal. ✉ *North end of marina* 🎟 *Donation* 🕒 *Mon.–Sat. 9–1 and 2:30–5:30.*

There's plenty to do and see in Xcaret.

OFF THE BEATEN PATH

Cenotes Kantún Chi. The Maya-owned and operated eco-park of Cenotes Kantún Chi has cenotes and a few beautiful underground caverns that are great for snorkeling and diving, as well as some small Mayan ruins. The place is low-key—a nice break from the crowds. Bring natural mosquito repellent. ⊠ *Carretera 307, Km 266, in front of Barceló Hotel* ☎ *984/873–0021* ⊕ *www.kantunchi.com* ☑ *Adults $59 (children $45) for cenote and cave tour and lunch; adults $20 (children $15) for access to cenote only* ☻ *Daily 9–5.*

BEACHES

Omni Beach. Although the marina is the main focus here, Puerto Aventuras' beaches are naturally stunning and seldom crowded. The main beach, Fatima Bay, commonly referred to as Omni Beach, stretches nearly 3 km (2 miles) south between Chac Hal Al condominiums and the Grand Peninsula residence. Its shallow, calm waters are kid-friendly. To the north is a smaller bay, known as Chan Yu Yum, used by guests of the Catalonia Resort. Both bays are good spots for swimming and snorkeling. You'll find more excellent beaches just south of Puerto Aventuras in the community of Xpu-Há. **Amenities:** food and drink. **Best for:** swimming. ⊠ *Behind Omni Hotel.*

NAVIGATING XCARET

You can easily spend at least a full day at Xcaret. The park is big, so it's a good idea to check the daily activities against a map of the park to organize your time. Plan to be in the general area of an activity before it's scheduled to begin—you'll beat the crowds and avoid having to run across the park.

Paamul Beach. Beachcombers, campers, and snorkeling snowbirds love Paamul (pronounced pah-*mool*), a crescent-shape lagoon 21 km (13 miles) south of Playa del Carmen with clear, placid waters sheltered by a coral reef. Shells, sand dollars, and even glass beads—some from the sunken, 18th-century Spanish galleon *Mantanceros,* which lies off nearby Akumal—wash up onto the sandy parts of the beach. (There's a sandy path into deeper water in front of the restaurant—on the rocks, watch out for sea urchins.) Sea turtles hatch here in June through September and July. ■**TIP➜** **If you'd like to stay on this piece of paradise, Hotel and Cabanas Paamul is a laid-back option.** **Amenities:** food and drink; toilets. **Best for:** snorkeling; swimming; walking. ✉ *Paamul Bay, Carretera 307 Cancún–Chetumal, Km 85, between Xcaret and Puerto Aventuras, Paamul.*

SPAS

Hard Rock Hotel Riviera Maya Spa. This destination spa at the Hard Rock Riviera Maya is the hotel's signature, a vast labyrinth of candlelit treatment rooms and pools for hydrotherapy, which guests can use all day when they book a spa package. The Mayan *temazcal* is the spa's big draw, but only resort guests have access to the spa. ✉ *Carretera 307, Km 72* ☎ *984/875–1100* 🌐 *www.hardrockhotels.com.*

WHERE TO EAT

$$ SEAFOOD
🍴 **Café Olé International.** The laid-back hub of Puerto Aventuras is a terrace café with a varied menu, including coconut shrimp and chicken with a chimichurri sauce made from red wine, garlic, onion, and fine herbs. If you and local fishermen get lucky, the nightly specials might include fresh-caught fish in garlic sauce. Cheesecakes and pies, all homemade by owner Gaylita, are delicious. There's live music and all-you-can-eat ribs on Sunday, Wednesday, and Friday in high season, as well as Spanish guitar on Thursday and Saturday. [$] *Average main: $10* ✉ *Across street from Omni hotel* ☎ *984/873–5125* ⏲ *Closed Sept. Closed Mon. during Oct.*

WHERE TO STAY

For expanded reviews, facilities, and current deals, visit Fodors.com.

$$$$ RESORT ALL-INCLUSIVE FAMILY
🏨 **Hard Rock Hotel Riviera Maya.** This 85-acre all-inclusive resort—previously the Aventura Spa Palace—is so big, and has so many activities, that you may have trouble finding a reason to leave. **Pros:** breakfast delivered to your door; access to neighboring golf course. **Cons:** lots of sales pitches for time-shares; beach is artificial. [$] *Rooms from: $547* ✉ *Carretera 307, Km 271, 3 km north of Puerto Aventuras* ☎ *984/875–1100, 800/346–8225* 🌐 *www.hardrockhotels.com* 🛏 *1,221 rooms, 45 suites* 🍽 *All-inclusive.*

$$$ RESORT
🏨 **Omni Puerto Aventuras.** Atop the main beach and in the center of the action the Omni is the focal point of Puerto Aventuras, but its low-key luxury is a cut above the town's other resorts. **Pros:** pretty beach; sushi restaurant; nearby marina with dolphins; decent golf course. **Cons:** food choices could be better; no elevator; extra charge for beach amenities. [$] *Rooms from: $350* ✉ *Calle Punta Celis* ☎ *984/875–1950* 🌐 *www.omnihotels.com* 🛏 *30 rooms* 🍽 *Breakfast.*

Continued on page 186

ANCIENT ARCHITECTS
THE MAYA

Visiting the Yucatán Peninsula and not touring any Mayan sites is like going to Greece and not seeing the Acropolis or the Parthenon. One look at the monumental architecture of the Maya and you might feel transported to another world. The breathtaking structures are even more impressive when you consider that they were built 1,000 to 2,000 years ago or more without iron tools, wheels, pulleys, or beasts of burden—and in terrible heat and difficult terrain.

El Castillo, Tulum.

THE ARCHITECTURAL PERIODS

Calakmul

PRECLASSIC PERIOD: Petén

Between approximately 2000 BC and AD 100, the Maya were centered around the lowlands in the south-central region of Guatemala. Their communities were family-based, and governed by hereditary chiefs; their worship of agricultural gods (such as Chaac, the rain god), who they believed controlled the seasons, led them to chart the movement of heavenly bodies. Their religious beliefs also led them to build enormous temples and pyramids—such as El Mirador, in the Guatemalan lowlands—where sacrifices were made and ceremonies performed to please the gods.

The structures at El Mirador, as well as at the neighboring ruin site of Tikal, were built in what is known today as the Petén style; pyramids were steeply pitched, built on stepped terraces, and decorated with large stucco masks and ornamental (but sometimes "false" or unclimbable) stairways. Petén-style structures were also often roofed with corbeled archways. The Maya began to move northward into the Yucatán during the late part of this period, which is why Petén-style buildings can also be found at Calakmul, just north of the Guatemalan border.

EARLY CLASSIC PERIOD: Río Usumacinta

The Classic Period, often referred to as the "golden age," spanned from about AD 100 to AD 1000. Maya civilization expanded northward and became much more complex. A distinct ruling class emerged and hereditary kings ruled over densely populated jungle cities, filled with increasingly impressive-looking palaces and temples.

During the early part of the Classic Period, Maya architecture began to take on some distinctive characteristics. Build- ers placed their structures on hillsides or crests, and the principal buildings were covered with bas-reliefs carved in stone. The pyramid-top temples had vestibules and rooms with vaulted ceilings; many chamber walls were carved with scenes recounting important events during the reign of the ruler who built the pyramid. Some of the most stunning examples of this style are at the ruins of Palenque, near Chiapas.

Palenque

Chicanná

MID-CLASSIC PERIOD: Río Bec and Chenes

It was during the middle part of the Classic Period (roughly between AD 600 and AD 800) that the Maya presence exploded into the Yucatán Peninsula. Several Maya settlements were established in what is now Campeche state, including Chicanná and Xpujil, near the southwest corner of the state. The architecture at these sites was built in what is now known as the Río Bec style. As in the earlier Petén style, Río Bec pyramids had steeply pitched sides and ornately decorated foundations. Other Río Bec-style buildings, however, were long, one-story affairs incorporating two or sometimes three tall towers. These towers were typically capped by large roof combs that resembled mini-temples.

During the same part of the Classic Period, a different architectural style, known as Chenes, developed in some of the more northerly Maya cities, such as Hochob. While some Chenes-style structures share the same long, single-story construction as Río Bec buildings, others have strikingly different characteristics—like doorways carved in the shape of huge Chaac faces with gaping open mouths.

LATE CLASSIC PERIOD: Puuc and Northeast Yucatán

Chichén Itzá

Some of the Yucatán's most spectacular Mayan architecture was built between about AD 800 and AD 1000. By this time, the Maya had spread into territory that is now Yucatán state, and established lavish cities at Labná, Kabah, Sayil, and Uxmal—all fine examples of the Puuc architectural style. Puuc buildings were beautifully proportioned, often designed in a low-slung quadrangle shape that allowed for many rooms inside. Exterior walls were kept plain to show off the friezes above—which were embellished with stone-mosaic gods, geometric designs, and serpentine motifs. Corners were edged with gargoyle-like, curved-nose Chaac figures.

The fusion of two distinct Maya groups—the Chichén Maya and the Itzás—produced another striking architectural style. This style, known as Northeast Yucatán, is exemplified by the ruins at Chichén Itzá. Here, columns and grand colonnades were introduced. Palaces with row upon row of columns carved in the shape of serpents looked over grand patios, platforms were dedicated to the planet Venus, and pyramids were raised to honor Kukulcán (the plumed serpent god borrowed from the Toltecs, who called him Quetzalcoátl). Northeast Yucatán structures also incorporated carved stone Chacmool figures—reclining statues with offering trays carved in their midsections for sacrificial offerings.

Uxmal

▼
Between 2000 BC and AD 100, the Maya are based in lowlands of south-central Guatemala, and governed by hereditary chiefs.

2000 BC   1000

PETÉN

PRECLASSIC

POSTCLASSIC PERIOD: Quintana Roo Coast

Although Maya culture continued to flourish between AD 1000 and the early 1500s, signs of decline also began to take form. Wars broke out between neighboring city-states, leaving the region vulnerable when the Spaniards began invading in 1521. By 1600, the Spanish had dominated the Maya empire.

Mayan architecture enjoyed its last hurrah during this period, mostly in the region along the Yucatán's Caribbean coast. Known as Quintana Roo Coast architecture, this style can be seen today at the ruins of Tulum. Although the structures here aren't as visually arresting as those at earlier, inland sites, Tulum's location is breathtaking: it's the only major Maya city overlooking the sea.

Tulum

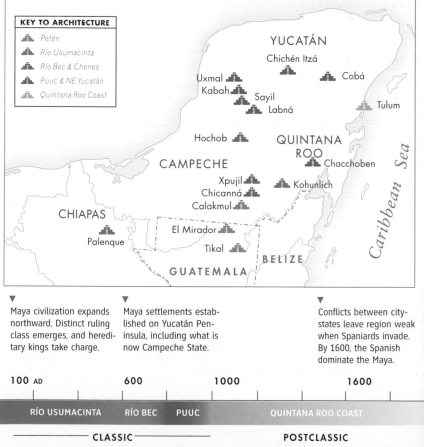

KEY TO ARCHITECTURE

- Petén
- Río Usumacinta
- Río Bec & Chenes
- Puuc & NE Yucatán
- Quintana Roo Coast

YUCATÁN

Chichén Itzá

Uxmal · Kabah · Sayil · Labná · Cobá · Tulum

Hochob

QUINTANA ROO · Chacchoben

CAMPECHE

Xpujil · Chicanná · Calakmul · Kohunlich

CHIAPAS · Palenque

El Mirador · Tikal

GUATEMALA · BELIZE

Caribbean Sea

▼ Maya civilization expands northward. Distinct ruling class emerges, and hereditary kings take charge.

▼ Maya settlements established on Yucatán Peninsula, including what is now Campeche State.

▼ Conflicts between city-states leave region weak when Spaniards invade. By 1600, the Spanish dominate the Maya.

| 100 AD | 600 | 1000 | 1600 |

RÍO USUMACINTA · RÍO BEC · PUUC · QUINTANA ROO COAST

CLASSIC · POSTCLASSIC

$ HOTEL 🏨 **Paamul Hotel and Cabañas.** This rustic resort with separate bungalows, hotel rooms, and campsites sits on a perfect white-sand beach, 12 miles south of Playa del Carmen. **Pros:** on the beach; some lovely views; nice open-air restaurant. **Cons:** need car to get around; breakfast not included. [$] *Rooms from: $95* ✉ *Carretera Cancún-Tulum, Km 85, 12 miles south of Playa del Carmen* ☎ *984/875–1053, 612/353–6825 from U.S.* 🌐 *www.paamulcabanas.com* 🛏 *12 suites, 10 cabanas, 220 RV sites, 30 campsites* 🍴 *No meals.*

NIGHTLIFE

Puerto Aventuras is far less happening than nearby Playa del Carmen or even sleepy Akumal. It's good for a sunset drink, but if you're looking for a party, head up the road to Playa.

Gringo's Cantina. Gringo's is a fun place to go for happy hour, karaoke, and free Wi-Fi. ✉ *On marina, across bridge from Dolphin Discovery* ☎ *984/105–1600, 303/719–0854 in U.S.*

SPORTS AND THE OUTDOORS

The reef here invites exploration, and there's fine diving and snorkeling, as well as the marina's dolphin center, where you can get in the water with a variety of sea creatures. On land there's tennis and golf at Omni Puerto Aventuras.

DOLPHIN SWIMS

FAMILY **Dolphin Discovery.** Dolphin Discovery lets you swim with dolphins in the closed-off waters of the marina. You can also get up close and personal with manatees, stingrays, and sea lions. Programs start at $79 and are available daily from 9 to 3:30. ✉ *On marina, Calle Bahia Xcacel* ☎ *998/193–3360 in Mexico, 866/393–5158 in U.S.* 🌐 *www.dolphindiscovery.com.*

SCUBA DIVING

Aquanuts. Aquanuts is a full-service dive shop that specializes in open-water dives, cenote dives, multitank dives, and certification courses. Dives start at $50, full courses at $445. ✉ *Calle Punta Celis, by marina* ☎ *984/873–5041, 877/623–2491 in U.S.* 🌐 *www.aquanutsdiveshop.com.*

XPU-HÁ

5 km (3 miles) south of Puerto Aventuras.

Located 20 minutes south of Playa del Carmen and 20 minutes north of Tulum, Xpu-Há is the perfect base to relax and get away from the crowds. The beach is startling white, with soft clean sand that is raked by the few boutique hotels and villas that dot the shores. Other than the Royal Catalonia Tulum, you won't find sprawling resorts taking over the area. This rather unknown stretch of paradise has recently brought in several beach clubs and restaurants, offering an alternative to the all-inclusive action. The downside however is that this hush-hush haven is now officially on the map.

GETTING HERE AND AROUND

Located between the towns of Puerto Aventuras and Akumal, Xpu-Há is at Km 265 off Carretera 307. The entrance is just south of Puerto Aventuras, after the Barceló Resort. Since Xpu-Há is simply a beach community comprised of hotels and villas, the closest services are in Puerto Aventuras to the north and Akumal to the south.

BEACHES

Chan Yu Yum. North of Tulum is a smaller bay, known as Chan Yu Yum, edging the Catalonia Royal Tulum. While it's marginally less protected than Omni Beach, it's also delightfully calm, with flat white sands melting into shallow waters great for snorkeling. Divers are likely to spot turtles, stingrays, toadfish, and perhaps even a nurse shark. Underwater currents can make diving a challenge here. **Amenities:** none. **Best for:** snorkeling; swimming. ✉ *Bahia Xcacel, near Catalonia Royal Tulum, off Carretera 307 at Km 264.5, Xpu-Há.*

La Playa. Located at Playa Xpu-Há, this beach club is open year-round from 11 to 6. Guests of nearby villas often come here for the plethora of amenities like showers, lockers, hammocks, umbrellas, and chaise longues. There is also a restaurant and a rental shop with snorkeling gear, wave runners, boogie boards, and kayaks. In full beach club tradition, you'll often have live music (Thursday–Sunday at 2:30), DJs, and a bar with swings instead of barstools. You can burn off your lunch with a game of volleyball, or opt for hair braids and henna tattoos. **Amenities:** food and drink; toilets; showers; water sports. **Best for:** swimming; walking; partiers. ✉ *Carretera 307, Km 265, Xpu-Há* ☎ *984/106–0024* 🌐 *www.laplayaxpuha.com* 🎟 *$10.*

Xpu–Há Beach. This stretch of powdery white sand is fairly isolated, other than the occasional villa and resort, including Royal Catalonia Tulum smack dab in the center. South of here are a few spots where you can grab a midday snack; La Playa Beach Club offers food, beach chairs, umbrellas, showers, lockers, hammocks, and volleyball. There are no hidden rocks in shallow areas, and the sand is like powered sugar, so many people come here to swim or snorkel, especially when the winds are calm. Resorts and beach clubs rake the sand each morning, making it a good place for an unobstructed stroll. Unlike many of the beaches that are blocked by resort security, this beach has public access off the main freeway at Km 265. **Amenities:** food and drink; showers; toilets; water sports. **Best for:** partiers; walking; swimming. ✉ *Carretera 307, Km 265, at entrance to La Playa Beach Club, Xpu-Há.*

WHERE TO STAY

For expanded reviews, facilities, and current deals, visit Fodors.com.

🏨 **Al Cielo Hotel.** On the powdery shores of Xpu-Há, this boutique inn has four chic rooms (named after the four elements) with hardwood floors, thatched roofs, and beds draped in white curtains. **Pros:** great restaurant; hospitable staff; excellent beach. **Cons:** Wi-Fi in restaurant only; not child-friendly; no TVs; beach facilities open to public. [$] *Rooms from: $160* ✉ *Carretera 307, Km 118, 1.5, Solidaridad, Xpu-Há* ☎ *984/840–9012* 🌐 *www.alcielohotel.com* 🛏 *4 rooms* 💳 *No credit cards* 🍴 *Multiple meal plans.*

$$$$ RESORT ALL-INCLUSIVE **Catalonia Royal Tulum.** This lavish, adults-only resort was designed around the surrounding jungle and has a great beach and good food for a resort in this price range, but it may not be the place for you if you don't want a nonstop environment. **Pros:** excellent beach; great diving classes; enthusiastic staff. **Cons:** pressure to join in activities; no kids under 18; no elevator; no pool bar. [$] *Rooms from: $388* ✉ *Carretera 307, Km 264.5, Xpu-Há* ☎ *984/875–1800* 🌐 *www.hoteles-catalonia.com* 🛏 *288 rooms* 🍴 *All-inclusive.*

$$$$ HOTEL Fodor's Choice ★ **Esencia Seaside Estate.** On 50 acres of jungle, this sprawling estate—once the home of an Italian duchess—has been converted into one of the most luxurious hotels in Riviera Maya. **Pros:** special discounts available through website; blackout shades; stunning beach; in-suite chefs; daily yoga. **Cons:** massages are pricey; not all rooms have ocean views; need a car to get around. [$] *Rooms from: $650* ✉ *Carretera 307, Km 265, Predio Rústico Xpu-Há lotes 18 and 19, Xpu-Há* ☎ *984/873–4830, 877/528–3490 in U.S.* 🌐 *www.hotelesencia.com* 🛏 *29 rooms* 🍴 *Multiple meal plans.*

$ B&B/INN **Organic Yoga.** It's all about yoga at this jungle property where five bungalows form a tiny village. **Pros:** reasonable rates; peaceful environment; organic garden. **Cons:** not on the beach; jungle bugs including the occasional scorpion; yoga classes are held at 8:30 am; four barking dogs on the property. [$] *Rooms from: $65* ✉ *Carretera 307, Km 256, 500 meters past Serenis Hotel, Xpu-Há* ✥ *Turn at dirt road next to Sirenis Hotel, follow signs to B&B* ☎ *984/117–1968* 🌐 *www.organicyogamexico.com* 🛏 *5 bungalows* 💳 *No credit cards* 🍴 *No meals.*

SPORTS AND THE OUTDOORS

KITE BOARDING

Morph Kiteboarding. These certified IKO instructors offer lessons starting at $225 that can be tailored for all levels. Based in Xpu-Há, they can pick you up at your hotel and go to the nearest kite-friendly location. ✉ *Carretera 307, Km 265, Xpu-Há* ☎ *984/114–9524* 🌐 *www.morphkiteboarding.com.*

SCUBA DIVING AND SNORKELING

Zero Gravity Dive Shop. This dive shop rents equipment and has a staff of experienced instructors that specialize in cave diving. ✉ *Carretera 307, Km 265, in front of Hotel Maeva, Xpu-Há* ☎ *984/840–9030 cell* 🌐 *www.zerogravity.com.mx* 🕒 *Open weekdays 8–10 and 4–6, Sat. 10–noon and 3–5.*

AKUMAL

37 km (23 miles) south of Playa del Carmen, 104 km (65 miles) south of Cancún.

In Mayan, Akumal (pronounced ah-koo-*maal*) means "place of the turtle," and this stretch of coast is a storied nesting ground, especially at Half Moon Bay. Akumal first attracted international attention in 1926, when explorers discovered the *Mantanceros*, a Spanish galleon that sank there in 1741. In the 1960s, diver Pablo Bush Romero established the Akumal Caribe resort as a place for his diving buddies to crash. The rest is history.

Today Akumal is an Americanized beach community, home to divers, fishermen, and laid-back expats from the U.S. and Canada. It's essentially a long string of upscale homes and condos strung along Akumal's three bays. Akumal Bay is the best base for visits with a good selection of hotels and restaurants and the best all-around beach for swimming and snorkeling. Half Moon Bay, just beyond, has decent snorkeling and more condos for rent, but the beach is narrow and rocky. Laguna Yalku is a protected snorkeling lagoon.

GETTING HERE AND AROUND
Akumal is an easy drive south from Puerto Aventuras or north from Tulum. The entrance to town is on the east side of the highway, so coming from the north you'll have to make a U-turn at the well-marked retorno. Coming from the south, exit at Km 264 off Carretera 307. From either direction, follow the signs to "Akumal Playa." You can also hire a taxi in Cancún—you can reduce your cost by sharing a ride with other passengers. Getting around is easy. There's only one road. It runs from the highway through the Arch—the town's gateway, at Club Akumal Caribe—and along Akumal Bay past Half Moon Bay to Laguna Yalku, a distance of about 10 minutes by car. Unlike many of the beach access roads blocked by resort security, this community entrance is open and can be entered even when a guard is stationed. Simply explain, "We're heading to the beach."

ESSENTIALS
Travel Services **TSA Akumal** ✉ *Plaza Ukana, Akumal Bay* ☎ *984/875–9030.*

EXPLORING
Akumal's tourist office is actually a small booth located in front of the Hekab Be library, on the main road before the Arch as you go into town.

FAMILY
Fodor's Choice
★
Aktun-Chen (*Indiana Joes*). Aktun-Chen is Mayan for "the cave with cenotes inside," and these amazing underground caves, estimated to be about 5 million years old, are the area's largest. You walk through the underground passages, past stalactites and stalagmites, until you reach the cenote with its various shades of deep green. There's also a canopy tour and one cenote where you can swim. This is a top family attraction, and one that's not as crowded or touristy as Xplor, Xel-Há, or Xcaret. ✉ *Carretera 307, Km 107, opposite Bahia Principe resort, between Akumal and Xel-Há* ☎ *998/881–9400* ⊕ *www.indiana-joes.com* ⚑ *$30 cave tour, $40 canopy tour, $30 cenote tour* ☉ *Mon.–Sat. 9–5.*

FAMILY
Hidden Worlds Cenotes Park. This park holds some of the Yucatán's most spectacular cenotes, made semi-famous by the 2002 IMAX film, *Journey into Amazing Caves*. You can explore these startlingly clear freshwater sinkholes, which are full of fantastic stalactites, stalagmites, and rock formations, on guided diving or snorkeling tours, or just splash into them on a zip line. To get to the cenotes, you ride in a jungle buggy through dense tropical forest from the main park entrance. You can also ride the sky cycle, a cable bicycle that glides over the abundant Mayan rain forest. Prices start at $35 for snorkeling tours, but the all-inclusive package is a better deal at $80. Two-tank diving tours are $130. Bring natural bug spray. ✉ *Carretera 307, 1.5 km (0.9 miles) south of Xel-Há, Xel-Há* ☎ *800/681–6755 from Mexico, 866/759–8726 from U.S.*

⊕ *www.rainforestadventure.com* ☉ *Daily 9–5; snorkeling tours at 9, 11, 1, and 3.*

FAMILY **Laguna Yal-kú** (*Yal-kú Lagoon*). Devoted snorkelers may want to walk or drive the unmarked dirt road to Laguna Yal-kú, a couple of miles north of Akumal in Half Moon Bay. A series of small mangrove-edged lagoons that gradually reach the ocean, Yal-kú is an eco-park that's home to schools of parrot fish in clear water with visibility to 160 feet in winter and spring. Entrance is $10 and you can rent snorkeling equipment in the parking lot for $10, a life jacket for $6, and a locker for $2. Sunscreen is not allowed, so bring a T-shirt to keep from getting sunburned. ⊹ *Located at end of main road that runs through Akumal, about 2 miles past town entrance* ☉ *Daily 8–5:30.*

FAMILY **Xel-Há.** Part of the Xcaret nature-adventure park group, Xel-Há (pronounced shel-*hah*) is a natural aquarium made from coves, inlets, and lagoons cut from the limestone shoreline. The name means "where the water is born," and a natural spring here flows out to meet the salt water, creating a unique habitat for tropical marine life. There's still enough here to impress novice snorkelers, although there seem to be fewer fish each year, and the mixture of fresh and salt water can cloud visibility. Low wooden bridges over the lagoons allow for leisurely walks around the park, and there are spots to rest or swim.

Xel-Há gets overwhelmingly crowded, so come early. The grounds are well equipped with bathrooms, restaurants, and a shop. At the entrance you'll receive specially prepared sunscreen that won't kill the fish; other sunscreens are prohibited. For an extra charge, you can swim with dolphins. There's also an all-inclusive package with a meal, a towel, a locker, and snorkel equipment for $79. Other activities like scuba diving, a sea trek, and an underwater walk, are available at an additional cost. Discounts are available when you book online. ⊠ *Carretera 307, Km 240, Xel-Há* ☎ *984/875–6000, 888/922–7381 in U.S.* ⊕ *www. xelha.com* ☉ *Daily 8:30–7.*

BEACHES

This community of divers and fishermen is a great place to get your feet wet. Beaches are safe, waters are calm, and there are roped-off swimming areas for children.

Akumal Bay. Akumal Bay is known for the sea turtles who swim in its waters, sheltered by an offshore reef. When you drag yourself away from the excellent snorkeling, there are plenty of palm trees for shade, as well as a variety of waterfront shops, restaurants, and cafés. If you continue on the main road, you'll reach Half Moon Bay and Laguna Yalkú, also good snorkeling spots. **Amenities:** food and drink, lifeguards, water sports. **Best for:** snorkeling. ⊠ *Enter at Hotel Akumal Caribe.*

X'cacel Beach. About 10 km (6 miles) south of Akumal, X'cacel Beach (also written Xca-Cel), has thick powdery sand and a nearby cenote that can be accessed through a jungle path to your right. To reach the beach from Carretera 307, turn at the dirt road that runs between Chemuyil and Xel-Há. The route is blocked by a guard who will charge you $2 to enter. Follow the dirt road that spills onto the white, sandy beach.

From May through November, this area is reserved for turtle nesting. One good resource for information is the website: www.locogringo.com/research/beaches/xcacel.html. **Amenities:** restrooms. **Best for:** snorkeling; solitude. ✉ *Carretera 307, Km 248.*

SPAS

Budha Gardens Spa. This small day spa in Akumal offers Swedish massage, reflexology, facials, body scrubs, wraps, manicures, and pedicures. After a day in the sun, try the popular Mayan clay mask, said to firm the skin and draw out impurities. Body scrub options range from mango-ginger to bamboo-walnut, while the cooling body wraps incorporate local ingredients like cucumber and lavender to rehydrate the skin. Each wrap and scrub is accompanied by a mini-facial and head massage. ✉ *Past Akumal Arch on main road, next to Hotel Club Akumal Caribe* ☎ *984/745–4942, 984/137–6947* 🌐 *www.budhagardensspa.com.*

4

WHERE TO EAT

$$ MEXICAN 🍴 **La Buena Vida.** With driftwood tables overlooking Half Moon Bay, swings at the lively bar and salsa music keeping things moving, this might be the perfect beach restaurant. The usual Mexican fare—quesadillas, empanadas, burritos, and fish tacos with handmade tortillas—is perfectly fine, but the food isn't the point. It's all about the location. Directly on the beach, this place takes full advantage with two big upstairs terraces with sweeping views of the water. Lounge chairs are scattered on the sand for customers' use, and there's a small pool to keep the kids busy while you have another margarita. Climb the ladder to the two-seater tower table, 15 feet above the sand, where your drinks are delivered in a bucket on a rope. [$] *Average main: $13* ✉ *North Akumal, main road, Lot #35, Half Moon Bay* ☎ *984/875–9061* 🌐 *www.labuenavidarestaurant.com.*

$$ SEAFOOD 🍴 **La Cueva del Pescador.** Dig your toes in the sand floor at this simple restaurant and enjoy the catch of the day. A crowd of easygoing expats hunkers down for the afternoon, feasting on octopus, shrimp, or conch ceviche prepared with lime juice and flavored with cilantro, with a generous helping of beer on the side. There's also great grilled garlic shrimp or a simple quesadilla. Servings and sides are generous, and prices are moderate. There's a pool table, too. [$] *Average main: $7* ✉ *Plaza Ukana, Main road, Akumal Bay* ☎ *984/875–9002* 💳 *No credit cards.*

$$ CAFÉ 🍴 **Turtle Bay Café & Bakery.** This funky café serves Akumal's best breakfast, with a vast menu spanning acai bowls, eggs Benedict, pancakes, and fruit plates. For lunch and dinner, you'll find blackened fish tacos, lamb burgers, and vegetable wraps. Set back from the little plaza, the garden is a pleasant place to sit and drink coffee (there's also free Wi-Fi), and its location by the ecological center makes it the closest thing Akumal has to a downtown. Smoothies, homemade ice cream, and fresh-baked goods like the chocolate peanut-butter cheesecake are tempting. If you fall in love with a local stray, the owner has set up an animal rescue program that will ship a pet directly to your home. The restaurant is open until 9 pm. [$] *Average main: $6* ✉ *Plaza Ukana, main road, Akumal Bay* ☎ *984/875–9138* 🌐 *www.turtlebaycafe.com* ⏲ *No dinner in Sept.*

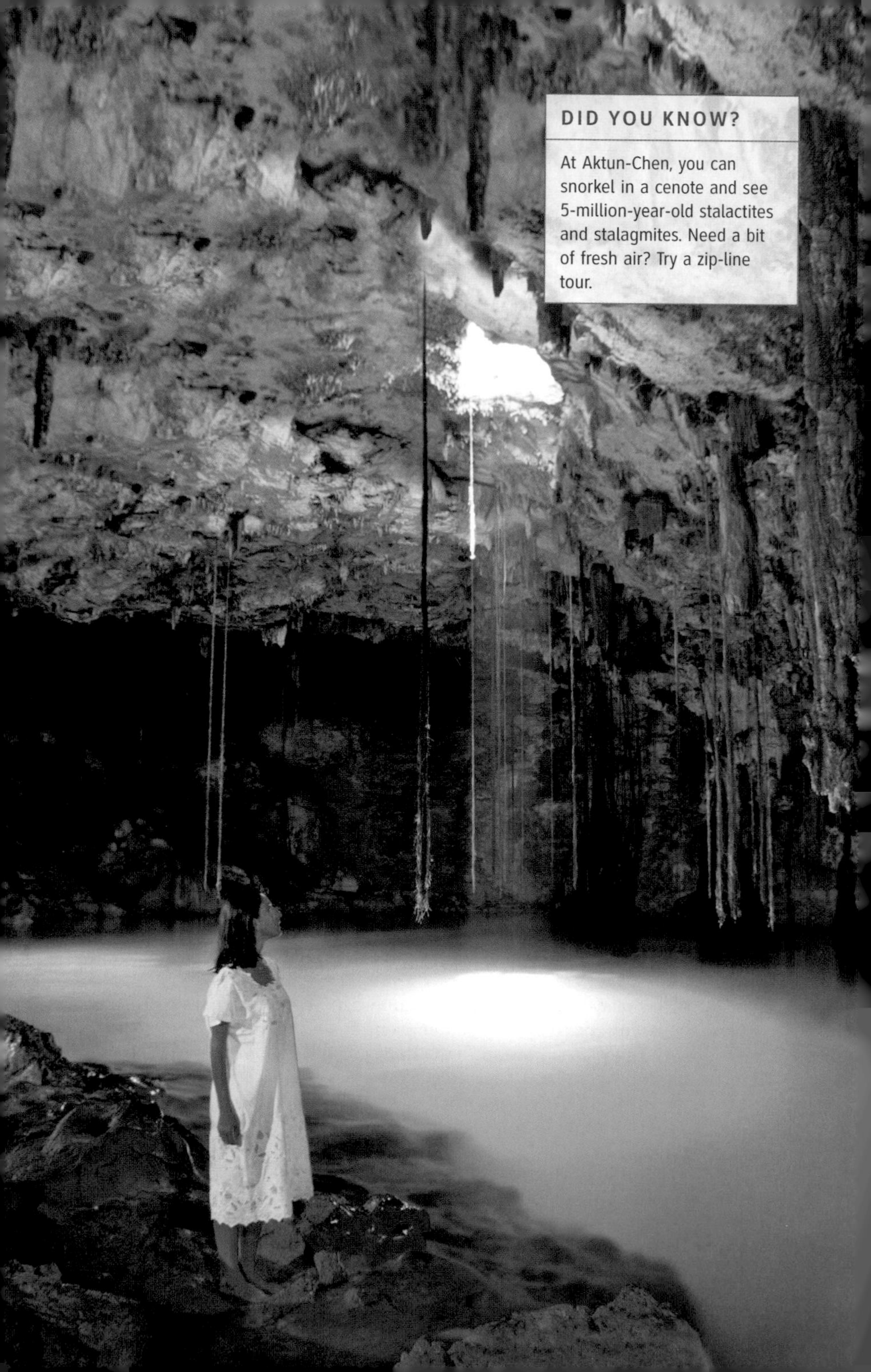

DID YOU KNOW?

At Aktun-Chen, you can snorkel in a cenote and see 5-million-year-old stalactites and stalagmites. Need a bit of fresh air? Try a zip-line tour.

WHERE TO STAY

For expanded reviews, facilities, and current deals, visit Fodors.com.

$$$$ RESORT ALL-INCLUSIVE **Grand Bahía Princípe.** This upscale all-inclusive is a mega-complex consisting of three hotels (Akumal, Cobá, Tulum, all of which have good food) with extensive shared facilities. **Pros:** on the beach; attentive staff; good food. **Cons:** beach is rocky; no Internet in rooms; some rooms are worn. [$] *Rooms from: $444* ✉ *Carretera 307, Km 250* ☎ *984/875–5000, 866/282–2442 in U.S.* 🌐 *www.bahiaprincipeusa.com* 🛏 *858 rooms* 🍴 *All-inclusive.*

$$ HOTEL **Hotel Club Akumal Caribe.** Back in the 1960s, Pablo Bush Romero established this resort as a place for his diving buddies to crash, and it still offers pleasant, if somewhat dated, accommodations and a congenial staff. **Pros:** reasonable rates; on the beach; easy snorkeling. **Cons:** basic decor; sometimes a bit noisy; no elevator. [$] *Rooms from: $150* ✉ *At Akumal Arch, main road, Akumal Bay* ☎ *984/206–3500* 🌐 *www.hotelakumalcaribe.com* 🛏 *21 rooms, 40 bungalows, 4 villas, 1 condo* 🍴 *Breakfast.*

$$ RESORT **Vista Del Mar.** Each small room in the main building here has an ocean view, a private terrace, and colorful Guatemalan-Mexican accents; next door are more expensive condos with Spanish-colonial touches. **Pros:** on beach; all rooms have Wi-Fi and ocean views; well-kept grounds. **Cons:** beach is a little rocky; beds aren't very comfortable; no meals. [$] *Rooms from: $95* ✉ *Half Moon Bay, Lot #40A, south end* ☎ *984/875–9060, 505/992–3333 in U.S., 866/425–8625 toll-free* 🌐 *www.akumalinfo.com* 🛏 *16 rooms, 16 condos* 🍴 *No meals.*

SHOPPING

Galería Lamanai. Galería Lamanai is a laid-back gallery under a palapa roof. There's a real mix of folk art and fine art from Mexican and international artists. ✉ *Club Akumal Caribe, Akumal Bay* ☎ *984/875–9055* 🌐 *www.galerialamanai.com.*

Mexicarte. Mexicarte is a little shop that sells high-quality crafts from around the country. ✉ *Next to Club Akumal Caribe, main road, Akumal Bay* ☎ *984/875–9115* 🌐 *www.akumalart.com.*

SPORTS AND THE OUTDOORS

BICYCLING

Akumal Guide. The small booth inside Hotel Club Akumal Caribe rents bikes for $8 as well as golf carts for $20 for four hours. Golf carts are a very popular way to get around Akumal. ✉ *Main road, inside Hotel Club Akumal Caribe* ☎ *984/875–9251, 984/875–9115* 🌐 *www.akumalguide.com.*

SCUBA DIVING AND SNORKELING

Akumal Dive Center. The Akumal Dive Center is the area's oldest dive operation, offering reef or cenote diving, fishing, and snorkeling. Dives cost from $40 (one tank) to $130 (four tanks); a three-hour fishing trip for up to four people runs $180. Take a sharp right at the Akumal arches and you'll see the dive shop on the beach. ✉ *Club Akumal Caribe, Akumal Bay* ☎ *984/875–9025* 🌐 *www.akumaldivecenter.com.*

FAMILY Fodor's Choice ★ **Akumal Dive Shop** (*TSA, Travel Services of Akumal*). This dive shop, which also operates as TSA Travel Agency, organizes daytime and sunset catamaran cruises for $95 per person. You can snorkel with the turtles ($25) or dive at two nearby cenotes ($140). Certification courses as well as specialized programs for kids are also available. ✉ *Plaza Ukana, North Akumal Bay* ☎ *984/875–9030* 🌐 *www.akumaldiveshop.com.*

TANKAH

19 km (12 miles) south of Akumal, 4 km (2.5 miles) north of Tulum.

If you plan on staying in the Cobá area, nearby Tankah is a good option, especially if you want to avoid the Tulum crowds. In ancient times Tankah was an important Mayan trading city. A number of small, reasonably priced hotels have cropped up here over the past few years, and several expats who own villas in the area rent them out year-round.

GETTING HERE AND AROUND

To reach the coastal road in Tankah, turn east off Carretera 307 at Km 237 (a faded green sign marks the turning point). At the end of the long, pitted road, turn left (north) where a string of villas and small hotels parallel the beach. Tankah is approximately 90 minutes south of Cancún. The closest Internet cafés, medical clinics, grocery stores, and emergency services are in Tulum.

BEACHES

Often overlooked by travelers, this spectacular stretch of coastline offers great snorkeling, diving, and best of all, isolation. What makes this area unique is the cenote that tunnels under the beach road and spills into the sea. The closest dive shops, however, are in Tulum, which means divers will have to organize their own equipment for undersea excursions.

Tankah Bay. Nestled in a protected cove, this wide stretch of beach is popular with divers and snorkelers due to the outer reef that keeps waters calm. The fine sand is perfect for a barefoot stroll, but the shallow waters have sharp rocks just below the surface. Just across the road from Casa Cenote Restaurant is Manatee Cenote, an underwater cave that spills from the mangroves into the sea. This freshwater pool, coupled with the outer reef, make Tankah a snorkeler's paradise. The main draw is that this area is relatively isolated because most sun worshippers tend to bask on the shores of Playa del Carmen. **Amenities:** food and drink; toilets. **Best for:** snorkeling; solitude; walking. ✉ *Tankah Bay.*

WHERE TO EAT

$$ ECLECTIC 🍴 **Restaurante Oscar y Lalo.** Though technically in Tulum, this wonderful palapa restaurant with a pebble floor and a peaceful garden is actually a couple of miles outside Tankah, alone on Carretera 307. The seafood is excellent here, although a bit pricey. Lalo's Special, a dish made with local lobster, shrimp, conch, and fish, and the chicken fajitas, prepared for 2 to 10 people, are standouts. The ceviche made of fresh fish and lobster, and the *caracol* (snails) with citrus juice are also exceptional. [$] *Average main: $14* ✉ *Carretera 307, Km 241* ✣ *Look for large billboard and Mayan sculptures* ☎ *984/127–1587 cell* 🌐 *www.oscarandlalo.com.*

WHERE TO STAY

For expanded reviews, facilities, and current deals, visit Fodors.com.

$$$ B&B/INN **Casa Cenote Hotel.** Located across from the cenote for which it's named, this peaceful property offers beach bungalows, a luxury villa, and rustic casitas. **Pros:** on the beach; close to cenote; excellent food; pet-friendly with extra deposit. **Cons:** need a car to get around; many services for bungalows only; Wi-Fi in common areas only. [$] *Rooms from: $175* ✉ *Interior Fraccionamento Tankah, Lote 32 Manzana 3, across from Cenote Manatee* ☎ *984/115–6996* 🌐 *www.casacenote.com* 🛏 *7 bungalows, 1 villa, 2 casitas* 🍴 *Multiple meal plans.*

$$$ HOTEL FAMILY **Jashita.** This sophisticated small beach hotel at the northern end of Soliman Bay has got style in spades, offers a surprisingly child-friendly atmosphere, and sits on a beautiful beach. **Pros:** kid-friendly, shallow bay; better facilities than you can get in Tulum; very private. **Cons:** mediocre and expensive restaurant; poor Wi-Fi; bay in some places too shallow for swimming; only seven rooms have ocean views. [$] *Rooms from: $380* ✉ *Bahia de Soliman, Tankah Rd IV, across Carretera 307 from Restaurante Oscar y Lalo* ☎ *984/139–5131 cell* 🌐 *www.jashitahotel.com* 🛏 *16 rooms* 🍴 *Breakfast.*

SPORTS AND THE OUTDOORS

Due to the outer reef, calm bay, and connecting cenote, Tankah has become a popular dive spot. The closest dive shop is Maya Dive Center; however, most dive shops along Riviera Maya can organize trips to Tankah.

Cenote Manatee (*Casa Cenote*). Directly across from Casa Cenote Hotel, this open lagoon (often referred to as Casa Cenote) is popular with cave divers because a freshwater tunnel—dropping below the main road—connects directly to the ocean. Here two ecosystems collide with both fresh and saltwater, offering a maximum diving depth of 26 feet. The constant currents draw in a variety of marine life including parrotfish, swimming crabs, moray eels, juvenile barracuda, and tarpon. Only experienced divers should enter the underwater cave since the distance between the cenote and ocean is dangerously long. There is a small parking lot but no facilities other than those at neighboring hotels and restaurants. ✉ *Interior Fraccionamento Tankah, Caribe Lote 32 Manzana 3, across from Casa Cenote Hotel* 🎟 *$5.*

Gorgonian Gardens. The Gorgonian Gardens, located about 60 feet below the outer reef, have made Tankah a particular destination for divers thanks to the offshore underwater environment. From southern Tankah to Bahía de Punta Soliman, the sand-free ocean floor has allowed for the proliferation of Gorgonians, or soft corals—sea fans, candelabras, and fingers that can reach 5 feet in height—as well as a variety of colorful sponges. Fish love to feed here, and so many of them swarm the gardens that some divers have compared the experience to being surrounded by clouds of butterflies. Although this underwater habitat goes on for miles, Tankah is the best place to access it. ✉ *In front of Tankah Inn, just south of Casa Cenote.*

Maya Dive Center. As Tankah's only dive shop, this outfitter offers diving and snorkeling trips to local reefs and cenotes. This is the only dive shop in the area to use a training pool for certification courses. ⊠ *Tankah Inn, Carretera 307, Km 234, Lote 16, Bahia Tankah Tres* ☏ *984/871–3333, 998/112–1805* ⊕ *www.mayadiving.com.*

TULUM

61 km (38 miles) southwest of Playa del Carmen.

It used to be that Tulum was simply known as a Mayan archaeological site and dusty little town with a few palapa huts scattered along a 7-mile stretch of luscious beach. No longer. Discovered by the international eco-set, Tulum now has whitewashed, solar-powered bungalow hotels that line the spectacular powdery white beach 2 km (1 mile) east of town. Chichi boutiques and organic jungle restaurants quickly followed. In the last few years, tourist dollars have opened a new hospital, a giant supermarket, and the town's first luxury resort, an anomaly in a protected beach town that still generates its own electricity. Locals speak of a battle for the town's bohemian soul, and although first-time visitors may not notice the changes, it's indisputable that Tulum's free-spirited hippie days are over.

Tulum is divided into three main areas: the downtown pueblo, south from the shore along Carretera 307 (here known as Avenida Tulum); the Mayan ruins to the north on the coast; and the beach (Zona Hotelera), which stretches from the ruins down along the Carretera Tulum-Boca Paila to the Sian Ka'an Biosphere Reserve.

The spectacular ruins here are the town's original attraction, and Tulum, which means "wall" in Mayan, is still the Yucatán Peninsula's most-visited Mayan site, attracting more than 2 million people annually. Even if you couldn't care less about the Maya, the site's location—above a sugar-white beach on an emerald cove—elevates it to the sublime.

The pueblo is an authentic jumble of food stalls, souvenir shops, budget hotels, and cheap restaurants, some catering to tourists, some to locals, and some to both. Although it's more appealing to stay at the beach, the town offers an authentic slice of Mexico, as well as some good bargain hotels for those on the strictest of budgets and restaurants. From here, walk the 2 km (1 mile) to the archaeological site entrance, rent a bike, or catch one of the shuttles that pass every few minutes. If you stay in town, you'll need a car or taxi to get to the beach.

A mile east of downtown on the Boca Paila road, Tulum's irresistible beach begins. (Technically there's beach all the way from the ruins down to Sian Ka'an, but the coast by the ruins, and south to Zamas restaurant, is a series of rocky coves. The endless powder-sand beach you came for is south of the bridge and police checkpoint after Zamas.) Miles of magnificent white sand sparkles before the aquamarine waves, backed by Robinson Crusoe–balconied eco-hotels on one side of the narrow road, and tropical hipster restaurants, yoga centers, and the odd spa on the other.

Tulum's ongoing transformation has brought new services to the pueblo and the beach area, and now there's a 24-hour hospital in town and a new Pemex gas station, OXXO convenience store, and Chedraui supermarket at the beginning of the beach road. There's no community power supply here, so eco-resorts rustic and chic make their own, with wind turbines, solar renewable energy, recycled water, and generators and/or candlelight—come prepared for low lighting and low water pressure. Some hotels draw water from nearby cenotes, which might result in a salty shower.

GETTING HERE AND AROUND
Tulum is a 20-minute drive from Akumal and a 45-minute drive from Playa del Carmen. You can hire a taxi from Cancún for approximately $80.

Tucan Kin has a direct shuttle service from Cancún airport for $24 per person one-way. Roberto Solis of Bob Transfers offers transportation between Cancún and Tulum for $85 one-way (up to five passengers).

Buses don't serve the hotel zone, so travelers must rely on taxis, cars, or bikes to get around. If you plan on driving, watch carefully for the large beach crabs that cross the roads after dark.

To reach Tulum's beachfront hotel area, head south on Carretera 307 and turn left (east) at the second stoplight in Tulum. Shortly after passing the fire station, you'll come to a "T" in the road. There you'll find dozens of signs directing travelers to hotels; the best beach is to the right, and the ruins are to the left.

Bus Contacts Tulum Bus Terminal. The main Bus Terminal for ADO, Mayab, OCC, ATS, and Oriente is in the center of downtown next to Charlie's Restaurant. ⊠ *El Centro.*

Taxi Contacts Tucan Kin. ☎ 984/871–3538 ⊕ *www.tucankin.com.* **Bob Transfers.** ☎ 984/133–5774 ✉ *bobviajes@hotmail.com.*

EXPLORING

Fodor's Choice ★ **Tulum.** Tulum is one of the few Mayan cities known to have been inhabited when the conquistadores arrived in 1518. In the 16th century it was a trade center, a safe harbor for trade goods from rival Mayan factions who considered the city neutral territory. The city reached its height when its merchants, made wealthy through trading, for the first time outranked Maya priests in authority and power. But when the Spaniards arrived, they forbade the Maya traders to sail the seas, and commerce among the Maya died.

Tulum has long held special significance for the Maya as a symbol of resistance and independence. A key city in the League of Mayapán (AD 987–1194), it was never conquered by the Spaniards, although it was abandoned by the Maya about 75 years after the conquest of the rest of Mexico. For 300 years thereafter it symbolized the defiance of an otherwise subjugated people, and it was one of the last outposts of the Maya during their insurrection against Mexican rule in the War of the Castes, which began in 1846. Uprisings continued intermittently until 1935, when the Maya ceded Tulum to the Mexican government.

■**TIP→** At the entrance to the ruins you can hire a guide for $25, but keep in mind that some of their information is more entertainment than historical accuracy. (Disregard that stuff about virgin sacrifices.)

Although you can see the ruins thoroughly in two hours, you might want to allow extra time for a swim or a stroll on the beach.

The first significant structure is the two-story **Templo de los Frescos**, to the left of the entryway. The temple's vault roof and corbel arch are examples of classic Mayan architecture. Faint traces of blue-green frescoes outlined in black on the inner and outer walls depict the three worlds of the Maya and their major deities, and are decorated with stellar and serpentine patterns, rosettes, and ears of maize and other offerings to the gods. One scene portrays the rain god seated on a four-legged animal—probably a reference to the Spaniards on their horses. Unfortunately, the frescos are difficult to see from the path to which visitors are restricted.

The largest and most-photographed structure, the **Castillo** (Castle), looms at the edge of a 40-foot limestone cliff just past the Temple of the Frescoes. Atop it, at the end of a broad stairway, is a temple with stucco ornamentation on the outside and traces of fine frescoes inside the two chambers. (The stairway has been roped off, so the top temple is inaccessible.) The front wall of the Castillo has faint carvings of the Descending God and columns depicting the plumed serpent god, Kuku-lcán, who was introduced to the Maya by the Toltecs. To the left of the Castillo, facing the sea, is the **Templo del Díos Descendente**—so called for the carving over the doorway of a winged god plummeting to earth.

A few small altars sit atop a hill at the north side of the cove, with a good view of the Castillo and the sea. ■**TIP**➔ To avoid the longest lines, be sure to arrive before 11 am. ⊠ *Carretera 307, Km 133, Tulum* ☎ *983/837–2411* ✉ *$5 entrance, $3 parking, $4 video fee, $1.50 shuttle from parking to ruins* ☉ *Daily 8–4:30.*

BEACHES

Tulum Beach. The 7 miles of Tulum's main beach are a tropical paradise of glassy water and powdery sand, set off from the jungle by dunes and, increasingly, low-slung bungalow hotels where the yoga set take their virtuous rest. It's divided by a bridge and rocky promontory into two main sections, similar to each other, although the farther south you go on the Carretera Tulum-Boca Paila beach road, the more secluded and lovelier it gets. The beach is bordered on the south by Sian Ka'an biosphere reserve, whose coast is more deserted yet. **Amenities:** food and drink; toilets; water sports. **Best for:** swimming; walking. ⊠ *Carretera Tulum-Boca Paila.*

Tulum Ruins Beach. Talk about a beach with a view! At Tulum's archaeological site, the Caribbean's signature white sand and turquoise waters are framed by a backdrop of Mayan pyramids. The small cove can get crowded, especially during peak season when travelers flock to the ruins for a day of sightseeing. The south end by the rocks tends to have more breathing room. Only those who purchase a ticket to the ruins can access this beach, unless of course you approach the shores by boat. **Amenities:** none. **Best for:** swimming. ⊠ *Carretera 307, Km 130.*

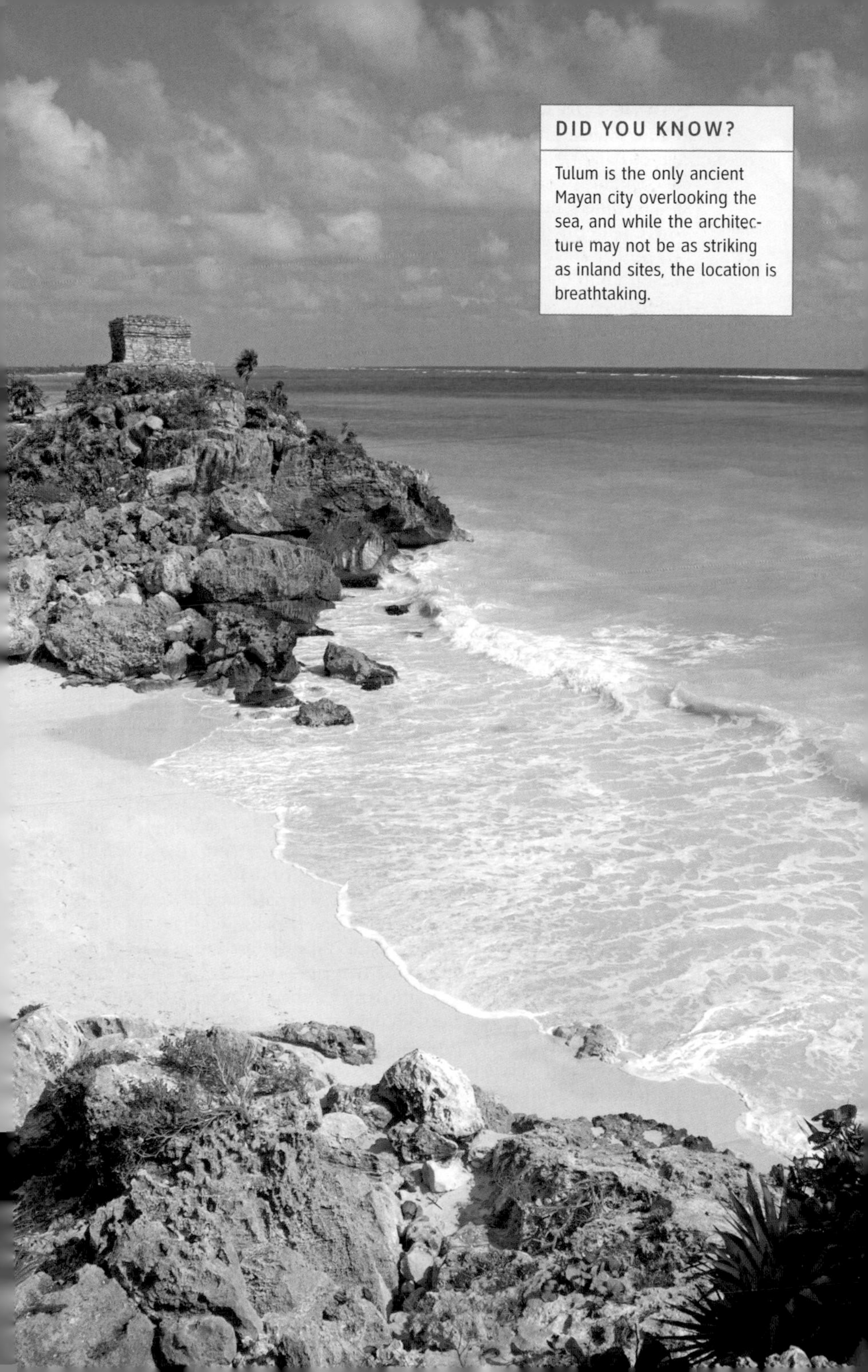

DID YOU KNOW?

Tulum is the only ancient Mayan city overlooking the sea, and while the architecture may not be as striking as inland sites, the location is breathtaking.

WHERE TO EAT

$$

ASIAN FUSION

✗ **Casa Jaguar.** This hipster hangout has a bohemian feel more reminiscent of Bali or Thailand than Mexico, but the eclectic cuisine and tropical cocktails (written on a chalkboard menu) are what keep this jungle spot on diners' most wanted list. Setting the scene is an über-chill garden where lanterns, birdcages, and dream catchers hang above candlelit tables. The smell of incense blends with a mélange of flavorful dishes like zucchini curry soup, squid ink risotto with mussels, and grilled fish topped with goat cheese, pine nuts, and passion fruit. The service is in line with the vibe, meaning that the staff is actually *tranquilo* as opposed to apathetic. $ *Average main: $25* ✉ *Carretera Tulum–Boca Paila, Km 7.5, Zona Hotelera* ☎ *984/155–2328 cell* ▬ *No credit cards.*

$

SEAFOOD

✗ **El Camello Jr.** By the time you get to this local favorite at the very end of Tulum's downtown strip, you'll think you've already left town. In fact, you've just arrived. This is Tulum's lunch time favorite, famed for the freshest seafood in town, and the jammed parking lot is testament to its enduring popularity. Fish or shrimp tacos are light and fresh, but the full splendor of the place is expressed by its whole grilled or fried fish, served with generous mounds of rice, beans, and plátanos. The lively scene and tropical ambience are a Mexican original. $ *Average main: $6* ✉ *Av. Tulum and Av. Luna, at back end of town* ▬ *No credit cards* ☉ *Closed Wed.*

$$

MODERN
MEXICAN

Fodor's Choice

★

✗ **El Tábano.** This jungle-side hangout founded in 2008 by Barcelona chef Laura Brea brings imaginative cuisine to a rustic, candlelit garden. You could spend the day here at a country-kitchen table: farm eggs and homemade bread with mango honey jam for breakfast; papaya tomato gazpacho for lunch; and fresh grouper in a *pipian* pumpkin-seed sauce or *chile ancho* stuffed with shrimp and nuts, served in a steaming clay pot, for dinner. Paying tribute to local blends is the wine list, on which 80% of the bottles are from Mexico. An international crowd of locals, expat residents, and in-the-know vacationers makes for a lively scene, especially at night. For large parties, book ahead. $ *Average main: $13* ✉ *Carretera Tulum-Boca Paila, Km 7* ☎ *984/134–3725 cell, 984/134–2706* ⊕ *www.eltabanorestaurant.com* ▬ *No credit cards.*

$$$

ECLECTIC

✗ **Ginger.** With its red walls, exotic menu, martini bar, and metropolitan vibe, this chic restaurant was the first to take Tulum dining to a whole new level. Flavorful starters include tropical ceviche, goat-cheese tart, and spinach salad with cherry tomatoes and bacon. Select from entrées like fettuccine al pesto with grilled peppers and portobello mushrooms or grouper fillet topped with passion fruit. Fresh herbs are grown on-site and the chef purchases fish directly from the local fishermen each morning. Save room for the sweet fruit flambé and vanilla ice cream. This is a great spot to relax with a martini, listen to chill-out music, and meet some locals. $ *Average main: $16* ✉ *Calle Polar Poniente, between Satelite and Centauro, next to Donususa* ☎ *984/116–4033* ⊕ *www.gingertulum.com* ☉ *Closed Sun. No lunch.*

$$$

ECLECTIC

Fodor's Choice

★

✗ **Hartwood.** New York chefs cooking New York food for New York prices—in a wood-fired jungle lot, open to the night sky—that's Hartwood. Big-city transplants Mya Henry and Eric Werner opened this solar-powered restaurant in 2011, and it has been drawing a full house

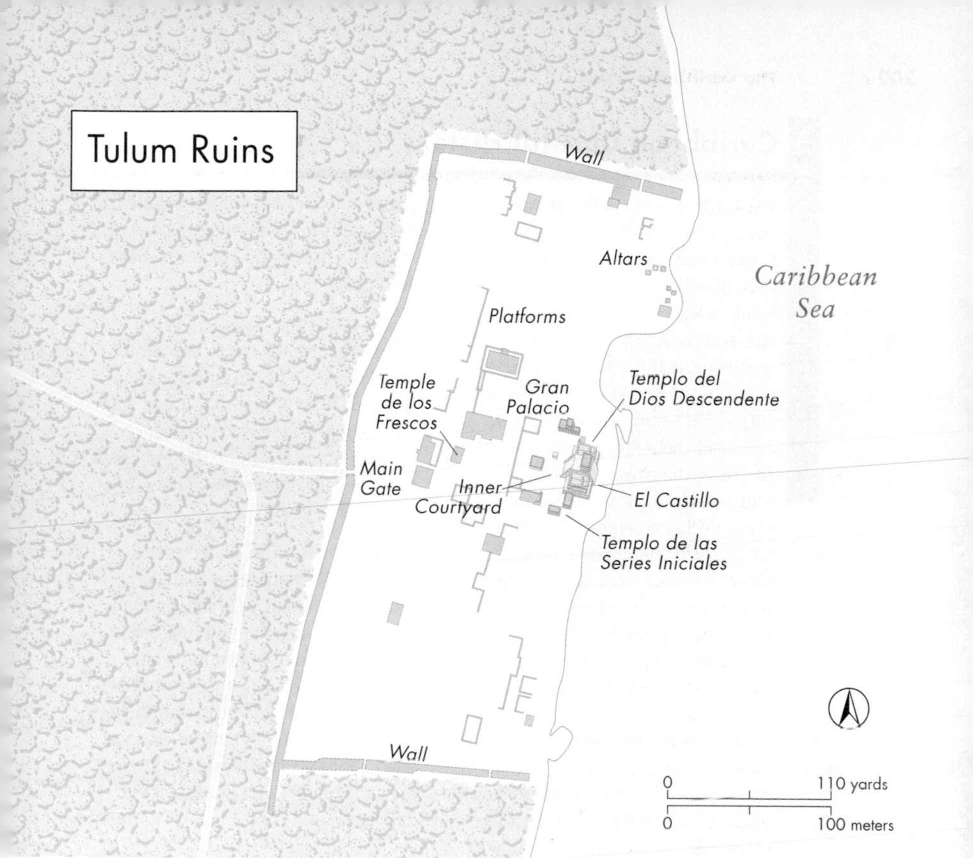
Tulum Ruins
Wall
Altars
Caribbean Sea
Platforms
Temple de los Frescos
Gran Palacio
Templo del Dios Descendente
Main Gate
Inner Courtyard
El Castillo
Templo de las Series Iniciales
Wall
0
110 yards
0
100 meters

and raves ever since. Try slow-roasted pork ribs, cooked overnight, or a marinated beet and Gorgonzola salad. Or go local with jicama, Caribbean lobster, or sea bass just a few hours out of the ocean. Chef Werner recently added farming to his list of talents, and he is now serving his own chipotle rabbit sausage. The setting of picnic tables on a white pebble floor is remarkably charming, as is the presentation of dishes served in cast-iron skillets and desserts in mason jars. The open kitchen and massive oven make for a dramatic, fiery show when the sun goes down. But in high season, get here when the dining room opens, at 6, or risk a New York–style wait, too. [$] *Average main: $25* ✉ *Carretera Tulum–Boca Paila, Km 7.6* 🌐 *www.hartwoodtulum.com* 💳 *No credit cards* 🕒 *Closed Mon., Tues., and Sept. 1–Oct. 15. No lunch.*

$$ MEXICAN 🍴 **Los Aguachiles.** The Tulum outpost of the Playa hipster cantina is at the edge of town, but it's worth the drive for a fresh, light take on traditional tacos and *mariscos* and seafood served with lots of lime, chile sauce, and creativity. Batter-fried shrimp on a bed of hydroponic lettuce, grouper with avocado and cucumber and lots of lime, and tacos de pescado are all good bets. After lunch, try your hand at the foosball table in back, but you can't while the night away here—it's only open from 12:30 to 6:30. [$] *Average main: $5* ✉ *Av. Tulum at Av. Palenque* ☎ *984/802–5482* 🕒 *Closed Mon.*

Caribbean Coastal History

The Mayan culture is the enduring backdrop for Mexico's Caribbean Coast. Archaeologists have divided this civilization, which lasted some 3,000 years, into three main periods: preclassic and late preclassic together (2000 BC–AD 100), classic (AD 100–1000), and postclassic (AD 1000–1521). Considered the most advanced civilization of the ancient Americas, the Maya are credited with several major breakthroughs: a highly accurate calendar based on astronomical study; the mathematical concept of zero; hieroglyphic writing; and extraordinary ceremonial architecture. Although the Maya's early days were centered on the lowlands in the south-central region of Guatemala, Mayan culture spread north to the Yucatán Peninsula sometime around AD 987. Tulum, which was built during this period, is the only ancient Mayan city constructed right on the water.

Until the 1960s, Quintana Roo (a Mexican territory, not a state) was considered the wildest coast in Central America. The Caste Wars of the Yucatán, which began in 1847 and ended with a halfhearted truce in 1935, herded hardy Maya to this remote region. With the exception of

chicleros (men who tapped zapote or chicle trees for the Wrigley Chewing Gum Corporation), few non-Maya lived here.

By the 1950s the Mexican government began giving tracts of land to the chicleros in hopes of colonizing Quintana Roo. At that time there were no roads. A few cocals, or coconut plantations, were scattered throughout the peninsula, headed by a handful of Maya families.

In 1967 the Mexican government decided to develop an international tourist destination, and was on the hunt for the location with the finest beaches, the most beautiful water, and the fewest hurricanes. A stretch of unpopulated sand at the northeast tip of the Yucatán Peninsula was the lucky winner. Soon after Cancún was born, Quintana Roo became Mexico's 31st state.

In 2000, the beaches south of Cancún were rebranded as the Riviera Maya. This 96-km (60-mile) region stretching south from Puerto Morelos to Tulum developed into one of the world's most popular beach destinations, with Playa del Carmen becoming the fastest-growing city in Latin America.

$$$ ✕**Mezzanine Thai.** People come from Playa del Carmen for the zingy
THAI   flavors of this authentic Thai restaurant. Recipes start with homegrown basil, chile, mint, and lemongrass, which are grown from seeds brought over from Thailand. The spiciness of the soups and curries (made with house-made coconut milk) are rated as "Tourist," "Expatriate," and "Truly Thai." For something a bit milder, try the sweet-and-sour chicken, fish, or shrimp. Also available are salads, Thai noodles, and grilled fish wrapped in banana leaves. The Asian parasols and red decor complete the setting. This place can get loud on Friday nights when a live DJ spins poolside. $ *Average main: $10* ✉ *Carretera Tulum–Boca Paila, Km 1.5, Zona Hotelera* ☎ *984/131–1596 cell* ⊕ *www.mezzanine. com.mx.*

$$$ MODERN MEXICAN

🍴 **Ziggy's Restaurant.** Named after the owner's dog, this restaurant has tables under a palapa roof and on the beach, making it the perfect place to sink your toes in the sand while you dine. Chef Jorge Hidalgo offers understated appetizers including tuna nachos (tuna tartare and avocado with tortilla strips) and coconut shrimp (dipped in piña colada and topped with mango). Veggie fans will love the creative salads made with locally produced ingredients like jicama, beets, and paprika-lemon vinaigrette. The fish is about as fresh as it gets, and the kitchen will even cook up your daily catch. By day, the menu focuses on lighter fare like sandwiches and wraps, and by night the attention turns to beef fillet with black truffles and short ribs cooked for eight hours. Above all, save room for the crème brûlée served in a pineapple. [$] *Average main: $20* ✉ *The Beach Tulum, Carretera Tulum-Boca Paila, Km 7, Zona Hotelera* ☎ *984/157–5569* 🌐 *www.thebeach-tulum.com.*

4

WHERE TO STAY

For expanded reviews, facilities, and current deals, visit Fodors.com.

$$$$ HOTEL Fodor's Choice ★

🏨 **Be Tulum.** Designed by owner-architect Sebastian Sas, this chic beachfront hotel is like stepping onto a beautifully executed canvas—each room is a pure work of art, with Brazilian wood floors, cowhide rugs, marble bathrooms, and outdoor showers. **Pros:** most upscale resort in Tulum; garden showers; excellent restaurant. **Cons:** no kids under 12; ground-level rooms get noise from above; only two rooms have ocean views. [$] *Rooms from: $403* ✉ *Carretera Tulum-Boca Paila, Km 10, Zona Hotelera* ☎ *984/132–6215* 🌐 *www.behoteles.com* 🛏 *20 rooms* 🍽 *Breakfast.*

$$$ HOTEL Fodor's Choice ★

🏨 **El Pez.** Perched on the shores of Turtle Cove, this chic boutique hotel has elevated rooms with private balconies that catch the ocean breeze. **Pros:** unlimited bottled water; gourmet breakfast included in the rate; saltwater pool. **Cons:** some rooms get street noise; several open-plan bathrooms don't have doors; beach not great for swimming. [$] *Rooms from: $230* ✉ *Carretera Tulum–Boca Paila, Km 6.4, at Turtle Cove, Zona Hotelera* ☎ *984/116–3357* 🌐 *www.tulumhotelpez.com* 🛏 *6 rooms, 6 cabanas* 🍽 *Breakfast.*

$$ RESORT

🏨 **La Vita e Bella Beachfront Bungalows.** Perched on sand dunes above the sea, this small Italian resort has lodgings that are rustic but also very comfortable. **Pros:** on the beach; laid-back atmosphere; nice restaurant. **Cons:** electricity is limited; mosquitoes at dusk; needs a renovation; Wi-Fi in common areas only. [$] *Rooms from: $135* ✉ *Carretera Tulum Ruinas, Km 1.5, Zona Hotelera* ☎ *984/151–4723* 🌐 *www.lavitaebella-tulum.com* 🛏 *22 bungalows* 🍽 *Breakfast.*

$$$ RESORT

🏨 **La Zebra.** On a pristine beach, the palapa rooms of this jungle-chic hotel have king-size beds draped in white satin. **Pros:** authentic Mexican food; on-site tequila bar; environmentally conscious; free salsa lessons 6 to 7 pm on Sunday. **Cons:** usually booked three months in advance; no Internet in rooms. [$] *Rooms from: $210* ✉ *Carretera Tulum–Boca Paila, Km 8.2, Zona Hotelera* ☎ *303/578–1301 from U.S., 984/115–4726* 🌐 *www.lazebratulum.com* 🛏 *16 rooms* 🍽 *No meals.*

$$$ HOTEL

🏨 **Mezzanine.** Music lovers will enjoy this small, hip hotel where DJs mix lounge and house music on the patio. **Pros:** Great Thai restaurant; DVD library; two-for-one margaritas daily from 1 to 4; rates drop

50% in low season. **Cons:** small pool area gets crowded; some rooms lack view; noisy on weekends; no kids under 16. $ *Rooms from: $220* ⊠ *Carretera Tulum–Boca Paila, Km 1.5* ☎ 984/136–9154 ⊕ *www. mezzaninetulum.com* ⟿ *7 rooms, 2 suites* �’❁❍ *No meals.*

$$$
HOTEL
🍴 **Playa Azul.** This beachfront confection brings together the best of Tulum's rapidly changing worlds, a solar-powered art-filled compound with killer margaritas and style to spare. **Pros:** live music Tuesday and Thursday nights; stylish rooms at reasonable prices; good restaurant. **Cons:** lots of stairs; booked solid in high season; only four rooms have ocean views. $ *Rooms from: $275* ⊠ *Carretera Tulum–Boca Paila, Km 8, Zona Hotelera* ☎ 984/157–4829 *cell* ⊕ *www.playaazultulum.com* ⟿ *22 rooms* ❁❍ *Breakfast.*

$$
HOTEL
🍴 **Zamas.** On the wild Punta Piedra (Rock Point), this hotel has rustic, freestanding bungalows with palapa roofs and ocean views as far as the eye can see. **Pros:** great restaurant; unspoiled views. **Cons:** rocky beach; some traffic noise; tiny rooms; Wi-Fi in restaurant only. $ *Rooms from: $195* ⊠ *Carretera Tulum–Boca Paila, Km 5, Zona Hotelera* ☎ 984/877–8523 ⊕ *www.zamas.com* ⟿ *24 cabanas* ❁❍ *No meals.*

NIGHTLIFE

Bar Pepenero. Located in the heart of downtown Tulum, this hookah bar has live music and strong cocktails like the "Pepenero Custom" made with local mezcal. It's open Monday through Saturday from 8 pm to 2 am. ⊠ *Av. Tulum, between Jupiter and Acuario Sur, Mza 4 Lote 1* ☎ 984/135–1093 ⊗ *Closed Sun.*

La Gran Mosca Verde. This hip little bar in downtown Tulum has a terrific mix of live music, local DJs, eccentric art, and cult classics projected on the big screen. The delicious tapas and creative cocktails make a nice accompaniment. Cash only. ⊠ *Calle Venus, between Orion Sur and Beta Sur, s/n Lote 19 Mz 33, El Centro* ☎ 984/151–5715 ⊗ *Closed Mon. and Tues.*

La Zebra. Get your hips ready for "Salsa Sundays" at this beachfront hot spot, where you can hear live music and enjoy cocktails made with their own sugar cane. You can brush up on your dance moves with free salsa lessons at 6 pm. ⊠ *Carretera Tulum–Boca Paila, Km 8.2, Zona Hotelera, Tulum* ☎ 303/578–1301 ⊕ *www.lazebratulum.com.*

Papaya Playa Project. Party people gather at this beachfront nightclub where DJs spin electronic and house music on Saturday nights. This place doubles as a hotel, but most people come here to simply kick off their flip-flops and dance among the trees. ⊠ *Carretera Tulum-Boca Paila, Km 4.5, Zona Hotelera* ☎ 984/116–3774 ⊕ *www. papayaplayaproject.com.*

SHOPPING

Tulum Farmers Market. From 2 to 5 on Saturday, there's a small farmers' market with live music at El Jardín de Frida Hostel. ⊠ *Av. Tulum at Av. Zebra, across from El Camello, Tulum.*

SPORTS AND THE OUTDOORS

BICYCLING

Punta Piedra Bike Rental. Punta Piedra Bike Rental is a small shop that rents equipment by the day. Boogie boards cost $5, bikes are $10, scooters are $40, and snorkel gear is $10. The owner, Felix, can also organize two-hour snorkeling tours for $30. Cash only. ⊠ *Carretera Tulum–Boca Paila, Km 4, Zona Hotelera* ☎ *984/157–4248 cell* ☉ *Daily 7:30–6.*

KITE SURFING

Extreme Control Kite School. Extreme Control Kite School offers all levels of kitesurfing lessons and the latest equipment. Led by IKO (International Kiteboarding Organization) instructor, Marco Cristofanelli, courses take place at Playa Esperanza, with the flattest conditions in Tulum. Their new kite shop and info center is located on Avenida Tulum in Tulum pueblo, one block from the HSBC bank. They are open on the beach from 9 am to sunset everyday unless there is absolutely no wind. Call to check the wind conditions ahead of time. ⊠ *Av. Tulum* ☎ *984/130–1596, 984/745–4555* ⊕ *www.extremecontrol.net.*

COBÁ

42 km (26 miles) northwest of Tulum.

Near five lakes and between coastal watchtowers and inland cities, Cobá (pronounced ko-*bah*) exercised economic control over the region through a network of at least 16 *sacbéob* (white-stone roads), one of which measures 100 km (62 miles) and is the longest in the Mayan world. The city once covered 70 square km (27 square miles), making it a noteworthy sister state to Tikal in northern Guatemala, with which it had close cultural and commercial ties. It's noted for its massive temple-pyramids, one of which is 138 feet tall, the largest and highest in northern Yucatán. Cobá is often overlooked by visitors who opt for better-known Tulum. This site is less crowded, giving you a chance to immerse yourself in ancient culture.

GETTING HERE AND AROUND

Cobá is a 35-minute drive northwest of Tulum, along a road that leads straight through the jungle. Buses depart to and from Cobá for Playa del Carmen and Tulum at least twice daily. Taxis from Tulum are about $20.

EXPLORING

Fodor'sChoice **Cobá Ruins.** Mayan for "water stirred by the wind," Cobá flourished
★ from AD 800 to 1100, with a population of as many as 55,000. Now it stands in solitude, and the jungle has overgrown many of its buildings— the silence is broken only by the occasional shriek of a spider monkey or the call of a bird. Most of the trails here are pleasantly shaded by overgrown jungle. Processions of huge army ants cross the footpaths as the sun slips through openings between the tall hardwood trees, ferns, and giant palms. Cobá's ruins are spread out and best explored by bike, for rent for about $3 a day. ■TIP➔ If you plan on walking (rather than exploring by bike), expect to cover anywhere between 5 and 6 km (3 and 4 miles).

The main groupings of ruins are separated by several miles of dense vegetation, so the best way to get a sense of the immensity of the city is to scale one of the pyramids. ■TIP→ Don't be tempted by the narrow paths that lead into the jungle unless you have a qualified guide with you. It's easy to get lost here, so stay on the main road, wear comfortable shoes, and bring insect repellent and drinking water. Inside the site, there are no restrooms and only one small hut selling water (cash only).

The first major cluster of structures, to your right as you enter the ruins, is the **Cobá Group,** whose pyramids are around a sunken patio. At the near end of the group, facing a large plaza, is the 79-foot-high temple, which was dedicated to the rain god, Chaac. Some Maya still place offerings and light candles here in hopes of improving their harvests. Around the rear, to the left, is a restored ball court, where a sacred game was once played to petition the gods for rain, fertility, and other blessings.

Farther along the main path to your left is the **Chumuc Mul Group,** little of which has been excavated. The principal pyramid here is covered with the remains of vibrantly painted stucco motifs (*chumuc mul* means "stucco pyramid"). A kilometer (½ mile) past this site is the **Nohoch Mul Group** (Large Hill Group), the highlight of which is the pyramid of the same name, the tallest at Cobá. It has 120 steps—equivalent to 12 stories—and shares a plaza with Temple 10. The Descending God (also seen at Tulum) is depicted on a facade of the temple atop Nohoch Mul, from which the view is excellent.

Beyond the Nohoch Mul Group is the **Castillo,** with nine chambers that are reached by a stairway. To the south are the remains of a ball court, including the stone ring through which the ball was hurled. From the main route, follow the sign to **Las Pinturas Group,** named for the still-discernible polychrome friezes on the inner and outer walls of its large, patioed pyramid. An enormous stela here depicts a man standing with his feet on two prone captives. Take the minor path for 1 km (½ mile) to the Macanxoc Group, not far from the lake of the same name. The main pyramid at Macanxoc is accessible by a stairway. ⊠ *42 km northwest of Tulum* ⊠ *$6; taxi-bike tours $10, bike rental $3* ☉ *Daily 8–5.*

OFF THE
BEATEN
PATH

Pac Chen. Pac Chen is a Maya jungle settlement of 125 people who still live in round thatch huts. There's no electricity or indoor plumbing, and the roads aren't paved. The inhabitants, who primarily make their living farming pineapple, beans, and plantains, still pray to the gods for good crops.

■TIP→ You can only visit Pac Chen on trips organized by Alltournative, an ecotour company based in Playa del Carmen. The "Coba Maya Encounter" includes transportation, entrance to Coba ruins, lunch, and Maya guides within the Pac-Chen village. Alltournative pays the villagers by the number of tourists it brings in, though no more than 80 people are allowed to visit on any given day. There's an additional $2 entrance fee per person. This money has made the village self-sustaining, and has given the people an alternative to logging and hunting, which were their main means of livelihood before.

The half-day tour starts with a trek through the jungle to a cenote where you grab onto a harness and zip-line to the other side. Next is the Jaguar cenote, set deeper into the forest, where you must rappel down the cavelike sides into a cool underground lagoon. You'll eat lunch under an open-air palapa overlooking another lagoon, where canoes await. The food includes such Mayan dishes as grilled achiote (annatto seed) chicken, fresh tortillas, beans, and watermelon. ☎ *877/437–4990 in U.S., 984/803–9999* 🌐 *www.alltournative.com.*

WHERE TO EAT

$ MEXICAN 🍴 **Ki-Janal.** You can't get any closer to the Cobá ruins than this two-story restaurant. Adding color to the palapa setting are Mexican blankets draped over wooden tables. Some of the more traditional selections include fish prepared Yucatán style, chicken in banana leaves, and cochinita pibil. You can also find soups, salads, and pastas. Plan to stay a while since the service isn't the best, but this is the only restaurant anywhere close to Cobá. [$] *Average main: $7* ✉ *To right of Cobá ruins entrance* 💳 *No credit cards.*

4

WHERE TO STAY

$$$ HOTEL 🏨 **La Selva Mariposa.** Located halfway between Tulum's beaches and the Cobá ruins, this jungle sanctuary provides the perfect escape for travelers wanting the best of both worlds. **Pros:** owners live on-site; peaceful retreat; delightful breakfast; bikes for exploring. **Cons:** two-night minimum stay; 20 minutes from the beach; advance reservations required; slow Wi-Fi. [$] *Rooms from: $150* ✉ *Carretera Tulum–Coba, Km 20, Macario Gomez* ✣ *On road to Cobá, turn right at Km 20 after first speed bump, just past small store with "SOL" sign. Follow signs to hotel* ☎ *984/133–3695* 🌐 *www.laselvamariposa.com* 🛏 *4 rooms* 🍽 *Breakfast.*

RESERVA DE LA BIOSFERA SIAN KA'AN

15 km (9 miles) south of Tulum to Punta Allen turnoff, 252 km (156 miles) north of Chetumal.

The pristine jungle wilderness of Sian Ka'an is a wildlife preserve, the second-largest reserve in Mexico after Reserva de la Biosfera Calakmul. It's both a shelter for thousands of species of wildlife, including jaguars and manatees, and a window to a time before resort development changed this coast forever.

GETTING HERE AND AROUND

To explore on your own, follow the beach road past Boca Paila to the secluded 35-km (22-mile) coastal strip of land that's part of the reserve. You'll be limited to swimming, snorkeling, and camping on the beaches, as there are no trails into the surrounding jungle. The narrow, rough dirt roads down the peninsula are filled with monstrous potholes, completely impassable after a rainfall. In rainy season, don't attempt it without a four-wheel-drive vehicle.

The archaeological site at Muyil is about 16 km (10 miles) south of Tulum (village and archaeological site) on Federal Highway 307, which

The ruins of Cobá are best explored by bike.

passes through the site. By car it's 145 km (90 miles) south of Cancún and 212 km (132 miles) north of Chetumal.

ESSENTIALS

Tours Visit Sian Ka'an. Local guide Aldo offers various tours of Sian Ka'an, including bird-watching, fly-fishing, snorkeling, and wildlife excursions. The popular Nature Encounter Tour includes a boat trip into the lagoons of Boca Paila and Campechen in search of crocodiles, birds, and manatees. ⊠ *Coastal road Tulum-Boca Paila-Punta Allen, Km 15.8* ☎ *984/141–4245, 984/108–8853* ⊕ *www.visitsiankaan.com.*

Visitor Information Sian Ka'an Visitor Center. Sian Ka'an Visitor Center is 9 km (6 miles) south of Tulum, just past the archway on the coastal road toward Boca Paila. Several kinds of tours, including bird-watching by boat and night kayaking to observe crocodiles, are offered on-site through the Sian Ka'an Visitor Center. The rickety observation tower offers the best view of the Sian Ka'an Biosphere—just don't look down. ☎ *998/887–1969 National Commission of Natural Protected Areas, 984/141–4245 cell at Visitor Center, 984/108–8853 cell at Visitor Center* ⊕ *www.cesiak.org.*

EXPLORING

FAMILY
Fodor'sChoice
★

Sian Ka'an. One of the last undeveloped stretches of coastline in North America, Sian Ka'an was declared a wildlife preserve in 1986, and a UNESCO World Heritage Site in 1987. The 1.3 million acre reserve accounts for 10% of the land in the state of Quintana Roo, and covers 100 km (62 miles) of coastline. It's amazingly diverse, covering freshwater and coastal lagoons, mangrove swamps, cayes, savannas,

Caste Wars

When Mexico won independence from Spain in 1821, there wasn't much for Maya to celebrate. They continued to be treated as second-class, "lower-caste" citizens, just as they had under centuries of Spanish rule, and the new government refused to return confiscated lands. In Valladolid in 1847, Maya rose up in a coordinated rebellion. Within a year, hundreds of Mexicans were dead, and the War of the Castes was on.

Help for the embattled Mexicans arrived with a vengeance from Mexico City, Cuba, and the United States. By 1850 the tables had turned, and as many as 200,000 Maya—nearly half the population—were killed. Survivors fled to the jungles and held out for decades, until government troops finally withdrew in 1915. The Maya controlled Quintana Roo from Tulum, their headquarters, but were finally forced to accept Mexican rule in 1935.

4

tropical forests, and a barrier reef. Hundreds of species of local and migratory birds, fish, animals and plants share the land with fewer than 1,000 Maya residents. The area was first settled by the Maya in the 5th century AD—the name Sian Ka'an translates to "where the sky is born." There are approximately 27 ruins (none excavated) linked by a unique canal system—one of the few of its kind in the Mayan world in Mexico. There's a $3 entrance charge for the park, but to see much of anything, you should take a guided tour.

Many species of the once-flourishing wildlife have fallen into the endangered category, but the waters here still teem with roosterfish, bonefish, mojarra, snapper, shad, permit, sea bass, and crocodiles. Fishing the flats for wily bonefish is popular, and the peninsula's few lodges also run deep-sea fishing trips.

■TIP→ Most fishing lodges along the way close for the rainy season in August and September, and accommodations are hard to come by. The road ends at Punta Allen, a fishing village whose main catch is spiny lobster, which was becoming scarce until ecologists taught the local fishing cooperative how to build and lay special traps to conserve the species. There are several small, expensive guesthouses. If you haven't booked ahead, start out early in the morning so you can get back to civilization before dark. ⊠ *Coastal Road Tulum-Boca Paila-Punta Allen, Km 15.8, just beyond Arco Maya (arch entrance)* ☎ *998/887–1969* ⊕ *www.cesiak.org.*

Muyil (*Chunyaxché*). This photogenic archaeological site just 15 km (9 miles) down the 307 from Tulum, at the northern end of the Sian Ka'an biosphere reserve, is underrated. Once known as Chunyaxché, it's now called by its ancient name, Muyil (pronounced moo-*hill*). It dates from the late preclassic era, when it was connected by road to the sea and served as a port between Cobá and the Mayan centers in Belize and Guatemala. A 15-foot-wide *sacbé*, built during the postclassic period, extended from the city to the mangrove swamp and was still in use when the Spaniards arrived.

The 1.3-million-acre Reserva de la Biosfera Sian Ka'an is now a UNESCO World Heritage Site.

Structures were erected at 400-foot intervals along the white limestone road, almost all of them facing west, but there are only three still standing. At the beginning of the 20th century the ancient stones were used to build a chicle (gum arabic) plantation, which was managed by one of the leaders of the War of the Castes. The most notable site at Muyil today is the remains of the 56-foot **Castillo**—one of the tallest on the Quintana Roo coast—at the center of a large acropolis. During excavations of the Castillo, jade figurines representing the moon and fertility goddess Ixchel were found. Recent excavations at Muyil have uncovered some smaller structures.

The ruins stand near the edge of a deep-blue lagoon and are surrounded by almost impenetrable jungle—so be sure to bring insect repellent. You can drive down a dirt road on the side of the ruins to swim or fish in the lagoon. The bird-watching is also exceptional here; come at dawn, before the site officially opens (there's no gate) to make the most of it. ⊠ *Carretera 307, 15 km south of Tulum* ⊕ *muyil.smv.org* 🖃 *$3* ⊙ *Daily 8–5.*

WHERE TO STAY

For expanded reviews, facilities, and current deals, visit Fodors.com.

$$$$ 🏨 **Boca Paila Fishing Lodge.** Home of the "grand slam" (fishing lingo for
RESORT catching three different kinds of fish in one trip), this charming fishing lodge has nine bungalows, each with air-conditioning, two double beds, couches, bathrooms, and screened-in porches. **Pros:** on beach; attentive staff; great fishing. **Cons:** not much to do in area besides fish; drinks

not included in price. $ *Rooms from: $886* ✉ *Boca Paila Peninsula* ☎ *724/935–1577 in U.S., 800/245–1950 for Frontiers, 998/185–3570* ⊕ *www.bocapaila.com* ⇨ *9 bungalows* ✵ *All meals.*

$$$$
RESORT
☖ **Casa Blanca Lodge.** This fishing lodge is on a rocky outcrop on remote Punta Pájaros Island, reputed to be one of the best places in the world for light-tackle saltwater fly fishing. **Pros:** remote location; comfortable rooms. **Cons:** minimum stay; far from anywhere else; drinks are not included in AI package. $ *Rooms from: $1256* ✉ *Punta Pájaros* ☎ *724/935–1577 in U.S., 800/245–1950 for Frontiers, 877/261-8867 from U.S.* ⊕ *www.casablancafishing.com* ⇨ *9 rooms* ✵ *All meals.*

THE COSTA MAYA

4

The coastal area south of Punta Allen is more purely Maya than anything in the resort-rich coast north to Cancún. Fishing collectives and close-knit communities carry on ancient traditions here, and the proximity to Belize lends a Caribbean flavor, particularly in Chetumal, where you'll hear both Spanish and a Caribbean patois. Although resort development is creeping in, a multimillion-dollar government initiative is attempting to support ecotourism and sustainable development projects here.

FELIPE CARRILLO PUERTO

156 km (97 miles) north of Chetumal.

Felipe Carrillo Puerto—the Costa Maya's first major town—is named for the governor of Yucatán in 1920, who was hailed as a hero after instituting a series of reforms to help the impoverished *campesinos* (peasants). Most (if any) travelers stop here as a midway point between Tulum and the beaches of Costa Maya. Although the town itself is of the muddy one-horse variety with little of visitor interest, Chacchoben, a little-explored archaeological site, isn't far.

GETTING HERE AND AROUND

You guessed it—Carretera 307 runs right through the center of town. Just drive straight and you can't miss it. Be aware that there are no gas stations between here and Chetumal, so make sure you gas up in town.

The 307 is known in town as Avenida Benito Juárez, and is the town's main drag. Taxis drive up and down the street if you arrive without transportation.

EXPLORING

As you enter the town, there's an HSBC bank complete with ATM located next to the Pemex gas station on the roundabout. The tourist information office is at the corner of Avenida Juárez and Avenida Santiago Pacheco Cruz.

Chacchoben. Excavated in 2005, Chacchoben (pronounced *cha*-cho-ben) is an ancient city that was a contemporary of Kohunlich and the most important trading partner with Guatemala north of the Bacalar Lagoon area. Several newly unearthed buildings are still in good condition. The lofty **Templo Uno,** the site's main temple, was dedicated to the Mayan sun god Itzamná, and once held a royal tomb. (When archaeologists found it, though, it had already been looted.) Most of the site was built around AD 200, in the Petén style of the early classic period, although the city could have been inhabited as early as 200 BC. It's thought that inhabitants made their living growing cotton and extracting chewing gum and copal resin from the trees. ✥ *From Carretera 307, turn right on Carretera 293 south of Cafetal, continue 9 km (5½ miles) passing Lázaro Cardenas town* 🌐 *www.chacchobenruins.com* 🎫 *$4; additional $3 to use video cameras* 🕒 *Daily 8–5.*

WHERE TO STAY

For expanded reviews, facilities, and current deals, visit Fodors.com.

$ HOTEL 🏨 **El Faisán y El Venado.** If you absolutely need a place to stay between Riviera Maya and the beaches of Costa Maya, then this simple three-story hotel, with rustic rooms accommodating up to three people (one room sleeps five), is really your only remotely acceptable option between the Riviera Maya and the Costa Maya. **Pros:** best place to stay in town; central location; strong a/c. **Cons:** basic rooms; staff speaks little English; Wi-Fi in common areas only; crowing roosters in the morning. [$] *Rooms from: $40* ✉ *Av. Benito Juárez, Lote 781* ☎ *983/834–0702, 983/834–0043* 🛏 *37 rooms* 🍴 *No meals.*

BACALAR

40 km (25 miles) northwest of Chetumal.

Founded in AD 435, Bacalar (pronounced *baa*-ka-lar) is one of Quintana Roo's oldest settlements. The mix of freshwater and salt water in the cenote-fed Laguna de Bacalar intensifies the color, which earned the lagoon the nickname "Lago de los Siete Colores" (Lake of the Seven Colors). Marking the entrance to Bacalar (Carretera 307 at Km 34) is Cenote Azul, a crystalline cenote that's 300 feet deep and 600 feet across. The water is clean and the diving is excellent here. Drive along the lakeshore for the affluent section of the town of Bacalar, with its waterfront homes.

GETTING HERE AND AROUND

Bacalar is 3½ hours south of Cancún and 30 minutes north of Chetumal. It's just off Carretera 307, south of Felipe Carrillo Puerto and Limones. If you're coming from Cancún, follow the well-marked signs toward Bacalar. Upon entering the town, you'll cross over two huge speed bumps. Pass the Catholic church on your right, take a left at the first corner, and continue straight to the town center; to your left will be the Fort of San Felipe. Northbound drivers should take Carretera 106 to 307 and enter at Km 34 marked by a sign for "Cenote Azul." Just past the cenote is a paved road that parallels Laguna de Bacalar and eventually leads to the town center.

ESSENTIALS

Although there are no banks in Bacalar, there's an ATM in the town square. Just past Km 22, turn left at the sign "Bacalar Salida 500m." Pass the white church and turn left. Make the first left again and you'll see the town square and the ATM on your right.

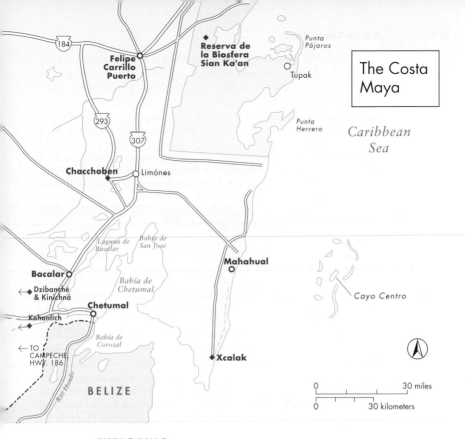

Caribbean Sea

Cayo Centro

0 ——— 30 miles

0 ——— 30 kilometers

EXPLORING

The alliance between sister cities Dzibanché and Kinichná was thought to have made them the most powerful cities in southern Quintana Roo during the Mayan classic period (AD 100–1000). The fertile farmlands surrounding the ruins are still used today as they were hundreds of years ago, and the winding drive deep into the fields makes you feel as if you're coming upon something undiscovered.

Dzibanché. Archaeologists have been making progress in excavating more and more ruins, albeit slowly. At Dzibanché ("place where they write on wood," pronounced zee-ban-*che*), several carved wooden lintels have been discovered; the most perfectly preserved sample is in a supporting arch at the **Plaza de Xibalba.** Also at the plaza is the **Templo del Búho** (Temple of the Owl), atop which a recessed tomb was found, the second discovery of its kind in Mexico (the first was at Palenque in Chiapas). In the tomb were magnificent clay vessels painted with white owls—messengers of the underworld gods. More buildings and three plazas have been restored as excavation continues. Several other plazas are surrounded by temples, palaces, and pyramids, all in the Petén style. The carved stone steps at **Edificio 13** and **Edificio 2** (Buildings 13 and 2) still bear traces of stone masks. A copy of the famed lintel of **Templo IV** (Temple IV), with eight glyphs dating from AD 618, is housed in the Museo de la Cultura Maya in Chetumal. (The original was replaced in 2003 because of deterioration.) Four more tombs were discovered at **Templo I** (Temple I). ⌨ *$4 (includes Kinichná)* ☽ *Daily 8–5.*

Fuerte de San Felipe Bacalar (*San Felipe Fort*). Fuerte de San Felipe Bacalar is a 17th-century stone fort, built by the Spaniards using stones from the nearby Mayan pyramids. It was originally constructed as a haven against pirates and marauding bandits, then was transformed into a Maya stronghold during the War of the Castes. Today the monolithic structure, which overlooks the enormous Laguna de Bacalar, houses government offices and a museum with exhibits on local history (ask for someone to bring a key if museum doors are locked). ☏ *983/832–6838 museum* ⌨ *$5* ☽ *Tues.–Thurs. and Sun. 9–7.*

Kinichná. After you see Dzibanché, make your way back to the fork in the road and head to Kinichná (House of the Sun, pronounced kin-itch-*na*). At the fork, you'll see the restored **Complejo Lamai** (Lamai Complex), the administrative buildings of Dzibanché. Kinichná consists of a two-level pyramidal mound split into Acropolis B and Acropolis C, apparently dedicated to the sun god. Two mounds at the foot of the pyramid suggest that the temple was a ceremonial site. Here a giant Olmec-style jade figure was found. At its summit, Kinichná affords one of the finest views of any archaeological site in the area. ⌨ *$4 (includes Dzibanché)* ☽ *Daily 8–5.*

Kohunlich. Kohunlich (pronounced *ko*-hoon-lich) is renowned for the giant stucco masks on its principal pyramid, the **Edificio de los Mascarones** (Mask Building). It also has one of Quintana Roo's oldest ball courts and the remains of a great drainage system at the **Plaza de las Estelas** (Plaza of the Stelae). Masks that are about 6 feet tall are set vertically into the wide staircases at the main pyramid, called **Edificio de las Estelas** (Building of the Stelae). First thought to represent the Mayan sun god, they're now considered to be composites of the rulers and important warriors of Kohunlich. Another giant mask was discovered in 2001 in the building's upper staircase.

Kohunlich was built and occupied during the classic period by various Mayan groups. This explains the eclectic architecture, which includes the Petén and Río Bec styles. Although there are 14 buildings to visit, it's thought that there are at least 500 mounds on the site waiting to be excavated. Digs have turned up 29 individual and multiple burial sites inside a residence building called **Temple de Los Viente-Siete Escalones** (Temple of the Twenty-Seven Steps). This site doesn't have a great deal of tourist traffic, so it's surrounded by thriving flora and fauna. ✉ *42 km (26 miles) west of Chetumal on Carretera 186* ⌨ *$4* ☽ *Daily 8–5.*

WHERE TO EAT

$$
SEAFOOD

✗ **Restaurant Cenote Azul.** Perched on the rim of the 300-foot-deep cenote, this palapa restaurant serves good chicken, pork, and fish dishes. House specialties include the seafood platter and shrimp kebab. Here you can linger over fresh fish and a beer while gazing out over the deep blue waters, or enjoy a swim off the dock. There's also a souvenir shop

The Laguna de Bacalar is known for the limestone formations along its shore.

popular with tour groups. $ *Average main: $10* ✉ *Carretera 307, Km 34* ☎ *983/834–2460* ⊕ *www.cenoteazul.com* ☾ *Daily 9–6.*

WHERE TO STAY

For expanded reviews, facilities, and current deals, visit Fodors.com.

$$$
B&B/INN
🛏 **Akalki.** Considered the most upscale property on Laguna de Bacalar, Akalki offers nine luxurious cabanas built over the water, each with a private dock and direct access to the enchanting turquoise waters. **Pros:** romantic setting; immaculate rooms; closest thing to a Bora Bora experience. **Cons:** rooms have electricity only at night; Wi-Fi in common areas only; food could be better; poor service. $ *Rooms from: $220* ✉ *Carretera 307, Km 12.5* ☎ *983/106–1751 cell* ⊕ *www.akalki. com* ⇶ *9 rooms* ⦿ *Multiple meal plans.*

$$$$
RESORT
ALL-INCLUSIVE
Fodor's Choice
★
🛏 **The Explorean Kohunlich.** At the edge of the Kohunlich ceremonial grounds, this ecological luxury resort gives you the chance to have an adventure without giving up life's comforts. **Pros:** attentive staff; excellent food; tours, meals and transportation included in room rate. **Cons:** expensive; no Internet; no children under 14. $ *Rooms from: $400* ✉ *Carretera Chetumal–Escarega, Km 5.6, on road to ruins* ☎ *55/5201–8350 in Mexico City, 877/397–5672, 800/343–7821* ⊕ *www.theexplorean.com* ⇶ *40 suites* ⦿ *All-inclusive.*

$$
B&B/INN
🛏 **Los Aluxes.** Right on the water's edge, Los Aluxes offers comfortable rooms and lovely views, but the staff have yet to fully comprehend the hospitality industry. **Pros:** quiet location; private dock; family-friendly. **Cons:** staff doesn't speak English; not all rooms have an ocean view; breakfast is toast and coffee only. $ *Rooms from: $90* ✉ *Av. Costera*

Bacalar No. 67 ☎ *983/834–2817* 🌐 *www.bacalarlagunazul.com* 🛏 *6 rooms* 🍴 *Breakfast.*

$$ HOTEL 🏨 **Rancho Encantado.** On the shores of Laguna Bacalar, 30 minutes north of Chetumal, these Mayan-themed casitas are uniquely decorated with murals and hammocks, and comfortably sleep four people. **Pros:** great location on lagoon; breakfast included; friendly staff; huge Jacuzzi; Wi-Fi in restaurant. **Cons:** some traffic noise; need car to get around; low water pressure; mosquitoes. [$] *Rooms from: $200* ✉ *Off Carretera 307, Km 24, look for turnoff sign* ☎ *998/884–2071, 877/229–2046 in U.S.* 🌐 *www.encantado.com* 🛏 *10 casitas, 6 suites* 🍴 *Breakfast.*

CHETUMAL

328 km (283 miles) southeast of Playa del Carmen.

At times, Chetumal feels more Caribbean than Mexican; this isn't surprising, given its proximity to Belize. A population that includes Afro-Caribbean and Middle Eastern immigrants creates a melting pot of music (reggae, salsa, calypso) and cuisines (Yucatecan, Mexican, and Lebanese). Although Chetumal's provisions are modest, the town has a number of parks on a waterfront that's as pleasant as it is long: The Bay of Chetumal surrounds the city on three sides. Tours go to the fascinating nearby ruins of Kohunlich, Dzibanché, and Kinichná, a trio dubbed the "Valley of the Masks."

Because this is the closest major town to Bacalar, Mahahual, and Xcalak, many neighboring residents come here to do banking and stock up on supplies. Traffic can get very congested. In the town of Chetumal itself, you will see very few tourists.

GETTING HERE AND AROUND

Chetumal's airport, Aeropuerto de Chetumal, lies on its southwestern edge. Interjet flies daily between Mexico City and Chetumal. Chetumal's main bus terminal, at Avenida Salvador Novo 179, is served mainly by ADO. Omnibus Cristóbal Colón has buses that run to Palenque and San Cristóbal. If you're driving here, be sure to fill up at the Pemex station in Felipe Carrillo Puerto, one of the few stations along this stretch of Carretera 307.

Bus Contacts ADO ☎ *983/832–5110* 🌐 *www.ado.com.mx.* **Bus Terminal** ☎ *983/832–5110.*

ESSENTIALS

There's an ATM at the bus station near the San Francisco Grocery Store. On Avenida Insurgentes, there's a bank and ATM in the center of the shopping mall.

Visitor Information Chetumal Tourist Information ✉ *Calles 28 de Enero and Reforma* ☎ *983/832–6647.*

EXPLORING

FAMILY **Museo de la Cultura Maya.** The Museo de la Cultura Maya, a sophisticated interactive museum dedicated to the complex world of the Maya, is outstanding. Displays in Spanish and English trace Mayan architecture, social classes, politics, and customs. The most impressive display is the three-story Sacred Ceiba Tree, a symbol used by the Maya to explain the relationship between the cosmos and the earth. The first floor represents the roots of the tree and the Mayan underworld, called Xibalba. The middle floor is the tree trunk, known as Middle World, home to humans and all their trappings. The top floor is the leaves and branches and the 13 heavens of the cosmic otherworld. ⊠ *Av. Héroes and Calle Mahatma Gandhi* ☎ *983/832–6838* ⊕ *www.secqr.gob.mx* ⊡ *$6* ⊙ *Tues.–Sun. 9–7.*

BEACHES

Chetumal Bay. Surrounding the bay of Chetumal are several grassy beach parks, including Punta Estrella and Dos Mulas. The water here is calm, if cloudy, and there's plenty of shade from trees and little palapa-topped picnic tables. (Because of maintenance and cleanliness problems, Dos Mulas is presently not recommended.) Punta Estrella offers parking, toilets, volleyball courts, and a small boat marina. **Amenities:** food and drink; parking (no fee); toilets. **Best for:** walking.

WHERE TO EAT

For expanded reviews, facilities, and current deals, visit Fodors.com.

$ ✕ **Restaurant Encuentro.** At this bright café, you can enjoy fresh salads,
CAFÉ pastas, sandwiches, and chicken dishes. Early risers can try a house omelet stuffed with *chaya* (tree spinach), tomatoes, and salsa verde. They also have 12 kinds of coffee. This is a great place to quickly escape the busy streets outside the restaurant. $ *Average main: $5* ⊠ *Av. Alvaro Obregón #193* ☎ *983/833–3013* ⊙ *Closed Sun.*

$$ ✕ **Sergio's Restaurant & Pizzas.** Locals rave about this restaurant's grilled
PIZZA steaks, barbecued chicken (made with the owner's special sauce), and garlic shrimp, along with smoked-oyster and seafood pizzas. There's a huge breakfast menu and a variety of lunchtime pasta dishes. This is one of the nicest restaurants in Chetumal and the staff is gracious. When you order the delicious Caesar salad for two, a waiter prepares it at your table. You can also order takeout or delivery, or come in for a snack and use the restaurant's free Wi-Fi. $ *Average main: $15* ⊠ *Av. Alvaro Obregón 182, at Av. 5 de Mayo* ☎ *983/832–2991, 983/832–0882* ⊕ *www.sergiospizzas.com.*

WHERE TO STAY

$$$ ⛫ **Los Cocos.** This large and "modern" hotel (by Chetumal's standards)
HOTEL has a pool in a pleasant garden, a boon on sweltering days, and clean, if not especially stylish, rooms. **Pros:** reasonable rates; strong water pressure; good location; free Wi-Fi in rooms. **Cons:** uncomfortable beds; loud a/c; staff speaks minimal English. $ *Rooms from: $90* ⊠ *Av. Héroes 134, at Calle Chapultepec* ☎ *983/835–0430* ⊕ *www. hotelloscocos.com.mx* ⇱ *134 rooms, 3 suites* ⛏ *No meals.*

MAHAHUAL

143 km (89 miles) northwest of Chetumal via Carreteras 186 and 307.

Sleepy Mahahual (also spelled *Majahual*) has something of a split personality. With a population of 600, it's a quiet, tiny little beachfront town with clear, calm waters, good snorkeling and diving, and not a whole lot to do. That's just the way its Mexican and expat U.S. and Canadian residents like it.

When the cruise ships are in port, however, the dozy town gets a locally unwelcome shot in the arm. Cruise passengers flood its beachfront palapa restaurants, beach clubs, and the boardwalk that fronts the town's few blocks; it's lively, but can be overwhelming. That's when locals and savvy overnight visitors retreat to the handful of delightfully remote beachfront hotels and inns on Mahahual's outskirts, waiting out the crowds in a hammock, beach book in hand.

GETTING HERE AND AROUND

To get here by car, take Carretera 307 to Highway 10, approximately 2½ km (1½ miles) past the dusty little town of Limones (you can't miss the road; it's marked Mahahual). Continue for 50 km (30 miles) until you reach the coast. Turn right at the lighthouse and follow the road into the town of Mahahual where a string of hotels and restaurants line the beach. For those staying at Almaplena Beach Resort, turn right at the paved road toward Xcalak and continue for 10 miles until you see a sign for Punta Herradura. Turn left on this bumpy road and follow the signs to the resort. Almaplena is halfway between Mahahual and Xcalak. To reach the port area of New Mahahual, turn left at Km 55, just past the mayor's office.

The beach road south of town is rough and potholed. After it rains driving here can be an adventure. If you're planning to drive south, check with locals for road conditions, and plan plenty of time.

Mayab offers bus service from Cancún to Limones, but you'll need to take a taxi or colectivo (shared van) from Limones to Mahahual. At various times throughout the day, there are yellow colectivos that go back and forth between Limones and Mahahual, but they fill up quickly since this is the main transportation for locals. In the worst-case scenario, you can take a taxi for $25 each way.

In both high and low seasons, Caribe is the only bus line offering daily transportation from Mahahual, but it only goes to Chetumal, with a brief stop in Limones. It departs Mahahual at 6:30 am and 3:30 pm.

There's a taxi stand at the corner of Avenida Mahahual and Calle Rubic. A full day of transportation, with a private driver, can be arranged for around $100. Otherwise, you can expect to pay around 10 pesos per kilometer. Additional taxis are parked around the soccer field. Always ask to see a rate card before agreeing to a price.

ESSENTIALS

Banks and Currency Exchange Most properties don't accept credit cards. There are six ATMs in town, as well as a small exchange booth in the orange building on the main beach road.

Visitor Information Although there isn't a visitor center, Fernando, owner of 100% Agave in town, is a true ambassador for Mahahual, and gladly offers advice on what to see and where to go.

BEACHES

The three cruise ships that stop here daily have made Mahahual's beach the liveliest place in town. Seaside restaurants dish out cerveza and ceviche, and several vendors offer boat tours and rental equipment like glass-bottomed kayaks. The main beach in the center of town has fine sand and glassy waters, great for swimming and snorkeling. Some hotel owners have opened beach clubs to cater to cruise passengers looking for a day (and a drink) in the sun.

BEACH CLUBS

Fodor's Choice ★ **Nacional Beach Club.** Many travelers stumble on this colorful beach club and end up staying past sunset. For just $10, you get a beach chair, umbrella, and access to the pool, showers, and changing facilities. Margaritas can be delivered to you beachside, or you can escape the heat by grabbing a bite in the enclosed patio. By day you can munch on tacos, enchiladas, and sandwiches; by night the menu expands to include delicious smoked fish or grilled shrimp (there's also an impressive vegetarian menu), but reservations are required at the restaurant. The $3 Coronas and free Wi-Fi make this a popular spot to while away the day. There's decent snorkeling right out front, and equipment available next door at Gypsea Divers. Movies are shown under the stars on Wednesday at 6. There are also three bungalows for rent if you feel like staying the night. **Amenities:** food and drink; showers; toilets. **Best for:** partiers; snorkeling; swimming. ✉ *Av. Mahahual, s/n Lote 4, Manzana 14, Mahahual* ☎ *983/834–5719* 🌐 *www.nacionalbeachclub.com* 🎫 *$10* 🕒 *Daily 8–5.*

Nohoch Kay Beach Club. This beachfront restaurant on the boardwalk doubles as a beach club, offering an open bar, lunch, beach chairs, umbrellas, kayaks, and snorkeling gear for a flat $40 fee per person. There are restrooms, showers, and an on-site massage therapist ready to work her magic for $30 per half-hour. The restaurant cooks up ceviche, tacos, sandwiches, and nachos, but most people opt for the fresh fish served with tortillas with lime and homemade tartar sauce. Between tanning sessions, you can head to the outer reef on a private catamaran for a snorkeling tour. Cruise passengers flock to this all-you-can-drink hot spot, meaning that if you want to be part of the action, you'll have to reserve in advance (cash only). **Amenities:** food and drink; showers; toilets; water sports. **Best for:** partiers; snorkeling. ✉ *Malecón, between Calles Liza and Cazón, Mahahual* ☎ *983/125–6610* 🎫 *$40.*

WHERE TO EAT

$ MEXICAN 🍴 **Nacional Beach Club.** Many travelers stumble on this colorful beach club and end up staying past sunset. For just $10, you get a beach chair, umbrella, and access to the pool, shower, and changing facilities. Margaritas can be delivered to you beachside or you can escape the heat by grabbing a bite in the enclosed patio. By day you can munch on tacos, enchiladas, and sandwiches and by night enjoy the delicious smoked fish or grilled shrimp (reservations are required for dinner). The $3 Coronas and free Wi-Fi make this a popular spot to while away the day. There are also three bungalows for rent if you feel like staying the night. [$] *Average main: $8* ✉ *Av. Mahahual* ☎ *983/834–5719* 🌐 *www.nacionalbeachclub.com* 🕒 *Daily 8–5.*

$ MEXICAN 🍴 **100% Agave.** Fernando's beloved palapa shack is a Mahahual institution, with a friendly, homey atmosphere that's made the restaurant a sort of ersatz visitor bureau. The affordable menu features Mexican and Yucatecan specialties with a generous splash of gringo—great food that's an even better bang for your buck. Should you be in the market for a margarita, don't be shy—this is the place for expert guidance on all things agave, as suggested by the name, and the man-size tequila bottle out front. You can even buy a bottle of Fernando's homemade tequila to go. If the indoor party scene isn't lively enough for you, head to the beachfront tables, where a DJ spins beats on the sandy dance floor. [$] *Average main: $8* ✉ *Calle Huachinango, between Coronado and Martillo; north of soccer field* ☎ *983/834–5609.*

WHERE TO STAY

For expanded reviews, facilities, and current deals, visit Fodors.com.

$$$ RESORT Fodor's Choice ★ 🏨 **Almaplena Resort.** As one of only two fully green eco-hotels in the area, this one also happens to be the most luxurious, with rustic-chic rooms designed with textiles from Chiapas, rugs from Michoacan, wood from Yucatan, and iron from Jalisco. **Pros:** stay four nights for the price of three; spotless rooms; great snorkeling at reef in front of hotel; stunning views from rooftop terrace. **Cons:** no TV; cash only; flat pillows; low water pressure; bland breakfast. [$] *Rooms from: $145* ✉ *Carretera Costera, Mahahual–Xcalak, Km 12.5, Majahual* ☎ *983/137–5070 cell* 🌐 *www.almaplenabeachresort.com* 🛏 *10 rooms* 💳 *No credit cards* 🍽 *Breakfast.*

$$ HOTEL 🏨 **Balamku.** This ecologically sensitive hotel 5 km (3 miles) south of town sits on a stretch of pristine private beach where you can lose all track of time. **Pros:** beachfront location; comfortable rooms; excellent breakfast; friendly Canadian owners. **Cons:** far from town; restaurant serves only breakfast and lunch; no air-conditioning; small and rocky beach. [$] *Rooms from: $95* ✉ *Carretera Federal Majahual-Xcalak, Km 5.7, Majahual* ☎ *983/732–1004* 🌐 *www.balamku.com* 🛏 *10 rooms* 🍽 *Breakfast.*

$ HOTEL 🏨 **El Caballo Blanco.** Named for the owner's son's boyhood *caballo blanco* (white horse), this stark-white property is the tallest in Mahahual, meaning that the view from the rooftop bar is spectacular. **Pros:** great views; fantastic restaurant; all rooms have balconies. **Cons:** small bathrooms; back room lacks full ocean view; meals not included. [$] *Rooms from: $75* ✉ *Av. Mahahual, Lote 1, Mza 12* ☎ *983/126–0319* 🌐 *www.hotelelcaballoblanco.com* 🛏 *7 rooms* 🍽 *No meals.*

$ HOTEL 🏨 **La Posada de los 40 Cañones.** This nautically themed hotel is adorned with anchors, wooden pathways, and queen-size beds that swing from ropes. **Pros:** reasonably priced rooms; covered parking; comfortable beds; good restaurant. **Cons:** no pool; reservations require nonrefundable payment; not all rooms have ocean view. [$] *Rooms from: $80* ✉ *Calle Huachinango* ☎ *983/123–8591* 🌐 *www.40canones.com* 🛏 *26 rooms* 🍽 *No meals.*

$$ B&B/INN 🏨 **Maya Luna.** This small inn on the beach, far from the boardwalk, is a quiet place to relax and enjoy the sand and the sun. **Pros:** beachfront

Mahahual is a lively little community with a wonderful beach.

location; nice restaurant open to the public; relaxed atmosphere. **Cons:** no a/c; 40-minute walk to town. $ *Rooms from: $85* ✉ *Carretera Mahahual-Xcalak, Km 5.2* ☎ *983/836–0905* ⊕ *www.hotelmayaluna. com* ↪ *4 rooms* ⊙ *Breakfast.*

$$
B&B/INN
Fodor's Choice
★

⊞ **Mayan Beach Garden.** Nineteen kilometers (12 miles) north of Mahahual, this solar-powered beachside B&B offers blessed isolation, with not another hotel for miles. **Pros:** optional all inclusive plan available; very good restaurant; use of bikes and snorkels. **Cons:** minimum three-night stay during high season; bumpy dirt road means 30-minute drive to town; only two rooms have a/c. $ *Rooms from: $140* ✉ *N. Carretera Costera Majahual–Punta Herrera, Km 20.5, 19 km north of Mahahual town* ☎☎ *983/130–8568, 206/905–9665 in U.S.* ⊕ *www. mayanbeachgarden.com* ↪ *2 cabanas, 5 rooms, 1 suite* ⊙ *Multiple meal plans.*

$$
B&B/INN

⊞ **Posada Pachamama.** This simple, charming little hotel is just across the street from the beach on Mahahual's main boardwalk. **Pros:** beachfront location; good rates; near restaurants and shops. **Cons:** no pool; tiny rooms; ground-floor rooms lack ocean view. $ *Rooms from: $80* ✉ *Calle Huachinango s/n* ☎ *983/834–5762, 253/397–1640 in U.S.* ⊕ *www.posadapachamama.net* ↪ *10 rooms* ⊙ *Breakfast.*

SPORTS AND THE OUTDOORS
ADVENTURE TOURS

Native Choice. Ivan and David's Native Choice tour company knows all there is to know about Cosa Maya sites Chacchoben, Kohunlich, and Dzibanché; they're experts on contemporary Maya culture, too.

✉ *Paseo del Puerto 1021, corner of Chinchorro, Nuevo Mahahual* ☎ *983/103–5955, 998/869–3346* ⊕ *www.thenativechoice.com.*

FISHING

Western Caribbean Fly Fishing School. Based out of Nohoch Kay Beach Club, this fly-fishing school offers trips to Sian Kaan Biosphere, Xcalak, Chetumal Bay or local cenotes for Tarpon and Snook. Fly-fishing instructor Nick Denbow leads beginners and experts through the fine arts of fly-tying and casting, and he custom-designs fishing trips for individuals and groups. ✉ *Nohoch Kay Beach Club, Malecón between Calles Liza and Cazón* ☎ *983/732–3144 cell* ⊕ *www. westerncaribbeanflyfishing.com.*

SCUBA DIVING

Dreamtime Dive Resort. Dreamtime Dive Resort offers snorkeling tours and night dives managed by some of the most experienced divers in the area, who handle the cruise-ship crowd, too. Single-tank dives cost $50; two-tank dives are $75. ✉ *Av. Mahahual, Km 2.5, south of town* ☎ *983/124–0235, 904/730–4337 in U.S., 983/700–5824 cell* ⊕ *www. dreamtimediving.com.*

Gypsea Divers. Owners Catherine and Abel offer single-tank dives for $60, two-tank dives for $75, and snorkeling trips for $25. Group discounts are available. ✉ *Av. Mahahual, next to Nacional Beach Club* ☎ *983/130–3714* ⊕ *www.gypseadivers.com.*

XCALAK

180 km (111 miles) southwest of Chetumal.

As the southernmost town in Quintana Roo, Xcalak (pronounced *ish-ka-lack*), is 11 km (7 miles) from the Belize border (by water), and has a little of both places in its local life. Spanish is still the primary language, although most people speak English, and you'll sometimes hear a Caribbean patois. Getting here is an adventure, since you first have to drive just short of the beach in Mahahual, and then cut over another 61 km (37 miles) to reach the entrance of Xcalak. From here, beach properties are down a rough and pitted road, but it's worth the effort. This remote area offers excellent saltwater fly-fishing for a variety of catches including tarpon, bonefish, and permit.

This national reserve is on the tip of a peninsula that divides Chetumal Bay from the Caribbean. Flowers, birds, and butterflies are abundant here, and the terrain is marked by savannas, marshes, streams, and lagoons dotted with islands. There are also fabulously deserted beaches, and a small town center comprised of bars, restaurants, and a few food shops. Although Xcalak has electricity, it's not very dependable. There is no air-conditioning and no phones, other than satellite cell phones for emergency. To book a hotel, email the property rather than call since you probably won't get through.

Visitor amenities are few, and the town itself lacks a nightlife; the hotels cater mostly to rugged types who come to bird-watch on Bird Island or to dive at Banco Chinchorro, a coral atoll and national park some two hours northeast by boat. This is also a great launching point for

Mayan Beach Garden Inn

day trips to Belize. Most hotels and businesses close down during hurricane season, so check ahead to make sure your destination is open.

Although there has been minimal coastal development of private homes, all construction near Xcalak is bound by stringent environmental laws. The entire coast in this area is a designated National Marine Park, which protects the natural beauty of this frontier village.

GETTING HERE AND AROUND

From Carretera 10 to Mahahual, turn right at the intersection 2 km (1 mile) before Mahahual and continue along the rough and tricky road until you reach Xcalak, about 37 miles. Pass the soccer field and turn left onto the bumpy beach road, now heading north toward "Zona Hotelera," a 14-km (9-mile) stretch of properties lining the beach. Your hotel will probably be within this main area.

On a map, the 55 km (34 miles) of bay separating Chetumal from Xcalak looks like an easy boat trip. Unfortunately, shallow sections of the bay make it impassable.

There is one bus each day between Xcalak and Chetumal. If you arrive in Xcalak without a car, don't rely on taxi service or local transportation. Consider staying close to town or in a hotel that offers bicycles.

As an alternative to renting a car, there's a five-hour route (first-class ADO), stopping incrementally at Puerto Morelos, Playa del Carmen, Tulum, Felipe Carrillo Puerto, Limones, and Chetumal. Visitors traveling to Xcalak can get off at Limones and take a two-hour taxi ride for about $70. Make note that all ADO and Caribe buses stop in Limones, where one can easily transfer to a north–south bus running from Cancún to Chetumal at all hours of the day.

SAFETY AND PRECAUTIONS

Make sure you have a full tank before you drive south. Although there is a Pemex gas station in Mahahual, it is sometimes closed for no apparent reason.

Unlike the trafficked roads along Riviera Maya, the two-lane stretch near Belize is seldom visited by tourists. It's always best to travel with a partner and to drive during daylight hours. Drive with caution and be careful of wild animals and potholes. Once you leave the paved road and enter Xcalak, the road goes from bad to worse. Be sure to rent a car that can handle pitted dirt roads.

BANKS AND CURRENCY EXCHANGE

There are no banks or ATMs in or near Xcalak, and because there are no phone lines, no one accepts credit cards. Bring plenty of cash for your entire stay. The closest ATMs are 64 km (40 miles) north in Mahahual, though they often run out of money. Another option is to try one of the ATMs in the village of Bacalar.

COMMUNICATION

No phones, no cell service—plan on being out of touch, or doing as the locals do and using email or Skype.

MEDICAL EMERGENCIES

Xcalak's growing expat community includes several nurses, who are always willing to help. There's a small clinic in the center of town; however, the "medic" (not always a doctor) is seldom around. Usually, a local can point you in the right direction for rudimentary first aid until you can reach the nearest staffed clinic in Bacalar. The closest small hospital (Carranza Clinic) is in Chetumal.

BEACHES

Playa Xcalak. Far from the bustling beaches of Riviera Maya, Playa Xcalak is remarkably tranquil. As the southernmost town on the Mexican Caribbean coast, Xcalak borders the Caribbean Sea to the east and Chetumal Bay to the west, creating a biodiverse ecosystem made up of coral reefs (15 miles of protected reef), mangroves, rivers, lagoons, and bays. Sections of the beach connect to a network of protected mangroves where manatees frequent. The white-sand beach stretches for miles, and the offshore reef of nearby Banco Chinchorro is great for snorkeling, diving, and fishing. However, much of the sand has been eaten away by past hurricanes, narrowing the shore. Although that makes strolling a chore, the isolated location means you'll likely be alone on the beach. Waters are pristine and placid, making this one of the area's best spots for swimming, kayaking, or just a day in the sun. **Amenities:** food and drink. **Best for:** snorkeling; swimming.

WHERE TO EAT

$$
SEAFOOD
Fodor'sChoice
★

╳ **The Leaky Palapa.** Nobody expected the kind of sophisticated flavors that the Leaky Palapa brought to town, but this little 11-table palapa restaurant is done up in twinkling lights and has quickly become *the* place to meet, enjoy a beer, and eat like kings. Feast on lobster bisque or the seared shrimp on bean cakes with tamarind salsa. Homemade pasta isn't the first thing you think of when you think tropical beach, but the ravioli with corn truffle will convince you. The menu changes weekly depending on what local fisherman bring to the dock. Canadian owners Linda and Marla believe in using local ingredients as much as possible. Opening hours (and months) vary so check their website before arrival. Ⓢ *Average main: $10* ✉ *Calle Pedro Moreno, just past light house, in big red house on left* ⊕ *www.leakypalaparestaurant.com* ⊟ *No credit cards* ⊘ *Closed Sept. and Oct.*

$$ ✕ **The Mayan Grill.** Unlike most restaurants in Xcalak, this beachside eat-
EUROPEAN ery is open daily for breakfast, lunch, and dinner. Start the morning with a ham and cheese O'Mayaletes (omelet) served with beans and potatoes. The child-friendly lunch menu offers everything from tacos and nachos to hotdogs and quesadillas. For something a bit more gourmet, drop by at night for delectable dishes like fresh lobster, shrimp brochettes, or chicken stuffed with poblano and cheese. Dinner prices include an appetizer, soup, entrée, and dessert. The open-air palapa, right on the water's edge, is a great place to spend the day. Ⓢ *Average main: $12* ✉ *Hotel Tierra Maya, Xcalak, 2 miles past soccer field on beach road* ☎ *983/839–8012 cell* ⊕ *www.tierramaya.net* ⊟ *No credit cards.*

$ ✕ **Toby's.** Near the entrance to Xcalak is this modest Mexican restau-
MEXICAN rant made up of a few plastic tables and chairs. Stop by for Toby's famous fajitas, fried fish, coconut shrimp, and chicken quesadillas. The place comes alive on Monday nights when locals gather for the daily special and live music. This is one of the few spots in town where Wi-Fi is available (free with food). Ⓢ *Average main: $8* ✉ *Leona Vicario s/n, across from parking lot and volleyball court* ⊟ *No credit cards* ⊘ *Closed Sun.*

WHERE TO STAY

For expanded reviews, facilities, and current deals, visit Fodors.com.

$$ 🏨 **Casa Carolina.** This small hotel is a wonderful place to stay if you
B&B/INN want to dive, snorkel, kayak, fly fish or just relax in one of the hammocks. **Pros:** on a nice beach; diving lessons available; kayaks and bikes available. **Cons:** no restaurant; no air-conditioning. Ⓢ *Rooms from: $110* ✉ *Carretera Majahual–Xcalak, Km 48* ⚓ *Beach road "Calle Costero," 2 kms north of Xcalak town* ☎ *610/616–3862 in U.S.* ⊕ *www.casacarolina.net* ⤵ *4 rooms* ⊟ *No credit cards* ⦿ *Breakfast.*

$$ 🏨 **Sin Duda Villas.** On a lovely beach, this property has several parts: a
B&B/INN house divided into three suites; two apartments; and one studio apartment set in the jungle. **Pros:** solar powered; all rooms have Wi-Fi; very private; credit cards accepted via PayPal. **Cons:** getting here isn't easy; owner's dogs may bark at night; no children under 10. Ⓢ *Rooms from: $90* ✉ *Xcalak Peninsula, 60 km (33 miles) south of Majahual, 5½ km (4 miles) north of Costa de Cocos* ☎ *415/868–9925 in U.S.* ⊕ *www. sindudavillas.com* ⤵ *3 rooms, 1 studio, 2 apartments* ⦿ *Breakfast.*

SPORTS AND THE OUTDOORS

XTC Dive Center. XTC Dive Center is the only full-service dive shop in Xcalak. In addition to recreational diving, they offer DAN and PADI scuba diving instruction. Two-tank dives cost $90, and snorkeling and boat trips to Belize can be arranged for groups of five people for

$250. The company also offers lessons in fly-fishing and is the only dive company licensed to take passengers to Chinchorro. Serious divers might be interested in renting one of the basic rooms attached to the property. Cash only. ⊠ *650 feet north of main bridge in Xcalak, Camino Costero Mahahual–Xcalak, Km 54* ☎ *983/120–5804 cell* ⊕ *www.xtcdivecenter.com.*

COZUMEL

WELCOME TO COZUMEL

TOP REASONS TO GO

★ **Dive one of the world's great reefs:** A rainbow of tropical fish, living coral, and other underwater creatures illuminates the 966-km-long (600-mile-long) Great Maya Reef, stretching from Cozumel to Central America.

★ **Slowing down:** Lounge poolside, stroll along a white-sand beach, or explore the gardens above and below the waters at Chankanaab. Or just grab a table at a sidewalk café and watch the world go by.

★ **Local food:** San Miguel's Plaza Central is a Sunday-evening hot spot for families and couples who gather for music and dancing. Visit during Carnival, the spring Fería del Cedral, or any national holiday, and you'll find parades, processions, and food stands with seasonal treats.

★ **Mayan sites:** Take a refresher course on Mayan culture past and present at the Museo de Cozumel, then explore the temples dedicated to Ixchel, the Mayan goddess of fertility and the moon, at San Gervasio.

1 **The Northwest Coast.** Broad beaches and the island's first golf course occupy the northwest tip of Cozumel. The sand gives way to limestone shelves jutting over the water; at hotels without big beaches, strap on your snorkel and climb ladders down the docks or rocks.

2 **San Miguel.** Though cruise ships loom over the piers and souvenir shops line the streets, Cozumel's only town still retains some of the flavor of a Mexican village. On weekend nights, musicians and food vendors gather in the main square and attract lively crowds.

3 **The Southwestern Beaches.** Proximity to Cozumel's best reefs makes the beaches south of San Miguel a prime destination for divers. A parade of hotels, beach clubs, commercial piers, and dive shops lines the shore here.

4 **The Southern Nature Parks.** Cozumel's natural treasures are protected both above and below the sea. At Faro Celarain, mangrove lagoons and beaches shelter nesting sea turtles. Chankanaab, one of Mexico's first marine parks, is superb for snorkeling. Parque Marino Nacional Arrecifes de Cozumel covers the coral reefs along the southwest edge of the island.

5 **The Windward Coast.** The rough surf of the Caribbean pounds against the limestone shore here, creating pocket-size beaches made for solitary sunbathing. The water can be rough, though, so pay attention to the tides, currents, and sudden drop-offs in the ocean floor.

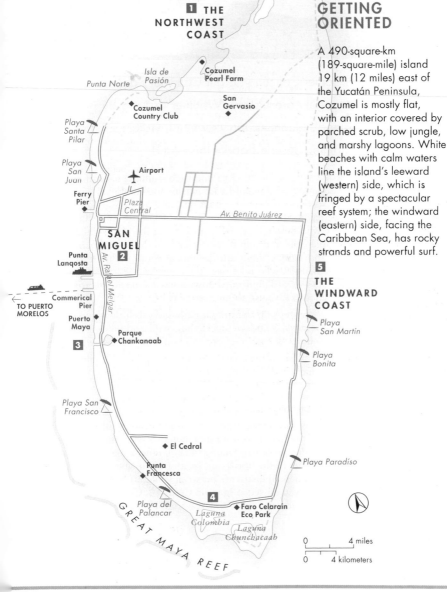

Punta Molas

1 THE NORTHWEST COAST

Punta Norte

Isla de Pasión

Cozumel Pearl Farm

San Gervasio

Cozumel Country Club

Playa Santa Pilar

Playa San Juan

Airport

Ferry Pier

Plaza Central

Av. Benito Juárez

SAN MIGUEL
2

Punta Langosta

Av. Rafael Melgar

Commerical Pier

TO PUERTO MORELOS

Puerto Maya

3

Parque Chankanaab

Playa San Francisco

El Cedral

Punta Francesca

Playa del Palancar

4

Laguna Colombia

Faro Celarain Eco Park

Laguna Chunchacaab

G R E A T   M A Y A   R E E F

GETTING ORIENTED

A 490-square-km (189-square-mile) island 19 km (12 miles) east of the Yucatán Peninsula, Cozumel is mostly flat, with an interior covered by parched scrub, low jungle, and marshy lagoons. White beaches with calm waters line the island's leeward (western) side, which is fringed by a spectacular reef system; the windward (eastern) side, facing the Caribbean Sea, has rocky strands and powerful surf.

5

5 THE WINDWARD COAST

Playa San Martín

Playa Bonita

Playa Paradiso

0 ————— 4 miles

0 ————— 4 kilometers

Updated by
Marie Elena
Martinez

It's not another Cancún yet, but Cozumel's days as a rustic divers' hangout are history. Whether arriving by plane or at the island's gleaming ferry terminal, visitors soon realize there's nothing deserted about this island.

That has its advantages. It's rare to find such stunning natural beauty, glass-clear aquamarine seas, and vast marine life combined with top-flight visitor services and accommodations, and as a result Cozumel's devotees are legion. Divers sharing stories of lionfish and sharks sit table-to-table with families tanned from a day at the beach club, while Mexican couples spin and step to salsa music in the central plaza. But the elephant in Cozumel's big and bountiful room is the throngs of cruise-ship passengers who take over the countless crafts and jewelry stores along the seaward boulevard downtown any day there are ships in port—which is to say, just about every day.

But take just a few steps off the beaten path and this little island offers big rewards. Deserted, windswept beaches, wild and vibrant natural parks, and 600 miles of coral reef are still yours for the discovering.

Just 19 km (12 miles) off the coast, Cozumel is 53 km (33 miles) long and 15 km (9 miles) wide, making it the country's third-largest island. Plaza Central, or just "la plaza," is the heart of San Miguel, directly across from the docks. Residents congregate here in the evening, especially on weekends, when free concerts begin at 8 pm. Heading inland (east) takes you away from the tourist zone and toward residential areas of town. Most of the island's restaurants, hotels, stores, and dive shops are concentrated downtown and along the two hotel zones that fan out on the leeward coast to the north and south of San Miguel. The most concentrated commercial district is between Calle 10 Norte and Calle 11 Sur to beyond Avenida Pedro Joaquin Coldwell. Cozumel's solitude-seeking windward side also has a few restaurants and one hotel.

PLANNING

WHEN TO GO

Peak Season: November; February and March. Late autumn and early spring bring the best weather, warm and dry—and with it, tourists in droves. You'll pay top dollar, but it may well be worth it if you're in search of uninterrupted sunshine.

Off-season: June–October; December and January. Weather conditions here are more extreme than you might expect on a tropical island, with chilly winters and steamy summers. June and September bring tropical rainstorms and in general summer is hot and humid. Prices are much lower out of season, and if you're a diver, the warm water and year's-best visibility might be enough to beat the heat. In winter, *nortes*—winds from the north—blow through, churning the sea and making air and water temperatures drop. If you visit during this time, bring a shawl or jacket for the chilly 65°F evenings. The windward side is calmer in winter than the leeward side, and the interior is warmer than the coast.

Sweet Spot: April and May. With a lull in tourist business and the perfect weather that precedes the rainy season, late spring might be your all around best bet.

GETTING HERE AND AROUND

AIR TRAVEL

A few national and international flights land at the Aeropuerto Internacional de Cozumel, 3 km (2 miles) north of San Miguel, but flights to Cancún are usually considerably less expensive. A small airline called Mayair offers flights between Cancún and Cozumel for about $70 each way, with luggage limited to 25 kilos (55 pounds) per passenger. A budget alternative is to take a bus from the Cancún airport to Playa del Carmen and then the ferry to Cozumel. If everything runs on schedule, the trip should cost less than $20 and take about three hours.

From the airport, take a *colectivo*, a van that seats up to eight, to your hotel; fares range from $7 to $20 per person depending on where you're going.

Contacts Mayair ⊠ *Cozumel Airport, Blvd. Aeropuerto at Av. 65* ☎ *997/872-3609 in Cancún* ⊕ *www.mayair.com.mx.*

BOAT AND FERRY TRAVEL

Passenger-only ferries to and from Playa del Carmen leave roughly every hour from early morning until late at night. The trip takes 45 minutes and costs about $14 to $15 each way. The lone car ferry leaves from Calica and costs $55 per car, $5 for each person after the driver.

Contacts Car ferry from Calica ☎ *987/872-7688.* **Mexico Waterjets** ☎ *984/879-3112 in Playa del Carmen* ⊕ *www.mexicowaterjets.com.* **Ultramar** ☎ *998/881-5890 in Cancún* ⊕ *granpuerto.com.mx.*

BUS TRAVEL

Bus service on Cozumel is basically limited to San Miguel, so you'll need a rental car or taxi to explore. Though it's tempting to drive on Cozumel's dirt roads (which lead to the least crowded beaches), most car-rental companies have a policy that voids your insurance once you leave the paved roadway.

CAR TRAVEL

If you want to explore the island (particularly the eastern side) at your own pace, you can rent a car.

Contacts CP Rentals ⊠ *Av. 10 Norte, between Calles 2 and 4* ☎ *987/878–4055.* **Hertz** ⊠ *Cozumel International Airport, Blvd. Aeropuerto* ☎ *987/869–8184* ⊕ *www.hertz.com.* **Thrifty** ⊠ *Cozumel International Airport, Blvd. Aeropuerto at Av. 70* ☎ *987/869–2957* ⊕ *www.thrifty.com.*

SCOOTER TRAVEL

Scooters are popular, but heavy traffic, potholes, and hidden stop signs make them a risky option. Mexican law requires all riders to wear helmets (it's a $25 fine if you don't).

If you do decide to rent a scooter, drive slowly, check for oncoming traffic, and don't ride when it's raining or you've been drinking. Scooters rent for about $25 per day or $15 for a half day, including insurance.

Contacts Ernesto's Scooter Rental ⊠ *Carretera Costera Sur, Km 4* ☎ *987/871–1223 mobile* ⊕ *www.ernestosrental.com.*

TAXI TRAVEL

Cabs wait at all the major hotels, and you can hail them on the street. The fixed rates run about $3 within town; $8 to $20 between town and either hotel zone; $10 to $30 from most hotels to the airport; and about $20 to $40 from the northern hotels or town to Parque Chankanaab or Playa San Francisco. The cost from the Puerta Maya cruise-ship terminal by El Cid La Ceiba to San Miguel is about $10.

ESSENTIALS

BANKS AND CURRENCY EXCHANGE

San Miguel is dotted with bank offices, and ATMs are abundant, including a few that dispense U.S. dollars. Some major hotels and resorts along the northern and southern hotel zones have ATMs on-site. Credit cards are readily accepted, as are U.S. dollars, although often at a disadvantageous exchange rate.

HEALTH AND SAFETY

Cozumel is very safe; the most trouble you're likely to get in has four wheels and a motor (drive carefully). If you plan to try water sports, make sure that your health or travel insurance has a sports rider.

TOURS

Tours of the island's sights, including the San Gervasio ruins, El Cedral, Parque Chankanaab, and the Museo de la Isla de Cozumel, cost about $50 per person and can be arranged through travel agencies; most larger hotels have an on-site travel agency or tour operator that conducts tours. Another option is to take a private tour of the island via taxi, which costs about $60 for a half day.

RESTAURANTS

At first glance, the food scene here is tourist-typical: fresh seafood, American beach-shack standards, and a rainbow of sweet and fruity cocktails. A handful of creative chefs, however, have started serving up more-sophisticated dishes.

HOTELS

You can book most Cozumel hotels online, but it's a good idea to shop around online for the best rates—hotels often use multiple sites. While online booking is convenient and often cheaper than by phone, the imperfect realities of the Internet suggest you'll do well to bring a printout of all receipts and confirmations, just in case.

HOTEL AND RESTAURANT PRICES

Prices in the restaurant reviews are the average cost of a main course at dinner or, if dinner is not served, at lunch; taxes and service charges are generally included. Prices in the hotel reviews are the lowest cost of a standard double room in high season, excluding taxes, service charges, and meal plans (except at all-inclusives). Prices for rentals are the lowest per-night cost for a one-bedroom unit in high season.

VISITOR INFORMATION

The website ⊕ *www.thisiscozumel.com* has up-to-date news items and info on all things Cozumel. They also book tours. The site ⊕ *www. cozumelmycozumel.com*, edited by full-time island residents, has insider tips on activities, sights, and places to stay and eat. There's also a bulletin board where you can post questions.

Contacts Cozumel Tourist Information Office ⊠ *Plaza del Sol, Calle 2 Norte #299-B* ☎ *987/872-7585* ⊕ *www.cozumel.travel.*

EXPLORING COZUMEL

Unless you want to stick around your hotel or downtown San Miguel for your whole stay, you'll do well to rent a car or a scooter. Most worthwhile sites, such as the island's Mayan ruins and pristine windward beaches, are only readily accessible with wheels. Taxi fares are astronomical, and after just a few trips a rental car is clearly a better deal.

San Miguel is Cozumel's only town. Wait until the cruise ships sail toward the horizon before strolling the *malecón*, or boardwalk. The waterfront has been taken over by large shops selling jewelry, imported rugs, leather boots, and souvenirs to cruise-ship passengers, but the northern end of the malecón, past Calle 10 Norte, is a pleasant area lined with sculptures of Mayan gods and goddesses that draws more locals than tourists. The town feels more traditional as you head inland to the pedestrian streets around the plaza, where family-owned restaurants and shops cater to locals and savvy travelers.

San Miguel's heart is the plaza, where families gather Sunday nights to stroll, snack, and dance to live music around the central *kiosko*, or bandstand. There are plenty of benches for watching the action. Facing the square is an artisan's market, a good stop for souvenirs.

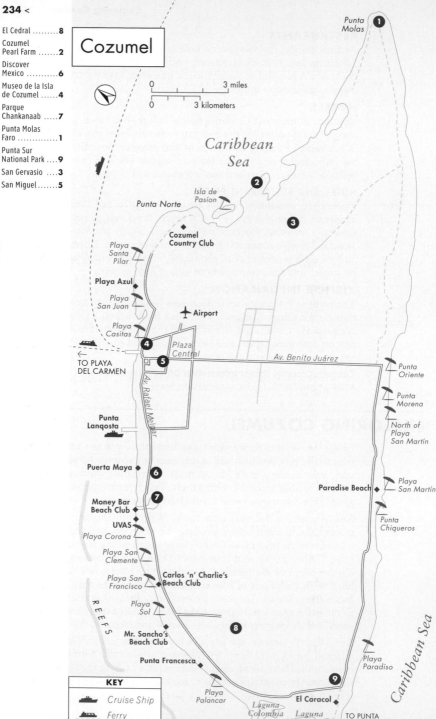

Cozumel

0   3 miles

0   3 kilometers

Caribbean Sea

Punta Molas ①

Isla de Pasión

②

Punta Norte

③

Cozumel Country Club

Playa Santa Pilar

Playa Azul ◆

Playa San Juan

✈ **Airport**

Playa Casitas

④

Plaza Central

⑤

Av. Benito Juárez

← TO PLAYA DEL CARMEN

Punta Oriente

Punta Morena

North of Playa San Martín

Av. Rafael Melgar

Punta Langosta

Puerta Maya ◆ ⑥

⑦

Paradise Beach ◆   Playa San Martín

Money Bar Beach Club ◆

Punta Chiqueros

UVAS ◆

Playa Corona

Playa San Clemente

Playa San Francisco

Carlos 'n' Charlie's Beach Club

Playa Sol

R E E F S

⑧

Mr. Sancho's Beach Club

Punta Francesca

Playa Paradíso

⑨

Playa Palancar

Laguna Colombia

Laguna Chunchacaab

El Caracol ◆

TO PUNTA CELERAIN FARO

Caribbean Sea

KEY

🚢 *Cruise Ship*

⛴ *Ferry*

Cozumel is a favorite cruise-ship destination.

TOP ATTRACTIONS

FAMILY

Fodor'sChoice

★

Cozumel Pearl Farm. Currently the only pearl farm operating in the Caribbean, the Cozumel Pearl Farm is on a beautiful private beach of white sand surrounded by turquoise waters and grows Caribbean pearl oysters over a period of eight years. Conceived as a project of research and development, this spectacular place opened its doors to visitors in early 2012. Small groups of up to 12 people a day can visit to discover how to grow a pearl, as well as snorkel and relax on the beach. Accessible only by boat, the farm will make you feel like a castaway on a desert island during the six-hour experience, which runs from 10 to 4. Transportation (from San Miguel Pier or other meeting point), gear, lunch, beer, and soft drinks are included in the price. ⊠ *Punta Norte* ☎ *987/119–9417, 984/114–9604 from U.S.* ⊕ *www.cozumelpearlfarm. com* ⚍ *$110.*

FAMILY

Museo de la Isla de Cozumel. Filling two floors of a former hotel, Cozumel's island museum has displays on natural history—the island's origins, endangered species, topography, and coral-reef ecology—as well as human history during the pre-Columbian and colonial periods. The photos of the island's transformation over the 20th and 21st centuries are especially fascinating, as is the exhibit of a typical Mayan home. Guided tours are available. The rooftop restaurant is open daily from 7 am to 11 pm. ⊠ *Av. Rafael E. Melgar, between Calles 4 and 6 Norte* ☎ 987/872–1475 ⚍ *$4* ⊙ *Mon.–Sat. 9–5, Sun. 9–4.*

QUICK
BITES

Restaurante del Museo. On the terrace off the second floor of the Museo de la Isla de Cozumel, the Restaurante del Museo serves breakfast, lunch, and dinner from 7 am to 11 pm. The Mexican fare is enhanced by a great waterfront view, and the café is as popular with locals as tourists. ☎ *987/872–0838.*

Parque Chankanaab. The National Park of Chankanaab, translated as "small sea," consists of a saltwater lagoon, an archaeological park, and a botanical garden, with reproductions of a Mayan village and Olmec, Toltec, Aztec, and Mayan stone carvings scattered throughout. You can swim, scuba dive, or snorkel at the beach; the park also offers dolphin encounters, which are a highlight for kids. There's plenty to see beneath the surface: underwater caverns, a sunken ship, crusty old cannons and anchors, and a sculpture of la Virgen del Mar (Virgin of the Sea), all populated by parrotfish and sergeant majors galore. To preserve the ecosystem, park rules forbid touching the reef or feeding the fish. You'll also find dive shops, restaurants, gift shops, a snack stand, and dressing rooms with lockers and showers right on the sand. ⊠ *Carretera Sur, Km 9* ☎ *987/872–4014* ⊕ *www.cozumelparks.com* 🖃 *$21* ⊗ *Daily 8–4.*

Punta Molas Faro (*Molas Point Lighthouse*). The lighthouse at Cozumel's northernmost point is a solitary, beautiful sight. The rutted road to Punta Molas is open for four-wheel-drive vehicles and dune buggies only. The scenery is awe-inspiring no matter how far you're able to go. Some dive boats travel out this way, providing a photo op from the sea.

San Gervasio. Surrounded by a forest, these temples make up Cozumel's largest remaining Mayan and Toltec site. San Gervasio was the island's capital and ceremonial center, dedicated to the fertility goddess Ixchel. The classic- and postclassic-style buildings and temples were continuously occupied from AD 300 to 1500. Typical architectural features include limestone plazas and arches atop stepped platforms, as well as stelae and bas-reliefs. Be sure to see the temple "Las Manitas," with red handprints all over its altar. Plaques in Mayan, Spanish, and English clearly describe each structure. ⊠ *Off Carretera Transversal* ✛ *From San Miguel, take cross-island road (follow signs to airport) east to San Gervasio access road; turn left and follow road 7 km (4½ miles)* ☎ *987/872–0093* 🖃 *$8* ⊗ *Daily 8–4.*

WORTH NOTING

FAMILY **Discover Mexico.** Want to see Mexico but can't be bothered to leave Cozumel? This theme park purports to show you the country's archaeological sites, important architectural landmarks, and cultures, all without leaving the island. The scale models of temples, pyramids, monasteries, and the Zócalo, Mexico City's main square, have kitsch value, but a slickly produced film about the country and high-quality folk art exhibits begin to touch on the real thing. An outdoor café serves tasty fruit sorbets and light meals, or reserve in advance for the daily tequila tasting. The gift shop has an array of beautiful Mexican folk art for sale. A combo entry ticket ($34 adults, $24 kids) includes admission to Parque Chankanaab. ⊠ *Carretera Sur, Km 5.5* ☎ *987/875–2820* ⊕ *www.discovermexico.org* 🖃 *$20* ⊗ *Mon.–Sat. 8–4.*

El Cedral. Spanish explorers discovered this site, once the hub of Mayan life on Cozumel, in 1518. Later it became the island's first official city, founded in 1847. Today it's a farming community with small, well-tended houses and gardens. Conquistadores tore down much of the Mayan temple, and the U.S. Army Corps of Engineers destroyed the rest to make way for the island's first airport during World War II. So there's little in the way of actual ruins apart from one small stone arch, but if you're in the market for souvenirs, vendors around the main plaza display embroidered blouses and hammocks. ⊠ *Off Carretera Sur ✛ Turn at Km 17.5 off Carretera Sur or Av. Rafael E. Melgar, then drive 3 km (2 miles) inland to site* ☒ *Free* ☉ *Daily dawn–dusk.*

FAMILY **Punta Sur National Park.** This 247-acre national preserve at Cozumel's southernmost tip is a protected habitat for numerous birds and animals, including crocodiles, flamingos, egrets, and herons. At the park's (and the island's) southernmost point stands the **Faro de Celarain,** a lighthouse that's now a museum of navigation. Climb the 134 steps to the top for the best view on the island. Spot crocodiles and birds from observation towers near **Laguna Colombia** or **Laguna Chunchacaab,** or visit the ancient Mayan lighthouse **El Caracol,** designed to whistle when the wind blows in a certain direction. Beaches here are wide and deserted, and there's great snorkeling offshore. Snorkeling equipment is available for rent, as are kayaks, and there are restrooms at the museum and by the beach. Leave your car at the Faro and take park shuttles or rental bikes to the beach. Without a rental car, expect to pay about $40 for a round-trip taxi ride from San Miguel. ⊠ *Southernmost point of Carretera Sur and coastal road* ☒ *$12* ☉ *Daily 8–4.*

BEACHES

Unlike the long, broad beaches of Cancún or the Riviera Maya, most of Cozumel's beaches are pockets of sand collected between sections of brittle limestone. The best sandy beaches are along the island's southern shores, although sea grass mars the underwater scenery. The windward coast has stretches of spectacular isolated beaches, but rough tides can make swimming dangerous.

LEEWARD BEACHES

Wide sandy beaches washed with shallow waters are typical at the far north and south ends of Cozumel's west coast. The topography changes between the two, with small sandy coves interspersed with limestone outcroppings. ■**TIP➔** Generally, the best snorkeling from shore is wherever piers or rocky shorelines provide a haven for sergeant majors and angelfish. However, shore diving and snorkeling took a hit with Hurricane Wilma in October 2005, from which they have not yet fully recovered. While they're improving gradually, you'll still find the greatest undersea life at the reef, reachable only by boat.

Isla de Pasión. The private Isla de Pasión lies a short boat ride off Punta Norte on the leeward coast and has one of Cozumel's loveliest beaches. Most guests reach the island on an organized tour (about $80 or more

Cozumel's History

Cozumel's name is believed to have come from the Mayan "Ah-Cuzamil-Peten" ("Land of the Swallows"). For the Maya, who lived here intermittently between about AD 600 and 1200, the island was not only a center for trade and navigation but also a sacred place. Pilgrims from all over Mesoamerica came to honor Ixchel, the goddess of fertility, childbirth, the moon, and rainbows. The mother of all other gods, Ixchel was often depicted with swallows at her feet. Maya women, who were expected to visit Ixchel's site at least once in their lives, made the dangerous journey from the mainland by canoe. Cozumel's main exports were salt and honey, which at the time were both considered more valuable than gold.

In 1518 Spanish explorer Juan de Grijalva arrived on the island in search of slaves. His tales of treasure inspired Hernán Cortés, Mexico's most famous Spanish explorer, to visit the following year. There he met Gerónimo de Aguilar and Gonzalo Guerrero, Spaniards who had been shipwrecked years earlier. Initially enslaved by the Maya, the two were later accepted into the community. Aguilar joined forces with Cortés, helping set up a military base on the island and using his knowledge of the Maya to defeat them. Guerrero, in contrast, died defending his adopted people, and the Maya still consider him a hero. By 1570 most Maya islanders had been massacred by the Spanish or killed by disease, and by 1600 the island was abandoned.

In the 17th and 18th centuries, pirates found Cozumel to be the perfect hideout. The notorious buccaneers Jean Lafitte and Henry Morgan favored the island's safe harbors and hid their treasures in Mayan catacombs and tunnels. By 1843 Cozumel had again been abandoned. Five years later, 20 families fleeing Mexico's brutal War of the Castes resettled the island, and their descendants still live there today.

By the early 20th century the island began capitalizing on its abundant supply of *zapote* (sapodilla) trees, which produce chicle, a chewy substance prized by the chewing-gum industry. (Now you know how Chiclets got their name.) Shipping routes began to include Cozumel, whose deep harbors made it a perfect stop for large vessels. Jungle forays in search of chicle led to the discovery of ruins, and soon archaeologists began visiting the island as well. Meanwhile, Cozumel's importance as a seaport diminished as air travel grew, and the demand for chicle dropped off with the invention of synthetic chewing gum.

For decades Cozumel was another backwater where locals fished, hunted alligators and iguanas, and worked on coconut plantations to produce *copra*, the dried kernels from which coconut oil is extracted. Cozumeleños subsisted largely on seafood, still a staple of the local economy. During World War II, the U.S. Army built an airstrip and maintained a submarine base here, accidentally destroying some Mayan ruins in the process. Then in the 1960s the underwater explorer Jacques Cousteau helped make Cozumel famous by featuring its reefs on his television show. Today Cozumel is among the world's most popular diving locations.

5

per person depending on the type of tour and transportation), but you can go on your own for $65 per person from the dock at the end of the dirt road to Punta Norte. The all-inclusive fee includes the round-trip boat ride, a buffet lunch, soft drinks, some alcoholic drinks, and use of the extensive facilities and amenities. You can easily spend a whole day here strolling the 2.5 mile-long beach, floating in the shallow water, swinging in a hammock, playing volleyball, indulging in a massage (for an extra fee), or even getting married in the island's chapel. This is a favorite stop for hordes of cruise-shippers, but the beach is long enough that you can escape the crowds. **Amenities:** food and drink; lifeguards; showers; restrooms. **Best for:** swimming; walking. ⊠ *Off Punta Norte* ☎ *987/105–9791* ⊕ *www.isla-pasion.com.*

Playa Casitas. Playa Casitas, a hugely popular locals' beach, has a restaurant, several large palapas for shade, a parking area, and a long stretch of white sand and calm water. It's fairly deserted on weekdays but completely packed on Sunday, the traditional day for family outings. **Amenities:** food and drink; restrooms; parking (free); showers. **Best for:** swimming. ⊠ *Carretera Norte at Blvd. Aeropuerto* ☜ *Free.*

Playa Palancar. South of the resorts, down a rutted and potholed road and way off the beaten path lies the serene Playa Palancar. The on-site dive shop can outfit you for trips to the famous Palancar Reef just offshore. There's also a water-sports center, a bar-café, and a long beach with hammocks hanging under coconut palms. **Amenities:** food and drink; showers; restrooms; parking (free); water sports. **Best for:** snorkeling; swimming. ⊠ *Carretera Sur, Km 19* ☜ *Free.*

Playa Santa Pilar. Playa Santa Pilar runs along the northern hotel strip and ends at Punta Norte. Long stretches of sand and shallow water encourage leisurely swims, but the privacy diminishes as you swim south past hotels and condos. Beach hotels have all the facilities you would need, but most are all-inclusive and don't allow nonguests on the premises, so if you're not staying at one, bring your own shade. **Amenities:** parking; restrooms (at hotels); showers (at hotels). **Best for:** solitude; snorkeling; swimming; walking. ⊠ *Carretera San Juan, just south of Punta Norte* ☜ *Free.*

Playa San Juan. Playa San Juan, south of Playa Santa Pilar, has a rocky shore with no easy ocean access. You can park on the roadside just south of the fence surrounding the ruins of the Sol Cabañas del Caribe hotel, which was destroyed by Hurricane Wilma. The winds can be strong here, so it's popular with kiteboarders. **Amenities:** none. **Best for:** solitude; snorkeling; windsurfing. ⊠ *Carretera Costera Norte, Km 5.1* ☜ *Free.*

BEACH CLUBS

Carlos 'n' Charlie's Beach Club. Carlos 'n' Charlie's Beach Club at Playa San Francisco is a rowdy, bawdy affair with a restaurant and bar where waiters break into song and draw customers into line dances. The food is typical of the chain—burgers, barbecued ribs, tacos—and the alcohol flows generously. While there's a wide array of water sports on offer, the water is shallow and not always clear, and the scene best suits youthful fun seekers. **Amenities:** food and drink; parking (free); showers. **Best**

for: partiers. ✉ *Carretera Costera Sur, Km 14* ☎ *987/564–0960 mobile* ⊕ *www.carlosandcharlies.com/cozumelclub* ☞ *Free* ☉ *Mon.–Sat. 9–4, Sun. 11–4.*

Money Bar Beach Club. The Money Bar Beach Club on the Dzul Ha reef is the most upscale spot with all the bells and whistles, from massage to kayaking. Activity packages (starting at $30) give you a buyout rate for meals, massage, even snorkel tours, or you can just paddle around and check out the angelfish before lunching à la carte under the peaked palapas. A water-sports center rents snorkel and scuba gear, kayaks, and small sailboats. Happy regulars and visitors come to sip frothy cocktails during the daily sunset happy hour and linger into the dark. There's live music on weekend nights, and happy hour from 5 pm to 7 pm daily. **Amenities:** food and drink; lifeguards; parking (free); showers; toilets; water sports. **Best for:** snorkeling; sunset; swimming. ✉ *Carretera Sur, Km 6.5* ☎ *987/869–5141* ⊕ *www.moneybarbeachclub.com* ☞ *Free* ☉ *Mon.–Thurs. 7 am–9 pm, Fri.–Sun. 7 am–10 pm.*

FAMILY **Mr. Sancho's Beach Club.** There's always a party going on at Mr. Sancho's Beach Club. Scores of vacationers come here to swim, snorkel, and drink buzz-inducing concoctions out of pineapples. Kids shriek happily as they hang onto banana boats dragged behind speedboats. Guides lead horseback and ATV rides along the beach and into the jungle, and the restaurant holds a lively, informative tequila seminar at lunchtime. Grab a swing seat at the beach bar and sip a mango margarita, get a massage, or settle into the 30-person hot tub. Lockers are available, and there are souvenirs aplenty for sale. **Amenities:** lifeguards; food and drink; toilets; parking (free); showers; water sports. **Best for:** partiers; swimming. ✉ *Carretera Sur, Km 15* ☎ *987/871–9174 mobile* ⊕ *www.mrsanchos.com* ☞ *Free* ☉ *Daily 9–5.*

FAMILY **Paradise Beach.** The club at Paradise Beach charges $2 for lounge chairs, but the $12 Fun Pass gets you all-day use of kayaks, snorkel gear, a trampoline, the large, heated swimming pool, and a climbing wall that looks like an iceberg in the water. Parasailing equipment and Jet Skis are available for rent. Food at the club's three bars is expensive, and there's a minimum per-person consumption of $10, but if you're lucky, Sunshine the resident parrot will open your beer for you with his beak. There's also Wi-Fi, if you must. **Amenities:** food and drink; parking (free); showers; toilets; water sports. **Best for:** partiers; swimming. ✉ *Carretera Sur, Km 14.5* ☎ *987/120–0027* ⊕ *www.paradise-beach-cozumel.com* ☞ *Free.*

Playa Azul. The Playa Azul Beach Club sits just north of the hotel of the same name and is under the same management. The beach is actually pockets of soft sand between limestone shelves; there's also a pool at the hotel that is open to beach club guests. The restaurant beneath a large A-frame palapa serves delicious ceviche and bountiful club sandwiches and fries, and there's free Wi-Fi to boot. A salsa band plays on Sunday afternoon and draws a crowd of fun-loving dancers—older couples, parents dancing with their kids, and friends of all ages boogying alone or together. **Amenities:** food and drink; parking (free); restrooms; show-

Punta Sur National Park is at Cozumel's southern tip.

ers. **Best for:** swimming; snorkeling; sunsets. ✉ *Carretera Norte, Km 4* ☎ *987/869–5160* ⊕ *www.playa-azul.com* ✈ *Free* ⊙ *Daily 9–5.*

Playa San Francisco. Playa San Francisco was one of the first beach clubs on the coast. The inviting 5-km (3-mile) stretch of sandy beach, which extends along Carretera Sur south of Parque Chankanaab at about Km 14, is among the longest and finest on Cozumel. Encompassing the beaches Playa Maya and Santa Rosa, it's typically packed with cruise-ship passengers in high season. On Sunday locals flock here to eat fresh fish. Amenities include two outdoor restaurants, a bar, dressing rooms, gift shops, beach chairs, restrooms, massage treatments, and water-sports equipment rentals. Divers use the beach as a jumping-off point for the San Francisco reef. In lieu of a fee, there's a $10 minimum purchase of food or drinks for adults. **Amenities:** food and drink; lifeguards; parking (free); showers; toilets. **Best for:** walking; swimming. ✉ *Carretera Costera Sur, Km 14* ✈ *Free ($10 minimum for food and drink).*

Uvas. Uvas started out with a sexy, South Beach–style attitude, but now it caters to small cruise-ship groups and independent tourists. Facilities include lockers, restrooms with showers, kayaks, on-site massages, and a dive shop. Fees vary with packages that include entrance, lunch, and additional activities. The basic entrance fee includes one drink and the use of beach umbrellas, lounge chairs, and other amenities. ■**TIP→** Phone or online reservations are required since the club tries to keep crowds away and limits the number of guests. **Amenities:** food and drink; water sports; lifeguards; parking (free); toilets; show-

The Quieter Side of Cozumel

Blazing-white cruise ships parade in and out of Cozumel like a regatta of floating apartment buildings. There's at least one on the horizon every day of the year; some days the island gets six. The day-trippers they carry pack the tourist-trap souvenir shops and bars on San Miguel's waterfront every afternoon, making the place feel more like a suburban shopping mall than a small Mexican town.

Luckily, there's plenty of Cozumel to go around. If you're fortunate enough to overnight on the island, try these tricks to avoid the crowds.

1. Keep a low profile. Stick close to the beach and pool when more than two ships are in port.

2. Time your excursions. Go into San Miguel for early breakfast and errands, then stay out of town for the rest of the day. Wander back after you hear the ships blast their departure warnings around 5 or 6 pm.

3. Dive in. Hide from the hordes by slipping underwater. But be sure to choose a small dive operation that travels to less-popular reefs.

4. Drive on the wild side. Rent a car and cruise the windward coast, still free of rampant construction. You can picnic and sunbathe on private beaches hidden by limestone outcroppings, and watch the waves roll in. Use caution when swimming, though, since the surf can be rough.

5. Frequent the "other" downtown. Most of Cozumel's residents live and shop far from San Miguel's waterfront. Avenidas 15, 20, and 25 are packed with taco stands, *papelerías* (stationery stores), and neighborhood markets. While driving here can be messy, park on a quieter side street and explore the shops and neighborhoods to see a whole different side of Cozumel.

ers. **Best for:** solitude; snorkeling; swimming. ⊠ *Carretera Sur, Km 8.5* ☎ *987/872–5876* ⊕ *www.playauvas.com* ⊒ *$8.*

WINDWARD BEACHES

The east coast of Cozumel presents a splendid succession of deserted rocky coves and narrow powdery beaches poised dramatically against the turquoise Caribbean. ⚠ Swimming can be treacherous here if you go out too far—in some places the strong undertow can sweep you out to sea in minutes. But the beaches are perfect for solitary sunbathing. Several casual restaurants dot the coastline; they all close after sunset.

Beyond Punta Oriente, the sandy road beside Mezcalitos leading to the wild northeast coast is sometimes open and sometimes gated—a shame, because the beaches here are superb. At this writing there were no tours to this part of the coast, and the road is too rutted for rental cars. Rumors abound as to this area's future—some say there will be a small-scale resort here someday, while others hope it will become an ecological reserve. A small navy base is the only permanent settlement on the road for now, though some of the scrub jungle is divided into housing lots.

North of Playa San Martín. About 1 km (½ mile) to the north of Playa San Martín the island road turns hilly and offers panoramic ocean views. Coconuts, a hilltop restaurant, is a prime lookout spot that also serves good food. The adjacent **Ventanas al Mar** hotel is the only one on the windward coast, attracting locals and travelers who value solitude. Locals picnic on the long beach directly north of the hotel. When the water's calm, there's good snorkeling around the rocks beneath the hotel, but steer clear if the water's rough. **Amenities:** food and drink; parking (free). **Best for:** solitude; snorkeling. ✉ *Carretera C-1.*

Playa de San Martín. Not quite 5 km (3 miles) north of Punta Chiqueros, a long stretch of beach begins along the Chen Río Reef. Turtles come to lay their eggs on the section known as Playa de San Martín. Soldiers or ecologists sometimes guard the beach during full moons in May and June to prevent poaching. This is a particularly good spot for swimming when the water is calm (and the turtles aren't nesting). Directly in front of the reef is a small bay with clear waters and surf that's relatively mild thanks to a protective rock formation. When the wind is blowing from the south, though, the water is best for kiteboarders and windsurfers. A restaurant, also called **Chen Río,** serves cold drinks and decent seafood. **Amenities:** food and drink; parking (free). **Best for:** swimming; windsurfing; solitude. ✉ *Carretera C-1, Km 43* ⌨ *Free.*

FAMILY **Punta Chiqueros.** Punta Chiqueros, a half moon-shaped cove sheltered by an offshore reef, is the first popular swimming area as you drive north on the coastal road. (It's about 12 km [8 miles] north of Faro Celarain Park.) Part of a longer beach that some locals call Playa Bonita, it has fine sand, clear water, and moderate waves. This is a great place to swim, watch the sunset, and eat fresh fish at the restaurant, also called Playa Bonita. **Amenities:** food and drink; toilets; parking (free). **Best for:** walking; sunsets; swimming. ✉ *Carretera C-1, Km 38.*

Punta Oriente. Punta Oriente is a typical windward beach—great for beachcombing but unsuitable for swimming. The beach has been nicknamed Playa Mezcalitos after the much-loved **Mezcalito Café,** which serves seafood and beer and can get pretty rowdy. Iguana's is the other restaurant option on this stretch of sand. **Amenities:** food and drink; parking (free). **Best for:** partiers; nudists; walking. ✉ *Carretera C-1, KM 49* ⌨ *Free.*

Punta Morena. Surfers and boogie-boarders have adopted Punta Morena, a short drive north of Ventanas al Mar, as their official hangout, and for good reason: great waves and a restaurant serving surfer-friendly burgers and fries. Camping is allowed; for the full experience, you can pick up a hammock, for sale by the side of the road, and string it up under the many shade-providing palapas. **Amenities:** food and drink; parking (free). **Best for:** surfing. ✉ *Carretera C-1, Km 46.*

WHERE TO EAT

Dining options on Cozumel reflect the island's laid-back attitude: breezy and relaxed, with casual dress and no reservations the rule. Most restaurants emphasize fresh ingredients, simple presentation, and amiable service. As befits an island, there's lots of fresh seafood on the menu; *pescado tixin-xic* (fish spiced with achiote and baked in banana leaves) is a regional specialty. However, regional Yucatecan cuisine is hard to come by except in a few tourist-area places. You're more likely to find standard Mexican fare like tacos, enchiladas, and huevos rancheros. For budget meals, head into the untouristed part of downtown, because they're few and far between in tourist areas. Although some restaurants are turning out creative cuisine to suit the most demanding of palates, most visitors say their best dining experiences are in small, family-owned restaurants that seem to have been here forever. While many restaurants accept credit cards, café-type places generally don't. ■**TIP→** Cab drivers are often paid to shill for restaurants, so take their dining suggestions with a grain (or two) of salt.

ZONA HOTELERA SUR

$$$$ ✕ **Alfredo di Roma.** The opportunity to dine graciously amid crystal and
ITALIAN candlelight (and blessedly cool air-conditioning) is just one reason to book a special dinner at Alfredo's. The pastas are made fresh daily, and cheeses are flown in from Italy so the chef can prepare the house special, authentic fettuccine Alfredo, at your table. The carpaccio, spaghetti with lobster, and Chilean sea bass in white wine and tomato sauce are all superb, and the wine cellar is the largest on the island. Book a table for early evening and enjoy the sunset view through wall-length windows. Diners not staying at the hotel must have advance reservations. $ *Average main: $22* ⊠ *Presidente InterContinental Cozumel, Carretera Chankanaab, Km 6.5* ☎ *987/872-9500* ⊕ *www.alfredodiroma.com.mx* ⌲ *Reservations essential* ⊘ *No lunch* ✢ *B4.*

SAN MIGUEL

$ ✕ **Casa Denis.** This little yellow house near the plaza has been satisfying
MEXICAN cravings for Yucatecan *cochinita pibil* (spiced pork baked in banana leaves) and other favorites since 1945, though locals tend to stop in for the cheap breakfast and lunch menus (8:30–1) that highlight tacos and empanadas. *Tortas* (sandwiches) are also a real bargain, and you'll start to feel like a local if you spend an hour at one of the outdoor tables, watching shoppers dash about. $ *Average main: $6* ⊠ *Calle 1 Sur 132, between Avs. 5 and 10* ☎ *987/872-0067* ⊕ *www.casadenis.com* ▬ *No credit cards* ✢ *B3.*

$$$ ✕ **Casa Mission.** Part private home and part restaurant (and owned by
MEXICAN the same family since the 1980s), this somewhat dated estate evokes
FAMILY a country hacienda in mainland Mexico. The on-site botanical garden has mango and papaya trees and a small zoo with caged birds. The setting, with tables lining the veranda, outshines the food, which caters to the tourist palate. Nonetheless, stalwart fans rave about huge platters of fajitas and grilled fish. It's a few blocks from the waterfront, so you may want to take a cab. Or, visit one of their two more-central sister restaurants, La Mission and Parilla Mission. $ *Average main: $18* ⊠ *Av. 55, between Calle Juarez and Calle 1 Sur* ☎ *987/872-1641* ⊕ *www.missioncoz.com* ✢ *D3.*

5

CLOSE UP

Island Dining

There's no shortage of dining choices on Cozumel, where restaurateurs from Mexico, the U.S., and Europe bring every visitor a taste of home. The narrow streets of San Miguel are filled with the aromas of grilling steaks and smoking shrimp, as waiters deliver platters of enchiladas and pizza to sidewalk tables and passersby eye the tables full of food, trying to choose where to eat. At rooftop restaurants groups gather over Italian feasts; along the shoreline, lobster and fresh fish are the catch of the day. All over the island, there is a bias toward tourist taste buds, and in fact it can be a challenge to find authentic regional cuisine. Yucatecan dishes such as *cochinita pibil* (pork with achiote spice), *queso relleno* (Gouda cheese stuffed with ground meat), and *sopa de lima* (lime soup) rarely appear on menus aimed at foreign visitors, but an easy hunt will find them at San Miguel's small family-owned eateries, often simply a cluster of wobbly tables in a tiny café.

Although there are a few restaurants serving fine cuisine, even the island's top chefs tend to emphasize natural flavors and simple preparations. The same spirit holds for the dining room, where casual clothes are the rule and a shirt with buttons qualifies as dress-up. (There are a few places where you can let your sartorial excellence shine.)

$ MEXICAN 🍴 **El Foco.** This local-favorite taquería stays open until midnight, or until the last customer leaves. The soft tacos stuffed with pork, chorizo, cheese, or beef are cheap and filling, and the graffiti on the walls and the late-night revelers provide the entertainment a block off the main square. [$] *Average main: $4* ✉ *Av. 5 Sur 13B, between Calles Adolfo Rosado Salas and 3 Sur* 💳 *No credit cards* 🕒 *No lunch* ✥ *B3.*

$$$ ITALIAN 🍴 **Guido's.** Chef Yvonne Villiger works wonders with fresh fish—if the wahoo with capers and black olives is on the menu, don't miss it. But Guido's is best known for its pizzas baked in a wood-burning oven, which tends to make sections of the indoor dining room rather warm. Instead, enjoy a pitcher of sangria in the pleasant, roomy courtyard. [$] *Average main: $19* ✉ *Av. Rafael E. Melgar 23, between Calles 6 and 8 Norte* ☎ *987/872–0946* 🌐 *www.guidoscozumel.com* 🕒 *No lunch Sun.* ✥ *C1*

$$$ MEXICAN Fodor's Choice ★ 🍴 **Kinta.** Both locals and visitors rave about this upscale spot, owned by personable chef Kris Wallenta, formerly of Guido's. It's easy to overlook the entrance (look for a bright orange facade on the west side of the street), but once you've discovered the blissfully air-conditioned dining room, romantic outdoor garden, and impressive menu, you'll likely return. When he's not at his newest restaurant, Kondesa, Wallenta rushes about the open kitchen, whipping up sophisticated interpretations of classic Mexican dishes. He updates the menu often and offers light selections for those craving less filling fare, but among the favorites are his savory black bean soup, a chile relleno filled with vegetable ratatouille and Chihuahua cheese, pork in a smoky *pasilla* chile sauce, and a tender filet mignon with *huitlacoche* (a corn truffle) and cheese.

Hand-crushed mojitos, fruity sangria, and virgin *limomenta* (lemonade with mint) add a refreshing lilt, and the *budín de la abuelita,* bread pudding with Mexican chocolate and *cajeta* (caramel sauce), is a fitting end to a stellar meal. [$] *Average main: $17* ✉ *Av. 5 #148, between Calles 2 and 4* ☎ *987/869–0544* 🌐 *www.kintacozumel.com* ⏲ *Closed Mon.* ✣ *C2*

$$$ MEXICAN Fodor's Choice ★ 🍴 **Kondesa.** You can't miss the hot pink and turquoise exterior of local chef Kris Wallenta's latest restaurant. The chill, lounge-y feel of the island's new hot spot, which features a palapa-covered bar that opens onto a dimly lit garden dining room, may cater more to the tourist set, but don't be fooled: this isn't a tourist trap. Wallenta excels at putting modern spins on classic flavors, and this menu centers on locally caught fish. Favorites include the *guak* trio, the *jikama* tacos, which change depending on the day's catch, the Kondesa *kakes,* which are an interpretation of crab cakes made with lion fish, and enchiladas, also filled with seafood. A full cocktail list complements any meal, so if you can't make it for dinner, stop in for a drink. The vibe can't be beat. [$] *Average main: $17* ✉ *5th Av. #456, between 5th and 7th* ☎ *987/869–1086* ⏲ *Closed Mon.* ✣ *A3*

$$ MEXICAN 🍴 **La Choza.** Locals get together for breakfasts of *migas* (scrambled eggs with bits of bacon and tortilla) and the daily lunchtime *comida corrida,* a set-priced meal of the day with a choice of appetizers and entrées. The à la carte menu, however, is almost double in price. Favorite dishes include *pollo con mole poblano* (chicken in a smooth, earthy chile sauce), chile relleno *de camarón* (chile stuffed with shrimp), and pork with pumpkin seed sauce. An array of *agua frescas* in flavors like hibiscus are served in massive goblets, and remember to leave room for the chilled avocado pie. [$] *Average main: $8* ✉ *Av. 10, between Calle Adolfo Rosado Salas and Av. 3* ☎ *987/872–0958* ✣ *B3.*

$$$$ ECLECTIC 🍴 **La Cocay.** This casually sophisticated dining room and garden is always full. The menu has a little bit of everything and changes frequently, but you can expect to find salads laced with fruits, pastas, and entrées like seared sashimi-grade tuna and steaks. Consider sharing several small plates from the tapas menu, such as the blue-cheese phyllo rolls with black-cherry sauce, salmon meatballs, and octopus with garlic. Also on offer are reasonably priced wines by the glass from Argentina, Chile, and Mexico. Though the service can run a bit on the slow side—and popular menu items tend to run out—everyone seems to leave happy. [$] *Average main: $25* ✉ *Calle 8 Norte 208, between Avs. 10 and 15* ☎ *987/872–5533* 🌐 *www.lacocay.com* ⏲ *Closed Sun. No lunch* ✣ *C1.*

$$$ ECLECTIC 🍴 **Le Chef.** This tiny, popular café and restaurant, featuring six indoor tables and six along Avenida Quinta's sidewalk, is an all-day affair. At breakfast, you can have a full meal for less than $10, while at lunch locals linger over the must-have lobster BLT sandwich, various soups, salads, or special pizzas. As the sun sets, Le Chef's ambience skews toward cozy as the lights dim and the menu expands to include a daily list of specials including various preparations of seafood and pasta. [$] *Average main: $16* ✉ *5th Av. #378, at Calle 5* ☎ *987/878–4391* ✣ *B3.*

$$$ MEXICAN 🍴 **Pancho's Backyard.** Marimbas play beside a bubbling fountain in the charming courtyard behind one of Cozumel's best folk-art shops.

Mopeds are a great way to explore the island.

Though Pancho's is always busy, the waitstaff is patient and helpful. Cruise-ship passengers seeking a taste of Mexico pack the place at lunch; dinner is a bit more serene. The American-style, English menu is geared toward tourists, but regional ingredients like smoky chipotle chile make even the standard steak stand out. Other stars include the cilantro cream soup and shrimp flambéed with tequila. [$] *Average main: $16* ✉ *Av. Rafael Melgar, between Calles 8 and 10 Norte* ☎ *987/872–2141* 🌐 *www.panchosbackyard.com* ⏱ *No lunch Sun.* ✣ *C1*

$$$$ STEAKHOUSE 🍴 **Pepe's Steak and Seafood House.** Once a kitschy, nautical-themed eatery, a recent renovation has given this popular second-story restaurant off San Miguel's main street a long-needed face-lift, as well as a steep rise in prices. The upstairs dining room's tall windows allow for fantastic sunset views, and classic cuts of meat including filet mignon, T-bone, and prime rib, please American palates, though some say the meat isn't up to steak-house standards. [$] *Average main: $33* ✉ *Av. Rafael E. Melgar and Calle Adolfo Rosado Salas* ☎ *987/872–0213* 🌐 *www.pepesgrillcozumel.com* ✣ *B3.*

$ ECLECTIC 🍴 **Rock 'n Java Caribbean Bar & Grill.** The extensive breakfast menu here includes whole-wheat French toast and cheese crêpes. For lunch or dinner try the vegetarian tacos or linguine with clams, or choose from more than a dozen salads. Pies, cakes, and pastries are baked on site daily. You can enjoy your healthy meal or sweet snack while enjoying a sea view through the back windows. Used books are piled on shelves along one wall, and the bulletin board by the front door is an interesting read—although with free Wi-Fi, your reading options are unlimited. New Rock 'n Java spots—Noodle Bar & Sushi and Tex-Mex Island Grill (both in the Mega Shopping Center)—round out the offering of this popular Cozumel brand. $ *Average main: $9* ⊠ *Av. Rafael E. Melgar 602-6* ☎ *987/872–4405* ⊕ *www.rocknjavacozumel.com* ✛ *A3.*

WINDWARD COAST

$$ ✕ **Coconuts.** The T-shirts and bikinis hanging from the palapa roof at this
MEXICAN windward-side hangout, which is known more for its views than for its cuisine, are good indicators of its party-time atmosphere. Jimmy Buffett tunes play in the background while crowds down cervezas and garlic shrimp. These may not be good enough to write home about, but they are good enough to keep the crowds coming. The scene is more peaceful if you choose a palapa-shaded table on the rocks overlooking the water. Be warned, the party closes at 6 pm when the sun sets. $ *Average main: $10* ⊠ *Carretera C-1, Km 43* ▭ *No credit cards* ☽ *No dinner* ✛ *C4.*

$ ✕ **Playa Bonita.** Locals gather on Sunday afternoons at this casual beach
MEXICAN café. The water here is usually calm, and families alternate between swimming and lingering over long lunches of fried fish. Weekdays are quieter, making it a good place to spend the day if you want access to food, drinks, and showers but aren't into the rowdy beach-club scene. $ *Average main: $8* ⊠ *East Coast Rd., Km 38 at Punta Chiqueros* ☎ *987/872–4868* ▭ *No credit cards* ☽ *No dinner* ✛ *C4.*

WHERE TO STAY

Small, one-of-a-kind hotels have long been the norm in Cozumel. Most of the island's hotels are on the leeward (west) and south sides of the island, but there's one peaceful hideaway on the windward (east) side. The larger resorts are north and south of San Miguel, while the less-expensive places are found in town.

ZONA HOTELERA NORTE

$$ ⊡ **Coral Princess Hotel and Resort.** Good snorkeling off the rocky shoreline
RESORT and a relaxed family feel makes this resort, which has both hotel rooms
FAMILY and apartmentlike units, a north-coast favorite. **Pros:** excellent snorkeling right off beach; decent, well-priced meals; family-friendly. **Cons:** can be noisy; some rooms lack bathtubs. $ *Rooms from: $108* ⊠ *Carretera Costera Norte, Km 2.5* ☎ *987/872–3200* ⊕ *www.coralprincess.com* ⊠ *142 rooms* ❖❘ *Breakfast* ✛ *B3.*

$$$$ ⊡ **Hotel B.** The latest entry in the northern hotel zone, this sleek boutique
HOTEL spot has quickly become the preferred lodging choice for a discerning crowd. **Pros:** on-site dive center; nice spa; sleek design; free Wi-Fi. **Cons:** rocky beach; sometimes inconsistent service. $ *Rooms from: $270* ⊠ *Playa San Juan, Km 2.5* ☎ *987/872–0300* ⊕ *www.hotelbcozumel.com* ⊠ *45 rooms* ❖❘ *No meals* ✛ *A3.*

$$$ ⊡ **Playa Azul Golf and Beach Resort.** Though some rooms have recently
HOTEL been renovated and feel bright and airy, most rooms in this resort are
ALL-INCLUSIVE unremarkable, even though all are complete with terraces and face the ocean. **Pros:** small and intimate feel; excellent spa; no greens fees for hotel guests. **Cons:** unheated pool and no hot tub; may be too quiet for some; lobby and most rooms feel dated; rocky beach. $ *Rooms from:*

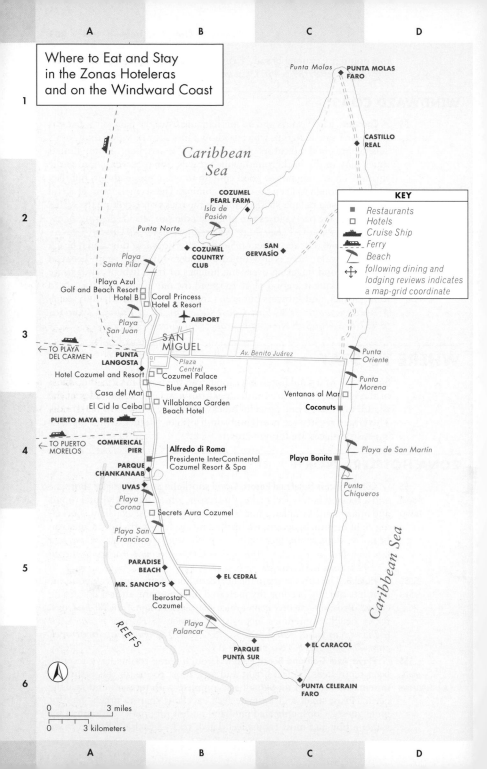

Where to Eat and Stay in the Zonas Hoteleras and on the Windward Coast

Caribbean Sea

Punta Molas

PUNTA MOLAS FARO

CASTILLO REAL

COZUMEL PEARL FARM
Isla de Pasión

Punta Norte

SAN GERVASIO

COZUMEL COUNTRY CLUB

Playa Santa Pilar

Playa Azul Golf and Beach Resort
Hotel B

Coral Princess Hotel & Resort

AIRPORT

Playa San Juan

SAN MIGUEL

← TO PLAYA DEL CARMEN

PUNTA LANGOSTA

Plaza Central

Av. Benito Juárez

Punta Oriente

Hotel Cozumel and Resort

Cozumel Palace

Blue Angel Resort

Punta Morena

Casa del Mar

Villablanca Garden Beach Hotel

Ventanas al Mar

El Cid la Ceiba

Coconuts

PUERTO MAYA PIER

← TO PUERTO MORELOS

COMMERICAL PIER

Alfredo di Roma
Presidente InterContinental Cozumel Resort & Spa

Playa Bonita

Playa de San Martín

PARQUE CHANKANAAB

UVAS

Punta Chiqueros

Playa Corona

Secrets Aura Cozumel

Playa San Francisco

PARADISE BEACH

EL CEDRAL

MR. SANCHO'S

Iberostar Cozumel

REEFS

Playa Palancar

PARQUE PUNTA SUR

EL CARACOL

Caribbean Sea

PUNTA CELERAIN FARO

0   3 miles
0   3 kilometers

KEY

- ■ Restaurants
- □ Hotels
- Cruise Ship
- Ferry
- Beach
- ↔ following dining and lodging reviews indicates a map-grid coordinate

$185 ✉ Carretera Costera Norte, Km 4 ☎ 987/869–5160 🌐 www.playa-azul.com 🛏 36 rooms, 16 suites, 1 house 🍴 Multiple meal plans ⊕ A3.

ZONA HOTELERA SUR

$$ B&B/INN 🏨 **Blue Angel Resort.** A complete makeover in 2009 turned this small, diver-friendly hangout into a real gem. **Pros:** friendly, repeat clientele; clean; close to town; great snorkeling, on-site PADI outfit. **Cons:** non-divers may feel out of place. [$] *Rooms from: $109 ✉ Carretera Sur, Km 2.2 ☎ 987/872–0819 🌐 www.blueangelresort.com 🛏 22 rooms 🍴 Breakfast ⊕ B3.*

$ HOTEL 🏨 **Casa del Mar.** Rooms at this diver-oriented hotel are bright with Mexican artwork, but those with sea-facing balconies are lighter and airier and don't cost that much more. **Pros:** good dive shop; optional, reasonably priced all-inclusive plan. **Cons:** air-conditioning weak in some rooms; nondivers may feel out of place. [$] *Rooms from: $79 ✉ Carretera Sur, Km 4 ☎ 987/872–1900 🌐 www.casadelmarcozumel.com 🛏 98 rooms, 8 cabanas 🍴 No meals ⊕ B4.*

5

$$$$ RESORT ALL-INCLUSIVE FAMILY 🏨 **Cozumel Palace.** Within walking distance of San Miguel, this luxurious all-inclusive hotel faces the water but lacks a beach. **Pros:** in-room hot tubs; on-site spa; good honeymoon hideaway. **Cons:** sales pressure by time-share reps; no beach. [$] *Rooms from: $389 ✉ Av. Rafael E. Melgar, Km 1.5 ☎ 987/872–9430, 877/325–1537 in U.S. 🌐 www.palaceresorts.com 🛏 175 rooms 🍴 All-inclusive ⊕ B3.*

$$ RESORT ALL-INCLUSIVE FAMILY 🏨 **El Cid la Ceiba.** This smallish pierside resort is a comfortable choice, with large condo-style rooms equipped with dining tables and kitchenettes. **Pros:** reasonably priced all-inclusive option available; good snorkeling offshore. **Cons:** massive cruise ships nearby mar sea view; pool scene can be rowdy. [$] *Rooms from: $135 ✉ Carretera Chankanaab, Km 4.5 ☎ 987/872–0844, 800/733–7308 toll-free in U.S. 🌐 www.elcid.com 🛏 60 rooms 🍴 Multiple meal plans ⊕ B4.*

$$ RESORT ALL-INCLUSIVE FAMILY 🏨 **Hotel Cozumel and Resort.** On sunny days in high season, families and revelers surround the enormous pool at this bright orange hotel, while activity directors enliven the crowd with games and loud music. **Pros:** 10-minute walk from town; near grocery stores and restaurants; 10 fully accessible rooms. **Cons:** rocky beach area; poolside entertainment sometimes loud and annoying; Wi-Fi access unreliable. [$] *Rooms from: $150 ✉ Carretera Costera Sur, Km 17 ☎ 987/872–9020 🌐 www.hotelcozumel.com.mx 🛏 181 rooms 🍴 Multiple meal plans ⊕ B3.*

$$$$ RESORT ALL-INCLUSIVE FAMILY 🏨 **Iberostar Cozumel.** Jungle greenery surrounds this all-inclusive resort at Cozumel's southernmost point. **Pros:** friendly, personal service; large pool area with plenty of lounge chairs. **Cons:** rocky beach; murky water; so-so food without much variety. [$] *Rooms from: $280 ✉ Carretera Chankanaab, Km 17, past El Cedral turnoff ☎ 987/872–9900, 888/923–2722 in U.S. 🌐 www.iberostar.com 🛏 300 rooms, 6 suites 🍴 All-inclusive ⊕ B5.*

$$$$ RESORT FAMILY Fodor's Choice ★ 🏨 **Presidente InterContinental Cozumel Resort and Spa.** The InterContinental really owns the luxury resort market on Cozumel, offering top-notch service, expansive lawns, pristine beaches, and spacious, modern rooms. **Pros:** secluded and spacious feel; high-quality beds and linens; iPod docking stations; impeccable service. **Cons:** overpriced restaurants;

Presidente InterContinental Cozumel Resort and Spa

timeshare pitches in the lobby; far from town. [$] *Rooms from: $295* ✉ *Carretera Chankanaab, Km 6.5* ☎ *987/872–9500, 800/327–0200* 🌐 *www.intercontinentalcozumel.com* 🛏 *183 rooms, 37 suites* 🍴 *No meals* ✥ *B4.*

> **WORD OF MOUTH**
>
> "This may be on the higher end of reasonable, but I've gone there twice for the snorkeling—Presidente InterContinental. I've booked it through Apple or Funjet or similar and stayed in one of the less expensive room options to get the great snorkeling right from the beach, which is right out of your hotel door. The resident iguanas are photogenic, too." —atravelynn

$$$$ RESORT ALL-INCLUSIVE **Secrets Aura Cozumel.** Now part of the Secrets brand, the elegant, all-inclusive Aura, raises the bar for the southern coast's string of swish beach properties. **Pros:** high-tech; luxurious amenities (rare on Cozumel); intimate, sophisticated ambience. **Cons:** far from town; offshore snorkeling not very good; no kids; some rooms not updated yet. [$] *Rooms from: $500* ✉ *Carretera Costera Sur, Km 12.9* ☎ *800/413–3886 in Mexico, 800/467–3273 in U.S.* 🌐 *www.secretsresorts.com* 🛏 *168 suites* 🍴 *All-inclusive* ✥ *B5.*

$ HOTEL **Villablanca Garden Beach Hotel.** The landscaped grounds here are lovely, as are most rooms, although there is a certain budget-hotel spareness to the place, as befits the price. **Pros:** lush gardens around pool; good value. **Cons:** no dressers in rooms, 2 miles from town. [$] *Rooms from: $85* ✉ *Carretera Chankanaab, Km 3* ☎ *987/872–0730* 🌐 *www.villablanca.net* 🛏 *45 rooms and suites, 1 penthouse, 3 villas* 🍴 *Multiple meal plans* ✥ *B4.*

SAN MIGUEL

$ HOTEL Fodor's Choice ★ **Casa Mexicana.** Although not on the beach, this distinctive and inexpensive hotel overlooks the waterfront in San Miguel; splurge on the waterfront rooms, which have comfortable balconies from which to enjoy the sea views. **Pros:** great downtown location near restaurants and shops; friendly staff (especially bartenders); substantial breakfast. **Cons:** no beach; tiny pool; some street noise. [$] *Rooms from: $95* ✉ *Av. Rafael E. Melgar #457, between Calles 5 and 7 Sur* ☎ *987/872–9090, 877/228–6747 from U.S.* 🌐 *www.casamexicanacozumel.com* 🛏 *90 rooms* 🍴 *Breakfast* ✥ *A3.*

$ B&B/INN **Hacienda San Miguel.** Guests at this small inn five blocks south of San Miguel's main plaza get discounts at Mr. **Pros:** quiet but central; plenty of great restaurants nearby; courtyard gardens make it feel like a private home. **Cons:** no parking; air-conditioning can be noisy; no pool. [$] *Rooms from: $94* ✉ *Calle 10 Norte #1500, at Av. 5* ☎ *987/872–1986* 🌐 *www.haciendasanmiguel.com* 🛏 *7 studios, 3 suites, 1 town house* 🍴 *Breakfast* ✥ *C1.*

WINDWARD COAST

$$ B&B/INN **Ventanas al Mar.** The lights of San Miguel are but a distant glow on the horizon when you look west from the only hotel on the windward coast. **Pros:** blissful solitude; long beach great for sunset walks. **Cons:**

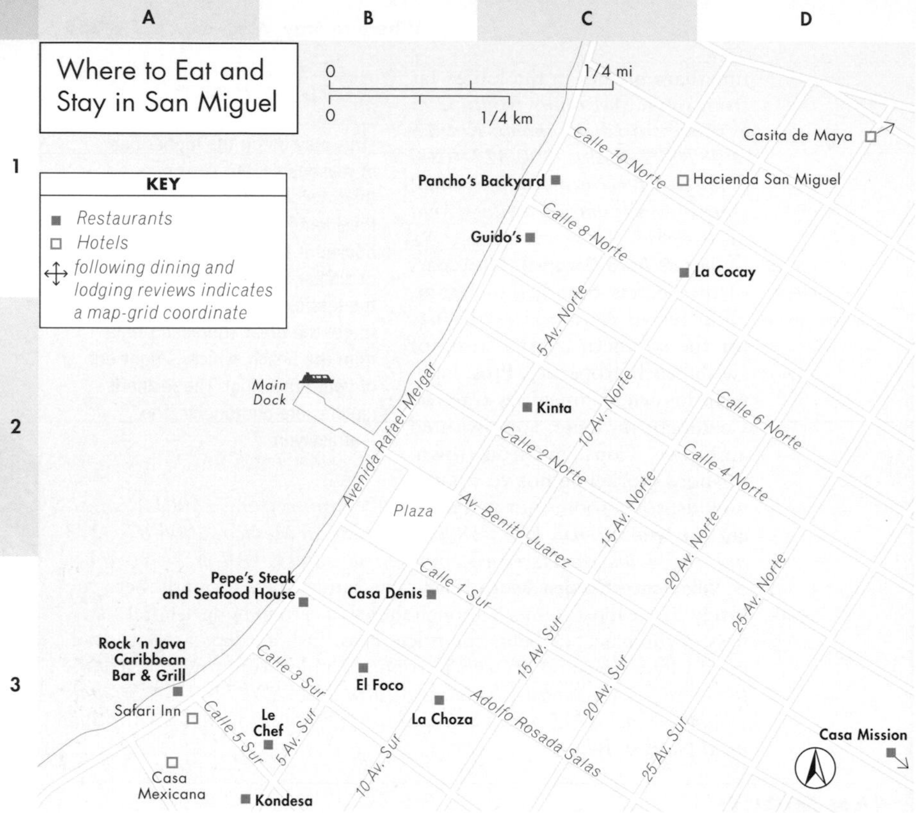
A
B
C
D
1
2
3
Where to Eat and Stay in San Miguel
0
1/4 mi
0
1/4 km
KEY
■ Restaurants
□ Hotels
✣ following dining and lodging reviews indicates a map-grid coordinate
Casita de Maya □
Calle 10 Norte
□ Hacienda San Miguel
Pancho's Backyard ■
Calle 8 Norte
Guido's ■
■ La Cocay
5 Av. Norte
Main Dock
Avenida Rafael Melgar
■ Kinta
10 Av. Norte
Calle 6 Norte
Calle 2 Norte
Calle 4 Norte
Plaza
Av. Benito Juarez
15 Av. Norte
20 Av. Norte
Pepe's Steak and Seafood House ■
Casa Denis ■
Calle 1 Sur
25 Av. Norte
Rock 'n Java Caribbean Bar & Grill ■
Calle 3 Sur
■ El Foco
15 Av. Sur
Safari Inn □
Calle 5 Sur
Le Chef ■
5 Av. Sur
■ La Choza
Adolfo Rosada Salas
20 Av. Sur
Casa Mission ■
□ Casa Mexicana
■ Kondesa
10 Av. Sur
25 Av. Sur

spotty electricity; limited food and drink options; driving not recommended on unlit road at night. [$] *Rooms from: $110* ✉ *East-coast road north of Coconuts, Carretera C-1, Km 43.5* ☎ *987/105–2684* 🌐 *www.ventanasalmar.com.mx* 🛏 *12 rooms, 2 suites* 💳 *No credit cards* 🍴 *Breakfast* ✣ *C4.*

NIGHTLIFE

If you're looking for a party, look elsewhere. Cozumel's already low-key nightlife shuts down by midnight, perhaps thanks to the many dive excursions leaving at the crack of dawn. The cruise-ship passengers mobbing the bars seem to drink enough for the whole island, and the rowdiest action sometimes takes place in the afternoon, when mojito-slinging revelers pull out the stops before reboarding. But if you're willing to shift the night action a few hours earlier, the excellent salsa bands playing a few bars and beach clubs will oblige. Join locals and resident expats for a few rounds on the dance floor and you'll be ready for bed at a relatively reasonable hour.

BARS

Carlos 'n Charlie's and Señor Frog's. The *Animal House* ambience at rowdy restaurant-bars Carlos 'n Charlie's and Señor Frog's includes loud rock music and a bar-dancing, bead-throwing, anything-goes drinking scene. ✉ *Av. Rafael E. Melgar #551 at Punta Langosta* ☎ *987/869–1647, 987/869–1658* ⊕ *www. carlosandcharlies.com.*

DLounge. For a more sophisticated scene with mojitos and great cigars, check out DLounge (formerly Havana Blue) in the flashy Forum shopping mall. ✉ *Av. Rafael E. Melgar and Calle 10 Norte, 2nd fl.* ☎ *987/869–5317.*

SPRING FESTIVAL

If you're here in April, tap your toes to some traditional dance during the **Fería del Cedral,** a fair held in the settlement of El Cedral near the last weekend in April. Park in dirt lots nearby or take one of many available taxis. To get here, turn at Km 17.5 off Carretera Sur or Avenida Rafael E. Melgar, then drive 3 km (2 miles) inland to the site.

5

Fat Tuesday. Lively, rowdy Fat Tuesday draws crowds day and night for frozen daiquiris, ice-cold beers, and blaring rock. ✉ *Av. Juárez 2, between Av. Rafael E. Melgar and Calle 3 Sur* ⊕ *fat-tuesday.cozumel.net.*

Love Cafe. The vibe at this beachfront palapa café is laid-back throughout the day, when it serves coffee and three meals. However, by night, live music is the draw. The local Red Eye Band plays four nights a week, and the owners bring in bands from other parts of Mexico regularly. It's open until midnight daily, cash only. ✉ *Playa Casitas, Av. Rafael Melgar, at Blvd. Aeropuerto* ☎ *987/107–1252.*

Viva Mexico. Viva Mexico sometimes has a DJ spinning Latin and U.S. dance music into the wee hours. There's also an extensive snack menu. This place is popular any time of day or night. The best seats are near the second-story railing overlooking the waterfront. ✉ *Av. Rafael E. Melgar, off Calle 7S* ☎ *987/872–0799.*

DANCE CLUBS

Tiki Tok. A tiki-themed bar by day, this locale is reborn as a dance club after dark. Local group Explosión Latina draws salsa aficionados of all stripes from 10:30 pm to 2 am Friday and Saturday, while a DJ spins hots from the 1970s and '80s, Latin, and reggaeton (a blend of West-Indian and Latin beats) the rest of the week. ✉ *Av. Rafael E. Melgar 13, between Calles 2 and 4 Norte* ☎ *987/869–8119* ⊕ *www.tikitokcozumel. com* ⊙ *Daily 10 am–4 am.*

LIVE MUSIC

Sunday evenings from 8 to 10, locals head for the *zócalo* (main square) to hear mariachis and local, Caribbean-style bands.

Hard Rock Cafe. The band at the Hard Rock Cafe rocks until 1 am nightly. Air-conditioning is a major plus. ✉ *Av. Rafael E. Melgar, between Av. Juárez and Calle 2, 2nd fl.* ☎ *987/872–5271* ⊕ *www.hardrock.com.*

Nothing beats live entertainment.

'Ohana. Skip the salsa and relax into some roots reggae at 'Ohana. This café-bar, serving three meals daily, is open Monday through Saturday, with a daily happy hour from 7 to 9 pm. ⊠ *Av. 5, between Calles 6 and 8 Norte* ⊕ *www.ohanacozumel.com.*

Playa Azul. The salsa band Aquino plays beneath the palapas on Sunday afternoon at Playa Azul. They're onstage from 3 to 4:30 pm, or whenever the spirit moves them. ⊠ *Playa Azul Hotel, Carretera Norte, Km 4* ⊕ *www.playa-azul.com.*

Cinepolis. On a sweltering afternoon, slip into the silver screen at Cinepolis. The modern, multiscreen theater shows current hit films in Spanish and English and has afternoon matinees and nightly shows. ⊠ *Av. Rafael E. Melgar 1001, between Calles 15 and 17 Sur* ☎ *987/869–0799* ⊕ *www.cinepolis.com.*

SHOPPING

Cozumel's main souvenir-shopping area is downtown along Avenida Rafael E. Melgar and on side streets around the plaza. You'll also find clusters of shops at **Plaza del Sol** (⊠ *East side of main plaza*) and **Vista del Mar** (⊠ *Av. Rafael E. Melgar 45, between Calles 5 and 7*). Tourist-trap malls at the cruise-ship piers sell jewelry, perfume, sportswear, and low-end souvenirs at high-end prices.

Most downtown shops accept U.S. greenbacks, and many goods are priced in dollars. To get better prices, pay with cash or traveler's checks—some shops tack a hefty surcharge on credit-card purchases. Shops, restaurants, and streets are always crowded between 10 am

A Ceremonial Dance

Women regally dressed in embroidered, lace-trimmed dresses and men in their best guayabera shirts carry festooned trays on their heads during the Baile de las Cabezas de Cochino (Dance of the Pig's Head) at the Feria del Cedral, held in El Cedral. The trays are festooned with trailing ribbons, *papeles picados* (paper cutouts), piles of bread and, in some cases, the head of a barbecued you-know-what.

The pig is a sacrificial offering to God, who is said to have saved the founders of this tiny Cozumel settlement during the 19th-century War of the Castes, when Yucatán's Maya rose up against their oppressors. The enslaved Maya killed most of the *mestizos* (those of mixed European and indegenous heritage) in the mainland village of Sabán. Casimiro Cárdenas, a wealthy young mestizo, survived while clutching a small wooden cross, and later promised he would establish an annual religious festival once he found a new home.

Today the original religious vigils and novenas blend into the more secular fair, which usually runs through the last weekend in April. Festivities include horse races, bullfights, and carnival rides, and food stands sell hot dogs, corn on the cob, and cold beer. Celebrations peak with the ritual dance, usually held on the final day.

The music begins with a solemn cadence as families enter the stage, surrounding one member bearing a multitiered tray. The circular procession proceeds, with participants showing off their costumes and offerings. Gradually the beat quickens and the dancing begins. Grabbing the ends of ribbons trailing from the trays, children, parents, and grandparents twirl in ever-faster circles until the scene becomes a whirl of laughing faces and bright colors.

and 2 pm, but slow down in the evening. Traditionally, stores are open from 9 to 1 (except Sunday) and 5 to 9, but those nearest the pier tend to stay open all day, particularly during high season. Most shops are closed Sunday morning.

■**TIP→** When you shop for souvenirs, be sure you don't buy anything made with black coral. Not only is it overpriced, it's also an endangered species, and you may be barred from bringing it to the United States and other countries.

MARKETS

FAMILY **Crafts Market.** There's a crafts market in town that sells a respectable assortment of Mexican wares. Practice your bartering skills—start low, compromise, smile—while shopping for blankets, T-shirts, hammocks, and pottery. ⊠ *Calle 1 Sur, behind Plaza del Sol building.*

Mercado Municipal. For fresh produce, fish, chiles, and a taste of local life in Cozumel, stop by the Mercado Municipal. It's open daily from 6:30 am to 3 pm. ⊠ *Calle Adolfo Rosado Salas, between Avs. 20 and 25 Sur* ☎ *987/872–0771.*

SHOPPING MALLS

Forum Shops. Forum Shops is a flashy marble-and-glass mall with jewels glistening in glass cases and an overabundance of eager sales clerks. Diamonds International and Tanzanite International have shops in the Forum and all over Avenida Rafael E. Melgar, as does Roger's Boots, a leather store. Should you be in the market for expensive cigars, there's a Havana Blue bar upstairs. Note: You will pay top dollar for all purchases. ⊠ *Av. Rafael E. Melgar and Calle 10 Norte* ☎ *987/869–1687.*

Puerta Maya. Puerta Maya is a pedestrian mall geared to cruise-ship passengers, with branches of many of downtown's most popular shops, restaurants, and bars. It's close to the ships at the end of a huge parking lot. ⊠ *Carretera Sur, Km 4, at southern cruise dock* ⊕ *www.puertamaya. com.*

Punta Langosta. Punta Langosta, a fancy multilevel shopping mall, is across the street from the cruise-ship dock. An enclosed pedestrian walkway leads over the street from the ships to the center, which houses several jewelry and sportswear stores, as well as chain restaurants like Carlos 'n' Charlie's, Starbucks, and Señor Frogs. ⊠ *Av. Rafael E. Melgar 551, at Calle 7* ⊕ *www.centrocomercial-puntalangosta.com.mx.*

SPECIALTY STORES

CLOTHING

Several trendy sportswear shops line Avenida Rafael E. Melgar between Calles 2 and 6.

Exotica. Exotica has high-quality sportswear and shirts with nature-themed designs. ⊠ *Av. Juárez, at plaza* ☎ *987/872–5880.*

Island Outfitters. Island Outfitters has Mexican crafts, high-quality sportswear, beach towels, and sarongs. ⊠ *Av. Rafael E. Melgar at plaza* ☎ *987/872–0132.*

Mr. Buho. Mr. Buho specializes in black-and-white clothes and has well-made guayabera shirts and cotton dresses. ⊠ *Av. Rafael E. Melgar, between Calles 3 and 5* ☎ *987/872–1601.*

CRAFTS

Balam Mayan Feather. At Balam Mayan Feather, artists create intricate paintings on feathers from local birds. ⊠ *Av. 5 and Calle 2 Norte* ☎ *987/869–0548.*

Galería Azul. At Cozumel's best art gallery, Galería Azul, Artist Greg Dietrich creates and shows his engraved blown glass along with paintings, jewelry, and other works by local artists. It's open Monday through Friday from 11 am to 7 pm and by appointment. ⊠ *449 Av. 15 Norte, between Calles 8 and 10* ☎ *987/869–0963* ⊕ *www.cozumelglassart. com.*

Los Cinco Soles. Los Cinco Soles is the best one-stop shop in Cozumel for crafts from around Mexico. Several display rooms, covering almost an entire block, are filled with clothing, furnishings, home-decor items, and jewelry. There are also branches at the Puerta Maya cruise pier and at the Punta Langosta shopping mall. ⊠ *Av. Rafael E. Melgar and Calle 8 Norte* ☏ *987/872–9004* ⊕ *www.loscincosoles.com.*

Shalom. Antiques and high-quality silver jewelry are the draws at Shalom. ⊠ *Av. 10 #25* ☏ *987/872–3783.*

Viva Mexico. Viva Mexico sells souvenirs and handicrafts from all over Mexico; it's a great place to find T-shirts, blankets, and trinkets. There are also branches at the Puerta Maya cruise pier, and on Avenida Rafael E. Melgar between Calles 4 and 6 Norte. ⊠ *Av. Rafael E. Melgar at Adolfo Rosado Salas* ☏ *987/872–5466.*

GROCERY STORES

Chedraui. The grocery store Chedraui is open daily from 7 am to 10 pm and also carries clothing, kitchenware, appliances, and furniture. ⊠ *Av. Rafael E. Melgar, between Calles 15 and 17 Sur* ☏ *987/872–5404.*

Mega. The superstore Mega is a supermarket, pharmacy, and department store all under one big roof. It has a huge enclosed parking lot and pretty much anything you would need for a short or extended stay on Cozumel. It's open daily from 8 am to 10 pm. ⊠ *Av. Rafael E. Melgar, at Calle 11.*

JEWELRY

Diamond Creations. Diamond Creations lets you custom-design pieces of jewelry from a collection of loose diamonds, emeralds, rubies, sapphires, or tanzanite. The shop and its affiliates, Tanzanite International and Silver International, have multiple locations along the waterfront and in the shopping malls—in fact, it's hard to avoid them. ⊠ *Av. Rafael E. Melgar Sur 131, at Calle 2* ☏ *987/872–5330* ⊕ *www. diamondsinternational.com.*

Luxury Avenue (Ultrafemme). Luxury Avenue (Ultrafemme) sells high-end goods including watches and perfume. ⊠ *Av. Rafael E. Melgar 341* ☏ *987/872–0025.*

Pama. Pama, near the pier, carries imported jewelry, perfumes, and glassware. ⊠ *Av. Rafael E. Melgar Sur 9.*

Sergio Bustamante. The renowned artist's wild sculpture and jewelry collections are sold at this store and gallery on Cozumel's main drag. ⊠ *Av. Rafael Melgar at Calle 4 Norte* ⊕ *www.sergiobustamante.com.mx.*

Tanya Moss. One of Mexico's most famous jewelry designers, Tanya Moss creates original silver and gold necklaces and earrings that have become collectibles for those in the know. There's also a branch at the Hotel Presidente InterContinental. ⊠ *Av. Rafael E. Melgar at Punta Langosta* ☏ *987/869–1612* ⊕ *www.tanyamoss.com.*

Van Cleef and Arpels. Innovative designs and top-quality stones are available at Van Cleef and Arpels. ⊠ *Av. Rafael E. Melgar Norte, across from ferry* ☏ *987/872–6540* ⊕ *www.vancleefarpels.com.*

SPORTS AND THE OUTDOORS

Water sports are naturally Cozumel's biggest draw, especially scuba diving, snorkeling, and fishing. Services and equipment rentals are available throughout the island, especially through major hotels and water-sports centers at the beach clubs.

FISHING

The waters off Cozumel teem with more than 230 species of fish, making this one of the world's best deep-sea fishing destinations. During billfish migration season from late April through June, blue marlin, white marlin, and sailfish are plentiful, and world-record catches aren't uncommon.

Most sportfishing boats are located in the Puerto Abrigo marina just north of San Miguel. Fishing boats are also located at **La Caleta**, the marina on the south side, beside the Presidente InterContinental resort. Most sportfishing companies are affiliated with dive shops and offer a full range of water activities.

You can charter high-speed fishing boats for about $420 per half-day or $600 per day (with a maximum of six people). Hotels can help arrange daily charters—some offer special deals, with boats leaving from their own docks.

RECOMMENDED CHARTER COMPANIES

Albatros Deep Sea Fishing. Albatros Deep Sea Fishing offers half- and full-day trips that include boat and crew, tackle and bait, and lunch (quesadillas or your own fresh catch) with beer and soda starting at $420 for up to six people. ⊠ *Puerto Abrigo Marina* ☎ *987/872–7904, 888/333–4643 toll-free in U.S. and Canada* ⊕ *www.albatroscharters. com.*

Ocean Tours. All equipment and tackle, lunch with beer, and of course the boat and crew are included in the norther hotel zone's Ocean Tours' full-day rates, which start at $650, half-day tours start at $440. Discounts for cash payments. ⊠ *Cozumeleno Beach Resort, Playa Santa Pilar s/n, North Hotel Zone, Km 4.5* ☎ *987/872–9530* ⊕ *www.cozumel-diving. net/oceanturl/.*

Sand Dollar Sports. Sand Dollar Sports does it all. From bottom-fishing to deep-sea fishing trips, as well as America's Cup regatta races and scuba and snorkeling trips, this outfit can satisfy all of your over- and underwater needs. ⊠ *Carretera Sur, Km 6.2* ☎ *987/872–0793* ⊕ *www. sanddollarsports.com.*

3 Hermanos. This oufit specializes in deep-sea and fly-fishing trips, with rates for a half-day deep-sea fishing trip starting at $350 (a full day runs $450). The company also offers scuba-diving trips, and their boats are available for group charters—a great way to snorkel and cruise at your own pace—for $400 for up to six passengers. ⊠ *Puerto Abrigo Marina* ☎ *987/107–0655* ⊕ *www.cozumelfishing.com.*

5

Continued on page 271

COZUMEL DIVING AND SNORKELING

First comes the giant step, a leap from a dry boat into the warm Caribbean Sea. Then the slow descent to white sand framed by rippling brain coral and waving purple sea fans. If you lean back, you can look up toward the sea's surface. The water off Cozumel is so clear you can see puffy white clouds in the sky even when you're submerged 20 feet under.

With more than 30 charted reefs whose depths average 50–80 feet and water temperatures around 24°C–27°C (75°F–80°F) during peak diving season (June–August, when hotel rates are coincidentally at their lowest), Cozumel is far and away the place to dive in Mexico. More than 60,000 divers come here each year.

Because of the diversity of coral formations and the dramatic underwater peaks and valleys, divers consider Cozumel's Palancar Reef (promoters now call it the Maya Reef) to be one of the top five in the world. Sea turtles headed to the beach to lay their eggs swim beside divers in May and June. Fifteen-pound lobsters wave their antennae from beneath coral ledges; they've been protected in Cozumel's National Marine Park for so long they've lost all fear of humans. Long, green moray eels still appear rather menacing as they bare their fangs at curious onlookers, and snaggle-toothed barracuda look ominous as they swim by. But all in all, diving off Cozumel is relaxing, rewarding, and so addictive you simply can't do it just once.

Hurricane Wilma damaged the reefs during her 2005 attack and rearranged the underwater landscape. Favorite snorkeling and diving spots close to shore were affected, and the fish may not be as abundant as they were in the past.

The reef is home to brain coral and huge sponges.

DIVE SITES

Cozumel's reefs stretch for 32 km (20 mi), beginning at the international pier and continuing to Punta Celarain at the island's southernmost tip. Following is a rundown of Cozumel's main dive destinations.

◣ Chankanaab Reef.
This inviting reef lies south of Parque Chankanaab, about 350 yards offshore. Large underground caves are filled with striped grunt, snapper, sergeant majors, and butterfly fish. At 55 feet, there's another large coral formation that's often filled with crabs, lobster, barrel sponges, and angelfish. If you drift a bit farther south, you can see the Balones de Chankanaab, balloon-shaped coral heads at 70 feet.

◣ Colombia Reef.
Several miles off Palancar, the reef reaches 82–98 feet and is best suited for experienced divers. Its underwater structures are as varied as those of Palancar Reef, with large canyons and ravines to explore. Clustered near the overhangs are large groupers, jacks, rays, and an occasional sea turtle.

◣ Felipe Xicotencatl (C-53 Wreck).
Sunk in 2000 specifically for scuba divers, this 154-foot-long minesweeper is located on a sandy bottom about 80 feet deep near Tormentos and Chankanaab. Created as an artificial reef to decrease some of the traffic on the natural reefs, the ship is open so divers can explore the interior and is gradually attracting schools of fish.

◣ Maracaibo Reef.
Considered one of the most difficult reefs, Maracaibo is a thrilling dive with strong currents and intriguing old coral formations. Although there are shallow areas, only advanced divers who can cope with the current should attempt Maracaibo.

◣ Palancar Reef.
About 2 km (1 mi) offshore, Palancar is actually a series of varying coral formations with about 40 dive locations. It's filled with winding canyons, deep ravines, narrow crevices, archways, tunnels, and caves. Black and red coral and huge elephant-ear, and barrel sponges are among the attractions. At the section called Horseshoe, a series of coral heads form a natural horseshoe

shape. This is one of the most popular sites for dive boats and can become crowded.

◣ Paraíso Reef.
About 330 feet offshore, running parallel to the international cruise-ship pier, this reef averages 30–50 feet. It's a perfect spot to dive before you head for deeper drop-offs. There are impressive formations of star and brain coral as well as sea fans, sponges, sea eels, and yellow rays. It's wonderful for night diving.

◣ Paseo El Cedral.
Running parallel to Santa Rosa reef, this flat reef has gardenlike valleys full of fish, including angelfish, grunt, and snapper. At depths of 35–55 feet, you can also spot rays.

◣ San Francisco Reef.
Considered Cozumel's shallowest wall dive (35–50 feet), this 1-km (1⁄2-mi) reef runs parallel to Playa San Francisco and has many varieties of reef fish. You'll need to take a dive boat to get here.

◣ Santa Rosa Wall.
North of Palancar, Santa Rosa is renowned among experienced divers for deep dives and drift

Chankanaab Reef

Young yellow sponges, Palancar Reef.

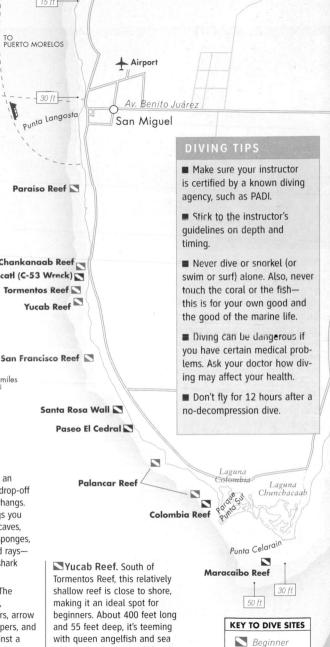

15 ft

TO
PUERTO MORELOS

TO
PLAYA
DEL CARMEN

+ Airport

30 ft

Av. Benito Juárez

Punta Langosta

San Miguel

Caribbean Sea

Paraíso Reef ◣

Chankanaab Reef ◣
Felipe Xicotencatl (C-53 Wreck) ◣
Tormentos Reef ◣
Yucab Reef ◣

San Francisco Reef ◣

0 _____ 3 miles

0 _____ 3 km

Santa Rosa Wall ◣

Paseo El Cedral ◣

◣

Palancar Reef ⟨

◣

◣

Colombia Reef

*Laguna
Colombia*

*Laguna
Chunchacaab*

*Parque
Punta Sur*

Punta Celarain

◣
Maracaibo Reef

30 ft

50 ft

DIVING TIPS

■ Make sure your instructor is certified by a known diving agency, such as PADI.

■ Stick to the instructor's guidelines on depth and timing.

■ Never dive or snorkel (or swim or surf) alone. Also, never touch the coral or the fish—this is for your own good and the good of the marine life.

■ Diving can be dangerous if you have certain medical problems. Ask your doctor how diving may affect your health.

■ Don't fly for 12 hours after a no-decompression dive.

KEY TO DIVE SITES

◣	Beginner
◣	Advanced

dives; at 50 feet there's an abrupt yet sensational drop-off to enormous coral overhangs. The strong current drags you along the tunnels and caves, where there are huge sponges, angelfish, groupers, and rays—and sometime even a shark or two.

◣**Tormentos Reef.** The abundance of sea fans, sponges, sea cucumbers, arrow crabs, green eels, groupers, and other marine life—against a terrifically colorful backdrop—makes this a perfect spot for underwater photography. This variegated reef has a maximum depth of around 70 feet.

◣**Yucab Reef.** South of Tormentos Reef, this relatively shallow reef is close to shore, making it an ideal spot for beginners. About 400 feet long and 55 feet deep, it's teeming with queen angelfish and sea whip swimming around the large coral heads. The one drawback is the strong current, which can reach two or three knots.

DIVE SHOPS AND OPERATORS

It's important to choose a dive shop that suits your expectations. Beginners are best off with the more established, conservative shops that limit the depth and time spent underwater. Experienced divers may be impatient with this approach, and are better suited to shops that offer smaller group dives and more challenging dive sites. More and more shops are merging these days, so don't be surprised if the outfit you dive with one year has been absorbed by another the following year. Recommending a shop is dicey. The ones listed in this chapter are well-established and recommended by experienced Cozumel divers.

Because dive shops tend to be competitive, it's well worth your while to shop around. Many hotels have their own on-site operations, and there are dozens of dive shops in town. **ANOAAT** (Aquatic Sports Operators Association; ☎ 987/872–5955) has listings of affiliated dive operations. Before signing on, ask experienced divers about the place, check credentials, and look over the boats and equipment.

(top) Felipe Xicotencatl (C-53 Wreck). (bottom) Coral, coral and more coral.

WHAT IT COSTS	
Regulator & BC	$15–$25
Underwater camera	$35–$45
Video camera	$75
Pro videos of your dive	$160
Two-tank boat trips	$60–$90
Specialty dives	$70–$100
One-tank afternoon dives	$35–$45
Night dives	$35–$45
Marine park fee	$2

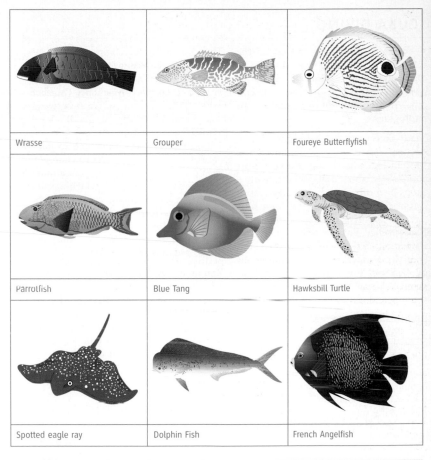

Wrasse	Grouper	Foureye Butterflyfish
Parrotfish	Blue Tang	Hawksbill Turtle
Spotted eagle ray	Dolphin Fish	French Angelfish

SNORKELING TIPS

Snorkeling equipment is available at nearly all hotels and beach clubs as well as at Parque Chankanaab, Playa San Francisco, and Parque Punta Sur. Gear rents for less than $10 a day. Snorkeling tours run about $60 and take in the shallow reefs off Palancar, Chankanaab, Colombia, and Yucab.

■ Never turn your back on the ocean, especially if the waves are big.

■ Ask about rip tides before you go in.

■ Enter and exit from a sandy beach area.

■ Avoid snorkeling at dusk and never go in the water after dark.

■ Wear lots of sunscreen, especially on your back and butt cheeks.

■ Don't snorkel too close to the reef. You could get scratched if a wave pushes you.

■ Be mindful of boats.

SCUBA DIVING

There's no way anyone can do all the deep dives, drift dives, shore dives, wall dives, and night dives in one trip, never mind the theme dives focusing on ecology, archaeology, sunken ships, and photography.

Many hotels and dive shops offer introductory classes in a swimming pool. Most include a beach or boat dive. Resort courses cost about $60–$80. Many dive shops also offer full open-water certification classes, which take at least four days of intensive classroom study and pool practice. Basic certification courses cost about $350, while advanced and specialty certification courses cost about $250–$500. You can also do your classroom study at home, then make your training and test dives on Cozumel.

DIVING SAFELY There are more than 100 dive shops in Cozumel, so look for high safety standards and documented credentials. The best places offer small groups and individual attention. Next to your equipment, your dive master is the most important consideration for your adventure. Make sure he or she has PADI or NAUI certification (or FMAS, the Mexican equivalent). Be sure to bring your own certification card; all reputable shops require customers to show them before diving. If you forget, you may be able to call the agency that certified you and have the card number faxed to the shop.

Keep in mind that much of the reef off Cozumel is a protected National Marine Park. Boats aren't allowed to anchor in certain areas, and you shouldn't touch the coral or take any "souvenirs" from reefs when you dive there. It's best to ʰt least three feet above the reef— ʰecause coral can sting or cut ʰo because it's easily damaged ʰry slowly; it has taken 2,000 ʰ their present size.

There's a reputable recompression chamber at the **Buceo Médico Mexicano** (✉ Calle 5 Sur 21B ☎ 987/872–1430 24-hr hotline). The **Cozumel Hyperbarics Chamber** (✉ San Miguel Clinic, Calle 6 between Avs. 5 and 10 ☎ 987/872–3070) is also a fully equipped recompression center. These chambers, which aim for a 35-minute response time from reef to chamber, treat decompression sickness, commonly known as "the bends," which occurs when you surface too quickly and nitrogen bubbles form in the bloodstream. Recompression chambers are also used to treat nitrogen narcosis, collapsed lungs, and overexposure to the cold.

You may also want to consider buying dive-accident insurance from the U.S.-based **Divers Alert Network** (DAN) (☎ 800/446–2671, 919/684–9111 emergency hotline ⊕ www.diversalertnetwork.org) before embarking on your dive vacation. DAN insurance covers dive accidents and injuries, and their emergency hotline can help you find the best local doctors, hyperbaric chambers, and medical services. They can also arrange for airlifts.

Diver on the Paradise Reef.

GOLF

Cozumel Country Club. The Cozumel Country Club has an 18-hole championship golf course, the work of the Nicklaus Design Group. The lush fairways amid mangroves and a lagoon have been declared an Audubon nature reserve, and it's a favorite spot for bird-watching, too. The greens fee is $169 before 12:30 pm and $105 after, and the fee includes a shared golf cart. Some hotels, including Playa Azul, offer golf packages here. ⊠ *Carretera Costera Norte, Km 6.5* ☏ *987/872–9570* ⊕ *www. cozumelcountryclub.com.mx.*

KITEBOARDING AND PADDLEBOARDING

De Lille Sports. Cozumel native Raul De Lille, former Olympic kiteboarding competitor and certified instructor, now offers lessons and sessions for both paddleboarding and kiteboarding, the former having become much more popular in Cozumel, where the conditions can be more ideal than for kiteboarding. Individual and group classes cost $150 to $250 for a two- to three-hour class. Tours take kiteboarders to various parts of the island where the winds are strongest. Multiday courses to learn how to paddle and kiteboard vary, inquire via website. ☏ *987/103–6711 cell* ⊕ *www.delillesports.com.*

SUP Cozumel. Free lessons come with paddleboard rentals at this company that operates off Casitas Beach. Rates are $25 for a one-hour rental, $40 for a half day, and $60 for a full day. Guided group tours are also offered throughout the day. ⊠ *Casitas Beach, Blvd. Aeropuerto* ☏ *987/101–6286* ⊕ *supcoz.com.*

SNORKELING AND SCUBA DIVING

Aldora Divers. Aldora Divers offers reef dives on fast boats and accommodations in Villa Aldora, a 12-bedroom inn just north of town. They also have trips to pristine dive sites and shipwrecks off the windward coast. ⊠ *Calle 5 Sur, between Av. Rafael Melgar and Av. 5* ☏ *987/872–3397, 210/569–1203 in U.S.* ⊕ *www.aldora.com.*

Aqua Safari. One of the island's oldest and most professional shops, Aqua Safari provides beginning and advanced PADI certification and daily introductory scuba courses. Owner Bill Horn has long been involved in efforts to protect the reefs and stays on top of local environmental issues. ⊠ *Av. Rafael E. Melgar 429, between Calles 5 and 7 Sur* ☏ *987/872–0101* ⊕ *aquasafari.com.*

Aquatic Sports and Excursions Cozumel. Sergio Sandoval gets rave reviews from his clients, many who are repeat customers. In addition to the usual excursions, he'll take you out for wreck dives, underwater photo safaris, or to hunt invasive lionfish. He also charters his boat for full- and half-day sport fishing trips. Two-tank dives run $75. ⊠ *Carretera Sur, Km 6.5* ☏ *987/112–5002, 987/111–1172 mobile* ⊕ *cozumeldivingwithsergio.com.*

Blue Angel. Blue Angel offers combo dive and snorkel trips so famili· who don't all scuba can still have fun together. Along with dive trip·

local reefs, they offer PADI courses. Two-tank dives run $79 plus tax. ✉ *Carretera Sur, Km 2.2* ☎ *987/872–1631* ⊕ *www.blueangelresort.com.*

Del Mar Aquatics. Del Mar Aquatics, in operation since 1987, offers PADI and DAN certified dive trips, certification courses, and fishing trips. ✉ *Casa Del Mar Hotel, Carretera Sur Km 4* ☎ *987/872–5949* ⊕ *delmaraquatics.com.*

Eagle Ray Divers. Eagle Ray Divers offers snorkeling trips and dive instruction. (The three-reef snorkel trip lets nondivers explore beyond the shore.) As befits their name, the company keeps track of the eagle rays that appear off Cozumel from December to February and runs trips for advanced divers to walls where the rays congregate. Beginners can also see rays around some of the reefs. ✉ *La Caleta Marina, near Presidente InterContinental Hotel* ☎ *987/872–5735, 866/465–1616 in U.S.* ⊕ *www.eagleraydivers.com.*

Fury Catamarans. Fury Catamarans runs snorkeling tours from its 45-foot catamarans. Rates begin at about $59 per day and include equipment and a guide, soft drinks, beer, margaritas, and a beach party with lunch. ✉ *Carretera Sur, Km 3.5, beside Casa del Mar Hotel* ☎ *987/872–5145* ⊕ *www.furycozumel.com.*

Fodor's Choice
★
Scuba Du. Dive magazines regularly rate Scuba Du among the best dive shops in the Caribbean, though it's one of the more expensive in Cozumel (two-tank dives are $89). Along with the requisite Cozumel dives, the company offers night dives and an advanced trip to walls off Punta Sur, as well as snorkeling and fishing trips. The Presidente InterContinental Hotel offers dive packages including lodging for guests. ✉ *Presidente InterContinental Hotel, Carretera Sur, Km 6* ☎ *987/872–9500, 310/684–5556 from U.S.* ⊕ *www.scubadu.com.*

SUBMARINE TOURS

FAMILY **Atlantis Submarine.** If you're curious about what's underneath Cozumel's waters but don't like getting wet, Atlantis Submarine runs 1½-hour submarine rides that explore the Chankanaab Reef and surrounding area. Subs descend about 100 feet down—deeper than most scuba dives go—but be warned: claustrophobes may not be able to handle the sardine-can conditions. Admission is $99 for adults ($89 online). All riders must be 36" tall and over 4 years old. ✉ *Carretera Sur, Km 4, across from Hotel Casa del Mar* ☎ *987/872–5671* ⊕ *www.atlantissubmarines. travel.*

YUCATÁN AND
CAMPECHE STATES

WELCOME TO YUCATÁN AND CAMPECHE STATES

TOP REASONS TO GO

★ **Visiting spectacular Mayan ruins:** Chichén Itzá and Uxmal are two of the largest, most beautiful sites in the region.

★ **Living like a wealthy hacendado:** You can stay in a restored *henequen* (sisal) plantation-turned-hotel and delight in its old-world charm.

★ **Browsing at fantastic craft markets:** This region is known for its handmade *hamacas* (hammocks), piñatas, and other local handicrafts.

★ **Swimming in the secluded, pristine freshwater cenotes:** These sinkholes, like portals to the underworld, are scattered throughout the inland landscape.

★ **The chance to taste the diverse flavors of Yucatecan food:** Mérida has 50-odd restaurants, which serve up local specialties like fish stews and ~~ated dishes~~

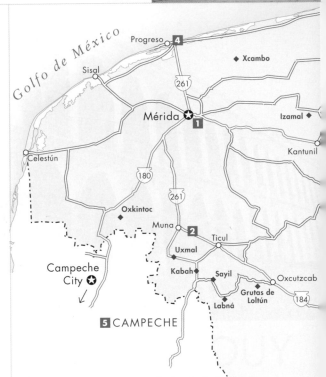

1 Mérida. Fully urban, and bustling with foot and car traffic, Mérida was once the main stronghold of Spanish colonialism in the peninsula. Tucked among the restaurants, museums, and markets are grand, old, beautifully ornamented mansions and buildings that recall the city's heyday as the wealthiest capital in Mexico.

2 Uxmal and the Ruta Puuc. South of Mérida, Uxmal is less well known

(and typically far less crowded) than Chichén Itzá, but beautiful. Many other smaller archaeological sites—some hardly visited—lie along the Ruta Puuc south of Mérida.

3 Chichén Itzá and the Mayan Interior. Yucatán's spectacular Mayan ruins are famous all over the world. The best-known, Chichén Itzá, draws thousands of visitors every year.

Isla Holbox

Río Lagartos
El Cuyo

Santa Clara
295

Teapa

176
Tizimín

281

X-can

Ek Balam   **180**

GETTING ORIENTED

Grutas de
Balancanchén

Pisté

Valladolid

3 Chichén Itzá

YUCATÁN

Yucatán State's topography has more in common with that of Florida and Cuba—with which it was probably once connected—than with central Mexico. Exotic plants like wild ginger and spider lilies grow in the jungles, and vast flamingo colonies nest at coastal estuaries. Human history is evident everywhere here—in looming Franciscan missions, thatch-roof adobe huts, and the majestic ruins of ancient Mayan cities. Campeche State, the Yucatán Peninsula's least-visited corner, is the perfect place for adventure. Its colonial communities have retained an air of innocence, and its protected biospheres, farmland, and jungles are relatively unspoiled. Campeche City, the state's most accessible spot, make⸻ a good hub for exploring other areas, many of w⸻ have only basic resta⸻ and primitive lodgi⸻

QUINTANA ROO

5 Campeche. The most happening town in this little-visited Mexican state is Campeche City, a colonial enclave with brightly painted buildings and the dreamy airs of bygone times. Elsewhere are Mayan villages where three-wheeled bike-taxis rule the road and women dress in embroidered *huipiles* (traditional white embroidered dresses). Far to the south, along the Guatemalan border, the Reserva de la Biosfera Calakmul is home to thousands of birds, butterflies, and plants—but hosts only about a dozen visitors a day.

4 Progreso and the Northern Coast. Outside the unpretentious town of Progreso, empty beaches stretch for miles in either direction—punctuated only by fishing villages, estuaries, and salt flats. Bird-watchers and nature lovers gravitate to rustic Celestún and Río Lagartos, home to one of the hemisphere's largest colonies of pink flamingos.

6

YUCATÁN CUISINE

Chefs in Mexico skillfully combine ingredients and techniques from the New World and Old, but the cuisines here vary dramatically from region to region. The flavors of Yucatán are subtle, unique, and not to be missed.

(*Above and top right*) Cochinita pibil's presentation can vary from restaurant to restaurant. (*Bottom right*) *Huevos motuleños.*

Regional culinary traditions in the country can be divided into four regions. Foods from the north have an unpretentious culinary tradition; here you'll find dishes that were originally served on ranches and haciendas. On both coasts, seafood takes center stage. The central region includes the area in and around Mexico City, where many of the country's most characteristic plates 〜o invented in convent kitchens during colonial times. 〜 the south, including the Yucatán, are singu-
〜o. This region was once a difficult area
〜ary traditions that developed on
quite different from those in
At the same time, centuries of
〜rade with Cuba, Europe (espe-
Orleans have left their mark on
〜ons. More recent Middle Eastern
〜ble.

AGUA

In the Yucatán's warm weather, nothing satisfies like a cool *aguas fresca* (fruit-infused water). One drink that you won't want to miss is *agua de chaya*. Chaya, sometimes called tree spinach, is a nutritious leafy green that's used in a wide variety of recipes, including soups, omelets, tamales, and a sweet agua fresca.

REGIONAL CUISINES

Visitors to the Yucatán often discover a wide variety of dishes they've never seen before. This is because Yucatán cuisine is not often served in Mexican restaurants north of the border, or even in other areas of the country. Here are some of the most typical dishes—all of them well worth a try.

Huevos motuleños. This is a popular breakfast dish that originated in Motul, a small town east of Mérida, where the ancient Mayan city of Zacmotul once stood. Eggs, sunny side up, are covered with black beans and cheese and served on a crispy tortilla. Other ingredients like red salsa, ham, and green peas are usually heaped on top. Fried plantains are often served on the side.

Sopa de lima. This soup is traditionally prepared with turkey, indigenous to the Yucatán, and includes pieces of tomatoes, sweet chile or green pepper, and lime juice. It's garnished with strips of lightly fried tortilla.

Queso relleno. Legend has it that in the 19th century a boat from Holland was forced to dock on the peninsula because of bad weather, and the people in Mérida were delighted with the cargo of Dutch cheese. From this trip, a typical Yucatecan dish made with Gouda or Edam cheese was born. A salty cow's-milk cheese is stuffed with spiced ground beef and served with

two sauces: a tomato-caper sauce and a milder creamy sauce.

Cochinita pibil. This is perhaps the most representative dish in the Yucatecan repertoire. The word *pibil* means "roasted in the hole," which describes just how this dish is classically prepared. The Maya used to roast venison in this way, but the Spanish introduced pork is now the standard. The meat is first marinated in a mixture of bitter orange juice (from the Seville oranges that grow in this region), *achiote* (an intensely peppery flavored paste that some describe as having a nutmeglike flavor, made from annatto seeds), oregano, salt, and pepper. Next, it's wrapped in banana leaves and placed in a hole lined with stones that have been heated with fire. The meat cooks slowly. These days, this dish is often made in a pot on the stove or slow-roasted in the oven. It's usually served in tacos with pickled onions called *cebolla en escabeche*.

6

Updated
by Marlise
Kast-Myers

In sharp contrast to the resort lifestyle of Cancún and Riviera Maya, the Yucatán and Campeche states cater to a more tranquil traveler who is looking to avoid the spring-break atmosphere. Here you'll find innumerable natural and historic wonders, including mangrove forests, unspoiled beaches, quaint colonial villages, and more than 50% of Mexico's bird species.

Unlike Quintana Roo, Yucatán and Campeche states have few international residents, and there's much less emphasis on beachside activities. With the largest indigenous population in the country, these states are defined by Mayan culture and traditions; the area's history, people, and food set it apart from the rest of Mexico.

One of Yucatán State's biggest draws is its capital, Mérida. As it's the hub of art and culture, locals and travelers alike gather in the town square for weekend performances. Izamal, the oldest town in the Yucatán, will take you back in time with its cobblestone streets, iron lampposts, yellow-painted buildings, and horse-drawn carriages. Near the state's eastern border, the budding cosmopolitan town of Valladolid offers excellent bird-watching and freshwater cenotes where you can explore underwater caves.

More than 2,000 Mayan ruins lie within these two states, but only a handful have been restored for tourism. Nestled amid rampant jungles are the magnificent archaeological sites of Uxmal, Kabah, Labna, Sayil, Dzibilchaltún, and Chichén Itzá, a UNESCO Natural World Heritage site. Roughly one hour southeast of Uxmal, the Grutas de Loltún show ⌐f human civilization dating as far back as 800 BC. At these natu-
⌐lluminated pathways meander past stalactites, stalagmites,
⌐ formations.

⌐vers, the beach town of Celestún serves as a natural habitat
⌐ds of pink flamingos. To combine wildlife and adventure,
⌐io Lagartos where you can kayak through the mangroves. Off
⌐ of Isla Holbox, diving with whale sharks is possible from June

through August. This small island, void of cars, is one of the area's best spots to relax and enjoy beach life. The laid-back beach community of Progreso (near Mérida) is another coastal favorite.

Campeche, the neighboring state, is more remote and less visited than Yucatán, and is known for its haciendas and colonial towns. The state's capital, by the same name, sits within a 26-foot wall that once served as a protective border against pirates in the 17th century. Today this harbor city is centered by colorful buildings and a charming plaza where people gather to admire the cathedral, browse the market, or enjoy *pan de cazon,* traditional shredded fish with black beans. For a mellow alternative, you can explore the coastline by boat or spend a day bird-watching at the Calakmul Biosphere Reserve.

PLANNING

WHEN TO GO
Rainfall is heaviest in the Yucatán between June and October, bringing with it an uncomfortable humidity. The coolest months are December to February, when it can get chilly in the evening, while April and May are usually the hottest. Afternoon showers are the norm June through September, and hurricane season is late September through early November.

As with many other places in Mexico, high season begins mid-November and continues until early April. The weeks around Christmas and Easter are peak times for visiting Yucatán State. Making reservations up to a year in advance is common. Fortunately the Yucatán doesn't get the spring-break crowds like Cancún, but you may still see a slight increase in travelers (and prices) from March to April and during August when most Europeans take their vacations.

Prices drop as much as 50% the day after Easter and will stay reasonably low until mid-December. Rates will increase around Thanksgiving, but in general, November is a great month to travel due to good travel deals and ideal weather.

If you can avoid Thanksgiving weekend, November is one of your best bets for good weather and affordable rates. This time of year, the rainy season is over, the humidity has faded, and temperatures are pleasantly cool. You also won't have to deal with holiday crowds, which means properties and airlines will most likely be offering discounted rates.

GETTING HERE AND AROUND
Mérida is the hub of the Yucatán Peninsula, and a good base for exploring the rest of the state.

AIR TRAVEL
Mérida's airport, Aeropuerto Manuel Crescencio Rejón, is 7 km (4½ miles) west of the city on Avenida Itzáes. Getting there from the down town area usually takes 20 to 30 minutes by taxi. Numerous airlir including Aerocaribe, Aeroméxico, and Mexicana fly from Can Mexico City, Villahermosa, and other cities. Continental flies dai¹ stop from Houston. Interjet offers flights to Mérida from sev'

locations including New York; Orange County, California; Miami; Las Vegas; and San Antonio.

BUS TRAVEL

For travel around the region, ADO and UNO have direct buses to many coastal cities and ruins from Mérida. They depart from the first-class CAME bus station. Regional bus lines to intermediate or more out-of-the-way destinations leave from the second-class terminal. City buses charge about 60¢ (6 pesos); having the correct change is helpful but not required.

Bus Contacts Autobuses de Occidente ⊠ *Calle 70, between 79 and 71, Centro, Mérida* ☎ *999/924–8391, 999/924–9741* ⊕ *www.ado.com.mx.* **CAME** ⊠ *Calle 71 No. 555, between Calles 69 and 71, Centro, Mérida* ☎ *999/924–8391.*

CAR TRAVEL

From Mérida, highways radiate in every direction. To the east, Carreteras 180 *cuota* and 180 *libre* are, respectively, the toll and free roads to Cancún. The toll road (which costs about $35 from Cancún to Mérida, ⊕ *www.sct.gob.mx*) has exits for the famous Chichén Itzá ruins and the low-key colonial city of Valladolid; the free road passes these and many smaller towns. Unless you want to explore these little villages, and nearly double your travel time, it is not recommended to travel on the free roads. Many are poorly marked, extremely dark at night, and dotted with potholes and speed bumps. The toll road, however, is nicely paved and void of detours. Heading south from Mérida on Carretera 261 (Carretera 180 until the town of Umán), you come to Uxmal and the Ruta Puuc, a series of small ruins (most have at least one outstanding building) of relatively uniform style. Carretera 261 north from Mérida takes you to the port and beach resort of Progreso. To the west, the laid-back fishing village of Celestún—which borders on protected wetland—can be accessed by a separate highway from Mérida.

■**TIP→** If you're independent and adventurous, hiring a rental car is a great way to explore. Daily rental rates are low, but full-coverage car insurance (by Mexican law) will cost you about $35 per day. Be sure to check the lights, windshield wipers, and spare tire before taking off. Carry plenty of bottled water, fill up the gas tank whenever you see a station, and try to avoid driving at night.

Contacts Avis ⊠ *Fiesta Americana, Calle 60 No. 319-C, near Av. Colón, Centro, Mérida* ☎ *999/925–2525, 999/920–1101* ⊕ *www.avis.com.*

RESTAURANTS

Expect a superb variety of cuisines—primarily Yucatecan, of course, but also Lebanese, Italian, French, Chinese, vegetarian, and Mexican—at ˜ry reasonable prices. Reservations are advised for the pricier res- ˜ on weekends and in high season. Beach towns, such as Pro- ̧artos, and Celestún, tend to serve fresh, simply prepared ́ regional cuisine of Campeche is renowned throughout ̧cialties include fish and shellfish stews, cream soups, shrimp ̧uid and octopus, and *panuchos* (chubby rounds of fried ̧covered with refried beans and topped with onion and shred- ̧ey or chicken).

Mexicans generally eat lunch in the afternoon—certainly not before 2. If you want to eat at noon, call ahead to verify hours. In Mérida the locals make a real event of late dinners, especially in summer. Casual, but neat, dress is acceptable at all restaurants. Avoid wearing shorts or casual sandals in the more expensive places, and anywhere at all—especially in the evening—if you don't want to look like a tourist. Although food servers at most local restaurants are kind and hospitable, they don't always show it like they do in the States. Be patient and realize that for many, the language barrier may cause them to be more reserved, but not necessarily unfriendly. ■TIP→ It's common practice for restaurants to include gratuity and tax in the total bill, so double check your bill before adding a tip.

HOTELS

Yucatán State has around 8,500 hotel rooms—a little over a third of what Cancún has. Try to check out the interior before booking a room, as the public spaces in Mérida's hotels are generally better kept than the sleeping rooms. Most hotels have air-conditioning, and even many budget hotels have installed it in at least some rooms—but it's best to ask ahead.

■TIP→ If you plan to spend most of your time enjoying downtown Mérida, stay near the main square or along Calle 60. If you're a light sleeper, however, opt for one of the high-rises along or near Paseo Montejo, about a 20-minute stroll (but an easy cab ride) from the main square.

Inland towns such as Valladolid and Ticul are good options for a look at the slow-paced countryside. There are several charming hotels near the major archaeological sites Chichen Itzá and Uxmal, and a growing number of small beachfront hotels in Progreso, which previously had only a couple of foreign-run bed-and-breakfasts. Campeche City has a few interesting lodgings converted from old homes (and in some cases mansions), as well as newer, large hotels along the *malecón* (boardwalk) and near the town center.

HOTEL AND RESTAURANT PRICES

Prices in the restaurant reviews are the average cost of a main course at dinner or, if dinner is not served, at lunch; taxes and service charges are generally included. Prices in the hotel reviews are the lowest cost of a standard double room in high season, excluding taxes, service charges, and meal plans (except at all-inclusives). Prices for rentals are the lowest per-night cost for a one-bedroom unit in high season.

TIMING

You should plan to spend at least five days in the Yucatán. It's best to start your trip with a few days in Mérida; the weekends, when streets are closed to traffic and there are lots of free outdoor performances, are great times to visit. You should also budget enough time to day-trip ' the sites of Chichén Itzá and Uxmal; visiting Mérida without trave' to at least one of these sites is like driving to the beach and not g out of the car.

6

MÉRIDA

Bustling streets, lively parks, a tropical version of the Champs-Elysées, endless cultural activities, and a varied nightlife: Mérida is the beating urban heart of the Yucatán. The hubbub of the city can seem frustrating—especially if you've just spent a peaceful few days on the coast or visiting Mayan sites—but as the cultural and intellectual hub of the peninsula, Mérida is rich in art, history, and tradition.

Most streets are one-way and the bus routes are not all that direct, so you're better off parking your car near the downtown main plaza and walking to the local sites and attractions. Most are located around the *zócalo* (main plaza), bordered by Calles 60–63. Using this as your starting point is a great way to get to know the layout of the city.

If you need extra orientation, be sure to stop in at the tourism offices, where you'll find friendly, helpful staff. A two- to three-hour group tour of the city, including museums, parks, public buildings, and monuments, costs $20 to $35 per person. Free guided tours are offered daily by the Municipal Tourism Department. These last about an hour and 45 minutes and depart from City Hall, on the main plaza, at 9:30 am Monday through Saturday. Or you can rent gear for a four-hour audio-guide tour for about $7. More information is available at ☎ 999/942–0000.

There have also been recent reports of vendors increasing the prices of their art and crafts by the hundreds, claiming that the value of their wares is far greater than it really is. Most vendors are honest, so just be sure to shop around and acquaint yourself with the kinds of crafts, and the levels of quality, that are available. Once you have an idea of what's out there, you'll be better able to spot fraud, and you may even have some fun bargaining.

■**TIP→** Most streets in Mérida are numbered, not named, and most run one-way. North–south streets have even numbers, which descend from west to east; east–west streets have odd numbers, which ascend from north to south. Street addresses are confusing because they don't progress in even increments by blocks, for example, the 600s may occupy two or more blocks. A particular location is therefore usually identified by indicating the street number and the nearest cross street, as in `` 64 and Calle 61," or "Calle 64 between Calles 61 and 63," which ``alle 64 x 61 y 63."

ERE AND AROUND

ıer fly into Mérida (you may have to connect in Cancún) ɔm the Cancún airport. The drive from Cancún is almost and takes at least four hours, so most people fly directly to ven if it costs a bit more.

BUS TRAVEL

Within Mérida, a fun way to get around, get a feel for the city layout, and hear some of its history is to spend some time on the red, open-roof, double-decker **Turibus.** You can buy your ticket ($10) onboard the bus, and can get on and off at seven stops as you please. The complete bus route is 1 hour and 45 minutes. Buses operate from 9:05 am until 9 pm, and stop at the Holiday Inn, Fiesta Americana, and Hyatt hotels (clustered near one another on Paseo Montejo), the Museo de Antropología e Historia, the old barrio of Izimná, the Gran Plaza mall (with its 250 stores), the Monument to the Flag, and finally the Parque de las Américas.

A second, smaller tour bus operator is the **Carnavalito,** which visits many of the same sites. The advantage to this tour is that it's given by real people (in both Spanish and English) as opposed to a recording, so you can ask questions. The disadvantage is that you can't get on and off the bus at will. The tour lasts around two hours, with a 20-minute break at a small shopping center where you can stretch your legs or buy something to drink. The colorful Carnavalito bus takes off from Parque Santa Lucía Monday through Saturday at 10 am, 1 pm, and 7 pm.

Contacts Carnavalito ☎ 999/927–6119, 999/928–7916. **Turibus** ☎ 999/920–7636, 55/5563–6693 in Mexico City ⊕ www.turibus.com.mx.

CARRIAGE TRAVEL

One of the best ways to get a feel for the city of Mérida is to hire a *calesa*—a horse-drawn carriage. You can hail one of these at the main square or, during the day, at Palacio Cantón, site of the archaeology museum on Paseo Montejo. Choose your horse and driver carefully, as some of the horses look dispirited, but others are fairly well cared for. Drivers charge about $15 for an hour-long circuit around downtown and up Paseo de Montejo, pointing out notable buildings and providing a little historic background along the way. An extended tour costs $22.

TAXI TRAVEL

Regular taxis in Mérida charge beach-resort prices, and most don't use meters. Taxis that do use meters have a sign that reads "taximetro" on the roof. These are recommended, because they offer a fair price.

TOURS

Mérida has more than 50 tour operators, and it could be said that they generally take you to the same places. Because there are so many reputable and reasonably priced operators, there's no reason to opt for the less predictable *piratas* ("pirates") who sometimes stand outside tour offices offering to sell you a cheaper trip and don't necessarily have much experience or your best interests at heart. If you enjoy walking, the **Mérida English Library** conducts home and garden tours (2½ hours costs $20) every Wednesday morning. Meet at the library at about 9:45 am.

Amigo Travel is a reliable operator offering group and private tour the major archaeological sites and also to Celestún, the town k for the massive flamingo colonies living in its river. Amigo has r accommodation packages and well-crafted tours, like their C and Yucatán combo, and has adopted a pace that allows you to actually enjoy the sites you visit.

If you don't have your own wheels but like the freedom afforded by traveling on your own, a great option for seeing the ruins of the Ruta Puuc is the unguided **ATS** tour that leaves Mérida at 8 am from the second-class bus station (Terminal 69, ATS line) on Friday, Saturday, and Sunday only. The tour stops for a half hour each at the ruins of Labná, Xlapak, Sayil, and Kabah, giving you just enough time to scan the plaques, poke your nose into a crevice or two, and pose before a pyramid for your holiday-card picture. You get almost two hours at Uxmal before heading back to Mérida at 2:30 pm. The trip costs $10 per person (entrance to the ruins isn't included) and is worth every penny.

EcoTurismo Yucatán has a good mix of day and overnight tours. Their Calakmul tour includes several nights' camping in the biosphere reserve for nature spotting, as well as visits to Calakmul, Chicanná, and other area ruins. The one-day biking adventure packs in biking as well as brief visits to two archaeological sites, a cave, a hacienda, and two cenotes.

Mérida English Library ⊠ *Calle 53 No. 524, between Calles 66 and 68, Mérida, Yucatán* ☎ *999/924–8401* ⊕ *www.meridaenglishlibrary.com.*

VISITOR INFORMATION

Contacts Municipal Tourism Department ⊠ *Calles 59, between Calle 52 and 50, Centro* ☎ *999/928-1966, 999/924-7381* ⊕ *www.merida.gob.mx.* **Municipal Tourist Information Center** ⊠ *City Hall, Calle 62, between Calle 61 and 63; ground floor of Palacio Municipal, Centro* ☎ *999/942-0000.*

EXPLORING

The *zócalo*, or main square, is in the oldest part of town—the Centro Histórico. On Saturday night and Sunday practically the entire population of the city gathers in the parks and plazas surrounding the zócalo to socialize and watch live entertainment. Cafés along this route are perfect places from which to watch the parade of people as well as folk dancers and singers. Calle 60 between Parque Santa Lucía and the main square gets especially lively. Restaurants here set out tables in the streets, which quickly fill with patrons enjoying the free tango, salsa, or jazz performances.

Every Sunday, from 8 am to 12:30 pm, downtown streets are closed for ~edestrians and cyclists. The route begins at the Parque de la Ermita, ~vels through the Plaza Grande, out on to the Paseo Montejo ~*ida.gob.mx/biciruta*).

ᴬCTIONS

ıtejo. Two Franciscos de Montejo—father and son—con- peninsula and founded Mérida in January of 1542, and they ~ stately "casa" 10 years later. In the late 1970s it was restored ~ɛr Agustín Legorreta, converted to a branch of Banamex bank, and now sits on the south side of the plaza. It's the city's finest—and oldest—example of colonial plasteresque architecture, a Spanish architectural style popular in the 16th century and typified by the kind of elaborate ornamentation you'll see here. A bas-relief on the doorway—the facade is all that remains of the original house—depicts Francisco de Montejo the younger, his wife, and daughter, as well as Spanish soldiers standing on the heads of the vanquished Maya. ⌧ *Calle 63, No. 506, Centro* ☎ *999/923–0633* ⊕ *www.museocasamontejo.com* ☼ *Tues.–Sat. 10–7, Sun. 10–2.*

Catedral de San Ildefonso. Begun in 1561 and completed 38 years later, St. Ildefonso is the oldest cathedral on the American continent (though an older one can be found in the Dominican Republic). It took several hundred Maya laborers, working with stones from the pyramids of the ravaged Mayan city, 36 years to complete it. Designed in the somber Renaissance style by an architect who had worked on the Escorial in Madrid, its facade is stark and unadorned, with gunnery slits instead of windows, and faintly Moorish spires. Inside, the black *Cristo de las Ampollas* (Christ of the Blisters) occupies a side chapel to the left of the main altar. At 23 feet tall, it's the tallest Christ in Mexico inside a church. The statue is a replica of the original, which was destroyed during the revolution in 1910, which is also when the gold that typically decorated Mexican cathedrals was carried off. According to one of many legends, the Christ figure burned all night yet appeared the next morning unscathed—except that it was covered with the blisters for which it's named. You can hear the pipe organ play at the 11 am Sunday Mass. ⌧ *Calles 60 and 61, Centro* ☼ *Daily 7–11:30 and 4:30–8.*

FAMILY **Centro Cultural de Mérida Olimpo.** Referred to as simply Olimpo, this is the best venue in town for free cultural events. The beautiful porticoed cultural center was built adjacent to City Hall in late 1999, occupying what used to be a parking lot. The marble interior is a showcase for top international art exhibits, classical-music concerts, conferences, and theater and dance performances. The adjoining 1950s-style movie house shows classic art films by directors like Buñuel, Fellini, and Kazan. There's also a planetarium with 90-minute shows explaining the solar system ($3, Tuesday through Saturday at 6 pm and Sunday at 11, noon, and 6; be sure to be there 15 minutes early, because nobody is allowed to sneak in once the show has begun). Next door there's a bookstore, and a wonderful cybercafé-restaurant. ⌧ *Calle 62, between Calles 61 and 63, Centro* ☎ *999/942–0000* ⊕ *www.merida.gob.mx/planetario* ⌧ *Free; $3 for planetarium* ☼ *Tues.–Sun. 9–3 and 5–7:30.*

Paseo Montejo. North of downtown, this 10-block-long street was *the* place to reside in the late 19th century, when wealthy plantation owners sought to outdo each other with the opulence of their elegant mansions. Mansion owners typically opted for the decorative styles popular in New Orleans, Cuba, and Paris—imported Carrara marble, European antiques—rather than any style from Mexico. The broad boulevard, lined with tamarind and laurel trees, has lost much of its f panache; some of the mansions have fallen into disrepair. Many used as office buildings, while others have been or are being r part of a citywide, privately funded beautification program

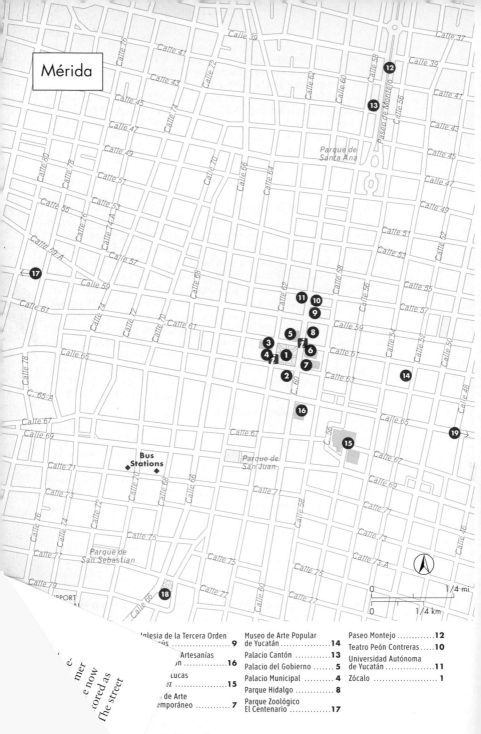

Mérida

Calle 39
Calle 37
Calle 41
Calle 43
Calle 45
Calle 47
Calle 49
Calle 51
Calle 53
Calle 55
Calle 57
Calle 59
Calle 61
Calle 65
Calle 65-A
Calle 67
Calle 69
Calle 71
Calle 73
Calle 75
Calle 77
Calle 79

Parque de Santa Ana

Parque de San Juan

Parque de San Sebastian

Bus Stations

AIRPORT

0   1/4 mi
0   1/4 km

is a lovely place to explore on foot or in a horse-drawn carriage.

Teatro Peón Contreras. This 1908 Italianate theater was built along the same lines as grand turn-of-the-20th-century European theaters and opera houses. In the early 1980s, the marble staircase, dome, and frescoes were restored. Today, in addition to performing arts, the theater houses the **Centro de Información Turística** (Tourist Information Center), which provides maps, brochures, and details about attractions in the city and state. The theater's most popular attraction, however, is the café-bar spilling out into the street facing Parque de la Madre. It's crowded every night with people enjoying the balladeers singing romantic and politically inspired songs. ⊠ *Calle 60, between Calles 57 and 59, Centro* ☎ *999/923–7354 Tourist Information Center, 999/924–9290, 999/923–7354 theater* ⊕ *www.culturayucatan.com* ☉ *Tourist Information Center daily 9–9.*

WORD OF MOUTH

"[Our] last day in Mérida was a Sunday, the best day in the city because the streets are closed—activities and vendors are all over the zócalo. The zócalo has free Wi-Fi which was pretty cool, so I was able check email on my iPhone and use Internet." —Nicci

Universidad Autónoma de Yucatán. Pop into the university's main building—which plays a major role in the city's cultural and intellectual life—to check the bulletin boards just inside the entrance for upcoming cultural events. The folkloric ballet performs on the patio of the main building most Fridays between 9 and 10 pm ($5). You'll easily find this imposing Moorish-inspired building, which dates from 1711, with its crenellated ramparts and arabesque archways. ⊠ *Calle 60, between Calles 57 and 59, Centro* ☎ *999/930–0900 operator, 999/924–6729 art and culture programming* ⊕ *www.uady.mx.*

Zócalo. Méridians traditionally refer to this main square as the Plaza de la Independencia, or the Plaza Principal. Whichever name you prefer, it's a good spot to start a tour of the city, watch dance performances, listen to music, or chill in the shade of a laurel tree when the day gets too hot. The plaza was laid out in 1542 on the ruins of T'hó, the Mayan city demolished to make way for Mérida, and is still the focal point around which the most important public buildings cluster. *Confidenciales* (S-shape benches) invite intimate tête-à-têtes, and lampposts keep the park beautifully illuminated at night. ⊠ *Bordered by Calles 60, 62, 61, and 63, Centro.*

WORTH NOTING

Aké. Aké, a compact archaeological site 35 km (22 miles) southeast of Mérida, offers the unique opportunity to see architecture spanning two millennia in one sweeping vista. Standing atop a ruined Mayan temple built more than 1,000 years ago, you can see the incongruous sight of workers processing sisal in a rusty-looking factory, which was built in the early 20th century. To the right of this dilapidated building are the ruins of the old Hacienda and Iglesia de San Lorenzo Aké, both constructed of stones taken from the Mayan temples.

Experts estimate that Aké was populated between around 200 BC and AD 900; today many people in the area have Aké as a surname. The city seems to have been related to the very important and powerful one at present-day Izamal; in fact, the two cities were once connected by a *sacbé* (white road) 43 feet wide and 33 km (20 miles) long. All that has been excavated so far are two pyramids, one with rows of columns (35 total) at the top, very reminiscent of the Toltec columns at Tula, north of Mexico City. ⊠ *Off Cancún-Merida toll road near Tahmek, 35 km southeast of Mérida* ⌦ *$3.50* ☉ *Daily 9–5.*

Ermita de Santa Isabel. At the southern end of the city stands the restored and beautiful Hermitage of St. Isabel. Built circa 1748 as part of a Jesuit monastery, also known as the Hermitage of the Good Trip, it served as a resting place for colonial-era travelers heading to Campeche. It's one of the most peaceful places in the city, with an interesting, inlaid-stone facade (although the church itself is almost always closed), and is a good destination for a ride in a horse carriage. Behind the hermitage are its huge and lush tropical gardens, with a waterfall and footpaths, which are usually unlocked during daylight hours. ⊠ *Calles 66 and 77, La Ermita* ⌦ *Free* ☉ *Church open only during Mass.*

Iglesia de la Tercera Orden de Jesús. Just north of Parque Hidalgo is one of Mérida's oldest buildings and the first Jesuit church in the Yucatán. It was built in 1618 from the limestone blocks of a dismantled Mayan temple, and faint outlines of ancient carvings are still visible on the west wall. Although a favorite place for society weddings due to its antiquity, the church interior is not ornate.

The former convent rooms in the rear of the building now host the **Pinoteca Juan Gamboa Guzmán,** a small but interesting art collection. The most engaging pieces here are the striking bronze sculptures of indigenous Maya crafted by celebrated 20th-century sculptor Enrique Gottdiener Soto. On the second floor are about 20 forgettable oil paintings—mostly of past civic officials of the area. ⊠ *Calle 59, between Calles 58 and 60, Centro* ☎ *999/924–5233, 999/924–9712* ⊕ *www. inah.gob.mx* ⌦ *$3* ☉ *Tues.–Sat. 9–5, Sun. 10–5.*

Mercado de Artesanías García Rejón. Although many deal in the same wares, the shops or stalls of the García Rejón Crafts Market sell some quality items, and the shopping experience here can be less of a hassle than at the municipal market. You'll find reasonable prices on palm-fiber hats, hammocks, leather sandals, jewelry, and locally made liqueurs. Persistent but polite bargaining may get you even better deals. ⊠ *Calles 60 and 65, Centro* ☉ *Weekdays 9–6, Sat. 9–4, Sun. 9–1.*

Mercado Lucas de Gálvez. Sellers of chiles, herbs, crafts, trinkets, and fruit fill this pungent and labyrinthine municipal market. In the early morning the first floor is jammed with housewives and restaurateurs shopping for the freshest seafood and produce. The stairs at Calles 56 and 57 lead to the second-floor Bazar de Artesanías Municipales, on either side, where you'll find local pottery, embroidered clothes, men's guayabera dress shirts, hammocks, and straw bags. Note that most prices are inflated, and vendors expect you'll bargain—one way to begin

6

is to politely request a discount. ⊠ *Calle 56, between Calles 65 and 67, Centro* ⊘ *Daily 5 am–10 pm.*

Museo de Arte Contemporáneo. Originally designed as an art school and used until 1915 as a seminary, this enormous, light-filled building now showcases the works of contemporary Yucatecan artists such as Gabriel Ramírez Aznar and Fernando García Ponce, as well as a variety of temporary exhibits. If you want to explore beyond the outside plaza, be sure to sign in first. ⊠ *Pasaje de la Revolución 1907, between Calles 58 and 60 on main square, Centro* ☎ *999/928–3236* ⊕ *www.macay.org* ⬙ *Free* ⊘ *Wed.–Mon. 10–5:30.*

Museo de Arte Popular de Yucatán. Facing the Plaza Mejorada, this museum is funded by the Banamex Cultural Foundation, and offers a comprehensive introduction to different kinds of Mexican art craft including ceramics, textiles, stone work, cardboard art, woodwork, and glass. Even if you don't want to see the whole museum, take a look in the gift shop, which sells shawls, baskets, dolls, and masks. Prices are a bit high, but so is the quality of the crafts; even if you don't buy anything here, a look around will inform your purchases at area markets. ⊠ *Calle 50 No. 487, between Calles 57 and 59, Centro* ☎ *999/928–5263* ⬙ *$2* ⊘ *Tues.–Sat. 10–6:30, Sun. 9–2.*

Palacio Cantón. The most compelling of the mansions on **Paseo Montejo,** this stately palacio was built as the residence for a general between 1909 and 1911. Designed by Enrique Deserti, who also did the blueprints for the Teatro Peón Contreras, the building has a grandiose air that seems more characteristic of a mausoleum than a home: there's marble everywhere, as well as Doric and Ionic columns and other Italianate beaux arts flourishes. The building also houses the air-conditioned **Museo Regional de Antropología,** which introduces visitors to ancient Mayan culture. Temporary exhibits sometimes brighten the standard collection. ⊠ *Paseo Montejo 485, at Calle 43, Paseo Montejo* ☎ *999/928–6719, 999/923–0557* ⊕ *www.inah.gob.mx* ⬙ *$4* ⊘ *Tues.–Sun. 8–5.*

Palacio del Gobierno. Visit the seat of state government to see Fernando Castro Pacheco's murals of the bloody history of the conquest of the Yucatán, painted in bold colors in the 1970s and influenced by the Mexican muralists José Clemente Orozco and David Alfaro Siquieros. On the main balcony (visible from outside on the plaza) stands a reproduction of the Bell of Dolores Hidalgo, on which Mexican independence rang out on the night of September 15, 1810, in the town of Dolores Hidalgo in Guanajuato. On the anniversary of the event, the governor rings the bell to commemorate the occasion. ⊠ *Calle 61, between Calles 60 and 62, Centro* ☎ *999/930–3101* ⬙ *Free* ⊘ *Daily 8–8.*

Palacio Municipal. The west side of the main square is occupied by City Hall, or Ayuntamiento, a 17th-century building trimmed with white arcades, balustrades, and the national coat of arms. Originally erected on the ruins of the last surviving Mayan structure, it was rebuilt in 1735 and then completely reconstructed along colonial lines in 1928. It remains the headquarters of the local government, and houses the municipal tourist office, where you can pick up free maps or rent a four-hour audio guide for about $7. ⊠ *Calle 62, between Calles 61 and*

63, Centro ☎ *999/928–2020* ⊘ *Palacio daily 9–8; Tourist Information Center weekdays 8–8, Sat. 9–1.*

NEED A BREAK?

El Colón Sorbetes y Dulces Finos. The homemade ice cream and sorbet at El Colón have been keeping locals cool since 1907. The tropical fruit flavors, like *chico zapote* (a brown fruit native to Mexico that has a flavor a little like cinnamon and comes from a tree that's used in chewing-gum production), served up in a pyramid-shape scoop are particularly delicious and refreshing. The shop also sells cookies and fresh candies—the meringues are exceptional. The Paseo Montejo branch has the same menu with both outdoor and indoor seating. The tables inside are under whirling fans that make it a comfortable spot to cool off on a hot afternoon, and the Paseo Montejo location makes it a great place to people-watch. ⊠ *Calle 62 No. 500, at Calle 59 and Calle 61, Centro* ⊟ *No credit cards.*

Parque Hidalgo (*Plaza Cepeda Peraza*). A half block north of the main plaza is this small cozy park, officially known as Plaza Cepeda Peraza. Historic mansions, now reincarnated as hotels and sidewalk cafés, line the south side of the park and at night the area comes alive with marimba bands and street vendors. On Sunday the streets are closed to vehicular traffic, and there's free live music performed throughout the day. ⊠ *Calle 60, between Calles 59 and 61, Centro.*

FAMILY **Parque Zoológico El Centenario.** Mérida's greatest children's attraction, this large amusement complex features playgrounds, inexpensive rides like motorized cars, small electric merry-go-round style rides, pony rides, a small train ($1) that circles the park, a rollerblading rink, and cages with more than 300 native animals as well as exotics such as lions, tigers, and bears. At the exit, there are snack bars and vendors. It also has picnic areas, pleasant wooded paths, and a small lake where you can rent rowboats. The French Renaissance–style arch (1921) commemorates the 100th anniversary of Mexican independence. ⊠ *Av. Itzáes, between Calles 59 and 65 (entrances on Calles 59 and 65), Centro* ☎ *999/928–5815, 999/945–0733* ⊕ *www.merida.gob.mx/centenario* ⊡ *Free* ⊘ *Tues.–Sun. 8–6.*

WHERE TO EAT

With more than 250 restaurants (not to mention the markets and street-food stands) there are plenty of dining options to choose from in Mérida. Regional dishes and Middle Eastern cuisine are staples, but the flavors and preparations don't stop there. You can even find places serving hamburgers and sandwiches if you're craving something familiar.

$$ **✕ Alberto's Continental Patio.** Though locals say this eatery has lost some
LEBANESE of its star power, it's still a dependable place for shish kebab, fried *kibbe* (meatballs of ground beef, wheat germ, and spices), hummus, tabbouleh, baba ghanoush, and other Lebanese dishes. The strikingly handsome dining spot is full of character, with an eclectic collection of antiques, paintings, and sculptures. The building itself dates to 1727, and is adorned with some of the original stones from the Mayan temple

it replaced, as well as mosaic floors from Cuba. Even if you choose to have dinner elsewhere, stop in for almond pie and Turkish coffee in the romantic, candlelit courtyard. [$] *Average main: $15* ✉ *Calle 64 No. 482, at Calle 57, Centro* ☎ *999/928–5367* 🕒 *No breakfast or lunch. Closed Sun.* ✥ *B6*

$$ MEXICAN Fodor's Choice ★ 🍴 **Amaro.** The romantic patio of this historic home glows with candlelight in the evening; during the day things look a lot more casual. Meat, fish, and shellfish are served here in moderation, but the emphasis is on vegetarian dishes like avocado pizza and *chaya* soup (made from a green plant similar to spinach), and healthful juices. Other local favorites include stuffed mushrooms, spinach lasagna, cochinita pibil, and butterfly chicken breast in a cream sauce. Prices are reasonable, and the service is always excellent. Amaro stays open until 2 am from Monday to Saturday. Expect live music in the open-air courtyard daily between 8:30 pm and midnight. [$] *Average main: $12* ✉ *Calle 59 No. 507, between Calles 60 and 62, Centro* ☎ *999/928–2451* 🌐 *www.restauranteamaro.com* ✥ *B6.*

$$ ITALIAN 🍴 **Café Lucía.** Music floats above black-and-white tile floors in the dining room of this century-old restaurant in the Hotel Casa Lucía near the main plaza. Meals are relatively heavy, like the steak cooked in sherry and the Fettuccini Lucia with cream, cheese, and mushrooms. Pizzas, salads, and calzones are the linchpins of the Italian menu, and pecan pies, cakes, and cookies beckon from behind the glass dessert case. Breakfasts are about half the price of the lunch and dinner menu so drop by early for a value meal. The original art on the walls is for sale, however the paintings by the late Oaxacan artist Rodolfo Morales are not, so don't bother asking. [$] *Average main: $12* ✉ *Calle 60 No. 474A, Centro* ☎ *999/928–0704* 🌐 *www.casalucia.com.mx* ✥ *B5.*

$ MEXICAN 🍴 **Eladio's.** Part bar, part restaurant, and part theater, this lively venue is often crammed with local families and couples. There's an ample dance floor and a free, supervised children's play area—you can also buy ceramic figures for them to paint while you dance. There's a full menu of tasty Yucatecan dishes like *papadzules* (hard-boiled eggs wrapped in warm tortillas and covered with a thick pumpkin-seed sauce) and sopa de lima. Free appetizers, which are actually just smaller portions of the dishes on the menu, come with your beer. From 2 to 6:30 pm there's live salsa, cumbia, and other Latino tunes, punctuated by stage-show–style talking. The attached sports bar offers 2-for-1 beers Monday through Friday. At 7:30 most families disappear, and singles and couples arrive to watch whatever football or boxing match is on TV. This place is known to get lively, loud, and hot. [$] *Average main: $7* ✉ *Calle 24 No. 101C, at Calle 59, Col. Itzimná* ☎ *999/927–2126* 🌐 *www.eladios.com.mx* ✥ *B1.*

$$ MEXICAN 🍴 **Gran Almendros.** This classic Yucatecan eatery has been a favorite with locals since the 1960s, when the owners opened their first restaurant in nearby Ticul. The Mérida branch—with its high colonial ceilings and elegant atmosphere—has been here since 1972 and many say, it's still the best place to eat in town. The *combinado yucateco* (Yucatecan combination plate) is a great way to try different dishes: cochinita pibil, *longaniza asada* (grilled pork sausages), *escabeche de Valladolid* (turkey

with chiles, onions, and seasonings in an acidic sauce), and *poc-chuc* (slices of pork marinated in sour-orange sauce and spices). In fact, they invented some dishes that have become Yucatecan classics, including the poc-chuc and the cheese soup, which is also spectacular. A live trio performs daily from 2 to 5. [$] *Average main: $15* ✉ *Calle 50A No. 493, between Calles 57 and 59, facing Parque La Mejorada, Col. Centro* ☎ *999/928–5459, 999/923–8135* 🌐 *www.restaurantelosalmendros.com.mx* ✣ *C6.*

$$ MEXICAN Fodor's Choice ★ 🍴 **Hacienda Teya.** Once a henequen-producing site dating back to 1683, this beautiful hacienda just outside the city serves some of the best regional food around. It has attracted some big names, like Vicente Fox (back when he was president, and would order the queso relleno to go) and even Hillary Clinton. Most patrons are well-to-do Méridians enjoying a leisurely lunch, so you don't want to wear your beach clothes. In fact, men wearing tank tops will be asked to change. It's open from noon to 6 daily, and a guitarist serenades the tables between 2 and 5 on weekends. Start with the sopa de lima; it's perhaps the most flavorful in the region. After a fabulous lunch of poc-chuc or cochinita pibil (both served with homemade tortillas), take a stroll through the gardens where peacocks roam. This restaurant has the largest wine selection in the Yucatán, and their desserts, like the award-winning flan, come with a complimentary digestif of rum, orange, and spices. If you find yourself wanting to spend the night, you can. The hacienda has six handsome suites ($$), which are often available on short notice, although they need to be reserved in advance over long weekends and holidays. [$] *Average main: $12* ✉ *Carretera 180, 12.5 km (8 miles) east of Mérida, Kanasín* ☎ *999/988–0800* 🌐 *www.haciendateya.com* ⏲ *No dinner. Closed Dec. 25–Jan. 1* ✣ *B6.*

$$$ MODERN MEXICAN 🍴 **Kuuk.** Kuuk, meaning "sprout" in Mayan, offers the most unique dining experience in Mérida. The cutting-edge menu features eight courses, each prepared using molecular gastronomy and fresh ingredients, most of which are grown on-site. Many of the Yucatecan dishes are cooked in the custom built "pibil" oven, a modernized version of the underground cooking method that gives food that smoky flavor. Although small, each course is a work of art, like the dollops of baby pumpkin sprinkled with goat cheese the texture of powdered snow. Each course will leave you scratching your head in bewilderment, including the transparent potatoes as thin as tissue paper and the onion soup paired with crispy onion and bacon orbs that melt in your mouth. Desserts are sprinkled with dehydrated berries, honey-soaked pumpkin seeds, and cilantro pieces that look more like Skittles. This place is chic in every sense of the word, from the cutlery and decor to the wine cellar and suave waiters dressed in black and grey. Plan to stay a while since the entire dining experience takes between two and three hours. ■ **TIP→ Lunch is served 1–5, the bar is open 5–7:30, and dinner is from 7:30 pm to 1 am.** [$] *Average main: $40* ✉ *Calle 30 No. 313, between Calles 37 and 39, San Ramon Norte* ☎ *999/944–3377* 🌐 *www.kuukrestaurant.com* ⏲ *Open Tues.–Sun., 1 pm–1 am* ✣ *C1.*

$$ MEXICAN 🍴 **La Casa de Frida.** Chef-owner Gabriela Praget puts a healthful, cosmopolitan spin on Mexican fare at her restaurant. This is a great place

6

La Casa de Frida serves foods from around Mexico.

to sample foods from around Mexico. Praget prepares all the dishes herself, and is usually on hand to greet guests. Traditional dishes like *chiles en nogada* (stuffed pepper in a walnut sauce) or duck in a dark, rich mole sauce (made with chocolate and chiles) share the menu with gourmet vegetarian cuisine: potato and cheese tacos, ratatouille in puff pastry, and crêpes made with *cuitlachoche* (a delicious truffle-like corn fungus). The dining room—a casual covered patio decorated with plants, copies of Frida Kahlo self-portraits, several Frida dolls, and other art—is a comfortable place to enjoy a leisurely meal. Don't be alarmed by "Coco," the owner's little white rabbit that hops between the tables. ■**TIP**➔ A 15% service charge is automatically added to your bill and credit cards are not accepted. $ *Average main: $11* ✉ *Calle 61 No. 526, at Calle 66, Centro* ☎ *999/928–2311* ⊕ *www.lacasadefrida. com.mx* ▭ *No credit cards* ☉ *No lunch Mon.–Sat. Closed Sun.* ✛ *A6*

$ ✕ **La Tradición.** This family restaurant is popular among locals—in fact,
MEXICAN many say it's their favorite restaurant in town. It's also one of the most formal places that serves the region's cuisine, but you'll still fit right in if you're wearing jeans. Proprietor Albino Medina is a third-generation chef and restaurant owner in his family. Dishes are prepared with a charcoal stove, like your grandma might have used (if you were from around here). The kitchen standards of cleanliness are so strict that the restaurant has received recognition from the Secretary of Tourism. Just about everything you'll try is tasty—including the *queso relleno* (hollowed-out cheese, stuffed with a pork-vegetable mixture) and the *cochinita pibil* (slow-roasted pork dish)—but you might not want to pass up the cream of chaya soup, since you won't find it in many other restaurants. La Tradición is open from 11 to 6. $ *Average main:*

$7 ✉ *Calle 60 No. 293, at Calle 25 next to Fiesta Americana, Col. Alcalá Martin* ☎ *999/925–2526* ⊕ *www.latradicionmerida.com* ◔ *No dinner* ✛ *B1.*

$$$ ✕ **La Tratto.** For the last 20 years, this
ITALIAN family-owned Italian restaurant has been a popular spot among locals. The bar is a nice place to have a drink and to watch the activity on the Paseo Montejo. Although the open design of the restaurant does make it a nice place to enjoy the cool evening weather, the food isn't spectacular, and prices are pretty high by Mérida standards. Still, the salads are generous, almost all of the thin-crust pizzas come with four cheeses, and there's usually some kind of deal on the excellent wine list (check their website for promotions). Happy hour is offered weekdays from 7 to 9 and Wednesday you'll find 2-for-1 deals on pastas. Early birds may want to look elsewhere because this restaurant opens at 7 pm. $ *Average main: $17 ✉ Paseo Montejo 479-C* ☎ *999/927–0434* ⊕ *www.panchosmerida. com* ◔ *No lunch* ✛ *C1.*

WORD OF MOUTH

"I chose to dine at La Casa de Frida specifically because I had read a review that praised its *chiles en nogada* . . . and I found it praiseworthy indeed! I began with an appetizer of crêpes with *cuitlachoche* that was so delicious that I couldn't bring myself to stop eating . . . unfortunately, I was too full to do proper justice to the chiles en nogada. Even so, just thinking of that evening brings back memories of that entrée and its intensely flavorful and rich walnut sauce—wow! My server always seemed to appear out of nowhere at exactly the right time." —kja

6

$$$ ✕ **Pancho's.** In the evening this patio restaurant is bathed in candlelight
MEXICAN and the glow from tiny white lights decorating the tropical shrubs. Much of the menu, as well as the decor, is geared toward tourists, and you can even buy a Pancho's T-shirt on your way out. Tasty tacos, fajitas, burritos, and other dishes will be pleasantly recognizable to those familiar with Mexican food served north of the border. Although you won't find authentic Yucatecan dishes, this is a great place to order the familiar and enjoy a lively atmosphere over a beer. Waiters—dressed in white muslin shirts and pants of the Revolution era—recommend the shrimp flambéed in tequila, and the tequila in general. Happy hour is weekdays 6–8 pm. $ *Average main: $15 ✉ Calle 59 No. 509, between Calles 60 and 62, Centro* ☎ *999/923–0942* ⊕ *www.panchosmerida. com* ◔ *No lunch* ✛ *B6.*

$ ✕ **Rescoldos.** This small, cozy Mediterranean bistro (whose name means
MEDITERRANEAN "burning embers") was the dream of Canadian owners Jake and Rae Ann. Food is served in a courtyard where Jake mans the Pompeii pizza oven that they converted from an old cement water cistern. Rae Ann puts her own spin on traditional Italian dishes like fried raviolis with apple and walnut and thick-crust pizza piled high with sausage, spinach and provolone. Equally satisfying are Greek selections like spanakopita bites and falafel. Vegetarians have plenty of options, including vegetable lasagna, roasted veggies, and a selection of tasty salads. Don't leave without trying the memorable homemade gelato. $ *Average main: $8 ✉ Calle 62 No. 366, between Calles 41 and 43, Centro* ☎ *999/286–1028*

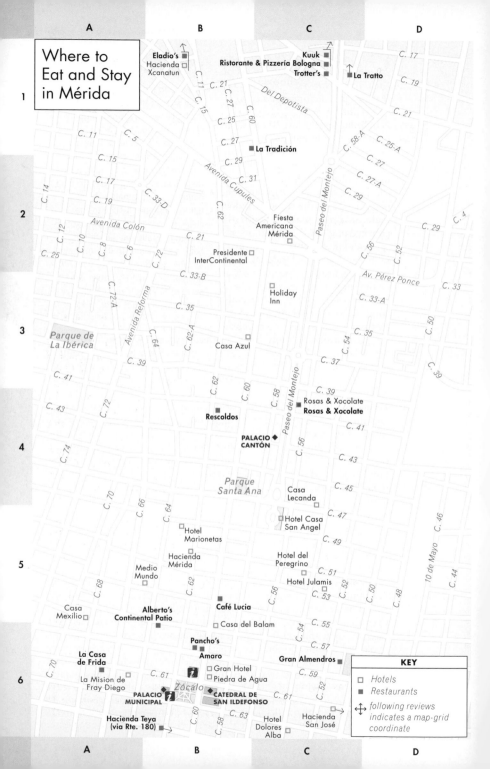

Where to Eat and Stay in Mérida

KEY

☐ Hotels
■ Restaurants
✛ *following reviews indicates a map-grid coordinate*

Eladio's
Hacienda Xcanatun

Kuuk
Ristorante & Pizzería Bologna
Trotter's
La Tratto

C. 17
C. 19
C. 21

Del Depotista

C. 11
C. 21
C. 27
C. 15
C. 25
C. 60

C. 11
C. 5
C. 27
La Tradición

C. 15
C. 29
C. 58-A
C. 25-A
C. 27

C. 17
C. 31
C. 27-A
C. 14
C. 19
C. 33-D
Avenida Cupules
C. 29

C. 62
Fiesta Americana Mérida
Paseo del Montejo
C. 29
C. 4

Avenida Colón
C. 21
C. 56
C. 52

C. 12
C. 10
C. 8
C. 6
C. 72
Presidente InterContinental
Av. Pérez Ponce
C. 33

C. 25
C. 33-B
C. 33-A

C. 72-A
Holiday Inn

Avenida Reforma
C. 35
C. 54
C. 35
C. 50

Parque de La Ibérica
C. 64
C. 62-A
Casa Azul
C. 37
C. 39

C. 39
C. 41
C. 62
C. 60
C. 58
Paseo del Montejo
C. 39
Rosas & Xocolate
Rosas & Xocolate

C. 43
C. 72
Rescoldos
C. 41

C. 74
PALACIO CANTÓN ◆
C. 56
C. 43

Parque Santa Ana
Casa Lecanda
C. 45

C. 70
C. 66
C. 64
☐ Hotel Casa San Angel
C. 47
C. 46

☐ Hotel Marionetas
C. 49

Hacienda Mérida
Hotel del Peregrino
10 de Mayo

C. 68
Medio Mundo
C. 62
C. 56
Hotel Julamis
C. 51
C. 52
C. 50
C. 48
C. 44

Casa Mexilio ☐
Alberto's Continental Patio
Café Lucia
C. 53
C. 55

☐ Casa del Balam
C. 54
C. 57

Pancho's
C. 59
C. 52
Gran Almendros

La Casa de Frida
Amaro

C. 70
La Mision de Fray Diego
C. 61
ℹ ☐ Gran Hotel
☐ Piedra de Agua

PALACIO MUNICIPAL ◆
Zócalo
◆ **CATEDRAL DE SAN ILDEFONSO**
C. 61

Hacienda Teya (via Rte. 180)
C. 60
C. 58
C. 63
Hotel Dolores Alba
Hacienda San José

🌐 *www.rescoldosbistro.com* 💳 *No credit cards* 🕒 *No lunch. Closed Sun. and Mon.* ✥ *B4*

$ ITALIAN 🍴 **Ristorante & Pizzería Bologna.** You can dine alfresco or inside at this beautifully restored old mansion, a few blocks off Paseo Montejo. Tables have fresh flowers and cloth napkins, walls are adorned with pictures of Italy, and there are plants everywhere. Most menu items are ordered à la carte; among the favorites are the shrimp pizza and pizza *diabola,* topped with salami, tomato, and chiles. The beef fillet—served solo or covered in cheese or mushrooms—is served with a baked potato and a medley of mixed sautéed vegetables. [$] *Average main: $9* ✉ *Calle 21 No. 117A, between Calle 24 and 28, Col. Izimná* ☎ *999/926–2505* 🕒 *Closed Tues.* ✥ *C1*

$$$ ECLECTIC 🍴 **Rosas & Xocolate Restaurant.** A tribute to the owner's mother Rosa, and to Mayan chocolate, this trendy restaurant is beautifully designed in hues of pink and brown, with long stem roses on every table. Choose from the formal dining room or the more casual open-air patio or rooftop bar. Chef David Segovia's culinary creations are categorized by "Land" and "Sea." The menu changes regularly but you might find top selections like rib eye with cardomom-seasoned eggplant or tuna with a black sesame crust. There is also a six-course tasting menu as well as a reasonably priced lunch menu offering pasta, burgers, and sandwiches. [$] *Average main: $25* ✉ *Paseo de Montejo #480, on corner of Calle 41, Col. Centro* ☎ *999/924–2992* 🌐 *www.rosasandxocolate.com* ✥ *C4.*

$$$ STEAKHOUSE 🍴 **Trotter's.** Mérida's most upscale eatery, this restaurant is beautifully designed with indoor-outdoor dining rooms separated by a glass wall. Although less formal, the outdoor patio is surrounded by lush vegetation, helping you forget that you are on a bustling avenue. Catering to foreigners and locals alike, the staff speaks perfect English and will gladly explain house favorites like the tuna steak with black pepper crust, or the Angus beef served with a side of rosemary potatoes or lime sautéed spinach. The starters alone make this place worth a visit; try the octopus carpaccio or foie gras. Although steaks are the specialty here, you'll also find plenty of delicious tapas and salads. [$] *Average main: $30* ✉ *Paseo Montejo and Calle 60 Norte, Paseo Montejo* ☎ *999/927–2320* 🌐 *www.trottersmerida.com* 🕒 *No dinner Sun.* ✥ *C1*

MARKET SNACKS

Parque Santa Ana. The simple market in Parque Santa Ana is a popular breakfast spot where you'll find locals happily starting their day with regional dishes and fresh juices at plastic tables. The tamales are good and the *tortas de cochinita,* pork sandwiches flavored with a few drops of sour-orange chile sauce, are heavenly. Most vendors here close around 1:30 in the afternoon, but some reopen to sell snacks between 7 pm and midnight. ✉ *Calle 60, between Calles 45 and 47, Centro.*

6

WHERE TO STAY

Mérida has a wide range of lodging choices, from old haciendas and converted colonial homes to big corporate hotels and small B&Bs. Generally, you'll find smaller hotels in the downtown area, within walking distance of most sights; nights are inevitably a little louder here, especially if your room faces the street. A few larger chain hotels around the Paseo de Montejo offer quiet rooms, and are still near major streets, and only a short ride from downtown.

For expanded reviews, facilities, and current deals, visit Fodors.com.

$$$$
B&B/INN
Fodor's Choice
★

Casa Azul. Declared a historical monument and Yucatán Heritage sight in 1982, this French-style "Blue House" has extraordinary antiques, luxurious fabrics, rose-filled bouquets, and superior service, making every guest feel like royalty. **Pros:** sterling service; modern comforts in historic colonial home; filtered tap water safe for drinking; conveniently located off Paseo de Montejo. **Cons:** small pool; some street noise; restaurant closed to nonhotel guests; no children under 12. $ *Rooms from: $300* ⊠ *Calle 60 No. 343, between 35 and 37, Centro* ☎ *999/925–5016* ⊕ *www.casaazulhotel.com* ↙ *8 rooms* ⊖| *Breakfast* ✛ *C3.*

$$
HOTEL

Casa del Balam. This pleasant and comfortable hotel has an excellent location two blocks from the zócalo in downtown's best shopping area. **Pros:** easy walk to many sights; spacious rooms; great restaurant service (particularly at breakfast). **Cons:** slow elevator; street noise can be a problem. $ *Rooms from: $120* ⊠ *Calle 60 No. 488, Centro* ☎ *999/924–2150, 800/624–8451* ⊕ *www.casadelbalam.com* ↙ *43 rooms, 8 suites* ⊖| *Breakfast* ✛ *B6.*

$$$
B&B/INN
Fodor's Choice
★

Casa Lecanda. As one of Merida's most luxurious and newest boutique hotels, this historic home has been completely restored with European grandeur in mind. **Pros:** within walking distance of town; designated parking area; excellent service; free airport transportation if you stay more than three nights. **Cons:** must reserve dinner 24 hours in advance; no windows in "Adriana" room; no children under 12; mosquitoes in common areas. $ *Rooms from: $200* ⊠ *Calle 47 No. 471, between 54 and 56, Centro* ☎ *999/928–0112* ⊕ *www.casalecanda.com* ↙ *7 rooms* ⊖| *Breakfast* ✛ *C4.*

$$
B&B/INN

Casa Mexilio. Built in the late 1800s for the sons of Vicente Solis Leon, this Venetian-inspired town house serves as an intimate hotel with antique furniture and colorful tile floors four blocks from the main square. **Pros:** pleasant courtyard; easy walk to downtown attractions; excellent room prices; free international calls. **Cons:** small bathrooms; rooms on upper floors can be a bit of hike; no children under 16. $ *Rooms from: $85* ⊠ *Calle 68 No. 495, between Calles 57 and 59, Centro* ☎ *999/928–2505, 888/819–0024* ⊕ *www.casamexilio.com* ↙ *10 rooms* ⊖| *Breakfast* ✛ *A5.*

$$$
HOTEL
FAMILY

Fiesta Americana Mérida. This posh hotel echoes the grandeur of the mansions on Paseo Montejo, and its spacious lobby—with groupings of plush armchairs where guests often lounge—is filled with colonial accents and gleaming marble. **Pros:** comfortable beds; tasty breakfast buffet; shopping area just downstairs; free kids club. **Cons:** a taxi ride away from downtown; very small bathtubs; some amenities cost extra. $ *Rooms from: $250* ⊠ *Av. Colón 451, Paseo Montejo* ☎ *999/942–1111* ⊕ *www.fiestaamericana.com* ↙ *323 rooms, 27 suites* ⊖| *Multiple meal plans* ✛ *C2.*

$$
HOTEL

Gran Hotel. Cozily situated on Parque Hidalgo, this legendary 1901 hotel has extremely high ceilings, wrought-iron balcony and stair rails, and ornately patterned tile floors. **Pros:** beautiful antique decorations;

in the middle of downtown bustle, sights, and shops. **Cons:** downtown noise; no elevator makes upstairs rooms quite a hike; no pool or restaurant; not easy to park in front, and parking is sometimes unavailable (check ahead if you are driving). [$] *Rooms from: $70* ✉ *Calle 60 No. 496, Centro* ☎ *999/924–7730, 999/923–0407* 🌐 *www.granhoteldemerida.com.mx* 🛏 *18 rooms, 7 suites* 🍴 *No meals* ✣ *B6.*

$$$ HOTEL **Hacienda Mérida.** This oasis in the city welcomes guests with a dramatic pool surrounded by pillared archways draped with white curtains. **Pros:** walking distance to city center; great service; one of the few luxury haciendas that allow children. **Cons:** slow Internet; breakfast not included in the rate; no restaurant. [$] *Rooms from: $149* ✉ *Calle 62 No. 39, between 51 and 53, Centro* ☎ *999/924–4363* 🌐 *www.hotelhaciendamerida.com* 🛏 *8 rooms* 🍴 *No meals* ✣ *B5.*

$$$$ HOTEL **Hacienda San Jose.** As one of the five haciendas in the Starwood Luxury Collection, this former cattle ranch (circa 1974) has fully restored guest rooms throughout its 25 lush acres. **Pros:** authentic hacienda experience; rooms have jungle Jacuzzis; every guest receives a complimentary 10-minute massage. **Cons:** cold pool; jungle setting might be too remote for some; difficult to find; 45 minutes from Merida. [$] *Rooms from: $550* ✉ *Carr Tixkobob-Tekanto, Km 30, Tixkokob* ☎ *999/924–1333* 🌐 *www.thehaciendas.com* 🛏 *15 rooms* 🍴 *Multiple meal plans* ✣ *C6.*

$$$$ HOTEL Fodor's Choice ★ **Hacienda Xcanatun.** The furnishings at this beautifully restored 18th-century henequen hacienda include African and Indonesian antiques, locally made lamps, and comfortable, oversized couches and chairs from Puebla. **Pros:** outstanding restaurant; expansive gardens; hotel hosts classical concerts monthly; two wheelchair-accessible rooms. **Cons:** a drive from the city; pricey; not suitable for children. [$] *Rooms from: $310* ✉ *Carretera 261, Km 12, 13 km (8 miles) north of Mérida* ☎ *999/930–2140, 888/883–3633* 🌐 *www.xcanatun.com* 🛏 *5 rooms, 13 suites* 🍴 *No meals* ✣ *B1.*

$$ HOTEL **Holiday Inn.** The most light-filled hotel in Mérida, the Holiday Inn has an open, center courtyard, and floor-to-ceiling windows throughout the colorful lobby and tiled dining room. **Pros:** spacious rooms; free high-speed Wi-Fi, nice breakfast buffet; pleasant courtyard. **Cons:** 1 mile from downtown; pool too small for serious swimming; gym is not well equipped. [$] *Rooms from: $130* ✉ *Av. Colón 498, at Calle 60, Paseo Montejo* ☎ *999/942–8800* 🌐 *www.holidayinn.com.mx* 🛏 *198 rooms, 15 suites* 🍴 *No meals* ✣ *C3.*

$$$ HOTEL **Hotel Casa San Angel.** The comfortable lobby of this small hotel has an open-air central courtyard with a fountain surrounded by plants and brightly painted walls of a tropical motif by local artist "Calocho" Millet. **Pros:** unique setting; comfortable rooms with spacious bathrooms; fantastic service. **Cons:** small pool; no children under 15; those with allergies might have issues with the two resident cats. [$] *Rooms from: $180* ✉ *Paseo de Montejo 1, Centro* ☎ *999/928–0800, 999/928–1155* 🌐 *www.hotelcasasanangel.com* 🛏 *12 rooms, 3 suites* 🍴 *No meals* ✣ *C5.*

$ B&B/INN **Hotel del Peregrino.** This recently restored old home is now a comfortable and inexpensive hotel with 13 spacious rooms decorated with heavy, carved wooden furniture. **Pros:** inexpensive; easy walk

downtown; gracious staff can arrange tours and Spanish tutoring. **Cons:** spacious but basic rooms; kitchen and lounge areas can get noisy, mediocre breakfast; off-site pool is a five-minute walk. [$] *Rooms from: $55* ✉ *Calle 51 No. 488, between Calles 54 and 56, Centro* ☎ *999/924–3007* 🌐 *www.hoteldelperegrino.com* 🛏 *13 rooms* 🍴 *Breakfast* ✣ *C5.*

$ HOTEL 🏨 **Hotel Dolores Alba.** If you can look beyond the plastic flowers, cement bed frames, and vending machines at reception, then this cheerful hotel can be quite a bargin, especially the rooms in the newer wing that have powerful air-conditioning, comfortable beds, and amenities like large TVs, balconies, and telephones. **Pros:** great room prices; nice pool; clean rooms; short walk to the zócalo. **Cons:** mediocre breakfast; Internet access in common areas only; loud a/c; no bathroom amenities. [$] *Rooms from: $60* ✉ *Calle 63 No. 464, between Calles 52 and 54, Centro* ☎ *999/928–5650* 🌐 *www.doloresalba.com* 🛏 *65 rooms* 🍴 *Breakfast* ✣ *C6.*

$ B&B/INN Fodor's Choice ★ 🏨 **Hotel Julamis.** With room rates just below the competition, this 200-year-old artist-owned hotel is a Mérida leader when it comes to value and service. **Pros:** remarkable rates; halfway between Paseo de Montejo and historic center; great views from the rooftop bar. **Cons:** no children under 12; credit cards not accepted. [$] *Rooms from: $69* ✉ *Calle 53 No. 475B, at corner of Calle 54, Centro* ☎ *999/924–1818* 🌐 *www.hoteljulamis.com* 🛏 *7 rooms, 1 suite* 💳 *No credit cards* 🍴 *Breakfast* ✣ *C5.*

$$ B&B/INN 🏨 **Hotel Marionetas.** Attentive proprietors Daniel and Sofija Bosco, who are originally from Argentina and Macedonia, have created this lovely B&B on a quiet street seven blocks from the main plaza. **Pros:** intimate feel; personal attention from proprietors and staff; courtyard and pool area are a calm escape from the bustling Mérida streets. **Cons:** reservations can be hard to come by in high season; restaurant only serves breakfast; no children under 12; pool is shaded by 1 pm. [$] *Rooms from: $100* ✉ *Calle 49 No. 516, between Calles 62 and 64, Centro* ☎ *999/928–3377, 999/923–2790* 🌐 *www.hotelmarionetas.com* 🛏 *8 rooms, 1 suite* 🍴 *Breakfast* ✣ *B5.*

$$ HOTEL 🏨 **La Mision de Fray Diego.** This former 1900s convent still retains its colonial charm within the elegant rooms and suites, each with high ceilings, arched doorways, and checkered tile floors. **Pros:** courteous staff; great restaurant; charming property; centrally located. **Cons:** a bit of climb to third-floor rooms; no children under 12; stairwell is not well lit at night. [$] *Rooms from: $140* ✉ *Calle 61, No. 524, between Calles 64 and 66, Centro* ☎ *999/924–1111* 🌐 *www.lamisiondefraydiego.com* 🛏 *20 rooms, 6 suites* 🍴 *Breakfast* ✣ *A6.*

$$ B&B/INN 🏨 **Medio Mundo.** This former house, run by a Lebanese-Uruguayan couple in a residential area of downtown, has been brightly painted and has Mediterranean accents and spacious rooms off a long passageway. **Pros:** great location; friendly staff; reasonable rates. **Cons:** guests' comings and goings can be noisy at night; no children under eight; Wi-Fi does not reach all rooms. [$] *Rooms from: $80* ✉ *Calle 55 No. 533, between Calles 64 and 66, Centro* ☎ *999/924–5472* 🌐 *www.hotelmediomundo.com* 🛏 *12 rooms* 🍴 *Breakfast* ✣ *B5.*

$$ HOTEL [hotel icon] **Piedra de Agua.** This converted 1842 mansion has been tastefully renovated for maximum comfort without compromising its historical charm. **Pros:** centrally located; communal computer for use. **Cons:** small bathrooms; street noise; gym needs more equipment; low water pressure. [$] *Rooms from: $160* ✉ *Calle 60 No 498, between 59 and 61, Centro* ☎ *999/924–2300* 🌐 *www.piedradeagua.com* ↩ *20 rooms* 🍴 *No meals* ✥ *B6.*

MAKING YOURSELF AT HOME

There are a few Internet agencies that can help you rent a home if you plan on staying in the area for a while. At 🌐 *www.bestofyucatan.com,* you can find some stunningly remodeled old Mérida homes, and haciendas remodeled by artists John Powell and Josh Ramos.

$$$ HOTEL [hotel icon] **Presidente InterContinental.** A salmon-color replica of a 19th-century French-colonial mansion, the Presidente is a bit of a hike from the main plaza, but sits right next to the Santiago church and public square, where a big, live band attracts whirling couples on Tuesday at 9 pm. **Pros:** spacious rooms; comfortable beds; helpful staff; good value. **Cons:** far from main plaza; extra charge for Internet. [$] *Rooms from: $230* ✉ *Av. Colon 500, between 60 and 62, Colonia Centro* ☎ *999/942–9000* 🌐 *www.intercontinentalmexico.com* ↩ *127 rooms, 4 suites* 🍴 *Multiple meal plans* ✥ *B2.*

$$$ B&B/INN [hotel icon] **Rosas & Xocolate.** This boutique hotel has been designed with romance and opulence in mind, with the theme of roses and chocolate carried throughout, from the building's pink exterior and the restaurant's brown chairs to the chocolate soaps in the bathrooms and the Belgium truffles in the gift shop. **Pros:** beautiful architecture; great breakfasts; remarkable showers and mattresses; well-equipped fitness gym. **Cons:** pool is small and in a very public area; no elevator; not suitable for children. [$] *Rooms from: $235* ✉ *Paseo de Montejo 480, at Calle 41, Centro* ☎ *999/924–2992* 🌐 *www.rosasandxocolate.com* ↩ *14 rooms, 3 suites* 🍴 *Breakfast* ✥ *C4.*

NIGHTLIFE

Mérida has an active and diverse cultural life, which features free government-sponsored music and dance performances many evenings, as well as sidewalk art shows in local parks. On Thursday at 9 pm Méridians enjoy an evening of outdoor entertainment at the **Serenata Yucateca.** At **Parque Santa Lucía** (Calles 60 and 55) you'll see trios, the local orchestra, and soloists performing compositions by Yucatecan composers. On Saturday evenings after 7 pm the **Noche Mexicana** (corner of Paseo Montejo and Calle 47) hosts different musical and cultural events. More free music, dance, comedy, and regional handicrafts can be found at the **Corazón de Mérida,** on Calle 60 between the main plaza and Calle 55. Between 8 pm and 1 am, multiple bandstands throughout this area (which is closed to traffic) entertain locals and visitors with an ever-changing playbill, from grunge to classical.

On Sunday, six blocks around the zócalo are closed off to traffic, and you can see performances—often mariachi and marimba bands or folkloric dancers—at Plaza Santa Lucía, Parque Hidalgo, and the main plaza. For a schedule of current performances, consult the tourist offices, the local newspapers, or the billboards and posters at the Teatro Peón Contreras or the Centro Cultural Olimpo.

BARS AND DANCE CLUBS

Mérida has always been a great city to walk in by day and dance in by night. Méridians love music, and they love to dance, but since they also have to work, many discos are open only on weekend nights, or Thursday through Sunday. ■TIP➔ Be aware that it's becoming commonplace for discos and restaurants with live music and "comedy" acts (geared toward young people) to invite customers onstage for some rather shocking "audience participation" acts. Since these are otherwise fine establishments, we can only suggest that you let your sense of outrage be your guide. Locals don't seem to mind.

Café Peón Contreras. This theater from 1908, which also serves as a café-bar, is one of the most happening nightspots in town. Tables spill onto the street, where locals gather to hear balladeers singing romantic songs. The drinks are expensive and the food is not worth mentioning, so only go if you want culture, live music, and an opportunity to splurge. ⊠ *Calle 60, between 57 and 59, facing Parque de la Madre, Centro* ☎ *993/924–7003.*

El Cielo. Popular with middle-aged professionals and the local *niños fresa* (which translates as "strawberry children," meaning upper-class youth), this indoor-outdoor lounge is a minimalist hot spot where you can drink and dance to party or lounge-music videos. It's open Wednesday through Saturday nights from 10 pm till 4 am. Thursday and Saturday there's a $12 cover charge for men ($4 for women), as well as an open bar until 11 pm. ⊠ *Prolongación Paseo Montejo, at Calle 25, Col. México* ☎ *999/944–5127* ⊕ *www.elcielobar.com.*

El Nuevo Tucho. El Nuevo Tucho has cheesy cabaret-style entertainment and comedy acts with no drink minimum and no cover. In fact, despite the music and comedy, this is not just a place for young people or for dancing. Families dine here as well. There's music for dancing in this cavernous—sometimes full, sometimes empty—venue. Drinks come with free appetizers. Plan for midday entertainment because this place closes at 2 pm on weekdays and at 5 pm on Saturday. ⊠ *Calle 60 No. 482, between Calles 55 and 57, Centro* ☎ *999/924–2323* ⊕ *www. eltucho.inmerida.com* ☉ *Weekdays 8–2, Sat. 8–5. Closed Sun.*

La Parranda. Location, location, location is the allure of this loud and colorful drinking establishment. Right in the heart of Plaza Grande, this tourist magnet offers live music and drinks served in plastic yard glasses. Despite the cheesy decor, it's still one of the best spots to grab a beer and watch Mérida in action. Check their website for weekly promotions. ⊠ *Calle 60 No. 502, between 59 and 61, Centro* ☎ *999/928–1691* ⊕ *www.laparrandamerida.com* ☉ *Daily 11 am–2 am.*

Mayan Pub. A pleasant atmosphere, flowing beer, and live music are what make this bar one of Merida's best-kept secrets (you might want to pass on the food). Grab a spot in the beer garden where you can listen to live reggae, rock, or jazz. A rather worn billiard table and occasional

The plaza outside Catedral de San Ildefonso is a popular gathering spot.

entertainment—such as belly dancers and fire spinners—draw in a decent crowd. ⊠ *Calle 62, No. 473, at corner of Calle 55, Centro* ☎ *999/968–7341* ⊕ *www.mayanpub.com* ⊙ *Wed.–Sun. 7 pm–2 am.*

Parque de Santiago. If dancing to the likes of Los Panchos and other romantic trios of the 1940s is more your style, don't miss this Tuesday-night ritual at Parque de Santiago, where older folks and the occasional young lovers gather for dancing under the stars at 8:30 pm. ⊠ *Calles 59 and 72, Centro.*

Slavia. Enormously popular and rightly so, the red-walled Slavia is an exotic Orientalist beauty. There are all sorts of nooks where you can be alone yet together with upscale Meridians. Ambient music in the background, low lighting, beaded curtains, embroidered tablecloths, mirrors, and sumptuous pillows and settees surrounding low tables produce a fabulous vibe that you won't find anywhere else in Mérida. ⚠ Double check your bill for fraudulent tax and tip charges because several customers have reported incidents recently. If smoking a hookah under Buddha's watchful eyes isn't your thing, check out the two other concepts the owner has opened on the same block—Cubaroo, a Latin-themed fusion restaurant and bar whose roof deck has spectacular views of the Monument to the Flag, and Tobago, a cozy replica of a Parisian café. ⊠ *Calle 29 No. 490, at Calle 58* ☎ *999/926–6587* ⊙ *Daily 7 pm–2 am.*

FOLKLORIC SHOWS
Paseo Montejo hotels such as the Fiesta Americana, Hyatt Regency, and Holiday Inn stage dinner shows with folkloric dances. Check with concierges for schedules.

Ballet Folklórico de Yucatán. The Ballet Folklórico de Yucatán presents a combination of music, dance, and theater every Friday at 9 pm at the university; tickets are $5. (Performances are every other Friday in the off-season, and there are no shows from August 1 to September 22 and during the last two weeks of December.) ⊠ *Calles 57 and 60, Centro* ☎ *999/923–1198.*

SHOPPING

Mérida has something for everyone when it comes to shopping, from the souvenir junkies to the most discriminating of market trollers. Crafts at reasonable prices can be found in the markets, parks, and plazas, and local art can be picked up at one of the many galleries, for the art scene here is burgeoning. If you're looking for a more standard shopping experience, or need to stock up on goods like new tennis shoes or a pair of jeans, there are also a few shopping malls in town.

MALLS
Gran Plaza. Mérida has several shopping malls, but the largest and nicest, Gran Plaza, has more than 200 shops and a multiplex theater. It's just outside town, on the highway to Progreso (called Carretera a Progreso beyond the Mérida city limits). ⊠ *Calle 50 Diagonal 460, Fracc. Gonzalo Guerrero* ☎ *999/944–7657* ⊕ *www.granplaza.com.mx.*

Pasaje Picheta. Tiny Pasaje Picheta is on the north side of the town square on Calle 61. It has a bus-ticket information booth and an upstairs art gallery, as well as souvenir shops and a food court. It's open 9 am to 11 pm daily. ⊠ *Calle 61, #516.*

Plaza Américas. Plaza Américas is a pleasant mall where you'll find more than 100 stores and eateries including Sears, McDonald's, and the Cineopolis movie theater complex. ⊠ *Calle 21 No. 331, Col. Miguel Hidalgo* ☎ *999/987–5611* ⊕ *www.plaza-lasamericas.com.*

MARKETS
Bazar de Artesanías. Sunday brings an array of wares into Mérida. Starting at 9 am, the Handicrafts Bazaar, or Bazar de Artesanías, sells lots of huipiles as well as hats and costume jewelry. ⊠ *Main square, Centro.*

Bazar de Artes Populares. As its name implies, popular art, or handicrafts, are sold at the Bazar de Artes Populares beginning at 9 am on Sunday. ⊠ *Parque Santa Lucía, at Calles 60 and 55, Centro.*

Bazar García Rejón. If you're interested in handicrafts, Bazar García Rejón has rows of indoor stalls that sell items like leather goods, palm hats, and handmade guitars. ⊠ *Calles 65 and 62, Centro.*

Mercado Municipal. The Mercado Municipal has lots of things you won't need, but which are fascinating to look at: songbirds in cane cages, mountains of mysterious fruits and vegetables, ladles made of hollow gourds (the same way they've been made here for a thousand years). There are also lots of crafts for sale, including hammocks, sturdy leather huaraches, and piñatas in every imaginable shape and color. ■**TIP→** Guides often approach tourists near this market. They expect a tip and won't necessarily bring you to the best deals. You're better off visiting some specialty stores first to learn about the quality and

Hamacas: A Primer

Yucatecan artisans are known for creating some of the finest *hamacas,* or hammocks, in the country. For the most part, the shops of Mérida are the best places in Yucatán to buy these beautiful, practical items— although if you travel to some of the outlying small towns, like Tixkokob, Izamal, and Ek Balam, you may find cheaper prices, and enjoy the experience as well.

One of the first decisions you'll have to make when buying a hamaca is whether to choose one made from cotton or nylon: nylon dries more quickly and is therefore well suited to humid climates, but cotton is softer and more comfortable (though its colors tend to fade faster). You'll also see that hamacas come in both double-threaded and single-threaded weaves; the double-threaded ones are sturdiest because they're more densely woven.

Hamacas come in a variety of sizes, too. A *sencillo* (cen-*see*-oh) hammock is meant for just one person (although most people find it's a rather tight fit), a *doble* (*doh*-blay), on the other hand, is very comfortable for one but crowded for two. *Matrimonial* or king-size hammocks accommodate two, and *familiares* or *matrimoniales especiales* can theoretically sleep an entire family. (Yucatecans tend to be smaller than Anglos are, and also lie diagonally in hammocks rather than end-to-end.)

For a good-quality king-size nylon or cotton hamaca, expect to pay about $35; sencillos go for about $22. Unless you're an expert, it's best to buy a hammock at a specialty shop, where you can climb in to try the size. The proprietors will also give you tips on washing, storing, and hanging your hammock. There are lots of hammock stores near Mérida's municipal market on Calle 58, between Calles 69 and 73.

---

types of hammocks, hats, and other crafts. Then you'll have an idea of what you're buying—and what it's worth—if you want to bargain in the market. Also be wary of pickpockets within the markets. ⊠ *Calles 56 and 67, Centro.*

SPECIALTY STORES
BOOKS
Mérida is a good destination for book-lovers.

Amate Books. A new branch of an old Oaxacan bookstore, Amate Books stocks books on all kinds of Mexican themes—from art and cooking to archaeology and language—in English. This cool building with high ceilings and old ceramic-tile floors is a beautiful setting in which to browse, meet people, and ask questions about local goings-on. ⊠ *Calles 60 and 51, No. 453* ☎ *999/924–2222* ☉ *Mon.–Sat. 10–8, Sun. 2–7.*

Librería Dante ⊠ *Calle 17 No. 138B, at Prolongación Paseo Montejo, Centro* ☎ *999/926–4566* ⊕ *www.editorialdante.com.*

Mérida English Library ⊠ *Calle 53 No. 524, between Calles 66 and 68, Centro* ☎ *999/924–8401* ⊕ *www.meridaenglishlibrary.com* ☉ *Mon.– Sat. 9–1.*

CLOTHING

Camisería Canul. You might not wear a guayabera to a business meeting as some men in Mexico do, but the shirts are cool, comfortable, and attractive. For a good selection, try Camisería Canul. Custom shirts take a week to tailor, in sizes 4 to 52. ⊠ *Calle 62 No. 484, between Calles 57 and 59, Centro* ☎ *999/923–0158* ⊕ *www.camiseriacanul.com.mx.*

Guayaberas Jack. Guayaberas Jack has an excellent selection of *guayaberas* (men's cotton or linen dress shirts) in 18 colors; they also sell typical women's cotton *filipinas* (house dresses), blouses, dresses, classy straw handbags, and lovely rayon *rebozos* (shawls) from San Luis Potosí. Guayaberas can be made to order, allegedly in less than a day, to fit anyone from a year-old baby to a 240-pound man, and anything in the shop can be altered or custom-made. Everything here is of fine quality, and is often quite different from the clothes sold in neighboring shops—the prices reflect this superior quality. The store has a small branch near the Fiesta Americana Mérida, but it doesn't have as much variety as the downtown location. You can browse and make purchases on their website as well. ⊠ *Calle 59 No. 507A, between Calles 60 and 62, Centro* ☎ *999/928–6002* ⊕ *www.guayaberasjack.com.mx.*

Mexicanísimo. Sleek, clean-lined clothing made from natural fibers for both women and men are available at Mexicanísimo. ⊠ *Calle 60 No. 496, at Parque Hidalgo, Centro* ☎ *999/923–8132.*

JEWELRY

Joyería Kema. Shop for malachite, turquoise, and other semiprecious stones set in silver at Joyería Kema. ⊠ *Calle 60 No. 502-B, between Calles 61 and 63, in front of Plaza Grande, Centro* ☎ *999/923–5838.*

LOCAL GOODS AND CRAFTS

Casa de Cera. This small shop sells signed collectible indigenous beeswax figurines. It's closed afternoons after 5 pm. ⊠ *Calle 74A No. 430E, between Calles 41 and 43, Centro* ☎ *999/920–0219.*

Casa de las Artesanías Ki-Huic. Visit the government-run Casa de las Artesanías Ki-Huic for folk art from throughout Yucatán. There's a showcase of hard-to-find traditional filigree jewelry in silver, gold, and gold-dipped versions. ⊠ *Calle 63 No. 503A, between Calles 64 and 66, Centro* ☎ *999/928–6676.*

El Aguacate. A great place to purchase hammocks is El Aguacate, a family-run outfit with many sizes and designs. It's closed Sunday. ⊠ *Calle 58 No. 604, at Calle 73, Centro* ☎ *999/289–5789, 999/928–6265* ⊕ *www.hamacaselaguacate.com.mx.*

El Hamaquero. The knowledgeable personnel at El Hamaquero will let you try out the hammocks before you buy. It's closed Sunday. ⊠ *Calle 58 No. 572, between Calles 69 and 71, Centro* ☎ *999/923–2117.*

El Mayab. For a multitude of hammocks, head to El Mayab. ⊠ *Calle 58 No. 553-A, at Calle 71, Centro* ☎ *999/924–0853.*

El Xiric. You can buy hammocks made to order—choose from standard nylon and cotton, super-soft processed sisal, Brazilian-style (six-stringed), or crocheted. You can also get Xtabentún, as well as jewelry, black pottery, woven goods from Oaxaca, T-shirts, and souvenirs. ⊠ *Calle 57-A No. 15 and 16, Pasaje Congreso, Centro* ☎ *999/924–9906.*

La Casa de las Artesanías. La Casa de las Artesanías is a government-run craft store offering all kinds of local crafts at fair prices. The tourism offices sometimes give out coupons for a 10% discount. There's a smaller branch in front of the Museo de Antropología e Historia on the Paseo de Montejo, but this main branch offers the best selection. ⊠ *Calle 63, No. 513, between Calles 64 and 66, Centro* ☎ *999/928–6676* ☉ *Mon.–Sat. 9–8, Sun. 9–1.*

Miniaturas. This shop sells a delightful and diverse assortment of different crafts, but specializes in miniatures. ⊠ *Calle 59 No. 507A, between Calles 60 and 62, Centro* ☎ *999/928–6503* ☉ *Closed Sun.*

SPORTS AND THE OUTDOORS

BASEBALL

Centro Deportivo Kukulcán. Baseball is played with enthusiasm between February and July at the Centro Deportivo Kukulcán. There are also tennis courts, soccer courts, and an Olympic pool. It's most common to buy your ticket at the on-site ticket booth the day of the game. A-league volleyball and basketball games and tennis tournaments are also held here. ⊠ *Circuito Colonias, Calle 6 No. 315, across street from Pemex gas station and next to Santa Clara Brewery, Col. Unidad Morelos* ☎ *999/940–4261.*

GOLF

FAMILY   **Club de Golf de Yucatán.** The 18-hole championship golf course at Club de Golf de Yucatán is open to the public. It's about 16 km (10 miles) north of Mérida on the road to Progreso; greens fees are about $100, carts are an additional $35, and clubs can be rented. The pro shop is closed Monday, but the golf course is open seven days a week. The club also has tennis courts, a swimming pool, a restaurant, mini-golf, and a play area for children. ⊠ *Carretera Mérida–Progreso, Km 14.5* ☎ *999/922–0053* ⊕ *www.clubdegolfyucatan.com.*

TENNIS

Estadio Salvador Alvarado. There are two cement public courts at Estadio Salvador Alvarado. The cost is $2.50 per hour during the day and $3 at night, after 6, when the courts are lighted. ⊠ *Calle 11, between Calles 62 and 60, Paseo Montejo* ☎ *999/925–4856.*

IZAMAL

68 km (42 miles) east of Mérida.

In the beautiful town of Izamal you may not find too many sights, but you'll almost certainly be taken by the town's color and carefully cared-for colonial architecture. Although unsophisticated, Izamal is a charming and neighborly alternative to the sometimes frenetic tourism of Mérida. Hotels are humble, and the few restaurants offer basic fare. For those who enjoy a quieter, slower-pace vacation, Izamal is worth considering as a base. The city has recently been refurbished, and the downtown area shines with remodeled buildings, new roads, and bright yellow paint that strikingly contrasts with the blue sky. Some of these efforts have been part of the city's current efforts to be named a UNESCO World Heritage Site.

One of the best examples of a Spanish colonial town in the Yucatán, Izamal is nicknamed "Ciudad Amarilla" (Yellow City), because its most important buildings are painted a golden ocher. It's also sometimes called "the City of Three Cultures," because of its combined pre-Hispanic, colonial, and contemporary influences.

GETTING HERE AND AROUND

The drive to Izamal from Mérida takes less than an hour. Take Highway 180 and follow the signs. Calesas are stationed at the town's large main square, fronting the lovely cathedral, day and night. The drivers charge about $5 an hour for sightseeing, and many will also take you on a shopping tour for whichever items you're interested in buying (for instance, hammocks or jewelry). Pick up a brochure at the visitor center for details.

ESSENTIALS

Visitor and Tour Information Izamal Tourism Department ⊠ *Calle 30 No. 323, between Calles 31 and 31-A, Centro* ☏ *988/954–1096.*

EXPLORING

Centro Cultural y Artesanal Izamal. Banamex has set up this small, well-organized popular art museum right on the main plaza. There are all kinds of high-quality crafts on display, from textiles and ceramics to papier-mâché and woodwork. You can also take home a souvenir from the gift shop. The center also has small café, a mini-spa that offers massages, and a pleasant patio at the foot of the Kabul pyramid. ⊠ *Calle 31 s/n No. 201, Centro* ☏ *988/954–1012* ⊕ *www.centroculturalizamal. org.mx* ☏ *$2* ⊙ *Tues.–Sat. 10–8, Sun. 10–5.*

Ex-Convento y Iglesia de San Antonio de Padua. Facing the main plaza, this enormous 16th-century former monastery and church of St. Anthony of Padua is perched on—and built from—the remains of a Mayan pyramid devoted to Itzámná, god of the heavens. The monastery's ocher-painted church, where Pope John Paul II led prayers in 1993, has a gigantic atrium (supposedly second in size only to the Vatican's) facing a colonnaded facade and rows of 75 white-trimmed arches. The Virgin of the Immaculate Conception, to whom the church is dedicated, is the patron saint of the Yucatán. A statue of Nuestra Señora de Izamal, or Our Lady of Izamal, was brought here from Guatemala in 1562 by Bishop Diego de Landa. Miracles are ascribed to her, and a yearly pilgrimage takes place in her honor. Frescoes of saints at the front of the church, once plastered over, were rediscovered and refurbished in 1996.

The monastery and church are now illuminated in a light-and-sound show of the type usually shown at the archaeological sites. You can catch a Spanish-only narration and the play of lights on the nearly 500-year-old structure at 8:30 pm Tuesday, Thursday, Friday, and Saturday—buy tickets ($4.50) on-site at 8.

San Antonio de Padua was built from the remains of a Mayan pyramid.

Diagonally across from the massive cathedral, the small **municipal market** is worth a wander. It's a lot less frenetic than markets at major cities like Mérida, and the kind of place where if you stop to watch how the merchants prepare their food, they may spend the time to let you in on their cooking secrets. .

Kinich Kakmó (*Kinich Kak Moo*). The Kinich Kakmó pyramid is the largest pre-Hispanic building in the Yucatán, and it's all that remains of the royal Mayan city that flourished here between AD 250 and 600. Dedicated to Zamná, Mayan god of the dew, the enormous structure is the largest of its kind in the state, covering about 10 acres. More remarkable for its size than for any remaining decoration, it's nonetheless an impressive monument, and you can scale it from the stairs on the south face for a view of the cathedral and the surrounding countryside. There is a $2 fee to use a video camera. 📷 *Free ☉ Daily 8–5.*

WHERE TO EAT

$ ✕ **Los Mestizos.** This humble restaurant has brightly painted walls; even
MEXICAN   the ceiling fans are painted bright orange. The "Combinado los Mestizos" on the dinner menu offers a taste of several regional specialties including *salbutes* and *panuchos*—both typical appetizers of fried cornmeal, the latter stuffed with beans—as well as chicken and turkey dishes. A far less common dish called *dzotobichay* is a tamale made with chaya leaves. There's a bit of a view of the church beyond the marketplace from the rooftop terrace. This is a great place to get an early start or wind up a long day of sightseeing. They're open daily from around

7 in the morning until 11 at night. $ *Average main: $7* ⊠ *Calle 33 No. 301, behind market, Centro* ☎ *988/954–0289* ▬ *No credit cards.*

$ ✗**Restaurante Kinich.** This is the most comfortable place to eat in town.
MEXICAN   The entrance has a small shop featuring a carefully selected and cleverly displayed collection of local folk art for sale. Beyond this, you enter a dining area with white tablecloths under a wide *palapa* (thatched roof), which is surrounded by plants and a burbling fountain, with a small hut in back, where women make tortillas the old-fashioned way—by hand. This is a great place to try local dishes as well—including locally made *longaniza*, a tasty grilled pork sausage. The sopa de lima is also excellent. The restaurant is open daily from noon until around 7 at night, but when there's a light-and-sound show downtown, it stays open until 10. $ *Average main: $8* ⊠ *Calle 27 No. 299, between Calles 28 and 30* ☎ *988/954–0489* ⊕ *www.kinichizamal.com.*

WHERE TO STAY

For expanded reviews, facilities, and current deals, visit Fodors.com.

$$$ ⛺ **Hacienda Sacnicte.** Three miles north of town, the hacienda (whose
B&B/INN   name means white flower) dates from 1811, but it's been restored to strike a perfect balance between the old and new with beautifully appointed suites and spacious bathrooms. **Pros:** rate includes delicious breakfast; thoughtful design; wonderful staff **Cons:** no refunds on cancellations; owners rarely on-site; pricey; not centrally located. $ *Rooms from: $300* ⊠ *Carretera a Tekal de Venegas, Km 5, Izamal, Yucatán* ☎ *999/222–6933* ⊕ *www.haciendasacnicte.com* ⤢ *10 suites* ❑ *Breakfast.*

$ ⛺ **Macanché.** Each artsy bungalow here has its own theme decor: the
B&B/INN   Asian room has a Chinese checkers board and origami decorations; the Safari room has artifacts from Mexico and Africa. **Pros:** full breakfast included; great room price; private yoga classes available; huge bathtubs. **Cons:** several blocks from central plaza; mosquitoes in common areas. $ *Rooms from: $70* ⊠ *Calle 22 No. 305, between Calles 33 and 35* ☎ *988/954–0287* ⊕ *www.macanche.com* ⤢ *15 bungalows, 2 houses* ❑ *Breakfast.*

$$ ⛺ **Romantic Hotel Santo Domingo.** Built on a 44-acre hacienda property,
B&B/INN   this hotel has freestanding rooms separated by carefully tended gardens
Fodor'sChoice   full of exotic plants and fruit trees. **Pros:** freestanding rooms provide
★   some privacy; owners offer transportation to Chichén Itzá; close to town center; cooking lessons available. **Cons:** no credit cards accepted; Wi-Fi in common areas only. $ *Rooms from: $90* ⊠ *Calle 18, between Calles 33 and 35* ☎ *988/967–6136* ⊕ *www.izamalhotel.com* ⤢ *10 rooms* ▬ *No credit cards* ❑ *Breakfast.*

SHOPPING

Hecho a Mano. On the other side of the square, Hecho a Mano is the only place in town to buy folk art from all over Mexico. There's something in every price category, including a growing collection of textiles. ⊠ *Calle 31-A No. 308, Centro* ☎ *988/954–0344.*

Uxmal is an example of the Puuc architectural style.

remote ruin sites, here you can buy food, drinks, and souvenirs at the entrance.

GETTING HERE AND AROUND

If you plan to drive, take Highway 180 south out of Mérida, and then get on Highway 261 in Umán. This will take you south all the way to Uxmal.

EXPLORING

Fodor's Choice ★ **Uxmal Ruins.** Although much of Uxmal hasn't been restored, the following buildings in particular merit attention:

At 125 feet high, the **Pirámide del Adivino** is the tallest and most prominent structure at the site. Unlike most other Mayan pyramids, which are stepped and angular, the Temple of the Magician has a softer and more-refined round-corner design. This structure was rebuilt five times over hundreds of years, each time on the same foundation, so artifacts found here represent several different kingdoms. The pyramid has a stairway on its western side that leads through a giant open-mouthed mask to two temples at the summit. During restoration work in 2002 the grave of a high-ranking Maya official, a ceramic mask, and a jade necklace were discovered within the pyramid. Continuing excavations have revealed exciting new finds that are still being studied.

West of the pyramid lies the **Cuadrángulo de las Monjas,** considered by some to be the finest part of Uxmal. The name was given to it by the conquistadores, because it reminded them of a convent building in Old Spain (*monjas* means nuns). You may enter the four buildings, each comprising of a series of low, gracefully repetitive chambers that look onto a central patio. Elaborate and symbolic decorations—masks, geometric patterns, coiling snakes, and some phallic figures—blanket the upper facades.

Heading south, you'll pass a small ball court before reaching the **Palacio del Gobernador,** which archaeologist Victor von Hagen considered the most magnificent building ever erected in the Americas. Interestingly, the palace faces east, while the rest of Uxmal faces west. Archaeologists believe this is because the palace was built to allow observation of the planet Venus. Covering 5 acres and rising over an immense acropolis, it lies at the heart of what may have been Uxmal's administrative center.

Apparently the house of an important person, the recently excavated **Cuadrángalo de los Pájaros** (Quadrangle of the Birds), located between the above-mentioned buildings, is composed of a series of small chambers. In one of these chambers, archaeologists found a statue of the royal, by the name of Chac (as opposed to Chaac, the rain god), who apparently dwelled there. The building was named for the repeated pattern of birds, which decorates the upper part of the building's frieze.

Today you can watch a sound-and-light show at the site that recounts Mayan legends. The colored light brings out details of carvings and mosaics that are easy to miss when the sun is shining. The show is performed nightly in Spanish, but earphones ($3) provide an English translation. ■TIP→ In the summer months, tarantulas are a common sight at the ruins and around the hotels that surround the ruins. *Site, museum, and sound-and-light show $19.50; show only $5; parking $2; use of video camera $4.50 (keep this receipt if visiting other archaeological sites along Ruta Puuc on same day)* ⊙ *Daily 8–5; sound-and-light show 7 pm in winter, 8 pm in summer.*

WHERE TO EAT

$ **✕ Cana Nah.** Although this large roadside spot mainly caters to the
MEXICAN groups visiting Uxmal, locals recommend it as the most formally established and hygienic eatery in the area, and the friendly owners are happy to serve small parties. The basic menu includes local dishes like lime soup and pollo pibil, and such universals as fried chicken and vegetable soup. Approach the salsa on the table with a bit of caution: it's made almost purely of habanero chiles. After your meal you can dive into the property's large rectangular swimming pool. There's a small shop as well, selling pieces of popular art including figurines of *los aluxes,* the mischievous "lords of the jungle" that Mayan legend says protect farmers' fields. $ *Average main: $8* ⊠ *Carretera Muna–Uxmal, 4 km (2½ miles) north of Uxmal* ☎ *999/109–7513* ▬ *No credit cards.*

WHERE TO STAY

For expanded reviews, facilities, and current deals, visit Fodors.com.

$$ **Flycatcher Inn.** Although branding itself as a boutique hotel, this prop-
B&B/INN erty is actually comprised of seven freestanding casitas, each brightly decorated with yellow walls and Mayan art. **Pros:** great base to explore the ruins; clean rooms; delicious breakfasts. **Cons:** no closets or drawers; no children under 6; no restaurant. $ *Rooms from: $80* ⊠ *Corner of Hwy. 261 and Calle 20, Santa Elena* ☎ *997/978–5350* ⊕ *www. flycatcherinn.com* ⤳ *7 rooms* ❏ *Breakfast.*

6

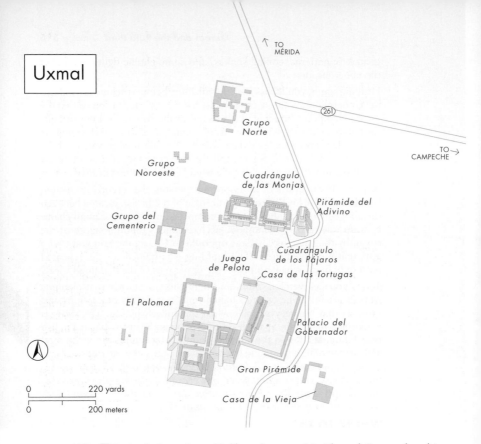

Uxmal

TO MÉRIDA

261

TO CAMPECHE

Grupo Norte

Grupo Noroeste

Cuadrángulo de las Monjas

Pirámide del Adivino

Grupo del Cementerio

Cuadrángulo de los Pájaros

Juego de Pelota

Casa de las Tortugas

El Palomar

Palacio del Gobernador

Gran Pirámide

Casa de la Vieja

0 ——— 220 yards
0 ——— 200 meters

$$$$ 🛏 **Hacienda Santa Rosa.** Halfway between Merida and Campeche, this
HOTEL 120-year-old hacienda once served as a nobleman's private estate. **Pros:**
romantic setting; quiet property; interaction with local communities;
great midway hotel between Merida and Campeche, 44 miles from
Uxmal ruins. **Cons:** pool is partly shaded; property is difficult to find;
expensive. ⓢ *Rooms from: $410* ✉ *Carr Merida-Campeche, Km 129,
Santa Rosa* ☎ *999/923–1923* ⊕ *www.thehaciendas.com* 🛏 *11 rooms*
🍴 *No meals.*

$$$ 🛏 **Hacienda Uxmal.** The first hotel built in Uxmal, this colonial-style
HOTEL building was looking positively haggard before a face-lift brought the
property back to life with rooms decorated simply but elegantly, each
fronted with wide, furnished verandas that face the pool. **Pros:** good ser-
vice; good restaurant; pretty gardens; interesting on-site activities. **Cons:**
Wi-Fi in common areas only; lacks true hacienda charm; slightly musty
rooms; tourists arrive by the busload. ⓢ *Rooms from: $190* ✉ *Carretera
261, Km 78* ☎ *997/976–2012, 800/235–4079* ⊕ *www.mayaland.com*
🛏 *54 rooms, 8 suites* 🍴 *No meals.*

$$$ 🛏 **Lodge at Uxmal.** The outwardly rustic, thatch-roof buildings here have
HOTEL red-tile floors, hand carved doors and rocking chairs, stained glass win-
dows, and local weavings. **Pros:** directly across from Uxmal entrance;
simple yet beautiful rooms; big pools; gracious staff. **Cons:** no room
phones; mosquitoes; expensive for rustic rooms. ⓢ *Rooms from: $150*

✉ *Carretera Uxmal, Km 78* ☎ *998/887–2495* 🌐 *www.mayaland.com* 🛏 *30 rooms, 10 suites* 🍴 *No meals.*

$ B&B/INN 🏨 **The Pickled Onion Hotel.** Owner Valerie Pickles has carved out a lovely little paradise with six bungalows and a wonderful restaurant on the outskirts of Santa Elena. **Pros:** food at restaurant is made from scratch; communal computer for use; amazing rates; wonderful owner. **Cons:** no Wi-Fi in rooms; no a/c; rustic setting is not for everyone. [$] *Rooms from: $45* ✉ *Carretera 261, between Uxmal and Kabah, just after Santa Elena Centro, Santa Elena* ☎ *997/111–7922* 🌐 *www.thepickledonionyucatan.com* 🛏 *6 rooms* 🍴 *Breakfast.*

KABAH

23 km (14 miles) south of Uxmal on Carretera 261.

Kabah. The most important buildings at Kabah, which means "lord of the powerful hand" in Mayan, were built between AD 600 and 900, during the later part of the classic era. A ceremonial center of almost Grecian beauty, it was once linked to Uxmal by a sacbé, at the end of which looms a great independent arch—now across the highway from the main ruins. The 151-foot-long **Palacio de los Mascarones,** or Palace of the Masks, boasts a three-dimensional mosaic of 250 masks of inlaid stones. On the central plaza, you can see ground-level wells called *chultunes,* which were used to store precious rainwater. The site officially opens at 8 am, but the staff doesn't usually show up until 9. ✉ *Off Mérida-Campeche road, 20 km south of Uxmal* 🎟 *$3.50* 🕒 *Daily 8–5.*

6

SAYIL

9 km (5½ miles) south of Kabah on Carretera 31 E.

Sayil. Experts believe that Sayil, or "place of the red ants," flourished between AD 800 and 1000. It's renowned primarily for its majestic **Gran Palacio.** Built on a hill, the three-story structure is adorned with decorations of animals and other figures, and contains more than 80 rooms. The structure recalls Palenque in its use of multiple planes, columned porticoes, and sober cornices. Also on the grounds is a stela in the shape of a phallus—an obvious symbol of fertility. 🎟 *$3.50* 🕒 *Daily 8–5.*

LABNÁ

9 km (5½ miles) south of Sayil on Carretera 31 E.

Eco Museo del Cacao. On a cocoa plantation between Xlapak and Labna, this museum highlights the history of cocoa and its relationship with the Mayan culture. Tours take place in traditional homes where you can learn about the cultivation of cocoa and the process of making chocolate. At the end, you'll be treated to a traditional Mayan drink, prepared with organic cocoa and local spices. ✉ *Km 20, Rte. Puuc, near ruins of Xlapak and Labna Yotholin, Ticul* ☎ *045 999/121–8839 cell* 🌐 *www.ecomuseodelcacao.com* 🎟 *$9* 🕒 *Daily 9–6.*

Grutas de Loltún is an extensive cave system.

Labná. The striking monumental structure at Labná (which means "old house" or "abandoned house") is a fanciful corbelled arch (also called the Mayan arch, or false arch), with elaborate latticework and a small chamber on each side. One theory says the arch was the entrance to an area where religious ceremonies were staged. The site was used mainly by the military elite and royalty. ⌧ *Off Hwy 261. Detour left at Km 30 by Interstate 31* ⌑ *$3.50* ⊙ *Daily 8–5.*

GRUTAS DE LOLTÚN

19 km (12 miles) northeast of Labná, down an unmarked road toward Oxkutzcab.

FAMILY **Grutas de Loltún.** The Loltún ("stone flower" in Mayan) is one of the largest and most fascinating cave systems on the Yucatán Peninsula. Long ago, Mayan ceremonies were routinely held inside these mysterious caves, and artifacts found inside date as far back as 800 BC. The topography of the caves themselves is fascinating: there are stalactites, stalagmites, and limestone formations known by such names as Ear of Corn and Cathedral. Illuminated pathways meander a little over a kilometer through the caverns, most of which are quite spacious and well ventilated (claustrophobics needn't worry). Nine different openings allow air and some (but not much) light to filter in. Moisture can make these paths somewhat slippery so be sure to wear shoes that grip. ■TIP→ You can enter only with a guide. Although these guides earn a very small salary, they mostly survive on tips—so be generous. Scheduled tours are at 9:30, 12:30, 3, and 4 (in Spanish), and 11 and 2 (in English). ⌑ *$10; parking $2* ⊙ *Daily 9–5.*

Yucatán's History

Francisco de Montejo's conquest of Yucatán took three gruesome wars over a total of 24 years. "Nowhere in all America was resistance to Spanish conquest more obstinate or more nearly successful," wrote the historian Henry Parkes. In fact, the resolute Maya, their ancestors long incorrectly portrayed by archaeologists as docile and peace loving, provided the Spaniards and the mainland Mexicans with one of their greatest challenges. Rebellious pockets of Mayan communities held out against the *dzulo'obs* (dzoo-loh-*obs*)—the upper class, or outsiders—as late as the 1920s and '30s.

If Yucatecans are proud of their heritage and culture, it's with good reason. Although in a state of decline when the conquistadores clanked into their world with iron swords and fire-belching cannons, the Maya were one of the world's greatest ancient cultures. As mathematicians and astronomers they were perhaps without equal among their contemporaries, and their architecture in places like Uxmal was as graceful as that of the ancient Greeks.

To "facilitate" Catholic conversion among the conquered, the Spaniards superimposed Christian rituals on existing beliefs whenever possible, creating the ethnic Catholicism that's alive and well today. (Those defiant Maya who resisted the new ideology were burned at the stake, drowned, and hanged.) Having procured a huge workforce of free indigenous labor, Spanish agricultural estates prospered like mad. Mérida soon became a thriving administrative and military center, and the gateway to Cuba and to Spain. By the 18th century, huge maize and cattle plantations were making the *hacendados* incredibly rich.

Insurrection came during the War of the Castes in the mid-1800s, when the enslaved indigenous people rose up with long-repressed furor and massacred thousands of non-Indians. The United States, Cuba, and Mexico City finally came to the aid of the ruling elite, and between 1846 and 1850 the Indian population of Yucatán was effectively halved. Those Maya who didn't escape into the remote jungles of neighboring Quintana Roo or Chiapas, or get sold into slavery in Cuba, found themselves, if possible, worse off than before the dictatorship of Porfirio Díaz.

The hopeless status of the indigenous people—both Yucatán natives and those kidnapped and lured with the promise of work elsewhere in Mexico—changed little as the economic base segued from one industry to the next. After the thin limestone soil failed to produce fat cattle or impressive corn, entrepreneurs turned to dyewood and then to henequen, a natural fiber used to make rope. After the widespread acceptance of synthetic fibers, the entrepreneurs used the sweat of local labor to convert gum arabic from the peninsula's prevalent *zapote* tree into European vacations and Miami bank accounts. The fruits of their labor can be seen today in the imposing French-style mansions that stretch along Mérida's Paseo Montejo.

6

TICUL

27 km (17½ miles) northwest of the Loltún Caves, 28 km (17 miles) east of Uxmal, 100 km (62 miles) south of Mérida.

One of the larger cities in the Yucatán (with a population of around 20,000) and a busy market town, Ticul is a good base for exploring the Puuc region—if you don't mind rudimentary hotels and a limited choice of simple restaurants. Many descendants of the Xiu Dynasty, which ruled Uxmal until the conquest, still live here. Industries include fabrication of huipiles (traditional dresses worn by indigenous women) and shoes, as well as much of the pottery you see around the Yucatán. It also has a handsome 17th-century church.

GETTING HERE AND AROUND

Ticul is an easy drive south of Mérida, along the Ruta Puuc. Follow México 180 from Mérida to Umán, where you'll get on the México 261 to Muná. From Muná, simply follow the signs to Ticul, by way of the México 184.

EXPLORING

Arte Maya. This ceramics workshop produces museum-quality replicas of archaeological pieces found throughout Mexico. The workshop also creates souvenir-quality pieces that are more affordable and more easily transported. ⊠ *Calle 23 No. 301 and 46, Carretera Tikul Muna at entrance to town, next to cemetery* ☎ *997/972–0901.*

Iglesia de San Antonio de Padua. This pretty, faded, red colonial church is typical of the Yucatán colonial churches. It has been weathered and ransacked on more than one occasion, but the Black Christ altarpiece is original. The best view might be from the outside, where you can take in the facade, including its three towers, and the slow pace of the town as families ride by in carts attached to bicycles and locals mill around in traditional Mayan dress. ⊠ *On zócalo, Centro.*

┌─── OFF THE
│ BEATEN
│ PATH

Mayapán. Those who are enamored with Yucatán and the ancient Maya may want to take a 42-km (26-mile) detour east of Ticul (or 43 km [27 miles] from Mérida) to Mayapán, the last of the major city-states on the peninsula that flourished during the postclassic era. It was demolished in 1450, presumably by war. It's thought that the city, with an architectural style reminiscent of Uxmal, was as big as Chichén Itzá, and there are more than 4,000 mounds, which might lend truth to this. At its height, the population could have been well more than 12,000. A half dozen mounds have been excavated, including the palaces of Mayan royalty and the temple of the benign god Kukulcán, where stucco sculptures and murals in vivid reds and oranges have been uncovered. ■**TIP→** The Mayapán ruins are a few miles south of the town of Telchaquillo, about 25 miles south of Mérida. Be sure you head toward the Mayapán ruins, and not the town of Mayapán, since they are far apart. ⊠ *Off road to left before Telchaquillo (follow signs)* ▣ *$4* ۞ *Daily 8–5.*

WHERE TO EAT

$ ✕ **El Príncipe Tutul-Xiu.** About 15 km (9 miles) from Ticul in the little town
MEXICAN   of Maní, this large, open restaurant under a giant palapa roof is a great place for lunch or an early dinner (it closes at 7 pm). Though you'll

find the same Yucatecan dishes here as elsewhere—pollo pibil, lime soup—the preparation is excellent and portions are generous. Best of all is the poc-chuc—little bites of pork marinated in sour orange, garlic, and chiles and grilled over charcoal. Ⓢ *Average main: $7* ⊠ *Calle 26 No. 208, between Calles 25 and 27, Mani* ☎ *997/978–4086, 997/978–4257* ⊕ *www.restaurantestululxiu.com.*

$ ✕ **Pizzería La Góndola.** The wonderful smells of fresh-baked bread and
PIZZA pizza waft from this small corner establishment between the market and the main square. Scenes of Old Italy and the Yucatán adorn bright yellow walls, clients pull their padded folding chairs up to yellow-tile tables, or take their orders to go. Pizza is the name of the game here, although tortas and pastas are also for sale. Although the restaurant is open daily, they close between 1 and 5. Ⓢ *Average main: $8* ⊠ *Calle 23 No. 208, at Calle 26A* ☎ *997/972–0112* ▭ *No credit cards* ☾ *No lunch.*

WHERE TO STAY
For expanded reviews, facilities, and current deals, visit Fodors.com.

$$$$ ⬚ **Hacienda Temozón.** These luxurious Starwood accommodations may
HOTEL seem far from any town or city, but they're actually quite close to the
Fodor'sChoice ruins of Uxmal, the Ruta Puuc, and even Mérida, which is just 45
★ minutes away. **Pros:** gorgeous grounds; beautiful rooms; massages can be arranged; shutters can darken the room for a late sleep-in. **Cons:** expensive meals at the restaurant; you'll need to drive to get to nearby ruins and cities; lukewarm showers. Ⓢ *Rooms from: $500* ⊠ *Carretera 261, Km 182, Temozón Sur, turn off is 4 km (2½ miles) south of Yaxcopoil* ☎ *999/923–8089, 888/625–5144* ⊕ *www.thehaciendas.com* ⇥ *28 rooms, 1 suite* ⦿ *No meals.*

$ ⬚ **Hotel Plaza.** While they get no points for creativity as far as their name
HOTEL is concerned, this hotel does have a convenient location about a block from the main plaza. **Pros:** downtown location; clean rooms. **Cons:** no frills; street noise and church bells might keep you up late or wake you early; 6% surcharge for paying with credit card. Ⓢ *Rooms from: $40* ⊠ *Calle 23 No. 202, between Calles 26 and 26A* ☎ *997/972–0484* ⊕ *www.hotelplazayucatan.com* ⇥ *38 rooms* ⦿ *No meals.*

CHICHÉN ITZÁ AND THE MAYAN INTERIOR

Although hordes of buses arrive daily at Chichén Itzá, dropping off groups of tourists only to whisk them away a few hours later, visiting the area this way is almost criminal. The area around the ruins is dotted with stunning cenotes, numerous smaller archaeological sites, and sleepy towns, which may make you feel like you've stepped back in time. The small town of Pisté is little more than an outpost—it's a place where visitors to Chichén Itzá can rest at small hotels. The picturesque town of Valladolid, the second-largest city in the state, is notable for its cenotes and a beautiful 16th-century church. Here, perhaps while enjoying a traditional ice cream in the central plaza, you notice that things seem to move at a slower pace.

6

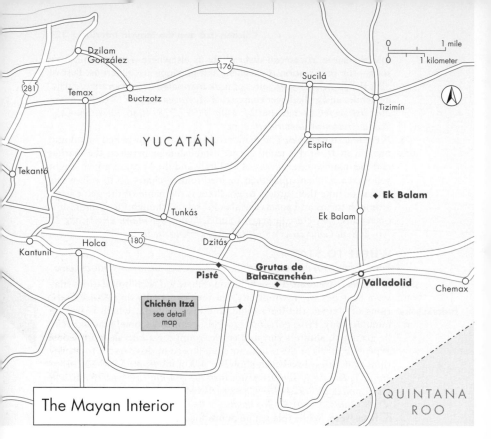

The Mayan Interior

GETTING HERE AND AROUND

Although you can get to Chichén Itzá along the shorter Carretera 180, there's a more scenic and interesting alternative. Head east on Carretera 281 through Tixkokob, a Maya community famous for its hammock weavers, and continue through Citilcúm and Izamal. From there, continue on through the small, untouristy towns of Dzudzal and Xanaba en route to Kantunil. There you can hop on the toll road or continue on the free road that parallels it through Holca and Libre Unión, both of which have very swimmable cenotes.

CHICHÉN ITZÁ

120 km (74 miles) east of Mérida.

Fodor's Choice **Chichén Itzá.** One of the most dramatically beautiful of the ancient Maya
★ cities, Chichén Itzá draws some 3,000 visitors a day from all over the world. Since the remains of this once-thriving kingdom were discovered by Europeans in the mid-1800s, many of the travelers who make the pilgrimage here have been archaeologists and scholars, who study the structures and glyphs and try to piece together the mysteries surrounding them. While the artifacts here give fascinating insight into Mayan civilization, they also raise many, many unanswered questions.

The name of this ancient city, which means "the mouth of the well of the Itzás," is a mystery in and of itself. Although it likely refers to the valuable water sources at the site (there are several sinkholes here), experts have little information about who might have actually founded the city—some structures, likely built in the 5th century, predate the arrival of the Itzás who occupied the city starting around the late 8th and early 9th centuries. The reason why the Itzás abandoned the city, around 1224, is also unknown. The role that this center then took is still being evaluated.

Of course, most of the visitors that converge on Chichén Itzá come to marvel at its beauty, not ponder its significance. Even among laypeople, this ancient metropolis, which encompasses 6 square km (2.25 square miles), is known around the world as one of the most stunning and well-preserved Mayan sites in existence.

The sight of the immense **El Castillo pyramid,** rising imposingly yet gracefully from the surrounding plain, has been known to produce goose pimples on sight. El Castillo (The Castle) dominates the site both in size and in the symmetry of its perfect proportions. Openjawed serpent statues adorn the corners of each of the pyramid's four stairways, honoring the legendary priest-king Kukulcán (also known as Quetzalcóatl), an incarnation of the feathered serpent god. More serpents appear at the top of the building as sculpted columns. At the spring and fall equinoxes, the afternoon light strikes the trapezoidal structure so that the shadow of the snake-god appears to undulate down the side of the pyramid to bless the fertile earth. Thousands of people travel to the site each year to see this phenomenon.

At the base of the temple on the north side, an interior staircase leads to two marvelous statues deep within: a stone jaguar and the intermediate god, Chacmool. As usual, Chacmool is in a reclining position, with a flat spot on the belly for receiving sacrifices.

On the **Anexo del Templo de los Jaguares** (Annex to the Temple of the Jaguars), just west of El Castillo, bas-relief carvings represent more important deities. On the bottom of the columns is the rain god Tlaloc. It's no surprise that his tears represent rain—but why is the Toltec god Tlaloc honored here, instead of the Maya rain god, Chaac?

That's one of many questions that archaeologists and epigraphers have been trying to answer, ever since John Lloyd Stephens and Frederick Catherwood, the first English-speaking explorers to discover the site, first hacked their way through the surrounding forest in 1840. Scholars once thought that the symbols of foreign gods and differing architectural styles at Chichén Itzá proved it was conquered by the Toltecs of central Mexico. (As well as representations of Tlaloc, the site also has a *tzompantli*—a stone platform decorated with row upon row of sculpted human skulls, which is a distinctively Toltec-style structure.) Most experts now agree, however, that Chichén Itzá was only influenced—not conquered—by Toltec trading partners from the north.

Just west of the Anexo del Templo de los Jaguares is another puzzle: the auditory marvel of Chichén Itzá's main ball court. At 490 feet, this **Juego de Pelota** is the largest in Mesoamerica. Yet if you stand at

Continued on page 332

The towering **El Castillo** pyramid, nearly 80 feet high, is the most striking structure at Chichén Itzá. Each side of the pyramid has 91 steps, which, with the addition of the topmost platform, equal 365, one for each day of the calendar year. At the vernal and autumnal equinoxes, thousands of people gather to watch as the shadow of the serpent god Kukulcán seems to slither down the side of the pyramid.

CHICHÉN ITZÁ

One of the most beautiful of the ancient Maya cities, Chichén Itzá draws some 3,000 visitors a day from all over the world. Since the remains of this once-thriving kingdom were discovered by Europeans in the mid 1800s, many of the travelers who make the pilgrimage here have been archaeologists and scholars who study the structures and glyphs and try to piece together the mysteries surrounding them. While the artifacts here give fascinating insight into the Maya civilization, they also raise many, many unanswered questions.

The name of this ancient city, which means "the mouth of the well of the Itzás," is a mystery in and of itself. Although it likely refers to the valuable water sources at the site (there are several sinkholes here), experts have little information about who might have actually founded the city—some structures, likely built in the 5th century, pre-date the arrival of the Itzás who occupied the city starting around the late 8th and early 9th centuries. The reason why the Itzás abandoned the city, around 1224, is also unknown.

Scholars and archaeologists aside, most of the visitors that converge on Chichén Itzá come to marvel at its beauty, not ponder its significance. This ancient metropolis, which encompasses 6 square km (2½ square mi), is known around the world as one of the most stunning and well-preserved Maya sites in existence.

(opposite) The main pyramid El Castillo is also called Temple of Kukulcán, (top) Carvings of ball players adorn the walls of the *juego de pelota*, (bottom) Maya statue.

MAJOR SITES AND ATTRACTIONS

Rows of freestanding columns where the roof has long since disintegrated

The sight of the immense **❶ El Castillo** pyramid, rising imposingly yet gracefully from the surrounding plain, has been known to produce goose pimples on sight. El Castillo (The Castle) dominates the site both in size and in the symmetry of its perfect proportions. Open-jawed serpent statues adorn the corners of each of the pyramid's four stairways, honoring the legendary priest-king Kukulcán (also known as Quetzalcóatl), an incarnation of the feathered serpent god. More serpents appear at the top of the building as sculpted columns. At the spring and fall equinoxes, the afternoon light strikes the trapezoidal structure so that the shadow of the snake-god appears to undulate down the side of the pyramid to bless the fertile earth. Thousands of people travel to the site each year to see this phenomenon.

At the base of the temple on the north side, an interior staircase leads to two marvelous statues deep within: a stone

jaguar, and the intermediate god Chacmool. As usual, Chacmool is in a reclining position, with a flat spot on the belly for receiving sacrifices. On the **❷ Anexo del Templo de los Jaguares** (Annex to the Temple of the Jaguars), just west of El Castillo, bas-relief carvings represent more important deities. On the bottom of the columns is the rain god Tlaloc. It's no surprise that his tears represent rain—but why is the Toltec god Tlaloc honored here, instead of the Maya rain god, Chaac?

That's one of many questions that archaeologists and epigraphers have been trying to answer, ever since John Lloyd Stephens and Frederick Catherwood, the first English-speaking explorers to discover the site, first hacked their way through the surrounding forest in 1840. Scholars once thought that the symbols of foreign gods and differing architectural styles at Chichén Itzá proved it was conquered by the Toltecs of central Mexico. (As well as representations of Tlaloc, the site also has a tzompantli—a stone platform decorated with row upon row of sculpted human skulls, which is a distinctively Toltec-style structure.) Most experts now agree, however, that Chichén Itzá was only influenced—not conquered—by Toltec trading partners from the north.

The flat part of a reclining Chacmool statue is where sacrificial offerings were laid.

It's believed that Mayan ball players had to pass some sort of ball through high stone loops.

Games may have ended with beheadings.

Just west of the Anexo del Templo de los Jaguares is another puzzle: the auditory marvel of Chichén Itzá's main ball court. At 490 feet, this ❸ **Juego de Pelota** is the largest in Mesoamerica. Yet if you stand at one end of the playing field and whisper something to a friend at the other end, incredibly, you will be heard. The game played on this ball court was apparently something like soccer (no hands were used), but it likely had some sort of ritualistic significance. Carvings on the low walls surrounding the field show a decapitation, blood spurting from the victim's neck to fertilize the earth. Whether this is a historical depiction (perhaps the losers or winners of the game were sacrificed?) or a symbolic scene, we can only guess.

On the other side of El Castillo, just before a small temple dedicated to the planet Venus, a ruined sacbé, or white road leads to the ❹ **Cenote Sagrado** (Holy Well, or Sinkhole), which was also probably used for ritualistic purposes. Jacques Cousteau and his companions recovered about 80 skeletons from this deep, straight-sided, subsurface pond, as well as thousands of pieces of jewelry and figures of jade, obsidian, wood, bone, and turquoise. In direct alignment with this cloudy green cenote, on the other side of El Castillo, the ❺ **Xtaloc sinkhole** was kept pristine, undoubtedly for bathing and drinking. Adjacent to this water source is a steam

TIPS

To get more in-depth information about the ruins, hire a multilingual guide at the ticket booth. Guides charge about $35 for a group of up to 7 people. Tours generally last about two hours. 🎟 $9.80 ☉ Ruins daily 8–5.

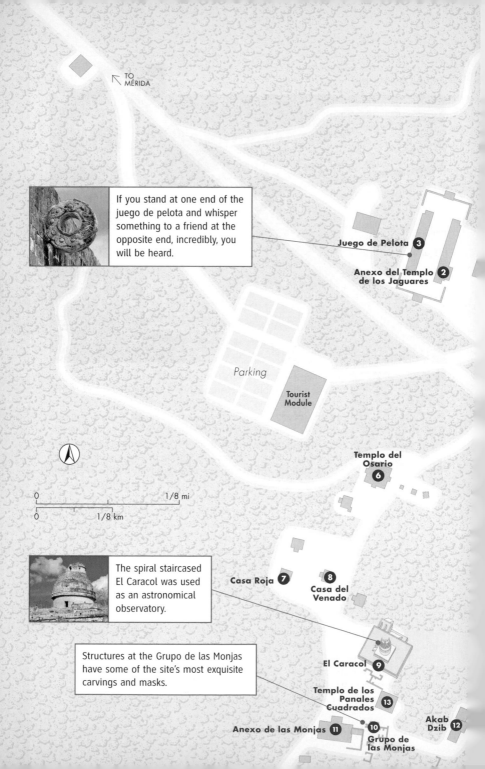

TO
MÉRIDA

If you stand at one end of the juego de pelota and whisper something to a friend at the opposite end, incredibly, you will be heard.

Juego de Pelota **3**

Anexo del Templo **2**
de los Jaguares

Parking

Tourist
Module

Templo del
Osario
6

0   1/8 mi
0   1/8 km

The spiral staircased El Caracol was used as an astronomical observatory.

Casa Roja **7**

8
Casa del
Venado

Structures at the Grupo de las Monjas have some of the site's most exquisite carvings and masks.

El Caracol **9**

Templo de los
Panales
Cuadrados **13**

Akab
Dzib **12**

Anexo de las Monjas **11**

10
Grupo de
las Monjas

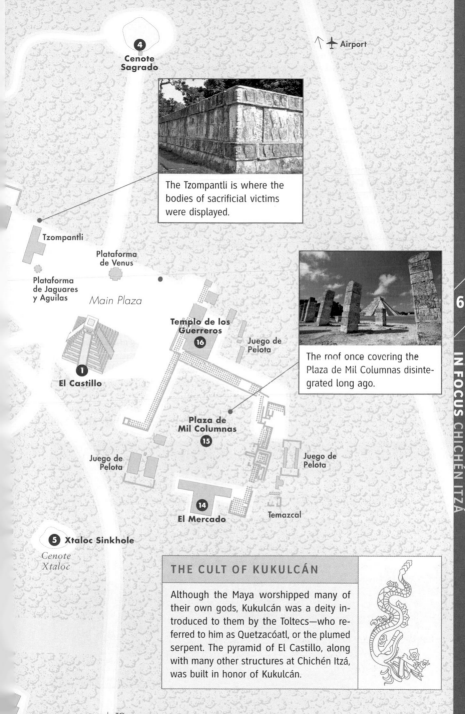

✈ Airport

The Tzompantli is where the bodies of sacrificial victims were displayed.

Tzompantli

Plataforma de Venus

Plataforma de Jaguares y Aguilas

Main Plaza

Templo de los Guerreros

16

Juego de Pelota

The roof once covering the Plaza de Mil Columnas disintegrated long ago.

1 El Castillo

Plaza de Mil Columnas

15

Juego de Pelota

Juego de Pelota

14 El Mercado

Temazcal

5 Xtaloc Sinkhole

Cenote Xtaloc

THE CULT OF KUKULCÁN

Although the Maya worshipped many of their own gods, Kukulcán was a deity introduced to them by the Toltecs—who referred to him as Quetzacóatl, or the plumed serpent. The pyramid of El Castillo, along with many other structures at Chichén Itzá, was built in honor of Kukulcán.

IN FOCUS CHICHÉN ITZÁ

TO OLD CHICHÉN ITZÁ

bath, its interior lined with benches along the wall like those you'd see in any steam room today. Outside, a tiny pool was used for cooling down during the ritual.

The older Mayan structures at Chichén Itzá are south and west of Cenote Xtaloc. Archaeologists have been restoring several buildings in this area, including the ❻ **Templo del Osario** (Ossuary Temple), which, as its name implies, concealed several tombs with skeletons and offerings. Behind the smaller ❼ **Casa Roja** (Red House) and ❽ **Casa del Venado** (House of the Deer) are the site's oldest structures, including ❾ **El Caracol** (The Snail), one of the few round buildings built by the Maya, with a spiral staircase within. Clearly built as a celestial observatory, it has eight tiny windows precisely aligned with the points of the compass rose. Scholars now know that Maya priests studied the planets and the stars; in fact, they were able to accurately predict the orbits of Venus and the moon, and the appearance of comets and eclipses. To modern astronomers, this is nothing short of amazing.

The Maya of Chichén Itzá were not just scholars, however. They were skilled artisans and architects as well. South of El Caracol, the ❿ **Grupo de las Monjas** (The Nunnery complex) has some of the site's most exquisite façades. A combination of Puuc and Chenes styles dominates here, with playful latticework, masks, and gargoyle-like serpents. On the east side of the ⓫ **Anexo de las Monjas** (Nunnery Annex), the Chenes facade celebrates the rain god Chaac. In typical style, the doorway represents an entrance into the underworld; figures of Chaac decorate the ornate façade above.

South of the Nunnery Complex is an area where field archaeologists are still excavating (fewer than a quarter of the structures at Chichén Itzá have been fully restored). If you have more than a superficial interest in the site—and can convince the authorities ahead of time of your importance, or at least your interest in archaeology—you can explore this area, which is generally not open to the public. Otherwise, head back toward El Castillo past the ruins of a housing compound called ⓬ **Akab Dzib**

The doorway of the Anexo de las Monjas represents an entrance to the underworld.

The Templo de los Guerreros shows the influence of Toltec architecture.

and the ⑬ **Templo de los Panales Cuadrados** (Temple of the Square Panels). The latter of these buildings shows more evidence of Toltec influence: instead of weight-bearing Mayan arches—or "false arches"—that traditionally supported stone roofs, this structure has stone columns but no roof. This means that the building was once roofed, Toltec-style, with perishable materials (most likely palm thatch or wood) that have long since disintegrated.

Beyond El Caracol, Casa Roja, and El Osario, the right-hand path follows an ancient sacbé, now collapsed. A mud-and-straw hut, which the Maya called a na, has been reproduced here to show the simple implements used before and after the Spanish conquest. On one side of the room are a typical pre-Hispanic table, seat, fire pit, and reed baskets; on the other, the Christian cross and colonial-style table of the post-conquest Maya.

Behind the tiny oval house, several unexcavated mounds still guard their secrets. The path meanders through a small grove of oak and slender bean trees to the building known today as ⑭ **El Mercado**. This market was likely one end of a huge outdoor market whose counterpart structure, on the other side of the grove, is the ⑮ **Plaza de Mil Columnas** (Plaza of the Thousand Columns). In typical Toltec-Maya style, the roof once covering the parallel rows of round stone columns in this long arcade has disappeared, giving the place a strangely Greek—and distinctly non-Maya—look. But the curvy-nosed Chaacs on the corners of the adjacent ⑯ **Templo de los Guerreros** are pure Maya. Why their noses are pointing down, like an upside-down "U," instead of up, as usual, is just another mystery to be solved.

Columns at Templo de los Guerreros.

one end of the playing field and whisper something to a friend at the other end, incredibly, you'll be heard. The game played on this ball court was apparently something like soccer (no hands were used), but it likely had some sort of ritualistic significance. Carvings on the low walls surrounding the field show a decapitation, with blood spurting from the victim's neck to fertilize the earth. Whether this is a historical depiction (perhaps the losers or winners of the game were sacrificed?) or a symbolic scene, we can only guess.

On the other side of El Castillo, just before a small temple dedicated to the planet Venus, a ruined sacbé, or white road, leads to the **Cenote Sagrado** (Holy Well, or Sinkhole), also probably used for ritualistic purposes. Jacques Cousteau and his companions recovered about 80 skeletons from this deep, straight-sided, subsurface pond, as well as thousands of pieces of jewelry and figures of jade, obsidian, wood, bone, and turquoise. In direct alignment with Cenote Sagrado, on the other side of El Castillo, the **Xtaloc Sinkhole** was kept pristine, undoubtedly for bathing and drinking. Adjacent to this water source is a steam bath, its interior lined with benches along the wall like those you'd see in any steam room today. Outside, a tiny pool was used for cooling down during the ritual.

The older Maya structures at Chichén Itzá are south and west of Cenote Xtaloc. Archaeologists have been restoring several buildings in this area, including the **Templo del Osario** (Ossuary Temple), which, as its name implies, concealed several tombs with skeletons and offerings. Behind the smaller **Casa Roja** (Red House) and **Casa del Venado** (House of the Deer) are the site's oldest structures, including m **El Caracol** (The Snail), one of the few round buildings built by the Maya, with a spiral staircase within. Clearly built as a celestial observatory, it has eight tiny windows precisely aligned with the points of the compass rose. Scholars now know that Maya priests studied the planets and the stars, in fact, they were able to accurately predict the orbits of Venus and the moon, and the appearance of comets and eclipses. To modern astronomers, this is nothing short of amazing.

The Maya of Chichén Itzá were not just scholars, however. They were skilled artisans and architects as well. South of El Caracol, the **Grupo de las Monjas** (The Nunnery complex) has some of the site's most exquisite facades. A combination of Puuc and Chenes styles dominates here, with playful latticework, masks, and gargoylelike serpents. On the east side of the **Anexo de las Monjas,** (Nunnery Annex), the Chenes facade celebrates the rain god Chaac. In typical style, the doorway represents an entrance into the underworld, and figures of Chaac decorate the ornate facade above.

South of the Nunnery Complex is an area where field archaeologists are still excavating (fewer than a quarter of the structures at Chichén Itzá have been fully restored). If you have more than a superficial interest in the site—and can convince the authorities ahead of time of your importance, or at least your interest in archaeology—you can explore this area, which is generally not open to the public. Otherwise, head back toward El Castillo past the ruins of a housing compound called

Akab Dzib and the **Templo de los Panales Cuadrados** (Temple of the Square Panels). The latter of these buildings shows more evidence of Toltec influence: instead of weight-bearing Maya arches—or "false arches"—that traditionally supported stone roofs, this structure has stone columns but no roof. This means that the building was once roofed, Toltec-style, with perishable materials (most likely palm thatch or wood) that have long since disintegrated.

Beyond El Caracol, Casa Roja, and El Osario, the right-hand path follows an ancient sacbé, now collapsed. A mud-and-straw hut, which the Maya called a **na**, has been reproduced here to show the simple implements used before and after the Spanish conquest. On one side of the room are a typical pre-Hispanic table, seat, fire pit, and reed baskets; on the other, are the Christian cross and colonial-style table of the post-conquest Maya.

Behind the tiny oval house, several unexcavated mounds still guard their secrets. The path meanders through a small grove of oak and slender bean trees to the building known today as **El Mercado.** This market was likely one end of a huge outdoor market whose counterpart structure, on the other side of the grove, is the **Plaza de Mil Columnas** (Plaza of the Thousand Columns). In typical Toltec-Maya style, the roof once covering the parallel rows of round stone columns in this long arcade has disappeared, giving the place a strangely Greek—and distinctly non-Mayan—look. But the curvy-nosed Chaacs on the corners of the adjacent **Templo de los Guerreros** are pure Maya. Why their noses are pointing down, like an upside down "U, " instead of up, as usual, is just another mystery to be solved. ■**TIP**➜ A light-and-sound show begins every night at 7 pm in fall and winter and at 8 pm in spring and summer. ⊠ *Off Hwy. 180* ⊕ *www.chichenitza.com* ⊡ *$10; parking $1* ⊗ *Daily 8–4:30.*

EK BALAM

30 km (18 miles) north of Valladolid, off Carretera 295.

Ek Balam. What's most stunning about the large Ek Balam ("black jaguar") site are the elaborately carved and amazingly well-preserved stucco panels of one of the temples, the **Templo de los Frisos.** A giant mask crowns its summit, and its friezes contain wonderful carvings of figures often referred to as "angels" (because they have wings)—but which more likely represented nobles in ceremonial dress.

As is common with ancient Mayan structures, this temple, styled like those in the region of Chenes in the northwest, is superimposed on earlier ones. The temple was a mausoleum for ruler Ukit Kan Lek Tok, who was buried with priceless funerary objects, including pearls, perforated seashells, jade, mother-of-pearl pendants, and small bone masks with movable jaws. At the bases at either end of the temple, the name of the leader is inscribed on the forked tongue of a carved serpent, which obviously didn't have the negative biblical connotation ascribed to the snake in Western culture today. A contemporary of Uxmal and Cobá, the city may have been a satellite city to Chichén Itzá, which rose to power as Ek Balam waned.

Another unusual feature of Ek Balam are the two concentric walls—a rare configuration in Mayan sites—that surround the 45 structures in the main part of the site. They may have provided defense, or perhaps they symbolized (more than provided safety for) the ruling elite that lived within.

Ek Balam also has a ball court and quite a few freestanding stelae (stone pillars carved with glyphs or images for commemorative purposes). New Age groups sometimes converge on the site for prayers and seminars, but it's usually quite sparsely visited, which adds to the mystery and allure. ■**TIP→ Ek Balam is one of the few Mayan sites where visitors are permitted to climb the structures.** ✉ *20 minutes from Carretera 295, toward Tizimin* 🎫 *$10* 🕓 *Daily 8–4:30.*

WHERE TO STAY

For expanded reviews, facilities, and current deals, visit Fodors.com.

$ HOTEL 🏨 **Genesis Ek Balam.** Close to the Ek Balam site, this simple retreat is modeled on the local dwellings of the region. **Pros:** eco-friendly; intimate atmosphere; cultural programs; close to the Ek Balam ruins. **Cons:** early morning crowing roosters; sometimes difficult to make reservations by phone; pitted road to hotel; those with allergies might have issues with the owner's dogs. [$] *Rooms from: $60* ✉ *Domicilio Conocido, turn left on last road before entrance to Ek Balam Ruins. Continue 2 km toward Ek Balam village and follow signs to Genesis* ☎ *985/100–4805, 985/101–0277* 🌐 *www.genesisretreat.com* 🛏 *9 cabins* 💳 *No credit cards* 🍴 *No meals.*

PISTÉ

46 km (29 miles) west of Valladolid, 116 km (72 miles) east of Mérida, 2 km (1½ miles) west of Chichén Itzá.

The town of Pisté serves primarily as a base camp for travelers to Chichén Itzá. Hotels, campgrounds, restaurants, and shops tend to be less expensive here than those at the ruins. Just outside the ruins is Zona Hotelera (Hotel Zone), comprised of three pricier properties: Villas Arqueológicas, Mayaland, and Hacienda Chichén Resort. Only the last property offers a true Mayan experience, is eco-friendly, and gives back to the local community.

EXPLORING

Parque Ik Kil (*"place of the winds"*). Across from the Dolores Alba hotel is the Parque Ik Kil. A $6 entrance fee is required if you want to swim in the lovely cenote here, open daily between 8 am and 6 pm. If you're going to eat in the adjacent restaurant, or sleep overnight, you don't need to pay the entrance fee. Lockers, changing facilities, showers, and life jackets are available ✉ *Carretera Mérida–Puerto Juárez, Km 122* ☎ *985/858–1525* 💳 *No credit cards.*

WHERE TO STAY

For expanded reviews, facilities, and current deals, visit Fodors.com.

$ HOTEL 🏨 **Dolores Alba.** The best low-budget choice near the ruins is this family-run hotel with a small motel feel, a longtime favorite of international travelers. **Pros:** close to ruins; transport to ruins is included (return is not included). **Cons:** restaurant leaves much to be desired; small rooms; furniture and linens look a little past their prime; weak Wi-Fi signal. $ *Rooms from: $60* ⊠ *Carretera 180, Km 122, 3 km (2 miles) east of Chichén Itzá* ☎ *985/858–1555* ⊕ *www.doloresalba.com* ↙ *30 rooms* ⦿| *Breakfast.*

$$ ⬚ **Hacienda Chichén Resort.** This refurbished hacienda with a butter-
HOTEL yellow exterior, has beautiful gardens and an inviting pool surrounded
Fodor's Choice by palm trees. **Pros:** designated cottages (gated) for travelers with pets;
★ short walk from ruins; beautiful gardens; amazing spa, 99% of the
staff are indigenous Mayans; on-site organic farm produces food and
herbs for restaurant and spa; hacienda serves as a community outreach.
Cons: pricier than other area hotels; restaurant food just OK; Wi-Fi in
lobby only; loud a/c. $ *Rooms from: $170* ⊠ *Carretera Mérida–Puerto
Júarez, Km 120, Zona Hotelera de Chichén Itzá cerca del Pueblo Pisté*
☎ *999/920–8407, 877/631–4005 in U.S.* ⊕ *www.haciendachichen.com*
↙ *28 rooms* ⦿| *No meals.*

$$ ⬚ **Hotel Chichén Itzá.** Just over 1½ km (1 mile) from the ruins in the town
HOTEL of Pisté, this two-story hotel surrounding a pool feels like a motel in a
very unlikely setting: a large grassy area edged with banana and other
tropical trees and flowers. **Pros:** minutes from ruins; big pool; kind staff.
Cons: mediocre food; room amenities vary (check out a few if possible).
$ *Rooms from: $80* ⊠ *Calle 15 No. 45* ☎ *985/851–0022, 800/235–
4079* ⊕ *www.mayaland.com* ↙ *44 rooms* ⦿| *Multiple meal plans.*

GRUTAS DE BALANCANCHÉN

*38 km (24 miles) west of Valladolid, 6 km (4 miles) east of Chichén
Itzá, 117 km (72 miles) east of Mérida.*

Grutas de Balankanché (*Balankanche Cave*). How often do you get
the chance to wander below the earth? The caves, translated as both
"throne of the jaguar caves" and "caves of the hidden throne," are dank
and sometimes slippery slopes to an amazing rocky underworld. The
caverns are lighted to best show off their lumpy limestone stalactites and
nichelike side caves. It's a privilege also to view in situ vases, jars, and
incense burners once used in sacred rituals. These were discovered in
the 1950s, and left right as they were. An arrangement of tiny *metates*
(stone mortars for grinding corn) is particularly moving. At the end
of the line is the underground cenote where Maya priests worshipped
Chaac, the god of rain and water. Wear comfortable, nonslip walking
shoes. The site has a sound-and-light show that recounts Mayan history.
The caves are 6 km (4 miles) from Chichén Itzá, and you can catch a
bus or taxi or arrange a tour at the Mayaland hotel. Although there's a
six-person minimum, the ticket vendor will often allow even a pair of
visitors to tour. Do not attempt if you're claustrophobic or have heart
or respiratory problems as the climb's steep and the caves are humid.
🎫 *$8.50, including tour and sound-and-light show* ☉ *Daily 9–5; tours
leave daily at 9:30, 11, 12:30, 2, 3, and 4 (English); 9, noon, 2, and 4
(Spanish); and 10 (French).*

VALLADOLID

Fodor's Choice ★ *161 km (100 miles) from Mérida, 44½ km (28 miles) east of Chichén Itzá.*

The second-largest city in the Yucatán State, Valladolid (vay-ah-do-*lid*), is a picturesque provincial town that's been growing popular among travelers en route to or from Chichén Itzá (or Río Lagartos, to the north). Francisco de Montejo founded Valladolid in 1543 on the site of the Mayan town of Sisal. The city suffered during the War of the Castes—when the Maya in revolt killed nearly all Spanish residents—and again during the Mexican Revolution.

Despite its turbulent history, Valladolid's downtown has many colonial and 19th-century structures. On Sunday evenings at 8 pm the city's orchestra plays elegant, stylized *danzón*—waltzlike dance music to which unsmiling couples (think tango: no smiling allowed) swirl around the bandstand of the main square. Valladolid is renowned for its *longaniza en escabeche*—a sausage dish made with pork, beef, or venison, served in many of the restaurants facing the square. In the shops and market you can also find deals on sandals, baskets, leather goods, and Xtabentún liqueur.

GETTING HERE AND AROUND
The drive from Mérida to Valladolid via the toll road (the tolls come to about $15) takes about two hours. The free road (México 295) cuts through several small towns where speed bumps, street repairs, and traffic can increase the travel time significantly. ADO and UNO have direct buses from Mérida to Valladolid, and other Mexican cities. They depart from the first-class CAME bus station. Most buses that come into Valladolid actually stop just outside of town, where you have to get on a second bus, a city bus. This is included in the price of your ticket.

Bus Contacts Autobuses de Occidente ☎ *999/924–8391, 999/924–9741* ⊕ *www.ado.com.mx.*

Visitor Information Municipal Tourist Information Center ⊠ *Palacio Municipal* ☎ *985/856–2529* ⊘ *Weekdays 8 am–9 pm, weekends 8–6.*

EXPLORING
Cenote Samula. Perhaps the most photographed cenote in the Yucatán, this sinkhole is across the road from Cenote X-Keken, about 5 km (3 miles) west of the main square. A narrow stairway leads to crystal-clear water where tree vines dangle overhead and hundreds of birds nest between the stalactites. Don't be alarmed by the tiny *Garra rufa* fish that nibble at your feet—they are actually eating away the dead skin cells. Guides offer tours for tips. ⊠ *On old highway to Chichén Itzá* 🖻 *$5.*

FAMILY   **Cenote X-Keken** (*Cenote Dzitnup*). Five kilometers (3 miles) west of the main square and on the old highway to Chichén Itzá, you can swim with the catfish in lovely, mysterious Cenote X-Keken, which is in a cave lighted by a small natural skylight. There are toilets and changing facilities but no lockers. Directly across the street from Cenote X-Keken is Cenote Samula, equally stunning with crystal clear water

CLOSE UP

Sacred Cenotes

To the ancient (and tradition-bound modern) Maya, holes in the ground—be they sinkholes, cenotes, or caves—are considered conduits to the world of the spirits. As sources of water in a land of no surface rivers, sinkholes are of special importance. Cenotes like Balancanchén, near Chichén Itzá, were used as prayer sites and shrines. Sacred objects and sacrificial victims were thrown in the sacred cenote at Chichén Itzá, and in others near large ceremonial centers in ancient times.

There are at least 2,800 known cenotes in the Yucatán. Rainwater sinks through the peninsula's thin soil and porous limestone to create underground rivers, while leaving the dry surface river-free.

Some pondlike sinkholes are found near ground level; most require a bit more effort to access, however. Near downtown Valladolid, Cenote Zací is

named for the Mayan town conquered by the Spanish. It's a relatively simple saunter down a series of cement steps to reach the cool green water.

Lesser-known sinkholes are yours to discover, especially in the area labeled "zona de cenotes." To explore this area southeast of Mérida, you can hire a guide through the tourism office. Another option is to head directly for the ex-hacienda of Chunkanan, 3 km (2 miles) from the town of Cuzama, about 30 minutes southeast of Mérida. Here former henequen workers will hitch their horses to tiny open railway carts to take you along the unused train tracks. The reward for this bumpy, sometimes dusty ride is a swim in several incredible cenotes.

Almost every local has a "secret" cenote; ask around, and perhaps you'll find a favorite of your own.

6

and hundreds of birds nesting between the stalactites. Guides offer tours for tips. 🕮 *$5.*

Cenote Zací. The large, round, and beautiful sinkhole at the edge of town, Cenote Zací, is sometimes crowded with tourists and local boys clowning it up; at other times, it's deserted. Leaves from the tall old trees surrounding the sinkhole float on the surface, but the water itself is quite clean. If you're not up for a dip, visit the adjacent handicraft shop or have a bite or a drink at the popular, thatch-roof restaurant overlooking the water. ⊠ *Calles 36 and 37* ☎ *985/856–0721* 🕮 *$1.50.*

Ex-Convento y Iglesia San Bernadino. Five long blocks away from the main plaza is the 16th-century, terra-cotta Ex-Convento y Iglesia San Bernadino, a Franciscan church and former monastery. The church was actually built over Cenote Sis-Há, which served as a clean water source for the monks. You can view the cenote through a grate in the well-house where much of the original stone still remains. ■**TIP→** If the priest is around, ask him to show you the 16th-century frescoes, protected behind curtains near the altarpiece. The lack of proportion in the human figures shows the initial clumsiness of indigenous artisans in reproducing the Christian saints. ⊠ *Calle 41-A* ☎ *985/856–2160.*

Iglesia de San Servacio. On the west side of the city's main plaza is the large Iglesia de San Servacio, which was pillaged during the War of the Castes.

WHERE TO EAT

$ MEXICAN 🍴 **La Cantina.** This colorful cantina, right on the main square, has brightly painted tables and chairs with sombreros that act as lampshades. The festive vibe is equally matched with the menu of lime soup, chicken fajitas, tacos, enchiladas, and *cochinita pibil* (slow-roasted pork) served with warm tortillas. Since it's open late, many locals drop by for a cocktail or Mayan-chocolate drinks. For a meal with a view, grab an outside table and watch Valladolid in action. It's open daily 7 am–11 pm. [$] *Average main: $7* ✉ *Calle 41 No. 202, Centro* ☎ *985/856–0999.*

$$$ MEXICAN FUSION Fodor's Choice ★ 🍴 **Taberna de los Frailes.** This "Tavern of the Monks" sits above Cenote Sis Ha and overlooks the ancient stonework of Convent of San Bernardino de Siena dating from 1552. Despite its historic location, the restaurant is equally known for its extraordinary Mayan cuisine and Yucatecan dishes like *tikin xic* (grilled snapper in annatto sauce), *pavo en relleno negro* (turkey medallions stuffed with pork and hard-boiled egg in Mayan pepper sauce), and *pechuga en pipian* (roasted chicken in pumpkin-seed sauce). For something light, try the grilled watermelon salad or *sikil pak,* a dip made from roasted pumpkin seeds, tomatoes, and Mayan spices. The three separate dining areas—garden lounge, stone cocktail bar, and palapa dining room—give the place an elegant and modern feel while still adhering to traditional Mayan architecture. [$] *Average main: $15* ✉ *Calle 49, No. 235, next to Convent of San Bernardino de Siena* ☎ *985/856–0689* 🌐 *www.tabernadelosfrailes.com.*

WHERE TO STAY

For expanded reviews, facilities, and current deals, visit Fodors.com.

$$ B&B/INN Fodor's Choice ★ 🏨 **Casa Tia Micha.** More than a century old, this colonial home has been beautifully transformed into a five-bedroom hotel that's owned and operated by "Micha's" grandchildren. **Pros:** homemade breakfast; friendly staff; clean rooms; secured parking. **Cons:** street noise; weak Wi-Fi signal. [$] *Rooms from: $80* ✉ *Calle 39 No. 197, between 38 and 40, Centro* ☎ *985/856–2957* 🛏 *3 rooms, 2 suites* 🍽 *Breakfast.*

$ HOTEL 🏨 **El Mesón del Marqués.** On the north side of the main square, this well-preserved, old hacienda house was built around a lovely, open patio and has clean and comfortable rooms with air-conditioning, Wi-Fi, and safes. **Pros:** great downtown location (just north of the main plaza); nice outdoor areas; 24-hour room service; free parking. **Cons:** food could be better; rooms lack the charm of the rest of the hotel; mostly shaded pool. [$] *Rooms from: $75* ✉ *Calle 39 No. 203, between Calles 40 and 42* ☎ *985/856–2073, 985/856–3042* 🌐 *www.mesondelmarques.com* 🛏 *80 rooms, 10 suites* 🍽 *No meals.*

SHOPPING

Yalat Arte Mexicano. On the main square, this small shop sells clothing, crafts, jewelry, pottery, and masks from southeast Mexico. ✉ *Calle 41 No. 204, between 40 and 42, Centro* ☎ *985/856–1969.*

You can swim in Cenote X-Keken (for a price).

PROGRESO AND THE NORTH COAST

Various routes lead from Mérida to towns along the coast, which are spread across a distance of 380 km (236 miles). Separate roads connect Mérida with the laid-back fishing village of Celestún, the gateway to an ecological marine reserve that extends south to just beyond the Campeche border. Carretera 261 leads due north from Mérida to the relatively modern but humble shipping port of Progreso, where Méridians spend hot summer days and holiday weekends. To get to some of the small beach towns east of Progreso, head east on Carretera 176 out of Mérida and then cut north on one of the many access roads. Although not as picturesque as the Rivera Maya coastline, beaches here are wide and generally shadeless with hordes of sunbathers visiting from Mérida during Holy Week and in summer. Fortunately, the beaches are nearly vacant the rest of the year.

The terrain in this part of the peninsula is absolutely flat. Tall trees are scarce, because the region was almost entirely cleared for coconut palms in the early 19th century and again for henequen in the early 20th century. Local people still tend some of the old fields of henequen, even though there's little profit to be made from the rope fiber it produces. Other former plantation fields are wildly overgrown with scrub, and are identifiable only by the low, white stone walls that used to mark their boundaries. Many bird species make their home in this area, and butterflies swarm in profusion throughout the dry season.

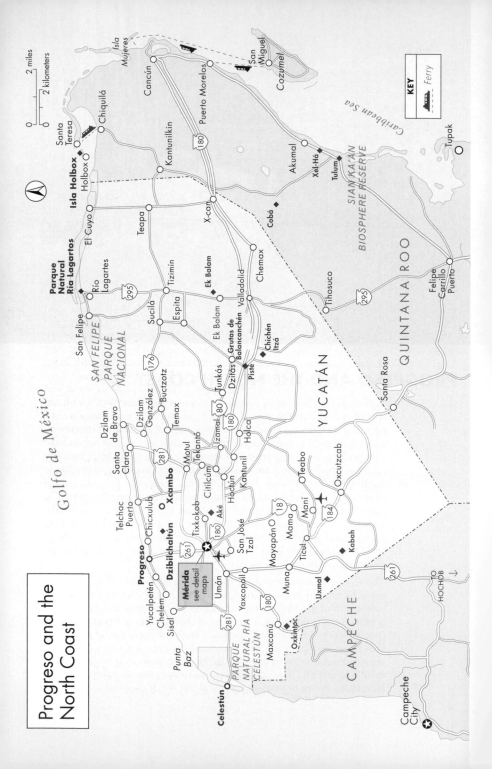

CELESTÚN

90 km (56 miles) west of Mérida.

This tranquil and humble fishing village sits at the end of a spit of land separating the Celestún estuary from the Gulf of Mexico.

GETTING HERE AND AROUND

Celestún is easily accessible by car, tour group, or bus. To go by bus, take one of the hourly second-class buses that depart from the Noroeste Terminal in Mérida (Calle 67 at Calle 50). The first bus departs at 6:15 am, and the last returning bus leaves Celestún at 8 pm. The fare costs about $6.50 round-trip. In the town of Celestún, your best bet is moto-taxi. These charge about 80¢ around town, and $1.20 to go out to the boats from the central plaza. Make sure you establish what the fare is before you get on, as sometimes drivers will try to charge foreign tourists significantly higher rates.

EXPLORING

Reserva de la Biósfera Ría Celestún. Celestún is the point of entry to the Reserva de la Biósfera Ría Celestún, a 220,000-acre wildlife reserve with extensive mangrove forests and one of the largest colonies of flamingos in North America. Clouds of the pink birds soar above the estuary all year, but the best months for seeing them in abundance are November through March. This is also the fourth-largest wintering ground for ducks of the Gulf-coast region, and more than 366 other species of birds, as well as a large sea-turtle population, make their home here. Conservation programs sponsored by the United States and Mexico protect the birds, as well as the endangered hawksbill and loggerhead marine tortoises, and other species such as the blue crab and crocodile. Other endangered species that inhabit the area are the ocelot, the jaguar, and the spider monkey.

The park is set among rocks, islets, and white-sand beaches. There's good fishing here, too, and several cenotes that are wonderful for swimming. Most Mérida travel agencies run boat tours of the *ría* (estuary) in the early morning or late afternoon, but it's not usually necessary to make a reservation in advance.

■TIP→ To see the birds, hire a fishing boat at the entrance to town (the boats hang out under the bridge leading into Celestún). A 75-minute tour for up to six people costs about $65; a two-hour tour, around $125. Although more expensive ($70 a person), local tour expert "Alex" specializes in ecotours and donates a portion of the proceeds to the Celestun Conservation Program (call Hotel Xixim to book a tour). Popular with Mexican vacationers, the park's sandy beach is pleasant during the morning but tends to get windy in the afternoon. And, unfortunately, mosquitoes gather in great numbers on the beach at dawn and dusk, particularly during the winter months, making a walk on the beach uncomfortable. Most hotels offer mosquito netting around the beds, but bring along a good cream or spray to keep the bugs away. ☎ 998/916–2100 *tours booked through Hotel Xixim.*

BEACHES

Celestún Beach. This quaint fishing village may not have the pristine beaches of the Caribbean, but it does have several kilometers of lovely coastline, perfect for long walks or collecting seashells. There are no crowds, even at the main beach in town, and the water is a pretty green-emerald color. The nicest stretch is at Hotel Xixim, home to three miles of white sandy beaches, where turtles nest from April through July and Bottlenose dolphins can be seen swimming. When winds are high, this isn't the best place to swim—but it's perfect for relaxing or kayaking (rentals at Hotel Xixim); the waters are usually tranquil until late afternoon. There are no lifeguards on duty, so be sure to ask hotel staff about rip currents and incoming swells. **Amenities:** kayak rentals at Hotel Xixim. **Best for:** walking; collecting shells; turtle-watching. ⊠ *Hotel Xixim, Municipio de Celestún Yucatán, Celestún.*

WHERE TO STAY

For expanded reviews, facilities, and current deals, visit Fodors.com.

$$
B&B/INN
⊡ **Celeste Vida Guest House.** Owned and operated by Canadian expats, this three-bedroom guesthouse is directly on the beach, making it one of the best values in town. **Pros:** isolated beach; less than a mile from town; gated property and secure parking area; stay seven nights for the price of six. **Cons:** mosquitoes can be a problem; no a/c; credit cards not accepted; nonanimal lovers might have an issue with rescued dogs on the property. $ *Rooms from: $85* ⊠ *49E Calle No. 12* ☎ *988/916–2536* ⊕ *www.hotelcelestevida.com* ⌧ *3 rooms* ⊟ *No credit cards* ⦵ *No meals.*

$$$$
HOTEL
Fodor's Choice
★
⊡ **Hotel Xixim.** On an old coconut plantation outside town, this hotel offers classy comfort in thatch-roof bungalows along a shell-strewn beach. **Pros:** on beach; garden showers; good service; breakfast basket delivered to your door. **Cons:** a drive from main plaza; no air-conditioning; mosquitoes at dusk; bland menu; Wi-Fi in common areas only. $ *Rooms from: $300* ⊠ *Camino Viejo a Sisal, Km 10* ☎ *988/916–2100, 800/400–3333 in U.S. and Canada* ⊕ *www.ecoparaiso.com* ⌧ *24 cabanas, 8 suites* ⦵ *Multiple meal plans.*

DZIBILCHALTÚN

16 km (10 miles) north of Mérida.

GETTING HERE AND AROUND

To reach Dzibilchaltún, head north on Carretera Mérida-Progreso. After 10 km (6 miles), turn right at the sign for the ruins, and continue another 3 km (2 miles) until you reach a village. Just after you pass the village, take your first right toward the ruins. To reach the archaeological site, follow the pathway past ancient Mayan stone sculptures. The entrance fee is about $8.

EXPLORING

FAMILY

Dzibilchaltún. Dzibilchaltún (dzi-bil-chal-*tun*), which means "the place with writing on flat stones," is not a place you'd travel miles out of your way to see. But because it's not far off the road, about halfway between Progreso and Mérida, it's convenient and, in its own small way, interesting. Although more than 16 square km (6 square miles) of land here is cluttered with mounds, platforms, piles of rubble, plazas, and stelae, only a few buildings have been excavated. According to archaeologists, the area may have been settled as early as 500 BC, and was inhabited until the time of the conquest. At its height, there were around 40,000 people living at the site.

Scientists find Dzibilchaltún fascinating because of the sculpture and ceramics from all periods of Mayan civilization that have been unearthed. Save what's in the museum, though, all you'll see is the tiny **Templo de las Siete Muñecas** ("temple of the seven dolls," circa AD 500), one of a half-dozen structures excavated to date. It's a long stroll down a flat dirt track lined with flowering bushes and trees to get to the low, trapezoidal temple exemplifying the late preclassic style. During the spring and fall equinoxes, sunbeams fall at the exact center of two windows opposite each other inside one of the temple rooms, which is an example of the highly precise mathematical calculations for which the Maya are known. Studies have found that a similar phenomenon occurs at the full moon between March 20 and April 20.

Dzibilchaltún's other main attraction is the ruined open chapel built by the Spaniards for the Indians. Actually, to be accurate, the Spanish forced Indian laborers to build it as a place of worship for themselves: a sort of pre-Hispanic "separate but equal" scenario.

One of the best reasons to visit Dzibilchaltún is **Xlacah Cenote,** the site's sinkhole, whose crystalline water is the color of smoked green glass and is ideal for cooling off in after walking around the ruins.

Finally, also consider a visit to the **Museo Pueblo Maya**: small, yet both attractive and impressive. The museum (closed Monday) holds the seven crude dolls that gave the Temple of the Seven Dolls its name, and outside in the garden rest several huge sculptures found on the site. Museo Pueblo Maya also traces the area's Hispanic history, and highlights contemporary crafts from the region.

The easiest way to get to Dzibilchaltún is to get a *colectivo* (taxi-van) or a regular taxi from Mérida's Parque San Juan or from the main dock in Progreso, depending on where you are staying. In Mérida, the *colectivos* depart whenever they fill up with passengers or you can take a regular taxi, which will cost about $15 one-way. A taxi from Progreso will cost about $70, which includes round-trip transportation and two hours at the ruins. ⊹ *North on Mérida-Progreso highway. After 11 km, turn right at sign and continue 3 km to entrance* ▱ *$12, including museum; parking $1.20; video fee $4* ☼ *Daily 8–5* ☼ *Museum closed Mon. Cenote closes at 4 pm.*

PROGRESO

16 km (10 miles) north of Dzibilchaltún, 32 km (20 miles) north of Mérida.

The waterfront town closest to Mérida, Progreso is not particularly historic. It's also not terribly picturesque; still, it provokes a certain sentimental fondness for those who know it well. On weekdays during most of the year the beaches are deserted, but when school is out (Easter week, July, and August) and on summer weekends it's bustling with families from Mérida. It's also started attracting cruise ships, and twice-weekly arrivals bring tourist traffic to town. Because this town is void of upscale hotels, it is recommended to overnight in neighboring Mérida at one of the nicer properties, and simply spend the day relaxing in Progreso.

Progreso's charm—or lack thereof—seems to hinge on the weather. When the sun is shining, the water appears a translucent green and feels bathtub-warm, and the fine sand makes for lovely long walks. When the wind blows during one of Yucatán's winter *nortes*, the water churns with whitecaps and looks gray and unappealing, and the sand blows in your face. Whether the weather is good or bad, however, everyone ends up eventually at one of the restaurants lining the main street, Calle 19, across from the oceanfront malecón. These all serve up cold beer, seafood cocktails, and freshly grilled fish. There's also a small downtown area, between Calle 80 and Calle 31, with small restaurants that serve simpler fare (like tortas and tacos), shops, banks, and supermarkets.

Although Progreso is close enough to Mérida to make it an easy day trip, several smaller hotels that have cropped up over the past few years make it a decent alternative and a great base for exploring the untouristy coast. Just west of Progreso, the fishing villages of Chelem and Chuburna are beginning to offer walking, kayaking, and cycling tours ending with a boat trip through the mangroves and a freshly prepared ceviche and beer or soft drink for about $33. This is ecotourism in its infancy, and it's best to set this up ahead of time through the Progreso tourism office. Experienced divers can explore sunken ships at the Alacranes Reef, about 120 km (74 miles) offshore, although infrastructure is limited. Pérez Island, part of the reef, supports a large population of sea turtles and seabirds. Arrangements for the boat trip can be made through individuals at the private marina at neighboring Yucaltepén, which is 6 km (4 miles) from Progreso.

GETTING HERE AND AROUND

Progreso is 32 km (20 miles) north of Mérida via México 261. To drive from Mérida, head north from the Paseo de Montejo and keep going north as you head out of town. It's a straight drive to the beach. Buses for Progreso also leave Mérida from Calle 62 No. 524, between Calles 65 and 67.

VISITOR INFORMATION

Progreso Municipal Tourism Office ⊠ *Casa de la Cultura, Calles 80, between Calle 31 and 33, Centro* ☎ *969/935–0104* ⊕ *www.ayuntamientodeprogreso.gob. mx.*

Pick up a shark jaw in Progreso.

BEACHES

Progreso Beach. Far from the pristine beaches of the Caribbean, Progreso's main beach runs several miles along the malecón (boardwalk). The main draw is its proximity to Mérida, a 30-minute drive from the coast, which often leaves the shores packed with tourists and locals during summer weekends and holidays. But the sand's gray, the water's murky, and the beaches are littered with beer bottles and dead fish. Water shoes are recommended because there are sharp and slippery rocks below the surface, making this a poor spot for diving or snorkeling. The beach is void of shade, so your best bet is to find refuge in one of the restaurants lining the malecón. Several restaurant owners rent beach chairs by the hour, but beware that Progreso's peddlers are relentless and will only leave once they receive a small tip. Despite its drawbacks, Progreso's waters offer a refreshing escape from the bustling city and provide the fish that's served in local restaurants. Although there are no public facilities, bathrooms are available at nearby restaurants. Cruise ships dock here about twice a week, so to avoid the crowds, walk along the beach toward the lighthouse. **Amenities:** food and drink; toilets. **Best for:** partiers; walking. ⊠ *Av. Malecón at Calle 28.*

WHERE TO EAT

$ ╳ **Eladio's.** This bar and restaurant is a branch of the classic and popu-
MEXICAN lar Mérida joint by the same name. Under a tall palapa on the beach you can enjoy the view and the breeze through tall windows facing the water. Live music in the afternoons (except Tuesday) adds to the party atmosphere. This place is extremely popular with cruise ship passengers who disembark in Progreso. Tasty appetizers are free with your

drinks, and there are plenty to choose from. This is a good place to try different Yucatecan dishes such as *longaniza asada* and *pollo pibil*. Fresh seafood dishes are also on the menu, but these don't come with the drinks. [$] *Average main: $7* ✉ *Av. Malecón s/n, at Calle 80, Centro* ☎ *969/935–5670* 🌐 *www.eladios.com.mx*.

$$ SEAFOOD 🍴 **Flamingos.** This restaurant facing Progreso's long cement promenade is a cut above its neighbors. Service is professional and attentive, and soon after arriving you'll get at least one free appetizer—maybe black beans with corn tortillas, or a plate of shredded shark meat stewed with tomatoes. The creamy cilantro soup is a little too cheesy (literally, not figuratively), but the large fish fillets are perfectly breaded and lightly fried. Breakfast is served after 7 am. There's a full bar, and although there's no air-conditioning, large, glassless windows let in the ocean breeze. [$] *Average main: $10* ✉ *Calle 19 No. 144-D, at Calle 72* ☎ *969/935–2122*.

WHERE TO STAY

For expanded reviews, facilities, and current deals, visit Fodors.com.

$ HOTEL 🏨 **Condhotel Progreso.** This small hotel is right across from the water and close to all of the restaurants along the malecón. **Pros:** inexpensive rooms; swimming pool. **Cons:** very sparse rooms; Wi-Fi in common areas only; uncomfortable beds. [$] *Rooms from: $50* ✉ *Calle 21 No.150, between Calles 66 and 68* ☎ *969/935–5079* 🛏 *51 rooms* 🍽 *No meals*.

$ HOTEL 🏨 **Playa Linda Hotel.** Directly across from the beach, this new hotel has clean rooms, incredible rates, and the best view in Progreso. **Pros:** great value; across from the beach; best option in Progreso. **Cons:** no restaurant; staff doesn't speak English; no amenities. [$] *Rooms from: $55* ✉ *Malecón and Calle 76* ☎ *985/858–0519, 999/220–8318* 🌐 *www.playalindahotel.com.mx* 🛏 *7 rooms* 🍽 *No meals*.

XCAMBO

32 km (20 miles) west of Progreso.

Xcambo. Surrounded by a plantation where disease-resistant coconut trees are being developed, the Xcambo (*ish*-cam-bo) site is a couple of miles inland following the turnoff for Xtampu. It's also in the hometown of former governor Victor Cervera Pacheco, who, it's rumored, gave priority to its excavation. Salt, a much-sought-after item of trade in the ancient Mayan world, was produced in this area and made it prosperous. Indeed, the bones of 600 former residents discovered in burial plots showed they had been healthier than the average Maya. Two plazas have been restored so far, surrounded by rather plain structures. The tallest temple is the Xcambo, also known as the Pyramid of the Cross. On a clear day you can see the coast, about a mile away, from the summit. Ceramics found at the site indicate that the city traded with other Mayan groups as far afield as Guatemala, Teotihuácan, and Belize. The Catholic church on the site was built by dismantling some of the ancient structures, and until recently locals hauled off the cut stones to build fences and foundations. ✉ *Between Progreso and Tel-*

chac Puerto, 3 km south of coastal road (turn off Progreso–Dzilam de Bravo Hwy. at Xtampu) ✉ *Donation* ☉ *Daily 8–5.*

PARQUE NATURAL RÍA LAGARTOS

115 km (71 miles) north of Valladolid.

FAMILY **Parque Natural Ría Lagartos.** This park, which encompasses a long estuary, was developed with ecotourism in mind—although most of the alligators for which it and the village were named have long since been hunted into extinction. The real spectacle these days is the birds. More than 380 species nest and feed in the area, including flocks of flamingos, snowy and red egrets, white ibis, great white herons, cormorants, pelicans, and peregrine falcons. Fishing is good, too, and the protected leatherback, hawksbill, and green turtles lay their eggs on the beach at night.

You can make the 90-km (56-mile) trip from Valladolid (1½ hours by car or 2 hours by bus) as a day trip (add another hour if you're coming from Mérida, or three hours from Cancún). There's a small information center at the entrance to town where Carretera 295 joins the coast road to San Felipe. Unless you're interested exclusively in the birds, it's nice to spend the night in Río Lagartos (the town is called *Río* Lagartos, the park *Ría* Lagartos) or nearby San Felipe. There's little to do except take a walk through town or on the beach, and grab a meal. Buses leave Mérida and Valladolid regularly from the second class terminals to either Río Lagartos or, 10 km (6 miles) west of the park, San Felipe.

The easiest way to book a trip is through Restaurante La Torreja, where you can also eat a delicious dinner of fresh seafood. Call ahead to reserve an English- or Italian-speaking guide through their organization, **Ría Lagartos Adventures** (☎ *986/862–0403,* ⊕ *www.riolagartosadventures.com*). This boat trip will take you through the mangrove forests to the flamingo feeding grounds (where, as an added bonus, you can paint your face or body with supposedly therapeutic white clay). A 2½-hour tour, which accommodates five or six people, costs $75. The 3½-hour bird-watching tour costs $90 (both per boat, not per person). You can take a shorter sunset trip for $50, or four-hour photography trip for $120. The night tour in search of crocs takes 2½ hours (one to four passengers, $90). You can also hire a boat ($20 for 1 to 10 passengers) to take you to an area beach and pick you up at a designated time.

Be aware that mosquitoes are known to gather at dusk in unpleasantly large groups in May, June, and July. So bringing along some spray to fend them off might be a good idea. ☎ *986/100–8390* ⊕ *www. riolagartosadventures.com.*

WHERE TO EAT

$ ✗ **La Torreja Restaurant.** Open since 1972, this palapa restaurant is
SEAFOOD directly across from the water, meaning you can watch the day's catch come straight from the docks. With its seashell-strewn floor and plastic tables, this place is far from fancy, but you're sure to leave satisfied. The menu features all the local specialties like ceviche, seafood soup, fish fillet stuffed with shrimp, and breaded seafood rolled into a ball and

deep fried. In season (July–December) you can order lobster and octopus cooked several different ways. Don't be surprised if owner Diego Núñez offers you a bird-watching tour; he and his family also operate Ría Lagartos Adventures across the street. $ *Average main: $9* ✉ *Calle 9 No. 105, on waterfront, 50 meters from lighthouse, Río Lagartos* ☎ *986/862–0452* ⊕ *www.riolagartosrestaurante.com.*

$ ✕ **Restaurante Isla Contoy.** Run by the amicable family that guides lagoon
SEAFOOD   tours, this open-sided seafood shanty at the dock serves generous helpings of fish soup, fried fish fillets, shrimp, squid, and crab. If you come with a group, order the combo for four (it can easily feed six, especially if you order a huge ceviche or other appetizer). The delicious platter comes with four shrimp crêpes, fish stuffed with seafood, a seafood skewer, and one each of grilled, breaded, garlic-chile, and battered fish fillets (usually grouper or sea trout, whatever is freshest). There are also a few regional specialties and red-meat dishes. It's open for breakfast, too, which is included in the room rate if you stay in one of their simple rooms at Punta Ponto Hotel on the beach. There's live music on Sunday. $ *Average main: $7* ✉ *Calle 19 No. 134, at Calle 14* ☎ *986/862–0000* ⊕ *www.riolagartosecotours.net16.net.*

WHERE TO STAY

For expanded reviews, facilities, and current deals, visit Fodors.com.

$ ☷ **Hotel Tabasco Río.** Right on the plaza, this hotel has a bright center
HOTEL   courtyard covered with skylights, allowing for light to shine on tables where breakfast is served. **Pros:** well-appointed rooms; hotel package can include meals and tours. **Cons:** not on water; uninspiring breakfast; Wi-Fi in common areas only. $ *Rooms from: $50* ✉ *Calle 12 No. 15, Río Lagartos* ☎ *986/862–0508* ⊕ *www.tabascoriohotel.com* ⇌ *19 rooms* ⭐️ *Breakfast.*

$$ ☷ **Hotel Villa de Pescadores.** By far the nicest hotel in Ría Lagartos, the
HOTEL   12 rooms have TVs, private balconies, water views, and colorful decor
Fodor's Choice   like paintings of local wildlife. **Pros:** great views; gracious owner; clean
★   rooms; best location in town; private parking lot. **Cons:** restaurant is closed for dinner in low season; no elevator; Wi-Fi in common areas only. $ *Rooms from: $70* ✉ *Calle 14, and Av. Malecon, Río Lagartos, Yucatán* ☎ *986/862–0020* ⊕ *www.hotelvilladepescadores.com* ⇌ *12 rooms* ⭐️ *No meals.*

$ ☷ **Punta Ponto Hotel.** The main draw here is the friendly, personal
HOTEL   attention the owners lavish on their guests. **Pros:** waterfront location; friendly staff. **Cons:** spartan accommodations; some street noise; rooms could use a makeover; credit cards not accepted. $ *Rooms from: $50* ✉ *Calle 9 Diagonal No. 140, Río Lagartos* ☎ *986/862–0509* ⊕ *www.hotelpuntaponto.com* ⇌ *9 rooms, 1 suite* ▭ *No credit cards* ⭐️ *Breakfast.*

ISLA HOLBOX

Fodor's Choice   *141 km (87 miles) northeast of Valladolid.*
★   Tiny Isla Holbox (25 km [16 miles] long) sits at the eastern end of the Ría Lagartos estuary and just across the Quintana Roo state line. A fishing fan's heaven because of the hordes of pampano, bass, barracuda,

and sharks just offshore, the island also pleases bird-watchers and seekers of tranquility. Birds fill the mangrove estuaries on the island's leeward side, whale sharks cruise offshore June through September, and sandy beaches are strewn with seashells. Although the water is often murky—the Gulf of Mexico and the Caribbean come together here—it's shallow and warm, and there are some nice places to swim. Sandy streets lead to simple seafood restaurants where the fish fillets, conch, octopus, and other delicacies are always fresh.

Isla's lucky population numbers some 2,000 souls, and in summer it seems there are as many biting bugs per person. Bring plenty of mosquito repellent. Many locals use baby oil as a natural repellent against no-seeums, also known as biting midges. There is Internet at most hotels and several ATMs on the island (some smaller businesses accept cash only).

There are less-expensive lodgings for those who eschew conventional beds in favor of fresh air and a hammock. Because it's a small island, it's easy to check several lodgings and make your choice. Hotel owners can help you set up bird-watching, fishing, and whale shark–viewing expeditions. Most restaurants serve fresh fish, but salmon and tuna are not local and were probably shipped in (and previously frozen) from Cancún.

GETTING HERE AND AROUND

To get to Isla Holbox from Río Lagartos, take Carretera 176 to Kantunilkin and then head north on the unnumbered road for 44 km (27 miles) to Chiquilá. From Cancún, take the 180 free road toward Mérida and pass through the small town of Leona Vicario. Follow the signs to Kantunilkin and continue 40 km (25 miles) until you reach the port town of Chiquilá. The drive from Cancún to Chiquilá takes about three hours depending on road conditions. The road is long and pitted with potholes, so avoid driving at night. You can park at 5 Hermanos, which has covered parking stalls for $4 a day (across from the port) and continue by ferry to the island. Schedules vary, but there are normally crossings on the hour from around 6 am to 7 pm. The fare is $4 and the trip takes about 35 minutes. Speed boats will take you to the island for double the price but will arrive in half the time. A car ferry makes the trip at 6 am daily, returning at 1 pm, but it's recommended to leave your car in Chiquilá and explore the island by golf cart. These little golf-cart taxis ply the island for about $15 an hour, or you can rent your own for $10 an hour. You may be able to negotiate a better price if you're renting for several hours or traveling in low season. Some hotels also offer complimentary bikes for guests. A rustic airport with a shell-bordered runway receives small airplanes, which can be booked

Isla Holbox is accessible only by ferry.

through Hotel Puerto Holbox. Round-trip airfare from Cancún to Isla Holbox costs $1,180 for a five-passenger Cesna.

WHERE TO EAT

$$ ✕ **Casa Nostra.** You can't get much closer to dining on the beach than
ITALIAN a meal at Casa Nostra, where water laps just below the tables on the sandy shore. The creative menu blends Italian, Mediterranean, and Caribbean cuisine, created by its Sicilian chef, Giuseppe Genovese (commonly known as "Beppe"). Recipes handed down through generations have made their way to this little palapa restaurant where locals gather for seafood pasta, grilled lobster, octopus salad, and fresh ceviche, all bathed in garlic and olive oil. Breads, sausages, and pizzas are made from scratch in the small kitchen where Beppe works his magic. The pizza topped with smoked ham, mozzarella, and arugula makes a perfect starter for two. This is the only spot on the island where you'll find authentic espresso, sorbet, and tiramisu. $ *Average main:* *$15* ✉ *Av. Morelos 231, at Hotel La Palapa* ☎ *984/875–2121* ⊕ *www. xperiencehotelsrestorts.com.*

$$ ✕ **El Sushi Holbox.** This tiny restaurant fills a void in island cuisine with
SUSHI the day's catch transformed into the sushi roll of your choice. Local favorites include the Holbox Rainbow made with shrimp, salmon, tuna, and sea bass. Nearly every roll is stuffed with cream cheese, an ingredient that makes the sushi far from authentic yet memorably tasty. Placing a sweet spin on the menu is the Banana Roll with shrimp, avocado, and cream cheese topped with fried banana and eel sauce. The restaurant, which is only open 5 pm–midnight, also serves Thai dishes and a full cocktail menu; the ginger margarita packs a punch. $ *Average main:*

$12 ✉ Av. Tiburón Ballena, top floor of Plaza El Pueblito ☎ 984/138–5571 ⏲ No lunch. Closed Mon.

$$ ECLECTIC 🍴 **Mandarina.** This restaurant and beach club, located on the ground floor of Casa Las Tortugas, has indoor and outdoor seating just feet from the sand. Chef Jorge Melul is a master baker and has become known on the island for his homemade breads, cakes, and pastas. Nearly every item on the menu is organic, with most ingredients coming from Mandarina's garden or nearby farms in neighboring Solferino. The daily catch is purchased directly from the local fishermen who dock on the shores. For a memorable meal, start with the shrimp tempura dipped in chipotle cream or homemade pesto. The fish, cooked in white wine and topped with spinach and pears, is light and satisfying. If it's just ambience you're after, head to the rooftop bar for a reasonably priced basil mojito or ginger margarita. [$] *Average main: $15 ✉ Casa Las Tortugas, Calle Igualdad s/n, Isla Holbox ☎ 984/875–2129 🌐 www.holboxcasalastortugas.com.*

$$ MEXICAN 🍴 **Restaurante Casa Lupita.** This is one of the more-formal dining options (i.e., the tables are not plastic) on the island, but you'll still feel right at home in jeans. The Spanish owners have decorated the walls with old, and sometimes rare, pictures of Isla Holbox in the 1940s. This is one of the few places in town where you can get Mexican dishes like *quesadillas de huitlacoche* (corn truffle), as well as some Spanish-inspired plates. In addition to salads, hamburgers, and vegetarian dishes, they also serve one of the most reasonably priced lobsters (around $30) in the area. The owners have a small hotel ($) above the restaurant with clean, colorful rooms. [$] *Average main: $15 ✉ Calle Palomino s/n, at Parque Central ☎ 984/875–2017 🌐 www.casalupitaholbox.com ⏲ Closed Sun.*

6

$$ SEAFOOD 🍴 **Zarabanda Restaurante.** Not far from the main square, this unpretentious family-run restaurant is one of the oldest (and most affordable) eateries on the island, and it's still considered one of the best places to try island-style food. There are quite a few tasty seafood dishes, including a huge *mariscada* for two that includes a fish fillet, a whole fish, a lobster, and octopus on a bed of shredded lettuce. The delicious seafood soup includes the freshest seasonal seafood and is an island classic. People come here for the food and not the ambience, so grab a seat at a plastic table, listen to the Mexican music, and take your pick from the extensive menu. [$] *Average main: $13 ✉ Calle Palomino s/n ☎ 984/875–2094 💳 No credit cards.*

WHERE TO STAY

For expanded reviews, facilities, and current deals, visit Fodors.com.

$$$ HOTEL Fodor's Choice ★ 🏨 **Casa Las Tortugas.** Boasting the best location on the island, this "bohemian-chic" hotel has 21 romantic rooms and one of the only spas on Holbox. **Pros:** on-site kite-surfing school; excellent location; organic restaurant; delicious breakfast included. **Cons:** not all rooms have ocean views; some staff members don't speak English; hotel is usually booked far in advance. [$] *Rooms from: $180 ✉ Calle Igualdad s/n, Hotel Zone, Isla Holbox ☎ 984/875–2129, 984/875–2468 🌐 www.holboxcasalastortugas.com 🛏 14 rooms, 7 suites 🍴 Breakfast.*

$$$ HOTEL 🏨 **Casa Sandra.** Rustic meets five-star at this boutique hotel, elegantly landscaped with winding pathways leading to two-story casitas draped

in bougainvillea. **Pros:** ayurveda treatments (holistic therapy from India); 500-thread-count Egyptian cotton sheets; plenty of hammocks for lounging; good restaurant. **Cons:** some rooms get kitchen noise; expensive restaurant; only two rooms have TV; weak Wi-Fi signal; not all rooms have ocean views. [$] *Rooms from: $239* ✉ *Calle de la Igualdad s/n, Hotel Zone, Isla Holbx, Quintana Roo* ☎ *984/875–2171* 🌐 *www.casasandra.com* 🛏 *15 rooms, 5 suites* 🍴 *Breakfast.*

$$$$ HOTEL Fodor's Choice ★ 🏨 **Hotel Las Nubes.** Opened in 2010, this beachfront hotel, named "the clouds," is remotely located on the northeast side of the island. **Pros:** unobstructed views; peaceful location; bikes for exploring the island. **Cons:** expensive; small beach; far from town. [$] *Rooms from: $300* ✉ *Paseo Kuka s/n, Esq. Calle Camaron, Zona Hotelera, Playa Norte, Isla Holbox* ☎ *984/875–2300* 🌐 *www.lasnubesdeholbox.com* 🛏 *19 rooms, 5 suites* 🍴 *Breakfast.*

$$$ HOTEL 🏨 **Hotel Villas Flamingos.** If you are looking for simplicity, tranquillity, and an eco-friendly property, then this is your place. **Pros:** eco-friendly property; nice pool; only beach house on the island. **Cons:** far from town; rustic design is not for everyone; rooms could use some upgrades. [$] *Rooms from: $250* ✉ *Calle paseo Kuka s/n, Hotel Zone, Isla Holbox* ☎ *984/875–2167* 🌐 *www.villasflamingos.com* 🛏 *17 rooms, 1 house* 🍴 *Breakfast.*

$$$ HOTEL 🏨 **Posada Mawimbi.** Known for its Mexican hospitality and relaxing vibe, this small hotel is made up of brightly painted beachside bungalows. **Pros:** inexpensive rooms; all rooms have a/c and safes; bilingual staff; suspended beach beds on ropes are great for relaxing. **Cons:** entryway rooms lack privacy; no room phones; no televisions. [$] *Rooms from: $145* ✉ *Calle Igualdad s/n* ☎ *984/875–2003* 🌐 *www.mawimbi.net* 🛏 *11 rooms* 🍴 *Breakfast.*

$$ HOTEL 🏨 **Villas Delfines.** This fishermen's lodge consists of 20 pleasant cabins on the beach. **Pros:** eco-friendly property; beautiful beach setting; nice Saturday grill (high season only). **Cons:** long walk into town; Wi-Fi in common areas only; slightly dated rooms. [$] *Rooms from: $130* ✉ *Domicilio Conocido* ☎ *984/875–2196* 🌐 *www.villasdelfines.com* 🛏 *20 cabins* 🍴 *Multiple meal plans.*

$$$ RESORT ALL-INCLUSIVE 🏨 **Villas HM Paraíso del Mar.** Despite the thatched roofs and rustic ambience, the rooms at the island's largest property are loaded with everything you could want to be comfortable. **Pros:** computers for guests to use; nice breakfast buffet; island's only all-inclusive property. **Cons:** some rooms lack ocean views; seaweed on the shores; Wi-Fi in common areas only. [$] *Rooms from: $228* ✉ *Av. Plutarco Elias s/n* ☎ *984/875–2062, 984/875–2077* 🌐 *www.hmhotels.net* 🛏 *52 rooms, 6 suites* 🍴 *Multiple meal plans.*

SPORTS AND OUTDOORS

SAILING

Sailing Isla Holbox. Two-hour sunset cruises can be arranged through Hotel Puerto Holbox. The 26-foot sailboat holds up to four passengers and is available for fishing trips or sunset excursions. Drinks and appetizers are included in the rate. ✉ *Hotel Puerto Holbox, Av. Pedro Joaquín Codwell s/n, Isla Holbox, Quintana Roo* ☎ *984/875–2157.*

SHOPPING

Artesanías Las Chicas. Sandra Thomson, a New York native who has lived on the island for years, runs Artesanías Las Chicas, a small shop with a delightful collection of art crafts. She carries everything from rings and mirrors to sophisticated hammocks and purses from all over Mexico. ⊠ *Domicilio conocido, Calle Igualdad* ☎ *998/875–2430.*

Plaza El Pueblito. This little collection of stores is the closest you'll get to a shopping mall on Isla Holbox. Tucked under a palapa roof are a dozen restaurants and boutiques selling clothing and handicrafts. There's even a small movie theater on the top floor, where films are shown nightly at 8 pm for $3. ⊠ *Av. Tiburón Ballena* ⊕ *www.elpueblitoholbox.com.*

CAMPECHE

Campeche City has to be one of the best-kept secrets in the Yucatán. Its beautifully preserved colonial district is brimming with historic sites, museums, cafés, and restaurants—all within easy walking distance of each other. Yet the city is far smaller and more easygoing than its Yucatecan cousin, Mérida. Its unique history—it was once a favorite target of seafaring pirates—has left its mark. Many of the protective walls that were built to safeguard the city's inhabitants are still standing, and the colorful colonial buildings were constructed with safety in mind; they're markedly less ornate than their counterparts elsewhere on the peninsula, with well-barred windows and impressively heavy-looking doors. The 18th-century fort at the south end of town lets you imagine Campeche's dangerous past, and is home to a fascinating collection of Mayan artifacts taken from many archaeological sites, the highlights being the relics of the ancient Maya ruler Gran Garra de Jaguar (Great Jaguar Claw), who presided over the city of Calakmul's rise and decline.

The city is the state's most accessible spot, and makes a good hub for exploring other areas, many of which have only basic restaurants and primitive lodgings. The Edzná archaeological site is a short detour south of Carreteras 180 and 188. ■**TIP→** You'll need at least rudimentary Spanish—few people outside the capital speak English. If you plan to venture off the beaten path, pack a Spanish-English dictionary.

CAMPECHE CITY

174 km (108 miles) southeast of Mérida via Mexico 180.

Campeche is a tranquil, picturesque town, where block upon block of buildings with lovely facades, all painted in bright colors, meet the sea. Tiny balconies overlook clean, geometrically paved streets, and charming old street lamps illuminate the scene at night.

In colonial days the city center was completely enclosed within a 10-foot-thick wall. Two stone archways (originally there were four)—one facing the sea, the other the land—provided the only access. The defensive walls also served as a de facto class demarcation. Within them lived the ruling elite. Outside were the barrios, with slaves from Cuba, and everyone else.

On strategic corners, seven *baluartes*, or bastions, gave militiamen a platform from which to fight off pirates and the other ruffians that continually plagued this beautiful city on the bay. But it wasn't until 1771, when the Fuerte de San Miguel was built on a hilltop outside town, that pirates finally stopped attacking the city.

■**TIP➔** Campeche's historic center is easily navigable—in fact, it's a walker's paradise. Narrow roads and lack of parking spaces can make driving a bit frustrating, although drivers here are polite and mellow. Streets running roughly north–south are even-numbered, and those running east–west are odd-numbered. The beautifully restored historic center has a perimeter stretching 2½ km (1½ miles).

GETTING HERE AND AROUND

Aeroméxico flies several times daily from Mexico City to Campeche City. Campeche's Aeropuerto Internacional Alberto Acuña Ongay is 16 km (10 miles) north of downtown. Taxis are the only means of transportation to and from the airport. The fare to downtown Campeche is about $9.

Within Campeche City, the route of interest to most visitors is along Avenida Ruíz Cortínez. The ride on a bus costs the equivalent of about 30¢. There are also fairly frequent buses to points all over the Yucatán Peninsula.

■**TIP➔** For trips between major destinations within the Yucatán Peninsula, purchase tickets with a credit card by phone through Ticketbus. Make sure to ask from which station the bus departs.

Campeche City is about 2 to 2½ hours from Mérida along the 180-km (99-mile) *via corta* (short way) on Carretera 180. The alternative route, the 250-km (155-mile) *via ruinas* (ruins route), on Carretera 261, takes three to four hours, but passes some major Mayan ruins.

You can hail taxis on the street in Campeche City, and there are also stands by the bus stations, the main plaza, and the municipal market. The minimum fare is $2; it's $2.50 from the center to the bus station and $10 to the airport (it's cheaper to go to the airport than from it). After 11 pm, prices may be slightly higher. There's a small fee, less than 50¢, to call for a cab through Radio Taxis.

Bus Contacts ADO ⊠ *Av. Patricio Trueba, at Casa de Justicia 237* ☎ *981/811–9910* ⊕ *www.ado.com.mx.* **Ticketbus** ☎ *800/009–9090 toll-free in Mexico, 55/5133–5133* ⊕ *www.boletotal.mx.*

Car-Rental Contacts Europcar ⊠ *Av. López Portillo, at Carretera Campeche-Chino, Col. Aeropuerto* ☎ *981/152–1172, 981/823–4083* ⊕ *www.europcar.com.mx.*

Taxi Contacts Radio Taxi ⊠ *114 23 Col. San Joaquin* ☎ *981/815–8888.* **Bancomer** ⊠ *Av. 16 de Septiembre 120* ☎ *981/816–6622* ⊕ *www.bancomer. com* ⊠ *Calle 8 No. 268, between 57 and 59* ☎ *01800/1122–610 in Mexico.* **Banorte** ⊠ *Calle 8 No. 237, between Calles 53 and 55* ☎ *981/811–4250* ⊕ *www.banorte.com.*

TOURS

You can take Xtampak Tours from Campeche to nearby ruins like Edzná, Calakmul, Balamku, and Uxmal. Prices for shared tours range from $20 per person (for a four-hour tour) to $95 per person (for a 12-hour tour). Some tours include guides and entry fees at the ruins, whereas others include transport only, so ask ahead about what's included in the package. Make your reservations a day in advance.

Contacts Xtampak Tours ⊠ *Calle 57 No. 14, Centro* ☎ *981/811–3559.*

VISITOR INFORMATION

Municipal Tourist Office ⊠ *Calle 55 No. 3, between Calles 8 and 10* ☎ *981/811–3989, 981/811–3990.* **State Tourism Office** ⊠ *Av. Ruíz Cortínez s/n, Plaza Moch Couoh, across from Gobierno, Centro* ☎ *981/127–3300* ⊕ *www. campeche.travel.*

EXPLORING

TOP ATTRACTIONS

Baluarte de la Soledad. This is the largest of the bastions, originally built to protect the **Puerta de Mar,** a sea gate that was one of four original entrances to the city. Because it uses no supporting walls, it resembles a Roman triumphal arch. It has comparatively complete parapets and embrasures that offer views of the cathedral, municipal buildings, and old houses along Calle 8. Inside is the **Museo de Arqueología Maya,** with artifacts that include a well-preserved sculpture of a man wearing an owl mask, columns from Edzná and Isla de Jaina, and at least a dozen well-proportioned Mayan stelae from ruins throughout Campeche. ⊠ *Calle 8, between Calles 55 and 57, Centro* ☎ *981/816–8174* 🎫 *$3* ☉ *Tues.–Sun. 9–5:30.*

Baluarte de San Carlos. Named for Charles II, King of Spain, this bastion, where Calle 8 curves around and becomes Circuito Baluartes, houses the **Museo de la Ciudad.** The free museum contains a small collection of historical artifacts, including several Spanish suits of armor and a beautifully inscribed silver scepter. Captured pirates were once jailed in the stifling basement dungeon. The unshaded rooftop provides an ocean view that's lovely at sunset. ⊠ *Calle 8, between Calles 65 and 63, Circuito Baluartes, Centro* 🎫 *Free* ☉ *Daily 9 am–8 pm.*

Calle 59. Some of Campeche's finest homes were built on this city street between Calles 8 and 18. At the end of Calle 59 is Puerta de Mar (Sea Gate), a main entrance to the historic city. Most of the homes here were two stories high, the ground floors serving as warehouses and the upper floors as residences. These days, behind the delicate grillwork and lace curtains you can glimpse genteel scenes of Campeche life. The best-preserved houses are those between Calles 14 and 18, and many closer to the sea have been remodeled or destroyed by fire. Campeche's INAH (Instituto Nacional de Antropología e Historia) office, between Calles 16 and 14, is an excellent example of one of Campeche City's fine old homes. Each month INAH displays a different archaeological artifact in its courtyard. Look for the names of the apostles carved into the lintels of houses between Calles 16 and 18.

DID YOU KNOW?

Mellow and almost completely unvisited by tourists, Campeche is a world unto itself. Campeche City's historic colonial district is a lovely place to stroll.

A STREETCAR NAMED EL GUAPO

Guided trolley tours of historic Campeche City leave from Calle 10 on the Plaza Principal on the hour from 9 to noon and 5 to 8. You can buy tickets ahead of time at the adjacent kiosk or once aboard the trolley. Be prepared to wait around, since the buses take off only when a minimum of eight people have bought their tickets. (Trips run less frequently in the off-season, and it's always best to double-check schedules at the kiosk.) The one-hour tour costs $8, and if English speakers request it, guides will do their best to speak the language. For the same price, the green "Guapo" ("handsome") trolley makes unguided trips to Reducto de San José at 9 am and 5 pm (also at 10, 11, and noon during vacation periods such as Christmas and Easter). You'll have only about 10 minutes to admire the view, though.

Casa Seis. One of the first colonial homes in Campeche is now a cultural center. It has been fully restored—rooms are furnished with original antiques and a few reproductions. Original frescoes at the tops of the walls remain, and you can see patches of the painted "wallpaper" that once covered the walls, serving to simulate European trends in an environment where wallpaper wouldn't stick due to the humidity. There is a small gift shop selling products from Campeche, and the Moorish courtyard is occasionally used as a space for exhibits and lectures. ⊠ *Calle 57, between Calles 10 and 8, Plaza Principal, Centro* ☎ *981/816–1782* ☜ *$1* ⊙ *Daily 9–9.*

Catedral de la Inmaculada Concepción. It took two centuries (from 1650 to 1850) to finish the Cathedral of the Immaculate Conception, and as a result, it incorporates both neoclassical and Renaissance elements. On the simple exterior, sculptures of saints in niches are covered in black netting to discourage pigeons from unintentional desecration. The church's neoclassical interior is also somewhat plain and sparse. The high point of its collection, now housed in the side chapel museum, is a magnificent Holy Sepulchre carved from ebony and decorated with stamped silver angels, flowers, and decorative curlicues. Each angel holds a symbol of the Stations of the Cross. ⊠ *Calle 55, between Calles 8 and 10, Plaza Principal, Centro* ⊙ *Daily 9–8.*

FAMILY **Fuerte de San Miguel.** Near the city's southwest end, Avenida Ruíz Cortínez winds its way to this hilltop fort with its breathtaking view of the Bay of Campeche. Built between 1779 and 1801 and dedicated to the archangel Michael, the fort was positioned to blast enemy ships with its long-range cannons. As soon as it was completed, pirates stopped attacking the city. In fact, the cannons were fired only once, in 1842, when General Santa Anna used Fuerte de San Miguel to put down a revolt by Yucatecan separatists seeking independence from Mexico. The fort houses the **Museo de la Arqueología Maya,** whose exhibits include the skeletons of long-ago Maya royals, complete with jewelry and pottery, which are arranged just as they were found in Calakmul tombs. Other archaeological treasures are funeral vessels, masks, many wonderfully expressive figurines and whistles from Isla de Jaina, stelae

Campeche's History

Campeche City's gulf location played a pivotal role in its history. Ah-Kim-Pech (Mayan for "lord of the serpent tick," from which the name Campeche is derived) was the capital of an Indian chieftainship here, long before the Spaniards arrived in 1517. In 1540 the conquerors—led by Francisco de Montejo and later by his son—established a real foothold at Campeche (originally called San Francisco de Campeche), using it as a base for the conquest of the peninsula.

At the time, Campeche City was the Gulf's only port and shipyard. So Spanish ships, loaded with cargoes of treasure plundered from Mayan, Aztec, and other indigenous civilizations, dropped anchor here en route from Veracruz to Cuba, New Orleans, and Spain. As news of the riches spread, Campeche's shores were soon overrun with pirates. From the mid-1500s to the early 1700s, such notorious corsairs as Diego the Mulatto, Lorenzillo, Peg Leg, Henry Morgan, and Barbillas swooped in repeatedly from Tris—or Isla de Términos, as Isla del Carmen was then known—pillaging and burning the city and massacring its people.

Finally, after years of appeals to the Spanish crown, Campeche received funds to build a protective wall, with four gates and eight bastions, around the town center. For a while afterward, the city thrived on its exports, especially *palo de tinte*—a valuable dyewood more precious than gold due to the nascent European textile industry's demand for it—but also hardwoods, chicle, salt, and henequen (sisal hemp). But when the port of Sisal opened on the northern Yucatán coast in 1811, Campeche's monopoly on gulf traffic ended, and its economy quickly declined. During the 19th and 20th centuries, Campeche, like most of the Yucatán Peninsula, had little to do with the rest of Mexico. Left to their own devices, Campechanos lived in relative isolation until the petroleum boom of the 1970s brought businessmen from Mexico City, Europe, and the United States to its provincial doorstep.

Campeche City's history still shapes the community today. Remnants of its gates and bastions split the city into two main districts: the historical center (where relatively few people live) and the newer residential areas. Because the city was long preoccupied with defense, the colonial architecture is less flamboyant here than elsewhere in Mexico. The narrow flagstone streets reflect the confines of the city's walls, and homes here emphasize the practical over the decorative. Still, government decrees, and an on-and-off beautification program, have helped keep the city's colonial structures in good condition despite the damaging effects of humidity and salt air. An air of antiquity remains.

and stucco masks from the Mayan ruins, and an excellent pottery collection. Although it's a shame that most information is in Spanish only, many of the pieces speak for themselves. The gift shop sells replicas of artifacts. ⊠ *Av. Francisco Morazán s/n, west of town center, Cerro de Buenavista* ☎ *981/821–0973* 🖵 *$3* ☉ *Tues.–Sun. 9–5:30.*

Malecón. A broad sidewalk, more than 4 km (2½ miles) long, runs the length of Campeche's waterfront boulevard, from northeast of the

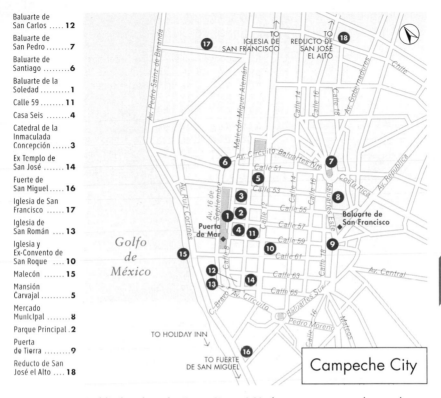

Campeche City

Debliz hotel to the Justo Sierra Méndez monument at the southwest edge of downtown. With its landscaping, sculptures, rest areas, and fountains lighted up at night in neon colors, the promenade attracts joggers, strollers, and families. (Note the separate paths for walking, jogging, and biking.) On weekend nights, students turn the malecón into a party zone, and families with young children fill the parks on both sides of the promenade after 7 or 8 in the evening, and stay out surprisingly late to enjoy the cool of the evening.

Parque Principal (*Plaza de la Independencia*). Also known as the Plaza de la Independencia, this central park is small by Mexican standards, though picturesque with a beautiful view of Catedral de la Inmaculada Concepción. In its center is an old-fashioned kiosk with a pleasing café-bar where you can sit and watch city residents out for an evening stroll and listen to the itinerant musicians that often show up to play traditional ballads in the evenings. ⊠ *Bounded by Calles 10, 8, 55, and 57, Centro.*

FAMILY **Puerta de Tierra.** The Land Gate, where Old Campeche ends, is the only one of the four city gates with its basic structure intact. The stone arch interrupts a stretch of the partially crenellated wall, 26 feet high and 10 feet thick, that once encircled the city. Walk the wall's full length to the **Baluarte San Juan** for excellent views of both the old and new cities.

Campeche's historic center is easy to explore on foot.

The staircase leads down to an old well, underground storage area, and dungeon. There's a one-hour light show accompanied by music and dance at Puerta de Tierra. Shows cost $4 and are Thursday–Sunday at 8 pm and daily in spring, summer, and Christmas vacation periods. ⊠ *Calles 18 and 59, Centro* ⊙ *Daily 9–5.*

WORTH NOTING

Baluarte de San Pedro. Built in 1686 to protect the city from pirate attacks, this bastion flanked by watchtowers now houses one of the city's few worthwhile handicraft shops. The collection is small but of high quality, and prices are reasonable. On the roof are well-preserved corner watchtowers. You can also check out (but not use) the original 17th-century toilet. ⊠ *Calles 18 and 51, Circuito Baluartes, Centro* ⊠ *Free* ⊙ *Daily 9–5.*

Baluarte de Santiago. The last of the bastions to be built (1704) has been transformed into the **X'much Haltún Botanical Gardens.** It houses more than 200 plant species, including the enormous ceiba tree, which had spiritual importance to the Maya, symbolizing a link between heaven, earth, and the underworld. The original bastion was demolished at the turn of the 20th century, and then rebuilt in the 1950s. ⊠ *Calles 8 and 49, Circuito Baluartes, Centro* ⊠ *$1 includes admission to Baluarte San Juan and Bastion de San Francisco* ⊙ *Daily 9–5.*

Ex-Templo de San José. The Jesuits built this fine baroque church in honor of Saint Joseph just before they were booted out of the New World. Its block-long facade and portal are covered with blue-and-yellow Talavera tiles and crowned with seven narrow stone finials—resembling both the roof combs on many Mayan temples and the combs Spanish women once wore in their elaborate hairdos. Next door is the **Instituto Campechano,** used for cultural events and art exhibitions. These events and exhibits are regularly held here Tuesday evening at 7 pm. At other times you can ask the guard (who should be somewhere on the grounds) to let you in. From the outside you can admire Campeche's first lighthouse, built in 1864, and perched atop the right-hand tower. ✉ *Calles 10 and 65, Centro* ☎ *981/816–2292 Instituto Campechano.*

Iglesia de San Francisco. With its flat, boldly painted facade and bells ensconced under small arches instead of in bell towers, the Church of Saint Francis looks more like a Mexican city hall than a Catholic church. Outside the city center in a residential neighborhood, the beautifully restored temple is Campeche's oldest. It marks the spot where some say the first Mass on the North American continent was held in 1517—though the same claim has been made for Veracruz and Cozumel. One of Cortés's grandsons was baptized here, and the baptismal font still stands. ✉ *Avs. Miguel Alemán and Mariano Escobedo, San Francisco* ☎ *981/816–2925* ◉ *Daily 10–7.*

Iglesia de San Román. Like most Franciscan churches, this one is sober and plain, and its single bell tower is the only ornamentation. The equally sparse interior is brightened a bit by some colorful stained-glass windows, and the carved and inlaid altarpiece serves as a beautiful backdrop for an ebony image of Jesus, the "Black Christ," brought from Italy in about 1575. Although understandably skeptical of Christianity, the Indians, whom the Spaniards forced into perpetual servitude, eventually came to associate this black Christ figure with miracles. As legend has it, a ship that refused to carry the holy statue was lost at sea, while the ship that accepted him reached Campeche in record time. To this day, the Feast of San Román—when worshippers carry a black-wood Christ and silver filigree cross through the streets—remains a solemn but colorful affair. ✉ *Calles 10 and Bravo, San Román* ☎ *981/816–3303* ◉ *Daily 7–1 and 3–7.*

Iglesia y Ex-Convento de San Roque. The elaborately carved main altarpiece and matching side altars here were restored inch by inch in 2005, and this long, narrow church now adds more than ever to historic Calle 59's old-fashioned beauty. Built in 1565, it was originally called Iglesia de San Francisco for Saint Francis. In addition to a statue of Francis, humbler-looking saints peer out from smaller niches. ✉ *Calles 12 and 59, Centro* ☎ *981/816–3144* ◉ *Daily 8:30–noon and 5–7.*

Mansión Carvajal. Built in the early 20th century by one of the Yucatán's wealthiest plantation owners, Fernando Carvajal Estrada, this eclectic mansion is a reminder of the city's heyday, when Campeche was the peninsula's only port. Local legend insists that the art-nouveau staircase with Carrara marble steps and iron balustrade, built and delivered in one piece from Italy, was too big and had to be shipped back and redone. These days the mansion is filled with government offices—you'll have to stretch your imagination a bit to picture how it once was. ✉ *Calle 10 No. 584, between Calles 51 and 53, Centro* ☎ *981/816–7419* 🖅 *Free* ◉ *Weekdays 9–2:30.*

Mercado Municipal. The city's heart is this municipal market, where locals shop for seafood, produce, and housewares in a newly refurbished setting. The clothing section has some nice, inexpensive embroidered and beaded pieces among the jeans and T-shirts. Next to the market is a small yellow bridge aptly named **Puente de los Perros**—where four white plaster dogs guard the area. ⊠ *Av. Baluartes Este and Calle 53, Centro* ⊙ *Daily dawn–dusk.*

FAMILY   **Reducto de San José el Alto.** This lofty redoubt, or stronghold, at the northwest end of town, is home to the **Museo de Armas y Barcos.** Displays in former soldiers' and watchmen's rooms focus on 18th-century weapons of siege and defense. You'll also see manuscripts, religious art, and ships in bottles. The view is terrific from the top of the ramparts, which were once used to spot invading ships. The "Guapo" tram ($7) makes the trip here daily at 9 am and 5 pm, departing from the east side of the main plaza. Visitors get about 10 minutes to admire the view before returning to the main plaza. ⊠ *Av. Escénica s/n, north of downtown, Cerro de Bellavista* ☎ *981/816–2460* ⛃ *$3* ⊙ *Tues.–Sun. 9:30–5:30.*

WHERE TO EAT

$ ✕ **Casa Vieja.** Whether you're having a meal or an evening cocktail, try
MEXICAN   to snag a table on this eatery's outdoor balcony for a fabulous view over Campeche's main plaza. You wouldn't know it from the tiny entrance on the main plaza, but the interior is large and inviting, and the brightly painted walls are crammed with eclectic art. The menu displays a rich sampling of Mexican dishes including coconut shrimp; chicken fajitas; *cochinita pibil* (a slow-roasted pork dish); and *pan de cazón* (shreaded fish with black beans and tortillas). In addition to pastas, salads, and regional food, you'll find a good selection of aperitifs and digestifs. The view (not the service) is the main draw. To get here, look for the narrow stairway on the plaza's east side. They're open from 8 am until midnight. Ⓢ *Average main: $13* ⊠ *Calle 10 No. 319 Altos, between Calles 57 and 55, Centro* ☎ *981/805–0021* ⊕ *www.casaviejacampeche. blogspot.com* ▬ *No credit cards.*

$ ✕ **Cenaduría Portales.** Campechano families come here to enjoy a light
MEXICAN   supper, perhaps a delicious sandwich *claveteado* of honey-and-clove-spiked ham, along with a typical drink such as the delicious *agua de chaya,* a mixture of pineapple water and chaya (a leafy vegetable similar to spinach). On weekends, try the *tamal torteado,* a tamale with beans, tomato sauce, turkey, and pork, wrapped in banana leaves—it's not listed on the menu but is available if you ask. Although the place opens at 6 pm, most people come between 8 and midnight. Mark your choices on the paper menu: for tacos, "m" means *maíz,* or corn; for tortillas, "h" stands for *harina,* or flour. The dining area is a wide colonial veranda with marble flooring and tables decked out in plastic tablecloths. There's no booze, but a couple of doors down there's a beer stall called Cervefrío that's open until around 9 pm. Ⓢ *Average main: $7* ⊠ *Calle 10 No. 86, at Portales San Francisco, 8 blocks northeast of Plaza Principal, San Francisco* ☎ *981/811–1491* ⊙ *No lunch.*

$ ✕ **Chocol Ha.** Follow your nose to this chocolate café, where the aro-
BAKERY   mas of French pastries and rich cocoa waft into the narrow streets of

Campeche. Tucked inside this stone-walled colonial building are small wooden tables and a collection of antiques, like a vintage cash register still used for store transactions. Drink recipes originated from the owner's research into Mayan traditions and her time spent with local families. Prepared with the purest form of organic cocoa, chocolate drinks are infused with such herbs as mint and chilies. Nonchocolate lovers can enjoy all-natural fruit juices made with jicama and piña. The crepes and cookies make nice accompaniments, and there is also a small gift shop selling locally made products and blocks of dark chocolate. $ *Average main: $3* ⊠ *Calle 59 No. 3, between Calles 12 and 14, Centro Historico* ☎ *981/811–7893* ◎ *No lunch. Closed Sun.*

$$
SEAFOOD
Fodor'sChoice
★

✕ **La Pigua.** This is the town's hands-down lunch favorite. The seafood is delicious and the setting is unusual: glass walls replicate an oblong Mayan house, incorporating the profusion of plants outside as a design element. As the sun goes down, candles adorn the white-linen tablecloths, and soft blue lighting illuminates the outside atrium. A truly ambitious meal might start with a plate of calamari, stone-crab claws, or *camarones al coco* (coconut-encrusted shrimp), followed by fresh robalo fish topped with puréed cilantro, parsley, orange, and olive oil. For dessert, the classic choice is *ate,* slabs of super-condensed mango, sweet potato, or other fruit or vegetable jelly served with tangy Gouda cheese. Larger groups can request one of the private dining rooms at the front of the restaurant. $ *Average main: $10* ⊠ *Av. Miguel Alemán 179A, Col. San Martin* ☎ *981/811–3365* ⊕ *www.lapigua.com.mx* ◎ *Sun.–Tues. noon–6, Wed.–Sat. noon–10.*

$
MEXICAN

✕ **Luz de Luna.** This small family-run restaurant is tucked inside an old colonial building brightly decorated with Mexican crafts and tabletops carved with scenes of pueblos. If you have trouble selecting from the enormous menu, just look at the top dishes photographed within its pages. Since most of the customers are tourists, you'll find familiar favorites like burritos, pasta, sandwiches, and fajitas. Grilled fish and steak are served with rice and shredded lettuce, as are the rolled tacos and enchiladas topped with red or green chili sauce. There are only five tables, but somehow this place can seem overwhelmingly busy on a packed night. Early risers might want to stop by for one of their breakfast crepes or French toast. Take note, this restaurant does not serve alcohol. $ *Average main: $9* ⊠ *Calle 59 No. 6, between 10 and 12, Centro Historico* ☎ *981/134–7158* ◎ *Closed Sun.*

$$
MEXICAN

✕ **Marganzo.** This is a local favorite and a great place to stop in for breakfast if you want to get an early start sightseeing (they are open 7 am–11 pm). Marganzo specializes in traditional Yucatecan dishes like *panuchos* (fried masa cakes stuffed with beans and piled high with shredded meat, lettuce, sour onions, and other toppings). Other signature dishes here include *queso relleno* (Dutch cheese stuffed with minced pork and beef), *chile mestizo* (poblano pepper stuffed with shredded meat), and beet-root carpaccio topped with goat cheese and toasted nuts. If you aren't sure what to order, ask to see their album menu of top dishes photographed and captioned in several languages. The waitresses, dressed in colorful skirts from the region, are very kind about explaining regional dishes to visitors. Note that you can try plain *agua*

6

de chaya here—in other restaurants the chaya-flavored water is often sweetened with pineapple. The lunch and dinner menus also offer good seafood options (and are finished off with a complimentary tamarind margarita). A guitar trio performs Tuesday through Sunday from 8 to 10:30 pm. [$] *Average main: $14* ✉ *Calle 8, No. 267, between Calles 57 and 59, Col. Centro* ☎ *981/811–3898* 🌐 *www.marganzo.com.*

$ ECLECTIC 🍴 **Solé.** This modern eatery on the Malecón is one of the most popular dining spots in town. Take a seat inside or grab a table on the patio overlooking the busy boulevard. The "wine wall" displays an extensive collection of boutique blends from Chile, Spain, and Argentina. Only the best cuts are served here, like Kobe beef hamburgers and tuna steak tacos. Sample their fondue and homemade pastas, including ravioli caprese with sundried tomatoes or spaghetti with shrimp. Despite the formal setting, this place is surprisingly easy on the wallet. If you're looking for some entertainment, head behind the restaurant to their attached karaoke bar. [$] *Average main: $9* ✉ *Calle 10 No. 400, at Victoria and Abasolo on the Malecón, Malecon* ☎ *981/881–5337* 🕓 *No lunch.*

WHERE TO STAY

For expanded reviews, facilities, and current deals, visit Fodors.com.

$$$$ HOTEL Fodor's Choice ★ 🏨 **Casa Don Gustavo.** This former 18th-century mansion is one of the historic masterpieces of Campeche. **Pros:** lovely restaurant; impeccable rooms; colonial touches. **Cons:** no children under 8 years of age; no spa services; small pool. [$] *Rooms from: $320* ✉ *Calle 59 No. 4, between Calles 10 and 8, Centro* ☎ *981/816–8090* 🌐 *www.casadongustavo.com* 🛏 *10 suites* 🍽 *No meals.*

$$$$ HOTEL 🏨 **Hacienda Puerta Campeche.** The 17th-century mansions that span nearly an entire city block were reconfigured to create this lovely Starwood property just across from the Puerta de Tierra, the old city's historic landmark. **Pros:** stunning surroundings; calm atmosphere; excellent restaurant. **Cons:** expensive; mosquitoes in common areas; not really a hacienda; shaded pool; lukewarm showers. [$] *Rooms from: $570* ✉ *Calle 59 No. 71, between Calles 6 and 18, Centro* ☎ *981/816–7508, 888/625–5144 in U.S. and Canada* 🌐 *www.thehaciendas.com* 🛏 *10 rooms, 5 suites* 🍽 *No meals.*

$$ HOTEL 🏨 **Hotel Castelmar.** This renovated hotel in the heart of the downtown area is an elegant and comfortable place to relax and enjoy Campeche. **Pros:** great downtown location; pretty building and rooms. **Cons:** street noise at night can be a problem; rooms vary; small bathrooms. [$] *Rooms from: $150* ✉ *Calle 61, between Calles 8 and 10, Centro* ☎ *981/811–1205* 🌐 *www.castelmarhotel.com* 🛏 *23 rooms, 3 suites* 🍽 *No meals.*

$$ HOTEL 🏨 **Hotel Francis Drake.** This small, yellow hotel sits right in the center of town and is one of the more affordable options if you can deal with such issues as street noise, tiny bathrooms, cold-water showers, and a weak Wi-Fi signal. **Pros:** helpful staff; good location; black-out curtains; breakfast included. **Cons:** windows in some rooms open above garage and exhaust enters the room; small bathrooms; traffic noise can be a problem at night; some rooms smell of strong cleaning products; cold-water showers. [$] *Rooms from: $90* ✉ *Calle 12 No. 207, between*

Calles 63 and 65, Centro ☎ *981/811–5626, 981/811–5627* 🌐 *www.hotelfrancisdrake.com* 🛏 *12 rooms, 12 suites* 🍴 *Breakfast.*

$$$ HOTEL 🏨 **Hotel Plaza Campeche.** Located in the historic center across from Plaza Street. **Pros:** designated parking area; spacious rooms; good location. **Cons:** small pool; no children under 13; street noise; rooms are slightly gaudy. [$] *Rooms from: $150* ✉ *Calle 10 and Circuito Baluartes, between 49-B and 49-C, Centro* ☎ *981/811–9900* 🌐 *www.hotelplazacampeche.com* 🛏 *65 rooms, 16 suites* 🍴 *No meals.*

NIGHTLIFE

In December, concerts and other cultural events take place as part of the Festival del Centro Histórico.

On Friday and Saturday nights there's lounge music at the Hacienda Puerta Campeche, and it's one of the nicest places in town to have a drink.

There are a few restaurant bars along the malecón. Locals like to show up around 10 pm to enjoy the cool evening air.

The Garage. Located in the back alley behind Restaurant Solé, this former garage comes alive with Karaoke music starting at 10 pm every Wednesday, Friday, and Saturday. The red leather chairs and disco ball add a '70s touch. ✉ *Calle 10 No. 400, at Victoria and Abasolo, Malecon* ☎ *981/811–5337* 🕐 *Closed Sun.–Tues.*

SHOPPING

Bazar Artesanal. This government-run bazaar offers a wide range of local crafts, including some items that are hard to come by, like bull horns carved into the shape of mirror frames, necklaces, and earrings, employing a dying artistic technique that only a small number of families in Campeche State still know. All the prices are fixed, so there's no need to bargain. ✉ *Plaza Ah Kim Pech, Col. Centro.*

SPORTS AND THE OUTDOORS

Fishing and bird-watching are popular throughout the state of Campeche.

Campeche Tarpon. Alejandro, and other local fishermen from Campeche Tarpon, can arrange fly-fishing excursions to nearby mangroves, flats, creeks, and lagoons. ☎ *981/120–4708, 888/777–5060 in U.S.* 🌐 *www.campechetarpon.com.*

Fernando Sansores. Contact Fernando Sansores at the Snook Inn to arrange area sportfishing or wildlife photo excursions. ✉ *Calle 30 No. 1, Centro, Champotón* ☎ *982/828–0018.*

Tarpon Town. This company offers the city's only fully licensed fishing tours, and they're experts in tailoring fishing trips to individual needs. ✉ *Marina Bahía Azul s/n* ☎ *1981/133–2135 cell* 🌐 *www.tarpontown.com.*

EDZNÁ

61 km (37 miles) southeast of Campeche City.

GETTING HERE AND AROUND
From Campeche, take Carretera 261 heading east toward Holpechén. The turnoff for Edzná is clearly marked about 55 km (34 miles) southeast of Campeche.

EXPLORING

Fodor's Choice ★ **Edzná.** A leaf-strewn nature trail winds slowly toward the ancient heart of Edzná. Although only 55 km (34 miles)—less than an hour's drive—southeast of Campeche City, the site sees few tour groups. The scarcity of camera-carrying humans intensifies the feeling of communion with nature, and with the Maya who built this once-flourishing commercial and ceremonial city.

Despite being refreshingly underappreciated by 21st-century travelers, Edzná is considered by archaeologists to be one of the peninsula's most important ruins. A major metropolis in its day, it was at a crossroads of sorts between cities in modern-day Guatemala, and Chiapas and Yucatán states, and this "out-of-state" influence can be appreciated in its mélange of architectural elements. Roof combs and corbeled arches are reminiscent of those at Yaxchilán and Palenque, in Chiapas; giant stone masks are characteristic of the Petén-style architecture of southern Campeche and northern Guatemala.

Edzná began as a humble agricultural settlement around 300 BC, reaching its pinnacle in the late classic period, between AD 600 and 900, and gradually waning in importance until being all but abandoned in the early 15th century. Today soft breezes blow through groves of slender trees where brilliant orange and black birds spring from branch to branch, gathering seeds. Clouds scuttle across a blue backdrop, perfectly framing the mossy, multistepped remains of once-great structures.

A guide can point out features often missed by the untrained eye, like the remains of arrow-straight sacbés. These raised roads in their day connected one important ceremonial building within the city to the next, and also connected Edzná to trading partners throughout the peninsula.

Edzná is one of the area's most important ruins. Here you'll see a smorgasbord of Mayan architectural styles. Roof combs and corbeled arches remind one of the early classical period and the giant stone masks are taken straight out of textbooks from the preclassical period.

The best place to survey the site is from 102-foot-tall **Pirámide de los Cinco Pisos,** built on the raised platform of the **Gran Acrópolis** (Great Acropolis). This five-story pyramid consists of five levels, terminating in a tiny temple crowned by a roof comb. Hieroglyphs were carved into the vertical faces of the 15 steps between each level, and some were recemented in place by archaeologists, although not necessarily in the correct order. On these stones, as well as on stelae throughout the site, you can see faint depictions of the opulent attire once worn by the Maya ruling class—quetzal feathers, jade pectorals, and jaguar-skin skirts.

DID YOU KNOW?

Edzná is one of the area's most important ruins. Here you'll see a smorgasbord of Mayan architectural styles. Roof combs and corbeled arches remind one of the early classical period and the giant stone masks are taken straight out of textbooks from the preclassical period.

In 1992 Campeche archaeologist Florentino García Cruz discovered that the Pirámide de los Cinco Pisos was constructed so that on certain dates the setting sun would illuminate the mask of the creator-god, Itzámná, inside one of the pyramid's rooms. This happens annually on May 1, 2, and 3, the beginning of the planting season for the Maya—then and now. It also occurs on August 7, 8, and 9, the days of harvesting and giving thanks. On the pyramid's fifth level, the last to be built, are the ruins of three temples and a ritual steam bath.

West of the Great Acropolis, the Puuc-style **Plataforma de los Cuchillos** (Platform of the Knives) was so named by a 1970 archaeological exploration that found a number of flint knives inside. To the south, four buildings surround a smaller structure called the **Pequeña Acrópolis.** Twin sun-god masks with huge protruding eyes, sharply filed teeth, and oversize tongues flank the **Templo de los Mascarones** (Temple of the Masks, or Building 414), adjacent to the Small Acropolis. The mask at bottom left (east) represents the rising sun, whereas the one on the right represents the setting sun.

If you're not driving, consider taking one of the inexpensive day trips offered by tour operators in Campeche. This is far easier than trying to get to Edzná by municipal buses. ✉ *Carretera 188, 18 km (11 miles) southeast of Cayal, via Carretera 261 east from Campeche City* 🎫 *$4* 🕓 *Daily 8–5; light show at 7 pm.*

WHERE TO STAY

For expanded reviews, facilities, and current deals, visit Fodors.com.

$$$$ HOTEL Fodor's Choice ★ 🏨 **Hacienda Uayamón.** Abandoned in 1913, this former hacienda was resurrected nearly a century later and transformed into a luxury hotel with an elegant restaurant. **Pros:** stunning grounds; beautiful, spacious rooms; bikes for use; bird-watching tours available. **Cons:** expensive; very difficult to find; weak Wi-Fi signal. [$] *Rooms from: $570* ✉ *Carretera Campeche-ZA Edzná, 20 km (12½ miles) northwest of Edzná* ☎ *981/813–0530, 888/625–5144 in U.S. and Canada* 🌐 *www.thehaciendas.com* 🛏 *10 suites, 2 deluxe suites* 🍴 *No meals.*

SANTA ROSA XTAMPAK

107 km (64 miles) from Campeche City, entrance at Carretera 261, Km 79. Travel 30 km (19 miles) down signed side road.

Santa Rosa Xtampak. A fabulous example of the zoomorphic architectural element of Chenes architecture, Xtampak's **Casa de la Boca del Serpiente** (House of the Serpent's Mouth) has a perfectly preserved and integrated zoomorphic entrance. Here the mouth of the creator-god Itzámná stretches wide to reveal a perfectly proportioned inner chamber. The importance of this city during the classic period is shown by the large number of public buildings and ceremonial plazas here. Archaeologists believe there are around 100 structures, although only 12 have been cleared. The most exciting find was the colossal **Palacio** in the western plaza. Inside, two inner staircases run the length of the structure, leading to different levels and ending in subterranean chambers. This combination is extremely rare in Mayan temples.

✉ *Dzibilchaltún–Chencho Rd., east of Hopelchén (watch for sign)* ✉ *$3* ☉ *Daily 8–5.*

HOCHOB

109 km (68 miles) southwest of Campeche City, 55 km (34 miles) south of Hopelchén, 15 km (9 miles) west of Dzibilnocac.

GETTING HERE AND AROUND

From Campeche, take Carretera 180 toward Holpechén and continue until you reach Federal Highway 261. Follow the road approximately 40 km (25 miles) toward Dzibalchen. Take the dirt road toward the town of Chencoh until you reach the site for Hochob, 14 km (8½ miles) ahead.

EXPLORING

Hochob. The small Mayan ruin of Hochob is an excellent example of the Chenes architectural style, which flowered from about AD 100 to 1000. Most ruins in this area (central and southeastern Campeche) were built on the highest possible elevation to prevent flooding during the rainy season, and Hochob is no exception. It rests high on a hill overlooking the surrounding valleys. Another indication that these are Chenes ruins is the number of *chultunes*, or cisterns, in the area.

Since work began at Hochob in the early 1980s, four temples and palaces have been excavated at the site, including two that have been fully restored. Intricate and perfectly preserved geometric designs cover the temple known as **Estructura II**, which are typical of the Chenes style.

The doorway represents the open mouth of Itzámná, the creator god, and above it the eyes bulge and fangs are bared on either side of the base. It takes a bit of imagination to see the structure as a mask, as color no doubt originally enhanced the effect. Squinting helps a bit: the figure's "eyes" are said to be squinting as well. But anyone can appreciate the intense geometric relief carvings decorating the facades, including long cascades of Chaac rain-god masks along the sides. Evidence of roof combs can be seen at the top of the building. Ask the guard to show you the series of natural and man-made chultunes that extend back into the forest. ✉ *Dzibalchén–Chencho Rd., southwest of Hopelchén on Hwy. 261* ✉ *$3* ☉ *Daily 8–5.*

CARRETERA 186 INTO CAMPECHE

Xpujil, Chicanná, Calakmul . . . exotic, far-flung-sounding names dot the map along this stretch of jungle territory. These are places where the creatures of the forest outnumber the tourists: in Calakmul, four- and five-story ceiba trees sway as families of spider monkeys swing through the canopy; in Xpujil, brilliant blue motmots fly from tree to tree in long, swoopy arcs.

The vestiges of at least 10 little-known Mayan cities lie hidden off Carretera 186 between Escárcega and Chetumal. You can see Xpujil, Becán, Hormiguero, and Chicanná in one rather rushed day by starting out early from Chetumal, Quintana Roo, and spending the night in Xpujil.

If you plan to visit Calakmul, spend the first night at Xpujil, arriving at Calakmul as soon as the site opens the next day. That provides the best chance to see armadillos, wild turkeys, families of howler and spider monkeys, and other wildlife.

GETTING HERE AND AROUND

From Chetumal on the coast of Quintana Roo, it's about 125 km (78 miles) to Xpujil. Carretera 186 is a two-lane highway in reasonably good condition. ■TIP→ Most hotels in the Xpujil area close around 11 pm. So, regardless of whether you have a reservation, you may find yourself locked out of all but the seediest lodgings if you show up late.

TOURS

Río Bec Dreams. Hotel owners Rick Bertram and Diane Lalonde, and the knowlegable archaeologist Dan Griffin, offer tours through their hotel Río Bec Dreams (⇨ see *Where to Stay below*). They're native English speakers and enthusiastic guides, and will give you a comprehensive trip around the local archaeological sites. They charge between $30 and $150, depending on the site. Be sure to book ahead, (in person or by email) since they juggle duties at their hotel with their tour schedules. ✉ *Carretera 186, Escarcega-Chetumal, Km 142* ✍ *info@riobecdreams. com* ⊕ *www.riobecdreams.com.*

Servidores Turísticos Calakmul. There aren't many good tour guides in the region. Some of the most experienced and enthusiastic are part of a community organization called Servidores Turísticos Calakmul. There are bicycle tours, horseback tours, and tours where spotting plants and animals are the main focus. All tours can be customized to meet your interests, including trips that span across several days with overnight stays in the jungle. If your Spanish is shaky, ask for Leticia, who speaks basic English and has years of experience as a guide. ✉ *Av. Calakmul, between Okolwitz and Payan, Xpujil* ☎ *983/871–6064* ⊕ *www. ecoturismocalakmul.com.*

XPUJIL

Carretera 186, Km 150, 300 km (186 miles) southeast of Campeche, 130 km (81 miles) south of Dzibilnocac, 125 km (78 miles) west of Chetumal.

GETTING HERE AND AROUND

From Chetumal, it's about 125 km (78 miles) to Xpujil. Carretera 186 is a two-lane highway in good condition, although it's not well lit so avoid driving at night. The ruins are just west of the town of Xpujil on Carretera 186. Interjet now offers flights to Chetumal from New York; Las Vegas; Orange County, California; and Miami.

Interjet Airlines ✉ *Chetumal International Airport, Prolong Av. Efrain Aguilar, Chetumal, Quintana Roo* ☎ *866/285–9525 toll-free from U.S., 800/011–2345 toll-free from Mexico* ⊕ *www.interjet.com.mx.*

EXPLORING

Xpujil. Xpujil (meaning "cat's tail," and pronounced ish-*poo*-hil) gets its name from the reedy plant that grows in the area. Elaborately carved facades and doorways in the shape of monsters' mouths reflect the Chenes style, while adjacent pyramid towers connected by a long platform show the influence of Río Bec architects.

Some of the buildings have lost a lot of their stones, making them resemble "day after" sand castles. In **Edificio I,** three towers—believed to have been used by priests and royalty—were once crowned by false temples, and at the front of each are the remains of four vaulted rooms, each oriented toward one of the compass points. On the back side of the central tower is a huge mask of the rain god Chaac. Quite a few other building groups amid the forests of gum trees and *palo mulato* (so called for its bark with both dark and light patches) have yet to be excavated. ✉ *West of town of Xpujil on Hwy. 186* 🎫 *$4* 🕒 *Daily 8–5.*

WHERE TO STAY

For expanded reviews, facilities, and current deals, visit Fodors.com.

$$ HOTEL 🏨 **Chicanná Ecovillage Resort.** Rooms in this jungle lodge are in two-story stucco duplexes with thatched roofs and are surrounded by lush gardens and tropical plants. **Pros:** convenient to several ruins in the Río Bec region; spacious rooms; pleasant balconies; eco-friendly design. **Cons:** restaurant food is just OK; unhelpful staff; Wi-Fi in reception area only; no a/c. [$] *Rooms from: $150* ✉ *Carretera 186, Km 144, 9 km (5½ miles) west of village of Xpujil* ☎ *01800/560–8612, 981/819–3298* 🌐 *www.chicannaecovillageresort.com* 🔑 *42 rooms* 🍴 *Breakfast.*

$ B&B/INN 🏨 **Río Bec Dreams.** From the moment you arrive at this hotel in the middle of the jungle, you'll be invited to pull up a chair at the bar, flip through books and magazines about the area, and swap stories with the owners and guests about your day and your interest in local ruins. **Pros:** laundry service; wonderful restaurant; owners are friendly, attentive, and excellent guides. **Cons:** some rooms lack private bathrooms; no a/c; reservations by email only. [$] *Rooms from: $70* ✉ *Carretera 186, Escarcega–Chetumal, Km 142* 🌐 *www.riobecdreams.com* 🔑 *4 jungalows, 3 cabanas* 💳 *No credit cards* 🍴 *No meals.*

BECÁN

Carretera 186, Km 145, 264 km (164 miles) southwest of Campeche City, 7 km (4½ miles) west of Xpujil.

Becán. An interesting feature of this once-important city is its defensive moat—unusual among ancient Mayan cities—though barely evident today. The seven ruined gateways, which once permitted the only entrances to the guarded city, may have clued archaeologists to its presence. Becán (usually translated as "canyon of water," referring to the moat) is thought to have been an important city within the Río Bec group, which once encompassed Xpujil, Chicanná, and Río Bec. Most of the site's many buildings date from between about AD 600 and 1000, but because there are no traditionally inscribed stelae listing details of royal births, deaths, battles, and ascendancies to the throne, archaeologists have had to do a lot of guessing about what transpired here.

You can climb several of the structures to get a view of the area, and even spot some of Xpuhil's towers above the treetops. Duck into **Estructura VIII,** where underground passages lead to small subterranean rooms and to a concealed staircase that reaches the top of the temple. One of several buildings surrounding a central plaza, Estructura VIII has lateral towers and a giant zoomorphic mask on its central facade. The building was used for religious rituals, including bloodletting rites during which the elite pierced earlobes and genitals, among other sensitive body parts, in order to present their blood to the gods. ⊠ *Off Hwy. 186 just west of Xpuhil* ⊠ *$4* ⊙ *Daily 8–5.*

CHICANNÁ

Carretera 186, Km 141, 274 km (174 miles) southwest of Campeche City, 3 km (2 miles) east of Becán.

Chicanná. Thought to have been a satellite community of the larger, more commercial city of Becán, Chicanná ("house of the serpent's mouth") was also in its prime during the late classic period. Of the four buildings surrounding the main plaza, **Estructura II,** on the east side, is the most impressive. On its intricate facade are well-preserved sculpted reliefs and faces with long twisted noses—symbols of Chaac. In typical Chenes style, the doorway represents the mouth of the creator-god Itzámná. Surrounding the opening are large crossed eyes, fierce fangs, and earrings to complete the stone mask, which still bears traces of blue and red pigments. ⊠ *Carretera 186, 5 miles west of Xpujil* ⊠ *$4* ⊙ *Daily 8–5.*

HORMIGUERO

272 km (169 miles) southwest of Campeche City, 14 km (9 miles) southeast of Xpujil.

Hormiguero. Bumping down the badly potholed, 8-km (5-mile) road leading to this site may give you an appreciation for the explorers who first found and excavated it in 1933. Hidden throughout the forest are at least five magnificent temples, two of which have been excavated to reveal ornate facades covered with zoomorphic figures whose mouths are the doorways. The buildings here were constructed roughly between 400 BC and AD 1100 in the Río Bec style, with rounded lateral towers and ornamental stairways, the latter built to give an illusion of height, which they do wonderfully. The facade of **Estructura II,** the largest structure on the site, is intricately carved and well preserved. **Estructura V** has some admirable Chaac masks arranged in a cascade atop a pyramid. Nearby is a perfectly round *chultun* (water-storage tank), and seemingly emerging from the earth, the eerily etched designs of a still-unexcavated structure.

Hormiguero is Spanish for "anthill," referring both to the looters' tunnels that honeycombed the ruins when archaeologists discovered them and to the number of large anthills in the area. Among the other fauna sharing the jungle here are several species of poisonous snakes. Although these mainly come out at night, you should always be careful of where you walk and, when climbing, where you put your hands. ⊹ *Hwy. 186 from Chetumal or Escarcega to Hwy. 180 toward town of Champoton, about 20 km* ⊠ *Free* ⊙ *Daily 8–5.*

RESERVA DE LA BIOSFERA CALAKMUL

Entrance at Carretera 186, Km 65, 365 km (227 miles) southwest of Campeche City, 107 km (66 miles) southwest of Xpujil.

Fodor's Choice   **Reserva de la Biosfera Calakmul.** Vast, lovely, green, and mysterious Calakmul may not stay a secret for much longer. You won't see any tour buses ★ in the parking lot, and on an average day, site employees and laborers still outnumber the visitors traipsing along the moss-tinged dirt paths that snake through the jungle. But things are changing. The nearest town, Xpujil, already has Internet service and a handful of restaurants and hotels. So if you're looking for untrammeled Mexican wilderness, don't put off a trip here any longer.

Calakmul encompasses some 1.8 million acres of land along the Guatemalan border. It was declared a protected biosphere reserve in 1989, and is the largest reserve of its kind in Mexico (Sian Ka'an in Quintana Roo is second with 1.3 million acres). All kinds of flora and fauna thrive here, including wildcats, spider and howler monkeys, hundreds of exotic birds, orchid varieties, butterflies, and reptiles. (There's no shortage of insects, either, so don't forget the bug repellent.)

The centerpiece of the reserve, however, is the ruined Mayan city that shares the name Calakmul (which translates as "two adjacent towers"). Although Carretera 186 runs right through the reserve, you'll need to drive about 1½ hours from the highway along a 60-km (37-mile) authorized entry road to get to the site. Structures here are still being excavated, but fortunately the dense surrounding jungle is being left in its natural state: as you walk among the ruined palaces and tumbled stelae, you'll hear the guttural calls of howler monkeys, and see massive strangler figs enveloping equally massive trees.

This magnificent city, now in ruins, wasn't always so lonely. Anthropologists estimate that in its heyday (between AD 542 and 695) the region was inhabited by more than 50,000 Maya. Archaeologists have mapped more than 6,800 structures and found 180 stelae. Perhaps the most monumental discovery thus far has been that of the remains of royal ruler Gran Garra de Jaguar (Great Jaguar Claw). His body was wrapped (but not embalmed) in a shroud of palm leaf, lime, and fine cloth, and locked away in a royal tomb in about AD 700. In an adjacent crypt, a young woman wearing fine jewelry and an elaborately painted wood-and-stucco headdress was entombed together with a child. Their identity remains a mystery. The artifacts and skeletal remains have been moved to the Museo de la Arqueología Maya in Campeche City.

Unlike those at Chichén Itzá (which also peaked in importance during the classic era) the pyramids and palaces throughout Calakmul can be climbed to achieve soaring vistas. You can choose to explore the site along a short, medium, or long path, but all three eventually lead to magnificent **Templo II** and **Templo VII**—twin pyramids separated by an immense plaza. Templo II, at 175 feet, is the peninsula's tallest Mayan building. Scientists are studying a huge, intact stucco frieze deep within this structure, so it's not currently open to visitors.

Arrangements for an English-speaking Calakmul tour guide should be made beforehand with Servidores Turísticos Calakmul, Río Bec Dreams, or through Chicanná Ecovillage near Xpujil. Camping is permitted at Km 6 with the Servidores Turísticos Calakmul after paying caretakers at the entrance gate. You can set up camp near the second checkpoint. Even if day-tripping, though, you'll need to bring your own food and water, as the only place to buy a snack is near the second entrance inside the museum. ■TIP→ You'll have to pay three entrance fees; $3 per person and $5 per vehicle to the owners of the first 20 km

6

(12.4 miles), which is private land, $5 per person to enter the reserve at the second gate located at the museum, and another $5 per person at the entrance to the ruins. ✉ *98 km (60 miles) east of Escárcega to turnoff at Cohuás, then 60 km (37 miles) south to Calakmul* 🎫 *$5 per car (more for larger vehicles), plus $13 per person* 🕓 *Daily 8–5; museum open 7–3.*

WHERE TO STAY

For expanded reviews, facilities, and current deals, visit Fodors.com.

$$$ HOTEL 🏨 **Hotel Puerta Calakmul.** This ecological retreat, just outside the entrance to Reserva de la Biosfera Calakmul—Mexico's largest tropical forest reserve—has gravel pathways that wind through the jungle to 15 private cabanas, each rustic in design with palapa roofs, tree stump nightstands, and parchment paper lampshades inlaid with leaves and bits of bark. **Pros:** closest accommodations to Biosfera Calakmul; peaceful setting; guided tours available. **Cons:** Wi-Fi in restaurant only; pricey for what you get; back cabanas get some freeway noise; credit cards not accepted. [$] *Rooms from: $180* ✉ *Km 98 Carretera Chetumal–Escarcega, Calakmul* ☎ *998/892–2624* 🌐 *www.puertacalakmul.mx* 🛏 *15 cabanas* 💳 *No credit cards* 🍴 *No meals.*

SPANISH VOCABULARY

	ENGLISH	SPANISH	PRONUNCIATION
BASICS			
	Yes/no	Sí/no	see/no
	Please	Por favor	pore fah-**vore**
	May I?	¿Me permite?	may pair-**mee**-tay
	Thank you (very much)	(Muchas) gracias	(**moo**-chas) **grah**-see-as
	You're welcome	De nada	day **nah**-dah
	Excuse me	Con permiso	con pair-**mee**-so
	Pardon me	¿Perdón?	pair-**dohn**
	Could you tell me?	¿Podría decirme?	po-dree-ah deh-**seer**-meh
	I'm sorry	Lo siento	lo see-**en**-toh
	Good morning!	¡Buenos días!	**bway**-nohs **dee**-ahs
	Good afternoon!	¡Buenas tardes!	**bway**-nahs **tar**-dess
	Good evening!	¡Buenas noches!	**bway**-nahs **no**-chess
	Good-bye!	¡Adiós!/¡Hasta luego!	ah-dee-**ohss**/**ah**-stah **lwe**-go
	Mr./Mrs.	Señor/Señora	sen-**yor**/sen-**yohr**-ah
	Miss	Señorita	sen-yo-**ree**-tah
	Pleased to meet you	Mucho gusto	**moo**-cho **goose**-toh
	How are you?	¿Cómo está usted?	**ko**-mo es-**tah** oo-**sted**
	Very well, thank you.	Muy bien, gracias.	**moo**-ee bee-**en**, **grah**-see-as
	And you?	¿Y usted?	ee oos-**ted**
	Hello (on the telephone)	Diga	**dee**-gah
NUMBERS			
	1	un, uno	oon, **oo**-no
	2	dos	dos
	3	tres	tress
	4	cuatro	**kwah**-tro
	5	cinco	**sink**-oh
	6	seis	saice

ENGLISH	SPANISH	PRONUNCIATION
7	siete	see-**et**-eh
8	ocho	**o**-cho
9	nueve	new-**eh**-vey
10	diez	dee-**es**
11	once	**ohn**-seh
12	doce	**doh**-seh
13	trece	**treh**-seh
14	catorce	ka-**tohr**-seh
15	quince	**keen**-seh
16	dieciséis	dee-**es**-ee-**saice**
17	diecisiete	dee-**es**-ee-see-**et**-eh
18	dieciocho	dee-**es**-ee-**o**-cho
19	diecinueve	**dee**-**es**-ee-new-**ev**-eh
20	veinte	**vain**-teh
21	veinte y uno/veintiuno	**vain**-te-**oo**-noh
30	treinta	**train**-tah
32	treinta y dos	train-tay-**dohs**
40	cuarenta	kwah-**ren**-tah
43	cuarenta y tres	kwah-**ren**-tay-**tress**
50	cincuenta	seen-**kwen**-tah
54	cincuenta y cuatro	seen-**kwen**-tay **kwah**-tro
60	sesenta	sess-**en**-tah
65	sesenta y cinco	sess-**en**-tay **seen**-ko
70	setenta	set-**en**-tah
76	setenta y seis	set-**en**-tay **saice**
80	ochenta	oh-**chen**-tah
87	ochenta y siete	oh-**chen**-tay see-**yet**-eh
90	noventa	no-**ven**-tah
98	noventa y ocho	no-**ven**-tah-**o**-choh
100	cien	see-**en**

ENGLISH	SPANISH	PRONUNCIATION
101	ciento uno	see-**en**-toh **oo**-noh
200	doscientos	doh-see-**en**-tohss
500	quinientos	keen-**yen**-tohss
700	setecientos	set-eh-see-**en**-tohss
900	novecientos	no-veh-see-**en**-tohss
1,000	mil	meel
2,000	dos mil	dohs meel
1,000,000	un millón	oon meel-**yohn**

COLORS

black	negro	**neh**-groh
blue	azul	ah-**sool**
brown	café	kah-**feh**
green	verde	**ver**-deh
orange	naranja	na-**rahn**-hah
pink	rosa	**ro**-sah
purple	morado	mo-**rah**-doh
red	rojo	**roh**-hoh
white	blanco	**blahn**-koh
yellow	amarillo	ah-mah-**ree**-yoh

DAYS OF THE WEEK

Sunday	domingo	doe-**meen**-goh
Monday	lunes	**loo**-ness
Tuesday	martes	**mahr**-tess
Wednesday	miércoles	me-**air**-koh-less
Thursday	jueves	hoo-**ev**-ess
Friday	viernes	vee-**air**-ness
Saturday	sábado	**sah**-bah-doh

MONTHS

January	enero	eh-**neh**-roh
February	febrero	feh-**breh**-roh

ENGLISH	SPANISH	PRONUNCIATION
March	marzo	**mahr**-soh
April	abril	ah-**breel**
May	mayo	**my**-oh
June	junio	**hoo**-nee-oh
July	julio	**hoo**-lee-yoh
August	agosto	ah-**ghost**-toh
September	septiembre	sep-tee-**em**-breh
October	octubre	oak-**too**-breh
November	noviembre	no-vee-**em**-breh
December	diciembre	dee-see-**em**-breh

USEFUL PHRASES

Do you speak English?	¿Habla usted inglés?	**ah**-blah oos-**ted** in-**glehs**
I don't speak Spanish	No hablo español	no **ah**-bloh es-pahn-**yol**
I don't understand (you)	No entiendo	no en-tee-**en**-doh
I understand (you)	Entiendo	en-tee-**en**-doh
I don't know	No sé	no seh
I am American/British	Soy americano (americana)/inglés(a)	soy ah-meh-ree- **kah**-no (ah-meh-ree- **kah**-nah)/ in-**glehs(ah)**
What's your name?	¿Cómo se llama usted?	koh-mo seh **yah**-mah oos-**ted**
My name is . . .	Me llamo . . .	may **yah**-moh
What time is it?	¿Qué hora es?	keh **o**-rah es
It is one, two, three . . . o'clock.	Es la una./Son las dos, tres . . .	es la **oo**-nah/sohnahs dohs, tress
Yes, please/ No, thank you	Sí, por favor/ No, gracias	**see** pohr fah-**vor**/ no **grah**-see-us
How?	¿Cómo?	**koh**-mo
When?	¿Cuándo?	**kwahn**-doh
This/Next week	Esta semana/ la semana que entra	**es**-teh seh-**mah**- nah/ lah seh-**mah**-nah keh **en**-trah

ENGLISH	SPANISH	PRONUNCIATION
This/Next month	Este mes/el próximo mes	**es**-teh mehs/el **proke**-see-mo mehs
This/Next year	Este año/el año que viene	**es**-teh **ahn**-yo/el **ahn**-yo keh vee-**yen**-ay
Yesterday/today/tomorrow	Ayer/hoy/mañana	ah-**yehr**/oy/mahn-**yah**-nah
This morning/afternoon	Esta mañana/tarde	**es**-tah mahn-**yah**- nah/**tar**-deh
Tonight	Esta noche	**es**-tah **no**-cheh
What?	¿Qué?	keh
What is it?	¿Qué es esto?	keh es **es**-toh
Why?	¿Por qué?	pore **keh**
Who?	¿Quién?	kee-**yen**
Where is . . . ?	¿Dónde está . . . ?	**dohn**-deh es-**tah**
the train station?	la estación del tren?	la es-tah-see-on del trehn
the subway station?	la estación del tren subterráneo?	la es-ta-see-**on** del trehn soob-teh-**rrahn**-eh-oh
the bus stop?	la parada del autobus?	la pah-**rah**-dah del ow-toh-**boos**
the post office?	la oficina de correos?	la oh-fee-**see**-nah deh koh-**rreh**-os
the bank?	el banco?	el **bahn**-koh
the hotel?	el hotel?	el oh-**tel**
the store?	la tienda?	la tee-**en**-dah
the cashier?	la caja?	la **kah**-hah
the museum?	el museo?	el moo-**seh**-oh
the hospital?	el hospital?	el ohss-pee-**tal**
the elevator?	el ascensor?	el ah-**sen**-sohr
the bathroom?	el baño?	el **bahn**-yoh
Here/there	Aquí/allá	ah-**key**/ah-**yah**
Open/closed	Abierto/cerrado	ah-bee-**er**-toh/ser-**ah**-doh
Left/right	Izquierda/derecha	iss-key-**er**-dah/dare-**eh**-chah

ENGLISH	SPANISH	PRONUNCIATION
Straight ahead	Derecho	dare-**eh**-choh
Is it near/far?	¿Está cerca/lejos?	es-**tah sehr**-kah/ **leh**-hoss
I'd like . . .	Quisiera . . .	kee-see-ehr-ah
a room	un cuarto/ una habitación	oon **kwahr**-toh/ **oo**-nah ah-bee-tah-see-**on**
the key	la llave	lah **yah**-veh
a newspaper	un periódico	oonpehr-ee-**oh**-dee-koh
a stamp	un sello de correo	oon **seh**-yo deh korr-ee-oh
I'd like to buy . . .	Quisiera comprar . . .	kee-see-**ehr**-ah kohm-**prahr**
cigarettes	cigarrillos	ce-ga-**ree**-yohs
matches	cerillos	ser-**ee**-ohs
a dictionary	un diccionario	oon deek-see-oh- **nah**-ree-oh
soap	jabón	hah-**bohn**
sunglasses	gafas de sol	**ga**-fahs deh sohl
suntan lotion	loción bronceadora	loh-see-**ohn** brohn-seh-ah-**do**-rah
a map	un mapa	oon **mah**-pah
a magazine	una revista	**oon**-ah reh-**veess**-tah
paper	papel	pah-**pel**
envelopes	sobres	**so**-brehs
a postcard	una tarjeta postal	**oon**-ah tar-**het**-ah post-**ahl**
How much is it?	¿Cuánto cuesta?	**kwahn**-toh **kwes**-tah
It's expensive/ cheap	Está caro/barato	es-**tah kah**-roh/ bah-**rah**-toh
A little/a lot	Un poquito/mucho	oon poh-**kee**-toh/ **moo**-choh
More/less	Más/menos	mahss/**men**-ohss
Enough/ too much/too little	Suficiente/ demasiado/muy poco	soo-fee-see-**en**-teh/ deh-mah-see-**ah**-doh/ **moo**-ee poh-koh

ENGLISH	SPANISH	PRONUNCIATION
Telephone	Teléfono	tel-**ef**-oh-no
Telegram	Telegrama	teh-leh-**grah**-mah
I am ill	Estoy enfermo(a)	es-**toy** en-**fehr**-moh(mah)
Please call a doctor	Por favor llame a un medico	pohr fah-**vor ya**-meh ah oon **med**-ee-koh

ON THE ROAD

Avenue	Avenida	ah-ven-**ee**-dah
Broad, tree-lined boulevard	Bulevar	boo-leh-**var**
Fertile plain	Vega	**veh**-gah
Highway	Carretera	car-reh-**ter**-ah
Mountain pass	Puerto	poo-**ehr**-toh
Street	Calle	**cah**-yeh
Waterfront promenade	Rambla	**rahm**-blah
Wharf	Embarcadero	em-bar-cah-**deh**-ro

IN TOWN

Cathedral	Catedral	cah-teh-**dral**
Church	Templo/Iglesia	**tem**-plo/ee-**glehs**- see-ah
City hall	Casa de gobierno	kah-sah deh go-bee-**ehr**-no
Door, gate	Puerta, portón	poo-**ehr**-tah, por-**ton**
Entrance/exit	Entrada/salida	en-**trah**-dah/ sah-**lee**- dah
Inn, rustic bar, or restaurant	Taverna	tah-**vehr**-nah
Main square	Plaza principal	plah-thah prin- see-**pahl**

DINING OUT

Can you recommend a good restaurant	¿Puede recomendarme un buen restaurante?	**pweh**-deh rreh-koh-mehn-**dahr**-me oon bwehn rrehs-tow-**rahn**-teh?
Where is it located?	¿Dónde está situado?	**dohn**-deh ehs-**tah** see-**twah**-doh?

ENGLISH	SPANISH	PRONUNCIATION
Do I need reservations?	¿Se necesita una reservación?	seh neh-**seh**-**see**-tah **oo**-nah rreh-sehr-bah-**syohn**?
I'd like to reserve a table . . .	Quisiera reservar una mesa . . .	kee-**syeh**-rah rreh-sehr-**bahr oo**-nah **meh**-sah . . .
for two people.	para dos personas.	**pah**-rah dohs pehr- **soh**-nahs
for this evening.	para esta noche.	**pah**-rah **ehs**-tah **noh**-cheh
for 8 pm	para las ocho de la noche.	**pah**-rah lahs **oh**-choh deh lah **noh**-cheh
A bottle of . . .	Una botella de . . .	**oo**-nah bo-**teh**-yah deh
A cup of . . .	Una taza de . . .	**oo**-nah **tah**-thah deh
A glass of . . .	Un vaso de . . .	oon **vah**-so deh
Ashtray	Un cenicero	oon sen-ee-**seh**-roh
Bill/check	La cuenta	lah **kwen**-tah
Bread	El pan	el pahn
Breakfast	El desayuno	el deh-sah-**yoon**-oh
Butter	La mantequilla	lah man-teh-**key**-yah
Cheers!	¡Salud!	sah-**lood**
Cocktail	Un aperitivo	oon ah-pehr-ee-**tee**-voh
Dinner	La cena	lah **seh**-nah
Dish	Un plato	oon **plah**-toh
Menu of the day	Menú del día	meh-**noo** del **dee**-ah
Enjoy!	¡Buen provecho!	bwehn pro-**veh**-cho
Fixed-price menu	Menú fijo o turistico	meh-**noo fee**-hoh oh too-**ree**-stee-coh
Fork	El tenedor	el ten-eh-**dor**
Is the tip	¿Está incluida la	es-**tah** in-cloo-**ee**-dah
included?	propina?	lah pro-**pee**-nah
Knife	El cuchillo	el koo-**chee**-yo
Large portion of savory snacks	Raciónes	rah-see-**oh**-nehs

ENGLISH	SPANISH	PRONUNCIATION
Lunch	La comida	lah koh-**mee**-dah
Menu	La carta, el menú	lah **cart**-ah, el meh-**noo**
Napkin	La servilleta	lah sehr-vee-**yet**-ah
Pepper	La pimienta	lah pee-me-**en**-tah
Please give me	Por favor déme	pore fah-**vor deh**-meh
Salt	La sal	lah sahl
Savory snacks	Tapas	**tah**-pahs
Spoon	Una cuchara	**oo**-nah koo-**chah**-rah
Sugar	El azúcar	el ah-**thu**-kar
Waiter!/Waitress!	¡Por favor Señor/ Señorita!	pohr fah-**vor** sen-**yor**/ sen-yor-**ee**-tah
Napkin	La servilleta	lah sehr-vee-**yet**-ah
Pepper	La pimienta	lah pee-me-**en**-tah
Please give me	Por favor déme	pore fah-**vor deh**-meh
Salt	La sal	lah sahl
Savory snacks	Tapas	**tah**-pahs
Spoon	Una cuchara	**oo**-nah koo-**chah**-rah
Sugar	El azúcar	el ah-**thu**-kar
Waiter!/Waitress!	¡Por favor Señor/ Señorita!	pohr fah-**vor** sen-**yor**/ sen-yor-**ee**-tah

TRAVEL SMART
CANCUN

GETTING HERE AND AROUND

■ AIR TRAVEL

Cancún is 4½ hours from New York and Chicago, 2½ hours from Miami, 4 hours from Los Angeles, and 3 hours from Dallas. Add another one to four hours if you change planes at one of the hub airports. Flights to Cozumel and Mérida are comparable in length, but are more likely to have a change along the way.

There are direct flights to Cancún from hub airports such as New York, Boston, Washington, D.C., Houston, Dallas, Miami, Chicago, Los Angeles, Orlando, Ft. Lauderdale, Charlotte, and Atlanta. From other cities, you must generally change planes. Some flights go to Mexico City, where you must pass through customs before transferring to a domestic flight to Cancún. This applies to air travel from both the United States and Canada, not to mention other countries. Charter flights, especially those leaving from Cancún, are notorious for last-minute changes. Be sure to ask for an updated telephone number from your charter company before you leave, so you can call to check for any changes in flight departures. Most recommend that you call within 48 hours of departure. This check-in also applies to commercial airlines, although their departure times are more regular. Their changes are usually due to weather conditions rather than to seat sales.

AIRLINE-SECURITY ISSUES

Transportation Security Administration. Transportation Security Administration has answers for almost every question that might arise. ☎ 866/289–9673 ⊕ www.tsa.gov.

AIRPORTS

Cancún Aeropuerto Internacional (CUN) is the area's major gateway, though some people now choose to fly directly to Cozumel (CZM). The inland Hector José Vavarrette Muñoz Airport (MID), in Mérida, is smaller but closer to the major Mayan ruins. Campeche and Chetumal

WORD OF MOUTH

"Arrival at Cancun [airport] is a zoo even to those of us seasoned in travelling to that area so I really think booking [an airport transfer] ahead of time will save you." — jette

have even smaller airports served primarily by domestic carriers. The ruins at Palenque and Chichén Itzá also have airstrips that handle small planes; there's an airport at Chichén (CZA), handling chartered flights, but most people fly into Cancún and travel to Chichén Itzá 1½ hours by bus or car.

In peak season, passenger waiting lines can be long and slow-moving; plan accordingly.

It's 20 to 30 minutes from the Hotel Zone to Cancún International or from downtown Mérida or Campeche to their airports. Allow 1½ hours from Playa del Carmen to the Cancún airport. The Cozumel airport is less than 10 minutes from downtown Cozumel.

Airport Information Contacts Aeropuerto Internacional de Mérida ⊠ *Carretera Mérida a Uman, Km 14.5, Mérida, Yucatán* ☎ *999/940–6090* ⊕ *www.asur.com. mx.* **Cancún Aeropuerto Internacional** ⊠ *Carretera Cancún-Chetumal, Km 22, Cancún* ☎ *998/848–7200* ⊕ *www.cancun-airport.com.* **Chetumal International Airport** ⊠ *Prolong Av. Efrain Aguila, Chetumal* ☎ *983/832–0898 General Administration for Civil Aviation.* **Cozumel Aeropuerto Internacional** ⊠ *Av. 65 and Blvd. Aeropuerto, Cozumel* ☎ *987/872–2081* ⊕ *www.asur.com.mx.*

GROUND TRANSPORTATION

As you exit the Cancún airport, transportation operators can be overwhelming as they eagerly wave signs and yell names to arriving passengers. If you're taking the bus, walk past the bar and toward the right where tickets are available from a small booth. There is a bus leaving every hour from Cancún Airport to downtown Cancún.

It's not uncommon to be told that you just missed the last bus, taxi, or van to your destination. This is actually a ploy to get you to use the transportation company that is "assisting" you. Ask around if you're not entirely sure. Always arrive with small bills for taxi or bus fare, otherwise you're liable to get ripped off. Check the identification of transportation operators and don't allow anyone to "help" you with your luggage. Many people perform this task on commission for specific transportation companies. Worse yet, they might end up disappearing into the crowd with your baggage.

Some of the major hotels send shuttles to pick up arriving guests; it's worth checking into before you arrive at the airport. Private taxis from the airport charge reasonable rates within Cancún, but will charge up to $60 or more to destinations in the Riviera Maya. Airport shuttle vans, which charge set rates based on your destination, sometimes take forever before filling up and getting under way. There are taxi and shuttle desks in the baggage-claim area; go to the ones with posted prices.

For round-trip transportation from the airport to the Riviera Maya, it's worth looking for a shuttle service, as a private taxi can be prohibitively expensive. Some of the shuttle services can be arranged beforehand via phone or the Internet. Cancún Valet rents per van, rather than per person, for up to 10 passengers, making it a good value for couples, families, and groups. Prices from the airport to the Hotel Zone, Playa del Carmen, and Tulum, as well as intermittent points are reasonable: $35 to Cancún ($65 round-trip) or $65 to Playa del Carmen ($125 round-trip), for example. Cancún Airport Transportation charges $35 per couple or individual, one-way, to the Hotel Zone ($55 round-trip) or $60 to Playa del

Carmen ($110 round-trip). Cancún Valet also rents cell phones for use in Mexico.

Contacts Cancún Airport Transportation ☎ *998/210–3317* ⊕ *www.cancuntransfers.com.* **Cancún Valet** ☎ *888/479–9095 toll-free from U.S., 998/848–3634* ⊕ *www.cancunvalet.com.*

FLIGHTS

You can reach the Yucatán by U.S., Mexican, or regional carriers. The most convenient flight from the United States is a nonstop on either a domestic or Mexican airline. Flying within the Yucatán is neither cost-effective nor convenient. Given the additional time needed for check-in, you might as well drive or take a bus to your destination, unless you're continuing on by plane.

Since all the major airlines listed here fly to Cancún—and often have the cheapest and most frequent flights there—it's worthwhile to consider it as a jumping-off point even if you don't plan on visiting the city. At this writing there are almost 200 flights that land daily at Cancún International Airport (CUN). Airlines that fly into Cancún include American, Aeroméxico, Air Canada, AirTran, Delta, Frontier, Interjet, JetBlue, Spirit, United, US Airways, and Virgin. American, Delta, Frontier, Interjet, and United also fly to Cozumel. Aeroméxico, Delta, Interjet, and United fly to Mérida. Mayair offers domestic flights from Cancún to Cozumel and Mérida. ■TIP➔ When you arrive at the airport, hang onto your FM-T form (tourist card) because you'll need it again on departure.

Airline Contacts Aeroméxico ☎ *800/237– 6639 in U.S. and Canada, 800/021–4000 in Mexico, 55/513–4000 in Mexico City* ⊕ *www. aeromexico.com.* **Air Canada** ☎ *888/247– 2262 in U.S., 800/719–2827 in Mexico* ⊕ *www. aircanada.com.* **AirTran** ☎ *800/247–8726, 678/254–7999* ⊕ *www.airtran.com.* **American Airlines** ☎ *800/433–7300 in U.S., 800/904-6000 in Mexico* ⊕ *www.aa.com.* **Delta Airlines** ☎ *800/221–1212 for U.S. reservations, 800/241–4141 for international reservations* ⊕ *www.delta.com.* **Frontier**

800/432–1359 ⊕ www.frontierairlines.com.
Interjet ☎ 866/285–9525 in U.S., 800/011–
2345 in Mexico ⊕ www.interjet.com.mx.
JetBlue ☎ 800/538–2583 in U.S., 800/861–
3372 in Mexico ⊕ www.jetblue.com. **Mayair**
☎ 998/881–9413 in Cancún, 987/872–3609
in Cozumel ⊕ www.mayair.com.mx. **Spirit Airlines** ☎ 800/772–7117 in U.S., 877/203–0891
in Mexico ⊕ www.spirit.com. **United Airlines**
☎ 800/864–8331 U.S. and Mexico reservations, 800/538–2929 international reservations
⊕ www.united.com. **US Airways** ☎ 800/428–
4322 ⊕ www.usairways.com. **Virgin America**
☎ 877/359–8474 in U.S., 877/359–8474 in
Mexico ⊕ www.virginamerica.com.

▌ BOAT AND FERRY TRAVEL

The Yucatán is served by a number of ferries and boats. Most popular are the efficient speedboats that run between Playa
del Carmen and Cozumel or from Puerto
Juárez, Punta Sam, and Isla Mujeres.
Boats also run from Chiquila to Isla Holbox. Smaller and slower boat carriers are
also available in many places.

Most carriers follow set schedules, with
the exception of boats going to the
smaller, less visited islands. However,
departure times can vary with the weather
and with the number of passengers. Visit-
cancun.com and travelyucatan.com have
information on water taxis and ferries,
though you should always confirm the
details before heading down to the docks.

▌ BUS TRAVEL

The Mexican bus network is extensive and
a great means of getting around. Service is
frequent, and tickets can be purchased on
the spot (except during holidays and on
long weekends, when advance purchase is
crucial). Bring something to eat on long
trips in case you don't like the restaurant
or market where the bus stops. Bring toilet tissue and wear a sweater, as the air-
conditioning is often set on high. Most
buses play videos or television until midnight, so bring earplugs if you're bothered

by noise. Smoking is prohibited on Mexican buses.

Mexican bus companies offer several
classes of service: first-class (*primera
clase*) and deluxe or executive-class (*de
lujo* or *ejecutivo*). Mexican buses are
generally punctual and have comfortable
air-conditioned coaches with bathrooms,
movies, reclining seats with seat belts, and
refreshments. They take the fastest route
(usually on safer, well-paved toll roads)
and make few stops between points. Less
desirable, second-class vehicles (*segunda
clase*) connect smaller, secondary routes;
they also run along some long-distance
routes, often taking slower, local roads.
They're tolerable, but are usually cramped
and make many stops. The class of travel
will be listed on your printed ticket—if
you see *económico* printed next to *servicio*, you've been booked on a second-class
bus. At many bus stations, one counter
will represent several lines and classes of
service, and mistakes do happen. ADO
(Autobuses del Oriente) is the Yucatán's
principal first-class bus company. Most
bus tickets, including first-class or executive and second-class, can be reserved in
advance in person at ticket offices. ADO
allows you to reserve tickets online 48
hours in advance. ADO, ADO GL (deluxe
service), and ADO Platino (luxury service), travel between the Yucatán and
Mexico City as well as other destinations
in southern Mexico, especially Oaxaca,
Veracruz, and Puebla.

ADO, along with other luxury liners like
Omnibus de Mexico and Primera Plus
travel the Yucatán loop of Cancún—Playa
del Carmen—Chetumal—Campeche—
Mérida—Cancún. If you're staying in
Riviera Maya, *colectivos* (mini-buses)
run along Carretera 307 from Cancún to
Tulum. Although affordable, traveling by
bus means you'll have to either walk or
organize additional transportation from
the bus stop.

Bus travel in the Yucatán, as throughout
Mexico, is inexpensive by U.S. standards,
with rates averaging $2 to $6 per hour

depending on the level of luxury (or lack of it). Schedules are posted at bus stations; the bus leaves more or less around the listed time. Often, if all the seats have been sold, the bus will leave early.

Typical times and fares on first-class buses are Cancún to Mérida: 4 hours, $45; Cancún to Campeche: 7 hours, $40; Mérida to Campeche: 2½ hours, $15; and Cancún to Mexico City: 23 hours, $130.

Bus Contacts ADO ☎ *01800/900–0105 toll-free in Mexico, 55/5133–2424* ⊕ *www.ado.com.mx.* **Omnibus de Mexico** ☎ *01800/765–6636 toll-free in Mexico* ⊕ *www.odm.com.mx.* **Primera Plus** ☎ *01800/375–7587 toll-free in Mexico* ⊕ *www.primeraplus.com.mx.*

▮ CAR TRAVEL

Renting a car is generally expensive in and around Cancún; if you're not traveling far afield, don't bother to rent, as you'll be able to arrange taxi service to nearby sights through your hotel.

However, taxis for longer trips—to Playa del Carmen, for instance—can get expensive, so renting a car for a day or two of exploring may be more economical. As a rule, avoid local agencies; stick with the major companies, because they tend to be more reliable. You can get the same kind of midsize and luxury cars in Mexico that you can rent in the United States. Economy usually refers to a small car barely fitting four passengers, which may or may not come with air-conditioning. Pancake-flat Yucatán makes for fairly easy driving, although side roads may have inadequate (or no) signage; four-wheel drive vehicles aren't necessary unless you plan on traveling to sites far off-the-beaten path in rainy season. Ask for a child's car seat when booking.

You won't need a car on Isla Mujeres or Isla Holbox, which are too small to make driving practical, nor in Playa del Carmen because the downtown area is quite small and the main street is blocked off to vehicles. Cars can actually feel like a burden in Mérida and Campeche City, because of the narrow cobbled streets and the lack of parking spaces. You'll need a car in Cozumel only if you wish to explore the eastern side of the island.

Car-rental agencies in Mexico require you to purchase CDW, or Collision Damage Waiver, coverage (starts at $16 per day), regardless of any coverage afforded by your credit-card company. Keep in mind that although you might have reserved a rental car for only $10 per day, full coverage insurance will cost you about $35 per day. Additional theft protection and personal injury policies are optional.

When renting a car, ask the agency for a "Tourist Traffic Card," which can be handed to police upon receiving a traffic violation. This voucher allows you to pay the ticket at the car-rental agency when you return the car, rather than having to spend several hours at the police station. It also helps eliminate corruption. Avis's Tourist Card actually serves as "payment" for two minor traffic violations. By presenting the card to authorities, the fine will be paid by Avis when you return the vehicle.

Be sure that you've been provided with proof of such insurance; if you drive without it, you're not only liable for damages, but you're also breaking the law. If you're in a car accident and you don't have insurance, you may be placed in jail until you're proven innocent. If anyone is injured you'll remain in jail until you make retribution to all injured parties and their families—which will likely cost you thousands of dollars. Mexican laws seem to favor nationals.

Even if you're absolutely certain you're fully covered by your credit-card company, we wouldn't recommend relying on it. Getting into a car accident in Mexico would be harrowing enough without having to navigate the bureaucracy of your credit-card company to clear things up with Mexican authorities. Make sure that your insurance covers the cost for an attorney and claims adjusters who will come to the scene of an accident. Buying insurance makes renting a car in Mexico one of the most expensive parts of the trip, but in this case it's better to be safe than frugal.

Before setting out on any car trip, check your vehicle's fuel, oil, fluids, tires, windshield wipers, and lights. It's even a good idea to check the stereo if you are planning a long road trip. Gas stations and mechanics can be hard to find, especially in more-remote areas. Consult a map and have your route in mind as you drive. Be aware that Mexican drivers often think nothing of tailgating, speeding, and weaving in and out of traffic. Drive defensively and keep your cool. When stopping for traffic or at a red light, always leave sufficient room between your car and the one ahead so you can maneuver to safety if necessary. On the highway, a left-turn signal in Mexico means the driver is signaling those behind that it's safe to pass. Blinking hazard lights means that traffic is stopped up ahead and to slow down. Always aim to be at your destination by sunset because most roads are pitted with potholes and are void of streetlights and signs. In Mexico the minimum driving age is 18, but most rental-car agencies have a minimum age requirement between 21 and 25; some have a surcharge for drivers under 25. Your own driver's license is acceptable; there's no reason to get an international driver's license.

GASOLINE

Pemex, Mexico's government-owned petroleum monopoly, franchises all gas stations, so prices throughout the Yucatán—and the country—are the same. Gas is always sold in liters. Some stations accept credit cards and a few have ATMs, but don't count on it—make sure you have pesos handy. When paying by credit card, don't be surprised if the gas attendant makes a photocopy of your passport since this is a normal practice. Overall, prices run slightly cheaper (around 30% less) than in the United States.

Ask for a *recibo* if you want a receipt. Premium unleaded gas (called *premium*), the red pump, and regular unleaded gas (*magna*), the green pump, are available nationwide. Fuel quality is generally lower than that in the United States and Europe, but it has improved enough so that your car will run acceptably.

There are no self-service stations in Mexico. Ask the attendant to fill your tank— *lleno* (YAY-noh), *por favor*—or ask for a specific amount in pesos to avoid being overcharged. Check to make sure that the attendant has set the meter back to zero and that the price is shown. Watch the attendant check the oil as well—to make sure you actually need it—and watch while he pours it into your car. Never pay before the gas is pumped, even if the attendant asks you to. Always tip your attendant a few pesos. Finally, keep your gas tank full, because gas stations are not plentiful in this area. If you run out of gas in a small village and there's no gas station for miles, ask if there's a store that sells gas from containers.

PARKING

A circle with a diagonal line superimposed on the letter *E* (for *estacionamiento*) means "no parking." A red curb means parking is restricted at all times, and a white curb is designated for loading and unloading only. A blue curb is for handicap parking, a green curb allows parking during specific hours, and a yellow curb means that the parking space is private. ■TIP→ If you're ticketed, your license plate will be taken to a nearby police station and will only be returned upon payment of the infraction. When in doubt, park your car in a parking lot instead of on the street; your car will probably be safer there anyway. Tip the parking attendant or security guard and ask him to look after your car. Never park your car overnight on the street. Never leave anything of value in an unattended car. Parking lots are plentiful, although not always clearly marked, and fees are reasonable—as little as $1 for a half day or up to $1 or more an hour. Sometimes you park your own car; more often, though, you hand the keys over to an attendant. There are a few (extremely few) parking meters in larger cities; the cost is usually about 10¢ per 15 minutes.

ROAD CONDITIONS

The road system in the Yucatán Peninsula is extensive and generally in good repair. Carretera 307 parallels most of the Caribbean Coast from Punta Sam, north of Cancún, to Tulum; here it turns inward for a stretch before returning to the coast at Chetumal and the Belize border. Carretera 180 runs west from Cancún to Valladolid, Chichén Itzá, and Mérida, then turns southwest to Campeche, Ciudad del Carmen, and on to Villahermosa. From Mérida, the winding, more scenic Carretera 261 also leads to some of the more off-the-beaten-track archaeological sites on the way south to Campeche and Escárcega, where it joins Carretera 186 going east to Chetumal. These highways are two-lane roads. Carretera 295 (from the north coast to Valladolid and Felipe Carrillo Puerto) is also a good two-lane road.

The *autopista*, or *carretera de cuota*, a four-lane toll highway between Cancún and Mérida, was completed in 1993. It runs roughly parallel to Carretera 180 and cuts driving time between Cancún and Mérida—otherwise about 4½ hours—by about 1 hour. Tolls between Mérida and Cancún total about $35, and the stretches between highway exits are long, sometimes as much as 75 miles. Be careful when driving on this road, as it retains the heat from the sun and can make your tires blow if they have low pressure or worn threads.

Many secondary roads are in bad condition—unpaved, unmarked, and full of potholes. If you must take one of these roads, the best course is to allow plenty of daylight hours and never travel at night. Slow down when approaching towns and villages—which you're forced to do by the *topes* (speed bumps)—and because of the added presence of children and animals, as well as adults. People selling oranges, candy, or other food will almost certainly approach your car.

MEXICAN DRIVERS

Mexicans are generally skilled drivers, but they do drive quite fast, even on twisting or extraordinarily dark roads. That said, Mexicans are in some ways more courteous than U.S. drivers—it's customary, for example, for drivers to put on their hazard lights to warn the cars behind them of poor road conditions, slow-downs, or upcoming speed bumps; oncoming cars may flash their lights at you for the same reasons.

ROADSIDE EMERGENCIES

The Mexican Tourism Ministry operates a fleet of some 1,800 pickup trucks, known as Angeles Verdes, or the Green Angels, an organization in existence since the early 1960s that assists motorists on major highways. Dial 078 from any cell phone or Telmex phone booth and your call will be routed to the Green Angels' dispatch office. The bilingual drivers provide mechanical help, first aid, radio-telephone communication, basic supplies and small parts, towing, and tourist information. Services are free, and spare parts, fuel, and lubricants are provided at cost. Tips are always appreciated, and are sometimes openly solicited.

The Green Angels patrol fixed sections of the major highways twice daily 8 am to dusk, later on holiday weekends. If your car breaks down, pull as far as possible off the road, lift the hood, hail a passing vehicle, and ask the driver to notify the patrol. Most bus and truck drivers will be quite helpful. Don't accept rides from strangers. If you witness an accident, don't stop to help since witnesses are often detained for questioning for long periods of time. Instead find the nearest official.

EMERGENCY SERVICE CONTACTS

Angeles Verdes ☎ *078 nationwide 3-digit Angeles Verdes and tourist emergency line, 91/5250–0123 Ministry of Tourism hotline.*

RULES OF THE ROAD

There are two absolutely essential points to remember about driving in Mexico. First and foremost is to carry Mexican auto insurance. If you injure anyone in an accident, you could well be jailed—whether it was your fault or not—unless you have insurance. Second, if you enter Mexico with a car, you must leave with it. In recent years the high rate of U.S. vehicles being sold illegally in Mexico has caused the Mexican government to enact stringent regulations for bringing a car into the country. You must be in your foreign vehicle at all times when it's driven. You cannot lend it to another person. Do not, under any circumstances, let a national drive your car. It's illegal for Mexicans to drive foreign-owned cars; if a national is caught driving your car, the car will be impounded by customs and you will receive a stiff fine. Newer models of vans, SUVs, and pickup trucks can be impossible to get back once impounded.

You must cross the border with the following documents: title or registration for your vehicle; a valid passport; a credit card (MC or V only); and a valid driver's license with a photo. You'll also need a temporary car-importation permit and an FM-T form (Tourist Card). The title-holder, driver, and credit-card owner must be one and the same—that is, if your spouse's name is on the title of the car and yours isn't, you cannot be the one to bring the car into the country. For financed, leased, rental, or company cars, you must bring a notarized letter of permission from the bank, lien holder, rental agency, or company. When you submit your paperwork at the border and pay the approximate $48 charge on your credit card, you'll receive a car permit and a sticker to put on your vehicle. The permit is valid for the same amount of time as your tourist visa, which is up to 180 days. You may go back and forth across the border during this six-month period, as long as you check with immigration and bring all your permit paperwork with you. If you're planning to stay and keep your car in Mexico for longer than six months, however, you'll have to get a new permit before the original one expires. In addition to the permit fee, your credit card will be charged a deposit based on the age of your car. This fee is to guarantee return of the vehicle to USA territory bond. If your car is older than 2000, you'll pay $200. Cars between 2001 and 2006 will be charged $300, and anything newer than 2007 will cost $400. This amount is refunded in full 24 hours after you cancel your permit, unless you have passed the expiration date or left your car in Mexico. Upon your departure from Mexico, the permit for temporary importation must be cancelled at Customs or you will not receive your refunded deposit.

One way to minimize hassle when you cross the border with a car is to have your paperwork done in advance at a branch of Sanborn's Mexico Auto Insurance; you'll find an office in almost every town on the U.S.–Mexico border. Average daily insurance rates are around $35. The fact that you drove in with a car is stamped on your tourist card, which you must give to immigration authorities at departure. If an emergency arises and you must fly home, there are complicated customs procedures to face.

When you sign up for Mexican car insurance, you should receive a booklet on Mexican rules of the road. It really is a good idea to read it to avoid breaking laws that differ from those of your country. If an oncoming vehicle flicks its lights at you in the daytime, slow down: it could mean trouble ahead. When approaching a narrow bridge, the first vehicle to flash its lights has right of way. One-way streets are common. One-way traffic is indicated by an arrow; two-way, by a double-pointed arrow. Other road signs follow the widespread system of international symbols.

Mileage and speed limits are given in kilometers: 100 kph and 80 kph (62 mph and 50 mph, respectively) are the most common maximums. A few of the toll roads allow 110 kph (68 mph). In cities and small towns, observe the posted speed limits, which can be as low as 20 kph (12 mph). Seat belts are required by law throughout Mexico.

Drunk-driving laws are fairly harsh in Mexico, and if you're caught you'll go to jail immediately. It's hard to know what the country's blood-alcohol limit really is. Everyone seems to have a different idea about it; this means it's probably being handled in a discretionary way, which is nerve-racking, to say the least. The best way to avoid any problems is simply not to drink and drive. Right turns on red are not allowed, and texting while driving is not permitted. Foreigners must pay speeding penalties on the spot, which can be steep. Minor traffic violations can be dismissed until you return your rental car by simply showing your "Tourist Traffic Card" available from most car-rental agencies.

If you encounter a police checkpoint, stay calm. These are simply routine checks for weapons and drugs; customarily they'll check out the car's registration, look in the backseat, the trunk, and at the under-carriage with a mirror. Basic Spanish does help during these stops, though a smile and polite demeanor will go a long way.

CONTACT

Sanborn's Mexico Auto Insurance
☎ 800/222-0158 ⊕ www.sanbornsinsurance. com.

SAFETY ON THE ROAD

Never drive at night in remote and rural areas. Although there are few *banditos* on the roads here, more common problems are large potholes, free-roaming animals, cars with no working lights, and road-hogging trucks. Getting assistance is difficult. If you must travel at night, use the toll roads whenever possible; although costly, they're much safer.

Some of the biggest hassles on the road might be from police who pull you over for supposedly breaking the law, or for being a good prospect for a scam. Remember to be polite—displays of anger will only make matters worse—and be aware that a police officer might be pulling you over for something you didn't do. Although efforts are being made to fight corruption, it's still a fact of life in Mexico. The $5 (and up) it costs to get your license back is definitely supplementary income for the officer who pulled you over with no intention of taking you down to police headquarters.

▮ CRUISE SHIP TRAVEL

Cozumel and Playa del Carmen (ships dock in Calica, south of town) have become increasingly popular ports for Caribbean cruises, and most recently Mahahual (popularly known as Puerto Costa Maya), Puerto Morelos, and Progreso (near Mérida) have been added to the list. Due to heavy traffic, Cozumel and Playa del Carmen have limited the number of ships coming into their ports. Cruise ships usually dock in Mahahual two to four times a week and in Puerto Morelos less often. Ships dock in Progreso twice weekly.

▮ TAXI TRAVEL

Taxis are ubiquitous in both big cities and midsize towns. The standard taxi is a midsize, four-door sedan. Drivers generally speak English, either enough to negotiate the fare or, in some cases, excellent enough for a lively discussion of national politics.

In addition to private taxis, many cities have bargain-price collective taxi services using minibuses and sedans. The service is called *colectivo* or *pesero*. Such vehicles run along fixed routes, and you hail them on the street and tell the driver where you're going. He charges you based on how far you're going on that route. Note that drivers often run out of change, so having change handy, and being able to pay the exact amount, can help make your ride smoother.

AIRPORT TAXIS

For safety, you should only take the authorized taxi service from most airports. Whenever possible, purchase the taxi vouchers sold at stands inside or just outside the terminal, which ensure that your fare is established beforehand. Check the taxi-zone map (it should be posted on or by the ticket stand) before you purchase your ticket and make sure your ticket is properly zoned.

FARES

A metered taxi has a taximetro, and if a cab has one, ask the driver what the rates are. Most taxis, particularly those in resort areas, are unmetered. Always confirm the fare before setting out. Major hotels post rate sheets, or you can ask a concierge or front-desk person what the rates should be. Note that even the posted rates are inflated, so always try to negotiate a slightly better price. Clearly, if any cabbie asks for more than the posted fare you're being grossly overcharged.

A surcharge of 20% to 40% may be added at night, usually after 11 pm.

If a driver doesn't know the address you give him, he'll radio either a dispatcher or other cabbie to get the info, or drive to the neighborhood and ask around. When you've negotiated the fare before starting, you needn't pay extra if the cabbie has to drive around a bit to find the address.

Tipping isn't customary, unless the driver helps you with your bags.

ESSENTIALS

■ ACCOMMODATIONS

The price and quality of accommodations in the Yucatán Peninsula vary from luxury resorts and coastal villas to seedy hostels and eco-friendly cabanas. Near Mérida and Campeche, many historic haciendas have been converted into luxury accommodations. You may find bargains while you're on the road, but if your comfort threshold is high, look for an English-speaking staff, guaranteed dollar rates, and toll-free reservation numbers. Mexico doesn't have an official star-rating system, but the usual number of stars (five being the ultimate) denotes the most luxury and amenities, while a two-star hotel might have a ceiling fan and TV with local channels only. "Gran turismo" is a special category of hotel that may or may not have all the accoutrements of a five-star hotel (such as minibars) but is nonetheless at the top of the heap, both in price and level of service and sophistication. All-inclusive hotels are a good option for families since the price of the room usually includes children's activities and meals.

APARTMENT AND HOUSE RENTALS

Local rental agencies can be found in Isla Mujeres, Cozumel, and Playa del Carmen. They specialize in renting out apartments, condos, villas, and private homes.

Rental Agency Contacts **Akumal Villas** ☏ 866/535–1324 ⊕ www.akumal-villas.com. **Caribbean Realty** ☏ 910/543–0019 in U.S, 984/873–5218 in Mexico ⊕ www.puertoaventurasrentals.com. **Cozumel Villas** ☏ 866/564–4427, 406/686–9169 ⊕ www.cozumelvillas.com. **Lost Oasis Property Rentals** ☏ 998/887–0951, 831/621–3749 in U.S. ⊕ www.lostoasis.net. **Real Estate Yucatán** ☏ 999/944–1315 ⊕ www.realestateyucatan.com. **Turquoise Waters** ☏ 877/254–9791 ⊕ www.turquoisewater.com. **Villas & Apartments Abroad** ☏ 212/213–6435 ⊕ www.vaanyc.com. **Villas International**

☏ 415/499–9490, 800/221–2260 ⊕ www.villasintl.com. **Villas of Distinction** ☏ 800/289–0900 ⊕ www.villasofdistinction.com.

HOTELS

Hotel rates are subject to the 10% to 15% value-added tax, in addition to a 2% to 3% hotel tax. Service charges and meals generally aren't included in the hotel rates. Make sure to ask if tax is included in quoted rates and take this into account when comparing properties.

High- versus low-season rates can vary significantly. In the off-season, Cancún hotels can cost one-third to one-half what they cost during peak season. Keep in mind, however, that this is also the time that many hotels undergo necessary repairs or renovations.

Hotels in this guide have private bathrooms with showers, unless stated otherwise; bathtubs aren't common in inexpensive hotels and properties in smaller towns.

Reservations are easy to make over the Internet. If you call hotels in the larger urban areas, there will be someone who speaks English. In more remote regions you'll have to make your reservations in Spanish. Be sure to book online hotel reservations at least two days in advance of your stay, and always print out your confirmation. Although major resorts are generally efficient at keeping up with online bookings, there's often a lag, and the reservation desks that handle such things may be closed on weekends. In more remote areas like Xcalak, you'll have to make reservations by email since most properties don't have telephones.

It's essential to reserve in advance if you're traveling to the resort areas during high season (mid-December through Easter) or holiday periods, and it's recommended, though not always necessary, to do so elsewhere during high season. Resorts popular with college students tend to fill up in the summer months and during spring-break season (generally March through April). Overbooking is a common practice in some parts, especially in Cancún. To protect yourself, get a written confirmation, via fax or email.

▌ COMMUNICATIONS

INTERNET

If you're traveling with your laptop, watch it carefully. The biggest danger, aside from theft, is the constantly fluctuating electricity in remote towns, which may eventually damage your hard drive. Although uncommon, you might consider investing in a Mexican surge protector (available at most electronics stores for about $50) that can handle the brownouts and fluctuations in voltage at "off grid" locations.

In Cancún free Wi-Fi is available in most large hotels, at least in public areas. Cost for an in-room connection starts at $25 per day. Yes, it's shocking, especially when in other parts of the country Wi-Fi is a free perk offered by many hotels. The cost for public Internet is as much as 10 pesos a minute (for those with super-fast connection). For slower connections, the charge is usually more like 10 pesos for 10 minutes.

PHONES

A few of Cancún's all-inclusive resorts are now offering free calls to the U.S. and Canada, but be sure to ask in advance. Calling cards usually keep costs to a minimum. Use your international calling card or purchase a Ladatel card to use at a pay phone—although hearing above ambient noise can be a problem. As expensive as international mobile phone calls can be, they're still usually a much cheaper option than calling from your hotel room. If you want to call a restaurant or local business, you can save money by simply walking to the concierge and asking the representative to make the call on your behalf.

The country code for Mexico is 52. When calling a Mexico number from abroad, dial the country code and then all of the numbers listed for the entry.

CALLING WITHIN MEXICO

Towns and cities throughout Mexico now have standardized three-digit area codes (LADAs) and seven-digit phone numbers. (In Mexico City, Monterrey, and Guadalajara the area code is two digits followed by an eight-digit local number.) While increasingly rare, numbers in brochures and other literature—even business cards—are sometimes written in the old style, with five or six digits. To call national long-distance, dial 01, the area code, and the seven-digit number.

Directory assistance is 040 for telephone lines run by Telmex, the former government-owned telephone monopoly that still holds near-monopoly status in Mexico. While you can reach 040 from other phone lines, operators generally don't give you any information, except, perhaps, the directory-assistance line for the provider you're using. For international assistance, dial 00 first for an international operator and most likely you'll get one who speaks English; tell the operator in what city, state, and country you require directory assistance, and he or she will connect you.

CALLING OUTSIDE MEXICO

To make an international call, dial 00 before the country code, area code, and number. The country code for the United States and Canada is 1, the United Kingdom 44, Australia 61, New Zealand 64, and South Africa 27.

The cheapest method for making local or long-distance calls is to buy a prepaid phone card and dial direct (⇨ see *Calling Cards*). Another option is to find a *caseta de larga distancia,* a telephone service usually operated out of a store such as a *papelería* (stationery store), pharmacy, restaurant, or other small business; look for the phone symbol on the door. These are few and far between in Cancún, however. Casetas may cost more to use than pay phones (a $5 flat fee in addition to long distance rates), but you have a better chance of immediate success. To make a direct long-distance call, tell the person on duty the number you'd like to call, and she or he will give you a rate and dial for you. Rates seem to vary widely.

Sometimes you can make collect calls from casetas, and sometimes you can't, depending on the individual operator and possibly your degree of visible despera tion. Casetas will generally charge 50¢ to $1.50 to place a collect call (some charge by the minute); it's usually better to call *por cobrar* (collect) from a pay phone—but be sure to avoid phones near tourist areas that advertise, in English, "Call the U.S. or Canada here!" These charge an outrageous fee per minute. If in doubt, dial the operator and ask for rates.

Access Code Contacts AT&T Direct
☎ *1800/225–5288 toll-free in U.S., 01800/288-2872 toll-free in Mexico* ⊕ *www.att.com.* **MCI WorldPhone** ☎ *01800/674–7000 toll-free in Mexico.* **Sprint International Access** ☎ *001800/877–8000 toll-free in Mexico, 817/698–4199 in U.S.* ⊕ *www.sprint.com.*

CALLING CARDS
In most parts of the country, pay phones (predominantly operated by Telmex) accept only prepaid cards (*tarjetas Lada*), sold in 30-, 50-, 100-, or 200-peso denominations at newsstands, pharmacies, minimarkets, or grocery stores. Coin-only pay phones are few and far between. There are pay phones all over the place—on street corners, in bus stations, and so on. They usually have two unmarked slots, one for a Ladatel (a Spanish acronym for "long-distance direct dialing") card and the other for a credit card. These are primarily for Mexican bank cards, but some accept Visa or MasterCard, though *not* U.S. phone credit cards.

To use a Ladatel card, simply insert it in the appropriate slot. To change instructions to English, push the ABC button on the left hand side of the dial pad. Dial 001 (for calls to the States) or 01 (for long-distance calls within Mexico) and the area code and number you're trying to reach. Local calls may also be placed with the card. Credit is deleted from the card as you use it, and your balance is displayed on a small screen on the phone.

MOBILE PHONES
If you have a multiband phone (some countries use frequencies different from those used in the United States) and your service provider uses the world-standard GSM network (as do T-Mobile, AT&T, and Verizon), you can probably use your phone abroad. Roaming fees can be steep, however: 99¢ a minute is considered reasonable, and you normally pay the toll charges for incoming calls. It's almost always cheaper to send a text message (usually 25¢ or less). If you have a laptop, the most affordable way to call is through Skype. If the person you are calling also has a Skype account, you can make international calls for free (through the Internet), or you can use the pay-as-you-go method.

If you just want to make local calls, consider buying a new SIM card (note that your provider may have to unlock your phone for you to use a different SIM card) and a prepaid service plan in the destination. You'll then have a local number and can make local calls at local rates. If your trip is extensive, you could also simply buy a new cell phone in your destination, as the initial cost will be offset over time.

■**TIP**➜ If you travel internationally frequently, save one of your old mobile phones or buy a cheap one on the Internet; ask your cell-phone company to unlock it for you, and take it with you as a travel phone, buying a new SIM card with pay-as-you-go service in each destination.

Mobile Phone Contacts Cancún Valet. Cancún Valet rents cell phones with rates at 69¢ per minute to/from the United States, Canada, and Europe. ☎ 888/479-9095 from U.S., 998/848-3634 from Mexico ⊕ www. cancunvalet.com. **Daystar.** Daystar rents cell phones at about $5.95 per day, with incoming calls at approximately 22¢ a minute and outgoing at $1.19. ☎ 877/820-7397 ⊕ www. daystarwireless.com.

TOLL-FREE NUMBERS
Toll-free numbers in Mexico start with an 800 prefix. To reach them, you need to dial 01 before the number. In this guide, Mexico-only toll-free numbers appear as follows: 01800/123-4567. Some toll-free numbers use 95 instead of 01 to connect. Some hotels will charge for 800 numbers made from guest rooms. The 800 numbers listed simply 800/123-4567 are U.S. numbers and generally work north of the border only. Those that do work to access a U.S. company from Mexico may or may not be free; those that aren't should give you the chance to hang up before being charged. Directory assistance is 040.

▌ CUSTOMS AND DUTIES

Upon entering Mexico, you'll be given a baggage-declaration form—you can fill out one per family. You'll also be given an FMT form (tourist card), to be stamped at immigration. Keep this card for the duration of your trip since you'll need to present it upon departure, or else you may be fined up to $80. Minors traveling without an adult must carry notarized written permission from a parent or guardian. Most airports have a random bag-inspection scheme in place. When you pick up your bags you'll approach

something that looks like a stoplight; hand your form to the attendant, press the button, and if you get a green light you (and the rest of your family) may proceed. If you get a red light, you may be subject to further questioning or inspection. You're allowed to bring in 3 liters of spirits or 6 liters of wine for personal use; 20 cartons of cigarettes, 25 cigars, or 200 grams of tobacco. You aren't allowed to bring firearms or ammunition, meat, vegetables, plants, fruit, or flowers into Mexico. Mexico also allows you to bring one cat, one dog, or up to four canaries into the country if you have these two things: (1) a pet health certificate signed by a registered veterinarian in the United States and issued not more than 72 hours before the animal enters Mexico; and (2) a pet-vaccination certificate showing that the animal has been treated for rabies, hepatitis, pip, and leptospirosis.

For more information or details on bringing other animals or more than one type of animal, contact a Mexican consulate. Aduana Mexico (Mexican Customs) has an informative website. You can also get customs information from a Mexican consulate; many major American cities as well as border towns have them. To find the consulate nearest you, check the Ministry of Foreign Affairs website, select Consular Services from the menu on the left, and scroll down.

Consulate Contacts Aduana Mexico ☎ 877/448-8728 ⊕ www.aduanas.gob.mx. **Ministry of Foreign Affairs** ☎ 202/728-1600 ⊕ portal.sre.gob.mx/usa. **U.S. Customs and Border Protection** ☎ 877/227-5511 from U.S. ☎ 202/325-8000 international callers ⊕ www. cbp.gov.

▌ EATING OUT

The restaurants we list are the cream of the crop in each price category.

⇨ For information on food-related health issues, see Health below.

MEALS AND MEALTIMES

Desayuno can be either a breakfast sweet roll and coffee or milk or a full breakfast of an egg dish such as *huevos a la mexicana* (scrambled eggs with chopped tomato, onion, and chiles), *huevos rancheros* (fried eggs on a tortilla covered with salsa), or *huevos con jamón* (scrambled eggs with ham), plus juice and toast or tortillas. Some cafés don't open until 8 or 8:30, in which case hotel restaurants are the best bets for early risers. *Panaderías* (bakeries) open early and provide the cheapest breakfast you'll find—a bag of assorted rolls and pastries will likely cost less than $1.

Traditionally, lunch is called *comida* or *almuerzo* and is the biggest meal of the day. Most restaurants start serving lunch no earlier than 1 pm and traditional businesses close between 2 pm and 4 pm for this meal. It usually includes soup, a main dish, and dessert. Regional specialties include *pan de cazón* (baby shark shredded and layered with tortillas, black beans, and tomato sauce) in Campeche; *pollo pibil* (chicken baked in banana leaves) in Mérida; and *tikinchic* (fish in a sour-orange sauce) on the coast. Restaurants in tourist areas also serve American-style food such as hamburgers, pizza, and pasta. The evening meal is called *cena*, which is sometimes replaced by *merienda* (a lighter meal between lunch and dinner).

Most restaurants are open daily for lunch and dinner during high season (December through April), but hours may be reduced during the rest of the year. It's always a good idea to phone ahead.

Unless otherwise noted, the restaurants listed in this guide are open daily for lunch and dinner.

PAYING

Most small restaurants do not accept credit cards. Larger restaurants and those catering to tourists take credit cards, but most establishments do not accept American Express.

⇨ *For guidelines on tipping, see Tipping below.*

RESERVATIONS AND DRESS

Regardless of where you are, it's a good idea to make a reservation if you can. In Cancún, for example, reservations are expected at the nicer restaurants. We mention them specifically only when reservations are essential (there's no other way you'll ever get a table) or when they're not accepted. Large parties should always call ahead to check the reservations policy. We mention dress only when men are required to wear a jacket.

Some restaurants accept online reservations, although it's always wise to confirm by phone.

WINES, BEER, AND SPIRITS

Almost all restaurants in the region serve beer and some Mexican label spirits. Larger restaurants have beer, wine, and spirits. Some of the more expensive all-inclusive resorts offer top-shelf international liquor brands but will only serve them if you specifically request the brands by name (otherwise, expect a hangover). The Mexican wine industry is relatively small, but notable producers include L.A. Cetto, Bodegas de Santo Tomás, Pedro Domecq, and Monte Xanic. As well as offering Mexican vintages, restaurants may offer Chilean, Spanish, Italian, and French wines at reasonable prices. You pay more for imported liquor such as vodka, brandy, and whiskey; some brands of tequila and rum are less expensive. Take the opportunity to try some of the higher-end, small-batch tequila—it's a completely different experience from what you might be used to. Some small lunch places called *loncherías* don't sell alcohol. Almost all corner stores sell beer, brandy, cheap wine, and tequila. Grocery stores carry all brands of beer, wine, and spirits. Liquor stores are rare and usually carry specialty items. You must be 18 to buy liquor, but this rule is often overlooked.

■ ELECTRICITY

Electrical converters are not necessary, because Mexico operates on the 60-cycle, 120-volt system. However, outlets at some of the older hotels have not been updated to accommodate three-prong and polarized plugs (those with one larger prong), so it's a good idea to bring an adapter.

■ EMERGENCIES

It's helpful, albeit daunting, to know ahead of time that you're not protected by the laws of your native land once you're on Mexican soil. However, if you get into a scrape with the law, you can call the Citizens' Emergency Center in the United States. In Mexico, you can also call INFOTUR, the 24-hour English-speaking hotline of the Mexico Ministry of Tourism (Sectur). The hotline can provide immediate assistance as well as general, nonemergency guidance. In Mérida and environs, contact the tourist police (☎ 999/930–3200 Ext. 40031), although getting an English speaker is hit or miss. In an emergency, call ☎ 060 from any phone.

Consulates and Embassies U.S. Consulate ☒ Calle 60 No. 338, Col. Alcala Martin, Centro, Mérida ☎ 999/942-5700. U.S. Consular Agency Cancún ☒ Blvd. Kukulcán Km 13, Zona Hotelera, Cancún ☎ 998/883-0272 ☉ Weekdays 8-1. By appointment only. U.S. Embassy ☒ Paseo de la Reforma 305, Col. Cuauhtémoc, Mexico City ☎ 01-55/5080-2000 ⊕ mexico.usembassy.gov.

General Emergency Contacts Air Ambulance Network ☎ 800/327-1966 in U.S., 01800/010-0027 in Mexico ⊕ www. airambulancenetwork.com. Angeles Verdes (Emergency roadside assistance in Mexico) ☎ 078. Citizens' Emergency Center ☎ 202/501-4444 from outside U.S., 888/407-4747 from within U.S. ⊕ www.travel. state.gov. Global Life Flight ☎ 01800/305-9400, 01800/361-1600 toll-free in Mexico, 800/831-9307 in U.S. and Canada ⊕ www. globallifeflight.com. INFOTUR ☎ 800/903-9200 toll-free in Mexico ⊕ www.sectur.gob.mx.

■ HEALTH

According to the U.S. government's National Centers for Disease Control and Prevention (CDC) there's a limited risk of malaria in certain rural areas of the Yucatán Peninsula, especially the states of Campeche and Quintana Roo. Dengue fever is also a limited risk along the Caribbean Coast. Travelers in mostly urban areas need not worry, nor do travelers who rarely leave artificial resort environs.

To safeguard yourself against mosquito-borne diseases like malaria and dengue, use mosquito nets (provided at most beach and jungle properties), wear clothing that covers the body, apply repellent containing DEET, and use spray for flying insects in living and sleeping areas. If you consider taking anti-malarial pills, remember that the side effects of some medications can be quite strong, and the current strain of Mexican malaria can be cured with the right medication. There's no vaccine to combat dengue.

HEALTH WARNINGS

National Centers for Disease Control & Prevention (CDC) ☎ 800/232-4636 international travelers' health line ⊕ www.cdc.gov/travel.

FOOD AND DRINK

In Mexico the biggest health risk is traveler's diarrhea caused by consuming contaminated fruit, vegetables, or water. The usual suspects are ice, uncooked food, and unpasteurized milk and milk products.

Drink only bottled water or water that has been boiled for at least 10 minutes, even when you're brushing your teeth. At restaurants off the beaten path, be sure to ask for *agua mineral* (mineral water) or *agua purificada* (purified water). When ordering cold drinks at questionable establishments, skip the ice: *sin hielo.* (You can usually identify ice made commercially from purified water by its uniform shape and the hole in the center.) Hotels with water-purification systems will post signs to that effect in the rooms; even then, be wary. Although salads in tourist-oriented areas have usually been hygienically prepared, when in doubt don't eat any raw vegetables that haven't been, or can't be, peeled (e.g., lettuce and tomatoes). In coastal towns like Celestún, the shrimp may be fresh, but it has been known to cause Montezuma's Revenge for travelers with sensitive stomachs.

REMEDIES

Mild cases of diarrhea may respond to Imodium (known generically as Loperamide or Lomotil) or Pepto-Bismol (not as strong), both of which you can buy over the counter. Keep in mind, though, that these drugs can complicate more serious illnesses. Drink plenty of bottled water or tea. Chamomile tea (*té de manzanilla*) is a good remedy, and it's readily available in restaurants throughout Mexico.

In severe cases, hydrate with Gatorade or a salt-sugar solution (½ teaspoon salt and 4 tablespoons sugar per quart of water). You can also balance out your pH levels by drinking a glass of water with a tablespoon of baking soda, which acts as a natural antacid. If your fever and diarrhea last more than three days, see a doctor—you may have picked up a parasite that requires prescription medication.

PESTS

It's best to be cautious and go indoors at dusk (called the "mosquito hour" by locals). An excellent brand of *repelente de insectos* (insect repellent) called Autan is readily available; don't use it on children under age two. If you want to bring a mosquito repellent from home, make sure it has at least 10% DEET or it won't be effective. If you're hiking in the jungle or near standing water, wear repellent and/or long pants and sleeves; if you're camping in the jungle, use a mosquito net and invest in a package of mosquito coils (sold in most stores). Isla Holbox is often riddled with tiny mosquitoes and "no-seeums" after the rains. Island locals use baby oil as a natural repellent. If you plan on visiting one of the many cenotes (subterranean water bodies) throughout the Yucatán, be sure to bring waterproof insect repellent.

Another local flying pest is the *tabaño*, a type of deer fly, which resembles a common household fly with yellow stripes. Some people swell up after being bitten, but taking an antihistamine can help. Watch out for the small red ants, as their bites can be quite irritating.

Scorpions also live in the region; their sting is similar to a bee sting. They're rarely fatal, but can cause strong reactions in small children and the elderly. Clean all cuts carefully (especially those produced by coral), as the rate of infection is much higher here.

The Yucatán has many poisonous snakes. The coral snake, easily identified by its black and red markings, should be avoided at all costs since its bite is fatal. If you're planning any jungle hikes, be sure to wear hard-sole shoes and stay on the path. For more remote areas, hire a guide and make sure there's an anti-venom kit accompanying you on the trip.

SUNBURN

More common hazards to travelers in the Yucatán are sunburn and heat exhaustion. The sun is strong here; it takes fewer than 20 minutes to get a serious sunburn. When practical, avoid the sun between 11 am and 3 pm. Wear a hat and use sunscreen, preferably something with zinc oxide. You should drink more fluids than you do at home—Mexico is probably hotter than what you're used to and you'll perspire more. Rest in the afternoon and stay out of the sun to avoid heat exhaustion. The first signs of dehydration and heat exhaustion are dizziness, extreme irritability, and fatigue.

TRIP INSURANCE

Whether you want comprehensive trip coverage, consider buying trip insurance with medical-only coverage. Neither Medicare nor some private insurers cover medical expenses anywhere outside the United States. Medical-only policies typically reimburse you for medical care (excluding that related to preexisting conditions), hospitalization abroad, and provide for evacuation. You still have to pay the bills and await reimbursement from the insurer, though.

Another option is to sign up with a medical-evacuation assistance company. A membership in one of these companies gets you doctor referrals, emergency evacuation or repatriation, 24-hour hotlines for medical consultation, and other assistance. International SOS Assistance Emergency and AirMed International provide evacuation services and medical referrals. MedjetAssist offers medical evacuation.

Medical Assistance Companies AirMed International ☎ 205/443–4840, 800/356–2161 ⊕ www.airmed.com. **International SOS Assistance Emergency** ☎ 215/942–8226 ⊕ www.internationalsos.com. **MedjetAssist** ☎ 1800/527–7478, 205/595–6626 ⊕ www.medjetassist.com.

Medical-Only Insurers International Medical Group ☎ 317/655–4500, 1800/628–4664 ⊕ www.imglobal.com. **International SOS** ☎ 215/942–8226 ⊕ www.internationalsos.com. **Wallach & Company** ☎ 540/687–3166, 800/237–6615 toll-free in U.S. ⊕ www.wallach.com.

▌ HOURS OF OPERATION

In well-traveled places such as Cancún, Isla Mujeres, Playa del Carmen, Mérida, and Cozumel, businesses generally are open during posted hours. In more off-the-beaten-path areas, neighbors can tell you when the owner will return.

Most banks are open weekdays 9 to 5, but some will exchange money only until early afternoon. Many are open Saturday until noon or 1 pm. Most businesses are open weekdays 9 to 2 and 4 to 7.

Some gas stations are open 24 hours, although those off main highways usually close from midnight until 6 am, or close even earlier.

Most museums throughout Mexico are closed on Monday and open 8 to 5 the rest of the week. But it's best to call ahead or ask at your hotel. Hours of sights and attractions in this book are denoted by a clock icon ☉.

The larger pharmacies in Cancún and Cozumel are usually open daily 8 am to 10 pm, and those in Cancún, Campeche, and Mérida have at least one 24-hour pharmacy. Smaller pharmacies are often closed on Sunday.

Tourist-oriented stores in Cancún, Mérida, Playa del Carmen, and Cozumel are usually open 10 to 9 Monday through Saturday and on Sunday afternoon. Shops in more traditional areas may close weekdays between 1 pm and 4 pm, opening again in the evening. They're generally closed Sunday.

▌ MAIL

Mail can be sent from your hotel or the *oficina de correos* (post office). Be forewarned, however, that mail service to, within, and from Mexico is notoriously slow and can take anywhere from 10 days to, well, never. Don't send anything of value to or from Mexico via mail, including cash, checks, or credit-card numbers.

SHIPPING PACKAGES

Hotel concierges can recommend international carriers, such as DHL, Estafeta, or Federal Express, which give your package a tracking number and ensure its arrival back home.

▌ MONEY

Because the value of the currency fluctuates, and since many businesses quote prices in U.S. dollars, most prices in this book are in dollars.

U.S. dollar bills (but not coins) are widely accepted in many parts of the Yucatán, particularly in Cancún and Cozumel, where you'll often find prices in shops quoted in dollars. However, you may get your change back in pesos. Many tourist shops and market vendors, as well as virtually all hotel service personnel, also accept dollars. Wherever you are, though, watch out for bad exchange rates—you'll generally do better paying in pesos. Hotels, restaurants, buses, and market vendors readily accept dollars but usually do not offer a good exchange rate. Many smaller businesses and most highway toll booths do not accept dollars. If you run out of pesos, then by all means use U.S. dollars, pay with a credit card, or make a withdrawal from an ATM.

ATMS AND BANKS

In 2010, Mexican authorities passed a law stating that foreign travelers may not exchange more than $1,500 U.S. dollars (cash) per person, per month into Mexican pesos. Mexican travelers are also limited to $1,500 U.S.D. cash per person, per month, with the added restriction of no more than $300 U.S.D. cash per day. Other methods of payment including credit cards, traveler's checks, and non-American foreign currencies are not affected by this new law.

When exchanging foreign currency at banks and hotels in Mexico, you must show your passport. Your own bank will probably charge a fee for using ATMs abroad; the foreign bank you use may also charge a fee. Nevertheless, you'll usually get a better rate of exchange at an ATM than you will at a currency-exchange office or even when changing money in a bank. Extracting funds as you need them is a safer option than carrying around a large amount of cash, but keep in mind that remote areas such as Xcalak near Belize don't have ATMs or banks, and businesses there don't accept credit cards.

▌**TIP→** PIN numbers with more than four digits are not recognized at ATMs in many countries. If your PIN has five or more numbers, remember to change it before you leave.

ATMs (*cajeros automáticos*) are now commonplace. Cirrus and Plus are the most frequently found networks. Rural towns, however, often lack banking facilities. Unless you're in a major city or resort area, treat ATMs as you would gas stations—don't assume you'll be able to find one in a pinch. In smaller towns, even when they're present, machines are often out of order or out of cash. Many, but not all, gas stations have ATMs. All airports have ATMs, but many bus stations do not.

Before you leave home, ask what the transaction fee will be for withdrawing money in Mexico (it can be up to $5 a pop). Ask your bank if it has an agreement with a Mexican bank to waive or charge lower fees for cash withdrawals. For example, Bank of America account holders can withdraw money from Santander-Serfin ATMs free of charge.

Be sure to also alert your bank's customer-protection division to let them know you will be using your card in Mexico—otherwise they may assume that the card's been stolen and put a hold on your account.

CREDIT CARDS

Throughout this guide, it's safe to assume that businesses accept major credit cards unless the service information reads ▬ *No credit cards.*

It's a good idea to inform your credit-card company before you travel to Mexico, especially if you don't travel internationally very often. Otherwise, the credit-card company might put a hold on your card owing to unusual activity—not a good thing halfway through your trip. Record all your credit-card numbers—as well as the phone numbers to call if your cards are lost or stolen—in a safe place, so you're prepared should something go wrong.

Note that some credit-card companies *and* the banks that issue them add substantial percentages to all foreign transactions. Check on these fees before leaving home, so there won't be any surprises when you get the bill.

Credit cards are accepted in most tourist areas. Smaller, less expensive restaurants and shops, however, tend to take only cash. In general, credit cards aren't accepted in small towns and villages. The most widely accepted cards are Master-Card and Visa; American Express is not widely accepted in Mexico except at large international chain hotels and resorts. When shopping, you can usually get better prices if you pay with cash.

In Mexico the decision to pay cash or use a credit card might depend on whether the establishment in which you're making a purchase finds bargaining for prices acceptable. To avoid fraud, it's wise to make sure that "pesos" or the initials M.N., *moneda nacional* (national currency) is clearly marked on all credit-card receipts, unless the charge was made in U.S. dollars.

CURRENCY AND EXCHANGE

Check with your bank, the financial pages of your local newspaper, or ⊕ *www. xe.com* for current exchange rates.

Mexican currency comes in denominations of 10-, 20-, 50-, 100-, 200-, 500-, and 1,000-peso bills. The latter are not very common, and many establishments refuse to accept them due to a lack of change. Coins come in denominations of 1, 2, 5, 10, 20, and 100 pesos. Many of the coins are very similar, so check carefully. Of the older coins you may

occasionally see a 10 or 20 or more often a 50 *centavo* (cent) piece.

Most banks only change money on weekdays until noon (though they stay open until 5), whereas *casas de cambio* (private exchange offices) generally stay open until 6 or 9 and often operate on weekends. Bring your photo ID or passport when you exchange money. Bank rates are regulated by the federal government but vary slightly from bank to bank, while casas de cambio have slightly more variable rates.

■**TIP**➔ Many shop and restaurant owners are unable to make change for large bills. Enough of these encounters may compel you to request billetes chicos (small bills) when you exchange money.

Currency Conversion Contacts XE.com ⊕ *www.xe.com.*

■ PACKING

Pack lightly, because you may want to save space in your suitcase for purchases. The Yucatán is filled with bargains on clothing, leather goods, jewelry, and other crafts. If you purchase pottery or ceramics, make sure they're carefully wrapped in your check-in luggage since TSA regulations prohibit these items from being in your carry-on.

Bring lightweight clothes, sundresses, bathing suits, sun hats or visors, and cover-ups for the Caribbean beach towns, but also pack a light jacket or sweater to wear in the chilly, air-conditioned restaurants, or to tide you over during a rainstorm or an unusual cool spell. For trips to rural areas or Mérida, where dress is typically more conservative and shorts are considered inappropriate, make sure you have at least one pair of slacks. Comfortable walking shoes with rubber soles are a good idea, both for exploring ruins and for walking around cities. Lightweight rain gear and an umbrella are a good idea during the rainy season. Cancún is the dressiest spot on the peninsula, but even fancy restaurants don't always require men to wear jackets.

Pack sunscreen and sunglasses for the Yucatán's strong sun. Other handy items—especially if you're using budget hotels and restaurants or going off the beaten path—include toilet paper, facial tissues, a plastic water bottle, and a flashlight (for occasional power outages). Snorkelers should consider bringing their own equipment unless traveling light is a priority; reef shoes with rubber soles for rocky underwater surfaces are also advised. To avoid problems at customs, bring your prescription drugs in the original, current pill bottle or with a current prescription. Don't count on purchasing necessary OTC or prescription meds (such as sleeping pills); the same brands are not always available in Mexico.

▌PASSPORTS AND VISAS

A tourist visa and valid passport are required for all visitors to Mexico traveling by air. If you're arriving by plane, the standard tourist visa forms will be given to you on the plane. They're also available through travel agents and Mexican consulates and at the border if you're entering by land. In addition to having your visa form, you must prove your citizenship.

▌TIP→ You're given a portion of the tourist card form upon entering Mexico. Keep track of this document throughout your trip: you will need it when you depart. You'll be asked to submit it, along with your ticket and passport, to airline representatives at the gate when boarding for departure. If you lose your tourist card, plan to spend some time (and about $80) sorting it out with Mexican officials at the airport before your flight home.

U.S. Passport Information U.S. Department of State ☎ 877/487–2778 ⊕ travel.state.gov/passport.

▌RESTROOMS

Expect to find reasonably clean flushing toilets and running water at public restrooms in the major tourist destinations and at tourist attractions. Toilet tissue and soap are usually, but not always, on hand. Although many markets, gas stations, bus and train stations, and the like have public facilities, you usually have to pay about 5 pesos for the privilege of using them. Some smaller hotels in Xcalak, Mahahual, and Isla Holbox have eco-friendly toilets, which utilize low water or sawdust for composting. Remember that unless otherwise indicated you should put your used toilet paper in the wastebasket next to the toilet. Many plumbing systems in Mexico still can't handle accumulations of toilet paper.

▌SAFETY

Unfortunately Mexico has seen a dramatic increase in violence—much of which is drug-related—over the past few years, but most of this has been concentrated along border zones and in less-touristy areas. The Yucatán remains one of the safest areas in Mexico.

Nevertheless, even in resort areas like Cancún and Cozumel you should use common sense. Make use of hotel safes when available, and carry your own baggage whenever possible unless you're checking into a hotel. Leave expensive jewelry at home, since it often entices thieves and will mark you as a *turista* who can afford to be robbed.

When traveling with all your money, be sure to keep an eye on your belongings at all times and distribute your cash and any valuables between different bags and items of clothing. Do not reach for your money stash in public. If you carry a purse, choose one with a zipper and a thick strap that you can drape across your body; adjust the length so that the purse sits in front of you at or above hip level.

There have been reports of travelers being victimized after imbibing drinks that have been drugged in Cancún nightclubs. Never drink alone with strangers, watch your drink being poured, and keep your eye on it at all times. Avoid driving on desolate streets, don't travel at night, and never pick up hitchhikers or hitchhike yourself.

Use ATMs during the day and in big commercial areas. Avoid the glass-enclosed street variety of banks where you may be more vulnerable to thieves who force you to withdraw money for them.

Cancún's Zona Hotelera (Hotel Zone) is a high-trafficked tourist area, making it extremely safe for those who want to relax at the beach or explore the string of shops and restaurants that line Boulevard Kukulcán. Security has recently increased on this main strip, which means you'll most likely see armed tourist police driving up and down the boulevard. There is also a security checkpoint that marks the entrance to the Zona Hotelera on Boulevard Kukulcán in front of Playa Delfines. Tourists are rarely stopped here. Less visited by tourists, El Centro (downtown Cancún) should be avoided late at night. An act of violence in 2010 resulted in the C4 Surveillance and Rescue Center installing video cameras in strategic points throughout the city. Additionally, an emergency 911 Call Center is now in place.

Bear in mind that reporting a crime to the police is often a frustrating experience unless you speak excellent Spanish and have a great deal of patience. If you're victimized, contact your local consular agent or the consular section of your country's embassy in Mexico City.

A woman traveling alone will be the subject of much curiosity, since traditional Mexican women do not generally choose to travel unaccompanied. Don't walk on deserted beaches alone, and make sure your hotel room is securely locked when you retire.

Part of the machismo culture is being flirtatious and showing off in front of *compadres*, and lone women are likely to be subjected to catcalls, although this is less true in the Yucatán than in other parts of Mexico. Although annoying, it's essentially harmless. The best way to get rid of unwanted attention is to simply ignore the advances. It's best not to enter into a discussion with harassers, even if you speak Spanish. When the suitor is persistent say "no" to whatever is said, walk briskly, and leave immediately for a safe place, such as a nearby store. Dressing conservatively may help—clothing such as halter tops or shorts may be inappropriate in more conservative rural areas. Never go topless on the beach unless it's a recognized nude beach with lots of other people. Mexicans, in general, don't sunbathe nude, and men may misinterpret your doing so as an invitation.

■TIP➔ Distribute your cash, credit cards, IDs, and other valuables between a deep front pocket, an inside jacket or vest pocket, and a hidden money pouch. Don't reach for the money pouch once you're in public.

BEACHES

Empty coastlines can be susceptible to car break-ins and theft. Most resorts notify beachgoers of coastal conditions by displayed colored flags. ■TIP➔ Don't swim when the black danger flags fly; red and yellow flags indicate that you should proceed with caution, and green flags mean the waters are safe. You will seldom see the green flag—even when the water is calm—so swim cautiously. Beware: Even the calmest-looking waters can have currents and riptides. Ignoring these warning flags has resulted in at least one tourist drowning each season.

If visiting isolated beaches, bring sunscreen and drinking water to avoid overexposure and dehydration. Take note that waves are most powerful during December, and that hurricane season lasts from June through November.

■ TAXES

An air-departure tax of around $50 is almost always included as part of your ticket; if for some reason, it's not included or only partially included, you must pay the remainder in cash at the airport. Check with your airline if you're not sure they included the tax in the ticket price.

Hotels in the state of Quintana Roo charge a 12% tax, which is a combined 10% Value Added Tax with the 2% hotel tax; in Yucatán and Campeche, expect a 17% tax, since the V.A.T. is 15% in these states.

Mexico has a value-added tax (V.A.T.), or IVA (*impuesto de valor agregado*), of 15% (10% along the Cancún–Chetumal corridor). Many establishments already include the IVA in the quoted price. When comparing hotel prices, it's important to know whether yours includes IVA and any service charge. Occasionally (and illegally) it may be waived for cash purchases; this is nothing for you to worry about.

Those who travel to Mexico by air or cruise ship are eligible to be reimbursed for the value-added tax they were charged on purchases made at stores throughout the country. There are, of course, some restrictions. You must have paid by credit card (from outside of Mexico), or cash, and your purchases must have totaled 1,200 pesos. While purchasing, you must show your passport and get a receipt and a refund form. Then you visit a kiosk at the Cancún airport to receive half of your refund in the form of a credit in pesos (to a max of 10,000 pesos) that can be applied to more shopping (no meals or hotel stays); the remainder will be credited to your credit card or bank account.

■ TIME

Mexico has three time zones. Baja California (*norte*) is on Pacific Standard Time. Baja California Sur and the northwest states are on Mountain Time. The rest of the country is on Central Standard Time, which is two hours ahead of Pacific Time. Cancún and all of the areas covered in this book are on Central Standard Time.

■ TIPPING

When tipping in Mexico, remember that the minimum wage is just a bit more than $5 a day and that many in the tourism industry don't earn much more. There are also Mexicans who think in dollars and know, for example, that in the United States porters are tipped $1 to $2 a bag. Many of them expect the peso equivalent from foreigners. Though dollars are widely accepted in Cancún and Cozumel, you should always tip using local currency whenever possible, so that service personnel aren't stuck going to the bank to exchange dollars for pesos.

What follows are some guidelines. Naturally, larger tips are always welcome: porters and bellhops, 10 pesos per bag at airports and moderate and inexpensive hotels and 20 pesos per person per bag at expensive hotels; maids, 10 pesos per night (all hotels); waiters, 15% to 20% of the bill, depending on service, and less in simpler restaurants (anywhere you are, make sure a service charge hasn't already been added, a practice that's particularly common in resorts); bartenders, 15% to 20% of the bill, depending on service (and, perhaps, on how many drinks you've had); taxi drivers, 5 to 10 pesos only if the driver helps you with your bags. Tipping cabbies isn't usual, and they often overcharge tourists when possible. Tip tour guides 50 pesos per half day, 100 for a full day; drivers about half as much. Gas-station attendants expect 3 to 5 pesos unless they check the oil, tires, and so on, in which case tip more; parking attendants, 5 to 10 pesos, even if it's for valet parking at a theater or restaurant that charges for the service.

▌ TOURS

Mayaland Tours leads custom tours as well as guided eight-day trips that hit the highlights of archaeology (Chichén Itzá, Uxmal, and the Ruta Puuc sites) with forays into Campeche and Río Lagartos. California Native includes guide service, accommodations, breakfast, and most lunches in its seven-day trip with stops at Mérida, Izamal, Chichén Itzá, Ek Balam, Uxmal, and Edzná. Originally organized by birders and naturalists, Ecoturismo Yucatán, based in Mérida, now leads a large variety of guided tours hitting peninsula highlights of archaeology and culture as well as specialized tours. EcoColors and Alltournative are recommended for sustainable adventure tours on the coast, offering archaeological and nature tours.

Recommended Companies Alltournative ⊠ *Carretera Federal Chetumal-Puerto Juarez, Km 287, in front of Playacar development (after Centro Maya and Hong Kong restaurant), Playa del Carmen* ☎ *984/803-9999, 877/437-4990 from U.S. and Canada* ⊕ *www.alltournative.com.* **California Native** ☎ *800/926-1140, 310/642-1140* ⊕ *www.calnative.com.* **EcoColors** ⊠ *Calle Camaron 32, Smz. 27, Cancún* ☎ *998/884-3667* ⊕ *www.ecotravelmexico.com.* **Ecoturismo Yucatán** ⊠ *Calle 3 No. 235, between 32A and 34, Col. Pensiones, Mérida, Yucatán* ☎ *999/920-2772, 999/920-2742* ⊕ *www.ecoyuc.com.mx.* **Mayaland** ☎ *998/887-2495 Cancún, 877/240-5864 in U.S.* ⊕ *www.mayaland.com.*

SPECIAL-INTEREST TOURS

ADVENTURE

Contacts Green Tortoise Adventure Travel ☎ *800/867-8647, 415/956-7500* ⊕ *www.greentortoise.com.* **TrekAmerica** ☎ *800/873-5872* ⊕ *www.trekamerica.com.*

ART AND ARCHAEOLOGY

Contacts Far Horizons Archaeological & Cultural Trips ☎ *800/552-4575, 415/482-8400* ⊕ *www.farhorizons.com.* **The Mayan Traveler** ☎ *888/843-6292, 281/367-3386* ⊕ *www.themayantraveler.com.*

BIKING

Contacts Backroads ☎ *800/462-2848* ⊕ *www.backroads.com.*

BIRD-WATCHING

ContactsEcoturismo Yucatán ⊠ *Calle 3 Nos. 235, between 32A and 34, Col. Pensiones, Mérida, Yucatán* ☎ *999/920-2772, 999/920-2742* ⊕ *www.ecoyuc.com.mx.*

DIVING

Contacts Scuba Travel Ventures ☎ *800/298-9009 toll-free, 619/456-9030* ⊕ *scubatravelventures.com.*

ECOTOURS

Contacts Alltournative ⊠ *Carretera Federal Chetumal-Puerto Juarez Km 287, in front of Playacar development (after Centro Maya and Hong Kong restaurant), Playa del Carmen* ☎ *984/803-9999, 1877/437-4990 from U.S.* ⊕ *www.alltournative.com.* **Ecoturismo Yucatán** ⊠ *Calle 3 No. 235, between Calles 32A and 34, Col. Pensiones, Mérida* ☎ *999/920-2772, 999/925-2187* ⊕ *www.ecoyuc.com.*

FISHING

Contacts Costa de Cocos ⊠ *2 km (1 mile) outside Xcalak* ⊕ *www.costadecocos.com.* **Fishing International** ☎ *800/950-4242, 707/542-4242* ⊕ *www.fishinginternational.com.* **EcoColors** ⊠ *Calle Camaron 32, Sm 27, Cancún* ☎ *998/884-9580 in Mexico, 998/884-3677 in Mexico* ⊕ *www.ecotravelmexico.com.*

LANGUAGE PROGRAMS

Contacts Institute of Modern Spanish ⊠ *Calle 15 Nos. 500B, between 16A and 18 Col. Maya, Mérida, Yucatán* ☎ *877/463-7432 in U.S., 999/911-0790 in Mexico* ⊕ *www.modernspanish.com.* **Spanish Institute of Mérida** ⊠ *Calle 60 No. 358, Col. Centro, Colonia Centro, Mérida, Yucatán* ☎ *999/925-4475, 866/511-5057 in U.S.* ⊕ *www.simerida.com.*

▌ VISITOR INFORMATION

ONLINE TRAVEL TOOLS

The official website for Mexico tourism has information on tourist attractions and activities, and an overview of Mexican history and culture. Yucatán Today and Loco Gringo have comprehensive information on nightlife, hotel listings, archaeological sites, area history, maps, and other useful information for travelers.

All About Cancún, Cozumel, and the Yucatán Peninsula ⊕ *www.yucatantoday. com,* ⊕ *www.locogringo.com.* Also try ⊕ *www. cozumelmycozumel.com,* ⊕ *www.islamujeres. info,* ⊕ *www.cancun.bz,* and ⊕ *www. travelyucatan.com.*

Tourist Board Offices Mexico Tourism Board ☎ *800/446–3942 in U.S. or Canada* ⊕ *www.visitmexico.com.*

INDEX

PHOTO CREDITS

Front cover: Maxine Cass [Description: Palapas on Cancun Beach]. 1, Kreder Katja/age fotostock. 2, Stuart Pearce/age footstock. 5, cancuncd.com. Chapter 1: Experience Cancun: 8-9, ESCUDERO Patrick / age fotostock. 10, Mike Liu/Shutterstock. 11(left), LipBomb/Flickr. 11 (right), GUILLERMO ALDANA/Mexico Tourism Board. 14, Cancun CVB. 15 (left), cancuncd.com. 15 (right), BRUCE HERMAN/Mexico Tourism Board. 16 (left), Curtis Kautzer/Shutterstock. 16 (top center), urosr/Shutterstock.16 (top right), Agnes Csondor/iStockphoto. 16 (bottom right), SEUX Paule / age fotostock. 17 (top left), Drimi/Shutterstock. 17 (bottom left), Alicia Navarrete Alonso/wikipedia.org. 17 (top-center), travelpixpro/iStockphoto. 17 (right), Scott Prokop/Shutterstock. 18 and 19 (left), Cancun CVB. 19 (right), BRUCE HERMAN/Mexico Tourism Board. 21(left),idreamphoto/Shutterstock. 21 (right), Alfredo Schaufelberger/Shutterstock. 22, aceshot1/Shutterstock. 23, Yarek Gora/iStockphoto. 24, Byron W.Moore/Shutterstock. 26, Chris Cheadle / age fotostock. Chapter 2: Cancun: 27, Victor Elias / age fotostock. 28 (top), Keith Pomakis/wikipedia.org. 28 (bottom), Joao Virissimo/Shutterstock. 29, David Davis/Shutterstock. 30, Cancun CVB. 31 (top), Thelmadatter/wikipedia.org. 31 (bottom), malias/Flickr. 32, aceshot1/Shutterstock. 42, JTB Photo / age fotostock. 45, Witold Skrypczak / age fotostock. 47, The Leading Hotels of the World. 52, JTB Photo/age fotostock. 69 (top and bottom), Aqua Cancun. 71 (top), Marriott International. 71 (bottom), The Ritz-Carlton Cancun Beach. 77, csp/Shutterstock. 78 (top left), Alfredo Schaufelberger/Shutterstock. 78 (bottom left), wikipedia.org. 78 (right), Casa Herradura/Brown-Forman. 79 (top left), csp/Shutterstock. 79 (bottom left), Alfredo Schaufelberger/Shutterstock. 79 (top center), Jesus Cervantes/Shutterstock. 79 (bottom center), Blaine Harrington / age fotostock. 79 (top right), Jesus Cervantes/Shutterstock. 79 (bottom right), Jesus Cervantes/Shutterstock. 79 (bottom), Smithsonian Institution Archives. 80 (top left), Eduard Stelmakh/Shutterstock. 80 (center left), svry/Shutterstock. 80 (bottom left), National Archives and Records Administration. 80 (top right), Andrew Penner/iStockphoto. 80 (bottom right), BlueOrange Studio/Shutterstock. 81 (top right), Patricia Hofmeester/Shutterstock. 81 (top left), Keith Dannemiller / Alamy. 81 (bottom left), csp/Shutterstock. 82 (left), The Patr.n Spirits Company. 82 (right), rick/Flickr. 83 (top left), Casa Herradura/Brown-Forman. 83 (bottom left), shrk/Flickr. 83 (right), Neil Setchfield / Alamy. 84, Hugo Cadavez/Flickr. 86, Jan Greune / age fotostock. 95, Cancun CVB. Chapter 3: Isla Mujeres: 97, Cancun CVB. 98 (left), Chie Ushio. 98 (top right), Bruce Herman/Mexico Tourism Board. 98 (bottom right), Stefano Morini/Cancun Convention and Visitors Bureau. 99, Nanako Inoue. 100, rj lerich/Shutterstock. 108-09, Alex Bramwell/iStockphoto. 111, Michael DeFreitas Central America / Alamy. 114, Chie Ushio. 122 (top), Courtesy of Casa de los Suenos. 122 (bottom), Casa El Pio. 125, Water-Frame / Alamy. 128, Chris Cheadle / age fotostock. Chapter 4: The Caribbean Coast: 131, Stuart Pearce / age fotostock. 132 (left), Bruce Herman/Mexico Tourism Board. 132 (right), Philip Coblentz/Brand X Pictures. 133, Stefano Marini/Cancun Convention and Visitors Bureau. 134, Viceroy Hotel Group. 135 (top), Banyan Tree Hotels & Resorts. 135 (bottom), Rosewood Hotels & Resorts. 136, Markus Sevcik/Shutterstock. 147 (top), Viceroy Hotel Group. 147 (bottom), amResorts. 151 (top), Almaplena Eco Resort & Beach Club.151 (bottom), Esencia Seaside Estate.156 (top), Fairmont Hotels & Resorts. 156 (bottom), Rosewood Hotels & Resorts. 160-61, Ken Welsh / age fotostock. 171, La Tortuga Hotel & Spa. 172, Corbis. 177, Banyan Tree Hotels & Resorts. 179, SEUX Paule / age fotostock. 181, Doug Plummer/age fotostock. 182, Jose Enrique Molino/age fotostock. 183 (left), Ales Liska/Shutterstock. 183 (right), Stefano Paterna/age fotostock. 184 (top), Ken Welsh/age fotostock. 184 (bottom) Qing Ding/Shutterstock. 185, Philip Coblentz/Brand X Pictures. 192, Cancun CVB. 199, Matty Symons/Shutterstock. 208, Nataliya Hora/iStockphoto. 210, david sanger photography / Alamy. 215, urosr/Shutterstock. 221, Stuart Pearce / age fotostock. 223, Linda Vermeulen/ http://www.mermaidskissgallery.com. Chapter 5: Cozumel: 227, B&Y Photography Inc. / age fotostock. 228 (top), Bruce Herman/Mexico Tourism Board. 228 (bottom), George Kirkaldie/Flickr. 229, eschipul/Flickr. 230, cancuncd. com. 235, Ron Buskirk / age fotostock. 237, Mark Newman / age fotostock. 240-41, Super-Stock/age fotostock. 244, SuperStock/age fotostock. 250, Alvaro Leiva / age fotostock. 254 (top & bottom), The Leading Hotels of the World. 258, Danita Delimont / Alamy. 260, SuperStock/age fotostock. 264, John Anderson / age fotostock. 265, cancuncd.com. 266 (top left), tslane888/Flickr. 266 (bottom left), pato_garza/Flickr. 266 (top right), tslane888/Flickr. 266 (bottom right), Mike Bauer/Shutterstock. 268 (top), sethbienek/Flickr. 268 (bottom), tubuceo/Shutterstock. 269 (bottom), Julie de Leseleuc/iStockphoto. 270, Jerry McElroy/iStockphoto. Chapter 6: Yucatán and Campeche States: 273, SEUX Paule / age fotostock. 274, GUILLERMO ALDANA/Mexico Tourism Board. 276, JTB Photo Communications, Inc. / Alamy. 277 (top), gonzalovalenzuela/Flickr. 277 (bottom), Hippietrail/wikipedia.org. 278, redsquarephoto/Shutterstock. 287, MAISANT Ludovic / age fotostock. 294, La Casa de Frida Restaurant. 300, Stuart Pearce / age fotostock. 304, Jose Peral / age fotostock. 310, Jo Ann Snover/iStockphoto. 314, Dmitry Rukhlenko/iStockphoto. 318, Stefano Paterna / age fotostock. 324, David Davis/Shutterstock. 325 (top), Corbis. 325 (bottom), Fedor Selivanov/Shutterstock. 326 (top), Bernard Gagnon/wikipedia.org. 326 (bottom), Richard Gillard/iStockphoto. 327 (top), Jos. A. Granados/Cancun CVB. 327 (top inset), Luis Casta.eda/age fotostock. 327 (bottom), Jo Ann Snover/iStockphoto. 328 (top), Sylvain Lapens.e-Ricard/iStockphoto. 328 (bottom), Fcb981/wikipedia.org. 329 (top), Philip Baird/anthroarcheart.org. 329 (bottom), Mexico Tourism Board. 330, Jo Ann Snover/iStockphoto. 331 (top), Markus Sevcik/iStockphoto. 331 (bottom), Deanna Bean/iStockphoto. 339, Alex James Bramwell/Shutterstock. 345, FRILET Patrick / age fotostock. 350, Adalberto R.os Szalay / age fotostock. 356, Strigl Egmont / age fotostock. 360, Targa / age fotostock. 367, Wojtek Buss / age fotostock. Back cover (from left to right): Zbiq/Shutterstock; cancuncd.com; The Leading Hotels of the World. Spine: Worachat Sodsri/ Shutterstock.

NOTES